THE RAILROADS OF THE CONFEDERACY

ROBERT C. BLACK III

THE UNIVERSITY OF NORTH CAROLINA PRESS

THE
RAILROADS
OF THE
CONFEDERACY

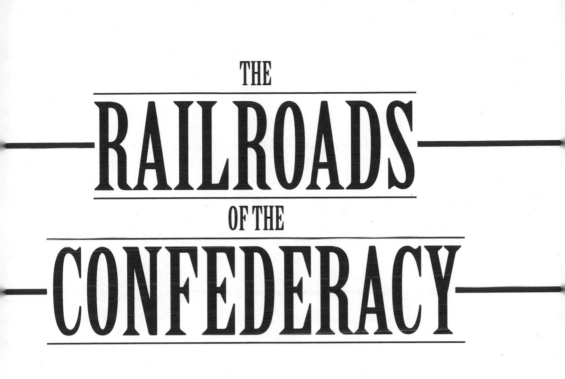

CHAPEL HILL AND LONDON

© 1998

THE UNIVERSITY OF NORTH CAROLINA PRESS

All rights reserved

MANUFACTURED IN THE UNITED STATES OF AMERICA

The paper in this book meets the
guidelines for permanence and durability of the
Committee on Production
Guidelines for Book Longevity of the
Council on Library Resources.

LIBRARY OF CONGRESS CATALOGING-IN-PUBLICATION DATA

Black, Robert C., 1914–
The railroads of the Confederacy / by Robert C. Black III.
p.   cm.
Originally published: Chapel Hill: University of North Carolina Press, 1952.
Includes bibliographical references and index.
ISBN 0-8078-4729-1 (pbk.: alk. paper)
1. United States—History—Civil War, 1861–1865—Transportation.
2. Railroads—Confederate States of America.
3. Confederate States of America. Army—Transportation.
I. Title.
E545.B55   1998
973.7—dc21   97-44268
CIP

02 01 00 99 98   5 4 3 2 1

For R.M.B.

WHO PROVIDED THE PATIENCE

CONTENTS

ILLUSTRATIONS

A DRAWING AND FACSIMILES

MAPS

FOREWORD

On June 18, 1861, Robert E. Lee addressed the critical role Confederate railroads would play over the next four years. "I consider it very important to the military operations within Virginia," he wrote, "that proper and easy connections of the several railroads passing through or terminating in Richmond or Petersburg should be made as promptly as possible. The want of these connections has seriously retarded the operations so far, and they may become more important." More than half a century later, historian Charles W. Ramsdell emphasized that the Confederacy never overcame the kinds of railroad-related troubles Lee had mentioned. "It would be claiming too much to say that the failure to solve its railroad problem was the cause of the Confederacy's downfall," stated Ramsdell in his pioneering article, "yet it is impossible not to conclude that the solution of that problem was one of the important conditions of success." Ramsdell's piece failed to inspire a full-scale scholarly treatment of the subject he had sketched in broad outline. In 1939 Douglas Southall Freeman listed "a study of the Southern railroads" as one of the Confederate topics most in need of book-length attention.[1]

Robert C. Black III closed this gap with *The Railroads of the Confederacy*, published in 1952 by the University of North Carolina Press.[2] Black's well-researched, comprehensive book expanded on many of the themes in Ramsdell's article and cited substantial evidence to reach similar conclusions. Did southern railroads figure prominently in the Confederacy's failure to secure independence? "To this question the author can only answer—yes," wrote Black.

"Railroad transportation in the Confederacy suffered from a number of defects, all of which played a recognizable part in the southern defeat." Insufficient mileage, gaps between key lines, inability to repair and maintain tracks and rolling stock, differences of gauge, and failure to build badly needed lines all hurt the Confederacy. Beyond such physical difficulties, argued Black, *"the Confederates by no means made the best use of what they had. It is men who are most at fault when a war is lost—not locomotives, or cars, or even economic geography. And in so far as railroad logistics were concerned, the Confederates committed two major sins: 1. Railroad owners, managers, and even employees were unwilling to make serious sacrifice of their personal interests. 2. The Confederate Government was loath to enforce the kind of transportation policy the war effort demanded."* In sum, the Confederacy lacked the "wholehearted public cooperation" and the "government coercion" necessary "to wage a modern war."[3]

Reviewers hailed *The Railroads of the Confederacy* as an impressive work. One called it "a superior historical monograph," adding that "Mr. Black has examined a technical subject with the understanding of an engineer." This historian also thought the illustrations and maps enhanced "the pleasure and value of the book." Other critics complimented Black's literary ability as well as his scholarship. "Dr. Black, exploring his entire subject with commendable thoroughness and neatly connecting his special problems with the broad stream of Confederate history," stated one scholar, "has written with such style that his book is outstanding for literary excellence." Another reviewer labeled the book "a notable literary achievement, as well as a solid contribution to Civil War history. From beginning to end it is a fascinating story of the administrative and operating problems faced by the South in its desperate attempt to supply and transport its armies, and at the same time to provide adequate rail service to keep its civilian economy alive and functioning."[4]

In the years since its publication, Black's book has attained the status of a classic title on the Confederacy. Two popular Civil War periodicals, in articles published in 1981 and 1996, included it on lists of the best books in the field.[5] A standard bibliography compiled during the mid-1960s described *The Railroads of the Confederacy* as "an able and detailed treatment of the management, difficulties, and significance of Southern railways, with emphasis on the railways themselves." Noted bibliographer Richard B. Harwell placed it among his two hundred essential titles on the Confederacy, calling it "a major contribution to Confederate economic history" that demonstrated how the "collapse of the Confederate railroad service was of immense importance in hastening the breakdown of the Confederacy." More recently, a major analytical bibliography termed it "a soundly documented study" that details how "Confederate military authorities failed to use effectively the valuable interior railroad lines scattered throughout the South that were available to support numerous campaigns."[6]

Although *The Railroads of the Confederacy* has remained the standard title for nearly half a century (a remarkable feat in a field that boasts a massive and rapidly growing literature), readers can consult several other books that illuminate facets of the subject. George Edgar Turner's *Victory Rode the Rails: The Strategic Place of the Railroads in the Civil War*, published a year after Black's book, supplies a narrative of notable military campaigns in which railroads played an important role. Interspersed among chronological chapters are treatments of rolling stock, government railroad policy, and movement by rail of sick and wounded soldiers. Less scholarly than Black's book, Turner's stresses Confederate inefficiency and failures: "Slow to recognize its railroad handicap, the Confederate government quarreled with its railroad men and did nothing to lessen that handicap. On the fateful day of Appomattox, the railroad system in the North was stronger than when the war began. Except for the lines taken over by the Federal army and rehabilitated for its military use, practically all the railroads of the South were a pitiable mass of wreckage."[7]

More specialized books explore individual states or railroads. The only study of a Confederate state is Angus James Johnston II's *Virginia Railroads in the Civil War*. Within a chronological framework, Johnston offers considerable analysis and gives attention to both Confederate-run lines and the development and operation of the U.S. Military Railroad's network in Virginia. He observes that "most Virginia railroad men in mid-1865 could look back with some degree of pride upon the part played by the state's railroads in the war." Yet he echoes Black in noting how, "as the war went on, shortcomings in various forms—deterioration, inflation, scarcity of men and material, corruption, particularism, attrition, contraction, and even disloyalty—took their toll." "As the railroads which were the very sinews of war grew flabby," concludes Johnston, "the fortunes of the Army of Northern Virginia speedily declined."[8]

Kenneth W. Noe's *Southwest Virginia's Railroad: Modernization and the Sectional Crisis* focuses on the Virginia and Tennessee Railroad as a factor in the economic, political, and military history of twenty-four Virginia counties from the late antebellum years to the end of the Civil War. Noe sees the railroad, which linked Lynchburg and Bristol, as a crucial "modernizing" force that helped tie a once isolated region to capitalist markets, encouraged the spread of slavery, and promoted secessionist sentiment as the sectional crisis reached its flash point in 1860–61. "In further commercializing Southwest Virginia, and linking it to Richmond's markets, the railroad had made the region more like the rest of Virginia and the South," comments Noe. During the Confederate years, Union armies made the railroad a major target: "Having brought greater commercialism, expanded slavery, and ultimately secession to the region, the railroad now would bring war and defeat." Noe's final two chapters assess the impact of the war on the railroad and on the people it served.[9]

Allen W. Trelease's *North Carolina Railroad, 1849–1871, and the Modernization of North Carolina* accords considerable attention to the wartime story of the longest and largest railroad in a vital Confederate state. In examining the NCRR, which ran from Goldsboro northwestward through Raleigh to Greensboro and eventually on to Charlotte, Trelease discusses managers and workers, problems related to maintenance and rolling stock, declining efficiency in carrying passengers and freight, and the line's role in supplying Lee's army. "So far as the NCRR was concerned," states Trelease, "the war accelerated a trend already evident by 1860: it was preeminently a north-south road rather than an east-west feeder of the state's own seaports as envisioned by many of its projectors. More specifically, it was a major link in one of the three railroad lines joining Virginia (including the Confederate capital at Richmond) with the rest of the Confederacy." Trelease charts the growing proportion of government business on the NCRR: military personnel accounted for 5 percent of passengers in 1860–61 and 65 percent in 1864–65; government freight receipts shot from 1.3 percent in 1860–61 to 57 percent in 1864–65. During the conflict, suggests

Trelease, "few southern railroads were more strategically placed or
played a greater role in determining the fate of the Confederacy."[10]

A pair of memoirs offers a personal dimension that compliments
the work by historians. Nimrod J. Bell's *Southern Railroad Man:
Conductor N. J. Bell's Recollections of the Civil War Era*, edited by
James A. Ward, recounts some of the author's wartime experiences
in Georgia, Tennessee, and the Carolinas. Carter S. Anderson's
Train Running for the Confederacy, 1861–1865: An Eyewitness Memoir,
edited by Walbrook D. Swank, details another conductor's service
on the Virginia Central Railroad. Bell and Anderson wrote long
after the fact, and their narratives are more useful for the impres-
sions they convey than for factual detail. Bell's is the more plain-
spoken of the two. "Railroading in time of war was almost as bad as
being in the army, for men were run day and night, Sundays not
excepted," he observed. The soldiers Bell's trains carried almost
certainly would have disagreed with this claim. He admitted that
they sometimes "would throw my grease buckets and my train
chains away. They did not like railroad men. I often heard them say
that railroad men ought to be in the army." Anderson often opted
for the more dramatic episode, as when he described a situation in
the summer of 1862: "My train came next and my engineer, John
Whalley, was signaled to pull down in place to load. To my horror,
I discovered that John was drunk, and that my fireman, John Wes-
ley, was dead drunk! We needed but little steam, however, as it was
mostly down grade all the way. I hope I may never again experience
such feelings as I then had. I had on board 2,000 soldiers, a train just
ahead, one immediately in the rear; overloaded, pouring rain, nearly night, engineer in liquor, no fireman; not a whistle allowed to be
sounded, not a bell allowed to be rung!"[11]

These half-dozen titles add detail and color to the solid foundation of Black's *Railroads of the Confederacy*. But Black's narrative
stands very well on its own. *Railroads of the Confederacy* is *the* indispensable place to begin any exploration of southern railroads en-
gulfed by war.

GARY W. GALLAGHER
PENN STATE UNIVERSITY
OCTOBER 1997

Notes

1. Robert E. Lee to Edmund T. Morris, June 18, 1861, in U.S. War Department, *The War of the Rebellion: A Compilation of the Official Records of the Union and Confederate Armies*, 128 vols. (Washington: Government Printing Office, 1880–1901), ser. 4, 1:394; Charles W. Ramsdell, "The Confederate Government and the Railroads," *American Historical Review* 22 (July 1917): 810; Douglas Southall Freeman, *The South to Posterity: An Introduction to the Writing of Confederate History* (New York: Charles Scribner's Sons, 1939), 200.

2. In 1987, the book was reprinted in paper and cloth editions by Broadfoot Publishing Company of Wilmington, North Carolina. Six years before the appearance of Black's book, Charles W. Turner published "The Virginia Central Railroad at War, 1861–1865" (*Journal of Southern History* 12 [November 1946]: 510–33), which provided an overview of one of Virginia's most important railroads. "Although every mile of its lines lay in the battle zone," wrote Turner, "and although it suffered greatly from loss of rolling stock, the Virginia Central Railroad, under its own officials and without coming under the control of the Confederate government, rendered great service to the Confederate cause. Beset by inflation, depreciation, and inadequate labor force, it nevertheless served as an important artery for Lee's army until Appomattox, and it was a strong factor in the success of the delaying actions of the Confederate forces in Virginia" (p. 533).

3. The quotations are from pages 294–95.

4. Harold Jaynes Bingham in *Mississippi Valley Historical Review* 39 (March 1953): 769; William S. Greever in *American Historical Review* 58 (April 1953): 652–54; Robert M. Sutton in *Journal of Southern History* 19 (May 1953): 246–48.

5. "Behind the Lines," *Civil War Times Illustrated* 20 (August 1981): 46–47 (a roster of 134 titles compiled with the advice of "over thirty consultants"); "The Civil War 200," *Civil War: The Magazine of the Civil War Society*, no. 55 (February 1996): 44–47 (which I selected after consultation with a number of specialists in the field).

6. Allan Nevins, James I. Robertson Jr., and Bell I Wiley, eds., *Civil War Books: A Critical Bibliography*, 2 vols. (Baton Rouge: Louisiana State University Press, 1967, 1969), 1:5 (entry by Archer Jones); Richard B. Harwell, *In Tall Cotton: The 200 Most Important Books for the Reader, Researcher, and Collector* (Austin, Tex.: Jenkins Publishing Company, 1978), 3; David J. Eicher, *The Civil War in Books: An Analytical Bibliography* (Urbana: University of Illinois Press, 1997), 289.

7. George Edgar Turner, *Victory Rode the Rails: The Strategic Place of the Railroads in the Civil War* (Indianapolis: Bobbs-Merrill, 1953), 376 [paperback reprint, Lincoln: University of Nebraska Press, 1991]. For an overview of the condition of southern railroads at the end of the war, see John F. Stover, "The Ruined Railroads of the Confederacy," *Georgia Historical Quarterly* 42 (December 1958): 376–88. "Four years of conflict had completely destroyed or crippled over half of the railroads of the South," noted Stover, "with a loss running into tens of millions of dollars." Yet by the end of the summer of 1865, "most of the railroads were operating, in at least some fashion, a major portion of their original routes" (376–77).

8. Angus James Johnston II, *Virginia Railroads in the Civil War* (Chapel Hill: University of North Carolina Press [for the Virginia Historical Society], 1961), 253–55. In alluding to disloyalty, Johnston likely had in mind the activities of Samuel Ruth, the Confederate superintendent of the Richmond, Fredericksburg

& Potomac Railroad's line between Richmond and Fredericksburg. For an excellent treatment of Ruth's efforts to undermine the Confederate war effort, see Meriwether Stuart, "Samuel Ruth and General R. E. Lee: Disloyalty and the Line of Supply to Fredericksburg, 1862–1863," *Virginia Magazine of History and Biography* 71 (January 1963): 35–109.

9. Kenneth W. Noe, *Southwest Virginia's Railroad: Modernization and the Sectional Crisis* (Urbana: University of Illinois Press, 1994), 108.

10. Allen W. Trelease, *The North Carolina Railroad, 1849–1871, and the Modernization of North Carolina* (Chapel Hill: University of North Carolina Press, 1991), 181, 177, 179.

11. Nimrod J. Bell, *Southern Railroad Man: Conductor N. J. Bell's Recollections of the Civil War Era*, edited by James A. Ward (DeKalb: Northern Illinois University Press, 1994), 12; [Carter S. Anderson], *Train Running for the Confederacy, 1861–1865: An Eyewitness Memoir*, edited by Walbrook D. Swank (Charlottesville, Va.: Papercraft Printing and Design, 1990), 10. Bell's memoir was originally published in 1896 as *Railroad Recollections for over Thirty-Eight Years*.

PREFACE

THIS BOOK HAS BEEN WRITTEN PRIMARILY BECAUSE THE AUTHOR has long desired such a volume, and no one has seen fit to produce it for him. An interest in the Civil War, persisting from boyhood, a passion for railroads that antedates even his earliest memories, and a service of three years in the U. S. Army Transportation Corps in the heart of the former Confederate States, finally conspired to drive him to his typewriter.

The author has been sufficiently exposed to the historical process to realize that history can never present the absolute truth, but the usual attempt has been made at impartiality. Though a northerner by birth, background, and education, his personal experience in the American South has come close to turning him into that most careless of enthusiasts—a converted Yankee. For this reason, he has endeavored not to bring any preconceived notions to bear and to allow the politicians and soldiers and railroaders of the Confederacy to speak for themselves. Whether he has succeeded therein is left to the reader.

All proper historical prefaces must contain acknowledgments of the aid received from others. But the author has not realized until now the real pleasure which is involved in the giving of academic thanks. The cooperation he received literally everywhere was a revelation. Especially gratifying to a mere taxpayer was the willingness and efficiency of a variety of public servants, both State and Federal, all of whom gave the lie to current traditions as to the energy and ability of those employed by government. Particular thanks are due the personnel of the War Records Division, National

Archives, and the Manuscripts and Photographs Divisions, Library of Congress, without whose help the information for this book could not have been compiled at all. Equally effective was the aid received from the several State departments visited, including the Virginia State Library at Richmond, the North Carolina Library and North Carolina Archives at Raleigh, the South Carolina Historical Department, Columbia, the Florida State Library, Tallahassee, the Alabama Department of Archives and History, Montgomery, and the New York State Library, Albany.

The help so willingly extended by private and semi-private organizations was as valuable as that afforded by official bodies. Miss India W. Thomas of the Confederate Museum, Richmond, proved cooperation itself, as did Mrs. Ralph Catterall of the neighboring Valentine Museum. Information of great value came streaming from the files of Miss Laura E. Armitage, Research Analyst of the Chesapeake & Ohio Railway Company, likewise at Richmond. In Washington, the author felt particularly privileged to receive the personal advice of that foremost expert upon both railroads and the War Between the States, Colonel Robert Selph Henry, of the Association of American Railroads, while at the Library of the Bureau of Railway Economics, Miss Elizabeth Cullen pitched in with her usual contagious enthusiasm. In South Carolina the delightful South Caroliniana Library, and especially the hospitable attendance of Mrs. Robert L. Meriwether, made the author's visit to Columbia a real pleasure. At the Georgia Historical Society in Savannah, Mrs. Lilla M. Hawes was graciousness itself. A pause of a single day at the Emory University Library produced a veritable avalanche of material. Nor must the days spent in the Columbia University Library, the Russell Sage College Library, the Library of Rensselaer Polytechnic Institute, the Public Library of Troy, New York, and the Engineering Societies Library of New York City, be permitted to go unacknowledged.

Though not visited personally, the Library of the University of Florida provided exceedingly valuable microfilms of selected portions of the David L. Yulee Papers. Mr. William D. McCain of the Department of Archives and History of the State of Mississippi and Mrs. W. O. Harrell of Jackson furnished a multitude of excerpts from the local press of the sixties. Thanks are likewise due Mr. E. A. Perkins of the Louisiana Historical Society for invaluable data. Practically the whole of the author's material upon the carriers of Texas he owes to the kindness of Professor Walter Prescott Webb and the really excellent notes unearthed by Miss Edith Parker of Austin. The aid of the University of North Carolina and especially of the gracious staff of the Southern Historical Collection and of Mr. William Y. Thompson, who searched a drab lot of material for information upon William M. Wadley, must likewise be acknowledged. From Richmond, Mr. Roy E. Appleman, Regional Historian of the National Park Service, furnished exceedingly welcome comments upon the move of Longstreet to Georgia in September, 1863. From the time-hallowed Charleston Museum came scarce information upon the railway wage scale in the first year of the war. Oddly enough, the principal resting place of Confederate railway time-tables was found to be the Boston Athenaeum, which extended its private facilities with great cordiality.

Space forbids an adequate listing of the nearly endless instances of aid on the part of private persons. But without the invaluable cooperation of Mrs. William Burt of Bolingbroke, Georgia, the story of Colonel Wadley could not have been told even in outline. Mr. Calder W. Payne of Macon, at the cost of enormous trouble, unearthed similarly indispensable information upon Lieutenant Colonel F. W. Sims. Dr. H. J. Eckenrode of Richmond produced a delightful mixture of technical advice and Virginia hospitality. A long conversation with Professor Milton S. Heath of the University of North Carolina proved most stimulating. It is a matter of deep regret that the author cannot herein personally acknowledge his debt of gratitude to the late Dr. Kathleen Bruce, but for his fellow graduate-student, Mr. Philip Ackerman of Fort Myers, Florida, he thankfully records similar unsolicited services rendered.

This preface cannot be concluded without reference to the unfailing help and inspiration of Professor Allan Nevins, under whose supervision this book has been written. Nor can the efficient services of Miss Rose Krugler and Mrs. C. F. Reynolds, who prepared the typed manuscript, be forgotten. Perhaps most of all the author is grateful to those who not only made his travels in quest of material seem like triumphal tours, but who bore with him during those months wherein he lost himself in the War Between the States. They know who they are.

ROBERT C. BLACK III

West Hartford, Connecticut
December, 1951

NUMERICAL KEY TO RAILROADS

1. Baltimore & Ohio
2. Alexandria, Loudoun & Hampshire
3. Orange & Alexandria
4. Winchester & Potomac
5. Virginia Central
6. Richmond, Fredericksburg & Potomac
7. Richmond & York River
8. Richmond & Petersburg
9. Richmond & Danville
10. South Side
11. Norfolk & Petersburg
12. Petersburg R.R.
13. Seaboard & Roanoke
14. Virginia & Tennessee
15. Piedmont R.R.
16. Raleigh & Gaston
17. Roanoke Valley
18. Wilmington & Weldon
19. Atlantic & North Carolina
20. North Carolina
21. Western North Carolina
22. Western R.R.
23. Atlantic, Tennessee & Ohio
24. Wilmington, Charlotte & Rutherford
25. Wilmington & Manchester
26. Cheraw & Darlington
27. Charlotte & South Carolina
28. King's Mountain
29. South Carolina R.R.
30. Greenville & Columbia
31. Spartanburg & Union
32. Laurens R.R.
33. Blue Ridge R.R.
34. Northeastern
35. Charleston & Savannah
36. Georgia R.R.
37. Augusta & Milledgeville
38. Western & Atlantic
39. Etowah R.R.
40. Rome R.R.
41. Central R.R. of Georgia
42. Macon & Western
43. Upson County
44. Macon & Brunswick
45. Southwestern R.R.
46. Muscogee R.R.
47. Augusta & Savannah
48. Savannah, Albany & Gulf
49. Atlantic & Gulf
50. Brunswick & Florida
51. Atlanta & West Point
52. Florida, Atlantic & Gulf Central
53. Florida R.R.
54. Pensacola & Georgia
55. Tallahassee R.R.
56. Alabama & Florida R.R. of Fla.
57. Alabama & Florida R.R. of Ala.
58. Montgomery & Eufaula
59. Montgomery & West Point
60. Tuskegee R.R.
61. Mobile & Girard
62. Mobile & Great Northern
63. Spring Hill R.R.
64. Mobile & Ohio
65. Mississippi, Gainesville & Tuscaloosa
66. Memphis & Charleston
67. Wills Valley
68. Nashville & Chattanooga
69. Winchester & Alabama
70. McMinnville & Manchester
71. Tennessee & Alabama
72. Nashville & Northwestern
73. Louisville & Nashville
74. Memphis, Clarksville & Louisville
75. Edgefield & Kentucky
76. East Tennessee & Georgia
77. East Tennessee & Virginia
78. Knoxville & Kentucky
79. Rogersville & Jefferson
80. Memphis & Ohio
81. Northeast & Southwest
82. Alabama & Mississippi Rivers
83. Cahaba, Marion & Greensboro
84. New Orleans & Ohio
85. Mississippi Central
86. Mississippi & Tennessee
87. Memphis & Little Rock
88. New Orleans, Jackson & Great Northern
89. Southern R.R. of Mississippi
90. Raymond R.R.
91. Jefferson & Lake Pontchartrain
92. Pontchartrain R.R.
93. Mexican Gulf R.R.
94. New Orleans, Opelousas & Great Western
95. West Feliciana R.R.
96. Clinton & Port Hudson
97. Baton Rouge, Grosse Tete & Opelousas
98. Vicksburg, Shreveport & Texas
99. Alexandria & Cheneyville
100. Texas & New Orleans
101. Eastern Texas R.R.
102. Buffalo Bayou, Brazos & Colorado
103. Houston Tap & Brazoria
104. Galveston, Houston & Henderson
105. Houston & Texas Central
106. Washington County R.R.
107. San Antonio & Mexican Gulf
108. Memphis, El Paso & Pacific
109. Southern Pacific
110. Manassas Gap
111. Alabama & Tennessee Rivers
112. Hungary Branch
113. Grand Gulf & Port Gibson

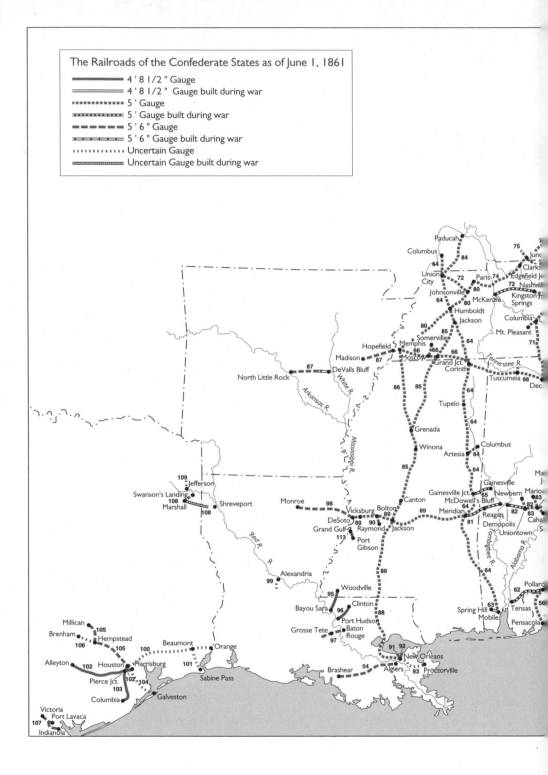

The Railroads of the Confederate States as of June 1, 1861

4' 8 1/2 " Gauge
4' 8 1/2 " Gauge built during war
5 ' Gauge
5 ' Gauge built during war
5 ' 6 " Gauge
5 ' 6 " Gauge built during war
Uncertain Gauge
Uncertain Gauge built during war

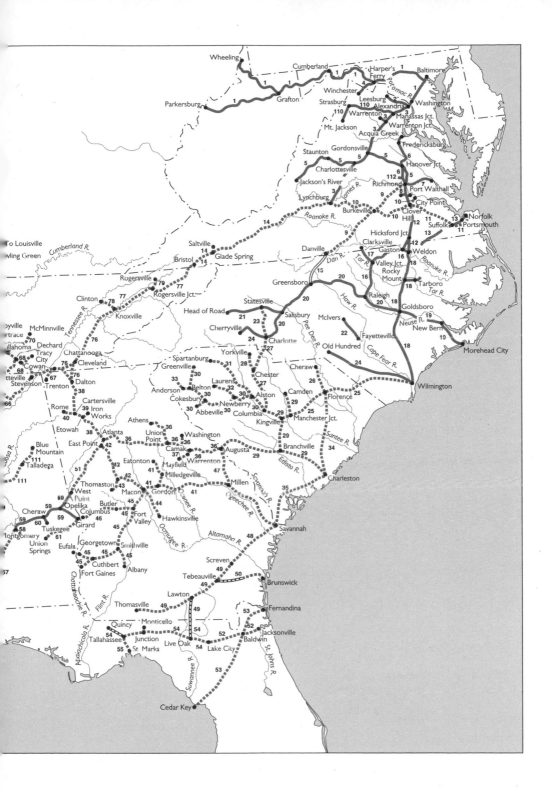

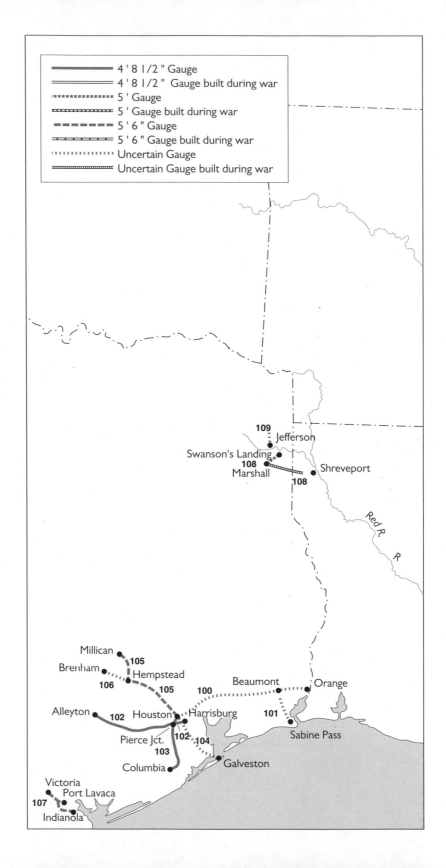

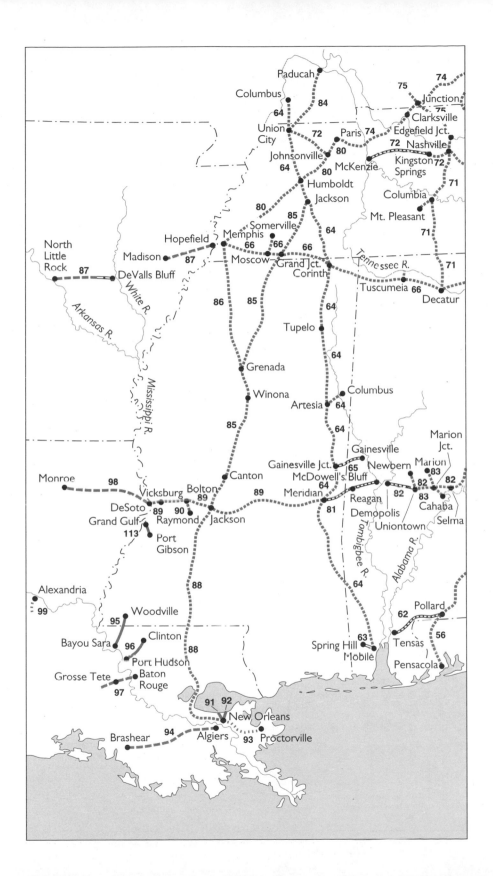

Paducah

Columbus

84

64

Junction 74

75

75

Clarksville

Union
City

72

Paris

74

Edgefield Jct.

Johnsonville

80

72

Nashville

64

McKenzie

Kingston
Springs

72

80

Humboldt

71

Jackson

Columbia

North
Little
Rock

87

80

85

Somerville

Memphis

64

Mt. Pleasant

Madison

87

66

66

Hopefield

66

71

DeValls Bluff

Moscow

Grand Jct.

Corinth

Tennessee R.

71

White R.

86

85

Tuscumeia

66

Decatur

Arkansas R.

64

Tupelo

64

Grenada

64

Mississippi R.

Winona

Columbus

Artesia

64

85

64

Marion
Jct.

Canton

Gainesville

Gainesville Jct.

65

Newbern

Marion

83

82

Monroe

98

Vicksburg

Bolton

McDowell's Bluff

64

82

83

82

DeSoto

89

89

Meridian

82

Cahaba

90

Raymond

Jackson

89

Reagan

83

Grand Gulf

89

81

Demopolis

Selma

113

Port
Gibson

Uniontown

Tombigbee R.

Alexandria

88

Alabama R.

Pollard

99

64

62

Woodville

Spring Hill

63

Tensas

56

95

Clinton

Bayou Sara

96

88

Mobile

Pensacola

Grosse Tete

Port Hudson

Baton
Rouge

97

91

92

Brashear

94

Algiers

93

New Orleans

Proctorville

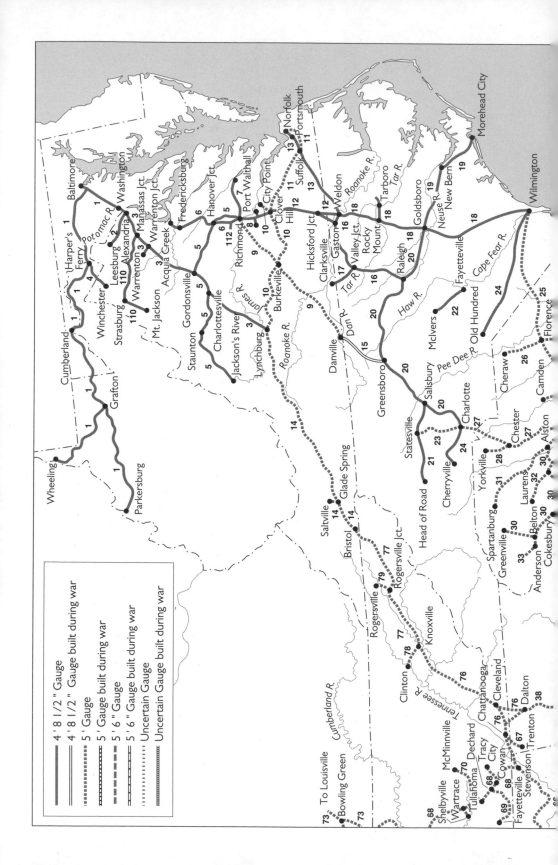

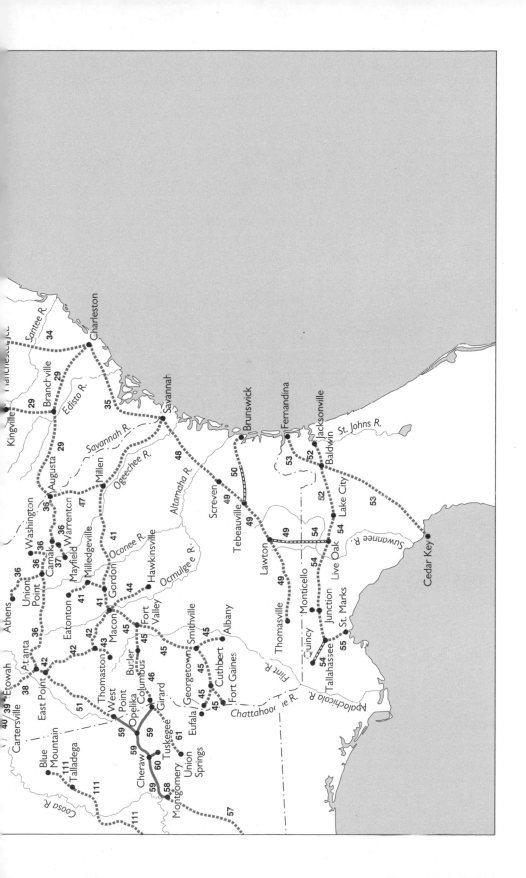

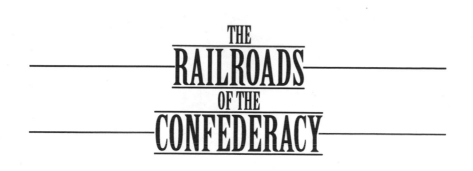

THE
RAILROADS
OF THE
CONFEDERACY

CHAPTER

~ 1 ~

Railroads through Dixie

"We know of no surer indication of the wealth and
enterprise of any people, than the extent of their railways."—J. D. B. DeBow.

UPON A BRISK AFTERNOON IN JANUARY, 1860, THE LITTLE TOWN
of Winona, Carroll County, Mississippi, found itself the scene of
unwonted activity. A murmur of excited talk rose from a crowd
of seven hundred people. The discord of an amateur brass band
echoed along the muddy streets, punctuated at intervals by the
hooting of locomotive whistles.

The occasion for all this was not, as might have been supposed,
a political canvass. This time Winona was celebrating the completion of the Mississippi Central Railroad, an event of no ordinary
significance to itself and to the back-country farmers of the region.
Following the driving of the last spike by the new company's
president, Mr. Walter Goodman, the music crashed on for hours,
and, before the ceremonies were pronounced at an end, the on-
lookers had partaken of "288 bottles of sparkling champagne, besides several barrels of other drink." [1]

Winona could face the morrow's headaches with stoicism. Cut
off for decades from the outside world, its citizenry had often cast
envious glances at the more fortunate planters of the Delta, whose
Father of Waters provided transportation as well as inundation. But
now the back country had its own route to New Orleans and the
sparkling Gulf beyond. Iron rails would furnish a royal highway
for King Cotton, and soon would make of rustic Winona another
Natchez. Nor was Winona alone in the contemplation of such

I

happy prospects. Everywhere through the Southern States men in frockcoats were discussing with animation the latest railroad project, or were toasting, with the best of Bourbon whiskey, the completion of a new link to prosperity. Spurred on by a growing sense of southern economic nationalism, but most of all by a simple desire to reduce shipping charges, southern leaders found themselves, early in 1860, in the midst of a well-matured railroad boom.

The possibilities of the steam locomotive had been early appreciated south of the Potomac and the Ohio,[2] but the Slave States had lagged conspicuously behind the North in its exploitation, and railway construction, upon an extensive scale, had failed to get underway until the decade of the fifties. But thereafter new lines etched their way across the spaces of the southern map so rapidly as to constitute a revolution.

The best-qualified observers did not know in 1860 exactly how many miles of primitive track curved across the American scene. The surviving reports everywhere show discrepancies. But upon one point they were agreed: the *relative* increase in railroad mileage between 1850 and 1860 was somewhat greater in the South than in the North. Where New England's lines reported a sturdy enough growth of 50 per cent and the system of the Middle Atlantic States was also doubled, the trackage of the South Atlantic States more than tripled, from 1,650 miles at the end of 1851 to 5,400 miles on January 1, 1861. More startling still was the growth announced for the Gulf region, new construction over the decade just ended having raised its mileage from 290 to 2,063. Most surprising of all were the statements coming from the South Interior States, where 55 miles of iron had grown to 2,666 in ten years. Only in the rapidly developing American "Northwest" could these figures be exceeded: here an already auspicious marriage of prairie and iron horse had proved so fruitful that 1,235 miles of line had swelled to an astonishing total of 10,333 on the eve of the Civil War. All in all, during the nervous decade between 1850 and 1860 some 22,000 miles of new railroad track had been traced across the face of America, nearly 7,000 of which was located within the seceding states—a respectable showing in view of a northern superiority in population of more than two to one.[3]

That the Cotton Kingdom was already well across the threshold of the railroad age was jubilantly announced by the New Orleans business journalist J. D. B. DeBow in May, 1860, when he reported that the South, including Missouri and Kentucky, contained 745 more miles of railroad than did Great Britain.[4] But figures based upon comparative mileage by no means told the whole story. Though the Southern States, in January, 1861, could claim an estimated railway mileage of 8,783 of a country-wide total of 31,168, the whole extent of southern iron, rolling stock, and other appurtenances reflected a *capital investment* of but $237,138,482, as compared with a national figure of $1,177,993,818. And Britain, whose railway development the incipient Confederacy was reputed to have surpassed so handsomely, had devoted an even larger sum to its "permanent way" and equipment. Comparisons of this kind should have served to dampen somewhat the enthusiasm of men like DeBow.[5]

Within the Southern States themselves, trackage was by no means spread evenly from the Potomac to the Rio Grande, nor was it everywhere of equal capacity. Herein time and history had played a part, but geography had played even more. Along the Atlantic coast the numerous rivers, often swift-running in their passage from the mountains to the sea, had never served as really satisfactory channels of trade. Thus it was hardly surprising that this region should display a relatively high degree of railway development. By 1861 Virginia led all of the Southern States in point of mileage. To be sure, the estuary system of the Chesapeake continued to provide transportation routes of local importance. But inland from the rapids of the James beside Richmond and the hills that hemmed in Alexandria, the Old Dominion reported a rail system of more than 1,800 miles. Second among the states of the coming Confederacy stood Georgia, with about 1,400. Even South Carolina could point to a mileage of nearly 1,000. Only North Carolina lagged somewhat; though they nursed ambitious projects, Tarheels had completed less than 900 miles of iron upon the outbreak of the War Between the States.[6]

If the Atlantic strip had wrestled for decades with inadequate rivers, the South that rimmed the Gulf enjoyed one of the finest systems of natural waterways in the world. This contrast in fluvial geography was nowhere better reflected than in railroad statistics. At a time when the cramped borders of South Carolina contained 1,000 miles of track, the much larger states of Alabama and Mississippi possessed, respectively, 643 and 797. Louisiana could boast of a mere 328, exceeding by but a single mile the figure for half-explored Florida. Less evidence still of the steam locomotive was to be seen in Arkansas and Texas. Very exceptional among the western states of the South was Tennessee, which, in January, 1861, claimed a surprising total of 1,284 miles of completed line.[7]

Even more varied was the picture in terms of capital investment. As might have been expected, the companies of Virginia, the leading southern state in point of mileage, represented the heaviest monetary outlay in the South—$69,580,696. But the railroad trackage and equipment of Georgia, the state next in rank, had absorbed only $27,632,690. Tennessee, plagued over a great part of its extent by tablelands and mountains, had spent close to $31,000,000 for its system of less than 1,300 miles. Without mountains Mississippi's 798 miles of iron had cost $22,986,370. In terms of capital investment per line mile, the leading southern state was swamp-bound Louisiana, with an average figure of $40,223. Virginia followed with $38,548. Next came Texas with a mean expenditure of $31,186 per mile; Mississippi with $28,841; and Alabama with $26,845. Tennessee had spent a trifle less than $24,000 per mile of track. The figures for the others declined variously, reaching $19,709 for Georgia, and, for thrifty North Carolina, an absolute low of $19,161.[8]

Of particular interest was the contrast between these data and the statistics of certain northern states. By 1861 the hills of Massachusetts were seamed by 1,314 miles of railroad of a book value of $45,500 per mile. New York had invested no less than $52,000 in each mile of its impressive network of 2,809 miles. The water-gaps of Pennsylvania cradled nearly 3,000 miles of iron, reportedly worth $151,529,629, a per-mile investment only a little less than that of New York. Even in Illinois, whose open spaces had invited so prodigious an extension of track during the preceding decade, existing companies had absorbed a respectable capital of $36,000 per mile. Against figures like these, the increasingly elaborate railroad map of Dixie lost something of its promise, and intelligent southerners had to admit privately that the Yankees, in quality of right of way and rolling stock, had far surpassed them.[9]

Nor had the Southern States achieved, on the eve of secession, any real trunk lines. What seemed at first a fairly well-developed railway system dissolved upon closer scrutiny into mere fragments. Many companies had been intended to serve only as feeders to some established waterway, or as routes of local trade. Even where, as in Georgia and Virginia, promoters dreamed of connections to the "Western Waters," the routes actually completed were frequently a nondescript sequence of separate roads. As late as the Confederate period, the average southern main stem seldom exceeded a length of 200 miles; the longest line under the control of a single company was that of the Mobile & Ohio, running from Mobile to Columbus, Kentucky, a distance of 469 miles. Even this was not completed until shortly after the outbreak of hostilities in 1861.[10]

Yet it was possible in 1861 to trace through the South the outlines of two major railroad routes, one complete, the other unfinished. In general they followed a basic southwest-to-northeast pattern imposed by the Appalachian Mountains. As indicated upon the accompanying sketch map, the southwestern terminus of the system lay in Mississippi and Louisiana; the northeastern anchor was Richmond, Virginia. The first of these lines involved a northerly passage through Corinth, Chattanooga, and Bristol; the second, and unfinished, route ran via Montgomery, Atlanta, Augusta, Wilmington, and Petersburg.[11] (Map on next page.)

Wandering in this fashion across the face of the South, these two "main" railway routes were only twice connected by lateral lines. The Mobile & Ohio Railroad joined Mobile and Meridian with the Memphis & Charleston road at Corinth, Mississippi, an obscure little town of which the world was presently to hear a great deal. In northwestern Georgia, where the Appalachian ranges sank briefly into low swells, the state-owned-and-operated Western & Atlantic linked Atlanta to Chattanooga. However, an important series of companies—the Macon & Western, the Central Railroad of Georgia, the Charleston & Savannah, and the Northeastern—did afford an alternate route east of Atlanta as far as Florence, South Carolina, by way of Macon, Savannah, and Charleston. Another by-pass, involving the South Carolina, the Charlotte & South Carolina, the North Carolina, and the Raleigh & Gaston roads, was available between Augusta and Weldon, North Carolina, by way of Columbia, Charlotte, and Raleigh. Equally important to the southern railroad picture was the Nashville & Chattanooga, which, in conjunction with the Louisville & Nashville, provided a route to Louisville and

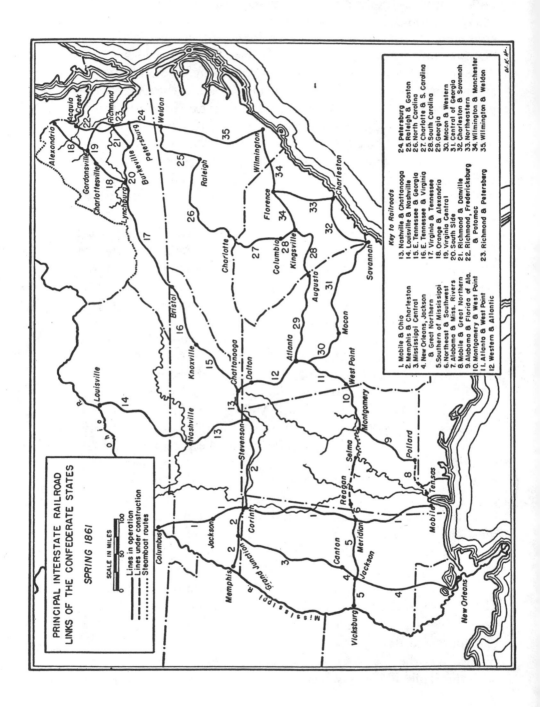

PRINCIPAL INTERSTATE RAILROAD
LINKS OF THE CONFEDERATE STATES

SPRING 1861

SCALE IN MILES

———— Lines in operation
—·—·— Lines under construction
·········· Steamboat routes

Key to Railroads

1. Mobile & Ohio
2. Memphis & Charleston
3. Mississippi Central
4. New Orleans, Jackson & Great Northern
5. Southern of Mississippi
6. Northeast & Southwest
7. Alabama & Miss. Rivers
8. Mobile & Great Northern
9. Alabama & Florida of Ala.
10. Montgomery & West Point
11. Atlanta & West Point
12. Western & Atlantic
13. Nashville & Chattanooga
14. Louisville & Nashville
15. E. Tennessee & Georgia
16. E. Tennessee & Virginia
17. Virginia & Tennessee
18. Orange & Alexandria
19. Virginia Central
20. South Side
21. Richmond & Danville
22. Richmond, Fredericksburg & Potomac
23. Richmond & Petersburg
24. Petersburg
25. Raleigh & Gaston
26. North Carolina
27. Charlotte & S. Carolina
28. South Carolina
29. Georgia
30. Macon & Western
31. Central of Georgia
32. Charleston & Savannah
33. Northeastern
34. Wilmington & Manchester
35. Wilmington & Weldon

the North. In northern Virginia the Richmond, Fredericksburg & Potomac and the Virginia Central–Orange & Alexandria combination furnished rail outlets to the Potomac, at Acquia Creek and Alexandria respectively.

In the western marches of the Cotton Kingdom, beyond the Mississippi, the only railroads were scattered and local. From Algiers and DeSoto, opposite, respectively, New Orleans and Vicksburg, two short lines with long names struggled hopefully toward the sunset; these were the New Orleans, Opelousas & Great Western, and the Vicksburg, Shreveport & Texas. With the coming of the war the former found itself at Brashear, a scant eighty miles from Algiers; the latter had only just reached Monroe, not halfway across upper Louisiana; both floundered equally in the swampy environment; nor was either to attain trunk-line status for many years.[12]

Along the river itself existed certain stray threads of track, of which nothing ever came. Only in Texas, whose terrain distinctly favored the locomotive over the steamboat, did the immediate future seem promising. Trackage already radiated from Houston like the spokes of a wheel, and additional construction was being pushed with much frontier enthusiasm and bombast. "The fact stands out plainly," exulted the Houston *Telegraph*, "that Houston is inevitably the railroad centre of Texas . . . a union depot is now talked of, and it would be well if the Harrisburg Company would allow the mists of local prejudice, that obstruct their mental vision, to clear off and view this matter in its proper light. A terminus here will be desirable in twelve months for their road. . ."[13] To which the "Harrisburg Company," more specifically the Buffalo Bayou, Brazos & Colorado, retorted in kind, many of its backers being Galvestonians. But such interurban squabbles served only to strengthen Texan optimism; local estimates of the railroad mileage within the state as of January 1, 1861, characteristically stretched the contemporary New York quotation from 328 to 399.[14]

Florida, like Texas, was still a frontier region, but, also like Texas, it contained a growing little system of roads, quite cut off from those of other states. Here in early 1861 the tracks of two companies were about to connect Jacksonville with Tallahassee, while the last spikes were being driven upon the Florida Railroad, joining Fernandina with Cedar Keys.[15] Already steps were being taken to bridge the flatwoods which separated these Florida projects from the nearest railroad in southern Georgia.

Everywhere through Dixie the railroad mania ran at flood tide. During the final ante-bellum year the forests of the Appalachians swarmed with surveyors and engineers as the states of the Atlantic seaboard strove to burst through their ancient mountain barriers. In addition to steady progress upon a long-anticipated road from Covington to the Ohio, Virginia had grading parties scattered along the famous route through Cumberland Gap, while her existing Richmond & Danville road had announced that it would embark upon a grandiose extension in the same direction.[16] In the Carolinas, dreams were more Olympian still. The Western North Carolina Railroad, a rustic carrier wandering westward through the Piedmont hills from Salisbury, proposed to assault the Blue Ridge in its most formidable portion.[17] Further to the south, the Spartanburg & Union and the Blue Ridge Railroad were considering other lines through skyland.[18] New schemes in Georgia attempted nothing so spacious, but a flurry of construction was going forward in the interior of the state. Florida dreamed of a complete line across her northern tier from Jacksonville to Mobile, while the swamps and savannahs of the half-explored peninsula already were ringing with axe and shovel as an extension of the Florida Railroad pushed southward toward Tampa Bay.[19] The Alabama Assembly of 1859-60 spewed railroad incorporation acts, while grading parties were making the dirt fly in many parts of that state.[20] The construction frenzy in Tennessee showed few signs of abating; in the spring of 1861 the finishing touches were being put upon exciting new links between Nashville and Memphis, and between Memphis and Louisville, and two or three companies asserted their intention of cutting boldly across the topographic grain of the Knoxville region.[21] In Mississippi the New Orleans, Jackson & Great Northern, in operation since 1858 over the 206 miles between New Orleans and Canton, now was pushing its roadbed toward Aberdeen and a connection with the Mobile and Ohio.[22]

But the construction boom had not yet produced in the Southern States a *system* of iron rails. Even the isolation of the Texas and Florida [23] roads did not tell the whole story. Serious gaps yawned elsewhere in the midst of what should have been continuous lines. Between Danville, Virginia, and Greensboro, North Carolina, a potential route through the Piedmont was broken sharply by a fifty-mile intermission, for the existence of which the narrow economic policy of certain North Carolinians was responsible.[24] Below Charlotte no direct line to Atlanta existed. The incomplete nature of the route across central Alabama already has been noted; Selma and Montgomery would remain unconnected, save by river, until 1870. An ambitious little road, the Alabama & Tennessee Rivers, extended northeastward from Selma, skirted a broken region known vaguely to contain coal seams, but had not yet achieved union with existing trackage in upper Georgia.[25] Everywhere through Dixie railroads were stretching iron fingers toward one another, but not yet everywhere had they joined hands.

More unsatisfactory still was the situation at a number of junction points. Even where roads possessed a common gauge (which was not always the case), their rails frequently enjoyed no physical contact. Though this was due in part to the inability of early promoters to foresee the advantages of integrated transportation service, the ridiculous practice had been often retained through the influence of teamster interests. In Virginia their efforts had produced a law which prohibited any railroad from laying its track in the avenues of a city without the express consent of its corporate authorities,[26] and as late as 1861 local liverymen had prevented the intersection of *any* of the five railroads entering Richmond. At Petersburg all north-south traffic was obliged to move painfully by horse-drawn vehicle through the streets.[27]

A similarly irritating prospect awaited the traveler at Augusta, Georgia, where the South Carolina and Georgia railroads remained unjoined to the Augusta & Savannah, though separated by a gap of only six hundred yards.[28] The entire width of the spacious city of Savannah intervened between the respective termini of the Central of Georgia and the Savannah, Albany & Gulf road.[29] Primarily because of bridging difficulties, the newly completed Charleston & Savannah abruptly ended on the river bank opposite Charleston, whence it conveyed passengers and freight to the city by wheezing ferry boat.[30] The two roads entering Montgomery, Alabama, were separated not only by a difference in gauge, but by a trek of several blocks across an area of bottomland, often inundated.

In the matter of gauge the southern carriers seem to have been little, if any, worse off than the roads north of the Potomac. A width of five feet was customary and remained so until the mid-eighties. Only in Virginia and North Carolina was the future standard gauge of four feet, eight and one-half inches commonly used, and even here the Virginia lines operating *east and west through the region south of the James*, together with at least three North Carolina companies, had adopted the conventional width of five feet.[31] The whole of Georgia, South Carolina, and Florida conformed to the southern norm, as did Tennessee and practically all of Mississippi. In Alabama, however, the Montgomery & West Point had been built to the four-foot, eight-and-one-half-inch gauge. But the situation did not become really kaleidoscopic until one crossed the Mississippi River. Here the New Orleans, Opelousas & Great Western, the Memphis & Little Rock, and the Vicksburg, Shreveport & Texas were constructed to an expansive standard of five feet, six inches. Some of the lesser enterprises of Louisiana, on the other hand, had utilized the conservative English measure of four feet, eight and one-half inches. In Texas there was a tendency toward the greater widths, but the Buffalo Bayou, Brazos & Colorado and the Houston Tap & Brazoria preferred the British gauge. Differences of this character were less felt, however, in a region of scattered railroads than they were further east.[32]

Though not so frequent as at times they have been pictured, these differences in the width of southern trackage were sufficiently disruptive. The common gauge of all the roads connecting Richmond with New Orleans by way of Knoxville and Chattanooga afforded, to be sure, a route of distinct promise. But elsewhere, most long-haul traffic had to be unloaded from cars of one standard and reloaded into cars of another. The ultimate in this kind of stupidity was furnished by the Roanoke Valley Railroad, a short line located primarily in southern Virginia. Under construction at the outbreak of the war, its two disconnected segments were actually being built to *two different gauges*. How the last spike of this hopeful project was to be driven, the management failed to explain.[33]

Such was the railroad system, if system it can be called, that was carried out of the American Union by the secession movement of 1860-61. Although it was rapidly growing, the traits of infancy still lay heavy upon it. A series of minor roads, constantly interrupted by differences of gauge or by sheer absence of physical connection, it presented but the shadow of the main lines of the future. The people of Winona, Mississippi, might gather in the January sunshine and toast the completion of the Mississippi Central, but the whole fabric of the Cotton Kingdom's transportation network remained unfinished.

CHAPTER

2

Of Tracks and Trains

I

IN COMMON WITH PIONEER LINES IN MANY PARTS OF THE UNITED
States, the railroads of the South were constructed through regions
that were still sparsely settled and would afford at first only a light
traffic. For this reason the southern carriers of 1861 were, with few
exceptions, lightly, if not carelessly, built. In an age without dyna-
mite, heavy grading was avoided wherever possible, and the typical
railroad of the Confederacy was carried upon the thinnest practicable embankment of raw earth. In level country a line was constructed as tangent; when it encountered hills, as in the Piedmont
region, it ran around them in a series of violent curves. In swampy
areas, very common near the coasts, the track was carried forward
occasionally upon dirt fills, but more often upon pile trestle work of
the crudest sort. Such a badly drained environment often involved
a more costly right of way than a hilly one; President John Screven
of the Atlantic & Gulf road in south Georgia complained in the
spring of 1861 that the excessive amount of trestle construction
upon his line was already becoming "an increasing source of ex-
hausting expense." [1] Stone or gravel ballast was seldom used. An
exception was the Virginia & Tennessee, which had embarked upon
an enterprising program that specified a layer of ballast beneath
every rail joint.[2] But nearly everywhere else the ties were laid with
little ceremony upon a base of native earth, and little effort was
expended upon drainage beyond the simplest kind of ditching.

Bridges were normally no more than elaborated wooden trestles
of spindly appearance and, occasionally, of terrifying height. Sometimes they were provided with stone abutments, sometimes not.

In the more important structures, the Howe Truss design was very popular. But even here the material used was timber, not iron, and nearly all the railroad bridges of the Confederacy were thus highly susceptible to serious damage either by freshet or by fire.

Raw material for crossties grew abundantly in the monotony of pine and oak and gum that bordered nearly every right-of-way. The cutting process, however, was expensive, being little mechanized, and the climate was not conducive to a long life for ties in the track. Virgil Powers, superintendent of the Macon & Western, reported shortly before the war that the life of ties on his road averaged only five years, as against eight or ten in colder climates.[3] Southern ties naturally varied in quality; among the best were those placed in the track of the New Orleans, Opelousas & Great Western; hewn from local cypress, they were 11 feet in length, or double the gauge of the road, and 12 inches in width. They were reported to have improved the road greatly.[4]

In 1861 the rail laid in southern track was commonly of rolled wrought-iron "T" section, varying in length from about 18 feet to 24 feet, or more, and weighing from 35 to 68 pounds to the yard.[5] Although such rail possessed neither the strength nor the stamina of the 110-150-pound steel rail of today, it did possess the advantage of being suitable for re-rolling, following which it could be returned to the track. But under conditions of heavy traffic, wrought-iron rail became seriously worn in less than a decade.[6]

"T" bar was not universal, however. Vestiges of a cruder era survived here and there in the form of "strap," "U," and "flanged" rail. The first was characteristic of the earliest years of American railroading and consisted merely of a thin iron strap, affixed along the upper surface of a "stringer" of wood. "U" and "flanged" rail were little more than sophisticated variations of the first and were likewise commonly attached to wooden stringers. By 1861 archaic track of this kind was largely relegated to sidings and similar structures, but it lingered here and there upon important main lines. Eleven and three-quarters miles of the Richmond, Fredericksburg & Potomac were of the strap variety, as were 41½ miles of the Richmond & Danville. Light "U" section upon stringers was the curse of 39 of the 151 miles of the Nashville & Chattanooga. Ten miles of similar road persisted upon the Georgia Railroad as late as 1859, while a goodly proportion of the Montgomery & West Point

consisted of stringer construction. Strap rail was especially susceptible to breakage, weighing only 18 to 24 pounds to the yard; "U"
rail seems to have averaged much heavier, attaining the respectable
weight of 60 pounds in the sidings of the Virginia & Tennessee, but
it frequently gave trouble by getting out of alignment. "T" bar had
thoroughly proved its superiority over the other types by 1861, and
the plans of every southern road called for its exclusive use in principal track as soon as possible.[7]

Photographs of the period indicate that the rails were spiked
directly to the ties without benefit of tie plates. At the joints they
were not connected, as today, by angle bars, but by a curious device called a "chair." This fastening of the sixties resembled the
chairs characteristic of present British railway practice, except that
the use of American chairs was confined to the rail joints and did
not serve primarily to fasten the rails to the ties. Chairs placed in
the track of the Macon & Western in 1859 were of "wrought iron
. . . weighing 12 lbs. each, and rolled to fit closely the tread of the
rail, making a firm, smooth joint."[8]

Up to 1861 freight and passenger traffic was insufficient to justify
double-tracking. Nor were the sidings, or "turnouts," as they still
were called, either numerous or extensive. On the Virginia & Tennessee, perhaps the most progressive carrier below the Potomac, a
main stem of 204 miles between Lynchburg and Bristol was served
by less than 10 miles of siding, a figure that included *all* yard facilities; and although its trains could pass at 35 points, the trackage
provided for the purpose averaged only about 900 feet in length.
The statistics for other roads reflect similar conditions. The Atlantic
& North Carolina, with 95 miles of line, possessed less than seven
miles of spur, yard, and passing track. For the 271 miles of the Memphis & Charleston, the siding figure was 20 miles. The Richmond,
Fredericksburg & Potomac reported less than five miles of secondary roadway for a main stem of 75 miles. Eight miles of subsidiary
iron were deemed enough for the nearly 200 miles of principal track
of the Nashville & Chattanooga. Everywhere in the Confederacy
the data for secondary track stood in awkward contrast to the
similar figures quoted for some of the northern carriers.[9]

Generally speaking, the investment in track materials represented
about one quarter of the usual construction expense. During the
year ending July 31, 1861, the Atlantic & Gulf, then building across

the easy distances of southwest Georgia, expended $922,839.43 upon grading, crossties, track-laying, and the like, while the bill for rails, chairs, and spikes amounted to $521,737.90. New wrought-iron rails were priced locally at about $50.00 per ton, spikes at three cents per pound. In north Georgia ties were to be had for forty cents each; in Virginia the cost was slightly higher.[10] But almost without exception the characteristic element was cheapness of construction; almost nowhere in Dixie did railway trackage exist that could be described by that stolid British idiom, "permanent way."

II

The heart and soul of any railroad is its motive power, and much would presently depend upon the little engines that rolled over southern rails in the winter of 1861. Angular of line and fragile of mechanism, their bulbous stacks pouring forth pungent clouds of pine smoke, they still stride vividly enough through the imagination of the mid-twentieth century by virtue of woodcut and ambrotype. Moreover, contemporary railroad reports contain much information concerning them, so that even today we can derive a surprisingly satisfactory picture of the little iron horses which were among the first of their breed to go to war.

The majority of the locomotives operating over the railroads of the Confederacy were of the "American" or 4-4-0 type. That is, the weight of the smoke box, cylinders, and huge extended cow-catcher was carried upon a leading swivel-truck of four wheels, while the remaining portion of the machine was carried upon four connected drivers. As its name implied, this class of power was a distinctively American development, whose beginnings and direction were conditioned primarily by the excessive curvature of American track. By the 1850's the type had settled down to a rough standard of size and power which persisted until after the War Between the States, with the result that the locomotives of the Confederacy were all very much alike and frequently were utilized interchangeably in freight and passenger service.[11]

There were, to be sure, exceptions. The Macon & Western possessed two "singles," having a pair of driving wheels only; two others were operating on the Seaboard & Roanoke. Upon the mountainous portion of the Virginia Central labored two special units having six drivers each; the Virginia & Tennessee owned four of similar type, plus a hissing leviathan boasting no less than *eight* driving wheels.[12]

It should not be imagined that anything approaching standardization or interchangeability of parts existed. Cylinder measurements, the size of drivers, boiler diameter, dimensions of firebox, gross weight, all were subject to a good deal of variation. Cylinders perhaps averaged 14 inches in diameter, with a stroke of about 22 inches. Driving wheels normally were between four and five feet in diameter, with a tendency toward the lower figure in mountainous districts and upon freight locomotives. Differences were greatest in the matter of weight. Power on the Virginia Central varied from 15 to 31 tons, on the Virginia & Tennessee from 23 to 33 tons, on the Seaboard & Roanoke from 9 to 22 tons. In Georgia the engines of the Macon & Western ranged from 14 to 25 tons; the engines of the Savannah, Albany & Gulf from 18 to 23.[13] These little locomotives may have looked alike, but their details were apt to be as individual as the names which shone so gaudily along their footrails.

Naming, incidentally, was the principal method of engine designation, not numbering. It was a picturesque practice, and served to bestow upon the units concerned a charming individuality. The names of states or of geographical features seem to have been especially popular. Many times, no doubt, the Louisiana stood wreathed in steam upon a Central of Georgia siding, as the Arkansas blasted by with ten or fifteen carloads of cotton. On the newly completed Charleston & Savannah the sharp wail of the Coosawhatchie, running easily along with a stubby passenger train, rang among the cypress swamps, while on the Nashville & Chattanooga the Tennessee, with sputtering valves and smoking brakes, crept down the long grade from Cowan Tunnel to the banks of its namesake river. Nearly as common were the names of men, particularly on the Georgia Central, which listed the C. T. Pollard, the W. M. Wadley, and the Isaac Scott, all of them commemorative of railroaders of local reputation. The Nashville road specialized in political figures, celebrating in gleaming brass the names of J. K. Polk, Andrew Jackson, Daniel Webster, and Henry Clay. Certain locomotives were presently to become the source of considerable embarrassment, being christened with designations like New Hampshire and United States, or even with the name of General Scott, the apostate. The time was near when these would be suitably changed to Confederate States, General Beauregard, and the like.[14]

In naming their engines, many companies freely indulged in flights of fancy. The North Carolina Railroad entered the field of Greek mythology, emerging with the Astron, the Ajax, the Cyclops, and the Midas. The Westward Ho and the Southward Ho were the pride, respectively, of the Virginia Central and the Charleston & Savannah. Picturesquely reminiscent of local scenery was the Virginia & Tennessee's Peaks of Otter. Most imaginative of all was the Flying Nelly of the Western & Atlantic, especially when its permanent assignment to switching service is considered.[15]

Though the elaborately painted driving wheels that rolled beneath the name plates appeared enormous, their actual dimensions were somewhat less than those in vogue upon modern steam passenger locomotives. Larger diameters were hardly required, for the average southern train of the sixties seldom exceeded a speed of 25 miles per hour. But the limiting factor was the track, not the locomotives; upon a line maintained to modern standards these little engines probably could have approached streamliner pace over short periods. The strength of Civil War track was seriously limited, and it curtailed, in turn, the proportions of the locomotives that were operated upon it.

Many details familiar today were absent from these engines of the sixties. No superheaters and feed-waterheaters served to eke out an extra margin of efficiency, nor were the lives of the crews made easier with power reverse gear and mechanical stokers, or safer with low-water alarms. Effete gadgets were held to a minimum. The cramped fireboxes, confined between the rear pair of driving wheels, were stoked laboriously with wood and by hand.[16] The swaying, banging tenders held little more than 1,000 gallons of water.[17] The cylinder valves, of the relatively inefficient "D" type, were commonly activated by motion of the "Stevenson Link" variety, which operated inside the frames and helped give the locomotives of the time their characteristically "clean" appearance.

Confederate railroad superintendents did not customarily measure the capabilities of their machines in terms of horsepower, or of "tractive effort at the drawbar." But a fair estimate of the abilities of Confederate locomotives can be derived from the trains they hauled, which seldom exceeded fifteen freight cars. The rolling stock of the sixties, when laden to their load limit of 16,000 pounds,[18] represented a weight of approximately 20,000 pounds, including tare, each. A train of fifteen fully laden cars would thus involve a total weight of 300,000 pounds, or 150 tons. Given such light loads as their normal operating limit, the "tractive effort" exerted could scarcely have surpassed the figure of 15,000 pounds.[19]

Typically American, even in the sixties, was the emphasis upon headlight and bell. The former represents one item of locomotalia which has not grown in stature with the years, for if the oil lamp that adorned the motive power of the Civil War was not so efficient as its electric descendant, it was incomparably more magnificent, as a glance at any engine picture of the time will show. On the other hand, of all the features of steam locomotive equipment, the bell has changed probably the least. Mechanical aid may now do its ringing, and the modern decline in human pride may have reduced its polish, but bell it essentially remains, and its presence upon a locomotive has ever been a distinguishing mark of North America.

III

Behind the engines, their link-and-pin couplers crashing and rattling, came the cars. In many respects they were very similar to their modern counterparts. This was especially true of freight equipment, for the vehicles which transported the supplies (and frequently the human reinforcements) of Braxton Bragg and Robert E. Lee resembled not a little those which only yesterday bore the raw materials for the first atomic bombs. They were smaller—it has been noted that their load limit was 16,000 pounds—and certain convenient refinements such as airbrakes and automatic couplers were conspicuous by their absence. But the differentiation of freight cars into the basic types we know today had already begun. In especially common use were boxcars (frequently called "house cars"), "platform" (i.e., flat) cars, and cars of a type we would classify as "gondola." Cattle cars had been introduced upon many roads. More exotic were the "dumping cars" of the Montgomery & West Point, described by the company as "working by cast iron arc—dumping wholeload," and the "hoisting car" in service upon the Charleston & Savannah. Specialization had proceeded upon the Savannah, Albany & Gulf, the

Montgomery & West Point, and the Seaboard & Roanoke until rolling stock was being specifically designed for maintenance service. Oddly enough, the now traditional caboose existed only locally and in rudimentary form. The Central of Georgia listed twenty-three "conductor's cars" in 1862, the Charleston & Savannah owned three, and the Montgomery & West Point, eight. But the statistics of many other roads make no mention of such equipment.[20]

The small "handcar" for routine maintenance had attained a hardly more sophisticated development. Some were propelled literally by hand. Others were pushed with poles. Still others were moved by means of a cranking device. All of them ultimately derived their motion at the expense of human sweat. But they seem to have been a more common feature of the railway than the caboose.

As might have been expected, rolling stock was constructed almost entirely of wood. Even bogie trucks were built partly of this material,[21] and metal commonly was utilized only in such appurtenances as couplers, springs, axles, and wheels. Persistent experimentation with *rubber* springs was carried on for years by the Montgomery & West Point.[22] A large proportion of the rolling stock of that road was so equipped.

It is probable that the passenger cars of the period were more crude in comparison with their modern descendants than were the freight cars. All were quite innocent of steam heat, electric lighting, or vestibules. Like the freight equipment, they were braked individually and by hand. Clouds of pitch-pine smoke, often complete with live sparks, of necessity accompanied every attempt at ventilation.

Aside from baggage, mail, and express cars (all of which were, by 1861, in common use), the passenger stock of the day was divided nearly everywhere into two classes. But the precise difference between "first-class" and "second-class" equipment is not clear from the record; nor did the passenger fares published by a wide variety of southern roads usually reflect the existence of a European stratification of railway travel. It seems probable that the second-class cars were reserved for the travel of slaves and free Negroes; but this supposition suffers embarrassment in the face of the rolling-stock statement of the North Carolina Railroad for 1860, which specified first-class, second-class and "servant's" cars.[23]

Sleeping cars, not yet in general use anywhere in the country, were almost unknown in the Slave States. In 1859 the Macon &

Western considered operating them upon night trains, but apparently never placed any in service until much later. Two sleepers, run under franchise by one E. H. Payne, were introduced upon the Memphis & Charleston during the winter of 1859-60. These were so "eagerly sought for by appreciative travelers" that the new service was expanded the following summer with a third car. The novel vehicles delighted the Memphis & Charleston. "We take pleasure," it declared, "in advertising the fact that they are conducted on a system of the most perfect propriety." The connecting Mississippi Central hastened to follow its example, placing "ELEGANT NEW SLEEPING CARS" in its night trains during the same year.[24] But nowhere else were southerners given the opportunity to enjoy the Alpine stimulation of an upper berth.

A considerable variety of motive power and rolling stock thus rattled over the rails of Dixie by 1861. But, comparatively speaking, there was not much of it. Nor was it evenly distributed. Certain companies were respectably outfitted with locomotives; others possessed so few that they hardly could risk regular operation. The most extensive collection below the Potomac was that of the South Carolina Railroad, which owned sixty-two. A close second was the Central of Georgia, with fifty-nine. The rosters of most companies were much smaller. The business of the Wilmington & Weldon was handled by twenty-three locomotives; sixteen were deemed sufficient for the traffic moving over the Orange & Alexandria. The Savannah, Albany & Gulf and the New Orleans, Opelousas & Great Western were limited to eleven engines each. At the bottom of the list were roads like the Florida, Atlantic & Gulf Central, with three, and the Macon & Brunswick, with a single unit.[25]

Southern locomotive statistics, as usual, failed to compare favorably with those of the North. The Western Railroad of Massachusetts possessed much less than half the line mileage of the Mobile & Ohio, but it owned nearly twice as many engines—seventy-two. With an equal length of line, the Marietta & Cincinnati had thirty-seven locomotives to the Virginia Central's twenty-seven. About 220 engines operated over the Pennsylvania Railroad between Philadelphia and Pittsburgh, a number greater than that of all the roads of the Commonwealth of Virginia. The number of locomotives upon the New York Central and the Erie was only slightly less.[26]

A similar story is told by the statistics for southern cars. Logically enough, those companies which owned the greatest amount of motive power also possessed the largest collection of freight and passenger equipment. Once more the South Carolina Railroad led the way with a total of 849 cars of all kinds. The Western & Atlantic listed 726. Closer to the southern average was the Southwestern with about 235. Many of the shorter roads possessed far fewer. Generally speaking, the ratio of passenger to freight equipment was low—less than 10 per cent. No southern figures, of course, could match those of the North, where the Delaware, Lackawanna & Western road alone could boast of more than 4,000 cars and where even a provincial carrier like the Michigan Central owned about 2,500.[27]

IV

Railroads have always been voracious consumers of fuel and supplies; those of the Confederacy were no exception. The items necessary to their operation, even in 1861, formed an impressive list, ranging from pig iron and spring steel to white lead, nails, varnish, and paper. Animal oils and tallow were utilized in large quantities as lubricants, for the petroleum industry had hardly made its appearance. Sperm oil fed the enormous headlights. Block tin was required for a multitude of bearings. Lumber was constantly needed at the car shops.

Every southern locomotive without exception burned wood as fuel; to this the marvelous smokestacks of the period owed their existence.[28] The cordwood stacked at intervals along every line represented, indeed, a large proportion of a carrier's running costs. The number of miles produced by the combustion of a single cord varied widely, even upon a single road, but it seems to have averaged between fifty and sixty. During the year ending September 30, 1861, the passenger engine Swiftsure of the Western & Atlantic ran 73½ miles for each cord consumed; the freight locomotive General, struggling with heavier loads, covered less than 33 miles with the same amount of fuel. The much better performance of freight power upon the Central of Georgia, often reaching 80 miles or more, was doubtless due to the easier terrain, although the results achieved upon the equally level Seaboard & Roanoke were less favorable. In any event, the money expended for wood was considerable. The Western & Atlantic purchased during its fiscal year 1861 more than

14,000 cords for a sum exceeding $26,000. The motive power of the Seaboard & Roanoke burned 1,900 cords at a cost of $4,700. The annual wood bill of the Macon & Western totaled nearly $12,000. Wood cost per engine mile varied rather widely, not only in consequence of different prices paid per cord, but because of the varying mechanical efficiency of locomotives. On the Macon & Western the figure stood in 1859 at 5.48 cents per mile. The New Orleans, Jackson & Great Northern two years later reported an average of 5.9 cents. The situation on the Southwestern road in Georgia was especially favorable; here the fuel cost per engine mile amounted to less than three cents.[29]

Locomotive wood, ordinarily, was provided by contract with local landowners. Some roads, like the Virginia & Tennessee, employed full-time agents to negotiate such agreements. It was the policy of this company to keep 30,000 cords on hand. The quality of the wood likewise had become a matter for attention. "The best wood must be carefully selected for the passenger trains," ran a rule of the South Carolina Railroad, "and the attendant must not allow it to be used for freight trains." Nor were the quantities to be secured from contractors, at reasonable prices, always dependable. By February, 1861, the Charleston & Savannah had deliberately purchased 6,713 acres of timberland, so that it might, if necessary, be independent of wood sellers. "There are railways in the South," commented its management, "which, in default of this foresight, have to employ wood trains to haul their wood from distances sometimes as far as 70 miles from their Depots." [30]

Fuel was a local product; it existed in the form of growing timber along nearly every southern right-of-way. Not so the hundred-odd other items of railroad supply. The rails which wound through the red oxide hills of the Carolina Piedmont were the product of the Yankee Adirondacks. Their fastenings were the issue, not of Birmingham, Alabama (no such municipality existed in 1861), but of Birmingham, Warwickshire. Locomotives from New Jersey, whale oil from New Bedford, boiler tubes from Pittsburgh—of such origin was the greater portion of southern railroad material on the eve of the Civil War.

There were exceptions to this rule, but they were so few as to be conspicuous. The famous Tredegar Iron Works at Richmond, Virginia, were capable of fulfilling almost any kind of metallurgical need. Under the management of Joseph Reid Anderson they already had manufactured more than forty locomotives. Further west, the Nashville Manufacturing Company had produced a scattering of engines in the early fifties. In Augusta, Georgia, the Forest City Foundry specialized in railroad car castings and possessed a capacity of fifty car wheels per day. The Atlanta Rolling Mill was especially adapted to the rolling of rail. Near Cartersville, Georgia, the Etowah Iron Works could boast of two pig iron furnaces, one rolling mill, and a nail factory; they not only could provide railroad bar iron, but represented the only facility south of Richmond capable of turning

Typical Confederate motive power, the American-Type locomotive Allegheny of the Virginia Central Railroad. Built in Richmond by the Tredegar Iron Works in 1856. Weight, without tender, 22½ tons. Diameter of drivers, 66 inches. Used in passenger and mail service throughout the War Between the States. Reproduced from an illustration in Kathleen Bruce, *Virginia Iron Manufacture in the Slave Era* (New York, The Century Company, 1931), taken in turn from a catalogue of the Tredegar Iron Works, Richmond, 1860.

out car axles. At Independence, Louisiana, a short distance north of New Orleans, the establishment of Gaston T. Raoul was building rolling stock upon a considerable scale.[31]

There likewise existed a scattering of minor facilities, which could be converted to light manufacture. Every railroad of consequence possessed locomotive and car shops for maintenance purposes, and these were capable of supplying a certain amount of new production. Indeed, a few southern roads had actually built, upon their own premises, a number of locomotives. The Richmond, Fredericksburg & Potomac had produced three such engines during the preceding decade. Early in 1859 the "firstclass passenger engine *Jno. McFar-land*" had emerged from the shops of the Richmond & Danville. The Montgomery & West Point had completed the previous year a single freight locomotive, which was appropriately christened the Native. Home-built motive power on the Central of Georgia had proved so successful that President R. R. Cuyler informed his stockholders in December, 1860, that it was "the aim of the President and Superintendent to avoid all purchases of these articles in the future." The latest product of the Central's shops, the 25-ton Thomas Purse, had attracted especially enthusiastic comment; the Savannah *Republican* noted that it embraced "several improvements, such as self-oiling its eccentrics, oiling of steam chests, opening and closing of cylinder cocks, all at the command of the engineer, while the machine is in motion, and thereby not endangering the lives of his assistants." Furthermore, it was "splendidly embellished with oil paintings of the Goddess of Liberty, views of the Savannah Exchange, embarkation of the Savannah Blues, etc., with two excellent portraits of the worthy citizen for whom the engine is named [a railroad director], all showing a high order of the fine arts." [32]

Many roads were building their own cars. From the shops of the South Side Company in Virginia came an especially impressive output, including passenger coaches, a baggage car, flat cars, box cars, and dump cars; the company also was experimenting with a new design of four-wheel truck with rubber springs. At Richmond the Virginia Central was evolving interesting plans for the production of all of its rolling stock. The Central of Georgia had completed a similar program. The Memphis & Charleston was erecting new shops at Huntsville, Alabama, and had announced its intention of building its own freight equipment thereafter. Most advanced of all was the Montgomery & West Point; *all* the cars belonging to that company had been manufactured in its shops at Montgomery, Alabama. As Professor Milton S. Heath has pointed out, the productive capacity of southern railroad-shop facilities in 1861 was very considerable and has heretofore been "almost entirely overlooked." [33]

But even the Central of Georgia shops represented nothing more than a series of assembly operations; there remained the question of where basic castings were to come from in the event the Southern States should find themselves isolated from the North, or from Europe. Furthermore, if the manufacturing potential of the infant Confederacy was scarcely adequate for the proper maintenance of its railroad system, what was to be the basis of production for purely military needs? In short, would the Tredegar and Etowah works prove themselves capable of supplying both rolling stock and guns?

CHAPTER

3

Of Men and Methods

"The General Superintendent, in preparing these
rules, would appeal to the manliness and gentlemanly
feeling of everyone in the Company's service under
his direction."—H. T. Peake of the South Carolina
Railroad in the preface to his company's book of
rules.
"The President and Directors should let it be understood that as far as it is practicable a preference shall
be given to native labor and talent in this great work
built by home labor and worked by home men."
—Report of Committee of Inspection, *Annual Report*, North Carolina Railroad, July 12, 1860.

I

JOHN S. BARBOUR, JR., WAS AN ARISTOCRAT. ERECT, SIX FEET IN
height, with severely chiseled features, graying hair, and sparkling
brown eyes, he looked the Virginia country gentleman that he was.
Born in Culpeper County of a family which long had been on terms
of social intimacy with Jeffersons, Madisons, and Lees, his first memories had been of the belling of foxhounds and of the distant hori-
zons of the Blue Ridge. His education had been the best the Old
Dominion could offer. He had suitably honored tradition by preparing himself for the bar. He was a dignified yet kindly man, and he
found early acceptance as a leader, socially, professionally, and po-
litically. A Democrat in the Jeffersonian rather than the Jacksonian
sense, he had served in the Virginia House of Delegates through
four consecutive sessions. Before his death he was to achieve the un-

26

questioned leadership of the Virginia Democracy and membership in both houses of the United States Congress. In 1861, forty-one years of age, he had been, for a decade, president of the Orange & Alexandria Railroad.[1]

As a railroad official, John S. Barbour, Jr., was hardly a unique phenomenon. Several railroad officers of the Confederate period could boast of similar background. Distinctly blue blood flowed through the veins of Edmund Fontaine of the Virginia Central. The lately deceased father of Peter V. Daniel, Jr., of the Richmond, Fredericksburg & Potomac, had sat upon the Supreme Court of the United States; the better local genealogies were crowded with Daniels, and Peter V., the younger, was a lawyer of recognized ability. John M. Robinson, superintendent of the Seaboard & Roanoke, was the son of Moncure Robinson, whose business successes alone could not have produced the carte blanche he held to Richmond drawing rooms. In North Carolina, William Shepperd Ashe of the Wilmington & Weldon came of a family which already had been enshrined in the name of the principal town of the lower Appalachians. The president of the Central of Georgia, Richard R. Cuyler, hailed similarly from the acceptable side of his tracks, and dwelt upon a beautifully situated plantation on the outskirts of Savannah.

But alongside the aristocrats were a number of self-made men of superior capacity. Perhaps the best known of these was the president of the Norfolk & Petersburg, William Mahone; of plain ancestry, his abilities were found, before the end of a fabulous career, to embrace not merely railroading, but military and political leadership as well. Among the slash pines of northern Florida, the iron of the Florida Railroad was presided over by a politician of the first magnitude, Senator David Levy Yulee. Conspicuous among the promoters of the New Orleans, Jackson & Great Northern had been Yulee's colleague, Judah P. Benjamin. Ablest railroad man of all was rugged, hard-working William M. Wadley, who was engaged early in 1861 in the construction of the Southern Railroad of Mississippi and the Vicksburg, Shreveport & Texas. He was to play an important role among the carriers of the Confederacy.

Except for a few outstanding figures like these, the human side of Confederate railroading at the outbreak of the War Between the States is difficult to reconstruct. For the day of the Confederacy was a period wherein railroad companies frequently chose not to publish information concerning their officers and employees; no railroad labor organization yet existed, and surviving statistics deal more often with the specifications of locomotives than with the personalities of the shadowy men who ran them.

A number of officials were northerners. Among them was Wadley, who had come to Georgia as a young man from New Hampshire. Another was Superintendent H. D. Whitcomb of the Virginia Central. S. L. Fremont, superintendent of the Wilmington & Weldon, was likewise a northerner by birth, but he had lived in North Carolina for most of his adult life, and he was soon to devote his engineering training to the construction of Confederate fortifications about Wilmington. Another Yankee turned southerner was G. W. R. Bayley of the New Orleans, Opelousas & Great Western. Less amenable, apparently, to the Confederacy were the officers of the Alexandria, Loudoun & Hampshire, who were accused in November, 1861, of being "worse than so many full-blood Yankees." [2]

Of the origins and sympathies of the rank and file much less is known. A heavy proportion had come from the North, but many of these were of an independent, roving character, wedded to their craft and utterly indifferent to political questions. It does not seem that they "went North" in very large numbers at the outbreak of hostilities. On the contrary, there exists much evidence that the railroad men of the Confederacy were as loyal to the cause of the South as any other similar element of the population.

Whatever the backgrounds of its officers and employees, the personnel organization of the average southern railway company reflected rudiments of modern practice. The Virginia & Tennessee, for example, employed a president, a general superintendent, a resident engineer, a treasurer, an auditor, a general freight agent, station agents, conductors, baggage masters, engineers, a master machinist, a number of journeymen machinists, car inspectors, section masters, and bridge carpenters, plus various watchmen, track laborers, and the like. Officers and employees of other roads were organized similarly.[3] Sometimes their designations differed; their duties did not. Especially noticeable was the very rudimentary development of what today are called traffic departments. Another interesting characteristic was the lack of any official bearing the title of "General Manager"; the roads of the Confederacy, seldom more than 200 miles in length, were not customarily divided into operating divisions, and a single superintendent was deemed sufficient for purposes of day-to-day administration.

The salaries of officers differed widely, but the wages of employees seem to have conformed to a rough standard. For the time and place, the rates of pay in vogue were not low, but certain peculiarities deserve notice. Very frequently the remuneration of a superintendent equaled, or even exceeded, that of a president; Superintendent Charles G. Talcott of the Richmond & Danville received $3,333.33 per annum, while President Lewis E. Harvie's salary was fixed at $3,000. Similar sums were paid to President Edmund Fontaine and Superintendent H. D. Whitcomb of the Virginia Central. Among the most highly rewarded railroad positions in the South was the superintendency of the Georgia Railroad, which carried a stipend of $6,943.62 in 1859. But upon newer and smaller lines, salaries were much less. President John D. Whitford of the Atlantic & North Carolina received only $2,000 while the sum of the salaries paid to the officers of the Raleigh & Gaston totaled $3,500.[4]

The compensation attached to subordinate positions was naturally lower, although the pay differential between officer and employee was smaller than it was later. Lesser officials, like treasurers, auditors, secretaries, and general freight agents, seldom enjoyed salaries of more than $2,500. The auditor of the Virginia & Tennessee received only $1,250. The treasurer of the Richmond & Danville was paid slightly more—$1,375. Seventy dollars per month was the usual wage of an accommodation train conductor on the Virginia Central; express passenger train conductors on the Richmond & Danville drew $81.25. The yardmaster and train dispatcher of the Central at Richmond earned a monthly stipend of no more than $60. Expert machinists did rather better, receiving a daily wage of between two and three dollars, or even more. In addition to the adulation of small boys, enginemen customarily were the recipients of seventy dollars per month.[5]

Especially interesting was railroad participation in that most peculiar of southern institutions, chattel slavery. Many lines actually owned considerable numbers of Negroes. Prior to emancipation the Nashville & Chattanooga had expended no less than $128,773.29 in the purchase of hands. In the summer of 1861 the stockholders of the Raleigh & Gaston appropriated $125,000 for the same purpose. At the end of 1859 the South Carolina road held 90 slaves, of a book value of more than $80,000. In Georgia, the Central, the Macon & Western, the Southwestern, and the Georgia railroads likewise owned a portion of their labor supply. Threescore blacks were the property of the Montgomery & West Point. Most startling of all was the case of the miniscule Baton Rouge, Opelousas & Gross Tete, which had invested $115,000 in slaves.[6]

Far more common, particularly in Virginia, was the hire of slave labor. The Virginia & Tennessee regularly employed more than three hundred, the Richmond & Danville nearly as many. Over a hundred toiled upon the Virginia Central. Richmond newspapers often carried the advertisements of local carriers, seeking the lease of surplus Negroes. The contracts between owners and railroads were executed with meticulous care, setting forth in detail the responsibilities of the lessee as to food, shelter, and clothing; copies thereof were deposited with the State Board of Public Works. The treatment of the slaves while working upon railroads seems to have met the better standards of the period; medical care was provided as a matter of course; in case of death, the owner was indemnified. In 1859 the Richmond & Danville paid no less than $1,379.44 to a master whose Negro had been accidentally killed while in the service of the company.[7]

Although the majority of colored hands performed the hard and menial tasks associated with routine maintenance of way, a surprising number filled positions requiring both skill and responsibility. Even the brakemen on passenger trains were frequently chattel Negroes. The colored fireman already was a feature of the southern scene, while certain mechanics proved so skillful that they commanded a wage (payable to their owners) of $140 per year, nearly double the sum demanded for the hire of a common slave laborer.[8] Slave personnel often manned complicated construction equipment. Strong black arms waited at wood stations to fill the tenders of passing trains. Roustabouts chanted upon freight-house platforms much as did their brethren along the river levees; but somehow they failed to establish themselves equally in the American legend. In truth, the long and honorable service of the American Negro upon the American railroad has too often been overlooked.

White or black, officer or employee, free citizen or slave, the typical railroader of the Confederate South worked hard, achieved varying rewards, and left few personal traces. The Barbours, the Mahones, the Ashes and the Yulees are better remembered for their political careers than for their enterprise with the steam locomotive. The reputation of men like Wadley lingers half-forgotten in obscure corners of the record. The names of G. W. R. Bayley, Walter Goodman, and a number of others merely survive here and there upon yellowing pages, no longer read. The memory of the great majority has vanished with the smoke of the trains they ran.

II

The North Carolina Railroad could boast of no faster schedule than that of the westbound mail. Following a noisy departure from Goldsboro every morning at half-past six, the little train coasted into Raleigh, some forty-eight miles away, at approximately nine-thirty. Forty-four miles farther its engine stood hissing in the noonday sun at Hillsboro. At three-thirteen it was solemnly inspected by the loungers of Greensboro. It lurched into Salisbury in deepening twilight and, if all went well, its headlight would sweep the houses of Charlotte at a quarter past nine. From Goldsboro it would have come 223 miles in a little less than fifteen hours.[9] Such was a typical day's run upon one of the larger railroads of the South in 1860. Including twenty-three intermediate stops, the mail rolled across the Tarheel State at an average speed of about fifteen miles per hour.

The time-cards of other roads were similarly lethargic. All over America they were slow, but nowhere more so than in Dixie. The principal passenger train of the Orange & Alexandria devoted more than eight hours to the 170 miles between Alexandria and Lynchburg. The Nashville & Chattanooga required nine hours and thirty minutes to negotiate 151 miles. Passenger trains of the South Carolina road were forbidden to exceed twenty miles per hour "unless greatly behind time, then not to exceed 25 miles per hour." The journey from New Orleans to Jackson, Mississippi, required a full day (or night). The fastest service in Dixie was afforded by the Louisville & Nashville, which sometimes attained speeds of forty miles per hour. But even so ardent a railroad booster as J. D. B. DeBow hesitated to endorse so radical a practice. "It was with some little nervousness," he declared after a trip over the road in the fall of 1860, "that we found ourselves dashing onward at this unusual speed—the rocking, and dancing, and jumping of the cars being little calculated to allay the feeling." [10]

Freight trains moved more slowly still. Their maximum speed upon the roads of South Carolina was fifteen miles per hour; the average for the state was reckoned at twelve. Freights were limited to about sixteen miles per hour upon the Western & Atlantic; their creeping progress necessitated a timing of twelve hours for the 138 miles between Chattanooga and Atlanta. Through service from Montgomery to Pensacola, established in the spring of 1861 over new track with easy grades, proved no speedier.[11]

Even when adhered to, passenger schedules remained full of pitfalls. In that day, as in this, they were subject to change without notice. Still worse was the absence of any system of standard time. Each railroad regulated its operations in accordance with a single specified clock, set to conform to the local mean solar time of some town or village. The Western & Atlantic might use Atlanta time, the connecting Georgia Railroad that of the meridian of Augusta. The trains of the South Carolina road were governed by the "clock at Charleston depot," while the affairs of the Richmond & York River were based upon the vagaries of the "Regulator at Mitchell and Tyler" in Richmond. So chaotic was the situation that a trouble-free cross-country journey presupposed mastery of the theory of longitude. "The inconvenience of such a system," commented a railway guide of the sixties, "must be apparent to all, but is most annoying to persons strangers to the fact." [12]

Though rail transportation in Dixie remained slow, it could not be accounted very safe. On the eve of the Civil War, the United States led the world in the matter of railway accidents; in the mid-fifties one out of every 188,000 revenue passengers upon American trains met a violent death, as against one in every 1,703,123 in France and one in every 6,680,324 in Great Britain. The season of 1860, to be sure, had shown improvement, only 57 citizens having met their end while traveling by train, as compared with a figure of 129 the previous year. But the record remained appalling enough, and when the sum of the employee dead was added to that of the passengers, the reckoning of those whose lives were sacrificed in the course of American railway operations in 1860 rose to 599.[13]

How much of the gruesome score should be credited to the south-

WILMINGTON & MANCHESTER RAILWAY.

THOS. D. WALKER, Pres.; J. P. ROBERTSON, Supt.; JOSEPH J. LING, Treasurer; and R. B. McRAE, Gen. Transportation and Ticket Agent, Wilmington, N. C. [March 1st.

Exp.	Mail.	Frs.	Mls.	STATIONS.	Mls.	Frs.	Mail.	Exp.
P.M.	A.M.			LEAVE ARRIVE			P.M.	A.M.
7 25	5 30			Wil. & Wel. R'way	171			
8 15	6 00			..Wilmington..	170	6 00	1 15	1 45
8 49	6 32		9	....Register's....	161		12 44	1 13
9 13	6 55	60	17	....Brinkley's....	153	5 40	12 21	12 51
9 42	7 23	90	27	....Maxwell's....	143	5 10	11 53	12 22
10 04	7 45	1 20	34	...Flemington..	136	4 80	11 31	12 02
10 35	8 17	1 50	44	....Whiteville....	126	4 50	11 02	11 31
11 05	8 45	1 80	53	.....Grist's....	117	4 20	10 36	11 05
11 17	8 56		57	...Cerro Gordo..	113		10 24	10 50
11 37	9 15	2 10	63	....Fair Bluff..	107	3 90	10 07	10 31
12 08	9 42	2 40	72	....Nichols'....	99	3 60	9 41	10 01
12 33	10 04	2 70	78	....Mullins'....	93	3 80	9 18	9 34
12 50	10 30	3 00	86	.... Marion	84	3 00	8 53	9 07
1 28	10 55	3 80	94	..Great Pee Dee..	76	2 70	8 26	8 35
2 03	11 26	3 60	101	... Mar's Bluff ..	69	2 40	7 54	8 01
2 28	11 50	3 90	107	.... Florence	63	2 10	7 35	7 41
3 03	12 19	4 20	119	..Timmonsville..	52	1 80	6 47	6 51
3 32	12 45	4 50	128	.... Lynchburg ..	43	1 50	6 20	6 20
4 00	1 10	4 80	137	.... Maysville....	34	1 20	5 57	5 54
4 28	1 36	5 10	146	.. Sumpterville ..	24	90	5 32	5 26
5 02	2 05	5 40	157	... Manchester ...	14	60	5 01	4 54
5 25	2 24	5 70	161	.... Wateree	9	30	4 39	4 33
6 15	3 05	6 00	171	.. Kingsville ..			3 50	3 45
A.M.	P.M.			ARRIVE LEAVE			A.M.	P.M.

ALABAMA & MISSISSIPPI RIVERS RAILWAY.

JAMES L. PRICE, Pres., Selma. W. R. BILL, Acting Supt., " [June 13.

Pass.	Mls	STATIONS	Mls	Pass.
A. M.		LEAVE ARRIVE		P. M.
8 30		..... Selma	30	3 30
9 20	12	Harrell's ⋈ Roads	18	2 50
9 30	14	Junc. C. M. & G. R.	16	2 30
10 15	17	...... Vernon ...	13	2 15
10 55	23	.... Bellevue	7	1 45
11 15	27	..Coffee Springs..	3	1 30
11 30	30	...Uniontown...		1 15
A. M.		ARRIVE LEAVE		P. M.

Fares, about 5 cents per mile.

Daily Stages connect at Uniontown with Greensborough, Demopolis, Lauderdale Springs, on the Mobile & Ohio Railway, and Southern Railway of Mississippi.

A branch road is being constructed from Uniontown in a northerly direction, 9 miles, to Newbern, with a prospect of being extended to Greensborough.

The Railway Connections of the Wilmington and Manchester Railway are the Wilmington & Weldon Railways (p. 234) at Wilmington; the Cheraw & Darlington Railway and North Eastern Railway (p. 237) at Florence; the Camden Br. of S. Carolina Railway at Wateree Junc., and the Col. Br. of S. Carolina Railway at Kingsville (p. 237). The standard time of this road is *eight minutes faster* than that of the S. Carolina.

SOUTH WESTERN AND MUSCOGEE RAILWAYS. [Sept. 6.

R. H. CUYLER, President, Savannah, Ga.   VIRGIL POWERS, Superintendent, Macon, Ga.
Muscogee Railway.—D. DRIFFIN, Pres., Columbus Ga.   GEO. W. ADAMS, Supt., Columbus Ga.

Macon to Albany & Columbus.					STATIONS.	Columbus to Albany & Macon.					
Mail.	Acc.	Mail.	Fares	Miles		Miles	Fares	Mail.	Acc.	Mail.	
P.M.	A.M.	A.M.			LEAVE ARRIVE			A.M.	P.M.	P.M.	
11 45	10 40	9 45			......Macon......	99	4 00	9 50	8 44	9 23	
12 23		10 26	50	12	....Echeconnee.....	87	3 50	9 12		8 38	
12 37		10 40		17	......Jackson's......	82		8 58		8 24	
12 53		10 58		21	......Powersville.....	78		8 46		8 12	
1 28		11 29	1 10	28	......Fort Valley.....	71	2 90	8 19		7 45	
1 20				7	Fort Valley	76				7 32	
1 58				9	..Marshallville..	69				7 07	
2 10				14	...Winchester....	67				6 57	
2 49				19	...Montezuma....	57				6 22	
2 59				21	...Oglethorpe....	55				6 12	
3 33				30	...Anderson....	46				5 40	
4 14				41	...Americus...	35				5 07	
4 45				50	...Sumter	26				4 32	
5 05				58	..Smithville*..	23				4 22	
5 50				65	....Wooton's..	11				3 87	
6 25	5 41			76	....Albany.....				1 40	3 00	
1 44		11 51	1 40	34	......Everett's....	65	2 60	7 54		7 19	
2 08		12 14	1 70	40	......Reynolds......	59	2 30	7 29		6 55	
2 25		12 82		45	......Thompson's...	54		7 15		6 41	
2 40		12 47	2 00	49	......Butler†....	50	2 00	7 05		6 32	
5 35		3 45	4 00	99	......Columbus......			4 00		3 45	
A.M.	P.M.	P.M.			ARRIVE LEAVE			A.M.	P.M.	P.M.	

AMERICUS BRANCH.

*Cuthbert Extension.—Leaves Cuthbert at 12 45 P. M. arrives at Smithville 8 13 P. M. Returning, leaves Smithville at 4 00 P. M. and arrives at Cuthbert 6 39 P. M. †Butler to Columbus, Muscogee Railway.

Typical southern passenger schedules, as they appeared in *Appleton's Railway Guide*, June, 1860. Note the confusing differences in time standards.

ern roads is difficult to determine. That their accidents were frequent the local newspapers bore abundant witness, but that the slaughter was so unrestrained as in the North remains questionable. The deliberation of southern trains bore a distinct advantage in the reduced impact of collisions. Indeed, the southern contribution to railroad vital statistics seems to have derived from incidents of individual misfortune rather than from large-scale disasters, as witness the following report of the Virginia & Tennessee for the year ending July 1, 1861:

"*September 3, 1860*—The down mail train, near Bedford's, ran over and killed a Negro man named NED, belonging to Mrs. Martha Lane; he was asleep on the track, and supposed to have been intoxicated, and was not seen by the engineer as the night was dark and stormy.

"*October 19*—Mr. J. M. Henderson in getting off the mail train at night, in a heavy rain at Christiansburg depot, slipped and got beneath the cars, and the lower part of his body was crushed. He survived the accident but a few hours and died during the night.

"*May 17*—BOB, a brakeman owned by Mr. M. H. Crump, fell from the freight train near Glade Spring, and broke one of his legs and died in a few days afterward." [14]

Every carrier endeavored by one means or another to eliminate accidents. "No passenger train will be permitted to run without a cord connecting the hindmost car with the bell of the engine," read Rule No. 3 for passenger engineers on the South Carolina Railroad. Speed on the same line was restricted to four miles per hour whenever there existed "a possibility of a collision with another train," and when a train was approaching a station or crossing Superintendent Peake required that "the whistle must be sounded for a quarter of a mile in advance." A "continuous whistle, or ringing the bell" was stipulated for cattle upon the line. Rude qualities of track made necessary a four-mile speed limit for freight trains when passing sidings, bridges, or trestle-work. Furthermore, the rule book quaintly concluded, "watchmen on bridges will be required to follow every train with a bucket and extinguish any coals that may have been dropped from the engine." [15]

Block signals, in the modern sense of the word, were unknown.

Chief Engineer G. W. R. Bayley of the New Orleans, Opelousas & Great Western did install, in 1857, a system of "safety Signals" at the five draw bridges located upon his line,[16] but almost everywhere else in the South the movement of trains still was governed solely by time-card and train-order. Even the telegraph had hardly yet made its appearance below the Potomac as a method of dispatching, although the Richmond & Danville boasted by the end of 1861 an organized telegraph department with a superintendent, six operators, and three messengers.[17] No effective automatic device existed to neutralize a mistake; no interlockings protected junction points. Even if enginemen received visual warning of imminent collision, the stopping of their trains remained, in the absence of the air brake, a distinct gamble. Railroading, indeed, was a hazardous business; and when President Charles H. Fisher of the North Carolina Railroad reported in the summer of 1860 that his line had never sustained a serious accident involving a passenger train, he ascribed the situation not so much to careful operation as to "the deliverance of a Higher Power."[18]

CHAPTER

~ 4 ~

Of Dollars and Cents

COTTON WAS KING ON THE CENTRAL OF GEORGIA. THROUGH THE
mild December days of 1860, trainload after trainload rumbled down
from the Piedmont hills to the port of Savannah; trackside platforms
sagged with the weight of hundreds of bales; and the chugging of
the engines sounded unceasingly through the pinewoods. Within
four weeks 32,234 bales had been offered for shipment; during the
following month, no less than 85,149 bales would jolt seaward. This,
however, the company regarded as routine; the previous winter it had
handled a total of 413,314 bales.[1] It was this way nearly every season,
for a railroad seldom fails to reflect, in the nature and volume of its
business, the economic basis of the territory it serves.

The other roads of the cotton belt presented a similar traffic picture. During the twelve months ending April 1, 1859, the Georgia
Railroad hauled more than 219,000 bales. In the course of 1860,
315,000 were carried to Charleston over the South Carolina road,
while 206,000 arrived in Macon behind the locomotives of the Southwestern. Though they were on the fringe of the cotton region, the
Memphis & Charleston carried 225,000 bales and the Western & Atlantic 24,000. Cotton overflowed to the North Carolina and Petersburg roads. Cotton laid iron rails through the back country; cotton
fired engines, paid superintendents and station agents, declared dividends to hundreds of stockholders. Cotton was King![2]

Yet its dominion was not absolute. Even on the Central of Georgia
there moved a respectable flow of other traffic, including wool,
hides, paper, lard, leather, tobacco, bacon, and forest products. Tobacco was an especially important item for the carriers of South Side
Virginia and the neighboring counties of North Carolina. The busi-

36

ness of the North Carolina Railroad in 1860 comprehended such varied articles as bran, green apples, feathers, beeswax, liquor (2,173 barrels), rags, salt, copper, and gold ore (over 1500 tons), machinery, molasses, wheat, and flour. Lumber made up the bulk of the eastbound tonnage upon the Seaboard & Roanoke, and its coastal-plain territory was further suggested by the important place occupied by lime and guano in its back-haul traffic.[3]

Revenues derived from freight customarily exceeded those received for the carriage of passengers. Of the $1,155,000 gross income enjoyed by the Georgia Railroad in 1859, less than $355,000 came from passenger fares. Travelers purchased $461,083.74 in tickets from the South Carolina Railroad in 1860, but shippers paid $968,672.76 in freight bills. Freight receipts on the Western & Atlantic exceeded those from passengers by nearly six to one. Only on the Memphis & Charleston and the Richmond, Fredericksburg & Potomac, among the more important roads, does passenger business seem to have yielded greater revenue than freight.[4]

Another feature of southern railroad operations, a feature pregnant with future woe, was its local nature. Northern lines already were beginning to enjoy the fruits of interchange. But in Dixie the advantages of the through freight car were only dimly perceived; and southern railway officials usually refused to permit their rolling stock to pass onto the iron of another line, even where a direct physical connection permitted. Freight moving over several carriers might have to be unloaded and reloaded three or four times. So unwieldy was the situation that Georgia roads received little traffic from the Mississippi Valley, much of it moving northward by river to the terminus of some eastern trunk line, thence to the seaboard, over a route perhaps a thousand miles longer.[5]

In truth, the rail carriers of the Slave States had not outgrown their initial function as feeders to water routes. The Richmond, Fredericksburg & Potomac fulfilled its name precisely, terminating nearly fifty miles short of Washington upon an arm of the Potomac called Acquia Creek, whence the company operated a line of steamboats to the Federal Capital. The Seaboard & Roanoke operated in conjunction with craft plying Chesapeake Bay. In February, 1861, the Atlantic & North Carolina inaugurated a special freight train to connect with a 600-ton steamer which ran semi-monthly from New York to Morehead City, while a tri-weekly coastal service was in effect between the western terminus of the New Orleans, Opelousas & Great Western and the ports of Galveston and Indianola in Texas. Stern-wheelers breasted the chocolate current of the Alabama River upon advertised schedules to connect the railroads at Selma with those entering Montgomery.[6] The real trunk lines of Dixie in the spring of 1861 were steamboat lines.

To be sure, there were signs that the provincial age of southern railroading was passing away. Inter-line cooperation in the form of trackage rights was evident here and there. The passenger trains of the Memphis & Charleston entered Chattanooga over the iron of the Nashville & Chattanooga for an annual consideration of $20,000. The rails of the Virginia Central between Gordonsville and Charlottesville carried the trains of the Orange & Alexandria to and from its newly completed Lynchburg segment. The Atlanta & West Point utilized the track of the Macon & Western between East Point and Atlanta at a yearly charge of $3,000. The Petersburg and the Seaboard & Roanoke roads appear to have operated between Garysburg and Weldon, North Carolina, under a cooperative trackage agreement.[7]

The rate structure, on the other hand, remained primitive. Fairly elaborate tariffs were published, even jointly by several roads, and there existed some differentiation between class and commodity rates. But tariffs, especially inter-line tariffs, appear to have been established with a splendid informality. Herein, of course, the South sinned no more grossly than did the North.

Long haul or short haul, the price demanded for railroad transportation was high. Cotton rates on the Southwestern Railroad in Georgia were reduced just sufficiently to divert traffic from the Flint and Chattahoochee rivers. A similar pattern existed upon the Mobile & Ohio, where the rate level rose steadily as the distance from Mobile increased, reaching $2.75 per 500-weight of cotton at Coonowah, Mississippi, 269 miles inland. Thence to Corinth, sixty miles farther, the rate experienced no further change, for at that point the Mobile & Ohio intersected the Memphis & Charleston, which furnished an alternative route direct to the Mississippi. The joint rate quoted upon pig iron from Cartersville, Georgia, to Savannah, via Atlanta and Macon, stood at about $7.00 per ton. The carriage of 100 pounds of groceries over 100 miles of the Virginia Central cost thirty-eight cents.[8] Nor were the possibilities of rate discrimination neglected; at the 1860 annual meeting of the North Carolina Railroad that ancient practice found itself enshrined in the minutes as follows: "*Resolved*, That the President and Directors of this Road be instructed to discriminate, in freights, on iron for the construction of the Western North Carolina Railroad, in favor of all iron landed at the Sea-Ports of our own State." [9]

Passenger fares were less chaotic, though relatively high. They varied from road to road, but averaged about four and a half cents per mile. The seven-hour, eighty-six-mile journey from Weldon, North Carolina, to Richmond cost four dollars, the hack ride between stations in Petersburg included. The price of a ticket from Charleston to Augusta was five dollars, from Memphis to Chattanooga, twelve dollars and a half. Travel on the Mobile & Ohio was less expensive, about four cents per mile. One of the highest passenger tariffs in the South was that of the Spartanburg & Union, in South Carolina, which charged its patrons five cents per mile; a journey over the Seaboard & Roanoke was equally exorbitant. The best travel bargain below the Potomac was offered by the Norfolk & Petersburg, with a straight three-cent fare.[10]

Through tickets could, by 1860, be purchased between all principal points, not only in the South, but throughout the United States. Often they involved rail-water combinations; sometimes, as between Vicksburg and Montgomery, they included a lurching intermission in a stagecoach. Even "commutation" tickets were available upon the Western & Atlantic, a book of twenty being sold at a 50-per cent discount. Most roads strenuously urged the purchase of tickets before boarding its trains. "Passengers getting on the cars," announced Superintendent Wadley of the Southern Railroad of Mississippi, "without procuring a ticket from the station where the Company is prepared to sell them, will be charged TEN CENTS extra for the first station, and five cents extra for every station thereafter to the place of stopping." [11] But not everywhere did management issue such Draconian directives. On the South Carolina road, the free baggage allowance of each passenger was limited to eighty pounds, but, said the rule book, no extra charge should be made if only a single trunk were taken, "nor for slight excess of weight, say fifteen or twenty pounds." [12]

II

The iron horse is a costly beast. Voracious of feed, requiring a specially-constructed roadway, always demanding the careful handling of scores of attendants, his purchase and maintenance have customarily exceeded the means of an individual owner. Railroading, as a result, is characteristically a corporate activity and has been so since the beginning. The industry as it existed in the ante-bellum South was no exception to the rule.

Indeed, it was the business of railroading that brought corporate organization, on an extensive scale, to the Southern States for the first time. The region was hardly prepared for it. Ordinary law-making machinery, even as late as 1861, proved hopelessly inadequate to the needs of the situation. State legislative calendars were choked with bills for the incorporation of new railway companies, or for the amendment of the charters of the old. The deficiencies of old-fashioned legal concepts became especially evident upon the map, where many of the new railroads were brought up short at state boundaries, delaying the development of effective trunk lines for decades. "It was the railroads that created the necessity for general incorporation laws." [13] But a purging of corporate channels was not to come until after the Civil War. Railroads remained local affairs in the South, local in outlook, and locally owned.

Especially significant was the matter of ownership. Despite the dearth of southern capital, despite the fabled lack of southern enterprise, the railroads of the section appear to have been owned and controlled to an extraordinary degree by southerners. There were, to be sure, exceptions. But enough evidence survives to point a tendency. Northern capitalists were simply not much interested in southern railroads in 1861. Their names hardly appear in the record, which, on the contrary, is heavily laden with figures of regional repute. Few companies published lists of their stockholders, *with addresses;* but where this was done, the preponderance of southerners is overwhelming. Of the sixteen thousand outstanding shares of the Atlantic & North Carolina, sixty-six were held outside of the State—two in New York, and the remainder in Philadelphia. The owners of the Nashville & Chattanooga were almost entirely Tennesseans; of more than two hundred thousand shares, only 3,127½ were held in the North. The Florida Railroad had issued 13,116 shares of stock, of which only 1,674 had gotten into northern hands by 1862. At the twenty-eighth annual meeting of the Richmond, Fredericksburg & Potomac, held in Richmond in May, 1861, *after* the outbreak of war, some 3,966 votes were accounted present, from a possible total of 5,784. Of the stock of the Southwestern Railroad in 1851, 1.4 per cent was held by non-residents of Georgia.[14] In instance after instance the equity-holders of southern carriers dwelt in the neighborhood, gentlemen of repute and rather moderate substance. They were not Yankees.

The exceptions were few. The majority of the shareholders of the Macon & Western were said to be northerners, although President Isaac Scott was a Georgian. Northern interests dominated the board of the Brunswick & Florida, a situation which presently was to cause singular repercussions. In scarcely another instance, however, were appreciable quantities of southern railroad stock contained in Yankee strong boxes.[15]

But if northern participation in southern companies was negligible, northern capital was not. In the absence of outside credit the iron horse could scarcely have gone striding across Dixie in 1861. A certain quantity of liquid wealth existed in commercial centers like Charleston, Savannah, Mobile, and New Orleans, but the rural planters possessed very little. It was seldom that new railroad shares were purchased outright by individuals; customarily they were floated on the installment plan, and if a multitude of railroad reports are to be believed, subscribers frequently failed to make good their obligations when due. Very often private investment was not made in money at all, but in land, cotton, or slave labor for the grading of roadbeds.[16] Resources of this sort would have been powerless to drive 9,000 miles of rails across the face of the South before the War Between the States.

Whence came the money? From the North and from Europe, but seldom directly. Between the banking parlors of London and New York and the freshly spiked iron of the latest southern railway there frequently intervened an active broker in the shape of State Government. In the South, Capitol Square assumed some of the functions of Wall Street.

The extraordinary role played by the various public agencies of the Southern States in the construction of railroad lines has received scant recognition from historians.[17] But its importance can scarcely be exaggerated. The subject can be treated here in its broadest aspects only. A thoroughly mercantilist union of governmental policy and private interest, it represented a kind of reduction, to a local level, of the "American System" once publicized by Henry Clay. It was grounded upon the theory that public authority should lend a helping hand to private enterprise in the furthering of schemes deemed socially desirable. For, contrary to tradition, "socialism" strode forth into the American wilderness at a very early date.

Beginning in the eighteen-thirties, aid was extended to railway companies in a number of ways. Straight cash subsidies, with few attached strings, were not unknown. More frequently a state would purchase the stocks or bonds of a new carrier, making payment in its own securities. Surveys were sometimes made free of charge by state engineers. Monopoly franchises were resorted to in great numbers, and varying degrees of tax exemption afforded. In Florida and in the Gulf and interior states, the roads were so lavishly plied with grants of public land that no less than 7,822,000 acres had been actually certified before secession; much of this, to be sure, was Federal largess, but most of it passed first through the hands of the states.[18]

This happy partnership of steam and government perhaps achieved its highest development in Virginia. Not only did the Old Dominion commonly subscribe three-fifths of the equity capital invested in her railroad companies, she had extended them loans to the sum of $3,904,918 by 1861. She had endorsed, or guaranteed, $300,000 of their bonds; she had constructed one railroad on her own account; and she was playing the major role in the building of another. Virginia directors dominated the board rooms of a majority of the carriers within her limits; her proxies wielded decisive influence at stockholders' meetings. All intrastate rates and fares were obliged to seek the approval of Richmond, while the State Board of Public Works carefully watched the financial condition of each carrier, even to the extent of specifying the format of its annual report. Railroading was no free enterprise in Virginia in 1861. It was not even private.[19]

The two-headed policy of state aid and state control likewise flourished in Florida. Here the state encouraged the growth of railways primarily by donations of land. Stripped of its complexities, the Florida method revolved about a State Internal Improvement

Fund, administered by a Board of Trustees, whose membership included the Governor, Comptroller, Treasurer, Attorney General, and Registrar of State Lands. With the money derived from land sales, the state, through the Fund, offered to guarantee the interest on the bonds of new railroads, provided the issues did not exceed a maximum of $10,000 per mile of line. As of January 1, 1863, public backing had been extended in this fashion to $555,000 of the certificates of the Florida, Atlantic & Gulf Central and to $1,616,000 of the obligations of the Florida Railroad. The loans of the Pensacola & Georgia fared as well. The trustees made few purchases of stock; the state held only $173,300.00 book value of such securities at the end of 1860. Its *direct* investment in railroad bonds amounted to even less.[20]

But if the directors of Florida carriers were hardly creatures of the Governor at Tallahassee, the acceptance of a public subsidy involved subjection to a real measure of public control. Rigid specifications were established for the trackage so aided, and no largess was extended until the right-of-way concerned had been minutely examined by the state engineer. A five-foot gauge, laid with at least 60-pound iron, was everywhere required, "connected continuously, so that cars, or trains of cars, can pass on all the routes indicated without changing freight." Such advanced practices as the interchange of rolling stock and uniform tariffs were insisted upon. Whenever the Improvement Fund found itself obliged to make good the interest upon a state-guaranteed bond, a specific portion of the stock of the delinquent company could be impounded by the trustees until proper reimbursement had been made. The Florida system could hardly be termed socialistic. But neither was it unrestrained free enterprise.[21]

In other parts of the South the story was much the same; public authority and private entrepreneur constantly joined hands to push forward the trackage from which so much good was expected. That they might be violating an American tradition seems to have worried them not at all. The people of Georgia even possessed in their state-owned-and-operated Western & Atlantic an example of pure collectivism. Moreover, the road had proved hugely successful, earning a net of $450,000, or 10 per cent upon its investment, in 1860. The North Carolina Railroad was practically an instrumentality of the state, which controlled seven of the eleven seats upon the board. The lines of twelve railroad companies seamed the map of South Carolina, "to every one of which," asserted the local comptroller general, "the State has by various acts of the General Assembly given aid, either by taking shares therein, or by the guaranty of their bonds, reserving as security to herself the first lein [sic] on the machinery and running stock of such roads." South Carolina, by the outbreak of the Civil War, had extended varied assistance to the sum of more than five millions.[22]

State paternalism, albeit of differing types, extended into every other southern commonwealth. Alabama endeavored to hasten the construction of the Tennessee & Coosa road through the difficult Cumberlands with an aid of $254,421 from her "3% Fund."[23] Louisiana had subscribed $1,355,000 to the stock of four railroads and held $592,000 of the bonds of three others. Of the twenty-four directors of the New Orleans, Jackson & Great Northern, three represented the interest of Louisiana and six were the delegates of the State of Mississippi. Most ambitious of all was the program of Tennessee, whose public subsidies had totaled by 1861 more than $17,000,000, including a loan of $10,000 for each new mile graded. The spirit of Tennessee entrepreneurs was further stimulated by the offer of liberal tax exemptions.[24]

But this was not all. So desirable seemed the rapid development of railways that the deluge of governmental assistance burst forth through other than state channels. Counties, cities, and towns mortgaged their futures so as to insure the entry of suitable trackage. The commercial spirit of Charleston became so aroused that the municipality had invested by 1856 nearly a million dollars in the distant properties of the Nashville & Chattanooga and the Memphis & Charleston; its total aid to railroads was reckoned in the same year at no less than three and one-half millions. By 1859 rival Savannah had underwritten at least six companies with sums totaling nearly $3,000,000. At the outbreak of the Civil War, even river-girt New Orleans had subscribed to railroad stock to the extent of $4,600,000. Mobile, by 1862, had devoted $1,000,000 to the purchase of Mobile & Ohio shares, while the Mobile & Great Northern could scarcely be accounted other than a public project of that city. Pensacola elected four of the five directors of the Alabama & Florida Railroad of Florida. No less than eighteen Virginia cities and towns endeavored to quicken the pace of railroad progress by means of stock purchase. Macon, Georgia, Knoxville, Tennessee, Vicksburg, Mississippi, Wilmington, North Carolina, all pledged their resources that the pant of the steam locomotive might be heard within their city limits. And the list could be greatly extended.[25]

Rural areas proved as enthusiastic. Two thousand five hundred of the 16,000 shares of the Atlantic & North Carolina were held by the Counties of Carteret, Lenoir and Craven. Various Louisiana parishes similarly brightened the hopes of the Vicksburg, Shreveport & Texas and the New Orleans, Opelousas & Great Western. From the picturesque brick courthouses of Virginia streamed subscriptions for railroad stock totaling well over a million dollars. Four Florida counties furnished $310,000 of the capital of the Pensacola & Georgia. Nearly every county in Tennessee granted some kind of aid to the railroads of that state. Only in Georgia and Arkansas did the county authorities hesitate to hold fistful of banknotes before the nose of the iron horse.[26]

It must not be supposed that public assistance was always provided in the form of currency. Very frequently state, county or municipality could furnish only its elaborately engraved bonds, which the roads were obliged to receive at par and then sell upon the open market. County aid in Virginia, North Carolina, Tennessee, and Mississippi came almost wholly in this form, and the same sort of assistance usually was proffered by local governments in Florida. Where actual cash was transmitted, the public agency concerned often resorted to the loan market to obtain it; Georgia did this in 1860 in order to speed the progress of the Atlantic & Gulf, and a large portion of the construction expenses of the Mobile & Great Northern was derived from the sale of a special bond issue of the City of Mobile.[27]

No precise information survives to indicate the source of all this money. It could hardly have been the South. A large amount must have been attracted from Yankee pockets. An equal sum, perhaps, was secured in Europe; bonds of the South Carolina Railroad, for example, of a face value of £2,000,000 and carrying the guarantee of the state, were held overseas in the summer of 1863. But of the importance of public assistance as a means of attracting this capital there is no question; probably 55 per cent of the total investment in the ante-bellum railroads of Dixie was made in this way. Indeed, the crude railroad trains of 1861 were matters of public concern in more than a broad sense.[28]

III

On May 10, 1859, was held at Augusta, Georgia, the Annual Meeting of the Georgia Railroad and Banking Company. It was an altogether happy affair, for it had been an extraordinarily satisfactory year along the line of the Georgia Railroad. Passenger revenue had produced $354,562; freight shipments, including 219,-218 bales of cotton, had brought in $800,058 more, making a total gross income for the transportation part of the corporation's business of $1,154,621. Expenses of operation had amounted to only $610,-258, giving an operating ratio of 52 per cent and a net operating profit of $544,363.[29]

The meeting excited no special comment in business circles. The panic of 1857 had long since passed; recovery for the Cotton Kingdom had been swift; and the carriers were sharing to the full the Indian Summer of the ante-bellum South. Railroaders had reason for optimism. The management of the Central of Georgia announced for 1860 an operating profit of $764,574.79. The results on the Memphis & Charleston, whose net *exceeded* expenses by more than $100,000 were even better. The treasurer of the Richmond, Fredericksburg & Potomac swam in a sea of dollars. In 1859 profits upon the capital investment of the Houston & Texas Central amounted to 14.20 per cent; the same figure for the Raleigh & Gaston stood at 9.76 per cent, for the Atlanta & West Point at 16.74 per cent. On many roads the dividends flowed like wine. The stockholders of the Macon & Western congratulated themselves upon an annual disbursement, per share, of nineteen dollars. The Southwestern paid thirteen dollars; the South Carolina, seven. The owners of the Wilmington & Weldon cashed drafts representing an annual distribution of eight dollars a share.[30]

Not every southern carrier, of course, could report such results. Dividends were confined in general to the older and better established companies. The shareholders of the New Orleans, Jackson & Great Northern received no checks, although their property already was netting more than a half-million dollars every year. Half-finished enterprises like the Opelousas road might make punctual payment upon their funded debt, but they could not yet afford to scatter profits among their owners. Scores of miles of cypress swamp had inflicted upon the Charleston & Savannah such heavy construction costs that it laid its last rail on October 26, 1860, and defaulted its first 7 per cent coupon on January 1, 1861. The Mobile & Ohio faced a future nearly as dark. Though its operating net nearly equaled its out-of-pocket expenses, the imminent maturity of a large part of its debt gave promise of an early visit to the courts. "No one regards the stock of any value," commented a planter from Clark County, Mississippi, in May, 1861, "except so far as it will enable its owner to make a trip free of passage to Mobile once a year." [31]

Although many southerners enjoyed the fruits of profitable railroad ventures, very few yet realized the opportunities that awaited the consolidation of little companies into unified systems. A beginning had been made in Georgia, where the Central and the Southwestern were controlled by common interests and shared a common president, Richard R. Cuyler. The same could be said for the Georgia Railroad and the Atlanta & West Point. The Montgomery & West Point exercised a voice in the affairs of the Alabama & Florida and the tiny Tuskegee road. A vague trend was establishing itself along the Atlantic seaboard, where the Wilmington & Manchester held sizeable blocks of the Wilmington & Weldon and the Charleston & Savannah, but the main stem of the present Atlantic Coast Line was scarcely a dream. Early in 1861, in an effort to minimize competition in the direction of Washington and Baltimore, the Seaboard & Roanoke bought up $20,000 of the stock of the Richmond, Fredericksburg & Potomac, but here, again, was only the start of a tendency. Beyond the mountains a basic link of the future Illinois Central system had recently been formed when the Mississippi Central absorbed the Mississippi Central & Tennessee.[32]

Here and there, railroads were learning how to quarrel. Along the border of Virginia and North Carolina the struggling little Roanoke Valley believed its rightful expansion was being checked by "the tyranny and power of other companies." Further north the smoldering rivalry of the Richmond, Fredericksburg & Potomac and the Virginia Central-Orange & Alexandria route had flared into a lawsuit which dragged endlessly and threatened to acquire political stature. But in most regions of the South the railroad net had not expanded sufficiently to arouse more than suspicious glances from one carrier to another.[33]

Indeed, in 1861 the railroads of Dixie had attained neither physical nor financial maturity. Buoyant, but ill-developed, they could normally have expected swift and happy growth. Instead they would learn to meet adversity.

CHAPTER

~ 5 ~

The Iron Horse Goes Forth to War

"Should the calamity of war be forced upon us, you will find that this much neglected Railway will be the cheapest and most formidable earthwork that could have been devised to give confidence and security at home and repel invasion from abroad."
—*Annual Report*, Charleston & Savannah Railroad, February 20, 1861.

I

IN THE PLEASANT WINTER SUNLIGHT THE BAND WAS PLAYING Dixie. Gaudy with color, the inaugural parade moved upward along the avenue to the immaculate white capitol on the hill, where already the elms were budding and a brightly dressed crowd stood waiting on the lawn behind the wrought-iron fence. Cannon boomed thunderously and people cheered. As the gilt hands of the capitol clock indicated precisely one, Jefferson Davis stepped to the front of the great portico to be sworn in as provisional president of the Confederate States of America. His inaugural address was described as "short, manly and pithy." Beneath blue skies the audience applauded, waved its kerchiefs and stovepipe hats, and dispersed as the citizens of a hopeful new nation.

Thus came to fruition the drift toward southern nationalism that had so disturbed the aged Jefferson more than forty years before. Perhaps the majority of men approved; all were a little bewildered. A very great proportion, now that the die was cast, were swept along in a vast ground swell of fervor, largely genuine.

Not even railroad companies were immune from the current

enthusiasm. On March 1, as the politicians asserted that there would be no war, the yet unfinished Mississippi & Tennessee Railroad offered the free use of its road to the State of Mississippi and to the Confederate States for military purposes. A similarly unselfish spirit stirred the Memphis & Ohio and the New Orleans, Jackson & Great Northern. The Opelousas road hastened to place its facilities at the disposal of the State of Louisiana. Following its completion on April 22, 1861, to Columbus, Kentucky, the Mobile & Ohio dedicated itself to the "support of southern commerce and the maintenance of southern institutions." [1] But such sacrificial gestures were not universal. As early as February, the General Assembly of Alabama felt it necessary to sweeten the cup of patriotism with an Act "to induce railroad companies in this State to carry troops and munitions of war for this State free of charge," wherein cooperative roads were to be exempted from all taxes "imposed by the laws of this State." The Florida carriers were merely handed a new regulation providing that "said Railroads shall be and remain free from toll or other charge upon the transportation of any property, or troops, of the State of Florida, or of any other Government legitimately succeeding to the powers, rights and privileges of the late United States." [2]

The vital role to be played by the steam locomotive in the coming struggle was hardly appreciated; after all, the previous war experience of American railroads had been slight. The conflict with Mexico had been waged hundreds of miles from the nearest American right-of-way, and it is not surprising that the carriers of the Confederacy should have cherished a deep misunderstanding of what was expected of them. Military preparations, marked by vast enthusiasm and an equally immense lack of coordination, went forward all about them; but for weeks southern railroaders went about their business much as usual. Feverishly engaged in the assembly of a workable political structure, the statesmen at Montgomery could offer little guidance. To be sure, an enactment of the Provisional Congress, signed by President Davis on February 26, had established a Quartermaster Department, which, as a photographic reproduction of the old United States organization, was charged with the transportation of troops and supplies. [3] But at first it possessed only paper personnel and paper facilities; it did not even have paper money. And so the first Confederate troop trains ran at the behest of local authorities. Among the earliest were those which puffed late in February over the Georgia roads between Dalton in the northern part of the state and Savannah.[4]

But at last the Confederate War Department emerged sufficiently from its inchoate state to act in the matter. A current feature of southern strategy was to overawe the diminutive Federal garrison at Fort Pickens near Pensacola; troops for the purpose were to be drawn from Louisiana, Mississippi, Alabama, and Georgia. First in a series of Confederate Secretaries of War, the enthusiastic but inept Leroy Pope Walker inaugurated the program by bickering with Governor Thomas O. Moore of Louisiana, who stoutly insisted that Confederate authority was responsible for the transportation of Louisiana volunteers beyond his borders. Walker soon found it awkward to defy the chief executive of a sovereign state; he presently gave way and dispatched to Louisiana one Captain John M. Galt with orders to muster the local troops into the Confederate service and to provide for their transportation to Pensacola. On the 19th of March, the captain departed,[5] his pockets stuffed with hastily prepared drafts upon the Confederate Treasury.

Similar difficulty marked the movement of the Georgia contingent. In the final week of March Walker completed plans for the departure of one thousand militia from Columbus, while Governor Joseph E. Brown simultaneously ordered them to rendezvous at Macon. This time the trouble was settled more easily. Walker had learned his lesson; the Georgia soldiers boarded the cars at Macon. Nor were the final arrangements unintelligent; a maximum of three hundred men were dispatched daily until all had been transported, thus preventing the indiscriminate jamming of troops into the Montgomery bottleneck.[6]

The most serious obstacle to the concentration of men at Pensacola was not, however, administrative, but physical. The Alabama & Florida Railroad of Alabama, over which many of the units were obliged to travel south of Montgomery, was not yet finished and the crossing of the gap brought vexatious delays. So serious, indeed, did the situation become that the State of Alabama advanced the road an emergency loan of $30,000 to hasten its completion. This proved sufficient; the last rails were spiked down on May 3 and a regular ten-hour passenger schedule inaugurated from Montgomery to Pensacola on the sixth. A single difficulty remained: the scarcity of Alabama & Florida rolling stock was found to be "a serious impediment to the rapid transportation of public supplies." [7] Nor could the matter be adjusted easily, for neither the Alabama & Florida of Alabama, nor its Florida counterpart, made connection with any other road of similar gauge.

II

The war that no one wanted came at last. The smoke of the first cannonade drifted over the Carolina marshes upon a pleasant April Sunday, while on the battery at Charleston an excited crowd lustily cheered its own doom. On the morrow a flurry of White House telegrams chattered out a plea for troops, and presently this first bloodless victory would wax into the most terrible conflict in American experience.

At Montgomery the harassed Confederate Government realized some of the implications. President Davis himself possessed a better than average military mind; he and his cabinet knew that their newborn nation stood deficient in manpower, in the sinews of war, and in the means to produce them. They knew the South was almost helpless upon the sea. In lieu of numbers and proper munitions, they affected, with a certain sincerity, to trust in southern skill, southern courage, and in God.

They appear to have placed less reliance upon another real advantage—the possibility of fighting upon interior lines. Given adequate inland transportation facilities, intelligently utilized, the Confederate States would find themselves in possession of a constant opportunity to "get there first with the most men." But though a vague appreciation of this must have penetrated the makeshift executive offices at Montgomery, it remained for the Postmaster General, the plain and capable John H. Reagan, to initiate the first deliberate effort to harness the iron horse for war. In April, 1861, he called a convention of key southern railroad officials, to meet at the little capital on the twenty-sixth. [8]

Reagan's purpose was logical enough; he desired to arrange definite mail contracts. Even after the outbreak of hostilities, the United States Post Office had continued to function throughout the seceded states, an astonishing situation which the Postmaster General of the Confederacy found as impracticable as it was embarrassing. He could scarcely bring it to an end without prior arrangements with the carriers.[9] But before the railway officers could arrive, so much difficulty had arisen over military transportation that the War Department became interested as well.

The convention met on schedule. Represented were nearly all the companies of the existing Confederacy, save those of Texas and Virginia, a total of four thousand miles of line. Conspicuous among the delegates were Richard R. Cuyler of the Central of Georgia, Charles T. Pollard of the Alabama & Florida and John Caldwell of the South Carolina road; there even appeared three well-known figures from states which had not yet seceded: Presidents William S. Ashe of the Wilmington & Weldon, William Johnston of the Charlotte & South Carolina, and Samuel Tate of the Memphis & Charleston. The Montgomery *Daily Mail* thought it a body "which for worth, ability and capital represented was perhaps the most distinguished that ever assembled in the South." [10]

The first order of business was a brief communication from the Secretary of War, containing a tentative plan for regulating the movement of troops and military supplies. It was a simple program, conceived in innocence: it strove to order the transportation needs of a warring people in just two paragraphs. It proposed first that soldiers should be carried at a fare of two cents per mile and that military freight should move at "half the regular local rates." Secondly, the roads were to receive payment in bonds or treasury notes of the Confederate States at par, if ordinary currency were not available. That was all, and the *Daily Mail* reported that the delegates extended their approval "with a unanimity almost without parallel in the history of conventions." In the freshness of their patriotism they attached a minimum of qualifying clauses; one provided that the new rates should go into effect on May 1, 1861; another stipulated that troops were to be transported at the official fare only upon presentation of "requisite authority" from the Quartermaster General, or "other proper officer of the Confederate States"; a third merely requested that the Quartermaster General designate the class of certificate to be used.[11]

The convention proved equally receptive to the wishes of Reagan. In a communication which "elicited high commendation from the various members ... for its perspicuity and grasp of the whole subject," the Postmaster General outlined a schedule of payments for carrying the mails that differed sharply from the old United States agreements. The rail carriers of the Confederacy were to be divided into three classes: "The great through lines connecting important points and conveying heavy mails," to receive an annual compensation of one hundred and fifty dollars per mile; completed railroads carrying heavy local mail, to be paid one hundred dollars per mile; and short, unimportant, or unfinished roads not carrying much mail, which were to be tendered fifty dollars per mile. Though these figures represented reductions in existing payments, the service was to be simplified for all concerned, and the costs thereof reduced, by discontinuing the *double* daily mails previously operated upon many routes. Payments were to be made, if necessary, in Confederate bonds or treasury notes. No specific time limitation was imposed; in any case, important changes would have to have congressional sanction. The whole of Reagan's proposal was promptly ratified by the delegates; they added only a recommendation that Sunday mails be dispensed with as soon as practicable and a clarifying section which limited mail deliveries to the precincts of their own depots. The substance of the program presently was enacted into law by the Provisional Congress.[12]

The purposes of the convention had been fulfilled in a single sitting, and the next day's session was devoted to the expression of mutual admiration on the part of the delegates and government leaders. Reagan visited the gathering in person, was hugely applauded, and responded "in a speech of great good sense and ability." The convention then waited in a body upon Jefferson Davis, to whom the railroaders pledged their personal support. The pleasure of the Chief Executive was manifest; his reply proved "very eloquent and interesting" and "produced a profound sensation among all the members." Following a brief final sitting, wherein Presidents R. R. Cuyler of the Georgia Central, C. T. Pollard of the Alabama & Florida, and John King of the Georgia road were constituted a central committee with powers to convoke a similar gathering at any time it seemed expedient, the convention broke up in an aura of cigar smoke and good feeling.[13]

Little more than a month elapsed before a second meeting was held. It was not, however, called by the "central committee," but by the presidents of the Memphis & Charleston and the Mississippi Central, Samuel Tate and Walter Goodman, and its agenda differed sharply from that of the April assembly. Secession not only had broken the political relationship of northerner and southerner; it had divided the American railroad net. Shattered were many traffic and other agreements between northern and southern companies, and it was primarily to settle the problems posed by this disruption that representatives from a majority of the Confederate lines crowded into a stuffy meeting room at Chattanooga, Tennessee, on June 4, 1861. The business of the convention occupied two days. The Montgomery resolution restricting Post Office contracts to the transit of mail from railhead to railhead was re-emphasized; but most of the other transactions dealt with non-governmental matters. A committee was appointed to "consider and report on the general welfare of Confederate States railroads." It was agreed that Confederate treasury notes should be received at par in payment of *all* transportation bills. A through passenger schedule (not train) of seventy-eight hours was arranged between New Orleans and Richmond, by way of Jackson, Grand Junction, Chattanooga, and Bristol. Steps were taken to establish a system of freight classification to be published in a common tariff, though the arrangement specifically omitted military traffic. Finally, the carriers agreed, as a group, to patronize "any" southern iron mill in preference to those located beyond the limits of the Confederacy.[14]

There were still other meetings that summer. In Virginia public opinion had hesitated long before taking its stand with the Confederacy, and the Old Dominion had not become a Confederate State in time for its carriers to send proper representatives to the Montgomery meeting in April. Yet it was becoming clear that Virginia would be a chief theater of military operations; already the youth and substance of the entire South were hopelessly crowding its trains. In the absence of any specific arrangement for their carriage, someone suggested a convention of the principal Virginia lines, to meet at Richmond on June 25. A number of delegates responded, quickly agreed to conform to the Montgomery rates in so far as the war traffic of the Confederate States was concerned, and as swiftly adjourned.

It soon was evident that they had been too hasty. The directors of the Virginia Central desired to receive Confederate bonds in payment for postal operations, but the convention had said nothing of the matter. Furthermore, many roads remained choked with an unprecedented volume of military traffic. At the request of his board, President Edmund Fontaine of the Virginia Central thereupon proposed a second meeting, and on July 19, ten officers of seven companies assembled at the stately Roman temple which now did double duty as Virginia's statehouse and as the capitol building of the Confederate States. This gathering considered things more carefully. It formally reaffirmed the Montgomery rates. It also followed the Montgomery precedent by receiving government bonds and treasury notes at par in payment for the transportation of military personnel, munitions, provisions, and the mails. It then went a step further. Two days before First Manassas, while the surrounding city lay in the grip of an unspeakable anxiety, the delegates pledged that their roads would grant precedence to troops and war matériel, even to the extent of stopping all civilian traffic.[15] From the Potomac to beyond the Mississippi a roughly standardized, if quite informal, relationship had now been achieved between the railroads and the central government.

III

Weeks before the first shells went whining across the valley of Bull Run, southern railroad officials knew that they were at war. On the nineteenth of April, 1861, to the immense indignation of President P. V. Daniel, the four steamboats of the Richmond, Fredericksburg & Potomac were seized at Washington by agents of the United States Government. Fearing further damage to his property, Daniel wrote lengthily to General Robert E. Lee, who had just been appointed commander-in-chief of the Virginia forces, outlining an elaborate scheme for the protection of threatened railroads. Lee thought sufficiently well of the idea to have it circularized among all the Virginia carriers. But other matters proved too pressing to permit his organizing railway-defense units under public auspices, and the Richmond, Fredericksburg & Potomac was obliged to raise and maintain its own guards, a policy which it followed for more than four months.[16]

Even more dangerous was the position of the lines entering Alexandria. From the windows of the Executive Mansion President Lincoln himself could see the smoke of their locomotives, while from their own cabs the Virginia enginemen could note the expanding rows of Union tents beyond the river. When the northern attack came, it would surely strike here.

Upon the secession of Virginia, President Barbour of the Orange & Alexandria excitedly organized a company of railroad guards for night duty along exposed portions of his line. He evidently expected that the men would quickly be mustered into the Commonwealth's service, but the State Advisory Council, in a report issued on May 21, declared the idea "inexpedient." The following day, however, it approved the payment of the force from public funds.[17]

The prospects of the Orange & Alexandria may have seemed foreboding, but the future of the little Alexandria, Loudoun & Hampshire was hopeless. Confined to a scanty territory between the Potomac and the upper Blue Ridge, and mercilessly exposed to attack from a number of directions, the Virginia authorities endeavored only to salvage as much of its property as they could. Just five days prior to the Federal seizure of Alexandria (May 24), General Lee instructed Lieutenant Colonel George H. Terrett, the local militia commander, to rescue its engines and cars by building a temporary connecting track across town to the rails of the Orange & Alexandria. Spurred by further reports of an imminent Federal descent, Lee reiterated his orders on May 22, but just how much of the equipment was saved is uncertain. Three weeks later similar orders to Colonel Eppa Hunton, commanding at Leesburg, directed the destruction of all the rolling stock that could not be removed, especially gondolas and flatcars.[18]

The motive power and cars of both the Orange & Alexandria and the Manassas Gap roads (whose trains entered Alexandria over Orange & Alexandria rails) were nearly all saved by removal to Manassas Junction and beyond. But eleven hundred tons of fine-quality imported rails, intended for the extension of the Manassas Gap line up the Shenandoah Valley, rails soon to become priceless, had to be left behind in an Alexandria warehouse, where they promptly fell into Federal hands.[19]

Worry over imminent loss and damage was by no means confined to railroad officials along the Confederate frontiers. In many places, especially where the Appalachians thrust a tongue of northern climate deep into the domain of King Cotton, there dwelt respectable numbers of Union sympathizers who looked upon the new Confederacy with an ill-concealed hostility. Of a fiercely independent, back-country type little given to restraint, certain of them proceeded to indulge their feelings in acts of sabotage. As early as the spring of 1861 a rail was removed surreptitiously from the track of the Southwestern road in Georgia, "by which the engine and three cars [of a passenger train] were precipitated down an embankment 23 feet high." No serious injuries, however, resulted, "which," commented Superintendent Virgil Powers, "was certainly providential." Early in July persistent rumors arose in the region of Chattanooga, Tennessee, that Union men were planning to burn a number of bridges on the Western & Atlantic, the Memphis & Charleston, and the East Tennessee & Georgia; E. B. Walker, Master of Transportation of the Western & Atlantic, was sufficiently alarmed to recommend that armed guards be posted at the structures concerned. Even in the pine forests of southern Alabama, there existed so much resentment that Samuel G. Jones, chief engineer of the Alabama & Florida, feared the malicious destruction of five key bridges.[20] That rumors of this kind were not unfounded, the future was to show abundantly.

IV

For many Confederate soldiers the war began as an excursion by rail in faultless spring weather. Within a fortnight passenger trains were appropriated by gay young men in heterogeneous uniforms, or in no uniforms at all, splendid specimens whose martial enthusiasms were exceeded only by their lack of knowledge as to their destinations. Upon the packed coaches, conductors faced a nightmare; in Virginia the chaos grew so vast that private citizens found it feasible to pose as recruits and enjoy extensive rides at the expense of the Commonwealth. So flagrant grew the practice that General Lee was obliged to issue a circular defining official travel and announcing that the State would not pay any transportation bills in the absence of regulation vouchers. Throughout May the Richmond papers carried repeated notices warning that those without competent orders would have to pay the ordinary cash fare upon the cars.[21]

Even worse was the disposition of many well-meaning military officers to interfere with the operation of trains. As early as the 25th of April President Daniel of the Richmond, Fredericksburg & Potomac strenuously urged that members of the Virginia State Forces be prohibited from molesting the regular crews. The requirements of ordinary safety made some regulation of the kind absolutely necessary, and on the following day General Lee's office ordered the practice stopped at once.[22] This alleviated, but did not permanently cure, the difficulty.

As it became obvious that the first Federal thunderbolt would be directed at Virginia, the southern authorities, State and Confederate, without special plan and by dint of sheer improvising, strove to gather an army to meet it. Every day fresh arrays of recruits came steaming over the James into Richmond. Lynchburg was selected as another point of concentration; as early as April 29 the Richmond *Examiner*, with a fine disregard of the most elementary principles of military security, noted that 10,000 men would soon be quartered there and pointed out quite candidly that they could thence be "thrown directly into Alexandria" over the line of the Orange & Alexandria whenever the necessity demanded. Although Lynchburg soon gave way to points like Manassas Junction and Centreville as a major place of assembly, full advantage continued to be taken of the railway route which led through it from Knoxville, Chattanooga, and other points south and west, and its days and nights were filled with the rumble of trains. The lines of eastern Tennessee proved, indeed, too convenient for their own good; summer had scarcely come before they began to collapse beneath floods of antique ordnance and excited volunteers. Hastily the afflicted carriers sought the aid of the Georgia-owned Western & Atlantic; and in a cooperative spirit he was presently to live down, Governor Brown provided three or four engines and about fifty cars to ease the strain. These appear to have been, for the time being, sufficient.[23]

For months a large proportion of the South's military transportation continued to be directed by individual states. Alabama even assumed, at least temporarily, the financial burden. Both Alabama and Tennessee issued travel requests and bills of lading, complete with Gothic capitals and visiting-card script. As late as October, 1861, Montgomery was employing special agents "for the transportation of clothing and supplies for Alabama volunteers in the Confederate Service in Virginia." By the end of the summer many of the railroads for their part were issuing special soldier's tickets for travel under orders; they included a separate coupon for every carrier concerned and resembled closely the kind of inter-line ticket in common use today.[24]

Railroads not only transported the first soldiers of the Confederacy to their first battles; they furnished a portion of their arms. Plagued by a thousand manufacturing deficiencies, the authorities turned early to locomotive and car shops for a multitude of critical items. The shooting had scarcely begun before the facilities of the Central of Georgia at Savannah found themselves finishing gun mounts for local defense; soon they were at work upon a wide variety of orders from the Confederate Government itself. By the end of the year the shops of the Richmond & Danville had produced thirty-five gun carriages. In November the Georgia Railroad was awarded a contract by the State of Georgia for the manufacture of six rifled field guns. Near Mobile the Whistler Shops of the Mobile & Ohio turned out mountings for both field and heavy artillery, while forges in the Atlanta shops of the Western & Atlantic flamed with the emergency production of gun barrels. If the South hardly yet realized the full importance of its rail carriers, they already were proving more vital than had been supposed.[25]

V

Of the first great collision upon the Plains of Manassas, July 21, 1861, little need be said; it may be studied in a hundred books. But it perhaps has been insufficiently emphasized that the southern victory was due in no small measure to the Manassas Gap Railroad, which succeeded in placing a respectable number of reinforcements upon the battlefield in the nick of time.

Immediately to the rear of the Confederate position lay the little station of Manassas Junction, whence the trains of the Manassas Gap line diverged westward from the iron of the Orange & Alexandria toward a convenient passage of the Blue Ridge and the corridor of the Shenandoah beyond. Behind the skyline of mountains waited the peppery General Joseph Eggleston Johnston with eleven thousand men, close to half the effective Confederate strength in northern Virginia. At Manassas Junction, facing northeastward toward Centreville and Alexandria, the self-esteeming Louisianian, P. G. T. Beauregard, had but few more. Although there was a certain faith in his military genius, he could scarcely be expected to withstand alone a Union force estimated at upwards of 35,000. The sole Confederate hope seemed to lie in *concentration*—by railroad.[26]

Just who planned the grand strategy of First Manassas is a matter of dispute, of little moment here. Johnston and Beauregard, however, both impatiently awaited the time when the army of the former might combine profitably with that of the latter. By July 17 the bustle and clamor among the Federal regiments among the Potomac hills made the imminence of an attack quite obvious, and late

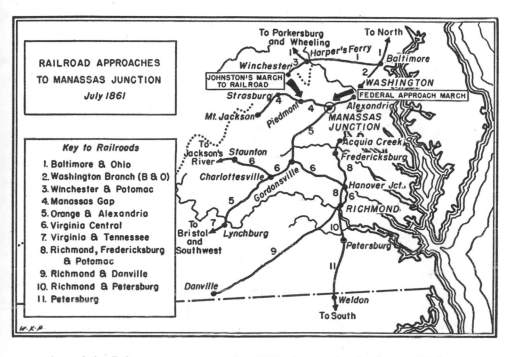

RAILROAD APPROACHES
TO MANASSAS JUNCTION
July 1861

Key to Railroads
1. Baltimore & Ohio
2. Washington Branch (B & O)
3. Winchester & Potomac
4. Manassas Gap
5. Orange & Alexandria
6. Virginia Central
7. Virginia & Tennessee
8. Richmond, Fredericksburg & Potomac
9. Richmond & Danville
10. Richmond & Petersburg
11. Petersburg

that night Johnston, encamped at Winchester in the lower Valley, was handed a telegram from Adjutant General Samuel Cooper in Richmond, ordering him to move at once to the support of the Confederate forces at Manassas.[27]

Just east of the Blue Ridge, at a little station appropriately called Piedmont, a smoking cluster of Manassas Gap trains stood waiting. Only the infantry were permitted aboard the cars, the five regiments of the brigade commanded by a certain Thomas J. Jackson being the first to lurch away. The Seventh and Eighth Georgia Regiments closely followed. Johnston himself departed with the next groups, consisting of the Second and Fourth Alabama and two companies of

the Eleventh Mississippi; he was set down upon the busy siding at
Manassas Junction at noon of the 20th, to be volubly assured by
railroad officials that the remainder of his foot-soldiers would arrive
during the same afternoon. But in this he was to be disappointed;
the capacity of the Gap road proved "inadequate and imperfect"
under the strain, and through the torrid hours of the following day,
as the concussion of battle shook the earth, Johnston's adjutant,
Major Thomas G. Rhett, was still working frantically to get the
arriving troops off the cars and into action. Of the rail-borne contingent, only two complete brigades, plus five regiments and two
companies from two others, had arrived upon the scene before the
sudden Federal rout put an end to the fighting.[28] But these had been
enough.

Less satisfactory still was the performance of the railroads leading
up from Richmond and Lynchburg. The carriers were not entirely
to blame. The first rumors of the Union advance had drifted into
the Confederate capital on July 17 before plans had been hurriedly
drawn to secure a daily northward flow of reinforcements. Under
the supervision of the local Richmond quartermaster, the Fifth
North Carolina was sent puffing off into the humid darkness on the
evening of Thursday, the 18th, but the infantry units of Hampton's
Legion did not get away until more than twenty-four hours later.
Priority telegrams flashed from the office of Adjutant General
Cooper to the quartermaster at Lynchburg, instructing him to
forward Barksdale's Mississippi regiment, together with every additional unit that might arrive at that point. The North Carolina troops
and Barksdale arrived at Manassas before the fighting began, but the
guns already were thundering before Hampton, following a nerve-
wracking ride of thirty hours in the overcrowded cars, detrained at
the Junction. With no further aid appearing in the form of additional troop trains, and with the day appearing to go in favor of the
North, Major Rhett telegraphed wildly to Richmond to rush all
available men, ammunition, and provisions, announcing that "a terrible battle" was raging. Cooper could only reply that further trains
would depart for the front "tonight and early tomorrow morning."
The Confederates on the slopes above Bull Run were left to win
with what they had.[29]

CHAPTER

~ 6 ~

Transportation Emergency—First Phase

I

Even before the near-disaster of first Manassas, it had become apparent that the Confederacy's use of railroad supply lines could not continue upon the existing informal basis without endangering the entire war effort. Of coordination there was none; everywhere local quartermasters entered into local arrangements with local railroads in the apparent belief that the doctrine of laissez faire could be successfully applied to the problems of military transportation. Quartermaster General Abraham C. Myers appeared too absorbed in other logistical difficulties to deal personally with the matter; and the routine distresses of the carriers too frequently engaged the attention, and wasted the time, of men like President Davis, the Secretary of War, and the Adjutant General. A broad control in the hands of a professional was clearly indicated.

And yet the Confederacy was never to exert an effective supervision over its railways. Paper controls would receive the grudging acquiescence of Congress, but neither the Davis Administration, nor the successive military officers it placed in charge of the carriers, ever carried them thoroughly into effect. Everyone concerned, from the President down, appeared smitten by a fatal hesitation.

To find a simple explanation for the difficulty is not easy. One can only read between the lines. Perhaps Jefferson Davis feared an unfavorable political reaction. His popularity was never universal. Robert Toombs considered him a "scoundrel" and a "false and hypocritical wretch," while a number of state governors, especially Brown of Georgia and Vance of North Carolina, bickered with him constantly. He suffered ceaseless attacks in Congress, especially in

63

the matter of appointments. His ancient enemy, Henry S. Foote, was on hand in the lower house, and let slip no opportunity to castigate the Administration—a process which seldom failed to draw applause from a large minority of the chamber. And yet it is doubtful that Davis refrained from a vigorous regulation of the carriers solely because he dreaded repercussions. A famous Davis trait was stubbornness.[1]

The real explanation probably lies in the excessive Confederate faith in the doctrine of States' Rights, which by the sixties had afflicted the southern mind for so long that men were confusing it with a multitude of other rights, regional, municipal, and even personal. Only a united people could have fought a successful war of secession, and the people of the Confederacy were not united. Too many endeavored to wage a *constitutional* war, wherein private interests were to remain inviolate. Too many endeavored to restrain the Confederate Government within the rigid bounds they formerly had prescribed for the Federal Government of the United States, and when the necessities of the conflict dictated an expansion of the central organization, they objected violently. They had toyed too long with Calhoun's theory of the concurrent majority. "It seems to me," declared Senator Louis T. Wigfall of Texas in 1863, "that the people do not properly realize the fact that their interests are identical with those of their Government." Yet, even when faced with practical considerations of the sternest kind, southerners continued to believe in what they chose to call States' Rights. And Jefferson Davis subscribed to the dogma almost as implicitly as the governors with whom he quarreled.[2]

No organization could appeal more logically to States' Rights doctrine than a southern railroad company. Nearly every carrier represented a state, county, or municipal interest of the most vital sort, and it was all too easy for individuals and localities to regard any interference by Richmond as a plot in behalf of a competitor. Given the theory of States' Rights as a fundamental axiom, the argument against centralized regulation of railroad affairs possessed real validity. In this, as in so many other things, Jefferson Davis found himself enmeshed in the strands of his own philosophy. As we shall see, he occasionally permitted its violation, but never to the extent necessary to get the best from his transportation system.

Indeed, the evil genius of the Confederate railroads lay not in the

Upper left, William Morrill Wadley. From a daguerreotype apparently taken shortly before the war. Courtesy of Mrs. William Burt, Bolingbroke, Georgia. *Upper right,* William Shepperd Ashe as he appeared in the 1850's. From an engraving in S. A. Ashe, *Biographical History of North Carolina.*

Lower left, General Alexander R. Lawton, Quartermaster General, C.S.A., August, 1863 —May, 1865. Library of Congress. *Lower right,* Frederick William Sims. From a photograph probably of the immediate postwar period. Courtesy of Calder W. Payne, Macon, Georgia.

Upper left, William Mahone, Major General, C.S.A., President of the Norfolk and Petersburg Railroad, military and political leader as well as successful railroad man. Note that he is wearing what is evidently a woman's dress converted into a uniform. Library of Congress. *Upper right*, General Jeremy F. Gilmer, Chief of the Army Engineer Bureau, C.S.A. Library of Congress.

Below, A Native Southerner. The freight locomotive Roanoke, of the Virginia & Tennessee Railroad. It was built by the Tredegar Iron Works, Richmond, Virginia, January, 1854. Cylinders, 16 x 24, drivers 54 inches, weight of engine about 21½ tons. The Roanoke stands here on a siding built of wooden stringer rail. From an ante-bellum photograph. Courtesy of H. E. Nichols, of the Norfolk & Western Railway, Bluefield, West Virginia.

makeshift administration at Richmond, or even in Davis himself. It derived from the nature of southern society, invertebrate and dis-unified, incapable of either cohesion or the management of large en-terprise. It found its true symbol in the ghost of John C. Calhoun.

On the other hand, the railway problem could not be simply ig-nored. On July 17, 1861, as the first hints of the impending Manassas battle were being whispered in the streets of Richmond, Davis com-missioned William Shepperd Ashe major and assistant quartermaster and placed him in charge of rail transportation to the Confederate armies in Virginia. It seemed an excellent selection. Born at Rocky Point, North Carolina, in 1814, of distinctly aristocratic parents, Ashe long since had proved himself a leader in both the business and political worlds. Following a year or two at Washington (now Trinity) College at Hartford, Connecticut, he returned to North Carolina and was admitted to the bar in 1836. Planting interests and a "social disposition" soon, however, led to the abandonment of ac-tive law practice, and his natural talents presently thrust him into politics. To the disgust of his Whiggish father, he became an ardent Jackson Democrat and as such was elected in 1846 state senator from New Hanover County. Thenceforth his rise was rapid. The canvass of 1848 sent him to the national House of Representatives, wherein his party loyalty became diluted by certain ideas of his own. As the slavery controversy deepened into the crisis of 1850, he so far de-parted from the principles of Old Hickory as to take his stand with the southern fire-eaters, making no attempt to conceal his belief in the right—and the desirability—of immediate secession. He also grew to be an especially close confidant of Senator Yulee of Florida.

Like many Democrats, Ashe was willing to support the Whigs in programs of internal improvement earmarked for his own district, and he continued his interest in the development of southeastern North Carolina when he left Congress in 1855. Already he had been elected, the preceding year, to the presidency of the Wilmington & Weldon Railroad, in which position he proved himself able and ag-gressive, cooperating with Yulee in the discussion of plans for a real southern rail system, and inaugurating through inter-line freight service without break of bulk from Charlotte to Wilmington. His outlook, however, remained circumscribed by the desire to serve the advantage of his own locality, and in 1858 he again entered the State Senate for the specific purpose of blocking a new railroad between

Greensboro and Danville, Virginia. He remained ultra-southern in his political views, and with the onset of the crisis of 1860 he at once joined the relatively thin ranks of the North Carolina secessionists. A leading member of the convention which finally carried the state out of the Union, he was still sitting in that body when the call to service came from Jefferson Davis. He at once departed for Richmond, a man in the prime of life, forty-six years of age, of stocky build, with hair still very black, and with dark eyes set in a friendly, somewhat heavy face.[3]

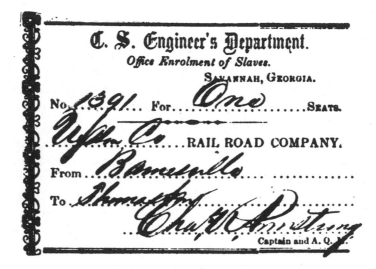

An Engineer's Department transportation request for official travel over the Upson County Railroad between Barnesville and Thomaston, Georgia. National Archives.

Setting up headquarters in Richmond, Ashe went to work with a will. As unofficial field assistants, he selected railroad officials of known ability. He introduced printed transportation requests, though Confederate stationery deficiencies and the personal tastes of local quartermasters were soon to find reflection in an extreme variation of their format. He induced the Virginia Central to operate *daily* through trains in each direction between the capital and its western terminus at Jackson's River. And in October there appeared for the first time some badly needed regulations to govern the transit of the sick and wounded from the army to the hospitals at Richmond.[4]

But Ashe was destined to meet early discouragement. The tendency of key government and army officials to deal personally with minutiae showed little sign of abatement, and they interfered constantly in Ashe's business.[5] Worse still, quartermasters and subsistence officers acquired the habit of using loaded freight cars as storehouses, a basic sin that doubtless will plague military logistics as long as the locomotive remains an engine of war. On September 18 the Government desired to send 1,000 barrels of flour to the front, but the Richmond agent of the Virginia Central complained that the authorities were holding practically all the rolling stock of his company at Manassas and at Millborough (the railhead for the Confederate forces in western Virginia), that only two cars remained in the Richmond yards, and that his freight depot was completely blocked up. There instantly exploded a telegraphic chain-reaction of charges, denials, and excuses, to and from Jefferson Davis, General Johnston, the new Acting Secretary of War Judah P. Benjamin, Commissary General L. B. Northrop, Quartermaster General Myers, and the local officers at Staunton and Millborough.[6] It was not until the 23rd that Major Ashe could inject his own comment. Amid the chatter of the telegraph, he had been quietly conferring with Superintendent H. D. Whitcomb of the Virginia Central. He admitted that recent delays to military freight could be blamed in part upon a scarcity of rolling stock, the irregularity of government shipments, and the lack of storage facilities at unloading points. But the heart of his report dealt with the unloading problem.

"I avail myself of this opportunity," he said, "to call your attention to the absolute necessity of having cars loaded with freight discharged as soon as practicable. Every moment's delay is felt more than any person who is not acquainted with railroad schedules can conceive of. This should not only be done at the various destinations of freight, but also here in Richmond."[7]

This effectively diagnosed the trouble and prescribed a cure, without the injection of personalities and ruffling of pride so characteristic of the armed forces of the Confederacy.

But despite all that Ashe and the railroad men could do, the traffic snarl between the capital and Manassas persisted throughout the autumn of 1861. Especially discouraging conditions obtained upon the single-track line of the Orange & Alexandria, over which the whole load had to pass from Gordonsville onward. Although a well-known Yankee railroader, Herman Haupt, later remarked that such a road "under intelligent management" should be able to maintain a force of 200,000, it remains doubtful whether any individual could be wholly blamed. The supply of an army by rail was a new experience to everyone concerned, and there is no question of the gross inadequacy of rolling stock and sidings.[8] And the time would come when the Confederate soldiers would look back nostalgically to the fall of 1861 as an age of plenty.

II

Of special concern to Major Ashe in the early months of the war were the roads that extended from Virginia southwestward into eastern Tennessee, northern Alabama, and northern Mississippi and afforded the only complete line of rail communication possessed by the Confederacy. Many of the links comprising the chain suffered from a characteristically southern poverty of rolling stock, and Ashe seems early to have approached the companies involved with proposals for the interchange of cars. But with the exception of the Virginia Central, the carriers clung to their own. By September the depots of East Tennessee were so choked with freight that Secretary of War L. P. Walker ordered the military seizure of the East Tennessee & Virginia "until every pound of freight for the army destined to Richmond and Manassas is sent from Knoxville to Bristol." But on the following day he was smitten by a sudden fear that his order would set off charges of military despotism. He backtracked—a fatal precedent.[9]

After the departure of Walker in September to the more rewarding environment of field service, his successor, Judah P. Benjamin, endeavored earnestly to unscramble the muddle. On September 23 the new Secretary directed the Quartermaster General to secure six engines "of at least 26 tons," and seventy boxcars, from the Western & Atlantic and Mobile & Ohio roads, if possible by contract, by impressment if necessary; and the next day Major Ashe, bearing orders to this effect, departed for the southwest. Having ascertained that the Mobile & Ohio and its connections were in no condition to lend any rolling stock, Ashe returned to Chattanooga, where he endeavored to borrow the equipment from the Georgia-owned Western & Atlantic. His bid met instant rejection. Moreover, when he proceeded to invoke his orders and seize the engines and cars, Governor Brown of Georgia burst into fury. Curt telegrams warmed the wires to Richmond, and within a few hours Secretary of War Benjamin was reading a crisp lecture upon the sovereign status of Georgia.[10]

The Secretary of War was nothing if not a diplomat. He furthermore faced real difficulties if he elected to match buffets with a champion of local privilege; the copiously scattered bread of southern political theory had returned to haunt its distributors, and Benjamin knew it. He quickly gave way. To Ashe went orders not to molest Georgia property; to the angry Governor went a mild and quite fruitless plea for cooperation. Brown remained adamant. When Ashe requested that he reconsider, the wires again vibrated with gubernatorial thunder: "If you seize our cars or engines I shall by military force, if necessary, make counter seizures." After that there remained nothing to do, unless Richmond chose to wage a shooting war with Milledgeville over seventy-six pieces of railroad equipment. The wheezing trains of the East Tennessee carriers had to labor on alone.[11]

Further dismal reports from beyond the mountains evoked only flutterings in the Confederate capital. In a letter to R. M. T. Hunter, then Secretary of State in Davis's cabinet, President Lewis Harvie of the Richmond & Danville submitted a "Proposed Through Freight Schedule" of five days and twenty hours between Richmond and New Orleans, via Knoxville, and strongly urged the creation of an inter-line freight-car pool; but nothing happened. A menacing advance of the Federal forces from western Virginia proved premature, but a worse danger presently loomed within the very mountain valleys through which the afflicted lines ran. During the first week of November, despite the fact that the southern authorities were not unaware of the plot, a number of bridges, including two on the Western & Atlantic near Chattanooga, were set afire, reportedly by Unionists under the direction of the notorious Parson Brownlow. This was a serious matter; in Richmond the preserver of official gossip, war clerk John B. Jones, confided to his diary that the burnings had an immediate effect upon the transmission of the men and munitions. The army promptly closed the door upon the stolen horse by stationing troops along the whole line between Chattanooga and Bristol.[12]

Repair of the wreckage was quickly begun, but the troubles of the

East Tennessee lines were hardly over. As the appointed guardians of the roads, the military still showed a disposition to interfere with their routine operations. This, of course, served chiefly to irritate railroad personnel and on December 2, President John R. Branner of the East Tennessee & Virginia dispatched a bitter telegram to Secretary Benjamin, wherein he threatened to cease operations if the practice continued.[13]

More blistering still was a joint outburst by Branner and President Campbell Wallace of the East Tennessee & Georgia. Declaring that "the movements of the trains and the control of the finances of the company are ordered by men incompetent, irresponsible and reckless—maybe very good military men, but certainly very bad railroad managers," they announced the suspension of all service after December 15. Benjamin, as was his wont, neutralized their wrath with soft words, and Wallace eventually apologized, explaining that he had been exhausted by overwork; he further commented that a misunderstanding between Major Ashe and Colonel Myers had delayed certain payments due on government transportation. But now his spirits had revived. "In two weeks," he promised, "I will have a better bridge than the one destroyed." [14]

Ashe was manifestly dropping from the picture. Discouraged by the lack of cooperation from the carriers, and particularly by his superiors' irritating habit of taking his responsibilities upon themselves, he was, in fact, losing all interest. After a well-meaning attempt to hasten the reconstruction of the Tennessee bridges in November, which led indirectly to the misunderstanding with Quartermaster General Myers just noted, the files saw him but seldom. In April, 1862, he withdrew from the frustrations of Richmond with the request that he be permitted to raise a battalion of artillery for field service. He met a hideous death the following autumn as the result of an accident upon his own Wilmington & Weldon. A man of real ability, he was not the last to suffer from a stifled spirit as Confederate coordinator of railroads.[15]

III

While the makeshift armies were reorganizing in the red dust of Northern Virginia, the strategic picture was coming slowly to a focus upon another portion of the Confederate frontier. Beyond the mountains, along a broad twilight zone paralleling the limits of Kentucky and Tennessee, was gathering a threat to the South that was ultimately to prove more decisive than the highly touted "On to Richmond" crusades of the East.

Here was a land of rivers, mainly navigable. Useful commercially, these streams quickly proved to be military menaces. Not only were they poorly arranged for purposes of southern defense and supply; their general courses lay in precisely those directions and places most helpful to Federal penetration. Nor could the South even command adequate facilities for their navigation; the outbreak of war found most of the steamboats removed safely from Confederate reach by their northern owners.[16]

There remained the railroads. Of these there existed a few, comprising a net which on paper seemed fairly adequate, but many of the lines remained in a crude state; nearly all of them, moreover, lay fully exposed to the raids of Union gunboats. Northward from Jackson, Tennessee, the brand new iron of the Mobile & Ohio extended to the Kentucky shore of the Mississippi at Columbus, while from the vicinity of Nashville the tracks of the Louisville & Nashville and of the Edgefield & Kentucky curved into the mid-section of the same state. From near Bowling Green the Memphis, Clarksville & Louisville and the Memphis & Ohio ran in a southwesterly direction through Memphis Junction, Clarksville, Paris, McKenzie, and Humboldt to Memphis, affording a tenuous link between the two principal north-south roads.[17]

In command of the scanty Confederate forces in this highly important region the Richmond authorities placed General Albert Sidney Johnston, reputedly the ablest officer in the whole of the southern service. Whatever may be said of Johnston's subsequent performance, his initial dispositions reflected a certain intelligence. He did examine the map and base his forces upon railroad lines. The terminus of the Mobile & Ohio at Columbus already had been occupied by that doughty fighting bishop, Leonidas Polk, with ten thousand men. To Bowling Green, far up the Louisville & Nashville and covering the divergence of the Memphis road, Johnston sent Simon Bolivar Buckner with a screen of four thousand; presently the little town would serve as the headquarters of twenty thousand troops under General William J. Hardee. Far to the east in the wild terrain of Cumberland Gap, Felix K. Zollicoffer loosely covered the carriers of eastern Tennessee. Between Columbus and Bowling Green, at least, the iron horse would stand at the service of the Confederates, affording the possibility of rapid concentration in the face of a Federal advance against either point.[18] But although the railroads did function as intended upon a minor occasion or two, no really adequate scheme for their coordination was ever developed.

Just what sort of control was adopted by the Confederate authorities in the west remains vague to this day, and it appears likely that the troops dependent upon the Louisville & Nashville and its connections were themselves not unaware of an administrative fog. Colonel V. K. Stevenson, president of the Nashville & Chattanooga road and currently serving as quartermaster in Nashville, acted upon one or two occasions as a kind of distributor of motive power and cars. Similar functions seem to have been performed, perhaps simultaneously, by Lieutenant John M. Hottel, late of Terry's Regiment of Texas Rangers; Hottel dealt likewise with the repair of locomotives and routine local management. At the end of the year, one G. B. Fleece was being employed as civilian superintendent, under military authority, of the southern portion of the Louisville & Nashville and its subsidiary, the Memphis, Clarksville & Louisville. But whatever the arrangements, the Confederate operations were seriously hampered by the usual dearth of rolling stock, while the constant shifting of units to and from Hardee and Polk evoked a generous measure of confusion.[19]

IV

Already it has been noted that no physical connection existed between the lines serving Richmond, or between the carriers entering Petersburg from south and north. An absurd situation in normal times, the outbreak of hostilities swiftly rendered it impossible. The closing of the gaps was earnestly favored by both the railroads and the army; as early as the first of May, 1861, preliminary surveys were being made in both cities by the Richmond city engineer, Washington Gill, probably at the instance of the companies. In June General Lee strongly endorsed the elimination of the Petersburg gap, asserting that desperately needed guns and ammunition taken from the navy yard at Norfolk were being seriously delayed in transit to the capital and points north. Rectification of the matter had become by this time so necessary that the Virginia Convention hastened to approve the work, although local opposition in both cities rallied sufficiently to insert a proviso forbidding the carriage of private freight over the connecting rails and requiring their removal after the war.[20]

Though at last in possession of the Commonwealth's blessing, the carriers had not the cash wherewith to commence the work. No funds being available from the state, the Richmond, Fredericksburg & Potomac and the Richmond & Petersburg turned to the Confederate Government for aid, offering to provide the desired trackage within three months in return for a subsidy of $60,000. Connections so constructed, explained President Daniel of the R. F. & P., would suffice for the transfer of cars and locomotives by horse power from any of the southern railroads to the railroads north of Richmond.[21]

The Richmond link seems to have been laid directly down Eighth Street between the Richmond, Fredericksburg & Potomac terminus at Eighth and Broad and the Richmond & Petersburg depot near Eighth and Canal. It never proved satisfactory because of the excessive gradient, nor did it provide an effective bridge to the rails of the Richmond & Danville because of the difference in gauge. Ill adapted though it was to the transfer of troops and military freight, the line was retained as an escape route across the city for rolling stock threatened by enemy action.[22]

The Petersburg project did better. The work was carried on under the supervision of Major Ashe, who appears in this instance to have been left strictly alone by his superiors. Even so there were delays; the contractor concerned undertook to provide a completed line by August 6, but it was not finished until later in the month. When placed in operation, however, it greatly expedited the flow of government traffic from the Carolinas into Richmond. The teamsters of Petersburg looked on sourly, but the link seems most seriously to have irritated the management of the Norfolk & Petersburg, whose yards it crossed, and a part of whose business it diverted.[23]

Ashe did not concern himself with Petersburg alone; during his regime he endeavored to eliminate discontinuities wherever they existed. For Savannah he urged the immediate junction of the Central of Georgia with the Savannah, Albany & Gulf. He repeatedly bewailed the 600 yards which separated the Augusta & Savannah from the other lines entering Augusta. He deplored the necessity of wagon transit across Montgomery, although the two principal roads serving that city had been built to separate gauges. State and municipal approval of the Georgia connections came slowly, but a start was made in the Montgomery matter in December, when the Alabama Assembly granted authority to the Alabama & Florida road to extend its track through the city to the depot of the Montgomery & West Point. Of the desirability of the Montgomery work there was no doubt. Already the Confederate Government was paying a monthly drayage bill of $2,000; worse still, the movement of a single regiment and its equipment from one station to the other consumed five hours. President Pollard of the Alabama & Florida promised to reduce this to a single hour, whenever the extension should be finished.[24]

Even more productive of paralysis were the trackless spaces which interrupted what should have been significant main routes. Most glaring of these, perhaps, was the incomplete sequence of roads running across central Alabama, between Meridian, just over the line in Mississippi, and Selma and Montgomery. The potential value of such a route had been noted as early as February, 1861, by Dr. Morris Emanuel, Vice-President of the Southern Railroad of Mississippi,[25] and he was echoed later in the spring by *DeBow's Review*. "No single proposition of internal improvement within the Confederate States," it declared, "is comparable in importance, viewed in a social, pecuniary, political, military or commercial light, to the rapid completion of this portion of the Main Trunk Line that is to bind together homogeneous States, and strengthen the hands of their people to achieve their magnificent designs." [26] During the fall the problem engrossed the attention of Major Ashe, who appears to have discussed it at length with officials of the Alabama & Mississippi Rivers Railroad, still unfinished between Selma and Demopolis and a key segment in the desired chain. "On the completion of this road," remarked Ashe, "the Government would have command of *two* continuous lines from the Mississippi to the Atlantic." A fortnight later, on December 13, he reported further that government freight was clogged at Memphis and Grand Junction and that tonnage from New Orleans would have to be diverted to the slow circuit via Meridian and Mobile Bay. Only twenty-three miles, he pointed out, of the direct Meridian-Selma line remained incomplete.[27]

Others were thinking similarly. On December 5 the State of Alabama advanced $40,000 to the A. & M. R. company to help push its rails westward. The previous August, furthermore, an Alabama congressman had introduced a bill "to aid in the completion of a railroad for war and defensive purposes," which seems to have had reference to the same project. Although legislation of this character had been deemed "inexpedient" at the time by a cautious Military Affairs Committee, the idea that the central Confederate authority should render assistance to uncompleted railroads of strategic significance was nevertheless gaining currency.[28]

The bridging of the Danville-Greensboro gap likewise stimulated an increasing discussion. It seems first to have been broached as a military measure by one B. M. Jones of Danville in a letter to General Lee early in May, 1861. The idea naturally awakened favorable echoes in Richmond & Danville circles; it was endorsed with enthusiasm at a meeting of its board on June 12, and was brought vigorously to the attention of Jefferson Davis by President Lewis Harvie on June 19. During the autumn Harvie continued to press the matter, and Davis finally was prodded into recommending government aid in a message to the Provisional Congress on November 18. But though the annual meeting of the stockholders of the Richmond & Danville, held in near-by Metropolitan Hall on December 12, pledged its cooperation, Congress by-passed the measure. A clamorous minority had discovered therein a monstrous threat to southern liberties. Pointing out that Article I, Section 8, Paragraph (1) of the Confederate Constitution prohibited bounties from the treasury "to promote or foster any branch of industry," they succeeded in delaying the legislation, despite the arrival of a booster message from the President's office four days later. But for all their constitutional scruples, the project refused to die, as will later appear. Its necessity was too apparent upon the map.[29]

More pressing still seemed the case of the little Mobile & Great Northern, which had bravely spiked down its first bar of English iron upon the east bank of the Tensas on March 28, 1861. The completion of the line to a junction with the Alabama & Florida at Pollard was first promised for September, then for October. But as the autumn breezes stirred the pinewoods, only half the track was finished, and though the balance of the required iron already lay piled in the Mobile customhouse, local financial resources, including those of the City of Mobile, were exhausted. An emergency loan of

$15,000, however, was all that was reckoned necessary to complete the work, and no one could deny its military value.

Calls for help, actively supported by an Alabama delegate in the Provisional Congress, elicited a surprisingly favorable response in Richmond. The $15,000 was at once provided from available Confederate funds, thus eliminating the need for tortuous legislation. Also surprisingly, the advance proved adequate, and the line was opened to traffic on November 15. A through schedule of fourteen hours was established to Montgomery; to Pensacola the running time averaged somewhat less. "The public will find this a cheap, comfortable and expeditious route," declared Superintendent Jordan, "with new Cars and Equipments." Perhaps even more to the point was the comment of General Braxton Bragg, who telegraphed from his headquarters in western Florida that the railroad was equal to 3,000 men at each end.[30]

A special problem, never solved in the course of the war, was the lack of railroad facilities between Texas and the remainder of the Confederacy. Correctly foreseeing the stoppage of coastwise sea travel, President Gentry of the Texas & New Orleans early recommended the establishment of a pony express system across the gap between railheads in Texas and Louisiana, but whether any such service was ever operated remains unknown. That a railroad might be pushed westward to the Sabine under Confederate auspices was proposed in the Provisional Congress as early as May, 1861, and a similar motion was offered by a Texas member, John Hemphill, on November 25, just as the Danville-Greensboro link was receiving its first serious attention. But, as has been noted, the political climate was not yet favorable to such legislation. Indeed, the isolation of Texas was not to end until some years after the collapse of the Confederacy.[31]

V

To the end of 1861 Confederate efforts to marshal the southern railways for war were merely tentative. Distracted by a thousand emergencies, the Government could devote little time to the matter, while the carriers themselves soon showed clearly that they expected help, not orders, from the authorities. There existed no reason why regularly scheduled government freights should not be run, asserted Harvie of the Richmond & Danville in October, "except that each railroad company wishes to control its own road in its own way, and make all others conform to its views." A single hesitant step in the direction of unified regulation was taken in July in the form of "a bill authorizing the President to regulate and take control of railroads in certain cases." Introduced by Conrad of Louisiana at the request of Major Ashe and the Secretary of War, the measure would have given Davis wide authority over the operations of the carriers and have permitted the seizure of recalcitrant roads. But such provisions were too explosive, and the delegates were happy to let them die.[32] Absorbed as they were in the defense of local liberties, no Confederate Congress was to approve so comprehensive a measure for nearly two years.

Few men, indeed, yet realized that the iron horse had become a military weapon of the first magnitude. But there were a few, both Federal and Confederate. "It cannot be ignored," declared a northern officer of increasing repute, "that the construction of railroads has introduced a new and very important element into war, by the great facilities thus given for concentrating at particular positions large masses of troops from remote sections and by creating new strategic points and lines of operation."[33] Perhaps the perception of George Brinton McClellan would have been less acute had he not been a railroad man himself.

CHAPTER

～7～

Profits, Losses, and Shortages

"Rail Road supplies are enormously high, and still
advancing and difficult to get at all. Labor is high;
trade and commerce nearly destroyed by our political troubles, so that it would be expecting too much
of the road to suppose that its income should even
be kept at what it has been or now is."—Report of
Superintendent John W. Lewis of the Western &
Atlantic Railroad to Governor Brown of Georgia,
October 1, 1861.

I

FOR THE FIRM OF JOHN A. LANCASTER & SON, LEADING STOCKHOLDERS
of Richmond, business was exceedingly dull. Specializing in local
bank, municipal, and railroad bonds and shares, they had lately received few inquiries and fewer orders. Of the fourteen railroad issues
in which they commonly dealt, only four had been traded during
the week ending May 2, 1861, and they all had been sold at prices
well below par. The clerks had little to do save stand at the windows
and watch the evolutions of the volunteer regiments in the street
outside.[1]

The business doldrums were by no means confined, that spring, to
the Lancaster office. With the country sinking into sectional war,
businessmen from Maine to Texas grew increasingly hesitant to risk
their capital. What would be the ultimate implications of secession,
no one could say. The infant railroad industry seemed especially
bewildered. Observers like the *Railroad Record* thought that the carriers of the cotton states might be injured by the outbreak of hostili-

78

ties but that an *internal* flow of cotton would develop to the North Atlantic ports upon the closure of the Confederate coastline. But however gross its misunderstanding as to what a conflict of the first order might involve, the *Record* assumed no Delphic attitude. "What changes may hereafter be produced, we know not," it admitted.[2]

Contrary to expectation, the business of a few companies soared briefly. Early in 1861 the planters along the Nashville & Chattanooga road endeavored to anticipate the Federal blockade by shipping all the cotton and other produce they possessed. The resulting traffic load attained such proportions that three of the company's passenger locomotives were transferred to freight service, while operating crews frequently worked thirty-six hours out of forty-eight. During April, in consequence of the crisis at Charleston Harbor, a large amount of business was diverted to the roads leading to Savannah.[3]

Nevertheless, for some months the initial fears seemed justified. The prodigious commerce upon the Nashville & Chattanooga proved but a powder flash; trade obstructions imposed by the Washington Government at Cairo in May and at Louisville in June brought a rapid decline in traffic. Equally brief was the boom upon the Macon & Western; its gross earnings had exceeded $40,000 in April, but tumbled to little more than $22,000 by June. The traffic of scores of other companies stagnated similarly. The total income of the South Carolina Railroad attained a figure of $1,499,637 in 1860; in 1861 it sank to $1,161,742. During the same period the receipts of the Richmond & Danville dwindled from $560,904 to $447,959, while the earnings of the Central of Georgia dropped from $1,700,000 to little more than $1,000,000. The list might be extended indefinitely.[4]

These depressing figures could be charged in great measure to shrinking private shipments. The volume of freight passing over the Seaboard & Roanoke diminished by nearly 100 per cent. In May, 1861, the *Annual Report* of the Mobile & Ohio ruefully noted the "complete prostration of business." "The condition of the country," complained the Richmond & Danville in December, "left but little for us to transport; and the low price of produce induced the farmers and planters to withhold from market the bulk of their crops." Especially severe was the plight of the cotton-carrying roads. Faced not only with a Federal blockade of increasing efficacy, but also with a Confederate regulation prohibiting the free export of the staple, cotton traffic upon the Central of Georgia declined from

413,000 bales to 260,000 bales in a single year. The decrease on the Montgomery & West Point was from 59,425 bales to 32,874; upon the Southwestern road, from 174,008 to 39,832.[5]

But as civilian business went down, military and other government traffic went up. On roads directly serving the theaters of military operations, army tonnage expanded at an unprecedented rate. From the spring of 1861 onward, the Virginia Central labored beneath the heaviest press of freight in its history. Many routes, especially those leading toward northern Virginia, reported a soaring passenger traffic of strongly military complexion. During the twelve months ending June 30, the Virginia & Tennessee carried nearly 130,000 individuals, an excess of 20,000 over the previous year. The volume of passengers seeking transportation over the North Carolina road doubled, and then tripled. Upon an overnight journey from Charleston to Columbia in July, a traveling bill collector "passed an almost sleepless night being cramped up by soldiers." Even in the case of the roads serving the interior, passenger traffic appears to have diminished very little, if at all.[6]

Increasing government business, however, by no means served to offset the loss of private traffic. For transporting the volunteers who crowded the windows of every passenger train, the carriers were receiving a fare averaging less than 50 per cent of that charged civilians, while until mid-autumn military freight was hauled at just half the ordinary local rates in effect. Moreover, war shipments tended to flow in one direction only, necessitating the handling of much empty equipment. Even with the fabulous growth of passenger business, only two or three roads could report an actual increase in receipts from this source. The gloomy prophecies of early spring seemed on the verge of fulfillment. And they were given further credence in October, when Superintendent Whitcomb of the Virginia Central estimated that the prices of ordinary railroad supplies had risen about 25 per cent, at a time when Confederate currency had as yet suffered little devaluation in terms of specie.[7]

The carriers, of course, struggled desperately to free themselves from this economic vise. The most obvious method was retrenchment—in salaries, in maintenance, in service, in dividends, occasionally in personnel. Of these, reductions in maintenance were particularly common, for many items of railway supply already had become extremely scarce in the Confederacy. Dividends were

Above, a typical certificate showing ownership of shares in the capital stock of a southern railroad. Note the locomotive and cars characteristic of the period. National Archives. "Thanks to soaring fares and rates, railroad profits became quite fabulous. War, in fact, no longer seemed a threat to owners of railroad securities—until they took their money to the county seat and endeavored to convert it into tangible goods."

Below, small-change "shin-plaster" issued by the South Carolina Railroad, April, 1864. Courtesy of the Southern Railway System. "Some of the railroad paper was elaborately engraved, with representations of locomotives pouring forth quantities of smoke over rural landscapes."

Above, an old drawing showing a Manassas Gap Railroad train carrying troops to the field of First Manassas. Library of Congress.

Below, Confederate track used by an emergency Federal hospital train. The Richmond & York River Railroad after the Battle of Seven Pines. In the same manner the road carried wounded Confederates. From a sketch "made on the spot." Library of Congress.

slashed in a number of instances. Of eleven railroads in South Carolina, only two made any distribution during 1861, and one of these, the South Carolina, seems to have paid nothing after June. The Virginia Central passed its usual spring dividend and asserted that it would restrict its fall payment to 3 per cent. The July dividend of the Petersburg road was cut from 5 per cent to 4. The elimination of various services was sometimes resorted to. Certain scheduled passenger trains were cancelled on the Virginia & Tennessee and the Richmond, Fredericksburg & Potomac. In the late autumn two lines entering the Confederate capital announced that their agents would no longer collect freight bills, while one of them, the Richmond & Petersburg, strictly limited the hours during which goods would be received at its depot. In Georgia the Western & Atlantic endeavored to reduce the salaries of its principal officers, a proposal which only met defeat in the State Senate. A common device was the reduction of train speeds. By October, 1861, a traveler from Savannah to Macon was obliged to ride from twenty minutes to a full hour longer than during the previous winter. Schedules between Augusta and Atlanta were lengthened even more severely. In July the Richmond, Fredericksburg & Potomac extended its running time from Fredericksburg to Richmond by more than twenty minutes, while in November the 104-mile journey from Charleston to Savannah absorbed six and three-quarters hours instead of the five and one-half hours in effect one year before. A similar tendency was evident upon the time-cards of other roads.[8]

In the face of declining civilian traffic, the carriers dared not try to expand the revenues derived therefrom by means of rate increases. For many months, indeed, most companies seem to have left their local rate structures strictly alone. But there was no such hesitation with reference to Confederate States business. At the Montgomery meeting, to be sure, the companies represented had agreed to transport government freight at one half the regular charges, but the pressures of a single wartime summer served as an effective solvent of patriotism. On the fourth of October representatives of the principal roads assembled once again at Chattanooga and blithely set up a new and more remunerative schedule of rates for government traffic. Shipments on Confederate account were divided into four classes: Ammunition, Live Stock, Stock Feed, and Miscellaneous. For ammunition a charge of forty-five cents per hundredweight per hundred miles was imposed; for livestock the rate was fixed at twenty dollars per carload per hundred miles; while a car of feed was to be moved a like distance for fifteen dollars. All other government freight was assessed at a rate of twenty cents per hundred miles. For hauls of less than one hundred miles no reduction was offered, "the labor and expense of loading and unloading, and the detention of the cars for the same, being as much for short as for long distances." [9]

Because there had been no clear understanding as to how the Montgomery rates should be determined in particular cases and because of the manifest advantages of uniformity, Quartermaster General Abraham C. Myers accepted the Chattanooga tariff; and in a printed circular, dated December 13, requested the adherence thereto of every railroad company in the Confederacy. The new basis, he thought, was liberal, "enough so to compensate Companies for the usual wear and tear in their rolling stock, and to induce its acceptance on their part." [10]

Just how liberal were the Chattanooga rates, Colonel Myers did not at first appreciate. But it became speedily apparent that the Government, in the case of many articles, was actually being charged more heavily than were private shippers. Over the 162 miles of the Wilmington & Weldon the existing rate for civilian consignments of pork and beef was thirty cents; under the Chattanooga plan, the Confederacy paid thirty-two and one-half cents. For citizens the rate on corn was ten cents per bushel; for the Government seventeen and one-half cents. Upon the Richmond & Petersburg line, twenty-two and one-half miles long, the new government rate upon a "large number" of articles was fixed at twenty cents—four cents higher than the ordinary tariff—while for the transportation of other items, including pig iron, coal, and corn, the Confederate States found themselves paying more than twice the normal charge. "It may be safely alleged," declared Myers' assistant, Lieutenant Colonel Larkin Smith, "that every Road, whether long or short, receives, under [the] plan, *more than individuals pay for the same transportation.*" But the Richmond authorities appear to have done nothing to remedy the situation; moreover, the impending tornado of inflation would presently whirl all ordinary freight rates skyward. [11]

To what extent the railroads endeavored to reduce expenses by laying off employees remains obscure; probably the expansion of military traffic on many roads precluded such a step. Indeed, railroad personnel could scarcely be classified as expendable. Upon the eve of disunion the whole number of the officers and employees employed by the carriers of the seceding states amounted to not quite 7,000, less than one-fifth the national total of 36,567, and little exceeding the figure for the State of New York alone.[12]

Furthermore, upon the outbreak of hostilities, a rather large number of railroad men, from a sense of duty if not of intelligence, abandoned their throttles for service as volunteers. In Virginia so many crowded the recruiting offices that Governor Letcher felt "constrained to order" each railway man in his state not to "leave his post for the purpose of engaging in military operations, without leave first obtained from the executive." From the Mississippi Central came a direct plea to Jefferson Davis, earnestly requesting that trained mechanics be released from the army and replaced by others; this the President endorsed to the Secretary of War with the remark that similar complaints had been received from other sources. "Our [Western & Atlantic] force has been greatly reduced," declared Governor Brown of Georgia to Richmond as late as March, 1862, "by volunteering for the service."[13]

The Government did take some action; a few railroad men, perhaps disillusioned already in the matter of military glory, were sent home from the camps. But the carriers thought the authorities niggardly, and moreover it became increasingly difficult to keep existing forces steadily at work. President Owen of the Virginia & Tennessee complained in November, 1861, that numbers of his most experienced hands had abandoned railroad service in favor of work in the government munitions factories at Richmond, which, he said, most unfairly were offering higher pay for a less strenuous day's labor. It did not take long for the War Between the States to assume most of the features of modern warfare.[14]

II

The onset of armed conflict not only brought distressing results to railroad balance sheets all over the South; it likewise served to quench much of the zeal for new construction. Even before the venerable Edmund Ruffin pulled the lanyard of the first gun in the war, and while there remained some hope that hostilities might be averted, an atmosphere of panic slowed the pace of grading gangs. As early as February 1, the Board of the Atlantic & Gulf announced that its track would not reach Bainbridge, Georgia, the proposed terminus of the road, within the time assigned for its completion. The arrival of the first train of the Vicksburg, Shreveport & Texas at Monroe, Louisiana, was proclaimed "with infinite pleasure" by the local press on January 31, but work westward toward the Texas line was reported "temporarily suspended by the pressure of the times." Progress upon new roads between Montgomery and Selma and Eufaula came suddenly to a stop. The San Antonio & Mexican Gulf, creeping inland from Matagorda Bay, was compelled to mark time at Victoria, Texas, a mere twenty-eight miles from salt water. The Western North Carolina awoke from its dream of conquest over the Blue Ridge to endeavor (unsuccessfully) to reach the Piedmont village of Morganton.[15]

In certain instances new iron continued to be pushed forward. The long-anticipated connection between Memphis and Louisville was triumphantly opened in mid-April, and the final spike of the Mississippi & Tennessee, linking Memphis with Grenada, was pounded home on July 4. In Texas the Texas & New Orleans possessed sufficient momentum to reach the Louisiana boundary at the Sabine by late spring, while the Houston & Texas Central inched into Millican and carried the track of its proposed Austin subsidiary from Hempstead as far as Brenham. The Brunswick & Florida, despite its northern ownership, managed to struggle forward through the Georgia flatwoods until in August its wavering rails joined the iron of the Atlantic & Gulf at the present site of Waycross. The year 1861 likewise saw the successful issue of the Mobile & Ohio and the Mobile & Great Northern projects. And for many other companies the suspension of construction seemed but an unpleasant interlude, which soon would pass away with the clouds of war.[16]

But in spite of retrenchments in service and maintenance, a growing military traffic, and the cancellation of plans for expansion, the "uncertainties of the times" hit a number of existing carriers hard. An early victim was the Orange & Alexandria. Others were the Charleston & Savannah and the Spartanburg & Union. In Alabama the Alabama & Tennessee Rivers Railroad, still far from finished and cursed through much of its length with a rugged terrain devoid of traffic, faced early bankruptcy. Yet a convenient life line lay at hand, of whose existence railway management was entirely aware: state assistance. President Barbour of the Orange & Alexandria, armed with the knowledge that the Commonwealth of Virginia could hardly permit the default of a company in which it held a heavy interest, focused his influence upon the State Assembly as early as March, 1861, and came away with a generous extension of the time wherein his line would be required to pay the interest overdue upon certain state loans. In Alabama the authorities were equally helpful. On February 7, 1861, the Montgomery legislature refloated the foundering Alabama & Tennessee Rivers road with a rebate of customs liabilities due upon imported rails held in the Mobile customhouse, moneys which the state was presuming to collect by virtue of its separation from the Federal Union. A little later the same lawmakers provided direct largess to the extent of $5,861.98.[17] In view of such cooperation it is doubtful if the railroad officers involved were so worried as they pretended.

III

Despite contemporary allegations, the secession of the Southern States had been hardly the result of an organized military plot. Indeed, a belief had persisted that an independent South could be established without bloodshed, and no Dixie Hitler had appeared to launch a program for hoarding strategic materials. Southern potentialities in the field of manufacture were, as has been pointed out, relatively slight. Thus the railroads of the Confederate States entered a first-class war with no extraordinary stockpile of supplies, nor with any hopeful prospect of meeting their needs from domestic sources. "In the whole Confederacy," declared the management of the Virginia & Tennessee in the autumn of 1861, "there is no manufacture of steel, locomotive, tire, or many other articles absolutely necessary."[18]

An especially pressing problem was an adequate supply of iron rails. By the first wartime summer these were being rolled, within the Confederacy, by only one mill—at Atlanta—and most of the scanty output appears to have been snatched up by the Navy Department for the plating of gunboats. Small stockpiles existed here and there in the hands of individual roads; in August the Southwestern Company in Georgia possessed 479 tons of good and 24 tons of worn iron, and the Virginia Central held in Richmond enough extra bar for a full ten miles of road, all of which had been earmarked for the extension of its line from Jackson's River into Covington. The Western & Atlantic managed to pick up 1,100 tons at Savannah at fifty dollars per ton.[19] But most of the available supply of rail lay piled in the warehouses of ports like Pensacola and New Orleans, iron caught in transit by the crisis. A large portion was the property of local railroads; the rest remained, technically, in hands of brokers, certain of them of northern residence and loyalty. Theodore Dehon, of 10 Wall Street, New York City, thus held in March, 1861, five hundred tons of light T-Section at New Orleans. Nervous over the prospect of open warfare between North and South, and perhaps unaware of the military importance of his goods, he advertised his willingness to deliver the same to any bona-fide purchaser "without delay." He quickly found a customer in the Macon & Brunswick, which tendered him its note for $42,000, a paper which, together with interest unpaid, remained in the hands of Mrs. Dehon as late as 1866. Other northerners were equally luckless. A railway project in northeastern Texas with some pretensions to a future, the Memphis, El Paso & Pacific, had contracted with Thomas C. Bates, likewise of New York, for its initial consignment of rail, which the outbreak of war found on deposit at New Orleans and in transit upon the Mississippi and Red rivers. This the Confederate Government permitted the company to retain without payment to Mr. Bates. Another 530 tons of Yankee ownership, though consigned to the Vicksburg, Shreveport & Texas, suffered direct Confederate seizure, the railroad, not the northern brokers, receiving ultimate compensation at the rate of sixty-five dollars per ton.[20]

A small additional amount was secured by the picturesque method of armed raid. This time the victim was the Baltimore & Ohio, which, like the Louisville & Nashville, had the misfortune to run through both seceding and non-seceding territory. Southern raiders, Stonewall Jackson and Turner Ashby among others, repeatedly occupied portions of the B. & O. and succeeded in carrying off respectable quantities of rail, as well as a variety of other equipment. The iron at first was given to the connecting Winchester & Potomac, but the little road proved so exposed as to be of small use to the southern war effort, and early in 1862 plans were made to move the precious bars further into the interior.[21]

An odd legacy of disunion was the problem of what to do about the customs charges ordinarily imposed upon imported iron and other railroad supplies of foreign origin. Secession left many loose threads, all of which could scarcely be picked up at once by an amateur government. In the absence of a Confederate tariff, the collection of import duties devolved at first upon the individual states. But the central authority retained constitutionally the right, if not the duty, of regulating foreign commerce, and as early as February 16, 1861, the Provisional Congress passed a bill providing for the free introduction of railway iron. A month later, however, additional legislation subjected "railroad rails, spikes, fishing plates, and chairs used in the construction of railroads" to an ad valorem impost of 15 per cent. This rate received confirmation in the General Confederate Tariff Act of May 21, 1861, to take effect the last day of August; a supplementary law, approved simultaneously, directed the refund of any excess that might have been paid by a railroad since the imposition of the low Confederate rate.[22]

The sudden termination of customs collection by Washington, the months of interregnum before a Confederate organization could function in its place, the temporary assumption of the duty by the states, the conflicting regulations derived therefrom, the varying acts emanating from a hastily organized Provisional Congress, all served to create bewilderment. A cargo of imported rails, intended for the Pensacola & Georgia, had lain in a Pensacola warehouse since the previous October; in March Governor John Milton of Florida suddenly ordered its delivery without payment of duty, an act of sturdy independence which led to a discrepancy in the accounts of the collector of the port of $7,884.81. The collector took such alarm that he immediately restored the old United States impost of 24 per cent. To withdraw additional iron from his warehouse, the Alabama & Florida road was obliged to pay an overage of $2,379.80 and the Mobile & Great Northern one of $1,110.22, the rectification of which required special congressional acts of reimbursement.[23]

As the Federal squadrons clustered more thickly off the few really navigable southern inlets, an ordinary bar of railroad iron grew to be a minor treasure. By the late fall of 1861, rail had become so valuable within the Confederacy that the owners of the Mexican

Gulf Railroad, a local enterprise half mired in the cypress swamps east of New Orleans, thought it more advantageous to tear up their line and advertise it for sale than to continue its operation; and were only restrained from so doing by a court injunction secured by the state.[24] To what lengths the Richmond Government would be ultimately driven by the scarcity of railroad track materials will become evident in due course.

IV

Southern motive power found itself in an even worse position than rail. There were not enough locomotives; there existed no real facilities for the manufacture of more, and companies so fortunate as to possess a surplus usually refused to lend their units to other lines. Carriers at a distance from routes of military traffic could nurse their engines along, thanks to a temporary decline in actual tonnage; upon the Central of Georgia, for example, fifty-five locomotives operated a total of 706,282 miles in 1861, as compared with a figure of close to 900,000 for the previous year. But though the Central probably enjoyed, with respect to locomotives, the most favorable position in the entire Confederacy, a decline in standards of maintenance became evident not only in the reduced luster of their brasswork, but in the statistics reflecting their thermal efficiency; where they covered 81 miles per cord of wood in 1860, they could operate only 79 miles in 1861. Reports from the neighboring Southwestern Railroad disclosed a similar tendency. Nor was the situation to improve—anywhere—until the day of the Confederacy was done.[25]

The Richmond authorities had endeavored to attack the locomotive problem very early in the war. Just before the Alexandria, Loudoun & Hampshire had been swallowed up within the Federal lines, two of its engines had been laboriously salvaged and, appropriately rechristened the General Beauregard and the General Johnston, had come into the possession of the Confederate Government. The first was sold to the Virginia Central, which already was reeling beneath the weight of its war traffic; the second, after repairs in the Virginia Central shops, went to the similarly overloaded Richmond, Fredericksburg & Potomac. More were secured in the autumn, thanks to the spoliations performed upon the Baltimore & Ohio by Stonewall Jackson and Turner Ashby. Aside from the nine miles of rail previously noted, their loot had included five well-furbished steam locomotives, plus $40,000 worth (U. S.) of machine tools and other materials removed from the Martinsburg shops. How the motive power was to be placed upon southern trackage was a problem—it could scarcely be routed via Washington, even under the personal escort of Ashby—and some discussion developed as to the feasibility of using the Baltimore & Ohio iron to build a military connection between Winchester, the terminus of the Winchester & Potomac, and Strasburg, on the line of the Manassas Gap Road. But the proposal ultimately was rejected by the War Department as impracticable, and presently a strange procession could be seen moving down the famous Valley Pike, as the five engines were dragged painfully southward behind multiple teams of horses. Under the direction of Thomas R. Sharp, veteran superintendent of the Charlotte & South Carolina and currently serving as a special agent of the Confederate Government, the locomotives arrived safely in Strasburg early in September, where they were hoisted onto Confederate rails. In the existing state of things they were worth at least a division of infantry.[26]

The Government likewise endeavored to secure motive power from roads not in serious straits and place it upon those whose need was greatest. Already described have been the experiences of Benjamin and Ashe with Governor Joseph E. Brown in the episode of the impressed Western & Atlantic equipment. Official pressure produced better results in the case of the Central of Georgia, which sold in the course of 1861 one passenger engine to the new Mobile & Great Northern and two freight locomotives to the Confederacy for distribution elsewhere. But the extent of the Central's self-sacrifice may be gauged by the fact that two of the three machines had recently been giving mechanical difficulty.[27]

The car situation was as bad. Like locomotives, cars seemed scarcest where they were most needed. Declared Superintendent H. D. Whitcomb of the Virginia Central: "The stock of cars is very deficient, and the number must be increased immediately or the patrons of the road will suffer for want of means of transportation for their produce to market. I suppose there is no road which is so deficient in this respect as yours. This has been more than apparent under the heavy transportation of the past three months, as it has been impossible to give the army transportation that prompt attention which is so necessary, to say nothing of the business that naturally belongs to the road." [28]

Needy lines, with the moral support of Richmond, tried constantly to borrow rolling stock from their connections, but with little success. That a "foreign" road would neglect equipment not its own was a southern railroad superstition of long standing and some justification. The treatment allegedly accorded the stock loaned in the summer of 1861 by the Western & Atlantic to the East Tennessee roads had abruptly terminated the cooperative attitude of Governor Brown, and when the officials of the Central of Georgia were asked to furnish twenty-two cars to the neighboring Charleston & Savannah, they released them only with a wry face. Early efforts of Major Ashe to organize through car lines for military traffic were hardly more successful. Forty-seven boxes and flats were wrung from the Richmond & Danville to transport heavy ordnance from the Tredegar Iron Works at the capital to the ports of New Orleans, Mobile, and Savannah, but the Danville management complained that many of the cars had been absent for two months at a time, and that the service had proved "very injurious" to them. Nothing like this, they intimated, must happen again. [29]

But though shortages loomed everywhere in the field of railroad supplies, adversity was not wholly unhealthful. As American railroad men, the officials of the Confederate carriers worked hardest at precisely those times they wailed the loudest. Certain of them performed prodigies. Witness the following report of Superintendent John M. Robinson of the Seaboard & Roanoke:

"Upon the breaking out of the war between the Confederate and United States the Seaboard Road, in common with many of the railways of the South, found itself cut off from the source upon which it had been heretofore dependent for supplies of almost every description. This led me to attempt the production of many articles from our own resources, and in many respects the attempt has succeeded in a manner which must be most gratifying to you [the stockholders]. I have heretofore used exclusively New Bedford whale oil as a lubricating material. The negroes employed by the Company have been fed upon bacon cured in Cincinnati. The Company has now erected a large smoke house, has killed and cured its own pork, from the refuse of which an oil has been prepared answering its purposes most admirably, as will be seen by the report of the Superintendent of Machinery. The bacon has been prepared at less cost than that which the Company has heretofore purchased, and the oil is obtained at so low a rate, and answers its purpose so admirably that I do not propose hereafter to use any other. The engine Norfolk is now running upon chilled tires made by ourselves, those purchased by me having failed to arrive in consequence of the blockade. Even the soap used by the Company is now made in its own shops." [30]

Initiative of this kind was, of course, exceptional, even in a beleaguered land where necessity already had become the mother of invention. Robinson was an above-average person. He will appear again in the Confederate transportation story.

Deficiencies in bacon and lubricating oil might be remedied by a combination of imagination and energy, but the dearth of metallic items—things like rails, boiler iron, cylinder castings, wheels and springs—could not be attacked so easily. Such articles could be turned out by only a handful of concerns, and these were hard pressed to fulfill the purely military orders which showered in upon them. In the face of all this, it seemed logical to call still another Southern Railroad Convention, this time to discuss the supply problem. The gathering, dominated by the Virginia lines, assembled at the Exchange Hotel, Richmond, on the morning of December 19, 1861. It accomplished very little. The members seemed appalled by the magnitude of their task, and they could think of nothing more effective than the creation of the usual committee to devise ways of securing supplies and to disseminate information concerning the same. Following the election of Edmund Fontaine of the Virginia Central as committee chairman, they returned with a certain relief to their private troubles. [31]

V

The year 1861 likewise produced a host of secondary difficulties. Particularly notable was the increase in accidents, especially upon roads subjected to heavy troop movements. On the night of June 27, a Mobile & Ohio northbound special, carrying sixty cavalrymen and their mounts, collided head-on with a southbound regular freight near Trenton, Tennessee. Twenty-five of the soldiers were injured, two critically. A Mobile newspaper reported that "the locomotives were stove against each other—or, as our informant expresses it: 'the smokestacks stood hugging,' defying all efforts at separation"; the conductor and enginemen of the special, it was said, had been so threatened by the soldiers that they took to the woods. Early in September a portion of a Virginia & Tennessee troop train broke loose upon a grade near Abingdon, Virginia, and without conductor or brakeman rushed backward down the line to smash into the locomotive of a following section. The disaster was blamed upon a broken coupling, and for this reason was deemed one "against which no foresight could provide." Tragedies of a routine nature also haunted the carriers, like that of the Confederate soldier who lay down to sleep one night upon the track of the Seaboard & Roanoke. The five fatalities upon the South Carolina Road do not appear to have been sufficiently spectacular to command more than local notice.[32]

Deaths increased, and so did taxes. The first months of the Confederacy had been financed chiefly by promissory notes; these the Government now endeavored to reduce by a special war tax, approved by the Provisional Congress in August, 1861, which imposed a levy of fifty cents upon each $100 valuation of a wide variety of property, railway securities included.[33] In many cases, particularly in Virginia, the roads assumed payment of the tax, perhaps for the convenience of the Treasury Department as much as for the benefit of their shareholders. But if this was hardly a direct tax upon the carriers, the governmental foot at least remained thereafter in the door.

A great inconvenience, especially to station agents, was the persistent dearth of currency. The financial earthquake set off by secession had played hob with normal issues of banknotes; Confederate money, ultimately so prolific, could not at once be distributed in adequate amounts; metallic currency quickly obeyed Gresham's law and disappeared from circulation. The railroads ultimately met the situation by the private issue of scrip of varied denomination and appearance; in most cases a minimum of five dollars in such bills had to be assembled by the bearer before a road would exchange it for Confederate money. Some of the railroad paper was elaborately engraved, usually with representations of locomotives pouring forth quantities of smoke over rural landscapes of obvious prosperity.[34]

Of petty exasperations there seemed no end. Georgia state transportation officers issued furlough permits so carelessly that local roads could hardly collect the payments due thereon. For months the Orange & Alexandria had guarded twenty bridges along its lines at its own cost; when approached, the Confederate War Department was loath to assume the expense. Again in Georgia, a shortage of salt produced a state freight embargo upon the article, filled with inconsistencies. The new government track connections at Richmond and Petersburg proved grossly inadequate; their use for the transportation of private freight was forbidden, and "several thousand tons" of goods had accumulated in the Weldon depot at Petersburg by the end of the year. But when a bill to authorize more permanent links was introduced into the Virginia House of Delegates in December, the vested interests of Petersburg fought back with desperation. Their opposition eventually crumbled and the bill passed both houses of the legislature early in February, 1862. Nevertheless in the absence of track materials at a reasonable price, the good Petersburgers could relax for four years more, secure from the threat of through freight trains, if not from the blast of Federal shells.[35]

Certain early effects of the war were bizarre. Across the coastal plain of Georgia, for example, ran the newly-finished track of the Brunswick & Florida. In its lack of rolling equipment and other essentials the little road did not differ from many other southern carriers, but it was exceptional in that its capital stock lay largely in northern hands. Moreover, the Yankee shareholders, who took a dim view of secession, refused to authorize board meetings or otherwise to carry on the corporate activities of the road. It was, indeed, a strike, of capital rather than of labor. The impasse continued through the summer of 1861 until, on September 25, the minority southern stockholders assembled at Brunswick and voted to turn the road over to the state for the duration of the war. As he considered the line "a means of public defense," Governor Brown agreed to intervene, and the company was seized by gubernatorial proclamation on October 7.[36] Nor did state management of the property prove ineffectual, for Joseph E. Brown could act with vigor in any matter restricted to the boundaries of his own commonwealth. Finding the rolling stock to consist of "the" engine, plus "one secondclass passenger, four boxcars and one handcar," he provided $5,000 of public funds for repairs, and, despite his recent fulminations to Major Ashe, an engine and several cars from the state road. For an additional consideration of $8,250 he wheedled yet another locomotive, the Augusta, and five boxcars from the Central of Georgia. Soon a rejuvenated Brunswick railroad was noisily engaged in transporting "troops and supplies to and from the coast." [37]

If the owners of the Brunswick & Florida refused to operate their railroad, the creditors of the Augusta & Savannah were loath to permit that carrier to pay its debts. Having enjoyed an exceedingly prosperous season or two, the company desired to reduce its obligations through the purchase of its outstanding bonds. But though the management offered par for them, the bondholders refused to part with their certificates, even in the face of a depressed market. The disappointed officers ascribed their stubbornness to "the deranged business of the country and the apprehensions felt by capitalists in regard to investments generally." If this was true, either human nature was working in reverse, or the Augusta & Savannah was considered a very sound venture indeed.[38]

For the railroads of the Confederate States, 1861 was, in fact, a distressing as well as a bewildering year. Bereft of much of their ordinary traffic, heavily strained by the demands of the military, plagued by shortages and a multitude of petty afflictions, railroad men could not be blamed for viewing the future with cynicism. Yet many of them were not without hope. A particularly optimistic note was struck in the February, 1862, report of Superintendent John M. Robinson of the Seaboard & Roanoke:

"In conclusion," he said, "it is to be hoped that the United States may soon be brought to perceive the folly of their attempt at subjugation of the Confederate States, that peace may be restored, and with it a return of the road to its legitimate business. In such an event the prospects of the Seaboard and Roanoke Railroad are of the most promising character, and under the guidance of the officers and employees, who during the past year have in general worked to my entire approbation, it cannot but prove a most successful enterprise." [39]

But the United States refused to perceive their folly—1861 was only the beginning.

CHAPTER

8

Colonel Myers Faces Chaos

"The necessity for some legislation for controlling military transportation on the railroads and improving their present defective condition forces itself upon the attention of the Government, and I trust you will be able to devise satisfactory measures for attaining this service."—Jefferson Davis to Confederate States Congress, Aug. 18, 1862.

I

DESPITE THE EFFORTS OF MEN LIKE ROBINSON, IT WAS EVIDENT BY the beginning of 1862 that railroad transportation within the Confederacy had sunk into an appalling state. Already it was openly charged that railway support of the war effort displayed gross ineptitude, if not worse. The military blamed the carriers; the carriers blamed the military and each other; and everyone cursed the Quartermaster Department. With the decline and fall of Major Ashe, there remained little of the first modest system of coordination. Worst of all, the dearth of railway supplies had become so bad that operating officials pondered whether or not they could keep their trains running. Basically the situation was compounded of two dilemmas. First, how was a smoothly running railroad net to be erected from a congeries of individual companies, of conspicuously local extent and prejudice, in the midst of a people whose notions of individual "rights" exceeded even the contemporary American norm? Secondly, how was the supply of the thousand and one articles necessary to the functioning of that net to be assured in a

95

land nearly devoid of heavy industry and now increasingly contained by a maritime blockade?

The southern attempts to solve these quandaries were hesitant, spasmodic, and largely ineffective. No really satisfactory answer to either problem was ever achieved. But though the efforts failed, they at least served to reveal much of the ultimate nature of the Confederate States of America.

II

Ever since the enthusiasms of First Manassas had died away in the face of blundering logistics, the Provisional Congress had ruminated over a reorganized system of military supply. By January, 1862, conditions in the field demanded real action, and on the 11th a special committee was appointed to investigate the abuses alleged. After "extensive visits" in the best congressional manner to various depots, installations, and departments, the members reported that the transportation of troops and supplies upon railroads and steamboats was already a responsibility of the Quartermaster General and that a paper system for the control thereof did exist. For the army they merely advised the erection of more and larger depots "at secure places near the fields of operation." But for the railroads they recommended a program of radical character. Pointing out that their deficiencies were to be blamed primarily upon the fragmentary nature of the Confederate net and upon the poor distribution of rolling stock, the committee proposed that direct military control be assumed over the routes leading through Richmond, Nashville, Memphis, and Atlanta to the several army headquarters. It was a bold program and not unintelligent. But it was too much for the southern legislative mind. It too seriously violated fundamental shibboleths concerning the evils of centralized government. The Provisional Congress, now in the final weeks of its existence, was content to let the report die quietly of neglect.[1]

For nearly two months thereafter, the transportation of men, food, and munitions to the Confederate armed forces was left largely to luck and to the vagaries of several hundred well-meaning military and railway officers. Quartermaster General Abraham C. Myers did issue, on February 10, a circular of instructions to govern the official travel of military personnel, which was distinctly superior to latter-day publications of the kind, being both clear and brief. But government rail transportation continued to depend in the main upon the efforts and cooperation of local quartermasters and local railway agents.[2]

Meanwhile there had assembled at Richmond a real Confederate Congress, complete with Senate and House of Representatives, constitutionally chosen by the southern people and resembling in nearly every respect the Congress of the United States, to which,

The Virginia Central Railroad transports flour for the Confederacy. National Archives.

indeed, many of its members had formerly belonged. Like all representative bodies it reflected a wide assortment of interests and superstitions, but it likewise contained some members who might, for the sake of their new country, break with the most sacred precepts of southern folklore. Its first session was not yet a month old before the railroad problem was brought to its attention.

On March 11, 1862, in the midst of the turmoil over recent defeats in Tennessee, Representative William W. Boyce of South Carolina introduced a resolution directing the House Committee on Military Affairs "to inquire whether further legislation is necessary to give increased efficiency to our interior lines of railroads." No action was taken upon this particular proposal, but the transportation problem grew so critical that on March 19 agreement was secured upon a much stiffer resolution sponsored by Peter W. Gray of Texas. A similar resolution, introduced by William B. Preston of Virginia, received the sanction of the Senate five days later.[3]

The House Committee was the first to report an actual bill, and this became the basis of the first attempt by the Confederate Congress to provide a real scheme of railroad regulation. Its clauses were enough to delight the strongest believer in centralized control. Very briefly, they provided for a "military chief of railroad transportation," with the rank of lieutenant colonel, to be appointed by the President from the railroad officers of the Confederacy on the basis of judgment, skill, and experience in practical transportation matters. As his immediate assistants a number of district military superintendents were to be selected, each to hold the rank of major and to be charged with the supervision of a specific portion of the railway system. The bill went further: it would invest *all* railroad officials with military rank *and military responsibilities*, to and including conductors, station agents, and section masters. It also required the establishment of through schedules for government freight and the interchange of cars under public control.[4]

This represented a real attack upon the problem. Just who was responsible for it remains obscure; the Confederate Congress and its committees usually deliberated in secret, and its official journal provides little more than an outline of events. Certainly the bill bore the imprint of an intelligent mind. Perhaps it was drawn by Ashe. Likewise in Richmond was the president of the Vicksburg, Shreveport & Texas, William M. Wadley, probably the leading railroad expert of the Confederacy.[5] But whoever did the thinking, the measure met the needs of the situation admirably. Certain of its ideas were to persist through the war.

The railroad bill was presented to the House on March 27 by William Porcher Miles of South Carolina. Many congressmen were appropriately appalled, and instantly the classic halls of the capitol were abuzz with opposition. An attempt to kill the measure on the spot indeed proved premature. But when the matter was taken up seriously on April 17, there burst forth a torrent of obstructive motions and it was ultimately abandoned to a thorough emasculation. Its twelve sections reduced to one, its stern requirements converted to a harmless provision for "consultations" between the Secretary of War and railroad officials, the bill at last was passed, but it now signified nothing. Even in so diluted a form, it drew a self-righteous protest from Augustus R. Wright of Georgia and Thomas J. Foster of Alabama, who declared it "subversive of, and in direct contravention to, the great and fundamental principles of State sovereignty." [6]

Thus denatured, the measure aroused little opposition in the

Senate, whose Committee on Military Affairs reported it without amendment on April 21. But it was the final day of the session and lack of interest committed the bill to oblivion. It was a small loss.[7]

The Confederacy thus entered the critical summer of 1862 with no special provision for the control of its railway. Even Major Ashe had departed, and responsibility for military transportation was back where it had been in the beginning—in the Quartermaster Department. But Quartermaster General Myers was a professional soldier, not a railroad man, and few of his subordinates, scattered from Manassas Junction to Brownsville, were transportation experts. Moreover, railroads were but one of his worries. Sometimes he could find time to consider them; more often he could not. Perhaps he did actually sponsor the peppering of rail-transportation circulars that appeared that summer. The auditing of railway bills certainly remained under his control, being carried on in Richmond by an immediate assistant, Lieutenant Colonel Larkin Smith. But much of the routine liaison between the army and the carriers, the ordering of troop trains and arguments over freight equipment, still devolved upon subordinates in the field.[8]

The Davis Administration, however, feared that a modification of the Quartermaster Department by executive fiat would produce embarrassing comments from press and public. The thankless responsibilities of the War Office were now discharged by George W. Randolph, who, like Benjamin before him, understood that a Confederate President was expected to refrain from administrative adventures. But Randolph likewise felt that something should be done about the railroad muddle. On August 12 he recommended to Davis, not that he should plunge like a bull through the fragile china of provincial sentiment, but that his office should be granted "right to control the operations of our railroads to some extent." A transportation czar, he said, would not be unwelcome, especially a man of experience upon whom *properly delegated* authority could be bestowed for the coordination of railway operations.[9]

This the President approved. On the eighteenth of August, Senators and Representatives again thronged the walks of Capitol Square, and when the usual message from the Chief Executive was read Randolph's recommendations as to railroads were faithfully included.[10] But the weather was hot and the members listened drowsily. As autumn came on, they did confer with the Quartermaster General on the subject, but Myers was strongly opposed to anything drastic; government control, he declared, would irritate railway personnel, cost more money than it was worth, and garble both public and private accounts; far better would be the adoption of the old scheme for a chief of transportation to "cooperate" with the carriers. Such a program, he hastened to add, would not require congressional action; indeed he did not see how his department's efficiency could be improved by further legislation.[11]

Myers found receptive ears; congressmen remained chary of the railroad question and were quite willing to leave its pitfalls to the executive. They heaved a sigh of relief and turned to other matters. But events soon were to show that they had not abandoned the field to Myers.

III

If railroad service in behalf of the southern military effort grew increasingly unsatisfactory during the period just described, the roads themselves were concurrently finding it difficult to furnish dependable transportation of any sort, either to the authorities or to private citizens. That they faced total collapse may be questioned, for the majority of companies, through the course of the war, never quite came to the end of their rope. Furthermore, southern railroad men remained fully aware of the possibilities inherent in public aid. Faced now with difficulties which they could hardly solve single-handed, they turned instinctively to Richmond for help.

By the beginning of 1862 a drumfire of pleas was sounding throughout the capital. Prodded no doubt by the Tennessee lines, former Governor Neill S. Brown wrote from Nashville suggesting that the War Department either subsidize the manufacture of locomotives and cars, or establish railroad supply plants itself. The Fontaine Supply Committee, the same which had been set up December 19, 1861, at the Exchange Hotel in Richmond, recommended a publicly sponsored cartel for the purchase of materials in Great Britain. Walter Goodman of the Mississippi Central, after an audience on January 25 with Jefferson Davis himself, covered several sheets of Spotswood Hotel stationery with an elaborate proposal for government rolling mills.[12]

Even the Provisional Congress, soon to be superseded, enjoyed no special immunity from railroad supply worries. A bill "to provide for the construction of rolling mills, locomotives, and engines for naval purposes" actually achieved a place on its calendar, but in the press of business preceding dissolution it was never voted upon.[13]

The Fontaine Supply Committee now determined to recall as many railroad officers as possible for further discussions. This latest convention gathered on February 5, 1862, in the chamber of the Richmond City Council and at once displayed more initiative than had the December meeting. Following discussions with Major I. M. St. John of the Army Ordnance Department, a specialist in the domestic resources of the South, the delegates endorsed the construction of new iron works within the Confederacy, to be financed in part with government, in part with railroad, money. They drew up a revised program for importations from abroad, and demanded the release of skilled labor from the army. They went further: they agreed that an immediate supply of iron could be provided *by tearing up secondary lines designated by the Secretary of War*. Such a project, plus a country-wide scrap-metal campaign, should, they thought, be placed under the jurisdiction of two officers chosen jointly by the carriers and the Government. Any disputes that might arise could be settled by the Chief of the Army Engineer Bureau.[14]

It was St. John who first suggested the removal of rail from unimportant lines in order that key routes might be maintained. Whether all the delegates approved of this specifically remains uncertain, but, in any case, St. John's recommendation was transmitted to the authorities along with the other resolutions. Perhaps no railway officer present was capable of regarding his own road as a secondary line; certainly it was easy to approve the destruction of the property of another. Whatever the reason, the Major's proposal escaped opposition. Yet from this single idea of an obscure ordnance officer was to develop an issue that would create a thousand grievances, that would dramatize with pitiless clarity a fatal weakness of the South, and that would play at least a minor role in the collapse of the southern war effort. For the time being, however, the rails of the most unimportant branch in the Confederacy were safe from seizure; the Davis Administration was too concerned at the moment with other problems to devote much time to the matter. The President read and approved the resolutions, but he took no action beyond forwarding the papers to the Provisional Congress for decision as to how far the Government should go in rendering aid to the roads.[15]

Though the new rolling mills were never to belch flame except in men's dreams, the Confederate States already were in the railroad equipment business. The locomotives and rolling stock salvaged the previous year from the Alexandria, Loudoun & Hampshire and the Baltimore & Ohio had been treated as public property.[16] But government participation in the distribution of rolling stock owed most to the genius of Generals Lee and Jackson, whose masterpiece at Second Manassas netted the South seven splendid locomotives of the United States Military Railroad in only slightly battered condition. The Confederate Senate quickly took cognizance of the loot with a resolution recommending the sale of the captured equipment "to main line railroads which may be most in need of engines and cars." Thanks to the efforts of President Barbour of the Orange & Alexandria and thirty of his employees, the captured equipment was taken across the bridgeless Rappahannock to safety, whence it was carried south in triumph.

The affair was to end, however, upon a sour note. It was decided that the machines should be disposed of by lot under the supervision of Captain Mason Morfit, local transportation quartermaster at Richmond. When the results were announced, the Orange & Alexandria had secured three of the seven units and the Virginia Central and Richmond & Danville two each. Barbour at once protested by telegraph, declaring that the Orange & Alexandria had not secured its proper share. By mail, he asserted that Secretary Randolph himself had promised that he might select whatever engines he needed, that he had chosen four, that the three he actually had received were not adapted to his line, that the Virginia Central and the Richmond & Danville, having rendered no assistance whatever in the salvage of the engines, did not deserve theirs, and that "really, after all the trouble I have taken," the entire incident had been unfair both to himself and to his company.[17]

Whatever the ethics of the case, it was actually too late to make any change. Captain Morfit declared in rebuttal that the Orange & Alexandria had so little need for additional motive power that it already had offered to rent, at high prices, two of its new machines. Both the Danville and the Central officers held legitimate government orders for the delivery of their share; they could scarcely be expected to give them up with good grace. And so the original distribution stood; certainly the Virginia Central received its portion, for it paid $50,000 to the Government that fall for the engines Hero and General Stuart. Presently the War Department filed the papers in the case and Barbour turned muttering to the routine management of his road.[18]

By one means or another a nearly continuous trickle of rolling stock and other railway supplies came into government hands in the course of 1862. Five locomotives were salvaged from the Louisville & Nashville, while at the end of November the Quartermaster Department also held sixteen freight cars and a small amount of bar iron. An additional engine or two appears to have been seized in the course of late autumn operations in northern Virginia. The role of the Department as a dealer in railroad equipment bade fair to become permanent. Before the end of the year, thanks to the machinery taken previously from the Baltimore & Ohio, Colonel Myers placed in operation at Raleigh, North Carolina, a fairly well equipped government locomotive shop for the restoration of whatever additional motive power the successes of southern arms might provide. In charge he put Thomas R. Sharp, the versatile Charlotte & South Carolina superintendent who had directed the passage of the first Baltimore & Ohio engines over the Shenandoah Turnpike, and who now was formally commissioned captain and assistant quartermaster.[19]

But the Confederate armies were not the only source of extra railway equipment. The fortunes of war had led, in the spring of 1862, to the abandonment of large segments of the Virginia frontier, and from the Manassas Gap Road and from the lines serving Portsmouth and Norfolk there came a motley parade of refugee rolling stock. The Manassas Gap moved what engines, cars, and shop machinery it could to Greensboro, North Carolina, whence much of it was released, for a suitable consideration, to other companies. The distribution was unfortunately limited by differences in gauge, but one of the Manassas engines found suitable employment on the North Carolina Railroad, while two more were welcomed to the congested iron of the Richmond & Petersburg. The half-truncated Richmond, Fredericksburg & Potomac and Seaboard & Roanoke likewise helped fill the equipment needs of neighboring lines. It was an ill wind that blew nobody good.[20]

IV

Behind the talk of government controls and schemes for securing railroad matériel, the ordinary routine of a quartermaster's bureaucracy continued without significant change. It was hardly an efficient operation. Its transportation phase still reflected a deep spirit of laissez-faire, and its effectiveness disintegrated in direct ratio to the distance from the Confederate capital. After the departure of Major Ashe, the distresses of the Virginia carriers fell upon the desk of Captain Mason Morfit, the Richmond transportation officer whose part in the Barbour locomotive squabble has been observed. Morfit was a Baltimorean of such pronounced secessionist sympathies that he had evaded incarceration in a Federal jail only by virtue of a swift scurry to the Confederate lines. His talents seem not to have fitted him for field service, but as an administrative officer he achieved a certain reputation. He was no Ashe, however, and in 1862 his sphere of influence did not extend south of the Roanoke. In North Carolina the regulation of military rail traffic was now the responsibility of John D. Whitford, president of the Atlantic & North Carolina. Over the greater part of the Confederacy, in fact, army railroad transportation was coordinated only by circulars. Even the paper forms utilized by individual quartermasters reflected a balkanized organization; some officers issued the most elaborate travel vouchers that have ever been seen on this continent; others furnished documents which had been overprinted upon the pages of old check books; still others confined themselves to freehand scrawls upon bits of scratch paper.[21]

One important duty did command the direct attention of the quartermaster general's office—the negotiation of rates and fares for military traffic. It was a thankless task. The carriers thought themselves the victims of a stingy government; some roads even refused to honor existing tariff agreements. In January, 1862, the Greenville & Columbia arbitrarily boosted its fare for military personnel to three cents per mile and its charges upon public freight to the regular commercial level. Aroused by soaring operating costs, the lust for additional revenue seemed to spread to other companies, until by late summer the hour was ripe for another in the endless series of railway conventions, this time for the avowed "rectification" of the whole government rate structure. Assembling at Columbia, South

Carolina, on September 4, the meeting wasted no time in professions of esteem for the "cause." A new tariff was discussed briefly, approved quickly, incorporated into crisp, businesslike phrases, and sent off to Colonel Myers. But when the document arrived in Richmond, the Quartermaster General received a pleasant surprise. The rates submitted remained almost unchanged from those adopted at the Chattanooga convention the previous October; increases were confined to fringe items like the travel of troops upon branch lines and the transportation of freight upon passenger trains.[22] Perhaps the high hopes occasioned by the Battle of Second Manassas were responsible. But this was to be the last time that a government official was to certify a tariff willingly. Soon the hard-bitten railroaders were citing the "fair and just" rates enjoyed by the Confederacy as an excuse for stiff increases for the private citizen. A leading Georgia road even subjected its ordinary rates to a surcharge of 50 per cent and canceled all deductions for carload lots.[23]

V

The Columbia Convention and the lofty statements of Colonel Myers as to the efficacy of his department did not alter the fact that in the autumn of 1862 a change was necessary in the routine liaison between the Confederacy and its rail carriers. The general situation afforded only a dreary repetition of 1861. Spasmodic efforts to set up through car lines served chiefly to irritate the roads, and the everlasting shortage of rolling stock was intensified by the eternal slowness of shippers and receivers in the loading and unloading of freight; early in December, War Clerk John B. Jones learned that a firm of Virginia flour contractors were keeping "whole trains" waiting for days, thus contributing both to the stifling of railroad traffic and to the soaring price of breadstuffs. Soon the carriers themselves were causing the Quartermaster General to forget that all was well in the best of possible relationships. In October a self-important freight conductor upon the South Side refused to pick up a rush shipment of ammunition intended for Knoxville, a delay of four days resulted, and complaints flowed upward to the Secretary of War. Whereupon Colonel Myers declared that "he had no control over the railroads," that Mr. Randolph knew it, that the whole matter was a nuisance, and that he could do nothing. By the following month the Quartermaster General was in the grip of a veritable inferiority complex with respect to his railroad duties. The East Tennessee & Georgia had arrived at another of its periodic crises, and President Campbell Wallace was calling lustily for fifty additional boxcars, plus two engines. Wallace asserted that these could be secured easily enough, if only the Government had the courage to seize them. But though the difficulties of the Tennessee company were brought repeatedly to the attention of Richmond, Myers could only reply that "he had no power" for assistance.[24]

The situation called for a new man and a new program. The man stood waiting. The program was never to achieve fulfillment.

CHAPTER

❧ 9 ❧

William M. Wadley

"The smith, a mighty man is he, . . ."—Henry Wadsworth Longfellow.

I

BETTER SUPERVISION WAS CLEARLY NECESSARY TO ASSURE THE military effectiveness of the railroads of the Confederacy, and the responsibility therefore now lay solely with the Davis Administration. Congress had taken no action; the executive had inherited the problem by default. But the program which the Government now brought forth represented nothing very new. It was not even adequate. Based upon the familiar idea of a government transportation coordinator, it amounted to no more than an expansion of the role of Ashe. This time, however, the central supervision was to be extended to all the roads of the Confederacy.

As the system involved no elaborate machinery, its success, if possible at all, would depend upon the person selected as superintendent. And it must be said that the Administration therein acted wisely, for its choice fell upon the man already mentioned as the ablest railroad official in the South.

II

William Morrill Wadley was a man of gigantic frame, rugged features, and huge capable hands. He possessed the head of a Vulcan, clean-shaven and muscular, set upon a leonine neck and surmounted by a shock of thick, unruly hair that once had been intensely black but now was streaked with gray. His eyes were calm and steady beneath thick brows. He moved slowly, but not quite ponderously, for

107

his carriage reflected the coordination of the athletically endowed. When he spoke, which was rather seldom, his words were crisp, and his tones held more than a hint of a twang. For like many southerners of the period, William Wadley was a Yankee.

Most of all, he was a typically American self-made man of the better type. He had been born in Brentwood, New Hampshire, in 1815, of plain but ancient Puritan stock that had migrated from England as early as 1623. Apprenticed at an early age to the blacksmith's trade, he quickly displayed an extraordinary ability in metalworking, and his labors at the forge, with occasional stints in the rocky New England fields, developed a naturally robust constitution into one of great strength; it is said that in later life he could twist an iron horseshoe with his bare hands. The vicissitudes that followed the death of his father in 1826 served chiefly to add to his moral fibre.

In 1834 he migrated to Georgia, which for some reason he regarded as a land of opportunity. Nor did his belief fail him. Landing in Savannah with hardly a dime in his pocket, he rose rapidly, first as a worker with his hands, then with increasing success as a director of the labor of others. With his outstanding mechanical and executive ability it was not long before he became involved in the construction and operation of the railroads which were just beginning to stretch their tracks inland, and by the mid-fifties he had become a recognized railroad expert. Wadley especially loved to act as a trouble-shooter, and during his young manhood he seldom remained long in the employ of a single company. Before the War Between the States he had moved from the Central of Georgia to the Western & Atlantic, back to the Central of Georgia, thence successively to the New Orleans, Jackson & Great Northern (which paid him the unheard-of salary of $10,000 per year), the Southern Railroad of Mississippi, and the Vicksburg, Shreveport & Texas. By 1861 Wadley was much more than a village blacksmith. But though he entered wholeheartedly into the life of the ante-bellum South, marrying a Savannah girl of good family and assuming the ordinary manifestations of respectability by the acquisition of land and slaves, he never quite shook off the imprint of the forge beneath the New Hampshire elms. His manner to the end possessed a certain brevity, his speech a certain abruptness, but he was highly respected, even beloved, by subordinates. Scrupulously fair in accordance with his own standards (which were high), he was aware of his superior talents, and he perhaps derived a secret satisfaction from a first-class business quarrel. And if he never lost himself in the fabled southern penchant for verbosity, he equally failed to absorb the southern flair for diplomacy and tact.[1]

III

The details of Wadley's appointment as railroad supervisor are obscure. But he was not unknown in Richmond, and there already had been serious talk of his assuming charge of the construction of the Selma-Meridian road. The superintendency of all government rail traffic seems first to have been tendered him early in November, 1862, while upon a business trip in Georgia. It is probable that he tentatively accepted on the spot, for on the fourteenth Secretary of War Randolph attempted to assuage the chronic worry of General Lee as to supplies with the information that Wadley was expected in Richmond on the twenty-third and that his experience and success in the management of railroads would bestow "great benefit." [2]

Wadley returned to his home in Louisiana only long enough to gather his personal belongings; he departed again on November 18 and soon was walking up the cobbled ascent of Ninth Street, Richmond, to the Confederate War Department. Whatever reservations he held as to the appointment quickly evaporated, and under orders dated December 3, 1862, he was officially charged to "take supervision and control of the transportation for the Government on all the railroads in the Confederate States." "I am sorry and yet I am glad," wrote his daughter Sarah in her journal, "for I know he can do a great deal of good for the country." [3]

By the terms of his orders, Wadley was appointed colonel and assistant adjutant general in the Army of the Confederate States. He was empowered to make contracts and to carry on negotiations with the carriers in behalf of the Government, to assume charge of whatever railroad personnel or equipment the Government might control and to call upon the Quartermaster and Commissary Departments for "cooperation." Finally, he was to report through the Adjutant and Inspector General to the Secretary of War.

His powers were hardly plenipotentiary; a colonel without subordinates, Wadley's activities perforce depended upon the good will of railway men and military personnel over whom he possessed no authority. It likewise will be remarked that the chain of command to which he was linked short-circuited the Quartermaster Department.

Quartermaster General Myers instantly emitted yelps of indignation, and indeed there was much to be said for the rationalizations he presently laid on the desk of the Secretary of War. His office had handled railroad contracts in the past and would retain the responsibility for the audit of railroad transportation bills in the future. Even under the new dispensation the routine problems of government rail traffic would remain in the hands of quartermaster officers. But Wadley's orders provided no effective administrative connection with the Quartermaster Department, and Myers predicted gloomily and with some logic that the arrangement would lead to "inconvenience, confusion and embarrassment." But dark, long-featured James A. Seddon, who had just inherited the uneasy swivel-chair of the War Office, paid little heed to his lamentations.[4]

Whatever he may have thought of the administrative fog with which he was surrounded, Wadley said nothing. He went vigorously to work and quickly made an impression. Soon the Secretary of War was talking of creating an entirely separate bureau for him. Though so imperial an expansion had to wait for a season, the Colonel was at least authorized to employ an assistant. He chose Captain Frederick William Sims of Savannah, an old friend and subordinate of Central of Georgia days. Sims had just been released from a northern prison camp, and, as a recently married man, seems to have made small complaint when detached from the First Regiment of Georgia Volunteers for transportation duty under his former superintendent. He was ultimately to play a major role in the Confederate railroad story.[5]

Almost the first official act of Colonel Wadley was to call another railroad convention. In a notice addressed "to the Presidents and Superintendents of all Rail Road Companies in the Confederate States," he announced his appointment as superintendent of government railroad transportation and selected December 15 as the date, and Augusta, Georgia, as the place, for the gathering. "It is to be hoped," remarked the Richmond *Daily Examiner*, "that the conference may devise some facilities for the transmission of freights which, for lack of system, have accumulated on the lines, greatly to the inconvenience of the Government and the public." [6]

With such sentiments Wadley agreed whole-heartedly. Although he had been wearing his colonel's stars for less than a fortnight, he already had abandoned the viewpoint of the usual railroad president, and was thinking in terms of a smoothly operating system of transportation for a warring power. He even endeavored to make the best of the ill-adjusted military structure of which he was a part, by taking with him from Richmond two quartermaster officers of known experience in the railroad field. [7]

Wadley's hopes must have soared when the conferees gathered at the Masonic Hall in Augusta. Forty-two delegates representing forty-one companies were present, including every important southern road lying east of the Mississippi River. As soon as the preliminaries were over, he arose and in crisp sentences outlined a carefully thought-out program for the improvement of rail transportation throughout the Confederacy. It was a simple plan, calling only for through train schedules and a real system of freight-car interchange. Having urged the delegates not to deliberate too hurriedly—"from my past experience in meetings of this character I am satisfied there is too much haste in bringing them to a close"— Wadley introduced the quartermaster officers, Major Wood and Captain Smith, and sat down. [8]

The convention responded by forming the inevitable committee to consider the proposal. But after its eight members had been selected, the delegates turned with ill-concealed eagerness to a subject which Wadley had meticulously avoided: the existing tariff for government business. This required the appointment of another committee, while a third group was charged with the arrangement of a through mail schedule from Montgomery to Richmond via the Carolinas.

As the delegates conversed through the evening in their hotel rooms, it became evident that the Government program was doomed. When the convention reassembled the following day and the Wadley-plan committee hesitantly submitted a scheme that differed little from the Colonel's own proposal, it met with swift rejection. That the interests of individual companies should be abandoned in favor of a car pool into which rolling stock should be indiscriminately poured was simply too much. A substitute resolution, adopted by a vote of twenty-five to eight, paid extravagant personal compliment to Wadley and pledged the usual "cheerful cooperation," but provided nothing of value.

Even more barren results emerged from the committee upon mail schedules; it failed to agree upon anything, though it had spent half the night drawing up manuscript time-tables. But the committee on government tariffs produced something very substantial; a passenger fare increase of one-half of one cent per mile, plus satisfying boosts through the whole schedule of government freight charges, and numerous restrictions upon special services. These the convention adopted with alacrity. Having thus protected themselves against inflation, and having directed the chair to appoint yet another committee to negotiate more favorable mail contracts, the meeting adjourned.

Wadley was thunderstruck. There was, of course, little he could do. As the trains carried the delegates homeward, he issued a circular letter wherein he begged the president of every road in the Confederate States to utilize his services as a coordinator and to direct his superintendent to furnish weekly reports upon local conditions. Wadley hoped he might thus organize a corps of unofficial "assistants" throughout the country.[9] But by the terms of his own orders, he could accomplish little without the support of the railway interests. And what he might expect from them already had been abundantly shown. As he departed for Richmond, he could not conceal his disappointment.

Wadley was entirely aware that the carriers were laboring under difficulties, and his report upon the Augusta fiasco did not confine itself to a recital of railroad sins. After recommending that the new government tariff *not* be accepted by the army, he carefully outlined the principal grievances of the carriers. Attempts by quartermasters to dictate local transportation policy, he pointed out, sapped the morale of overworked operating personnel. He particularly deprecated the haphazard employment of government labor in the transshipment of freight at junction points. He emphasized the problem of railway supplies, which he blamed not only upon the lack of raw materials, but also upon the scarcity of mechanics. "There is not a railroad in the country which has an efficient force today," he concluded, "and the power vested in the enrolling officer is seriously diminishing even the small number of men left to perform duties upon roads, the success of which is of the first importance to the Confederacy." [10]

Wadley was not without influence in Richmond. Hardly had his recommendations come to the attention of the Secretary of War when they were being issued to all commands of the army in the form of general orders. Doubtless Wadley practically dictated them, for they reflected the ideas and, indeed, the prejudices of a railroad man. Military officers were again forbidden to interfere with the operation of trains. Meticulous procedures were prescribed for the ordering of special trains. Of particular interest were new regulations placing the conscription of railroad men under Wadley's control. If the efficacy of Confederate edicts had not seriously diminished as the distance from Richmond increased, these might well have had a happy effect. [11]

Though he thoroughly appreciated the railroad point of view, and was prepared to do his part to redress their legitimate grievances, Wadley also was ready to advocate their subjection to government orders. The response to his post-Augusta circular proved disappointing. "I beg leave to state," wrote the president of the Charleston & Savannah, "that although the officers of this road will take pleasure in cooperating with you, to the *fullest extent*, yet it is not intended thereby to place the control of the road in other hands, than where the Charter and the voice of the stockholders have signified such management should be held—namely in the President and Board of Directors." [12] From the tone of other rail executives it was evident that they, too, would heed the "voice of the stockholders" rather than the appeals of a distracted government.

How far Wadley was prepared to go in his recommendation of public control is not entirely clear. Certainly he was opposed to any program wherein every turn of every wheel would have to await official approval. He appears to have had in mind a plan similar to that adopted by the United States in the course of the Second World War, whereby the carriers were permitted to carry out certain broad policies by themselves, but under the threat of coercive action in case of failure. Just what he told General Cooper or Secretary Seddon on the subject is unknown. But when Congress gathered for its third session on January 12, 1863, the presidential message urged "the control of the roads under some general supervision, and resort to power of impressment." [13]

IV

Wadley did not linger in Richmond. The big, capable blacksmith from the New Hampshire village felt ill at ease in an office chair; moreover, in the absence of subordinates he was obliged to assume personal charge of each transportation crisis as it arose. Both railroads and government remained in an astonishing state of maladjustment, and for the greater part of his brief military career Wadley followed successive emergencies hither and yon over the Confederacy, from the James to the Mississippi and back again.

His first crisis took him to the Carolinas. Repeated acts of sabotage had again disrupted the East Tennessee railroads; two years of conflict had seriously reduced the resources of Virginia; and the bulk of the food supplies for Lee's army now had to crawl over the tortuous iron that linked Augusta and Savannah with Columbia, Raleigh, Weldon, and Richmond. Furthermore, Federal moves along the Carolina coast had induced a heavy cross-current of army traffic toward Charleston and Wilmington. The resulting strain was too much for the roads concerned; by the third week in January the salt meat ration of the Army of Northern Virginia was down to one-quarter pound per man, and Lee's commissary had no sugar whatsoever to issue in its place. Frantic dispatches from Fredericksburg were supplemented by equally gloomy messages from the South, where Generals G. W. Smith and P. G. T. Beauregard feared the carriers would be unable to concentrate troops to meet an assault. Beauregard declared that five extra locomotives "with attendant cars" were needed at once between Charleston and Wilmington. Smith had not even a constructive suggestion. "Railroads are an uncertain reliance," he observed. "They will worry me out of my life, yet, I think." [14]

Invested only with the authority to request the cooperation of others, Wadley appeared in eastern North Carolina early in January. In local charge of government rail traffic he found Major John D. Whitford, president of the Atlantic & North Carolina and a man of some reputation for efficiency. But Whitford was officially attached to the Quartermaster Department and actually had been taking his orders direct from General Smith; when Wadley attempted in his blunt New England manner to direct his activities, he resigned. The mollification of Whitford consumed precious time, and hardly had Wadley gotten him into a happy mood again when a dispatch arrived from the Quartermaster General summarily dispensing with Whitford's services. Thanks to vigorous representations from Smith direct to the Secretary of War, Whitford was retained, but in the meantime more than a fortnight had passed with no visible increase in the flow of freight.[15]

In the course of a month Wadley journeyed to Raleigh, to Goldsboro, to Charleston, and back to Raleigh. Neither the battered rolling stock and crammed depots that he saw, nor the pessimistic talk that he heard, were calculated to raise his spirits. Every train and platform swarmed with government agents, whose mission was to pester railway employees into expediting specific shipments. They succeeded only in frustrating one another and in irritating station and train crews. Wadley thought their number would "form a full regiment." Railroad officers were in an especially evil mood; when approached with suggestions for a better service, they countered with complaints and excuses, many of them justified.[16]

Wadley, in fact, was seriously discouraged. Like Ashe before him, he considered that his efforts were going for naught in the face of an unintelligent policy. "Under existing circumstances," he informed the Adjutant General, "I can do but little toward expediting Government transportation, and I see no way that I can better the condition of things." To the Secretary of War he reported that everything on the North Carolina Railroad was "in the utmost confusion" and that the Wilmington & Weldon would give him no satisfactory answer concerning the transportation of corn. And to his family he wrote that his duties were "very arduous and very annoying" and that only his sense of duty was preventing his resignation.[17]

Though armed only with the power of giving unwelcome advice, Wadley could at least renew his previous recommendations. Let the roads have mechanics and supplies, he urged, and then let Congress pass a stiff railway act. Of these he considered the first the more important, for a mere law without assistance in the form of men and materials would be "of no use." "I do not make these remarks in a captious spirit," he concluded, "but to improve this branch of the public service, which I consider of vital importance." [18]

He was, of course, right. But the provision of "mechanics and supplies" was even more difficult in 1863 than in 1862. When his proposals were forwarded to General Lee with the suggestion that a greater number of railroad men be detailed from the ranks, they met with a grave refusal; if the Wilmington & Weldon Railroad lacked manpower, so did the Army of Northern Virginia.[19] As for supplies, that was a problem the Confederacy was never wholly to solve. Nor was Congress yet disposed to support Wadley with appropriate legislation.[20]

Wadley never ceased to advocate a government program for railway supplies and a congressional enactment for railway control. But in the absence of both he could do little. He especially opposed the regulation of the carriers in detail by local military officers. If Congress would not give him an effective law, if the Administration would not provide him with a suitable organization, he preferred that the railroads should stay in the hands of railroad men. It was his policy quickly to distribute government rolling stock among the carriers; during the early months of 1863 he sold the five renovated Louisville & Nashville locomotives to four needy roads at prices ranging from $18,000 to $25,000. To the Georgia Railroad he furnished sixteen freight cars for $600 each. But if the interchange of equipment could not be worked out upon a satisfactory master plan, he preferred that it should not be done at all.[21]

He retained the government facilities at Raleigh. Engines, cars, and a wide variety of miscellaneous material drifted continually into military hands; nearly always they needed repair. Moreover, the installation would afford some basis for a country-wide supply program, if ever it should be authorized. He placed Captain Sims in charge, but Captain Sharp of the Quartermaster Department stayed on for a time as advisor, associate, and liaison officer.[22]

Though his orders had said nothing of an organized staff, Wadley, by methods more informal than was customary even in the Confederate Army, already was gathering a corps of subordinates. Besides Sims, he now possessed a working arrangement with Major

Whitford in eastern North Carolina. With Whitford came the services of W. H. Harvey, who divided his time between expediting military shipments through Goldsboro and superintending what remained of the Atlantic & North Carolina Railroad. The force was presently increased by the unofficial accession of Lieutenant J. M. Hottel, whom we already have met at Bowling Green, Kentucky; though supposedly associated with the Commissary Department as a transportation agent, his theft by Wadley was regularized early in May.[23] Presently Wadley's organization was being called a "Rail Road Bureau." The name appeared upon sundry orders as early as March; by May it headed the Colonel's official stationery. Wadley appeared well on the way to the assembly, from nothing, of a recognized establishment.

Nevertheless his efforts were availing the Confederacy little. Early in the spring he was called to Mississippi, where unparalleled congestion had stifled the flow of food, munitions, and reinforcements to the ill-fated forces of General Pemberton. Though Wadley labored night and day, it was largely in vain. The shortage of rolling stock was indeed no worse than elsewhere. But the cooperation of the Mississippi railroads was especially reluctant; certain of Pemberton's orders had given offense. Moreover, local staff officers had fallen into the Confederate habit of tinkering with the arrangements of others. As the trains crept half-heartedly into Jackson and Vicksburg, disaster already hung over the blossoming countryside.[24]

Meanwhile the movement of supplies to the Army of Northern Virginia showed little improvement. From the dismal reports on his desk Secretary Seddon estimated that in three months no more than 400,000 pounds of meat had reached Richmond from the large commissary reserves in Atlanta. General Lee wrote soberly that sheer famine would soon render it impossible for him to maintain his position. Seriously alarmed, Seddon begged Wadley to arrange for through freight service "on all the leading lines," to operate on regular schedules like passenger trains, a thing which the carriers had already refused to provide. The situation even attracted the attention of Congress; Senator Edward Sparrow of Louisiana accused the roads of a whole catalogue of sins, citing the Petersburg company as an especially gross offender. Spurred by complaints, the Quartermaster Department actually induced the lines connecting Charlotte, North Carolina, and Petersburg, Virginia, to operate special army supply trains, but only by accepting, in so far as they were concerned, the Augusta tariff. Herein it was, of course, infringing upon Wadley's territory without prior agreement.[25]

V

As Wadley returned slowly from Vicksburg across the ragged Confederate landscape, his troubles remained unsolved. That the railroads were receiving no significant amounts of supply stuffs was only too apparent; through cracked car windows he could see engine after engine standing cold upon the sidings, their wrought-iron tires worn nearly away, while the locomotives that dragged him toward the capital breathed like consumptives. The crews drawled pessimism; bearings were practically unobtainable, they told him; nowadays a hotbox was no longer an incident, but a disaster. When at last his train crept gingerly over the James, he reached for his carpetbag with a worried frown.

Railway personnel were exaggerating their afflictions only slightly. Though the Confederate dollar still was worth twenty-five cents in terms of gold, the price of lumber suitable for buildings and rolling stock had quintupled. The cost of nails had increased twenty times, of illuminating oil ten times, of glass about fifteen times. At Augusta, Georgia, the leading manufacturers of car castings in the Confederate States possessed a capacity of fifty wheels per day. In February, 1863, they could produce no more than fifteen; there was insufficient rolling stock in the area to insure a full supply of raw materials, and a suitable increase in rolling stock was rendered impossible by the scarcity of wheels. In Virginia the carriers again petitioned the War Department for aid in the purchase of English supplies. After some hesitation, Seddon furnished the services of Captain John M. Robinson, whose lubrication of Seaboard & Roanoke motive power with homemade pig grease already has been noted, and who now was serving as an engineer officer in southwest Virginia. Robinson duly ran the blockade, his pockets crammed with cotton futures. A man of imagination, he appears to have been rather successful in the purchase of suitable articles, though Daniel of the Richmond, Fredericksburg & Potomac regretted that he had secured no shop machinery. As for the car wheel dilemma, thirteen railroads sought the aid of the War Department, and, after Richmond had proved uncooperative, of the General Assembly of Georgia. Milledgeville came through with a recommendation that the state-owned Western & Atlantic furnish the Augusta foundry with "special facilities of transportation," but the legislative goodwill seems never to have achieved translation into extra ton-miles.[26]

Harried by complaints, the Secretary of War now turned to the ancient instrument which already had failed Wadley and the carriers alike. Early in April he called a convention of the railway managers of the Confederacy, to meet at Richmond on the twentieth.

The affair was carefully planned. On the evening of the 13th Seddon conferred personally with Wadley, following which the transportation chief drew up detailed memoranda of the needs and capacities of every line of importance between the Rapidan and the Mississippi. The figures were blunt. Best off were the Mobile & Ohio, Central of Georgia, and Georgia roads, which could haul *800 tons* of freight daily; in most serious plight were the North Carolina, the Wilmington & Manchester, the Wilmington & Weldon, and the Richmond & Danville, each of which was limited to a load of *200 tons, or less* per day. To insure a minimum performance, Wadley estimated that an additional thirty-one engines and 930 cars would be required. Moreover, he reckoned the deterioration of *existing* rolling stock at 25 per cent. "I am only surprised that the roads of the country have been able to keep up the present standard," he added.[27]

Promptly on the morning of April 20, Wadley appeared before the railroad representatives and from carefully written notes outlined a "proposed agreement between R. R. Co's & Government." The carriers at once countered with a program of their own. There was little difference between the two; both advocated government aid in the purchase and manufacture of supplies; both called for the coordination of rail service in behalf of the government. As was natural, Wadley stressed coordination, while the railroads emphasized the aid. But the Colonel this time was careful not to ask anything too drastic. To be sure, the government position suffered inevitable erosion, and the convention failed to provide machinery adequate to the crisis, but Wadley remained an important influence throughout the meeting, and when the delegates departed the following evening, the resolutions they forwarded to the Secretary of War were inscribed in his own handwriting.[28]

These resolutions were interesting, for they represented the very limit to which the roads could be induced, with soothing syrup, to go. In essence they gave formal recognition to a "Railroad Bureau," recommended its moderate expansion, and suggested that it supervise the extension of public aid to the carriers. The assistance expected was clearly enumerated; it also was distinctly provided that the Government was to abstain from direct control of railway operations. The industry viewpoint was further emphasized by four recommendations, which (1) called for the importation of European skilled labor, (2) made the standard plea for the prompt unloading of cars, (3) urged more stringent prohibitions against military interference with the running of trains, and (4) proposed, for perhaps the only time in American history, the diversion of as much traffic as possible to inland waterways.[29]

Though the Richmond Convention adjourned in a happier personal atmosphere than had the Augusta meeting, its resolutions and recommendations meant very little, and both Wadley and Seddon knew it. It was whispered at the War Department that an annual production of 49,500 tons of rail would be necessary to maintain southern tracks, but both the Tredegar and Atlanta ironworks, if devoted exclusively to the purpose, could manufacture no more than 20,000 tons. President Daniel of the Richmond, Fredericksburg & Potomac feared that even the convention's report would not be adhered to, just as the resolutions of the Richmond supply meeting of 1862 never had been put into execution.[30]

VI

The war was now in its third spring. The Executive Department had failed to work out a solution to the transportation question, and it was painfully clear that railroad cooperation would never voluntarily exceed the limits imposed by personal interest. It was time for Congress to provide the Administration with a club.

The Senate already was fashioning such a weapon. Bill S. 112, "to facilitate transportation for the Government," had been introduced on April 7 by Louis T. Wigfall of Texas and had proceeded lethargically through the usual routine. It had, by April 20, emerged unscathed from the Committee on Military Affairs, and was ready for general consideration. However, Seddon's railroad convention was in session and the senators postponed debate until its results were known. The meeting having produced nothing of consequence, discussion was resumed on April 25. But the provisions of the bill were thought so extreme that the Senate gathered behind closed doors, and after a brief wrangle the members were only too glad to postpone action again in favor of a resolution requesting "the Secretary of War to communicate, in writing,... whether any, and if so what, additional legislation, in his opinion, is required to render more efficient the transportation of army supplies over railroads." [31]

Mr. Seddon responded with alacrity. His reply was in the hands of Senator Wigfall the following morning. Doubtless it had really come from the pen of Wadley, for the message went straight to the point. The railroads, it declared, were "patriotic," but exceedingly jealous of each other and of their "rights." They were too much under the influence of "the selfish instincts inherent in money-making corporations," and frequently catered to speculators rather than to the Government. Worst of all was the impossibility of relying upon the best laid plans for the transport of provisions and munitions. As for a suitable remedy, Seddon spoke directly for Wadley: the power of regulation should be vested in a single agent of the Government. And if his directives were willfully disobeyed, the Executive should possess specific authority to seize the offending carrier. [32]

Having again barred the door of their chamber, the senators acted swiftly. There was some heated opposition, but it was overwhelmed. On April 27, the bill was passed by a vote of 11 to 6. Three days later it was given the endorsement of the House by a majority equally large. It received the presidential signature on the first of May. [33]

Wadley now had his railroad law. It was a sufficiently stern enactment. It gave the Executive power to require any carrier to devote its facilities to the support of the army, except for "what may be requisite for the running of one train for passengers in each twenty-four hours." It obliged railroads to adhere to through schedules prescribed by the Government. It ordained the country-wide distribution of motive power and cars. It provided for the impressment of those roads which refused to cooperate, and it authorized the taking of rails, shop machinery, or other movable property from the premises of one company to insure the proper maintenance of another. It was, in fact, a thoroughly satisfactory law, except for one thing. It mentioned neither the Railroad Bureau, nor Wadley, and it placed the entire supervision of the carriers in the hands of the Quartermaster General.[34]

Nor was Congress content merely to frustrate the blunt New England blacksmith. The day after the railroad bill became law, the Senate formally relieved him of his duties as railway coordinator.

By the terms of the Confederate Constitution and of subsequent legislation, President Davis was empowered to appoint military officers solely "by and with the advice and consent of the Senate." When Wadley was first commissioned in the late fall of 1862, Congress had not been in session, and when it reassembled in January, it did not, for some reason, receive his name. Indeed, his formal appointment did not reach Davis's desk until April 23, 1863, and the President did not forward it to the Senate until April 30.[35]

Congress was on the eve of adjournment, and Wadley's appointment was thrust hastily into a small mountain of names awaiting action by the Committee on Military Affairs. The committee gave the greater part of the pile little more than a cursory glance; most of those nominated were given a routine benediction. But not Wadley. With a handful of others, he was specifically disapproved. And though Senator George Davis of North Carolina endeavored to protect him by moving that his case be postponed until the following session, the Senate sustained their committee's recommendation. Back to President Davis they sent the nomination with their formal refusal "to advise and consent to the appointment of William M. Wadley, to be assistant adjutant general, with the rank of colonel." [36]

The question naturally arises: "Why?" The author can only answer that he does not know. As already noted, much of the work of the Confederate Congress was carried on in secret, and the records of committee meetings, if kept at all, are nowadays singularly scarce. Wadley maintained no diary at the time, and he seems to have spoken little of his rejection in later years. In explanation of so astonishing an action, not a scrap of direct evidence has yet appeared.

His appointment can hardly have been disapproved upon grounds of incompetence. To be sure, he had accomplished little, but no one else could have done more under the circumstances. Also, he was cast aside just as the legal barriers which had so hampered him had been removed. That he was one of the outstanding railway experts of the South no one could gainsay.

Wadley's descendants have supposed that his rejection was due to his New England background.[37] This may have been so; by 1863 Richmond was ringing with criticism of the "Yankees" who filled responsible positions in the southern government and army. Perhaps his New Hampshire manner had given offense; Wadley never had lost his native tendency to come directly to the point; he called spades shovels; and his sharp phrases must have rasped in many southern ears.

On the other hand, his dismissal may have represented business revenge. The chairman of the Senate Military Affairs Committee was Edward Sparrow of Louisiana; and it was in Louisiana that Wadley was engaged in railway development immediately before the war. Moreover, the control of his Vicksburg, Shreveport & Texas had been the occasion of much financial jealousy, and there is food for thought in the fact that he had been placed upon the road by certain Georgia interests of slight local popularity.[38]

Whatever the reason, Wadley's rejection stood. Following the half-hearted efforts of Senator Davis, no one stepped forward as his champion. Neither the President, nor Seddon, chose to extend more than their regrets, but there is no evidence that he then or afterward complained of shabby treatment. The news may well have brought a feeling of relief. He was tired and discouraged. Perhaps already he realized that railroads would never provide the means of southern victory.

He lingered in Richmond nearly a month, settling the affairs of his bureau and offering solid advice to the man who he had reason to believe would be his successor. Not until all was in meticulous order did he bid his farewells to Mr. Seddon and General Cooper. He was still dressed in Confederate gray when he descended Ninth Street to the Petersburg station for the last time.

❧ 10 ❧

Expanding Difficulties

"The supply of the rolling stock and machinery of
our several Rail Roads, and the condition of their
roadbeds is such that, unless measures are taken to
meet their necessities, the days of transportation by
rail in the Confederacy are numbered."—Joint Committee Report to Georgia General Assembly, April
11, 1863.

I

As Wadley labored fruitlessly and the Davis Administration hesitated and convention followed convention in barren sequence, the progressive anemia from the Federal blockade steadily
was denying nourishment to the railroads of the South. Sea power
had hobbled the iron horse.

Not a single new rail was produced in the Confederacy after
1861. Very few were ever imported. Over existing iron the trains
rumbled without respite, compressing the railheads and battering
the joints. The deterioration in track was now evident everywhere.
The situation was especially serious on those lines where lingered
the old-fashioned strap rail; even so important a route as the Richmond & Danville was cursed with five miles of it, and by March,
1863, that part of the road was accounted entirely unsafe. On the
South Side road the main-line iron had become so mashed that the
management was obliged to replace the worst sections with two
miles of rail taken from its City Point branch. The Richmond &
Petersburg similarly robbed Peter to pay Paul with the iron of its
Port Walthall spur. For its new bridge over the Ashley River, the

Charleston & Savannah could secure only a few eroded bars deemed unsuitable for use even in the side tracks of the South Carolina road. A portion of the Southern of Mississippi's line between Jackson and Vicksburg was in such critical condition that a total suspension of operation was expected daily; about twenty miles of its rail had been in use for nearly twenty years.[1]

There remained the possibility of rerolling worn iron and returning it to the track. A respectable amount of Central of Georgia rail was so processed in the course of 1862. But so completely were the rolling mills of the South monopolized by the orders of the Navy and War Departments that it was seldom indeed that Confederate trackage could thus secure a fresh lease on life. Very fortunate were companies like the Wilmington & Weldon, which possessed limited facilities for the repair of its own rail.[2]

Rolling stock exhibited similar dilapidation. Motive power was in especially evil condition; proper boiler flues could hardly be purchased; chilled tires had become absolutely unobtainable. Labor for ordinary repairs seemed to have vanished. Thermal and mechanical efficiency declined steadily. The miles operated per cord of wood decreased on the Southwestern Railroad from 84½ in 1861 to 67 7/10 in 1863. The average performance for the Central of Georgia had been 81 in 1860 and 79 in 1861; in 1862 it was 75, and in 1863, 60. Everywhere master mechanics were submitting gloomy reports; on the Montgomery & West Point were neither flues nor tires; on the Virginia Central hopeful experiments with homemade chilled tires had failed utterly. The motive power of the Richmond & Danville had so degenerated by the spring of 1863 that President Harvie feared that freight service would have to be reduced to a tri-weekly basis. At the same time only six of the twenty-six locomotives of the North Carolina Railroad could be classified as "good order."[3]

The car situation was almost as bad. In December, 1862, the Charleston & Savannah, now a vital element in the defense of the South Carolina coast, possessed only forty-four boxcars, of which nine were not in operating condition. The troop-carrying capacity of the whole road was reckoned at only 4,325. Losses occurred in the wake of every major military movement; approximately twenty Virginia Central freight cars were missing following the southern withdrawal from Manassas and Winchester in the second spring of the war. Governor Brown of Georgia, perhaps with exaggeration, estimated late in 1862 that his beloved Western & Atlantic already had lost 180 cars while on loan in the Confederate service.

Even in the comparative safety of the interior, the supply and condition of freight equipment was causing concern. Best equipped, perhaps, of all the carriers in the South was the Central of Georgia; but by the end of 1862 it had suffered a net decrease of forty-five cars, including twenty which had been modified for the transportation of coal and sold to the Confederate Navy Department for $10,000, and for which no payment had been received. Of the company's total roster of 729, one-half had been drawn onto connecting roads by various military emergencies and had not been returned. The neighboring Macon & Western suffered similarly; in 1859 it owned 170 freight cars; in 1863 it possessed only 141.[4]

When rolling stock could be wrung from prehensile officials and placed in service upon foreign roads, the dissatisfaction of the owning lines was increased enormously by the lack of any comprehensive system of per diem, or rental payments. The Central of Georgia complained that it was receiving no compensation whatever for the hundreds of its cars that in 1862 had been scattered over nearly every road of five-foot gauge from Alabama to Virginia. The same absence of an effective accounting led the following year to a bitter exchange between Superintendent Rowland of the Western & Atlantic and President Campbell Wallace of the East Tennessee & Georgia. So casual were the auditing procedures of the Western & Atlantic that no full settlement was ever reached. "I know it will be difficult for you to render out a correct account for car rent," Wallace wrote at last in despair, "but *come as near to it as you can.*"[5]

Facilities for the repair and replacement of cars were better than those for locomotives—but not much better. Car bodies could be produced in the Confederacy upon a fairly large scale, but metallic parts grew increasingly critical. Here the problem posed by the shrunken output of wheels and axles was bad, but the supply of springs was even worse. In the whole Confederacy, steel of quality suitable for the purpose could be produced by a single concern—the Tredegar Iron Works at Richmond—and its output had been suspended by the end of 1861. In the face of such conditions it is little wonder that the market price for rolling stock that still would roll expanded at a rate that exceeded even the natural redundancy of Confederate currency. In December, 1862, the Central of Georgia sold ten boxcars; exactly a year later the money received therefor would not have purchased "half the same number of wheels." [6]

Even fuel became scarce. Unlike metallic supplies, this was primarily a labor problem, for the Confederacy did possess, if nothing else, a flourishing growth of timber. But whereas a well-distributed population of backwoodsmen ordinarily could be counted upon to cut and stack wood at trackside, the lanky, drawling axemen now had gone—some into the army; some into the munitions factories; some no one knew where. The truth of the matter was that it was no longer worth a man's effort to engage in such work. Even the owners of half-idle plantations were loath to furnish slaves for the purpose, a tendency that was especially marked in regions close to the Federal lines.

By the end of 1862 the railroads generally were forced to offer stiffly increased prices for fuel. During the last peacetime year, cordwood on the Central of Georgia had cost $37,315.50; while in 1863 a reduced consumption required an expenditure of nearly $60,000. But even the payment of inflated prices failed to keep tenders filled. Whole companies of Georgia militiamen were detailed in the fall of 1863 to cut wood for the state-owned Western & Atlantic. Six months earlier the situation on the Virginia Central had grown so critical that General Lee personally begged for impressed Negro labor. "The necessities of the road are immediate," he wrote the Secretary of War, "and I see no other way of supplying them." Ordinary firewood became so scarce that existing stocks suffered serious pilferage, and in Richmond the authorities issued sharp orders forbidding all persons, civilian or military, to interfere with railroad fuel. [7]

There existed hardly an item that was not in short supply. Despite the example of the corporate swine of the Seaboard & Roanoke, rail executives were increasingly plagued by the lack of lubricating and illuminating oils. In 1859 these had cost the Macon & Western $2,570; in 1863 they required an expenditure of $32,-689.74; and in 1864 the necessary disbursement soared past the $75,000 mark, figures which much more than reflected the depreciation of Confederate currency. The Montgomery & West

Point, by means of persistent newspaper advertising, besought housewives to help keep its trains running with salvaged kitchen fat. The lighting of passenger cars and depots on the South Side Railroad cost, in 1863, a sum nearly equal to the whole income derived from the company's mail contract.[8]

Even building materials became unobtainable, and trackside structures grew shabby. In Richmond the new shops of the Virginia Central could not be roofed for lack of slate. At Raleigh, the depot facilities of the North Carolina road became so dilapidated that the *Weekly Register* took note thereof in an editorial entitled "A Shocking Bad Railroad Platform": "... Such a hog-wallow as is presented by the platform we have never before seen. Daily is presented the spectacle not only of men, but of delicate women and children wading over their ankles in red clay mire, in their entrance to and departure from the cars. Such a railroad platform is a disgrace to the Company to which it belongs and to the Capital of the State...."[9]

Indeed, the railways of the seceded states were assuming an aspect of decrepitude that was to be matched by American carriers in no other American war.

II

The human shortages of the South were nearly as serious as the material. Just what caused the evaporation of the small, but adequate, pool of railroad labor, no one seemed able to agree; some blamed the army; a few pointed to the munitions plants with their generous wages; many blamed "the war." An important element was doubtless the rigid pay scale maintained by most companies; until the fall of 1862 railroaders received no conspicuous increase in pay to offset the accelerating cost of living. But concessions had eventually to be granted. In December, 1862, the Georgia Assembly permitted Governor Brown to raise wages and salaries upon the state-owned Western & Atlantic up to 50 per cent; under the new schedule the machinists in the Atlanta shops received from four to five dollars per day for a six-day week. A year later, when the Confederate paper dollar possessed a value of five cents in terms of gold, soaring price levels necessitated a further substantial boost. "The officers and employees cannot live at [present] rates," asserted Brown, "and I shall be unable to work the Road much longer if I am not permitted to increase their pay." The scale of the Virginia Central likewise remained without change for nearly two years. None of its men received a dime's increase until 1863, though the paper money in their pay envelopes depreciated by more than two-thirds. But at least it may be said of the company's officers that they refrained from expanding their own remuneration during the same period, and they received, when the time came, proportionately smaller increases.[10]

A favorite bone of contention was the draft. As the first instance of general military conscription in the history of Anglo-Saxon peoples, the Confederate act of April 16, 1862, occasioned an enormous amount of criticism, of which the share of the railroads was by no means the least. Actually the new regulations were consciously circumspect with railroad employees. The law provided for their deferment at the option of the Secretary of War; and their immunity was further confirmed by a special act of April 21, which stipulated that persons "in actual service on railroad routes of transportation" were to be exempted from enrollment.[11]

Yet the experience of the carriers with conscription was not a happy one. From the beginning, the administration of the law was marked by misunderstanding. Certain draft officials disregarded the special sanctity of railroad men. In Georgia the irascible Brown hastened to throw protective wings about his Western & Atlantic, declaring that the state road "must suspend operations if all between eighteen and thirty-five are taken away." In July he ordered all of the railroad men of the state into militia units in an active duty status and sent them back to their throttles.[12]

Despite the excess zeal of a few enrolling officers, the first draft did not rob the railroads of appreciable numbers of men. As of August 12, 1862, the War Department had sifted the forces of 6,222¼ miles of line; had exempted 5,718 employees outright; and had deferred ("detailed" was the Confederate term) 413 more. It was not until after the sobering action at Sharpsburg-Antietam that the Government showed signs of treating the carriers less generously. In October Congress reduced the broad exemptions of April 21 to specific categories of railroad personnel. Thereafter outright freedom from conscription was to be enjoyed only by "the president, superintendents, conductors, treasurer, chief clerk, engineers, managers, station agents, section masters, two expert track hands to each section of eight miles, and mechanics in the active service and employment of railroad companies, not to embrace laborers, porters and messengers." [13]

Even this was more liberal than in the North, where preliminary draft legislation had extended no special exemption whatever to rail workers, enginemen excepted. But the southern roads were not satisfied. They continued to demand that former employees be released from the ranks. To this many of the men concerned were by no means averse, but discharges were few and grudging. By the latter part of 1862 even normal employee attrition had reduced the carriers to an uncomfortable plight. "If the necessary number of railroad hands cannot be detailed," commented one superintendent, "our only resource will be to employ negroes to keep up the track and do much of the mechanical work." [14]

Southern railroad management had no objection to the employment of colored labor. Negro status and pigment furnished the best kind of exemption from military conscription. Their services were sought with special eagerness by the Virginia roads, which placed frequent advertisements in the Richmond press begging slaveowners to release their hands upon attractive terms. The Virginia & Tennessee called for no less than five hundred. "Persons resident adjacent to the enemy's lines," it hinted, "will find it to their interest to hire their hands on this road as it is remote from the seat of war, and consequently their negroes will be safe from escape to, or capture by, the enemy." But most planters were loath to respond. Indeed, the police of Negroes under railroad hire was not always sufficient to prevent runaways. Before long a number of companies were driven to purchase additional blacks, the Virginia Central buying during the first nine months of 1863 no less than thirty-five.[15]

In the long run, the use of colored labor failed to solve the personnel problem. Despite conspicuous examples to the contrary, slaves could not provide the technical skills of which the railroads stood most in need. The Negro population of the Confederacy proved a resource of no little value. But for the railroads it was not enough.

III

Confederate railroads continued to suffer annoyance at the hands of army officers. A leading purveyor of the bureaucratic fleabite was General John C. Pemberton, whose military misfortunes were presently to make the Mississippi village of Vicksburg famous. Meeting difficulty in concentrating a food supply for his forces, Pemberton on December 12, 1862, forbade the Mobile & Ohio Railroad to transport corn or bacon for private persons within his department until further notice. Instantly food prices soared in Mobile. The railroad objected strenuously; two of Pemberton's adjutants issued clarifying orders which proved mutually contradictory; and the quarrel spread by telegraph to Generals S. B. Buckner and Joseph E. Johnston; but Pemberton remained adamant. Sooner or later, however, the American aptitude for evading troublesome regulations came to the rescue. Doubtless with the connivance of Mobile & Ohio employees, food began to flow again from the prohibited area. An especially ingenious shipment was gleefully reported in the Montgomery *Daily Advertiser* of March 8, 1863, as follows:

GENERAL PEMBERTON BEAT

"A good dodge was recently played off on General Pemberton and his officers, who, by their acts, are apparently trying to starve out the city of Mobile.... The story is as follows: A gentleman wanting meat, purchased it up the road, but knowing that it would be confiscated if found, he procured a common pine box about six feet long, made to resemble a coffin, such as are commonly used to transport the dead. He filled this box with good sound bacon, which he found at reasonable prices in Mississippi, and then marked his dead body thus:

" 'John *Shoat*
            32nd Alabama Regiment
                Mobile, Ala.'

"The shoat, or shoats, came to hand without trouble, and in good order." [16]

In the long run the carriers worried less over the vagaries of the military than over taxation. By 1863 it had become obvious that the war would last longer than the southern capacity to finance it with bonds and treasury notes. On April 24 Jefferson Davis gave his approval to a law which imposed, for the first time, a tax upon incomes, corporate as well as individual.

By the peacetime standards of the twentieth century the Confederate emergency imposts of 1863 seem mild. Starting at 5 per cent for incomes in excess of five hundred dollars, they gradually increased to a peak of 15 per cent at the ten thousand dollar level. Joint stock corporations were obliged to pay in addition 10 per cent of their net annual earnings; in this case, however, the stockholders concerned were not required to pay a personal tax upon the dividends they received.[17]

Though such an impost was hardly confiscatory, many railroads made their payments with ostentatious ill-grace. In Georgia, where local jealousy perhaps exceeded the southern average, railroad enterprise was especially outraged. The Georgia Railroad obeyed the law, but only after its directors had solemnly resolved that the tax should be met "in the spirit of patriotism, but not as a gesture of surrender of actual exemption by charter." The Central road likewise paid under protest, with similar remarks as to its corporate sanctity.[18]

Confederate revenue agents were bumptiously eager to receive their money promptly, but government disbursing officers were frequently late and parsimonious. Sometimes they ran out of paper. "I have seen Captain Smith," reported a clerk employed by the Richmond, Fredericksburg & Potomac. "He says the Confederate States are not paying accounts now [June, 1862]. Reason, *no funds*." More often still, the government was tardy in the audit of railroad accounts, or niggardly over controversial items thereon. Railroads everywhere held bills past due from the Confederate States. When the pipsqueak Mississippi, Gainesville & Tuscaloosa submitted a statement totaling $16,559.40, the quartermaster at Mobile would authorize the payment of only $13,679.43. The New Orleans, Jackson & Great Northern appears to have received no money at all on its government account after May, 1862; and the final payment had not been in currency, but in Confederate bonds of dubious future. Similar treatment of the Western & Atlantic served as the inspiration of another of Joseph E. Brown's tirades.[19]

The Georgia governor himself was at times a burr in the railroad bed. When a salt famine and then a crop failure threatened the well-being of his constituents, he seized forty freight cars, together with a half dozen locomotives, from the *private* roads of the state, and sent them off to the salt-beds of southwestern Virginia, whence most of them never returned. In an effort to eliminate speculation he ordered successive embargoes upon cotton, leather, cloth, clothing and shoes moving out of the state, a policy that served chiefly to create confusion for the carriers. The roads thenceforth were damned by the speculators on one hand and regarded with suspicion by state officials on the other. Nor. was the situation confined to Georgia. All over the South the criticism of railroads was becoming a habit among the honest and the dishonest alike.[20]

The dilemmas of railroading in a beleaguered land nearly devoid of industrial capacity brought loud complaints from railroad officers, but it must be said that they faced their troubles squarely. Many, like John Robinson, were born improvisers. In 1862 the Central of Georgia turned out hand-wrought spikes upon its own premises; by the following year it had established brand new car and locomotive shops in Macon to replace its original facilities at Savannah, converted into military arsenals at the beginning of the war. Likewise in Macon the Macon & Western performed a miracle of loaves and fishes when it assembled two complete engines which were dubbed, with appropriate optimism, the Victory and the Sunshine.[21]

Most companies, of course, confined themselves to the conservation of existing physical plant. The techniques of retrenchment were limited only by human ingenuity and the patience of shippers, but the most popular method continued to be the reduction of train speeds. Schedules were again lengthened on the Virginia Central. In South Carolina the usual rate of passenger trains had been about twenty miles per hour; by 1863 it had been reduced to an average of fifteen. The superintendent of the South Side road reported in the same year that speeds upon his own and upon connecting lines had declined by "nearly one-half." In December, 1860, Mobile & Ohio passenger trains had run from Mobile to Meridian, Mississippi, 134 miles, in slightly more than seven hours; in the spring of 1863 they consumed ten hours and twenty minutes. The speed of freight trains appears to have declined equally; in South Carolina in 1863 the fastest freight service offered by any road averaged no more than twelve miles per hour.[22]

Certain companies made repeated efforts to pierce the Federal blockade. The Robinson mission was but one of a series of such attempts. The favorite method was to purchase cotton upon railroad account and exchange it either overseas or within the Union lines. Importations from Europe upon this basis do not appear, however, to have achieved significant proportions. A number of Georgia carriers did organize in the spring of 1863 a "Rail Road Steam Ship Company," to be financed by the sale of "middling cotton at 20¢ per pound." But the fleet of racing steamers that was to bear English rails and locomotive tires through the midst of the Federal navy never materialized.[23]

<h1 style="text-align:center">IV</h1>

If the carriers were doomed to physical decline, their monetary prospects seemed quite otherwise. If costs mounted, railway management found it a simple matter to boost rate levels in proportion, at least upon private business. If it seemed difficult to find steel springs, it was easy to make up a shortage of Confederate dollars.

After the first year, the price of civilian railway transportation exhibited an almost uninterrupted rise. No road was immune from the process; the record is filled with examples. Between January and November, 1863, non-government rates upon the South Side road were raised by 50 per cent. The Mississippi, Gainesville & Tuscaloosa, twenty-two miles in length, quoted in September, 1862, a passenger fare of one dollar and a freight rate of twenty cents per hundredweight; in October the passenger fare was doubled, while the freight rate rose to fifty cents. The following year the Mobile & Ohio published an astonishing schedule of charges, including a levy of $18.75 upon the shipment of a 125-pound box of tobacco from Mobile to Enterprise, Mississippi, and of $30 upon a bale of sheeting between Mobile and Brooksville; the public reaction was so explosive that the new rates were hastily suspended. But this seems to have been an exceptional case; though shippers complained, the railroads declared that their prices were relatively no higher than those demanded for other goods and services, and patrons ordinarily had no recourse but to pay the additional charges.[24]

Thanks to soaring fares and rates, railroad profits soon became quite fabulous, many companies enjoying an operating ratio of less than 50 per cent. During the year ending May 31, 1863, the Atlantic

& North Carolina, over whose half-abandoned line the armies waged fitful warfare, grossed $190,623, of which $152,054 was accounted "net profit." During the same period the Alabama & Florida of Alabama cleared over $380,000, after meeting all fixed charges and the Confederate income tax. The Virginia & Tennessee reduced its funded debt from $2,231,185 to $1,844,000, and paid off the entire amount it owed to the State of Virginia. The treasuries of the principal Georgia roads were crammed with Confederate paper. The Mississippi & Tennessee, though repeatedly despoiled by raid and counter-raid, reported a profit of over $140,000 for the two years between October, 1862, and October, 1864.[25]

A number of companies declared prodigious dividends. In November, 1862, the stockholders of the Wilmington & Weldon received a payment of 11 per cent and were handed disbursements of 10 per cent in both April and July of the following year. During 1863 the Petersburg Railroad distributed $653,403, which represented *60 per cent* of the book value of its ordinary shares. The dividend rate of the South Carolina road was far more conservative—only 12 per cent—but the Wilmington & Manchester was making quarterly payments that averaged 7½ per cent each. War, in fact, no longer seemed a threat to owners of railroad securities—until they took their money to the county seat and endeavored to convert it into tangible goods.[26]

V

The Confederate railroads might shower their shareholders with paper currency, but they were becoming less and less reliable as channels of trade. When the autumn of 1862 found the woodyards of Richmond nearly empty, and the Virginia Board of Public Works appealed to the carriers entering the city to rush emergency shipments of fuel, the response was a variety of excuses. Throughout the South exasperated shippers were complaining of impossible service. In December, 1862, the Montgomery & West Point was forced to impose a partial freight embargo, whereby no more than *two* carloads of civilian freight were to be dispatched from Montgomery in a single day, and an elaborate waiting list of shipments was set up at the company's offices. But even this proved insufficient, and on January 17, Superintendent Cram announced that the registry book had been closed because the freight already listed could not possibly move before the first of February. Government freight, he explained, must receive preference at all times; but he did establish a rough priority system in favor of "salt and family and plantation supplies" consigned to local stations.[27]

The press of passenger business continued to amaze everyone. An official of the Central of Georgia noted not only the "large number of soldiers transported for State and Confederate States," but also the throngs of "other persons visiting friends in the armies in Virginia and on our coast." The Confederate citizenry enjoyed every discomfort and harassment of railroad passenger travel in wartime, including the queues at the ticket offices, the heavy atmosphere of crowded waiting rooms and the dearth of places to sit. As was to be expected, they grumbled loudly and placed the blame upon a variety of persons and situations.

Passenger inconvenience appears to have reached its highest development upon the main lines. In 1861 the South Carolina Railroad carried 213,763 persons and missed its advertised connections ten times; in 1863 its trains transported 475,805 individuals and were conspicuously late twenty-four times. But on the 32-mile Laurens Railroad the passenger load increased from 6,000 to 8,500 only, while no serious lapses were charged against the little carrier in the matter of promptness.[28]

CHAPTER

∾ 11 ∾

Concentrations

"Railroads are at one and the same time the *legs* and the *stomach* of an army."—Brigadier General J. H. Trapier, C.S.A., December 26, 1861.

I

WHILE WADLEY WAS ORGANIZING HIS FRUITLESS RAILROAD Bureau, and while Congress was evading and then passing an adequate railroad law, the smoke of the steam locomotive was merging increasingly with that of the guns. The year 1862 was not two months old before the process had fairly begun. In the midst of a February of torrential rains and sudden blizzards, the southern fortresses of Henry and Donelson fell with disconcerting ease, laying bare the approaches into central Tennessee. The whole Confederate frontier between the mountains and the Mississippi disintegrated. In the Cumberland River the Federal forces now possessed an unobstructed highroad to Nashville, while in the Tennessee River they controlled a route that led them into the heart of the Confederacy. Northern supremacy upon the western waters was obvious. To counter it the South had only its railroads.

Before the February debacle, the trans-Appalachian armies of the Confederacy had been badly scattered—in Arkansas, in western Kentucky, at Bowling Green, in the region of Cumberland Gap, at New Orleans and at Pensacola. So suddenly did disaster strike that for the moment all efforts were devoted to saving the pieces. It was as instruments of salvage that the railroads of the west received their real baptism of fire.

Even while Fort Donelson remained in southern hands, the Confederate command was preparing for the worst. In the second week of February, Hardee's regiments were withdrawn from Bowling Green, but so hastily that the Louisville & Nashville could carry away only the heavier guns and military stores; the fourteen thousand troops were obliged to trudge toward Nashville through the vilest kind of weather. Further west the Confederates hurried out of Kentucky and across half of Tennessee, leaving torn and smoking railroads behind them. More serious still, the Tennessee capital had become a vast depot for Confederate matériel of all kinds. Quiet preparations were already afoot to move the supplies into the interior, but more rolling stock was required than the two roads leading south from the city could provide, and Joseph E. Brown was appealed to for the loan of Western & Atlantic equipment. Even the Georgia governor was impressed by the gravity of the crisis, and on February 12, he directed the transfer of a number of locomotives and cars to the Nashville & Chattanooga road.[1]

It was to no avail. The Nashville track was in frightful condition; it allegedly contained no less than 1,200 broken rails; and on February 15 Superintendent Rowland of the Western & Atlantic ordered his trains home. At Chattanooga the Fifth Georgia Regiment, quite evidently out of control, seized a string of his passenger cars and subjected them to thoughtless abuse. "Officers and Men were nearly all tight," Rowland declared.[2]

When on February 16 came news of the capitulation of Donelson, panic raced through the streets of Nashville. At the railroad stations throngs of citizens fought for space upon the cars. Major V. K. Stevenson, president of the Nashville & Chattanooga company and the quartermaster responsible for the government stores in the city, could be found nowhere; rumor said that he had departed upon a special train, accompanied by his personal belongings. Panic soon degenerated into violence, and though the first Union patrols did not appear for a week, the absence of proper planning for the loading and departure of trains prevented the salvage of mountains of matériel. On the last day a serious washout blocked all traffic over the Chattanooga road. A few cool heads, like General John B. Floyd and, especially, Nathan Bedford Forrest, labored prodigiously to reduce the chaos, but even they could not prevent losses of the first magnitude. The criminal waste at Nashville was in fact as serious a disaster as the loss of the river fortresses had been.[3]

II

The collapse in Tennessee had come chiefly because the Confederates had violated one of the basic principles of strategy. With inferior numbers they had endeavored to defend all places at all times and had failed to *concentrate*. This was a major sin, as men like Forrest realized. But the authorities at least were quick to grasp the lesson. Even before calamity had run its course, the southern forces were being drawn together from a score of points, some as widely separated as Florida, Kentucky, and New Orleans.[4]

There was at first some uncertainty as to where the Confederate units should gather. Jackson, Tennessee, was momentarily considered, as was Chattanooga. But simple geography quickly determined otherwise. Fundamentally, a southern rail-borne army faced an invader primarily water-borne. And though a locomotive could go where a steamboat could not, the peculiar course of the Tennessee, as it looped southward into Alabama, was conducting the Federals straight to the vicinity of the only trans-Confederate railroad route in existence. "The Memphis & Charleston Road is the vertebrae of the Confederacy," observed ex-Secretary of War Walker, and Secretary Benjamin was obliged, by the logic of the map, to agree. "The railroad line from Memphis to Richmond must be defended at all hazards," he wired Robert E. Lee a few days later.[5]

And so it happened that the Confederates assembled at the point where the valley of the Tennessee approached, at right angles, the main line of the Memphis & Charleston. Here in the northeast corner of Mississippi lay the little town of Corinth, where the Memphis road, extending from east to west, crossed the north-and-south-running Mobile & Ohio. Corinth had enjoyed a quiet past; even the Mobile & Ohio was still a newcomer. But now the fame of Corinth was for a brief season to span the world. Regiment after regiment was drawn to it as if by a magnet.[6]

It seemed for a time as if they would be too late. Even the weather was anti-Confederate; the same heavy rains which provided the North with unobstructed river channels, had washed away important sections of track in Mississippi, Alabama, and Georgia. Richmond directed the northward movement of all troops at Pensacola on February 18, but the first units found it impossible to depart by rail until March 4. Even then the operation of trains was restricted to the daylight hours, and certain regiments had to march overland as far as Mobile Bay. The shipment of heavy ordnance involved still greater difficulties. Track conditions remained so bad, and rolling stock so scarce, that most of the Pensacola stores never saw Corinth at all, being dumped in hastily provided depots at Pollard and a number of other Alabama points. The last southern regiment did not leave Pensacola until the night of May 9.[7]

Even when bridges had been rebuilt and embankments strengthened, the trains carried the Confederates to Corinth slowly enough. Administrative chaos was partly to blame; Richmond was far away, and the assembly of the Confederate armies devolved upon four or five different commanders located at widely separated and constantly fluctuating points. To the east was Albert Sidney Johnston, struggling to extricate the flotsam and jetsam of the Nashville fiasco from middle Tennessee. First at Mobile and then at Jackson, Tennessee, was Braxton Bragg. General Beauregard set up headquarters at Jackson, then gravitated to Corinth. Deep in Arkansas Van Dorn strove desperately in the face of incomplete railways to get his troops across the Mississippi. Johnston was presumed to be in overall charge, but the telegraph proved a poor substitute for centralized staff work.

Steps were taken, of course, to hasten the inflow of men and supplies. General Bragg, in command of the "Second Grand Division" of Beauregard's Army of the Mississippi, placed the railroads within his jurisdiction under the control of his chief quartermaster, and sufficient personnel were detailed to provide a guard of one commissioned officer and five enlisted men upon each passenger train. But the effort achieved little; the railroads concerned extended far beyond the geographic limits of Bragg's authority, and his guards were quite untrained. An inspecting officer reported that they had little effect upon traveling soldiers, who misconducted themselves with gusto. A few days later Bragg himself admitted that the railroads were utterly deranged. Wood and water stations stood abandoned; employees did not receive their regular pay and refused to work; engineers and conductors were either exhausted, or "being northern men, abandoned their positions, or managed to retard and obstruct our operations." And the temper of the railroaders hardly

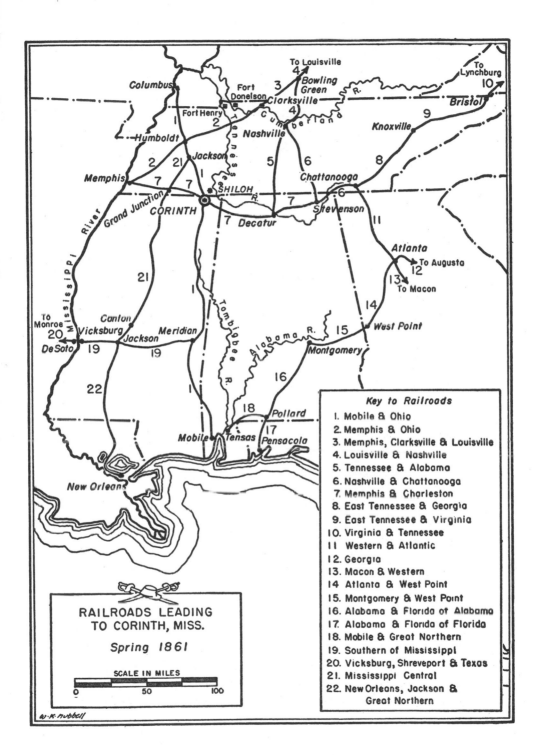

RAILROADS LEADING
TO CORINTH, MISS.

Spring 1861

SCALE IN MILES
0   50   100

Key to Railroads
1. Mobile & Ohio
2. Memphis & Ohio
3. Memphis, Clarksville & Louisville
4. Louisville & Nashville
5. Tennessee & Alabama
6. Nashville & Chattanooga
7. Memphis & Charleston
8. East Tennessee & Georgia
9. East Tennessee & Virginia
10. Virginia & Tennessee
11. Western & Atlantic
12. Georgia
13. Macon & Western
14. Atlanta & West Point
15. Montgomery & West Point
16. Alabama & Florida of Alabama
17. Alabama & Florida of Florida
18. Mobile & Great Northern
19. Southern of Mississippi
20. Vicksburg, Shreveport & Texas
21. Mississippi Central
22. New Orleans, Jackson &
     Great Northern

improved when their living quarters were repeatedly seized by irresponsible bands of soldiers.[8]

Yet the job was done. Whole brigades, most of them from Pensacola, came up the line of the Mobile & Ohio. From New Orleans, the New Orleans, Jackson & Great Northern and the Mississippi Central brought nine regiments and four batteries of artillery. Out of Tennessee at last, Albert Sidney Johnston loaded unit after unit upon the Memphis & Charleston and sent them puffing westward toward the rendezvous. The Mobile & Ohio, despite damage to one of its bridges by a Federal raiding party, carried in the elements of General Polk's command from the northwest. To be sure, Bragg complained from Corinth that the troops were arriving too slowly and without adequate supplies. Thousands of barrels of flour remained in storage at Chattanooga and one hundred carloads of provisions stood immobile at Stevenson, the junction of the Nashville & Chattanooga and Memphis & Charleston roads. But by March 29 the concentration upon Corinth had been nearly completed, and Johnston at last assumed command of the combined armies.[9]

It had not been an easy task. To keep the Memphis & Charleston steadily at work General Johnston seized "a large number" of Western & Atlantic cars, which subsequent Federal advances cut off from their parent road. Packed into ill-ventilated freight equipment, the soldiers cut the sides and roofs to pieces. Railway forces suffered endless interference at the hands of well-meaning quartermaster officers, who commandeered their trains, upset schedules, and violated operating rules. Nevertheless, the railroad compared favorably with the river as a mover of armies. In less than two months it had gathered nearly forty thousand men from points as distant as five hundred miles and had delivered them precisely where their presence would do the most good. When on April 3 the Confederates marched out of Corinth toward Pittsburg Landing, their number nearly equaled the Federal forces encamped along the river bluff.[10]

In less than a week they returned through the mud, carrying with them eight thousand wounded. Their commander was dead. Within three days northern troops were to sever the line of the Memphis & Charleston at Huntsville. But the iron horse had not failed. Fortune and the vagaries of the southern leadership had failed the iron horse.

III

When the Army of the Mississippi walked unmolested from the field of Shiloh, it lost the trunk railroad line of the Confederacy. Tactically the battle had been a draw, but strategically it remained a southern defeat of the first order. Never thereafter would a Confederate locomotive run through from Chattanooga to Memphis.

But the loss of Huntsville and of the Memphis & Charleston Railroad was initially the result of faulty intelligence, and, it appears, of the Union sympathies of certain Memphis & Charleston personnel. At dawn on April 11, without specific warning, a large Federal force under General O. M. Mitchel came pouring into the little town and within a few moments the yards, shops and general offices of the railroad were in their possession, including 18 locomotives, 100 freight and six passenger cars. Suspicion pointed to one Larcombe, a railroad telegraph operator, and to the assistant superintendent, A. J. Hopper, who had been instructed to move the rolling stock to Corinth some days before. It was whispered that even greater personalities were involved.[11]

Over a distance of one hundred miles, southern control of the road collapsed. Union detachments encamped beside the rails as far east as Stevenson, and were reported to be pressing toward the line farther west. Frenzied Confederate attempts to rush motive power and rolling stock to safety brought only confusion and further losses. Even in eastern Tennessee, wild rumors told of advancing hordes of abolitionists, and reinforcements moving up through Georgia toward Corinth were hastily stopped at Chattanooga.[12]

But the most dangerous Federal thrust was the Andrews Raid. As one of the more spectacular of the war's episodes, the events of the twelfth of April, 1862, have been retold so many times that they will bear only brief mention here. On a drab and rainy morning, twenty-one Federal soldiers disguised as civilians and led by Captain James J. Andrews, stole the locomotive, General, and several cars of a northbound Western & Atlantic passenger train as it stopped for breakfast at Big Shanty, Georgia.[13] The raiders intended to proceed up the line to Chattanooga, burning bridges and blowing up tunnels, thus rendering the road useless for a long time to come. The plan was a good one and probably would have worked successfully except for three things: the wet weather, which made arson difficult;

unanticipated meetings with extra trains, which involved long explanations; and finally the incredible determination of W. A. Fuller, conductor of the train from which the General had been stolen. For one hundred miles this bulldog of a man gave chase to the thieves, continuing at times on foot, and so closely did he press the Federals that they were able neither to damage the road seriously, nor to refuel their locomotive. At last, completely out of wood and water, the General was abandoned at the Tennessee state line, the Andrews party vainly attempting to escape through the woods.[14]

Although the raid was a failure, its implications were sufficiently frightening. "The mind and heart shrink back appalled at the bare contemplation of the awful consequences which would have followed the success of this one act," declared the editor of the Atlanta *Southern Confederacy*. "We doubt if the victory of Manassas or Corinth [!] were worth as much to us as the frustration of this grand *coup d'etat*." Governor Brown hurriedly placed two companies of militia on the road, and thenceforth, day and night, its sixteen principal bridges lay beneath the eyes of sentry details.[15]

With the northern strip of Alabama in enemy hands, the Confederates could do no more than pick up the pieces and concentrate again—largely by rail. Once more troops flowed toward Corinth, especially from the direction of Memphis, where Van Dorn had at last crossed the Mississippi. The Memphis & Charleston brought four of his brigades in as many days. Presently Johnston's successor, Beauregard, could count close to fifty thousand men behind the Corinth entrenchments, while daily through his headquarters floated the sound of clanging bells as the trains rolled in with additional food and munitions.[16]

And yet Corinth now seemed less a strategic base than a dangerous salient. On the melancholy retreat from Shiloh, Beauregard had been handed news of the loss of Island Number Ten, in the Mississippi River. Soon Memphis itself would lie at the enemy's mercy. To the east the railway for whose protection his army had first come to Corinth was gone. But to his rear the Mobile & Ohio ran down the length of Mississippi, promising shorter communications and the possibility of defense in depth. Beauregard was worried. On April 29 he ordered much of the railroad stock in Memphis removed to Granada, Mississippi. And on May 25, after a conference with his generals, he decided to evacuate Corinth.[17]

The withdrawal was meticulously planned. But the inevitable shortage of cars invalidated the most careful orders; large numbers of men were so ill that they could not march with their units, while the station platforms presently were piled with the surplus baggage of an amateur army. By the morning of May 29 the congestion was such that General Bragg was directed to take charge of the loading operations. "I find trunks enough here to load all trains for a day," he reported. "They are being piled for burning, and great is the consternation." The major traffic load fell upon the Mobile & Ohio, but at least seven trains, filled with military stores, were ordered westward over the Memphis & Charleston to Grand Junction, for transfer to the iron of the Mississippi Central. Someone held them at Corinth until four o'clock on the morning of May 30, by which time Confederate detachments to the west of the town had complied with orders to burn all the bridges of the neighborhood. The rear-guard could do nothing save put the torch to all seven trains with their contents. The loss to the Memphis road alone came to four engines and "over thirty" cars.[18]

Yet on the whole the steam locomotive had served the evacuation well. How a train was run back and forth during the final hours to the accompaniment of enthusiastic cheers, giving the Union pickets the impression that large reinforcements were arriving, is a familiar story. Certainly no such quantities of supplies as were saved could have been carried away without railroads. President Tate of the Memphis & Charleston, with his remaining employees and equipment, followed the army into exile, finally settling at Marion, Mississippi, on the line of the Mobile & Ohio a short distance north of Meridian. Here he erected temporary shops, and presently the Memphis & Charleston was back in business, repairing engines and rolling stock and leasing equipment to other lines. Nineteen of its locomotives and eighty-three of its cars ultimately found their way into the eastern Confederacy. Tate himself found employment as military superintendent of the Selma-Meridian project.[19]

IV

For the South, the spring of 1862 was a season of withdrawal before heavy Federal thrusts. At points as widely separated as New Orleans, Memphis, Florida, and North Carolina, the story was the same. The railways of the invaded regions invariably played a double role—as instruments of salvage and as victims of spoliation.

The experience of the New Orleans, Jackson & Great Northern was typical. One night in late April, an overwhelming Federal fleet churned up the lower Mississippi, while the sky shook with the futile flamings of the Confederate forts along the shore. In New Orleans there was disbelief, and then panic, as the realization dawned that the troops which might have defended the city now were far away at Corinth. There was a rush to the Jackson railroad station, where the cars were found to be already in military hands. Through four hideous days perspiring soldiers lifted ton upon ton of government stores aboard every piece of rolling stock they could find. Train after overladen train departed from the city beneath towering clouds of wood smoke. When the enemy at last stepped ashore to take possession, the Jackson railroad company found much of its equipment safe and sound amid piles of rescued public property at Pontchatoula, forty-eight miles inland. It likewise found itself without a principal terminus.[20]

Very similar was the experience of the Atlantic & North Carolina in March, 1862. It, too, endured a period of terror in the evacuation of Newbern, where a bevy of United States gunboats leisurely shelled its rolling stock, an episode spiced by the fact that most of the cars were crammed with munitions. No one was injured, however, and the entire equipment of the road was gotten safely away, with the exception of seven cars. But the Atlantic & North Carolina found that it, too, had become a rump carrier.[21]

In Virginia also the Confederates were receding. Tidal rivers that reached into the interior, disturbing reports as to the size of the enemy army, the exposed position of Richmond—all stimulated the decision to withdraw from the old front before Manassas. By early March the movement was under way.

This time there was no lack of railway equipment. Up from Gordonsville steamed practically all of the engines and cars of the Virginia Central, while from the Valley came most of the Manassas Gap stock. There were, in fact, too many trains for the single-track Orange & Alexandria, which swiftly became clogged into rigidity. Fifty-one miles separated Manassas Junction from Gordonsville, but some trains consumed thirty-six hours enroute from one to the other. As was his habit, General Joseph E. Johnston forwarded sharp complaints to Richmond. Terming the management of the Orange & Alexandria "wretched," he advised that he had been obliged to destroy huge grain and subsistence stores because of the impossibility of depending upon the promises of the railroad officials. A great deal of personal property had also to be left behind, though Johnston admitted that his army "had accumulated a supply of baggage like Xerxes' myriads." [22]

Following the appearance of McClellan on the Peninsula, the Confederate armies in Virginia and North Carolina were drawn steadily inward to cover the capital. They moved, more often than not, by rail. In North Carolina nine carriers organized, on April 1, two pools of stand-by rolling stock, one at Raleigh and the other at Goldsboro, wherewith ten thousand men could be rushed to any point on their lines in twenty-four hours. Nothing so elaborate was immediately required, but the carriers leading toward Richmond bore northward a steady flow of men and supplies. In early May the evacuation of Norfolk and Portsmouth saw two additional railroad companies, the Norfolk & Petersburg and the Seaboard & Roanoke, serve successively as avenues of escape and as victims of abandonment. Both lost half of their lines, but a portion of their iron was successfully removed. The military took special care to save the rolling stock, which Robert E. Lee regarded as more precious than army stores. [23]

Though the spring of 1862 thus brought distress to a number of Confederate railroads, their services had not been in vain. East and west, southern withdrawals had been not so much retreats as concentrations, so that by June there existed two major aggregations of southern power—one in Mississippi and one in Virginia; each poised like a compressed steel spring. Against them the still essentially water-borne Union armies advanced in confidence. Once more the Confederates based their plans primarily upon railroads.

CHAPTER

~ 12 ~

Wartime Construction Programs

I

THE OPERATION OF RAILROADS IN THE CONFEDERATE STATES MAY have seemed a thankless task, but the problems incident to the extension of new lines were appalling. Labor was scarce; iron was scarcer; and stockholders, for all their profits, hesitated to assume risks. Yet four extensive construction projects were undertaken within the Confederacy in the midst of the war, of which two were completed before the end came. None of these efforts involved the building of more than a connecting link, and only one became later a route of real importance. It was solely as avenues of military supply that they could be undertaken at all.

II

A special concern of the Confederate authorities, already mentioned in its earlier stages, was the elimination of the gap between Danville, Virginia, and Greensboro, North Carolina. It was an obvious military need. Forty miles of grading through rolling country would provide a new line southwestward from Richmond to the upper Carolinas and beyond. It also would afford relative immunity from raids, an advantage not possessed by existing routes below the James. It has been observed that President Davis advocated public assistance for the scheme as early as the fall of 1861, only to see his recommendation by-passed by a stubborn Congress. But the advantages of the idea were so clear that little more than a month had passed before it was again the subject of discussion in Capitol Square.[1]

The opponents of the measure continued to resist, again citing the

148

bogy of central government. In Congress they resorted to delaying tactics; in public they strove with some success to influence the press. "The precedent of government aid to railroads," asserted the Richmond *Semi-Weekly Examiner,* "is dangerous, difficult to be confined within proper limits, and liable to abuses and corruptions, especially in a legislative body which envelops its proceedings with secrecy." But sentiment for the project swiftly became overwhelming. Even in North Carolina, where powerful interests had long feared that such a route would divert the commerce of the western section of the state into Virginia, the State Convention approved on February 8, 1862, a charter for a "Piedmont Railroad Company," provided that the same be certified by the legislature of Virginia. The document granted the Confederate States the unlimited right to subscribe to the company's stock, and conferred similar powers upon any corporation of North Carolina or Virginia. Two days later Congress itself gave in, authorized the President to contract for a suitable connection between the Richmond & Danville and North Carolina railroads, and appropriated $1,000,000 in Confederate bonds for the purpose. The new company attained legal status on March 27, when the Virginia legislature gave it formal sanction.[2]

Nevertheless, it was May before a satisfactory construction agreement could be hammered out between the Confederate Government and the Richmond & Danville; and it was June before the Piedmont Railroad Company was fully organized. Stripped of its subordinate clauses the final arrangement provided that a subsidy of $1,000,000 in 8 per cent Confederate obligations would be given the Richmond & Danville Company, which in turn would undertake the construction and operation of the new line. The Richmond & Danville pledged as security an equal amount of its own 8 per cent bonds, the interest thereon not to become payable until eighteen months after the completion of the Piedmont road. The Danville company also was authorized to acquire any amount of Piedmont stock.[3]

By ordinary standards this hardly involved an excessive grant of public funds, and if the Danville railroad profited handsomely, it was less at the expense of the taxpayers than by virtue of economic luck. To the end of 1863 southern financial sentiment grew constantly more inflationary without quite abandoning the belief that military victory would be followed by a sound reorganization of the Confederate monetary structure. In such an atmosphere the public snapped up the securities of recognized railroad operations at steadily increasing premiums, and the market naturally exhibited an added zest when the road in question held in its treasury a pile of government paper, paying 8 per cent, while its own collateral certificates were subject for the time being to no interest at all. The demand for Richmond & Danville issues became so brisk that the directors were able to retain the 8 per cent governments unsold, while they financed their subsidiary with the sale of a brand-new series of 6 per cent bonds, which investors gobbled up at prices ranging from 133 to 248. For a face value of $500,000 issued, the company had received no less than $934,395.66 by the end of 1863. It is no wonder that the management took occasion "to congratulate the stockholders that a work of so much importance to the public interests of the Confederacy . . . could be completed under so many obstacles and so many difficulties at so small a sacrifice." [4]

But easy financing did not mean easy building. In spite of the congratulations offered the stockholders of the Richmond & Danville, the Piedmont extension was not completed until May, 1864, and its operations thenceforth were to be carried on under the most heartbreaking conditions. It was simple, under Confederate conditions, to pick dollars out of the air. To conjure up the physical apparatus of a railroad was not.

Of all the phases of construction, the selection of a route proved the easiest, for the charter had thoughfully left the entire responsibility therefor to the Confederate Government. On March 4, 1862, the War Department delegated the task to Captain Edmund T. D. Myers, a young engineer officer and son of the Quartermaster General. He had been engaged in the development of defenses along the lower James, where his embrasures are still clambered over by visitors to the site of Jamestown. It was a happy choice. Myers was a man of vigor and had the good fortune to be left strictly alone. His reconnaissance was finished early in April, and when the Piedmont Company was formally organized on June 11, he had already chosen Danville and Greensboro as the termini and had run a formal survey between them via Reidsville. [5] Myers, in fact, so impressed the Richmond & Danville interests that they offered him the position of chief engineer and chief of construction. On June 16 the War Department obliged by detailing him officially to that duty. [6]

In an atmosphere of optimism Myers dispatched a bevy of agents into the countryside to secure teams, carts, tools, and Negro laborers. He also issued scores of advertisements, inviting outside bids upon any portion of the work. But the planters of the neighborhood were extraordinarily loath to part with their slaves, or to sell their wagons and tools. The mails brought not a single bid, and when Myers appealed to a well-known railroad contractor in Georgia, he was given a quotation of fifty cents per cubic yard of grading, a figure so outrageous that the Piedmont directors refused to consider it.[7]

Soon the Piedmont board was dipping into Richmond & Danville funds for the outright purchase of slaves. But by mid-August they had secured only seventy-one, and at an average price of $1,141 each. Moreover, the Negroes manifested an emphatic distaste for construction labor; by the end of the year, nearly one-third of them had run away, of whom several were severely wounded in the process of recapture, while seventeen were still at large. "Under these circumstances," concluded the management, "every motive of humanity and every incentive of policy forbid the further prosecution of the work by purchased slaves." [8]

No solution to the labor problem was ever reached during the construction of the Piedmont Railroad. Two responsible contractors submitted acceptable proposals by midsummer of 1862, but they, too, encountered an unfavorable labor market. The company itself repeatedly raised its bid for slave hire until by October it was paying twenty-two dollars per month and keep for a single able-bodied Negro. But only a few were sent in, and Captain Myers could report only nominal progress.[9]

The War Department now intervened directly. Estimating that a minimum construction force should number 2,500, it made strenuous efforts to wring the slaves from a reluctant citizenry. Virginia cooperated with a state law authorizing the impressment of as many Negroes as were necessary to finish the road within her own borders, but this was of limited help, as 90 per cent of the line lay in North Carolina. Furthermore, there sat in the governor's chair in Raleigh the vigorous and picturesque Zebulon Vance, whose views upon state sovereignty were those of a sophisticated Joseph E. Brown. Two Secretaries of War, Randolph and Seddon, tried successively to secure his cooperation, but the sturdy governor refused to budge. With immense candor he admitted that his state really did not want the road. He also inquired why the Government could not protect the existing lines through Weldon. His most sarcastic thrust came when Seddon requested a change of gauge for the road from four feet, eight and one-half inches to five feet, so as to match the Richmond & Danville. "In regard to the gauge of the road," he wrote, "I have to say that the proposition to make it conform with the Virginia road had been disposed of in the negative before yours was received." [10]

The labor situation on the Piedmont Railroad was bad, but its matériel problem was worse. It was constantly plagued by the universal deficiency in rails. On May 24, 1862, nearly three weeks before the official birth of the new company, President Harvie of the Richmond & Danville informed Secretary Randolph that iron would be the principal bottleneck and suggested a number of places where the Government might impress it. Harvie also endeavored to smuggle track materials through the blockade, probably by means of the Robinson mission, although for reasons of security he published no details.[11]

By the beginning of 1863, a considerable amount of grading had been finished, but scarcely a bar could be had through ordinary channels. The Tredegar Works daily cast a pall of smoke over Richmond, but so confined were they to military production that they could not turn out a single section. A few railroad companies still possessed limited stocks, but they had long since learned to hoard them. There remained only the alternative of government seizure, and to this the Administration, very reluctantly, turned. On January 7 Jeremy F. Gilmer, Chief of the Engineer Bureau at Richmond, handed Captain Myers written authority to appropriate 50 per cent of the unlaid iron of the Western North Carolina, Raleigh & Gaston, Atlantic & North Carolina, and Virginia Central roads, together with all of the iron of the moribund Roanoke Valley, of the Port Walthall branch of the Richmond & Petersburg, and of the York River road beyond the Pamunkey. Gilmer emphasized that the War Department was in earnest. "The enemy seem to be systematically threatening our great lines of communication," he explained, "and your link may in consequence become one of vital consequence." Nevertheless each taking of private property was resisted with stubbornness, and the first rails did not arrive in Danville until April. The Roanoke Valley long sheltered its disused and rusting track with a court injunction. Materials came in so slowly that the frantic Richmond & Danville formally memorialized Congress for a special impressment law, and when the desired action was not forthcoming, disgustedly abandoned the entire field of iron purchase to the Government.[12]

Thereafter Captain Myers was forced to lean upon the War Department for even his routine needs. Not only did the greater portion of his rails and labor derive from public sources; he likewise looked to Richmond for his blasting powder, axes, and shovels. The Piedmont Company paid for all these items at impressment prices, but by the middle of 1863 Myers himself had grown thoroughly impatient with its timidity in the face of rising costs. The whole project, he wrote General Gilmer on July 6, should be taken over by the Engineer Bureau, lock, stock and barrel. Gilmer fully agreed, provided that the Richmond & Danville was willing, and forwarded the papers to the Secretary of War with a vigorous endorsement. Mr. Seddon merely filed them.[13]

Nevertheless, as 1863 drew to a close, 35½ miles of embankment already wound through the hills, while work trains were clattering over 28 miles of completed track. Myers had turned in what was, all things considered, a creditable performance.[14]

III

Nearly as vital as a rail connection from Greensboro to Danville was the completion of the line across central Alabama. The South managed to cling to the roads of the Atlantic seaboard for years; but the sole existing *through* route to the Mississippi Valley, the Memphis & Charleston, was lost for good in the spring of 1862, and its alternative, the long detour via Mobile, hardly afforded an adequate artery for the defense of the State of Mississippi and of the enormous reaches of the Confederacy west of the river.

In the early spring of 1862 a nearly complete line already existed between Selma, in the heart of Alabama, and Monroe, in north-central Louisiana, a line whose continuity was interrupted only by the Mississippi River ferry at Vicksburg and by a relatively short stretch from a point a few miles east of Demopolis, Alabama, to Meridian, Mississippi. Even here, grading was partly finished and track had been put down in a few places. At Demopolis, however, the

Tombigbee River remained unbridged.[15] This new deep-southern route was divided among a number of separate companies. West of Meridian were the Southern Railroad of Mississippi and the Vicksburg, Shreveport & Texas. To the eastward, construction was being shared between the Northeast & Southwest Railroad and the Alabama & Mississippi Rivers Railroad. For the time being the former carrier planned only to build 27 miles to Reagan, Alabama, whence the tracks of the latter would extend the rest of the distance to Selma. In 1862 only the Alabama & Mississippi Rivers had completed a part of its segment and was actually operating trains.[16]

Compared with the Danville-Greensboro project, which faced more than forty miles of jumbled country, the Selma-Meridian route appeared to offer no extraordinary difficulties. Not only did much of it lie within the rich and nearly level terrain of the Black Belt; grading was in large measure finished. The principal problem was iron. Another was the growing cost of labor. But only a slight subsidy appeared necessary. Instead of the $1,000,000 deemed indispensable to the Piedmont road, Secretary of War Benjamin thought a loan of $150,000 would suffice.[17]

In Congress the Selma-Meridian bill encountered the same sort of opposition, and at the hands of substantially the same individuals, as did the Danville measure. Conspicuous among them were Robert Barnwell Rhett of Charleston and the entire delegation of Georgia, all of whom represented existing railroad interests which the new line would in part by-pass. But congressional approval was ultimately forthcoming and the bill received the presidential signature on February 15.[18]

Unfortunately, the law was carelessly drawn; it approved the loan of $150,000 to the Alabama & Mississippi Rivers Railroad Company for the completion of a line between Selma and Meridian, while that company in fact did not contemplate building beyond Reagan and the connection with the Northeast & Southwest road aforementioned. The Government does not seem to have realized the existence of the latter carrier until April.[19]

There likewise occurred a lengthy negotiation with the directors of the Alabama & Mississippi Rivers Railroad. One of them declared that $150,000 was not enough and that at least $500,000 would be required. It was not until Richmond had extended a flat remission of import duties upon rails that the company agreed to cooperate.

On April 23 its board formally accepted the loan, issued a ten-year promissory note in favor of the Confederate Government, executed a mortgage upon its *entire* property between Selma and Reagan, and even posted bond, individually and collectively, for the repayment of the debt.[20]

Before the final agreement was signed, Secretary Randolph had determined to appoint a government agent to supervise operations on the spot. Though President Charles T. Pollard of the Alabama & Florida Railroad of Alabama recommended Wadley as a suitable choice, Randolph selected A. S. Gaines of Demopolis, a civil engineer of local repute. Gaines was instructed to push the work as rapidly as possible, to arrange for the operation of through trains, to provide for a suitable ferry service across the Tombigbee until a bridge could be finished, and, finally, to insure the cooperation of carriers concerned. The last chore promised special woe, as the Government had not yet seen fit to deal with the Northeast & Southwest Railroad at all. What Richmond had done was to lend money to another corporation to build its line.[21] And another thing had been forgotten. Even with a complete new railroad from Selma to Meridian to Vicksburg, and (beyond the Mississippi ferry) to Monroe, the Confederate States still would not possess a perfect central artery. The forty miles between Selma and Montgomery bore not a single rail; there was only the Alabama River, whose brown current afforded at best a poor substitute for what the fighting South really needed—a through, unbroken, interior line of railroad over which men and supplies could be forwarded without break of bulk from Virginia to the Mississippi.

Nevertheless, a finished route west of Selma would be of inestimable value. Gaines acted at once. Rail sufficient to finish the segment between Meridian and Reagan was lost with the Federal capture of New Orleans at the end of April, but the diligent agent already had made a survey of emergency sources. The Cahaba, Marion & Greensborough, a bankrupt short line which intersected the Alabama & Mississippi Rivers Railroad a short distance west of Selma, was found to possess four hundred tons of new iron, plus four hundred kegs of spikes, while on the Montgomery & Eufaula, the building of which had scarcely begun, he discovered a substantial hoard of track materials and a brand-new locomotive. By the latter part of June Gaines had actually secured from the Cahaba company 55,367 pounds of spikes, 3,810 pounds of bolts and nuts, 17,636 pounds of fish bars, and 1,276 sections of rail. This, he advised, was not the whole of his expected take.[22]

But Gaines's industry was exceeded by Confederate shortages. Despite the loan and the impressed supplies, the work progressed with a profound deliberation. President G. G. Griffin of the Alabama & Mississippi Rivers asserted that only one-third of the spikes necessary to complete the road were at hand. Furthermore, the tires of certain of his locomotives had become dangerously worn. Griffin's excuses, doubtless, were exaggerated only slightly. But in mid-June the patience of the local military suddenly ended. General Braxton Bragg, the newly appointed commander of the Army of Mississippi, personally intervened.[23]

Whatever were the deficiencies of Bragg as a leader of troops in the field—and they were many—it cannot be denied that he was a successful organizer. Among other things his appreciation of railroads as channels of military supply far exceeded the Confederate average. In June of 1862, his command was based upon Tupelo in northeastern Mississippi, where it lay licking the wounds received in the recent Shiloh-Corinth campaign. Tupelo afforded a desirable position, for the trains of the Mobile & Ohio could unload directly into its supply depots. But its natural connection with the east, by way of the line of the Memphis & Charleston, had been lost. Bragg had only to glance at the map to realize the importance of the half-finished Selma-Meridian route, and as he read the dispatches telling of its creeping progress, his impatience soared.

On the morning of June 24 there appeared at the offices of the Alabama & Mississippi Rivers Railroad at Demopolis Captain P. H. Thompson, an engineer officer upon Bragg's staff, bearing orders for the seizure of the property. Thompson feared trouble, but the company met him half-way. The prestige of the army would, it thought, assure the cooperation of contractors and suppliers. "If the Government wants the road in time to be available for war purposes," remarked President Griffin, "then as matters stand the plan of General Bragg of completing it under military authority is the only available one." [24]

In the end it was Bragg who hesitated. He possessed no special authority to take over the line, and he was not unaware of the existence of Gaines. Immediate seizure was for the moment suspended, while the General wrote at enormous length to Adjutant General Cooper in Richmond, explaining the strategic value of the connection and emphasizing the weaknesses of the Alabama & Mississippi Rivers Railroad. "I cannot present in too strong language the mischief that must result from further reliance on this company," he concluded. The response of the War Department was confusing, to say the least. Secretary Randolph authorized Bragg by telegraph to take charge of the work, but cautioned him that the only funds available were those already appropriated by the Congress. Ten days later, Adjutant General Cooper forwarded explicit instructions *not* to seize the railroad, or any material, on the ground that such action was illegal. But even if Cooper's orders were to be deemed legitimate in the face of the previous authorization of the Secretary of War, they arrived at Tupelo too late. A *modus vivendi* already had been worked out with Gaines, and Bragg had appointed Samuel Tate, president of the Memphis & Charleston, as general military superintendent of the Selma-Meridian project.[25]

Tate was a railroad man of such ability that his reputation rivaled that of Wadley. Through the whole of the summer and fall he bustled about Alabama and the states adjoining, nosing out accumulations of rail and fastenings like a bloodhound. With Gaines he had no difficulty; each superintendent, far from resenting a rival, appears to have welcomed the other as a valuable aide. But the work was not without its irritations. The matter of the Northeast & Southwest Railroad came at last to a head. The vague terms of the Confederate subsidy were of little help, and to get the track down quickly Tate was driven to use $20,000 of his own Memphis & Charleston funds. Before the problem could be disposed of, it was to reach the desk of President Davis himself. The impressment of iron from recalcitrant owners proved even more unpleasant; by the time the last rails were laid, Tate had been variously and publicly described as stupid, unfair, and the knowing agent of a criminal plot.[26]

Even with Tate in charge, construction proceeded slowly enough. No sooner had a supply of rails been obtained than the planters who had furnished slaves abruptly withdrew them to bring in the harvest. Pressed by Richmond, Governor J. G. Shorter of

Alabama commissioned former governor A. B. Moore to investigate. In due time the latter returned through the autumn mud to report that the labor situation was greatly improved, but that the track would not be finished for some weeks. "The trip along the road was very rough," he remarked, "and I had to take it on horseback nearly to Meridian." [27]

It was not until December 10 of 1862, that Gaines could inform the Secretary of War that the work had been completed. Even so, there still was no bridge to carry the trains over the Tombigbee, necessitating several miles of steamboat travel between Demopolis and McDowell's Bluff. The section east of the river lacked rolling stock, and Gaines warned that notice of large troop movements should be given far in advance. He and Tate were to be congratulated, but they hardly had provided the major artery that the South so desperately needed. [28]

IV

As the Alabama & Mississippi Rivers Railroad marched painfully and imperfectly forward, the little city of Selma remained completely unconnected by rail with any road lying to the east. A ceremonious start had once been made upon a line to Montgomery, but the work had not, as a local citizen expressed it, "made much progress yet." Much further advanced was the Alabama & Tennessee Rivers Railroad, which was in regular operation to Blue Mountain, 134 miles to the northeast. But even this road afforded no through passage. The closest iron was at Rome, Georgia, fifty miles from Blue Mountain over broken country. [29]

It was not, of course, very long before the need of a bridge line to the east, as well as to the west, of Selma was seriously felt. A rejuvenation of the Selma-Montgomery undertaking failed to attract much interest, but by the late summer of 1862, an animated discussion had developed as to the best ways and means of extending the Alabama & Tennessee Rivers into northwest Georgia. The talk spread to Richmond, and the inevitable subsidy bill was introduced into the Confederate House of Representatives on August 20. [30]

As in the case of the Piedmont and Selma-Meridian enactments, the Rome-Blue Mountain project was carefully advertised as a

matter of military necessity. It was likewise attacked on constitutional grounds by those whose economic interests it seemed to
threaten. When the route via Rome received favorable comment,
an outraged howl arose from the rival town of Dalton, and stiff
representations were forwarded to President Davis by that community's founder and chief citizen, the venerable Duff Green. In
the House, the bill encountered parliamentary barriers of formidable proportions, and two messages from Davis in its behalf were
required before it finally became law on October 2. Moreover, the
measure emerged with a number of strings attached. It favored no
specific railroad company, and the appropriation, limited to an
exact maximum of $1,122,480.92 in Confederate 8 per cent bonds,
was to be awarded to the lowest responsible bidders only. All new
construction and appurtenances were to be mortgaged to the Confederate States, while the work was to be finished in not more than
ten months. Precise clauses prescribed the manner of repayment.
Sternest of all was the requirement which obliged the railroads concerned to pay 8 per cent interest from the very beginning.[31]

Rigid as these specifications were, two companies at once expressed their willingness to accept them. From Rome the Georgia
& Alabama Railroad already had graded a line to the Alabama
boundary, and on October 20 its directors unanimously assented
to the Government's terms. Two weeks later the Alabama Assembly authorized the Alabama & Tennessee Rivers road to build
eastward under Confederate supervision to a junction at the state
line.[32]

A railroad having thus been committed to paper, the contractors
at once encountered the standard difficulty with rail and fastenings.
The War Department pledged itself to exert "its utmost powers"
to get them, and it placed an army engineer, Captain L. P. Grant,
in direct charge of the work. But as the weeks and months went
by and the grading gangs pushed forward through the soggy red
clay, absolutely no iron was forthcoming. After more than a year,
not a bar had been spiked down. There were periodic military
pronouncements as to the value of the road, and there occurred
more than one discussion as to suitable sources of rail. But to the
end of the war the Rome-Blue Mountain connection never became
more than a series of naked cuts and fills.[33]

V

Far beyond the Mississippi, and separated from the last threads of the main southern railway net by a hundred miles of prairie and bayou, the enormous mass of Texas sprawled in splendid isolation. The Lone Star State was different. Its enthusiasm for secession was as intense as that of any comparable area, and indeed it was in Texas that the spark of resistance lingered longest after Appomattox. But Texas never seemed to play a major role in the southern war effort. It simply was too remote. The Federal blockade and the lack of a connecting railroad kept it apart until the end.*

It was natural that an attempt should be made to bridge the gap. The example of the Piedmont and Selma extensions by no means went unnoticed west of the Mississippi, and as early as March 1, 1862, the usual bill to authorize Confederate aid was introduced by a Texas Congressman, Caleb C. Herbert. Louisiana interests at once sprang to the aid of the proposal; and on March 22 the Common Council of New Orleans pronounced the road "a military necessity of the first class" and officially requested the Louisiana delegation in Richmond to lend their energetic support.[34]

The bill attracted the inevitable denunciation. After a lengthy confinement in the House Military Affairs Committee, it escaped defeat by a margin of just four votes. In the Senate it was at first rejected entirely, and was passed only after a personal appeal by the grim and commanding Louis T. Wigfall.[35]

The final enactment closely resembled those dealing with other railroad links. It provided $1,500,000 in Confederate bonds for the construction of a railroad from New Iberia, Louisiana, to Orange, Texas. It required a mortgage contract, and especially emphasized the military character of the undertaking. It was less careful in its geographic specifications, as existing track west of New Orleans extended only to Brashear City, not New Iberia.[36]

Events followed in a familiar sequence. Secretary Randolph selected one Jacob Paine as government supervisor of the project. Rails, spikes, and chairs could be neither begged nor borrowed, and steps were taken to seize them. All of which led to nothing. Just ten days after Davis had affixed his signature to the act, New

* See "A Note on Texas Railroads," Appendix.

Orleans fell, and Mr. Paine, after due consideration, "thought it impracticable to construct the road." The scheme lingered longest in the subconsciousness of the Confederate Senate. Five months later, it actually requested the President to provide information as to the "progress of the work." [37]

VI

Early in November, 1861, there detrained at the depot of the Northeastern Railroad at Charleston a tall, erect figure in military dress who strode rapidly through the crowded train-shed. It was Robert E. Lee, whom President Davis had just sent to take command of the department of South Carolina, Georgia, and Florida. He attracted little attention, for the local citizenry had hardly heard of him.

Lee's orders emphasized the improvement of the defenses of Charleston and other places along the coast. But he soon realized that the key to the situation lay not so much in fortifications as in the ability to transfer troops and supplies from one point to another. Existing coastal railways seemed to serve the purpose, but he was distressed to note that they did not form a system of through lines. At Charleston the Ashley River remained unbridged. At Savannah the Savannah, Albany & Gulf was as yet unconnected with the other roads entering the city. At Augusta the rails of the Augusta & Savannah were still separated from those of the South Carolina and Georgia companies.

Before Lee departed in March to his Virginia destiny, he endeavored to eliminate all of these deficiencies. He especially urged the construction at Augusta, not only because of the limited work necessary, but because of the importance of the place as a distribution point. When the city council proved uncooperative, Lee appealed directly to Governor Brown, hinting broadly that the cost would be assumed by the Confederate Government. With respect to the half-finished Ashley River crossing, he likewise intimated that Richmond might cooperate financially. [38]

Lee's successor in the Department, John C. Pemberton, repeatedly urged the closure of the troublesome gaps. To Augusta he sent Brigadier General Thomas F. Drayton with instructions to confer directly with the Mayor. He particularly endorsed government help for the Savannah connection, for he coveted the Savannah, Albany & Gulf rolling stock. "This road is doing very little business," he reported, "and might readily spare some of its equipment to other roads not so well supplied. If the war continues, we shall need every locomotive in the Confederacy." To Isaac W. Hayne, a member of the South Carolina Executive Council, he described the Ashley bridge as "emphatically a military necessity" and pledged all the assistance in his power if the state would subsidize its completion.[39]

The forces of local interest and inertia at last gave way. Slowly —very slowly—the picturesque old discontinuities were erased. In the course of 1862 South Carolina provided $35,000 to insure the completion of the bridge at Charleston, and by the end of the year the work was finished, save for the draw and approaches. The first train passed nervously across a few months later. At Savannah trackage was extended briskly enough as soon as the War Department had made an advance of $6,000. Presently even the Augusta & Savannah was laying government rail along Washington Street, Augusta, to a junction with the South Carolina road.[40]

But despite the happy issue at Charleston, Savannah, and Augusta, the Confederacy was hardly finished with the railroad junction problem. The two roads serving Selma possessed no satisfactory means of interchange until 1863. Montgomery long remained a notorious center of congestion, and the delays experienced in the transshipment of government property across the city became so bad on one occasion that President Davis dispatched thither his personal aide, Colonel William Preston Johnston, to investigate. And even where the rails of different companies did join, operating officials remained extraordinarily loath to permit the uninterrupted passage of their rolling stock.[41]

VII

It must not be supposed that the Confederate Government served as purveyor of unlimited aid to the railroad industry of the South. The funds advanced were loaned, not donated, and were confined always to works of military value. Constitutionally restrained from subsidizing ordinary enterprise, both Executive and Congress were extremely chary of involvement in any private venture. The list of disappointed railroads was therefore a long one. Among those to return from Richmond with empty hands were the Memphis & Little Rock, the Eastern Texas, the Vicksburg, Shreveport & Texas, the Wilmington, Charlotte & Rutherford (which desired not money but shovels), and the Western North Carolina. Likewise turned down was a Virginia undertaking of long standing, the Covington & Ohio.[42]

Even state and local governments had become stingy. In March, 1862, the city of Raleigh refused to subsidize a hitherto cherished railroad to the coal fields of Chatham County, and what little progress was made came as a result of the purchase of stock (with protective restrictions) by the State of North Carolina. Attempts to secure the aid of Virginia for the extension of the Virginia Central over the last miles into Covington evoked only a flurry of correspondence. The fact that the Pensacola & Georgia utilized existing subsidy machinery to build westward from Tallahassee to Quincy, Florida, was merely an exception to prove a rule.[48] The truth was that the South had not the resources for active railroad construction. The dreams of 1860 remained for the most part among the notes of surveyors, or as gullied embankments that already were sprouting grass.

CHAPTER

～ 13 ～

Frederick W. Sims

I

WHEN COLONEL WADLEY DESCENDED THE NINTH STREET HILL that June morning of 1863 to re-enter civilian life, his works did not tumble into ruins behind him. Congress had, of course, failed to sanction his Railroad Bureau and had placed the execution of the recent railroad act in the hands of the Quartermaster Department. But the senators and representatives had then dispersed in the face of a Richmond summer, leaving the heat and the initiative to the Executive. In so far as the transportation problem was concerned, the Administration now turned at once independent and conservative. It preserved the Railroad Bureau, but it refrained from invoking the new railroad law.

Why the government of Jefferson Davis should have proceeded in this manner is, to say the least, puzzling. The legislature, the chief sounding board of the "local rights" viewpoint, had itself provided the Executive with an adequate weapon; yet the Act of May, 1863, lay unused in an obscure pigeonhole. It is easy to blame Davis, in whom the ultimate responsibility rested, but it is less easy to explain why he thus failed to act. The Confederate President was not unaware of the importance of the steam locomotive—witness his sponsorship of railroad extension while Secretary of War under Franklin Pierce. Why he should now fail to harness the iron horse is little less than astonishing. Perhaps, in the very crisis time of the Confederacy, the southern religion of individual rights overbore even his southern nationalism and his sense of military logistics.

But the Administration did extend tacit approval to Wadley by appointing as his successor his principal assistant and protégé.

164

Rail Road Bureau Richmond May 27th 1863

Hon James A Seddon
    Secy of War
        Richmond Va
            Sir

                    The Railroad property which came
into my hands by virtue of my appointment consisted of:
    3 Locomotive Engines, from Louisville & Nashville Railroad.
    16 Freight Cars
    105 Tons Iron
and a lot of laid rails on Government track at Augusta.
The following disposition has been made of them.

    1 Locomotive Engine sold to Charlotte & South Carolina RR $ 18.000.
    1   "   "   "   " Memphis & Charleston   " $ 22.500.
    2   "   "   "   " Wilmington & Manchester   " $ 42.500.
    1   "   "   "   " Virginia & Tennessee   " $ 25.000.
    8 Freight Cars   "   " Georgia Rail Road $ 4.800
    8   "   "   "   "   " $ 4.800.
    105 Tons bar Iron   "   "   "   &c.
                                                    $117.616.

The proceeds have been turned over to the Quarter Master General
All the property at Raleigh is in the hands of Capt I.R. Sharpe A.Q.M. or
he has the necessary receipts   I remain, Sir;
                            Very respectfully
                                Your obt servant
                                    Wm. M. Wadley
                                            A.A.G.

P.S. The laid rails at Augusta will be turned over to my successor.

Colonel Wadley turns over his Railroad Bureau property to Secretary of
War Seddon at the time of his dismissal. National Archives.

Hardly had the Colonel's bulky figure disappeared down Ninth Street, when orders were issued directing Captain F. W. Sims to assume his duties and "to execute the same to the like extent with his predecessor, reporting through the Adjutant and Inspector General to the War Department." [1]

Frederick William Sims was a man of parts. Unlike Wadley, he was no Yankee. Born in the north Georgia village of Washington on October 18, 1823, he had passed the greater part of his childhood and youth in Macon, where his father was mayor in 1842. During his young manhood he served as a "transporting agent" on the Central of Georgia and became acquainted with Wadley, acquiring the viewpoint of a railroad man. But Sims did not make transportation his life's work; he enjoyed the stimulation of varied activity, and in 1856 removed to Savannah, where, in partnership with James R. Sneed, he purchased the respectable old Savannah *Republican* and settled down to a newspaper career. [2]

Sims was an inveterate "public spirited citizen," serving constantly upon boards and committees. From the year of his arrival in Savannah, he joined enthusiastically in the activities of the Union Society, which then, as now, sponsored the Bethesda Orphanage for boys, one of the oldest functioning philanthropic institutions in the United States. He also devoted himself to the affairs of the Massie School. Nor did he eschew politics. No fire-eater, he associated himself with the "American" party in the presidential campaign of 1856, and upon taking over the *Republican* was elected vice-president of the Savannah Fillmore Club. By 1858 his multifarious affairs pressed so heavily upon him that he turned the active direction of the paper over to Sneed. Around the tables of scores of board meetings he met all the representative men of Savannah, among them Wadley and a leading lawyer named Alexander R. Lawton. [3]

When confronted with the crisis of 1860-61, Sims reacted moderately. He did not at first enter military service, but in September, 1861, finally donned the uniform of the Oglethorpe Light Infantry. His prestige in the city was such that he was almost immediately elected captain of Company B, in which capacity he underwent bombardment in Fort Pulaski and was carried north as a prisoner of war, probably to Fort Columbus, Ohio. His release through exchange in the autumn and his subsequent detail as assistant to Wadley have been noted.[4]

When he assumed his duties as supervisor of railroad transportation, Captain Sims was just entering the prime of life. Not quite forty years of age, he already had displayed marked administrative ability. Though inferior to Wadley as a transportation expert, he had absorbed the basic principles of his predecessor. He also possessed an attribute which Wadley did not share—a well-developed gift of gab. Sims enjoyed people; Wadley enjoyed railroads. Wadley had a tendency to look facts in the face; Sims possessed, on occasion, the Confederate ability to forget unpleasant realities. Of the two chiefs of the Railroad Bureau, Sims had much the happier time.

When Sims's very real abilities are considered, it seems strange that he has become so shadowy a figure. Even among the quiet squares of Savannah he has been almost forgotten. He was a rather large, homely man, of medium complexion, with heavy features; yet his personality must have been pleasing. Between the lines of his correspondence we glimpse an active, gregarious person, quick, intelligent, and much given to talk in the easy manner of mid-Georgia. All things considered, F. W. Sims represented the administrative branch of the Confederate Army at its best.

II

When Sims succeeded Wadley in June, 1863, he found that the meticulous New Englander had left everything in order. Nevertheless the Railroad Bureau was little more than a promising framework. It boasted, besides Sims, of an officer personnel of two. In immediate charge of the carriers of North Carolina was John D. Whitford, with headquarters at Goldsboro; on loan from the Commissary Department, and currently in Richmond for purposes of liaison was J. M. Hottel. With this staff Sims was to accomplish four missions: the expediting of Army shipments by rail, the apportionment of rolling stock and supplies among the several lines, the coordination of certain major troop movements, and the negotiation of tariffs for government business. The Bureau still had no control over the transportation activities of quartermaster officers in the field, and indeed in many areas local commanders had developed little railway offices of their own. Since the previous December, General Bragg's Army of Tennessee had maintained a one-man bureau in the person of Major John W. Goodwin (formerly assistant superintendent of the Mobile & Ohio), while a similar arrangement was evolving under General Joseph E. Johnston in Mississippi. The officer currently responsible for the management of military railroad traffic through Richmond, Major D. H. Wood, was answerable to the Quartermaster General alone. Worst of all, the Bureau possessed no representative at the turntable of the Confederacy—Atlanta.[5]

Throughout the rest of 1863 and into 1864 Sims strove to put meat upon the bones of his organization. An early concern was an increase in his own rank; Wadley had held a full colonelcy, while Whitford, who was supposed to be his subordinate, was already a major. This was quickly rectified, however; Sims received his majority in July, with date-in-grade preceding Whitford's. In December he was promoted to lieutenant colonel and, what is more, was easily confirmed in the Senate. He also acquired a more adequate staff through the assignment of officers from other units. To Atlanta he sent Major Thomas Peters, formerly chief quartermaster of Polk's Corps, Army of Tennessee. Hottel he placed at Montgomery, and later at Atlanta as Peters' assistant. For a time he controlled the activities of Major Mason Morfit, who was stationed successively at Wilmington, North Carolina, and Petersburg. But most helpful of all was the early transfer of his office to the Quartermaster Department, where it should have been from the beginning.[6]

At last there existed a chain of administration between Sims and the thousand-and-one quartermasters scattered over the Confederacy. In August, 1863, the unstable Myers was removed from his post as quartermaster general and replaced by none other than Alexander R. Lawton, Sims's old friend of Union Society days. Lawton was a professional soldier as well as an attorney, having graduated from West Point in 1839, and he even had enjoyed a season of practical railroad experience as president of the Augusta & Savannah from 1849 to 1854. He had served with distinction in the field during the first two years of the war, suffering major wounds at Sharpsburg. His replacement of Myers by presidential fiat aroused a political storm of major proportions, but no superior could have been more satisfactory to the chief of the Railroad Bureau.[7]

By the autumn of 1863 Sims's feet began to touch ground. In June his headquarters had been Box No. 1062 at the Richmond post office, but now he possessed a permanent office on the third floor of Belvin's Block on Twelfth Street. There remained some things that he could not directly control, such as the audit and payment of railway bills. But relief from such details could be an advantage. With the other branches of the Quartermaster Department his relations seem to have been singularly cordial.[8]

Like Wadley, Sims was no armchair administrator; both he and his assistants traveled continually throughout the eastern half of the Confederacy. From October 15, 1863, to the middle of December he was absent from Richmond five times for periods that varied from one to fifteen days. Hottel covered Alabama and eastern Mississippi, while Peters became a well-known figure in north Georgia. If vigor alone could have unraveled the railroad dilemma, Sims's Bureau might have done it. But it was not enough. Wadley had been vigorous, too.[9]

III

During the months he had served as Wadley's assistant, Sims's chief responsibility had been the Confederate railroad repair shop and equipment pool at Raleigh. It never left him. As the war continued, and as the carriers faced ever-increasing necessities with decreasing means, their appeals to the Government grew more vociferous, and it was the Railroad Bureau that usually was given the task of conjuring from the air such items as tires, frames, trucks, wheels, and whole locomotives. However impossible the situation, Sims made the effort. When in June, 1863, the Army of Northern Virginia went surging northward to its highwater mark, he saw to it that salvage officers followed in its wake, nosing out railway material.[10] And though the Confederates returned from Gettysburg too soon for the collection and shipment of much loot, he somehow contrived to make capital of the southern disasters in the west.

By the early summer of 1863 Union armies had knifed so repeatedly through northern and western Mississippi that the unhappy region was practically abandoned by the southern military command. Within this tortured zone lay sizeable amounts of rolling stock, including some which had been brought south from previously invaded areas in Tennessee. If left where they were, these engines and cars would serve only as convenient objects of destruction. On the other hand, farther east, in regions of unquestioned Confederate control, their presence would be a godsend.

That Sims was the first to suggest the movement of the threatened equipment is uncertain. But as early as June 10 he was writing the Secretary of War, requesting the aid of the Quartermaster Department in the undertaking. Indeed the task was of a magnitude far beyond the resources of his organization. The Selma-Meridian link, though leading in precisely the desired direction, was in so incomplete a state as to be of no use whatsoever. Even the route through Mobile presented serious obstacles: the rolling stock would have to be carried by water over twenty-five miles of Mobile Bay and the Tensas River; no connecting trackage yet existed between railheads at Montgomery; while the Montgomery & West Point road, over which the equipment would have to pass to the eastward, was of a narrower gauge than that of the locomotives and cars in question.[11]

Sims's appeal seems to have caught Quartermaster General Myers in one of his happy moods, for the helpfulness of his department left little to be desired. But the operation proceeded slowly enough. On June 24 Captain Hottel departed for Alabama to expedite matters, but not until winter was the last locomotive carried east. The modification of the Mobile ferry steamers required weeks; the track across Montgomery, built at last by the Eufaula road at a cost of over eleven thousand dollars, was not finished until the latter part of September, and special trucks to carry the refugee units over the narrow-gauge Montgomery & West Point were not ready until after the middle of October. Everywhere progress was hindered by late-summer outbreaks of malaria.[12]

Worse still was the human obstacle. Alabama railroaders watched the procession with shameless lust. Superintendent Jordan of the Mobile & Great Northern crowded the wires with pleas for a certain passenger engine. The Alabama & Florida secured a court injunction restraining the removal from its rails of three choice Mobile & Ohio locomotives, named Dart, Javelin, and Perseverance; the proceedings dragged on for weeks, while the desperately needed power remained immobile. Those units which succeeded in running the gauntlet were met by a swarm of representatives from the eastern carriers, each striving to get his hands upon the treasure in advance of his colleagues. G. J. Fulton of the Atlantic & Gulf demanded five engines. The officers of the Wilmington & Manchester stewed over the fate of the Dart, Javelin, and Perseverance, but in the meantime made off with two other machines, plus forty cars. From Atlanta the Western & Atlantic called for three engines. The Richmond & Danville declared that if it did not receive its fair share, it would cease converting its existing stock for use on the Piedmont road. By year's end the pile of telegrams on Sims's desk, pleading, cajoling and threatening, was inches thick.[13]

No figures have survived to indicate the total of equipment removed from Mississippi. Perhaps thirty locomotives were secured; the number of cars must have been much larger. They eased the situation in Georgia and the Carolinas, but as Sims himself pointed out, the evil day had merely been staved off. The Government had been able to provide them solely by virtue of the contraction of Confederate territory. During the same autumn, no less than fifty other southern locomotives stood useless for want of tires. "Is it any wonder that transportation is deficient?" queried Sims. "Is it not rather a wonder that we have any transportation by rail at all?"[14]

IV

When he could find time for reflection, Sims could see no reason for changing the fundamental program of his predecessor. In so far as transportation was concerned, he had been wholly Wadley-trained. Like Wadley, he insisted that unless something was done to increase the flow of ordinary supplies to the carriers, there could be no real hope for improvement. With Wadley, he opposed the *careless* ordering of rolling stock from one line to another, noting that cars had been "run from point to point without attention and only found rest in total destruction, utterly lost to their owners." But neither he nor Wadley thought that a satisfactory system of interchange could be established by the railroads themselves.[15]

In the negotiation of tariffs for government traffic his experience likewise paralleled that of his teacher. Within a fortnight of his assumption of office, he received a peremptory letter from Georgia's

Governor Brown, asserting that if the quartermaster in Atlanta did not validate the Augusta tariff within thirty days, the state-owned Western & Atlantic would cease to furnish transportation to the Confederate States. Sims could do no more than acquiesce. His first major railroad convention also found him practically helpless, with the carriers doing the dictating. When the meeting assembled at the General Passenger Depot in Macon on the morning of November 25, 1863, Sims still hoped that a general discussion of mutual problems might develop. But President Cuyler of the Central of Georgia announced blandly that "the object of the meeting [was] for the purpose of considering the propriety of advancing the present rates paid by the Government for transportation." In a few hours it was all over. Freight rates and certain classes of passenger fares were sharply increased, while demurrage and other rules were rewritten with an emphasis upon stringency. While Sims maintained a discreet silence, the delegates concluded by passing resolutions critical of the deliberation with which the Government paid its bills.[16]

The Macon Convention hardly represented the whole railroad industry of the South. Present were the officers of only nineteen companies of a total mileage of 2,938. Many roads were either uninterested, or too deeply involved at home. Sims soon found it convenient to deviate from official rate structures and deal directly with individual carriers; in September, 1863, he concluded in this fashion an agreement with the Norfolk & Petersburg, whereby the company undertook to handle all public traffic offered for a fixed payment of nine thousand dollars per month. At other times he would approve special rates to supplement the ordinary government tariff. Not infrequently single carriers saw fit to increase their charges unilaterally without notice; Governor Brown protected the interests of his Western & Atlantic in this manner in November, 1863, the advance being exactly 100 per cent upon all classes of Confederate freight. The Government stood helpless before any determined railroad interest; to protect itself it possessed nothing save the impressment statute and the railroad variant of May 1, 1863, neither of which it cared or dared to invoke.[17]

Although the Railroad Bureau never established a universal system of freight car interchange, it did try to concentrate equipment in regions of special strain. When moved about for this purpose, rolling stock was commonly kept together in trains, consisting of locomotive and twelve or fifteen cars, a practice which helped reduce straying. For months the Government kept two or three of these trains in regular operation between Georgia points and the port of Wilmington to insure the shipment of the cotton with which imported military supplies were paid for. The Ordnance Bureau asserted that even more equipment should be devoted to this work, but the officers of neighboring railroads grumbled that the trains were needed for vital service upon their own tracks. "We need help," telegraphed the superintendent of the Western & Atlantic in December, 1863, "Do you intend the Tennessee army shall suffer from want of food? Answer." [18]

The situation was not improved when army officers seized the equipment for their own purposes, and inefficient operations at the wharves sometimes clogged depots at intermediate points. On one occasion trackside facilities at Charleston were crammed with one thousand bales of government cotton, while seventeen loaded cars belonging to the Central of Georgia stood for days across the river from Wilmington. The paralysis was evident as far inland as Macon and Augusta; the Charleston & Savannah declared a cotton embargo; and Superintendent Adams of the Central refused to permit his trains to operate beyond Charleston. The whole affair was complicated further by another corn shortage in Virginia.[19]

An especially difficult problem at the Bureau was the draft of railway employees into the army. Heretofore bona-fide railway workers had been relatively safe, but as the military situation deteriorated, the conscription authorities assumed an increasingly stern attitude. On September 5, 1863, Colonel J. S. Preston, Chief of the Bureau of Conscription, ordered a census of all white males engaged in railroad service in Virginia, North Carolina, South Carolina, and Georgia; and in December Jefferson Davis informed the House of Representatives that exempted railroad men of draft age within those states totaled 2,316, with the implication that here was a reservoir of manpower that might be tapped.[20]

Railway operating officials soon learned that a word from Sims carried weight at the Conscription Bureau, and almost daily there came appeals for his intercession. Dire consequences were frequently threatened because of loss of personnel. "I have heard nothing from application," wired the president of the Wilmington,

Charlotte & Rutherford. "I shall lose the hands unless something is done for me and [will] be compelled in self defense to stop supplies of wood for [the] Charlotte Q. M. and Naval post.... Answer me." Demands also came in for the detail of former employees already in the ranks.[21]

V

Sims was capable of accomplishing much with a little, and his natural good-humor was seldom disturbed. Yet he remained quite aware that things were by no means going well. The responsibilities of the Railroad Bureau were always rather ill-defined. A notable area of competition was General Northrop's Commissary Department, which maintained representatives of its own at principal railroad points and which, in August of 1863, had gone so far as to designate President Cuyler of the Georgia Central as an independent transportation czar over all of southern Georgia.[22] But a defective administrative machine can always be rebuilt. Thus, as the rains of a new winter slashed at the windows of his office in Belvin's Block, Sims pondered the lessons of the preceding months and incorporated them into a scheme for a new and improved Railroad Bureau.

His plan envisaged an office coordinated with the Quartermaster Department, but independent of the Quartermaster General. It would be directed by a chief, having the rank of colonel, with a staff of assistants, one to be stationed in each Confederate State. The basic functions of this dream bureau were to differ little from those which Sims already had assumed, but its powers were to be specifically defined by Congress. His real aim was to secure for himself a greater certitude of action. As to the personnel of the organization, his suggestions were most meticulous. "The business," he remarked, "can only be managed by one who has been *educated to it*, and it is to this extent a specialty differing from any element heretofore entering into military operations. The importance of properly managing transportation, thus rapidly concentrating troops or supplies, can only be manifest to those whose daily business enables them to see the difficulties arising from a want of control of the movement of trains." [23]

This represented Sims's sole serious excursion into the field of bureaucratic imperialism. He took care not to forward it through channels; perhaps he feared that his friend, the Quartermaster

General, who recently had helped secure his lieutenant-colonelcy, might look askance at a request for independence. Instead, he injected it directly into the Confederate House of Representatives through an unofficial entrance. An intimate friend, President Bentley Hasell of the Charleston & Savannah Railroad, was the nephew of Lewis Cruger, a leading Treasury official and lobbyist. When approached, Cruger was glad to draw up a draft "Bill for establishing a Railroad Bureau," incorporating the gist of Sims's ideas, and submit it to Chairman W. P. Miles of the House Military Affairs Committee.[24]

Though irregular, the affair came to a harmless ending; if Congress actually heard of it, it failed to find a place on the calendar. Certainly Lawton seems never to have suspected anything, and Sims never pressed his scheme. There was work enough to do; through what remained of the Confederacy the engines were gasping with the agony of the war effort.

CHAPTER
～ 14 ～

Steam Cars to Glory

I

IN MAY, 1862, THE CONFEDERATE STATES SEEMED TO FACE IM-minent defeat. New Orleans had fallen. Union troops threatened to overrun eastern North Carolina. Enemy columns had penetrated into Alabama. Federal gunboats lorded it over great stretches of the Mississippi. Richmond itself had become a besieged citadel.

A feeling of doom fell upon the Virginia railroads. The York River line had ceased operation and had discharged its train crews; over its eastern portion northern motive power puffed smartly. Since April the Richmond & Danville had been quietly dismantling its shops and carrying the machinery to Danville, and its departing trains daily bore throngs of civilian refugees. In its yards, a loco-motive stood hissing day and night, ready to make off with the government treasure. The Richmond, Fredericksburg & Potomac sent its records to Lynchburg for safe keeping. Both the R. F. & P. and the Virginia Central were warned by Secretary Randolph to move their rolling stock across town to the Petersburg station; the Virginia Central hastened to lay temporary rails directly up the Broad Street hill and managed, thanks to flying starts, to force a number of its engines up the appalling gradient to the Eighth Street connecting track. Late in May Federal patrols cut both roads north of Ashland.[1]

Though prepared for the worst, the railroads continued to func-tion in behalf of a last-ditch Confederate defense. On the night of May 28 eighty cars of the Richmond & Petersburg clattered up the line, bringing more than four brigades of Huger's command. Three days later President Dudley of the York River road as-

sembled all the railway men he could find to help bring in the
wounded from Seven Pines. Presently his track was serving as a
runway for mobile artillery.[2]

Richmond, in 1862, lay upon the rim of a rough circle of railroads that ran southwest to Burkeville, then west to Lynchburg,

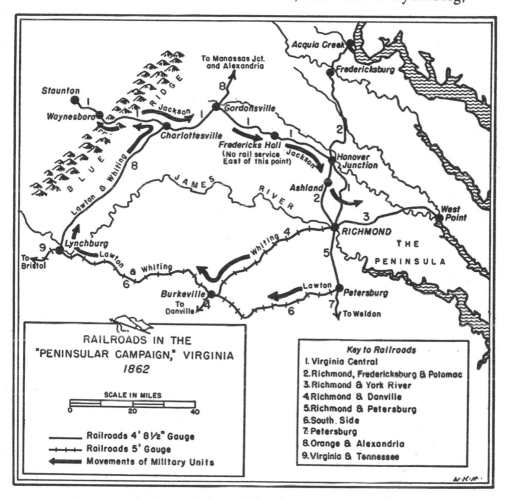

RAILROADS IN THE
"PENINSULAR CAMPAIGN," VIRGINIA
1862

SCALE IN MILES

———— Railroads 4' 8½" Gauge
++++++ Railroads 5' Gauge
◀━━━ Movements of Military Units

Key to Railroads
1. Virginia Central
2. Richmond, Fredericksburg & Potomac
3. Richmond & York River
4. Richmond & Danville
5. Richmond & Petersburg
6. South Side
7. Petersburg
8. Orange & Alexandria
9. Virginia & Tennessee

northeast to Charlottesville and Gordonsville, and finally east and
south, by way of Hanover Junction, to the capital again. From
Charlottesville the Virginia Central penetrated the Shenandoah
Valley, whence the dispatches of Stonewall Jackson were providing the War Department with its sole morsels of good news. The
situation obviously afforded the means either of reinforcing Jack-

son, whose troops were seriously outnumbered, or of bringing Jackson to Richmond, whose defenders faced equally heavy odds.

Joe Johnston now lay wounded in a secluded house on Church Hill, and fate had placed the direction of the Confederate armies in Virginia in the hands of Robert E. Lee. The new commander saw opportunity on the map, but he likewise was conscious of a dilemma. Ought he concentrate in the Valley, which led straight to the back door of Washington, or should he mass his forces directly against McClellan? At first he did neither; and with a caution that was hardly in character endeavored to evade the choice by ordering westward a handful of troops from the quiet Petersburg sector.[3]

Then luck, which for months had abandoned the Confederacy, returned in an unexpected manner.

On June 9 and 10 telegrams from the Valley brought news of the twin victories at Cross Keys and Port Republic. Lee acted instantly. He proposed that two additional brigades be detached from the Richmond front and hurried to Jackson, who then might find himself in a position to annihilate all the Federal forces beyond the Blue Ridge. The idea received the immediate approval of President Davis, and on June 11 six thousand men under General W. H. C. Whiting were quietly withdrawn from the line facing McClellan and marched through the Richmond streets to the Danville station.[4]

Abruptly reports of a disquieting kind drifted up the hill to the War Department. The Petersburg contingent, four thousand strong, under General Lawton, had not yet departed. By a misunderstanding every surplus car of the Richmond & Danville and the South Side roads had been sent off to Lynchburg, whence they slowly were returning, laden with Union prisoners of war for exchange. At Lynchburg an unimaginative quartermaster refused to release the freight equipment standing idle in the yards. The Richmond & Danville furnished an erroneous schedule to the South Side, while officers of the South Side incurred the wrath of Secretary Randolph by discussing the whole affair openly by telegraph. Nor could the move be diverted to the Virginia Central; its line had been broken by the enemy near Hanover Junction. Furthermore, the Federal captives were beginning to arrive and, from their camp upon Belle Isle in the James, could not help but see the trainloads of Confederate troops departing westward. Worry over this situation, declared Superintendent Bird of the

South Side Railroad, "put me to bed, where I am still very sick." [5]

Somehow, thanks to equipment borrowed from the Norfolk & Petersburg, all units got away. Whiting's troop trains were duly noted by the Federals; it could not be avoided. Lee, in fact, began to realize that the situation might be used to confuse the enemy; Whiting and Lawton should remain only temporarily in the Valley, while the Federals were permitted to believe that the transfer was permanent. With Whiting's infantry rode a scattering of civilians, quite unseen by the Union soldiers—employees of the Virginia Central, who presently would bring back toward Richmond not only the commands of Whiting and Lawton, but Jackson's whole army. [6]

Confederate folklore has long maintained that the shift of Whiting and Lawton to the Shenandoah was planned from the beginning as a brilliant stratagem. The story is still told that whole trainloads of troops were shunted up and down the Richmond & Danville tracks opposite Belle Isle to display them to the Federal exchangees. John Esten Cooke refers to the incident with relish, and he is seconded by so competent an observer as G. F. R. Henderson. But if the complaints of South Side Superintendent Bird can be believed, the operation was actually marked by vast confusion, and if the troop trains halted adjacent to the prisoner-of-war camp, they did so less by design than by delay. As Douglas Freeman has pointed out, Lee's handling of the affair is commendable chiefly in that he recognized the possibility of a ruse in a movement which had been designed for no such purpose. [7]

The five-foot Richmond & Danville and South Side carried the soldiers westward as far as Lynchburg, where a change of cars was necessitated by the narrower gauge of the Orange & Alexandria. But by the evening of June 15 the troops were entering Charlottesville, and on the following day the laboring engines of the Virginia Central dragged Lawton's first elements through the Blue Ridge. [8]

Neither Lawton nor Whiting lingered long in the pleasant environment of the Shenandoah. Their regiments still were pouring from the cars at Waynesboro when Jackson received discretionary orders from Lee, instructing him to turn toward the capital whenever the time seemed ripe. It already was. His tactics had so dazzled his opponents that they had withdrawn far down the Valley. On the seventeenth he put his army into motion toward the east. [9]

The move of Stonewall Jackson to the defense of Richmond was carried out with such secrecy that its details are difficult to follow. Many of his own staff remained baffled until they were nearly in hearing of McClellan's guns. The general seems to have confided only in his chief quartermaster and in H. D. Whitcomb, Superintendent of the Virginia Central, leaving even his division commanders fuming in helpless curiosity. Unfortunately, the railroad proved of limited help; because of Federal raids, its trains could operate only to Fredericks Hall, fifty miles short of his destination; and much of its rolling stock had been marooned in the capital. Whitcomb could scrape together no more than two hundred cars. But superintendent and general together worked out a series of "leap frog" moves, whereby the troops marched parallel to the track, to be picked up and carried forward by returning empty equipment. Much of the baggage, which under Jackson was hardly excessive, moved by road. In this fashion, and despite the delays incident to grossly inadequate sidings and Jackson's insistence upon a solemn keeping of the Sabbath, the whole force had, by June 24, been carried to the end of the undamaged portion of the Virginia Central. On June 25 it was at Ashland preparing for action.[10]

In the long run McClellan was not routed; the Confederate command, Jackson included, made mistakes. Nevertheless, a rail-based power, operating upon interior lines, had forced the retreat of a superior opponent supplied by water. Perhaps among those who noted this phenomenon was Braxton Bragg, who on June 27 had assumed command of the western department, with headquarters at Tupelo, Mississippi.

II

In the summer of 1862 occurred the largest single Confederate troop movement by rail. Thanks to the steam locomotive, the long-battered Army of the Mississippi would march almost, if not quite, to glory.

Triumphant in captured Corinth, the Federal army proceeded to thrust a fluid extension eastward along the line of the Memphis & Charleston. Under the command of General Don Carlos Buell, it moved so slowly in the Alabama heat, that Braxton Bragg remained for long uncertain of its objective. But at Knoxville General Kirby Smith concluded, correctly, that Buell planned the occupation of eastern Tennessee. Instantly his telegraph operators were pounding out calls for reinforcements. Smith's messages were supplemented by appeals from the Governor of Tennessee.[11]

With a large portion of the Memphis & Charleston already in Union hands, the newest key to the Confederate lines of communication was Chattanooga, where the railroads extending southwestward from Virginia met the Western & Atlantic running into the interior of Georgia. Now that the Memphis line was gone, this route afforded the best remaining artery between Richmond and the lower Mississippi Valley. Both Bragg and Smith realized this. The latter hastened to mass at Chattanooga every man he could spare, while Bragg already recognized an opportunity—a swift movement around the point of Buell's advance and a blow upon the heart of the Union communications system far away in central Kentucky. But how could he reach Chattanooga before Buell?

The answer was railroads. Nevertheless, the journey via Mobile seemed woefully circuitous, while the Meridian-Selma line was still unfinished. All Bragg would risk, for the moment, was a trial move by a small unit.[12]

On June 27 the General ordered McCown's division, approximately three thousand men, detached from Van Dorn's old Army of the West and shipped to Chattanooga. Routed via Mobile, Montgomery, and Atlanta, the transfer involved a journey of no less than 776 miles over six railroads; furthermore, the passage of Mobile Bay, and the narrow gauge of the Montgomery & West Point road, prohibited the use of through trains. But the operation was carefully planned. Quartermasters at the principal junction points were alerted. At Atlanta cooked rations were held in readiness. Only a single difficulty arose; independent orders from Richmond had likewise put some Alabama troops in motion toward Chattanooga, and congestion developed between Montgomery and Atlanta. Nevertheless, the first trainloads of McCown's westerners reached Chattanooga on July 3, just six days after their movement orders had been issued.[13]

This opened Bragg's eyes as never before to the capabilities of the iron horse, and his increased confidence found official expression two weeks later when he appointed Major J. W. Goodwin his "Military Superintendent of Railroads."[14] Already he was planning the greatest of his campaigns. Buell still floundered among the Cumberlands, but had proceeded far enough to indicate that his objective indeed was Chattanooga. For Bragg the time for action had come. On July 21 General Hardee and the whole Army of the Mississippi were ordered to east Tennessee.[15]

This was no test. Field returns reckoned the effective strength of Hardee's command as 31,193 officers and men. Even with the example of McCown before them the Confederates dared not place the whole weight of the movement upon rails. All horse-drawn elements—artillery, cavalry, engineers, and wagon trains—were directed to move overland. But practically the whole of the infantry, complete with field equipment and regimental supplies of ammunition, were entrusted to the railroads. Their number could not have been less than twenty-five thousand.[16]

Goodwin doubtless had warned the carriers of what was coming; certainly the flow of troops was well organized. Bragg wisely refrained from ordering a movement en masse. Scattered regiments stationed at Mobile and Pollard (and thus well along the road to Chattanooga) were sent forward first; from Tupelo the main body was dispatched by divisions. Before boarding his train, each man was handed seven days' cooked rations; commissary officers waited on the station platforms at Mobile, Montgomery, and Atlanta with additional supplies. This minimized delays by reducing the incentive to forage. Officers were especially careful to maintain discipline at junction points, where a single diversion to the fleshpots could disrupt the whole schedule.[17]

On July 23 the first Mobile & Ohio train pulled out of Tupelo with a portion of Cheatham's division. Bragg and his staff left the following day. Withers' division came next. For a week Tupelo enjoyed scarcely an hour of repose; its days were filled with a clanging of bells and its nights with a clashing of couplers and the cough of locomotives. By July 29 Jones's command was preparing to leave, as was Hardee himself. Already the job had been practically done. Just two days before, the first units from Mobile and Pollard had steamed into Chattanooga, and soon a procession of troop trains came curving around Missionary Ridge and into the city.[18]

For the time being, the whole complexion of the war in the west had been changed in favor of the Confederacy. Bragg's command even acquired a new name—Army of Tennessee. And if the general

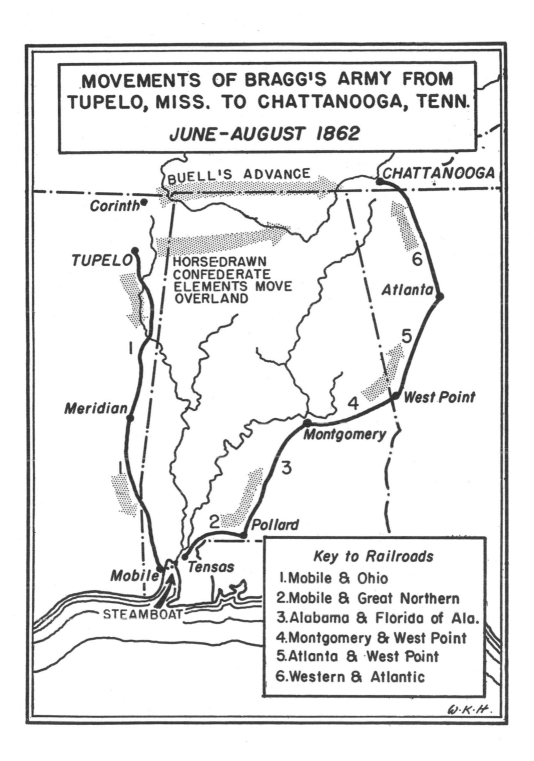

MOVEMENTS OF BRAGG'S ARMY FROM
TUPELO, MISS. TO CHATTANOOGA, TENN.
JUNE–AUGUST 1862

BUELL'S ADVANCE

CHATTANOOGA

Corinth

TUPELO

HORSE-DRAWN
CONFEDERATE
ELEMENTS MOVE
OVERLAND

6

Atlanta

5

Meridian

4

West Point

Montgomery

3

2   Pollard

Mobile   Tensas

STEAMBOAT

Key to Railroads
1. Mobile & Ohio
2. Mobile & Great Northern
3. Alabama & Florida of Ala.
4. Montgomery & West Point
5. Atlanta & West Point
6. Western & Atlantic

W.K.H.

subsequently was to fritter away great opportunities amid the Kentucky blue grass, that was hardly a reflection upon the military potentialities of the railroad.

III

By the autumn of 1862 the compressed springs of Confederate concentration had spent their force. The North recovered quickly. In Virginia Lee managed to beat back the next onrush at Fredericksburg, but at the New Year's eve action of Stone's River, Bragg achieved only a stalemate. In May, 1863, Lee at Chancellorsville wrecked the reputation of yet another Union general, but once more he failed to destroy the enemy army. On July 3 the Army of Northern Virginia further exhausted itself in the hideous charge up Cemetery Ridge. The following day Vicksburg capitulated, though only, be it noted, after its rail communications had been severed. In Tennessee Bragg had retreated to Chattanooga, and soon the northern flood was again lapping along the escarpments of the Cumberlands, precisely where it had been twelve months before.

And then the steam locomotive, and the persistent advantage of interior lines, gave Braxton Bragg, and perhaps the Confederacy, a second chance.

During much of the summer, while the latest Union commander, General W. S. Rosecrans, maneuvered his divisions in the complicated terrain, Bragg sat in Chattanooga and cried for reinforcements. It was not until the first days of September that he realized the enemy intended a movement around his left flank and an assault upon his only line of rail communication to the interior of Georgia. Aware at last of his peril, Bragg hastily evacuated Chattanooga on the 6th and moved uncertainly southward through the ridge country where flowed a creek called Chickamauga.[19] Meanwhile the help he needed was on its way.

That the First Corps of the Army of Northern Virginia might be detached and sent by rail to Georgia seems first to have occurred to the Corps' own commander. In his memoirs General Longstreet even asserts that he divulged the scheme to Secretary Seddon before discussing it with Lee. More important, however, is the fact that Lee, after some hesitation, gave the proposal his blessing. He journeyed to Richmond and, on September 6, just as Bragg abandoned Chattanooga, personally directed Quartermaster General Lawton to proceed with the arrangements.[20]

Lee's original movement orders appear to have gone the way of many other Confederate documents. Missing, too, is the initial transportation plan which Lawton apparently worked out with the Commanding General prior to the latter's return to the army at Orange Court House.[21] What was said in the course of their conversation can be surmised only by the fragmental evidence which has survived concerning the move itself. Doubtless Major Sims was consulted in many matters of detail. Certainly, when the essentials of the operation had been decided, it was he who was charged with their execution.

Sims faced no easy task as he returned to his office in Belvin's Block. Four days before, the Federal capture of Knoxville had severed the rail artery through eastern Tennessee, and any troops for Bragg had now to take the roundabout alternatives through the Carolinas, Augusta, and Atlanta. The Piedmont road remained unfinished. Southward from Richmond, and as far as Hicksford, Virginia, the entire load would have to be placed upon the single-track Richmond & Petersburg and Petersburg roads. From Hicksford, or from Weldon, North Carolina, two separate routes were available to Kingsville, South Carolina, one via Wilmington and Florence, the other via Raleigh, Charlotte, and Columbia. Beyond Kingsville the best available trackage was single again the remainder of the distance through Augusta and Atlanta. The mileage from Richmond to Atlanta by way of Wilmington was 705; through Charlotte, it totaled about 775. Both involved the iron of six railroad companies.

Moreover, Atlanta was not Longstreet's destination. Bragg lay somewhere up the line of the Western & Atlantic, but his movements were such that the ultimate detraining point could not be fixed in advance. Nor was this all. Bragg's was not the only command in serious straits. Cries for assistance sounded up the coast from Charleston, which had been under attack all summer. Lawton's instructions called for the diversion thence of at least two brigades. Also in the wind was a cross-movement of South Carolina militia from Columbia.

Sims went to work at once. Before midnight of the 6th, sheaves of messages had been hurried from his desk to the telegraph operators, and, by the following day, engines were snorting over both the Carolinas as every piece of serviceable equipment was hurried to designated junction points. Sims took pains to divide the load between the Wilmington and Charlotte routes, but through trains could not be extensively used because of differences in gauge. Inevitably, administrative difficulties developed, and one road (the Richmond & Petersburg) raised its charges for the special service it was asked to provide. But carrier cooperation proved, on the whole, excellent; for thirteen days the South Carolina company, which had to carry practically the entire movement west of Kingsville, suspended all but a skeleton of its ordinary services, while a number of superintendents and agents proved extraordinarily faithful about forwarding passing reports to Richmond.[22]

Of the details of the actual movement, little is known. It is not even clear to what extent the troops used rail transportation over the first leg between Orange Court House and Richmond, for Sims's responsibility seems to have been confined to the roads south of the capital. The first elements perhaps left Lee's Army as early as September 8, though Longstreet, writing after a lapse of thirty years, declared that "it was not until the ninth of September that the first train came to Orange Court House to start with its load of troops." However, it seems that a number of regiments did travel into Richmond by rail, for War Clerk Jones noted them swinging through the streets before writing up his diary on the evening of the ninth. The distance from Orange to Richmond exceeded sixty miles, much more than a single day's march.[23]

As to the reshuffling of units that occurred as they arrived in the capital, the record is more complete. On August 31, 1863, the First Corps consisted of three infantry divisions—McLaws', Hood's, and Pickett's—of four brigades each. Each division on paper should have contained approximately 10,000 officers and men, but all of them were greatly under strength, especially Pickett's, which had by no means recovered from the third day at Gettysburg. Even in Hood's organization, brigades of a presumed strength of about 2,500 could claim from 1,200 to 2,000 effectives only. Moreover, it was known that many of the men suffered from combat fatigue.[24]

After a good deal of discussion, Pickett's Division was left behind in Richmond. Its condition may be measured by the fact that its place was filled by *two* rested brigades from the Richmond defenses—Jenkins' and Wise's. Moreover, a brigade of Hood's Division—Anderson's Georgians—exhibited so low a morale that Longstreet dared not take it with him into its home state for fear of mass desertions. It presently found itself enroute to Charleston, accompanied by Wise's command.[25]

It must not be supposed that the soldiers were permitted to dawdle in Richmond. Lee and Longstreet carried out their weedings and diversions upon units in transit, and from September 9 onward a constant succession of troop trains rumbled off over the James. By ten o'clock that evening the leading regiment of Benning's Brigade was entering Raleigh; four days later, soldiers were passing that point in so steady a stream that opposing schedules on the North Carolina road were running more than twelve hours late. Through Charlotte there traveled on September 14 seventeen hundred men, plus twelve carloads of horses; on the fifteenth, five hundred men; on the seventeenth, two thousand men. By September 20 the whole wave had passed on southward. Upon the coastal route, Anderson's Brigade was beyond Wilmington on the evening of the twelfth, and its first train already was booming across the Santee swamps, not fifty miles from Charleston. Fourteen hours previously the sleepy privates of Benning's advance regiment had watched the village of Kingsville, South Carolina, slip behind them in the dawn.[26]

It was not a luxurious journey. Few obtained seats in passenger cars; most were crammed into and upon every conceivable variety of freight equipment—box, flat, coal, and stock. Temperatures were warm, and bayonets and axes speedily removed the outer sheathing of the boxcars. After that the accommodations, though crowded, seemed pleasant enough. Nor was there any lack of diversion. "They were not slow to pass jokes at the expense of the civilian passengers on our train," wrote a northbound traveler who encountered one of the regiments at a Virginia siding. At many stations pretty girls offered them country delicacies and blushed attractively at the whoops of appreciation which their presence invariably stimulated. Indeed, it was with difficulty that certain South Carolina and Georgia groups could be kept on the cars at all.[27]

There occurred but two untoward incidents. The infantry still were tramping across Richmond when Lee received the alarming intelligence that the New York *Herald* of September 9 had published the full details of the movement, including even the information about Wise's and Jenkins' brigades.[28] Actually neither Lee nor Longstreet had occasion for worry; they evidently had not personally examined the September 9 *Herald*, for it contained no mention whatever of the departure of the First Corps. The preceding day it had published a vague rumor that a portion of Lee's army was going south, but in succeeding issues it gravely stated that Lee was receiving reinforcements from Bragg! Its pages did not reveal the true situation until September 14.[29]

More serious was the rioting in Raleigh on the night of September 9, wherein a Georgia regiment of Benning's Brigade was alleged to have sacked the offices of the *Standard*. Immediately the touchy Zebulon Vance was cramming the wires with expostulations, threatening to withdraw his state from the Confederacy, to recall all North Carolina troops "to the defense of their homes," and, what was worse, to destroy the bridges upon the local railroads. The Governor subsided only after orders had been issued requiring the troops to pass around Raleigh without stopping. No further trouble seems thereafter to have arisen.[30]

Precisely which route was utilized by each unit remains uncertain. Benning, of course, was sent via Raleigh, Charlotte, and Columbia. Jenkins' command appears also to have traveled that way, for a notice in the *Tri-Weekly South Carolinian* of September 13 directed all furloughed members of his organization to report to their units at Columbia. Kershaw's Brigade took the coastal route via Wilmington, as did Wofford's. As the troops bore southward, Sims sought to relieve the pressure upon the single line beyond Kingsville by diverting twelve hundred men to the roundabout passage through Charleston and Savannah.[31]

At dusk on September 12, the first elements of Benning's Brigade came pounding up the Georgia Railroad into Atlanta. Their ride from Richmond had occupied the greater part of four days. For the moment they proceeded no further; many lacked shoes; all required rationing and a clarification of their orders. From Atlanta onward, transportation arrangements were in the hands, not of Sims, but of Colonel J. P. Jones of Bragg's staff, assisted by Colonel M. H. Wright, the local Atlanta commander. Bragg had directed

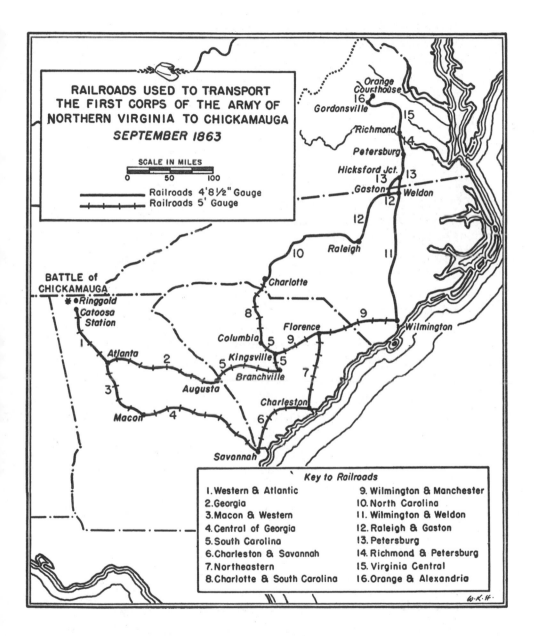

RAILROADS USED TO TRANSPORT
THE FIRST CORPS OF THE ARMY OF
NORTHERN VIRGINIA TO CHICKAMAUGA
SEPTEMBER 1863

SCALE IN MILES

0   50   100

——————— Railroads 4'8½" Gauge
+++++++ Railroads 5' Gauge

Orange Courthouse

Gordonsville   16

Richmond   15

Petersburg   14

Hicksford Jct.   13
                    13
Gaston   Weldon
            12

12

Raleigh   11

10

Charlotte

BATTLE of
CHICKAMAUGA

Ringgold
Catoosa
Station

8

9

Wilmington

Florence
Columbia   5   9
        5
Atlanta

1

2   Kingsville   5
        5
Branchville   7
Augusta

3

Macon   4   6
        Charleston

Savannah

Key to Railroads

1. Western & Atlantic   9. Wilmington & Manchester
2. Georgia   10. North Carolina
3. Macon & Western   11. Wilmington & Weldon
4. Central of Georgia   12. Raleigh & Gaston
5. South Carolina   13. Petersburg
6. Charleston & Savannah   14. Richmond & Petersburg
7. Northeastern   15. Virginia Central
8. Charlotte & South Carolina   16. Orange & Alexandria

W·K·H·

that the incoming troops be dispatched up the Western & Atlantic immediately upon arrival, but many units had to pause long enough to draw last-minute requirements from the city's quartermaster and commissary stores. The revictualling of Benning required more than forty-eight hours, and it was Robertson's command, thirteen hundred strong, that was first to depart on the evening of September 14. Thereafter the stream of reinforcements flowed northward with little interruption.[32]

They had come in the nick of time. Already the bewildered divisions of Bragg and Rosecrans, each striving to entrap the other, were about to blunder into contact along the line of the Chickamauga. At Catoosa Station, a wooden platform beside the Western & Atlantic four miles below Ringgold, two of Bragg's supply officers supervised unloading operations, and hurried the trains back down the line. Delays were relatively few; since the abandonment of Chattanooga, the Western & Atlantic had become essentially a military railroad, and the difficulties which did develop were of military origin. "Troops are being forwarded as fast as we can get cars," reported Colonel Wright from Atlanta. "Two trains of empty cars were seized [by local commanders] at Resaca yesterday and not allowed to come down, and it interferes greatly with movement of troops. Please have cars promptly returned."[33]

Three brigades, Robertson's, Benning's, and Law's, 4,500 men in all, had arrived by the morning of September 18. The smoke of their trains, hanging heavy in the gaps below Ringgold, reassured Bragg greatly—perhaps too greatly. Parts of Kershaw's Brigade arrived at intervals through the afternoon and into the night; Longstreet himself, having left Richmond four days previously with his staff and eight carloads of horses and baggage, detrained at two o'clock the following morning. But four more infantry brigades had still to come up; the artillery, under Alexander, was hardly out of Virginia. Yet on the nineteenth, before even the arrived elements could be properly incorporated into his alignment, Bragg had so exposed his army that the Battle of Chickamauga broke out by spontaneous combustion. Back at Catoosa the platform was being cleared for the arrival of Humphreys' Brigade, which still was jolting northward through the hills when a skirmish between Nathan Bedford Forrest and the Federal Brannan brought on the fighting. Humphreys did not see action until the following day. Wofford's and Jenkins' commands were close behind, but both became lost in the confusion of the rear areas and ultimately saw only the corpse-littered field after the enemy had withdrawn.[34]

Almost ninety years after the event, it is difficult to estimate the number of men involved in the transfer of Longstreet's Corps to Georgia. In the early stages of the movement, Major Sims telegraphed the superintendent of the South Carolina road to prepare for the passage of twenty thousand troops between Kingsville and Augusta, but the numbers actually carried appear to have been much less, perhaps as few as twelve thousand. Of these only about six thousand saw action at Chickamauga; four of the eight infantry brigades, and all of the artillery, arrived upon the battlefield after the fighting was over.[35]

And yet this longest and most famous Confederate troop movement by rail greatly influenced the outcome of Chickamauga. The Virginia soldiers served conspicuously, especially upon the second day, when their flanking charges broke through the Union right and drove it in disorder from the field. And if Bragg failed to press the ensuing Federal rout, that, once more, was no fault of the railroads, which for the second and last time had enabled him to strike with a rough equality of numbers.[36]

CHAPTER

~ 15 ~

The Iron Horse Stumbles

I

THOUGH BRAXTON BRAGG GAVE SCANT RECOGNITION TO THE RAIL-ways which had helped make his victory possible, their contribution did not pass without remark. Sims had special reason to be pleased, and for some time thereafter his correspondence was sprinkled with references to the "patriotism" of the roads. At Columbia, the *South Carolinian* devoted an editorial page to the South Carolina company, noting that "the late pressure on the road was met with admirable preparation and carried out with entire success." [1] Yet the performance of the steam locomotive in the movement of troops did not always elicit applause. Even before the triumphant journey of Longstreet, embarrassing lapses had occurred.

There was the transfer in December, 1862, of Stevenson's Division from the Army of Tennessee to Pemberton's command in Mississippi. Involving nine thousand men, it was, of course, a major task, and the loss of the Memphis & Charleston made necessary an appallingly circuitous routing: Murfreesboro, Tennessee, to Chattanooga, to Atlanta, to Montgomery, to Mobile, to Meridian, and thence across central Mississippi to Jackson. But the trip consumed more than *three weeks*, the division wagon train, dispatched across country, being on the road only a little longer. Reasons for the delay are obscure, but the military blamed the carriers. [2]

In the Carolina low country the roads were so conspicuously inefficient that the authorities launched an investigation. One movement of brigade size had been forty hours on the road between Charleston and Wilmington—209 miles. The journey of three regiments from Wilmington to Savannah in February, 1863, proved even more chaotic. "Three hours after the arrival of the 25th [Georgia] Regiment at the depot at Wilmington," reported the officer in command, "the train upon which [it] was placed attempted to leave, but in consequence of the weakness of the engine could not proceed." After the train crew had cut off three of the cars, the locomotive managed to struggle from the station, but presently broke down completely. The troops crept into Florence, 107 miles from Wilmington, twenty-seven hours later. Neither they, nor the unit following, reached Savannah until one o'clock of the morning of the third day. The experience of the Third Regiment was the most irritating of all. First the men were kept waiting upon the Wilmington platform from noon on February 5 until two o'clock the following morning. Next they were placed in two trains, wherein they sat equally immobile until nine-thirty. Having at length departed, they spent the following twenty-three and one-half hours upon the road to Florence. Just fifty-five hours after they had first assembled at the Wilmington depot, the tired soldiers entered Charleston. A rest stop being imperative, they were not to arrive in Savannah until midnight of the eighth.[3]

Wilmington came to be, increasingly, a center of congestion. Its rail facilities were divided by an unbridged river. A heavy proportion of the Confederacy's coastwise railway traffic passed through the place, together with the freight unloaded from blockade-runners. By the winter of 1864 the commander of the city's defenses estimated that reinforcements were requiring twice as long to reach him as a year previously and three times as long as at the beginning of the war.[4]

II

It was with respect to their freight service that the carriers gave greatest cause for complaint. As early as January, 1862, the Tredegar Iron Works and the Atlanta Rolling Mill worked overtime to produce plating and machinery for an emergency ironclad, then building in the Mississippi River for the defense of New Orleans, but the railroads forwarded the material so slowly that it did not arrive until a few days before the evacuation of the city. In the early spring of 1863, General John C. Pemberton experienced constant trouble with the carriers. The Southern Railroad, he thought, catered too much to private interests, and he accused the New Orleans, Jackson & Great Northern of immobilizing large accumulations of military stores by refusing to return some Mississippi Central equipment which had strayed onto its rails. The arrival of twelve cars of government corn in Vicksburg in a single day was regarded as quite extraordinary. In his post-surrender apologia, Pemberton directly accused the management of the Southern of selfishness and non-cooperation. Yet it was the Confederate failure to protect the road that did most to doom Vicksburg, for it was useless after the Federal capture of Jackson on May 14. In June, after Grant had wrecked a large portion of its line, Joseph E. Johnston explained that an attempt to raise the siege would be futile, as he had not wagons enough to leave the remaining railroads for more than four days.[5]

Private citizens complained as loudly as the military. It was said that the railroads reserved their favors for speculators (i.e., competitors), and the air grew warm with charges that railroad employees took advantage of the war to milk individual shippers. Doubtless some fire existed to bring forth so much smoke, but some of the tales were fantastic. Reported the Columbus (Miss.) *Republic*:

"A little incident came to our knowledge of a certain party, who had purchased a large amount of wool and a trifle over one thousand dollars' worth of sugar. The wool was especially valuable and the sugar was also to be got through. After some manoeuver on the part of the owner, he got a car and loaded it up, paying handsomely for the same, putting the sugar in sacks. When the car came to be switched on the track, the switchman demanded his part and received, we believe, $40. Soon after, the engineer came along and declared that he never would take that wool and sugar through without half the sugar. It was given him. Soon after, the conductor came along and stated that the wool would go, but he must have the other half of the sugar. There was no appeal, and the other followed the first. The wool came through. The owner had also paid freight in advance for both wool and sugar."[6]

But the most persistent critic of railroad freight service was General Braxton Bragg. His *bête-noire* was the Western & Atlantic, which for nearly two years served as the principal supply channel of the Army of Tennessee. Friction with its management became chronic, and this in turn led to a memorable series of exchanges with Joseph E. Brown.

The first incident of note occurred in March, 1863, when Bragg learned that the road had refused to forward certain ordnance equipment from Atlanta. He at once informed Superintendent Rowland that he regarded this as grounds for seizure; Rowland ran squalling to the Governor, who promptly took offence. "If General Bragg seizes the Road," he told Rowland, "take every officer, conductor, engineer and agent off of it, and stop operations until his superiors have learned him his duty." The dispute was quickly carried to Richmond. Unless Bragg changed his attitude, President Davis was warned, Brown would be obliged to repel his "unwarrantable aggressions" by force. Though Bragg was a favorite at court, Davis characteristically hesitated to challenge a sovereign state. His reply was almost too conciliatory. He assured Brown that he would endeavor to prevent aggression by Confederate officers, and instructed Bragg to avoid such collisions in the future.[7]

When handled with kid gloves, Governor Brown could be quite cooperative. Approached hat in hand by Bragg's chief of staff, he even promised to establish through supply trains from Americus to Chattanooga. But it swiftly became clear that a helpful attitude was not enough to get stores over the road. After Chickamauga, Bragg endeavored to liberate East Tennessee (and reopen its railroads) by dispatching Longstreet's corps against Knoxville; in doing so he succeeded chiefly in reducing his strength in the face of an imminent Federal attack and in scattering more of the engines and cars of the Western & Atlantic.[8]

This ended the brief reconciliation of Bragg and Brown. Because of the poor service allegedly provided, Bragg on November 15 declared that his army soon would be starved out. Though the warehouses of central Georgia bulged with fodder, his horses were wasting away for want of it. Two entire infantry battalions, he added, had remained stranded in Atlanta "whilst passenger trains loaded with citizens have left that city twice every day."[9] The Governor responded with a recital of woes. Rolling stock was short. Neither machinists nor materials were to be found. Those employees who remained were "worked down and almost worn out." In conclusion he again recommended that the military commandeer private equipment rather than the stock of the Western & Atlantic.[10]

Late in November the Confederates were hurled in defeat from Missionary Ridge and Lookout Mountain. But the subsequent resignation of Bragg and the appointment of General Joseph E. Johnston to the command of the Army of Tennessee failed to ease the transportation crisis. Indeed, Johnston's first comment seemed like an echo of Braxton Bragg. "The railroad from Atlanta," he wired from Dalton, Georgia, "does not supply our wants; ... if it does not supply us, we cannot defend this portion of the State." Brown's excuse this time was a lack of fuel; he likewise demanded "two good engines and trains of cars in place of eight or ten lost and destroyed by the military." Other reasons advanced for the plight of the Western & Atlantic were the slowness of connecting roads, their lack of equipment, unfavorable weather, and the loss of stock cars carried off by the army.[11]

Although Western & Atlantic freight trains were consuming thirty-six hours upon the 100-mile journey from Atlanta to Dalton, part of the blame could be placed upon the Confederate quartermasters. Loaded cars often were left untended upon sidings, where they suffered serious pilferage; worse still was the loss of equipment-availability caused by such carelessness.[12] Inevitably the Railroad Bureau was drawn into the case. Sims visited Atlanta in November, and Hottel had been in constant personal touch with the situation. Each thought the assertions of Brown, Bragg, and Johnston exaggerated. Because he failed to second the military viewpoint with enthusiasm, Hottel soon found himself in bad odor with Johnston, who demanded his transfer. Sims for his part ridiculed the Governor's figures as to losses of rolling stock. In a report to General Lawton on February 9 he estimated that seven freight trains of twelve cars each could be run daily from Atlanta to Dalton, which would mean theoretically an inflow of 21,000 bushels of corn every twenty-four hours. The road possessed, he concluded, "plenty of cars .... if any degree of energy is exhibited in loading and unloading and moving them promptly." [13]

Throughout the discussion the temper of Governor Brown had steadily simmered, and when on March 7 Jefferson Davis reproved him by telegraph, warning that "constant effort will be required to replace [equipment] losses by repairing and building new engines and cars," it blew sky-high. "You do not mention," retorted Brown, "where the material to be used in repairing and building new engines and cars is to be had." And then came perhaps the finest effort of a long practice of sarcasm: "I trust the management of the State Road will not suffer by comparison with the management which lost us New Orleans, and opened the Mississippi to the enemy, which lost us Fort Donaldson [sic] and gave them Nashville, which kept the Army too weak, divided between Vicksburk [sic] and Tennessee, 'till we lost both and which opened Georgia to attack by dividing our Army at Missionary Ridge in ... the ... face of the enemy." [14]

Although written in passion, a certain accuracy lurked beneath these lines. But the Governor neglected to mention his own reluctant support of the common cause as a factor in the declining fortunes of the Confederacy. He came closest to the truth in his original inquiry: "Where is the material to be had?"

III

In the summer of 1863 occurred a partial failure of the Virginia grain crop. The weather was not wholly to blame. Two years of campaigning had already seriously lowered the productiveness of the Shenandoah Valley and other areas, and the Confederate armies had all but disposed of the Commonwealth's normal cereal reserves. In the early autumn an intelligent officer in the Army Commissary Department pointed out that subsistence for Lee's forces must henceforth depend upon the production of Georgia, Alabama, and Mississippi.

The food-raising potential of the lower South has sometimes been overlooked by historians of the Civil War. But it seems not to have escaped the Davis Administration, which deliberately encouraged the diversion of cotton acreage to corn. Precise figures are scarce, but the program was an undoubted success. The Confederacy produced 4,500,000 bales of cotton in 1861; by 1863 production had declined to less than 500,000 bales. Travelers in a broad region from central Mississippi to mid-Georgia were astonished at the sea of maize which met the eye. With the development of this Confederate corn belt came a concomitant growth of the pig population. By 1864 Alabama had become a major bacon producer; 500 tons of it were reported in government storage there in April of that year.[15]

As carriers of local grain, the railways of Virginia and adjacent regions had functioned fairly well. But for long-haul movements on a large scale, the roads were not prepared. Between the fields of southwest Georgia and the Army of Northern Virginia lay over 700 miles of worn iron, operated by a half-dozen companies, and at each junction point existed a hundred opportunities for pilferage. As early as September there was a deficiency of nearly fifty thousand bushels between the amount of corn shipped from Columbus, Georgia, and the amount received at Richmond. At Orange Court House General Lee reported that the railroad was bringing him no more than one thousand bushels per day, not nearly enough to bring up his exhausted horses. In July the Richmond & Petersburg had carried 2,283 bushels into the capital; in September it brought less than half that amount. In January, 1864, its trains unloaded less than five hundred.[16]

The use of coastal vessels was too restricted by geography and the blockade to be of use. By winter things had become desperate not only for the Army but for the population of war-swollen Richmond. A mere *one thousand bushels* of an estimated ninety thousand shipped from Columbus had arrived in the capital. From Orange, Lee accused the railroad companies of an "irresponsible attitude" and requested permission to dispatch military officers over Virginia and North Carolina to seize food and railroads alike. At the end of February came the news that his army possessed bread sufficient for a single day.[17]

Commissary General Northrop thought the railroads should withdraw their passenger trains and devote their facilities to war supplies. Bragg, who had sought shelter under the presidential wing as a military advisor, recommended that William Wadley be recalled and made a transportation czar. Some intimated more directly that the Railroad Bureau could stand a reorganization. Others believed that the civilian population of Richmond should be removed. Still others confined themselves to denunciation, like diarist Jones, who especially loved to eviscerate the Quartermaster Department and the Southern Express Company.[18]

Only Sims came to the defense of the carriers. In a lengthy report on February 22 he dismissed the current babel of criticism with all the contempt of a professional railroad man. "It is not at all unusual," he began, "for persons to suppose that they can manage railroads with much more ability than those who have them in charge. It is still more unusual to find such professions supported by facts." There was, he insisted, but one way to improve the situation—the *permanent* detail of machinists from the army to serve not only in shops and roundhouses but likewise in manufactories of railway supplies. "I am willing to do all that I can do," he concluded, "but to improve transportation without men and materials is the requisition of the Egyptian taskmaster. Give me the men and you shall see advantages from them. Refuse and I can promise nothing." [19]

This was blunt, perhaps insubordinate. One can hear Wadley speaking between the lines. But Sims was not the man to brood. Down at Belvin's Block he continued to sift through the telegrams that told of bottlenecks from the James to the Chattahoochee, and to suggest—for he possessed little more power than that—ways to eliminate them. North of Augusta were fifteen locomotives and two hundred freight cars of the lot brought from Mississippi; these he ordered about the country as far as their five-foot gauge and the acquisitiveness of railway officials permitted. Despite a dislike of the Commissary Department which he found difficult to conceal, he was intelligent enough to endorse Northrop's proposal for reducing passenger service, and on March 12 he was given authority to stop passenger trains on any railroad upon which forage or subsistence was experiencing delay. Sims at once canceled a number of schedules, including every night run on the South Carolina road. Perhaps he was permitted to wave the half-forgotten railroad law of May 1, 1863, over the heads of the carriers, for they seem to have cooperated cheerfully enough. And he did succeed in unblocking a part of the congestion. As spring came, Lee's "miserables" were not quite too hungry to stand off yet another season of Union assaults. [20]

CHAPTER

~ 16 ~

The Treasure Hunt for Iron

"The iron was wanted more than anything else but men."—John B. Jones, August 11, 1863.

I

ONE APRIL MORNING IN 1862 STEPHEN R. MALLORY, THE ROTUND and able Secretary of the Navy of the Confederate States, signed an order seizing the rails and fastenings of the Hungary Branch Railroad. It was a routine act; the Hungary Branch was no more than a spur, leading from the main line of the Richmond, Fredericksburg & Potomac to some coal pits of dubious value; moreover, the road with mines appertaining belonged to a northern company. Mallory, in search of iron for armor plate, was proceeding entirely within the bounds prescribed by existing Confederate law. But the incident created a minor explosion. Even so early as the spring of 1862 the Navy Department was not alone in thinking iron more precious than gold. Writing to Jefferson Davis in behalf of a number of Virginia carriers, President Daniel of the Richmond, Fredericksburg & Potomac loudly complained that the railroads needed the rail more than did any hypothetical fleet.[1]

The Hungary incident was but a prelude; competition for inadequate stocks of iron was to continue throughout the war. Moreover, an appalling fact presently dawned on Mr. Daniel, his colleagues, and the Government: *iron was so short that even the railroad system of the Confederacy could be maintained only by destroying its own substance.*

This posed a real dilemma. It involved more than an unpleasant choice as to which lines should suffer destruction; there was a human obstacle. The owners of companies designated as iron mines were normal men. At the outbreak of the war they pledged their resources to the southern cause, but now, when called upon to make a real sacrifice, they hesitated. Soon they were offering a variety of reasons why their particular roads should not be despoiled. When pretexts failed, they grew angry, and like certain of their revolutionary ancestors turned to elaborate discourses upon the sins of tyrannical government. Occasionally they approached open rebellion.

This did not mean that the railway interests of the South were less patriotic than those of the North. But it did reveal certain fundamental weaknesses of the Confederacy itself. The regime of Jefferson Davis, even after it had been formalized in the cold rain of Washington's birthday, 1862, remained a makeshift structure. It could not acquire overnight the kind of prestige that the Federal Government of the United States had developed over a period of nearly eighty years. Lincoln came to the presidency of a going concern; Davis did not. When faced with opposition, Lincoln could crush it ruthlessly and at once. Davis too frequently could not.

II

When first confronted with a railway iron shortage, the South endeavored to muddle through. Impressment laws of a general nature, authorizing the confiscation of private property (with compensation) in cases of military necessity, had been passed by the Confederate Congress, but the actual seizure of a railroad in order to build or to repair another was at first left to the judgment of subordinate officers on the spot. It was such a local order that set off the first of the major railroad iron squabbles.

The Alabama & Florida Railroad of Florida was the pride of the city of Pensacola. It had been constructed by virtue of copious municipal aid and at the beginning of 1862 extended northward from its parent city to a connection with the Alabama & Florida Railroad of Alabama at a collection of shanties known as Pollard, just north of the Florida boundary. Pensacola's railroad had been designed expressly to neutralize the advantages of the rival port of Mobile, which theretofore had flourished at the mouth of an extensive system of navigable waterways such as Pensacola could not hope to duplicate.

In the early spring of 1862 the Confederate forces about Pensacola Bay were withdrawn for service elsewhere. Northern troops began to flow into the resulting vacuum, and it soon became obvious that a part of the railroad would have to be destroyed to prevent its use by the Federals. Even the directors of the company advocated that the rails be torn up as far as Pine Barren Creek, twenty-seven and a half miles north of Pensacola.[2]

But when the military commenced to pry up the iron *beyond* Pine Barren Creek and to re-lay it upon the Alabama & Mississippi Rivers Railroad connection and as extra sidings upon the Mobile & Great Northern, the management of the Florida road objected. Five of the directors, meeting in exile at Pollard, besought the Secretary of War to "stay the hand of the destroyer," and President O. M. Avery hastened to Richmond to lay his case before the Government in person.[3]

Avery was a thorough gadfly. He cherished the belief that the stripping of his line was the doing of the city of Mobile, and upon his arrival at the capital he so informed the Secretary of War. He did make some impression, for Randolph later expressed his disapproval of the seizures of so much rail. More satisfactory still was the reaction of Secretary of the Navy Mallory, who called the affair a "damned outrage." But perhaps Mallory was biased; Pensacola was his residence.[4]

Avery did not, however, confine himself to denunciation. During the early summer of 1862, he combed the lower South for alternative rail for the military to seize. In July he collided with his emotional twin, the Governor of Georgia, from whom he endeavored to secure a small amount of state-owned iron. Brown's reply was curt. "The State," he telegraphed, "has none she does not need and none to sell." But Avery did succeed in discovering some caches of material. He even prepared a report upon the railroads of Alabama, wherein "unnecessary" lines were carefully designated.[5]

In the meantime Samuel Tate had been appointed military superintendent of the Selma-Meridian project. On July 12 he impressed an additional twenty-eight miles of the Florida company's rail and ordered it shipped off to Meridian. Avery's wrath was savage, but

Richmond Va
23ʳ April 1863

Hon James A Seddon
    Sect'y of War
        Sir
            I learn from G J Pollard Esq
Prest of the Montgomery & West Point Railroad that
there is some hesitency on the part of Gen Buc:
:kner, in ordering rails removed from the Roads
indicated by you, from which the Montgomry &
West Point Road should be supplied. I beg
again to urge the great necessity for prompt
action in this matter, and would respectfully
suggest that, of the three Roads indicated,
the Ala & Fla Road of Fla would be much
the most convenient, and that the rails from
the other two Roads should be kept to supply
Roads West of the Ala River.
            I am Sir Very Respectfully
                Your Obt Servt
                    Wm. M. Wadley
                        A A Gen

William M. Wadley notes "the hesitancy on the part of Gen. Buckner, in ordering rails removed from the roads indicated . . . from which the Montgomery & West Point should be supplied." National Archives.

Tate persisted. Speed was of the essence, he declared; no iron in Mississippi could be had without pulling up roads then in daily use by the Confederate armies, while the material available in Georgia could not be shipped except at prohibitive expense. "I honestly believe," he concluded, "that this [Florida] road will not need their iron until the war is over." [6]

The authorities, for once, stuck to their guns. They refused to return the iron, nor was Avery's cup of woe yet filled. In April, 1863, Richmond ordered the seizure of additional rail for the repair of the Montgomery & West Point. Avery squalled lustily, insisted that his rump railway was indispensable to the defense of the Confederacy and shed crocodile tears over the plight of the west Florida citizenry. "The plot seems to thicken," he wrote bitterly. "The enemies of Pensacola are no doubt exulting at the apparent success of their schemes for her ruin." [7]

The Alabama & Florida indeed could take small comfort in the monetary recompense it secured. In February, 1864, Congress voted to compensate the road, but in the form of 8 per cent bonds and in amounts corresponding to the market price of the iron as of the dates seized. As the major impressments had occurred in 1862, the redundancy of the currency reduced to a pittance the real value of the securities when received. [8]

III

Like those who tore up track to build other track, Secretary of the Navy Mallory himself remained a persistent pilferer of railway iron. And though it was well known that without armor plating the South could not hope to disperse the maritime blockade, he faced the same sort of opposition as did Tate. [9] In June, 1862, for example, an agent of the Navy Department impressed 1,100 tons of unused rail and fastenings belonging to the Atlantic & Gulf road in southern Georgia. The acting president of the company, a tough individualist named Hiram Roberts, objected vehemently. When the navy representative persisted, pointing out that the iron was badly needed in Atlanta for the manufacture of ship's armor, he flatly refused to transport it thither over his line. Before the case could be disposed of it had reached, as did so many minor Confederate difficulties, the cabinet of Jefferson Davis. [10]

In the course of time, however, Mallory did secure a fair amount of iron from scattered railroad sources. Several hundred tons were taken from the Atlantic & North Carolina east of the Neuse River. In southeast Georgia, the derelict Brunswick & Albany yielded sixty miles of rail in the fall of 1863, although Governor Brown made off with 350 of the approximately 4,000 tons involved, while a large proportion of the residue never left Georgia. In North Carolina the Department stumbled upon 4,224 bars, all unlaid, in the hands of the Western Railroad and, in the course of the negotiations therefor, secured the cooperation of none other than Zebulon Vance. Indeed, without the iron provided by railroads, there would have been no "rebel rams." [11]

IV

By the autumn of 1862 the Confederacy swarmed with the impressment agents of a dozen different departments, offices, and commands, each laying claim to available stocks of railroad iron like a quarrelsome prospector. It was obvious that procurement of the metal should be regularized, but the Government as usual let matters drift until they became quite impossible. It was not until January 22, 1863, that a directive of the Adjutant and Inspector General's Office created a "commission to examine and advise on what Railroads in the Confederate States the iron on their tracks can best be dispensed with." [12]

By the terms of the order, the use of impressed rail was specifically limited to the construction of public vessels, the building of railroad connections designated by Congress as necessary to military operations, and the repair of other roads considered essential. Seizures from an important road were forbidden, and if new iron was taken from any source, it was to be exchanged if possible for used rails suitable for rerolling. To the commission were appointed Colonel Wadley and Major I. M. St. John (who first had suggested the seizure of railroad iron just a year before), together with an officer to be designated by the Navy Department. In February Colonel Jeremy F. Gilmer, Chief of the Army Engineer Bureau, was substituted for Wadley, but the original directive otherwise remained unchanged.[13]

Although the Iron Commission survived to the end of the war, its personnel suffered much fluctuation. For some time the Navy representative was George G. Hull, superintendent of the Atlanta & West Point Railroad. But St. John appears not to have served actively for more than a few months, and the press of other duties soon obliged Gilmer to withdraw from the chairmanship in favor of Colonel C. F. M. Garnett. A Captain Walker served briefly and died; in November, 1862, he was replaced by Major Minor Meriwether, an engineer officer who had served in the Western Department at Fort Pillow and Island Number Ten. Meriwether was ultimately to head the commission. At the end of September, 1864, the membership was further increased by the addition of Captain E. T. D. Myers, who had at last completed the Piedmont Railroad.[14]

The responsibilities of the Iron Commission were both advisory and executive. On March 28, 1863, it submitted to the Secretary of War an exhaustive survey of Confederate railways (save those of Texas), with recommendations as to the lines thought suitable for destruction. In this category it listed 173¾ miles of track from which the rails could be removed at once, 263 miles which might be torn up under certain conditions, and an additional 94 miles to be taken only as a last resort. The already considerable mileage in northern hands it briefly classified as "inaccessable." [15]

Having completed their basic study, the commissioners devoted themselves primarily to actual impressment. "You will endeavor to negotiate the purchase of the iron on satisfactory terms, introducing the condition of replacing the rails at the termination of the war, in lieu of immediate compensation for them, whenever practicable," read the instructions given Major Meriwether. If a carrier refused to sell, he could impress, but with careful attention to the limitations of existing law. The Commission was allowed to use legal assistance and also could employ such subordinate agents as it deemed necessary.[16] If a fair bargain could not be struck with a railroad company, the rail was seized at the specific impressment prices published periodically by the Adjutant and Inspector General's Office in Richmond. During the early fall of 1863 impressed railroad iron of "good" quality was paid for at a rate of $190 per long ton. This was, of course, greatly beneath the price obtainable in the free market, but it is significant that the War Department usually preferred to pay a moderate premium for an amicable sale, rather than save money and create resentment by resorting to impressment at the outset.[17]

Although the Commission never ceased to serve the interests of the Navy Department, it was from the first practically an agency of the Army Engineer Bureau. Soon its activities outgrew even the impressment of track material. In August, 1863, it superintended the seizure and distribution of the *locomotives* of Avery's Alabama & Florida road, and by the following year it was duplicating the activities of the Railroad Bureau in the operation of a general railroad equipment pool, which dispensed such varied items as rails, spikes, chairs, wrought-iron and cast-iron scrap, steel car springs, motive power, rolling stock, switch stands, grading tools, skillets, and ovens.[18] The rivalry of bureaucrats being the most intense in the world, this entry of the Iron Commission into a field already occupied by the Railroad Bureau was productive of a good deal of inefficiency and of eventual hard feeling.

A special concern of the Commission was a supply of rail and fastenings for the government-sponsored military connections. A large portion of the iron required for the Piedmont Railroad was taken from the York River and the Roanoke Valley roads. In the spring of 1864 Meriwether, just elevated to the rank of lieutenant colonel, personally directed one of the drives to complete the Rome-Blue Mountain link. He later turned to the Selma-Meridian undertaking, where the Tombigbee River bridge still remained unfinished.[19]

A seat on the Confederate Iron Commission was hardly comfortable. Railroad interests fought bitterly for their property, and it was seldom that the Commission secured their cooperation save at bayonet point. The local courts were almost universally hostile, and the threatened carriers quickly discovered the possibilities of injunction proceedings. "I shall need . . . a force to seize the iron despite injunctions with which I know I shall be plentifully served," wrote Meriwether to General Leonidas Polk in May, 1864. "I conversed with the Secretary of War upon the subject of disobeying writs of injunction, and seizing iron in such cases by military force. He said that in *his* position he could not give the order, but that the Generals Commanding could do so, and signified that it would meet his tacit approval." Occasionally even tacit approval was not forthcoming. In the summer of 1863 the Laurens Railroad in South Carolina protested the seizure of its rails so vigorously that the whole matter was quietly dropped. For impressment not only stimulated the wrath of railroaders; it frequently set off explosions among the citizenry.[20]

V

We have seen that certain steps already have been taken to bridge the gap that separated the railroads of Florida from those of the remainder of the Confederacy. In the early spring of 1861 construction had been started by the Savannah, Albany & Gulf–Atlantic & Gulf road southward from Lawton, Georgia, and by the Pensacola & Georgia northward from Live Oak, Florida, each company to build to the state line. Even after the outbreak of the war, grading was continued through the slash-pine forests, and by the end of 1862 the roadbed was substantially complete. Whereupon progress was stalled for lack of rail, which, as usual, was found to be unobtainable from any ordinary source.[21]

The Georgia-Florida connection never was cited as a military necessity by Congress, nor did it ever receive direct government assistance. Nevertheless, its strategic value was obvious. Its early completion would be "of the greatest advantage," declared Robert E. Lee in December, 1861, and the commanding General of the Department of Middle and East Florida, Brigadier General John H. Trapier, gave hearty endorsement to Lee's view.[22] As the war dragged on, the desirability of the road grew increasingly clear. Florida produced considerable foodstuffs, especially beef, of which the Confederate armies were desperately in want, while the state itself remained uneasily aware that, devoid of the means of rapid reinforcement, it lay helpless before a serious Federal attack.

Diagonally across the neck of the peninsula, from Fernandina to Cedar Keys, ran the 155-mile Florida Railroad. Already it had suffered partial destruction, its extremities having been torn up as an obstacle to enemy advance. In terms of rolling stock, it was perhaps the poorest road of its size in the Confederacy. But it was the special pride of its president and principal stockholder, ex-United States Senator David Levy Yulee.

Yulee was a man of Portuguese and Jewish descent, of Presbyterian faith, and of thoroughly southern prejudices. He was perhaps the most notable living Floridian. Only fifty-three years old in the summer of 1863, he could look back to nearly thirty years of public life. He had been a delegate to the Florida constitutional convention of 1838, territorial representative in the Federal Congress and United States senator from 1845 to 1851 and again from 1855 until 1861. He was accounted a southern fire-eater during the crisis of 1850, but 1860-61 found him distinctly calmed by age, experience, and that maturity of outlook which is induced by expanding wealth. Next to politics his chief love was the promotion of railroads.[23] And it was to Yulee's favorite line that the Government began to look for the rail with which to complete the Lawton–Live Oak undertaking.

That the Florida Railroad might serve as a convenient iron mine seems first to have occurred to Governor John Milton of Florida. In the late winter of 1862, just as the ends of Yulee's road were being dismantled, he seriously discussed the idea with the neighborhood Confederate military command. For the time being the influence of Yulee, supported by a legal injunction, buried the matter. But in May, 1863, to the Senator's consternation, the Governor suddenly resurrected the entire issue.[24]

Milton differed from a number of other southern state executives in that he frequently cooperated with Richmond; he was rather proud of this and especially enjoyed comparing himself favorably with Joseph E. Brown and Zebulon Vance. Indeed, he violently disliked opponents of the Davis regime, and his greatest horror was to have Florida classed with Georgia and North Carolina as an "Opposition State."[25] Milton had reason to fear that Yulee would be utterly stiff-necked with respect to his rails. He nevertheless approached Brigadier General Joseph Finegan, then in command of the Military District of East Florida and a personal friend of the ex-Senator. "I will not permit myself to believe," he wrote with tongue in cheek, "that he will not cheerfully yield the iron, or anything else that he owns or controls, to sustain the Confederate States in their defense."[26]

As an intermediary Finegan was most unsatisfactory. He informed Yulee of Milton's wishes, but announced concurrently his personal opposition to the removal of the rails. He pointed out that certain Confederate units depended upon the road for supplies and reported that he currently was using heavy guns mounted upon flatcars in the vicinity of Fernandina. Finegan thereafter ceased serving as ambassador, and the argument assumed a battledore and shuttlecock aspect, with Milton and Yulee as the principals.[27]

Yulee opened the game by declaring that the company possessed no legal power to give up its rail. Milton countered by securing formal authority therefor from the State Internal Improvement Board, transmitting it to Yulee with the ironic remark that he would like to extend his personal approval to the "patriotic effort" which the sale of the iron would represent. "I have not the right," retorted Yulee, "to make free with the property of others, nor to seek merit for a generous patriotism at another's cost." "Railroad companies have no claims paramount to the general safety," Milton responded, "Gentlemen of wealth and social and political position should not permit themselves to be wedded to schemes of personal ambition." Wouldn't it be better, he asked, if those Floridians still at home were to "report themselves for duty to Brigadier General Finegan and fight, bleed, and die in the achievement of the Independence of the Confederate States, rather than engage in a neighborhood fight for a little railroad iron?"[28]

To this Yulee only bristled. "I do not perceive," he wrote on June 19, "any probable utility in an extended correspondence upon the subject to which [your letter] relates." He would, he warned, use every legal resource to prevent the theft of a single bar. Filled now with indignation, the Governor countered with a savage letter. "I am sadly humiliated by the senseless or *treacherous* jargon of conflicting local interests in the State," he declared, "and by the grovelling, debasing and shameless desire manifested for the accumulation of wealth, regardless of personal honor and the general welfare.... I know no man in Florida under more obligations than yourself to rise superior to personal considerations and local interests."[29]

Yulee's rage was by now satanic, but he was too intelligent to insult the Governor. By remaining circumspect, he enjoyed for the moment the last word. But his pen shook as he wrote his final reply to Milton: "In the present agony of our country, I have no taste, nor inclination, for a correspondence of the tone and nature to which you invite me."[30]

Meanwhile the Confederate War Department had taken notice.

By September, 1863, both the Engineer Bureau and Secretary Seddon were committed to the Florida connection in principle, though specific approval did not come until December. Thereafter, events seemed to shape up rapidly. Arrangements were made to devote a portion of the iron from the Brunswick road, now in Government storage at Tebeauville, Georgia, to the completion of the new line as far as the Florida boundary. And then, for two whole months, the Confederate war office hesitated before the open defiance of Yulee.[31]

In the end it was the military crisis culminating in the Battle of Olustee that drove Richmond to action. The fight, which took place on February 20, 1864, was a distinct Confederate success, but could not be turned into a Union rout for lack of men. "Had the gap between Lawton and Live Oak been filled by a line of railroad connecting the two points," lamented Beauregard, "the reinforcements I was sending . . . would have arrived in time . . . and the enemy would at once have been driven out of Florida." This was sufficient argument. On March 4 the Engineer Bureau directed Major Meriwether of the Railroad Iron Commission to proceed south and complete the work in the shortest possible time.[32]

Meriwether took with him a junior officer of Engineers, Lieutenant Jason M. Fairbanks, and a civilian agent named J. H. Burns. They found the opposition completely prepared. As Meriwether and Fairbanks were gathering labor, Yulee quietly retained the services of every recognized lawyer in the eastern part of Florida, including the local Confederate States district attorney. Having thus carried off all of the legal ammunition in sight, he secured from the Suwanee Circuit Court, then sitting in Gainesville, an injunction restraining Fairbanks, Burns, Meriwether, and the Secretaries of War and Navy from taking either his rail or fastenings. The papers were served upon Fairbanks and Burns on April 27, just as they were scattering their laborers over Yulee's right of way.[33]

Fairbanks carried his difficulties first to Meriwether and then to Major General Patton Anderson, the latest in the numerous company to command the Military District of Florida. Meriwether instructed Lieutenant Fairbanks to pay no attention to the court but General Anderson passed the dilemma upstairs to Departmental Headquarters at Charleston. When Charleston replied that nothing must prevent use of the iron, the General supplemented Fairbanks' force with a military guard and summarily impressed sufficient locomotives and flatcars to carry the iron to Live Oak. He also issued orders that the Lieutenant was to be protected from interference by anyone. Meriwether, whose respect for local courts was small, conferred briefly with two stray attorneys in Tallahassee and quitted the state.[34]

Fairbanks carried out his instructions. By May 28 his laborers had ripped up nearly three miles of rail, when he was handed a curt notice from Judge Dawkins of the Suwanee Court directing him to show cause why he and Burns should not be attached for contempt. The unfortunate young officer found himself in a quandary: if he failed to heed the summons, he faced imprisonment by the Florida judiciary; if he responded, he faced court-martial. Following a conference with General Anderson, he concluded that a military tribunal would be the worse of two evils. He instructed his gangs to keep on tearing up Senator Yulee's track.[35]

On June 8 Judge Dawkins ordered the arrest of Fairbanks and Burns. Burns could not be found, but the sheriff discovered Fairbanks standing outside General Anderson's headquarters at Lake City. To the order placing him under arrest, the Lieutenant responded by reading aloud the order for his protection within the hearing of the provost guard. Instantly he was surrounded by a wall of bayonets, and the sheriff had no alternative but report his inability to secure the prisoner.[36]

Judge Dawkins was naturally outraged, and he at once appealed to Governor Milton "to vindicate the majesty of the law." Nevertheless he personally favored the construction of the Live Oak line, even at the expense of the Florida Railroad, having issued his first injunction only to assure a fair hearing for all concerned. Milton, of course, had been placed in a highly embarrassing position. As a collaborator with Richmond, it was most unpleasant to proceed against the agents of the central administration. Coached by Dawkins, he privately assured the military of the success of a motion for the dissolution of the injunction, if properly pressed.[37]

After much scurrying and caterwauling, all concerned, except Yulee, appealed to Richmond. The Administration was in no mood for a constitutional row. Late in July the War Department dispatched an attorney to Florida to enter a regular plea for the dissolution of the injunction. Everyone, save Yulee, sighed with relief. The case presently reached the Confederate States District Court for the Eastern District of Florida, which at once upheld the right of the Confederate Government to impress the iron.[38]

As Yulee looked on in helpless wrath, the demolition of the Florida Railroad was resumed. As with every similar undertaking, however, work progressed more slowly than had been anticipated; promised at first for September, the Live Oak–Lawton extension remained unfinished for months, a Federal raiding party having occupied and then destroyed the physical connection with the Florida road at Baldwin. The link was ultimately completed, but the Confederacy was in its death agony when the last spike was pounded home on March 4, 1865.[39]

CHAPTER

~ 17 ~

The Downgrade Steepens

"The greatest favor that could be conferred on the road—if public wants permitted—would be the privilege of quitting business until the end of the war." —*Annual Report*, Georgia Railroad, May 10, 1864.

I

FOR THE RAILROADS THEMSELVES, 1864 SERVED CHIEFLY TO UNDERscore old difficulties.

Supply costs tell the story clearly. They did not precisely follow the gold value of the Confederate dollar—which averaged four cents through much of 1864—but their tendency was always upward. The price of iron rail had risen in May, 1864, by 1,000 per cent. Car wheels, which had cost fifteen dollars each in 1860, now brought more than thirty times as much. Before the war the Richmond, Fredericksburg & Potomac had paid five cents per pound for boiler plate; the market now demanded one dollar. As late as 1862 the wood bill of the Western & Atlantic had been $33,104.21; in 1864 it was $228,732.75. The Mississippi Central possessed hardly a pick or a shovel; to get them it appealed again and again for permission to trade cotton with the enemy. In Virginia lubricants were obtainable only at a price fifty times higher than pre-war. Far away in Texas the single locomotive of the Houston Tap & Brazoria wore out completely, and the road was operated thenceforth with oxen, which performed the fifty-mile journey from Houston to Columbia in about three days.[1]

A few companies continued to perform wonders with limited

214

shop equipment, and at intervals an overworked factory would find time to produce a widow's mite of supplies. Early in 1864 the Tredegar Works delivered to the Virginia Central a number of cast iron locomotive tires, which were pronounced "equal in quality to any heretofore received from the United States." The same road bored 444 car wheels on its own premises. Alabama carriers undertook to manufacture their own lubricants, using a process based upon a widely available southern commodity, grain alcohol. Here and there a small foundry arose, capable of a limited production at high prices. A Montgomery firm even offered delivery of round bar iron suitable for car axles, but announced that precedence would be given those orders which were accompanied by cash.[2]

The manpower situation worsened steadily. On the Virginia Central, Negroes ran away or were captured by the enemy; fuel contractors and their teams were drafted into the Army. Operation of the line was continued only by sending military details into the woods to cut cordwood and crossties. Repeated advertisements testified to the shortage of slave labor on the Richmond & Danville, Piedmont, and Richmond & Petersburg lines.[3]

But the most serious problem was the conscription of experienced employees. By the end of 1863 southern manpower was so visibly on the wane that the Confederate Congress talked of drafting all able-bodied railroad workers under the age of forty-five and replacing them with older men and disabled soldiers. This was too much even for the Government's good. The presidents of the Richmond, Fredericksburg & Potomac and the Richmond & Petersburg lobbied frantically against the measure, and in a lengthy printed memorial declared correctly that such a law would end the remaining ability of the carriers to support the war effort. In conclusion they pointed out that it required one thousand wagons and drivers, and four thousand horses, to transport in five days what a railroad train could carry in one. Evidently Congress was impressed, for the proposal died in committee.[4]

Nevertheless, new legislation presently raised the military age limit to fifty and tightened the exemption regulations for railroaders. Thereafter employees were not to exceed in number the miles of road devoted to military transportation. Furthermore, those exempted were to be reported by name and description, were to be certified as indispensable, and were forbidden to leave their posts without forfeiting their status. Superintendents were directed to submit monthly personnel reports to the Conscription Bureau.[5]

This law endeavored to strike a balance between two irreconcilable interests, but it satisfied no one. If the measure was fully carried out, said the management of the Georgia Railroad, it would "paralyze business." President Webb of the North Carolina road feared he might have to cease operations entirely. Colonel Sims, as usual, took the railroad point of view, declaring that a rigid application of the law would cripple transportation everywhere in the Confederacy. He asserted inferentially that the ultimate decision in the matter of exemptions should rest with the Railroad Bureau, not with the Bureau of Conscription. The choice, he added, was between enforcement of the law and the survival of the carriers. Reading this, Secretary Seddon recommended that the situation be studied by an officer "not committed to consider primarily the railroad interest." [6]

The enforcement of so rigorous a law occasioned much confusion and no little dishonesty. There even arose a class of self-recommended "mechanics," who sought an exemption from every road within reach. Worse still, the carriers began brazenly to raid each other's personnel. Upon one occasion Superintendent Hugh Rice of the North Carolina road lost so many men to the Orange & Alexandria and the South Side that he threatened to cease running entirely, and it required all of Sims's cajolery to keep him in line.[7]

Despite the howls of railroad officials and a few cases of injustice, the Government did endeavor to administer the draft machinery impartially. During the year ending February 1, 1865, the Conscription Bureau exempted outright 4,747 railroad men of military age and "detailed" 849 additional employees for special reasons. This was quite generous, especially when it is remembered that the entire railroad force of the seceding states had totaled, in 1860, less than 7,000. Nevertheless, the woes of the carriers were not imaginary. The quality of their employees declined markedly, while the exemption figures failed to include a variety of fringe occupations, woodcutting particularly.[8]

Though the railway workers of the Confederacy now found themselves in a superficially favorable labor market, their lot was not enviable. Their wages rose rapidly, but the cost of living soared even higher. In the autumn of 1864 a Virginia Central conductor received a monthly wage of $270, a mere pittance at a time when the cost of groceries had increased from sixty to eighty times. The annual salary of the general freight agent was only $4,200. Management was quick to realize that workers would accept relatively low pay in order to escape the conscription officer, though it should be noted that the salaries of officials still enjoyed a proportionately smaller expansion. Indeed, expert mechanics often were carrying home more currency than were the superintendents under whom they worked. But early in 1864 the ten-dollar daily wage of Western & Atlantic shopmen represented less than fifty cents in terms of gold, and it is clear that *real* wages on other roads were as small.[9]

II

Facing unheard-of demands with disintegrating physical plants, the railroads could do no more than they had done previously—increase charges, and decrease service. Surviving time-tables of the war's final year everywhere reflect greatly lengthened schedules (which, if the comment of travelers is to be believed, were rarely met). Before 1861 the 80-mile ride from Montgomery to Columbus, Georgia, had occupied hardly a morning; it now took all day. In less than eight months the running time of the South Side road between Petersburg and Lynchburg was extended by an hour and a quarter. In June, 1864, the fastest train on the Wilmington & Manchester covered the 171 miles between Wilmington and Kingsville at an average velocity of ten and one-quarter miles per hour.[10]

No carrier, including those publicly owned or controlled, hesitated to pass on its swollen expenses to the general public. Every new tariff seemed more outrageous than the last. The inflation of freight rates indeed often exceeded the inflation of money. From Petersburg to Ivor, Virginia, the distance was thirty-six miles; but in March, 1864, the Norfolk & Petersburg demanded five dollars to carry a sack of salt between the two points. Yet President William Mahone, who in the midst of an increasingly successful military career never neglected his railroad, complained in April (when a gold dollar was worth twenty-one paper dollars) that his freight tariff was too low—only twenty-nine times higher than before the war. In July, a time of relative currency stability, the Virginia Central was demanding an increase over its entire list of 100 per cent. Other lines, notably the Orange & Alexandria, quoted rates as stiff as Mahone's. To ship a cord of firewood sixty-one miles from Lynchburg to Charlottesville cost $10.50. A like charge was imposed upon a single ton of coal. And in September the rate on both was raised to $11.00.[11]

Passenger fares were no less astronomical. In April, 1864, civilian tickets on the Norfolk & Petersburg cost twenty cents per mile, and the Virginia Board of Public Works was not slow to permit the other roads of the state to raise their charges to similar levels. Elsewhere in the Confederacy the story was much the same. To ride from Weldon to Raleigh, ninety-seven miles, cost in the autumn of 1864 twenty-two dollars; other North Carolina routes charged nearly as much. By June, 1864, fares were rising so rapidly throughout the South that W. Alvin Lloyd ceased publishing them in his *Southern Railroad Guide*. But as the end approached, even railroad charges failed to keep pace with currency depreciation. Just before Appomattox, with the Confederate dollar worth less than two cents in specie, the surviving carriers of Virginia were collecting a mere *forty cents* per mile from their regular revenue passengers.[12]

Even government tariffs were by no means immune from inflation. At the last general railroad convention of the Confederacy, held at Columbia on April 13, 1864, Colonel Sims had again to listen quietly while freight rates upon Confederate property were boosted by 50 per cent, and passenger fares to about six cents per mile. And though the carriers made no further general increase, individual lines insisted upon "adjustments." These secondary advances were especially common in Virginia, where in October the charge upon subsistence stores was fixed arbitrarily at one-half the ordinary civilian rate, and moved upward with it. In the Carolinas, Georgia, and Florida, on the other hand, the Columbia schedule remained in force (the Muscogee and Wilmington & Manchester roads excepted) as late as January, 1865.[13]

Mushrooming rates naturally evoked a good deal of grumbling. An impressment commissioner in North Carolina exclaimed that nothing demanded more vigorous action than "the rapaciousness and greed of the railroad companies of our country." The carrier interest, including the Railroad Bureau, were quick to retort that if private rates were reduced, the government tariff would have to go up. In South Carolina, a great outcry arose when the roads of the state announced they would accept only limited liability for freight transported and no liability at all for shipments refused. But in the last analysis neither shipper nor legislator could stand against the inflationary deluge; like chips upon a flood they were swept onward toward the final cataract.[14]

III

A favorite grievance of the growing company of railroad-baiters was the enormous paper profit that most carriers continued to enjoy. Superficially, their balances resembled financial versions of the Arabian Nights. A tiny fragment of a railroad, the Atlantic & North Carolina, incurred in the course of its fiscal year 1863-64 an operating expense of $100,720.44, but could report a "net profit" of $215,066.87. It already had wiped out more than a quarter of its outstanding debt to the State of North Carolina. After meeting all current expenses, the Southwestern Railroad in Georgia was clearing over a million dollars per annum. The Mississippi & Tennessee, which possessed practically no right of way by 1864, leased its equipment to other companies and pocketed nearly $75,000 during the first nine months of that year. Dividends matched profits. Though its line ran directly through a major theater of operations, the Petersburg road paid more than $300,000 in the final year of the war. In the same period the stockholders of the South Carolina Railroad received close to a million dollars, or 16 per cent upon the book value of their investment. A single disbursement of the Raleigh & Gaston, paid on August 1, 1864, amounted to 15 per cent.[15]

Yet there were those who had abandoned the illusion that paper money represented wealth. "The [fact] is," remarked President John P. King of the Georgia Railroad, "the Road is running at a heavy loss. It has made no *real* profit for the past two years and is making nothing now.... We say no *real* profit, for it would require much more than all reported profits to place the Road and outfit in the same condition they were in on the first of January, 1861." This was the naked truth. "From whence do we get the surplus revenues reputed during the past two years?" asked Super-intendent Whitcomb of the Virginia Central. "I answer unhesi-tatingly, from *Capital*." Many of the bondholders of the Alabama & Florida Railroad of Alabama took a similarly shrewd measure of the future when, after 1863, they deliberately withheld the coupons due and payable in Confederate money. Not until 1865 did they present them, for payment *in the currency of the United States*.[16]

Part of the paper in railway treasuries was removed by taxation. In February, 1864, Congress expanded the income tax, adding a surtax of 25 per cent upon profits exceeding one-quarter of the capital investment of railroad, banking, communication, and trans-portation companies. Though this would have made a twentieth-century American smile, carrier officials were aghast. At the Columbia convention of April 13 they formed a committee to memorialize Congress and denounced the impost as "oppressive class legislation." Oddly enough, they suggested as an alternative a *capital* levy upon the whole wealth of the country.[17]

Even after taxes and dividends, many lines still possessed whole bales of currency. A favorite method of getting rid of such de-teriorating money was the purchase of Confederate "Cotton Loans" —twenty-year securities payable in specie or in cotton at the option of the Government. In the fall of 1863 the Virginia Central bought $134,000 worth at a stiff premium. As late as the following summer the management of the Raleigh & Gaston still regarded the issues as attractive. The North Carolina road was even more patriotic, investing in several types of Confederate loans, not all of which possessed so solid a basis as a future cotton crop. Stockholders of the Nashville & Chattanooga, now operating a locomotive and car rental service in the absence of any trackage they could call their own, were astute as well as public-spirited, purchasing 1,420 bales of cotton for export. Unfortunately their president, Colonel V. K. Stevenson (who had allegedly fled Nashville via special train) proved sharper still. With a system of dummy contracts that would have done credit to a modern tax evader, he contrived to divert the cotton to his own speculative ends. At the close of the war the unhappy stockholders found nothing left save an array of com-plicated figures.[18]

Railroad profits were essentially imaginary, but the decline of railroad safety was very real indeed. Several accidents in a single day were not unknown upon heavily burdened lines. On the Western & Atlantic, April 13, 1864, brought a freight wreck near Acworth, Georgia, and a passenger derailment above Big Shanty. In consequence of the number of collisions, the Alabama Assembly in December passed a law requiring *all* trains to stop within fifty feet of junctions with other lines, "the train of the eldest road to have the privilege of crossing first." The North Carolina Railroad continued to attribute its freedom from major disasters to "the blessing of God." [19]

Many travelers waxed bitter over the trials of wartime journeys. A ride on a Confederate passenger train was now less comfortable than a wagon drive, and but little faster. "We broke down only once between Kingsville and Wilmington," wrote the diarist, Mary Boykin Chesnut, in November, 1863, "but between Wilmington and Weldon [we collapsed] so effectually as to have to remain twelve hours at that forlorn station." Mrs. Chesnut likewise noted the general bad manners of her fellow-passengers. The inevitable querulous female entered her car, denounced the odor of the military personnel therein, and endeavored (successfully) to occupy a double seat. In the confusion one of Mrs. Chesnut's lunch baskets was relieved of two fried chickens. Mrs. Chesnut, however, was fortunate; a fortnight previously passengers on the Petersburg Railroad had suffered larceny upon a far grander scale. Such affairs, said the Richmond *Examiner*, were becoming "alarmingly frequent." [20]

IV

In the interior of the Confederacy the carriers were slowly disintegrating; but in those regions where Federal troops could penetrate, they were being literally torn to pieces. Union cavalry thrusts perfectly supplemented the strangle hold of the blockade.

The prospect was nowhere more gloomy than in Mississippi. From the fall of Vicksburg onward, most of the state lay open to enemy raiders. By the end of the summer of 1863 much of the New Orleans, Jackson & Great Northern lay in ruins. Fire and sledge hammer had damaged the remnants of the Mississippi & Tennessee and the Mississippi Central in a score of places. An especially bold incursion by Colonel E. F. Winslow attempted in August to carry off a whole collection of locomotives and cars which had been gathered at Canton, Winona, and Grenada; thanks to the destruction of certain bridges, the Federals could not make away with their loot, but they did succeed in kidnapping twenty-five enginemen and shop mechanics. Thereafter, the M. & T. could be run only in segments. Upon the lower section two locomotives remained in operating condition, and schedules were limited to fifteen round trips per month. Beyond the bridgeless Tallahatchie,

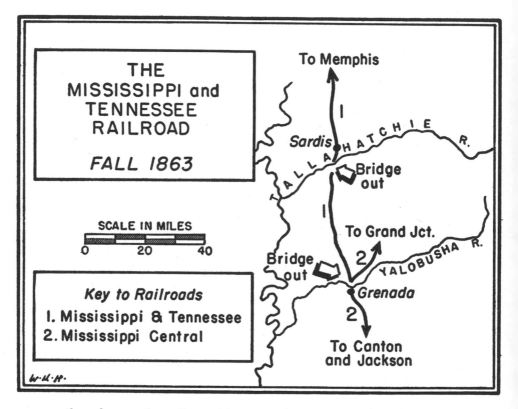

THE
MISSISSIPPI and
TENNESSEE
RAILROAD

FALL 1863

SCALE IN MILES
0   20   40

Key to Railroads
1. Mississippi & Tennessee
2. Mississippi Central

To Memphis

Sardis

Bridge out

To Grand Jct.

Bridge out

Grenada

To Canton and Jackson

and as far north as Senatobia, operations were reduced to "a line of horse cars." Past Senatobia the rusting iron lay under constant northern surveillance.[21]

Following the catastrophe of Vicksburg, the direction of Confederate military operations in Mississippi had fallen wholly into the hands of General Joseph E. Johnston. Though an able commander, Johnston remained throughout the war a pessimist of the first order. In July of 1863, in one of his black moods, he suddenly ordered the destruction of all the engines and cars remaining at

Canton and other points, in order to prevent their capture by the enemy. Such an act would have injured the Confederates more than the Federals, for much of the equipment subsequently was included with the rolling stock moved east for use in Georgia and the Carolinas. Johnston's scheme was stopped only by the frantic objections of Walter Goodman, president of the Mississippi Central, whose soul revolted at the loss of his equipment. Goodman was full of alternatives. It would be much better, he declared, if the rolling stock could be removed, and even if this were not feasible, the detachment of certain indispensable parts like side rods and journal boxes would render them useless to an invader. Though conceived in selfishness, these proposals contained much hard sense. When Johnston's famous stubbornness forced an appeal to the Administration, Secretary Seddon quickly saw the point. A telegram from Richmond called off the destruction.[22]

On every exposed salient of the Confederacy, Union flying columns slashed at every railroad within reach. By midsummer of 1863, their depredations forced the Vicksburg, Shreveport & Texas to cease operations entirely. In the spring of the same year the raid of Colonel Streight, driving upon the factories and depots of Georgia, came within an ace of cutting the Western & Atlantic, a disaster which only the capture of his force of 1,600 by the redoubtable Forrest prevented. When Governor Brown wrote to President Davis that the destruction of the Western & Atlantic "would seriously affect the operations of our army in Tennessee," he was putting it mildly. Though the authorities were slow to furnish the mounted guards the Georgia governor requested, they did take steps to insure the functioning of the road. Portable bridge frames, similar to those already in service upon the line, were prepared by the Atlanta engineer office and held in readiness. A number of other Georgia roads took alarm and organized their employees into military companies.[23]

Nor were the eastern marches of the Confederacy free from the Federal probe. Train crews upon the vital route north of Wilmington often glanced anxiously at the eastern horizon, whence blue-uniformed raiders had come more than once. In May of 1864, a torrent of Federal cavalry under Sheridan swept over the Virginia Central in the vicinity of Trevilian's Station. In June, Kautz and Wilson pounded deep into southern Virginia, a region hitherto immune from molestation, and tore to pieces a large portion of the Richmond & Danville between Burkeville Junction and the Staunton River. The damage was repaired, but not until a large force of laborers had been diverted from necessary finishing touches upon the Piedmont connection, and much of the iron of the Charlotte and Statesville road had been taken up for re-laying. Moreover, the northerners had thoughtfully demolished a number of trackside tanks, and the repair trains had to be supplied with water pumped by fire-engines loaned by the Richmond City Council.[24]

In the meantime, the relentless Grant had crowded the Army of Northern Virginia into Petersburg. Though the Confederates recovered themselves and the war of movement jelled into siege operations, the Federals on August 17 severed the Petersburg Railroad below the city, and thrust their way through the hills for several miles beyond. The direct connection with Wilmington was gone. Above the capital the Richmond, Fredericksburg & Potomac and the Virginia Central had been put practically out of action. No trains ran to the Valley over the Central until the first of July; beyond Staunton, thanks to the operations of the Federal General Hunter, no repairs could be undertaken at all. "We cannot hope, with the materials we have on hand, or are likely to get, to survive a similar disaster," commented Superintendent Whitcomb. As for the Fredericksburg road, it was little more than a ghost line, leading through a desolate country to nowhere.[25]

Two railroads remained: the South Side and the Richmond & Danville, the former drawing upon a limited though important hinterland, the latter connected with the Deep South by the single-track Piedmont road, half completed in the nick of time. But soon the Federal power would be cutting even the lower South to ribbons. By the final spring the *effective* Confederacy would be reduced to a tall gray general, a few thousand soldiers in rags, and a handful of locomotives struggling over warped and breaking iron.

↬ 18 ↬

The Failure of a Bureaucracy

"Of all the difficulties encountered by the administrative bureaus, perhaps the greatest has been the
deficiency in transportation."—James A. Seddon,
April 28, 1864.

I

LIEUTENANT COLONEL SIMS WAS A MAN WHO LIKED TO ESCAPE
office routine and face his problems on the spot. Journeying southward from Richmond in April, 1864, he personally could watch
the supply trains trailing their smoke across the Carolina fields, and
at successive interchange points could hear the direct assurances of
railway officials that everything possible was being done to move
subsistence stores. Yet he was not wholly content. More than once
he observed entire trains filled with private property of a specula-
tive nature. And the congestion of government freight upon trackside platforms bespoke trouble.[1]

The cancellation of a few passenger schedules had improved
matters, and back in Richmond Quartermaster General Lawton
breathed easier. But neither he nor anyone else was really satisfied.
The loss of the East Tennessee route had thrown an impossible
burden upon the seaboard lines. Supplies consigned even to southwestern Virginia now had to pass circuitously up the coast. "It is
truly lamentable," wrote Lawton, "to realize the necessity of transporting corn from Georgia, almost round the Confederacy, to a
point near the border of Georgia again."

Commissary General Northrop was even less happy. Though
receipts of grain had increased, the situation remained critical.

General Bragg echoed his pessimism. Secretary Seddon remembered the railroad act of May 1, 1863, and recommended that the carriers be placed once and for all under a system of government regulation. Even so faithful a spokesman of the railroad interest as Sims thought the time had come for genuine action. "That the railroads should come under military control I am becoming every day more satisfied," he informed Lawton. "There seems to be a desire to work for the road's interest rather than to sacrifice all convenience for the country's cause." [2]

There already existed good precedent for the use of the 1863 law. In January, in part because of Federal raids, the East Tennessee & Virginia had been placed under a government superintendent. Yet President Davis hesitated. Even in the face of a desperate situation he appears to have feared the consequences of such a step. He continued to place his hopes in a program of "cooperation" with the roads rather than in compulsory management by the War Department. [3]

Davis perhaps held back for political reasons; too sharp a use of the curb upon the tender mouth of southern constitutional belief might have upset the Confederate wagon. But to neglect the control of military transportation could be in the long run quite as disastrous. The trains somehow continued to operate, but the movement of foodstuffs alone strained their capacity to the limit. When a shipload of naval armor slipped into Wilmington, the iron lay rusting on the docks for weeks, and even Secretary Seddon pointed to the greater importance of food and fodder as the reason for the delay. When General Bragg asked the Richmond & Danville to move six hundred horses from Richmond to Burkeville, Virginia, he was told that the whole road already was devoted to forwarding grain supplies. Yet army and civil population alike continued to complain of lack of food. [4]

The carriers themselves realized that Davis dared not crack the whip, and they cooperated only when self-interest, or a transient patriotic impulse, moved them. From July, 1863, onward, volunteer units of Virginia Central employees repeatedly saw action in the Richmond fortifications. But while they were dodging Federal rifleballs, their company was engaged in an unseemly squabble with the Confederate Post Office Department and for a time refused to carry the mails. An aroused public opinion was required to bring disputants together, and then only when the Government offered concessions not enjoyed by other roads.[5]

Relations between the carriers and the Confederate Post Office Department were never, in fact, very happy. Disrupted train schedules meant disrupted mails. Diversion of rolling stock to military use brought chaos to many postal routes, and fantastic delays were experienced by even government dispatches. The army attempted to alleviate the situation in 1862 with a directive requiring troop trains to carry mail cars, but this was of little help, for such trains could hardly wait for connections. Moreover, the railroad mail contracts of 1861 were not generally revised until *February, 1865*, and even then the payments were ridiculously small. First-class roads, for example, were now to receive $225.00 per mile per annum, instead of $150.00 as theretofore. Payments to second-class roads were boosted from $100.00 to $150.00 and for third-class roads from $50.00 to $75.00, all, of course, in paper currency. In the face of such stinginess, it is little wonder that railroad cooperation with the postal authorities grew continually more sullen.[6]

II

What finally caused the resuscitation of the 1863 law was the case of the Piedmont Railroad. With the Knoxville-Chattanooga route gone for good, and with the increasing threat to the lines running through Petersburg and Weldon, the supreme importance of the line was more evident than ever. Nevertheless, the undertaking progressed very slowly, and as late as May 7, 1864, there remained a gap of four and one-half miles between iron and iron. Criticism of the contractors and even of Captain Myers arose, but chiefly to blame was the scarcity of labor and, particularly, of rail, much of which ultimately was pried from the half-abandoned Roanoke Valley road at prices as high as two hundred dollars per ton.[7]

Even before its completion the Piedmont line had become a primary channel of supply, the space between the advancing rails being bridged by wagons. And for all its slowness, the work never ceased. The last bar was hammered into place about May 22, and by May 25 a few experimental trains had crept over the whole road. To the Army of Northern Virginia, struggling to maintain a front between Grant and Richmond, its value was incalculable, and after the Union lines had severed the old route to the south below Petersburg, the connection meant literally the difference between continued resistance and early collapse. Indeed, it is hardly too much to say that the Piedmont Railroad added months to the length of the Civil War.[8]

The Piedmont Railroad, at last completed, furnishes transportation between Danville, Virginia, and Greensboro, North Carolina, for one horse. National Archives.

Yet the new line gave little satisfaction. On the map, it was a completed railroad, but there the resemblance ceased. It was opened without depots or platforms, and its sidings were insufficient even by southern standards. It possessed no proper water stations and no supplies of cordwood whatever. Its rolling stock consisted of modified Richmond & Danville equipment, plus two locomotives and twenty cars taken from the Virginia Central by military authority. Frequently it had to borrow stock from the North Carolina road; the Richmond & Danville could provide no emergency help because of its wider gauge.[9] It is little wonder therefore that the slightest overload brought paralysis. When, in December, General Hoke's division was shifted from Richmond to the defenses of Wilmington, the first brigade (Hagood's) required *three days* to traverse the forty-eight miles between Danville and Greensboro, and Hoke disgustedly ordered the remainder of his command to march down the country roads rather than risk further delay. He likewise accused the Piedmont officials of "incapacity and want of attention" and strenuously urged government seizure of the line. He was echoed by two senators of prominence, James L. Orr of

South Carolina and Herschel V. Johnson of Georgia, who experienced personal delay while enroute to their homes for Christmas.[10] Reports like these so disturbed the War Department that it at last exhumed the railroad act of May 1, 1863, and ordered the seizure of the road.

What happened next is not clear; it is certain only that the impressment was not carried out. Perhaps the order was issued primarily to frighten the offending line. Perhaps President Davis interposed. In any event, things continued much as before. Late in January, 1865, it was reported that corn and salt in "immense quantity" had been left exposed beside its track in mud and rain. The quartermaster depot at Charlotte contained eight hundred barrels of soap, but Lee's army had none. A collision upon the road deepened the gloom. Lieutenant Colonel Sims wrote that its inadequacy was "a source of anxiety and alarm," [11] and suggested that the Government lease the property, a proposal which the management was polite enough to discuss before rejecting. He next pressed for the establishment of a line of through cars from Charlotte to Danville, to run over North Carolina tracks as far as Greensboro, and in February he placed two additional locomotives upon the road. Secretary Seddon thought much of the congestion could be eliminated by widening the Piedmont gauge to conform to that of the Richmond & Danville and appealed once more to Governor Vance in the matter. The Governor again failed to budge, and indeed it is difficult to see how the change would have been of great advantage, for it would merely have shifted freight interchange from Danville to Greensboro. But neither suggestions nor limited practical aid increased the flow of freight. On February 5, 1865, forty-nine Richmond & Danville cars stood idle in the Danville yards awaiting the arrival of supplies from the south. Two days later the number had risen to sixty-one, while in the trenches before Petersburg Lee's soldiers were starving.[12]

The Danville-Greensboro connection may have been unsatisfactory, but no other building project, save the Florida connection, was even finished. A flurry of enthusiasm for the Rome-Blue Mountain scheme broke out in the spring of 1864; Samuel Tate pointed out that the line would place the southern armies in Mississippi and north Georgia within thirty-six hours of each other and asserted that the work could be completed in ninety days if the Government had the courage to take rail from other roads. But by mid-June the advance of Sherman had rendered the project meaningless. In October Lieutenant Colonel Meriwether of the Iron Commission considered that even a partial extension of track to Jacksonville, Alabama, would not be worth the trouble and expense.[18]

The Selma–Meridian line was, of course, finished except for the Tombigbee bridge. Work upon the structure continued through 1863 under the supervision of Tate, but though Meriwether had a "high opinion" of the Memphis & Charleston president, the task never seemed to approach completion. In March, 1864, it was delegated directly to Meriwether, but with the announcement that it could not be finished before midsummer. There were constant labor shortages; planters had grown weary of furnishing hands at low rates. In the end, even Meriwether, who was accounted a capable engineer, fared no better than Tate.[14]

The tensions of 1864 did bring forth a rash of schemes for railroad connections, all ostensibly for military purposes. The Mobile & Girard, which the war had killed in embryo, now wanted the Government to build its line for it and carefully pointed out that the necessary rail could be secured from "certain roads which are of little public importance." In June Congress talked of subsidizing a new line between Fayetteville, North Carolina, and Florence, South Carolina. Of more evident value was a proposal of General W. H. C. Whiting for a bridge over the Cape Fear River at Wilmington. But the Engineer Bureau reported dolefully that the idea was impracticable because (1) it would require "much material and labor," (2) it would connect roads of different gauge, (3) the through route via Petersburg had been broken, and (4) the presidents of the two Wilmington carriers refused "on direct appeal" to give any aid.[15]

III

The railroad iron problem was never solved; it merely changed its emphasis. To normal attrition was now added an increasing destruction by enemy action. As early as January, 1864, the picture had become so dark that the Engineer Bureau recommended the diversion of all Naval iron to railroad use. Secretary Seddon, in a gloomy report to President Davis on April 28, expressed similar alarm. The Wilmington & Manchester showed especially serious wear, and by August it was feared that without new bar it could continue in operation for no more than three months.[16]

The Iron Commission, it must be said, tried earnestly to ease the situation. But almost to the end it faced the same old impasse: the railroads selected as sources of track material would go to any length to retain their rail, and in the absence of special legislation the Government hesitated to enforce the Commission's findings. The obstreperous O. M. Avery fought Colonel Meriwether as enthusiastically as he had opposed Samuel Tate, though by this time his Alabama & Florida Railroad of Florida had been reduced to five miles. In his April report to Davis, Secretary Seddon lamented the delays incident to such tactics and urgently recommended that the iron be taken by military force *before* any disagreements were subjected to time-consuming procedures in the courts. In the fall he again complained of the situation—this time with a certain bitterness:

"In order to maintain the more important roads," he said, "and sometimes to construct others demanded by imperious military considerations, it is absolutely necessary to withdraw from local or branch roads their rails and equipments. Although such necessity may be manifest and acknowledged by all, it is rare the proprietors of the special road whose property is thus sought to be appropriated are prepared to acquiesce in its selection for the sacrifice. Each local corporation finds abundant reasons for further delay or special exemption in its own case, and on them base justification for refusal to sell, and the interposition of all possible legal obstructions to seizure by impressment." [17]

But Davis found it hard to swing the axe; he preferred to wait for ironclad legislative approval. A bill providing for the impressment of railroad iron and *rolling stock* occasioned some animated debate in both houses of Congress in the late spring of 1864, but ultimately was consigned to the table. When the members returned to the drab and besieged capital in November, the President's message again urged specific action on the subject, but the statesmen bickered and dawdled. Time had run out when in February, 1865, they at last eased Davis's fears with a renewal of the stiff railroad legislation that had been provided nearly two years before.[18]

IV

During 1864 the Confederate Railroad Bureau reached its apogee. Lieutenant Colonel Sims continued active as always. In June the completion of the Piedmont road and the nearly simultaneous raid damage to the Richmond & Danville took him off to Danville. Midsummer saw him at Columbia, Augusta and Wilmington. The chaos that followed Sherman's capture of Atlanta carried him as far as Selma, Alabama.[19]

He did acquire the services of two new officers. The responsibilities of Major Whitford in North Carolina had grown so heavy that Captain John M. Robinson, former superintendent of the Seaboard & Roanoke, and more recently the purchasing agent of the Virginia carriers in Great Britain, was made supervisor of railroad transportation between Wilmington and Richmond. Robinson assumed his new duties in May. A few days later Sims extended his practical operations far into Mississippi with the acquisition of Major George Whitfield, who was given the direction of military rail traffic beyond the Alabama River.

Whitfield (who is not to be confused with Whitford) brought with him an experience in western transportation dating back to 1861. He likewise nursed a profound dislike for the Quartermaster Department, an obsession which already had moved him to submit his resignation. "When the war began," he had written the Secretary of War in January, "I had some character for honesty and integrity, and I do not wish to loose [sic] it by remaining longer in the Quartermaster's Department." In reality Whitfield's record had been so good that his commanding general, Leonidas Polk, recommended his retention, and Seddon finally assigned him to Sims in order to keep his services. But with all his abilities, Whitfield was a distinct egocentric. In his first letter to Sims he demanded unlimited traveling expenses, asserting (probably correctly) that his current hotel bills alone were exceeding his army per diem pay three or four times over. He was a vigorous man, but his correspondence often reeked with self-congratulation.[20]

Meanwhile Sims had lost Major Thomas Peters, his principal officer in Atlanta. This probably disturbed him little, for the two never had worked very smoothly together. Peters was not inefficient—Meriwether of the Iron Commission regarded him as "worth more than any ten men"—but he was an elderly man and perhaps resented the brashness of his superior. Orders dated May 7, 1864, appointed him chief quartermaster on the staff of General Leonidas Polk, and following that fighting clergyman's decapitation by a shell at Pine Mountain he was placed in a similar position under General S. D. Lee. He remained on rail transportation duty, principally at Selma, Alabama, to the end of the war.[21] Peters' duties in Atlanta devolved upon his assistant, the Texas Major, J. M. Hottel. Hottel seems to have cut something of a figure in the little metropolis, maintaining a suite of four rooms and, if his expense vouchers are to be believed, a span of private horses. But he took care not to allow his western expansiveness to interfere with his duties, and his relations with Sims remained cordial.[22]

Though Sims retained his responsibility for the negotiation of government tariffs, he never directly controlled the audit and payment of railroad accounts. For the carriers east of the Chattahoochee River, this duty continued in the hands of Major C. Maurice Smith at Richmond; west of the Chattahoochee the work seems to have been handled by local quartermasters. To the end of 1864 Smith was assisted only by a Captain John Frizzell, seven hundred miles away in Georgia. Nor could he claim the undivided services of even this distant helper, as Frizzell was subject also to the Railroad Bureau. Thanks to the intervention of Sims, the overworked Smith at last secured for his Richmond office one captain and one civilian clerk, but the fall of the Confederacy was by then hardly three months away.[23]

The functions of the Railroad Bureau never were perfectly defined. Particular confusion arose as a result of Union raids upon the Mobile & Ohio, the necessary repairs being carried out by Engineer personnel, but under the supervision of Major Whitfield. Work of this sort came to occupy a large part of Whitfield's time, but though he requested a repair gang of his own, the War Department ordained that rebuilding operations should remain a responsibility of the Engineers. In a subsequent interview with General Gilmer, Sims found the Chief of the Engineer Bureau "very crusty about the matter" and responded with some heat that his own organization would not assume charge of any repairs in the future. To Major Peters he wrote sarcastically that requests for railroad rebuilding "should thereafter be addressed to the Engineers, they [being] presumed to be capable of completing such work more rapidly than others."[24]

To the end Colonel Sims never could bring himself to consistently favor what seemed to many a logical policy—the unrestricted interchange of rolling stock by all of the carriers. Herein he was perhaps more conservative than Wadley. "Cars never get the proper attention when from under the owner's eye," he told General Lawton in the spring of 1864, "and with the present scarcity it is the true policy to husband them with care. The experience of the world is against it, and if the time ever comes when it is pursued you may rely upon it that all improvement in, or certainty of, transportation is destroyed." He did persist in pressing for the release of mechanics from the army, but his suggestion was deemed so impracticable that no reply was made to it.

Sims's principal contribution to the theory of military rail transportation was a proposed consolidation of existing companies into a single, integrated system. He actually endeavored to sponsor the amalgamation of the three roads connecting Wilmington and Richmond, but without success. The stockholders of the Richmond & Petersburg resolved unanimously "to do everything in [their] power to carry out the wishes of the government but respectfully prefer that the business be permitted to remain under their own control and management." As for Sims's suggestion that *all* rail carriers should be united into a single organization, General Lawton passed it to the Secretary of War like a hot biscuit; and Mr. Seddon as quickly immobilized it in one of his pigeonholes.[25]

In February, 1864, the Bureau arranged the initial shipment of Federal prisoners from Virginia to the new and soon to be notorious camp at Andersonville, Georgia. The captives numbered more than twelve thousand. To minimize congestion, Sims limited departures to a single daily trainload of four hundred. To discourage escape they were routed inland via Petersburg, Gaston, Charlotte, Columbia, and Augusta. Though the prisoners were crammed into half-ruined boxcars which afforded little protection from the weather, the journey probably was a lesser ordeal than their subsequent confinement. Thereafter the flow of unhappy northerners never entirely ceased. Late in June, as the enemy closed in upon Richmond and Petersburg, a particularly heavy mass was dis-

Account of Sales of public property, under direction of the Rail
Road Bureau during the Quarter ending 31 March 1864 viz:

<u>Sold to the South Side Rail Road Company</u>;

200 pairs Car Wheels ^{400} on Axles ^{200}	@ $160	$32.000.00	
114.420 pounds Iron (Scrap) viz			
40.560 lbs @ 20^t	$8112.00		
65.670 " " 15^t	9850.50		
8190 " " 5^t	409 50	18.372.00	
15.270 pounds Springs (steel car)	@ 50^t	7.635.00	
	Total	$58.007.00	

Raleigh N C
Jany 30. 1864

[signature]

I certify that the above account of Sales is correct and just
and that the property was sold to facilitate Rail Road trans
=portation
    J. W. Mirs
    Lt Col & Quartermaster
        in Charge

The Railroad Bureau helps out the South Side Railroad. (See statement on
next page.) National Archives.

patched from Virginia, this time by way of the new Piedmont road.[26]

Most flourishing of the Bureau's activities was its trade in rolling stock and supplies. In both volume and variety this business displayed a remarkable development until nearly the end of the war. The spring of 1864 saw refugee equipment still being moved east from Mississippi and Alabama, of which the greater part seems to have been distributed to the Richmond & Danville. In February the Bureau sold to the Virginia Central one "planing, tongueing and grooving machine," for one thousand dollars, and two locomotives —the Hero and the President—for $43,494.05. Other sales were at similarly low figures. In March the Richmond & Petersburg secured three engines with tenders at a bargain price of $35,000. On January 30 the Railroad Bureau's Raleigh warehouse dispensed to the South Side road for $58,007.00 a great mass of miscellaneous material, including 200 pairs of carwheels, 114,420 pounds of scrap iron and 15,270 pounds of springs. Two days previously an even larger accumulation of supplies had gone to the Charlotte & South Carolina. During the final year even the Iron Commission disposed of much of its track salvage through Colonel Sims; in March, 1864, he received therefrom over a thousand iron rails, 1,052 chairs, and 19,800 spikes.[27]

The Bureau even supervised the manufacture of new equipment. Its total orders from the Tredegar Iron Works reached $400,000. Late in May, 1864, one Ira Van Pelt of Petersburg was building eight cars, for which the Bureau had agreed to provide wheels; in January, 1865, Sims contracted with John D. Gray of Columbus, Georgia, for the production of an unlimited number of boxcars. The terms were grim: costs plus 25 per cent. And when the Selma Iron Works undertook to provide the metal parts, it demanded a cash advance of $100,000.[28]

Whether in the time remaining to the Confederacy Mr. Gray turned out a single car the record does not say. It matters little. Within three months the southern defense had fallen to pieces, and with it the cost-plus contract, Railroad Bureau, War Department, and whole Confederate Government. Sims had failed. Yet it cannot be said that his Bureau had performed discreditably. If he nursed certain old-fashioned ideas, it must be remembered that they were compatible with the railroad ideology of his time and place. The seeds of southern disaster were hardly his, for if the carriers did not support the war effort with their whole strength, it was because they ran through a land of little industrial capacity and because the Davis Government dared not risk placing them under effective harness.

CHAPTER

~ **19** ~

Hard Faith and Soft Iron

I

THE ANCIENT TECHNIQUES OF ANIMAL AND FOOT TRANSPORT WERE by no means neglected in the Confederacy, but the most important southern medium of concentration remained the steam railroad. Destroy the South's ability to keep its trains running, and the military potential of the Confederacy would suffer a mortal wound. That the North realized this as early as 1862 is evident from the campaigns of that year. Indeed, much of the strategy of the war can be viewed as a Federal attack upon, and a Confederate defense of, a series of railroad junctions. Corinth was one. Vicksburg, a river port to be sure, but also a river crossing, was another. The position of Chattanooga was obvious. The greatest example of all, if we may except Atlanta, was Richmond.

By 1864 the Union strategy had assumed as its objective not merely the defeat of the southern armies in battle, but the destruction of the southern ability to make war. A most promising means to this end was the occupation and destruction of Confederate railroad lines. No one appreciated this better than the man who early in March found himself in command of the Union armies in the west, William Tecumseh Sherman.

II

Already that winter Sherman had thrust deep into the enemy country for the purpose of disrupting the remaining rail net of eastern Mississippi. Here, near the edge of a prairie region, highly productive of the grain that the Confederacy now prized above

238

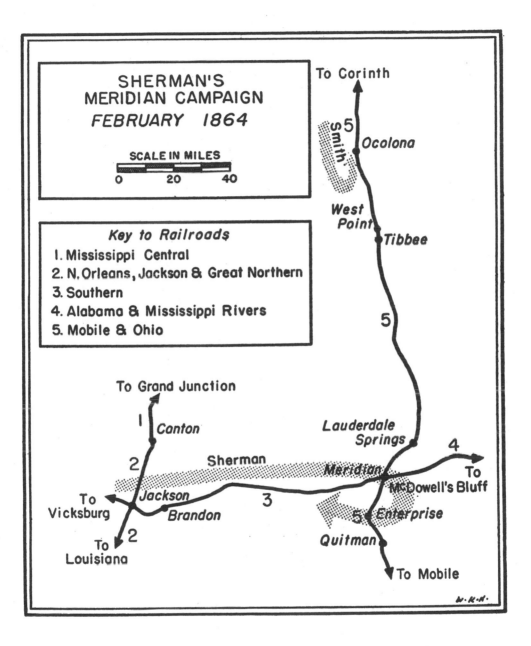

SHERMAN'S
MERIDIAN CAMPAIGN
FEBRUARY 1864

SCALE IN MILES

0   20   40

Key to Railroads
1. Mississippi Central
2. N. Orleans, Jackson & Great Northern
3. Southern
4. Alabama & Mississippi Rivers
5. Mobile & Ohio

To Corinth

Smith

5

Ocolona

West Point

Tibbee

5

Lauderdale Springs

To Grand Junction

1   Canton

2

Sherman

4

Meridian

To McDowell's Bluff

To Vicksburg

Jackson

Brandon

3

5   Enterprise

2

Quitman

To Louisiana

To Mobile

W·K·H·

cotton, stood the village of Meridian. Though its population totaled no more than eight hundred, it was the transportation center of an enormous area. Up from Mobile curved the Mobile & Ohio, to bisect the place and continue northward toward West Point, Tupelo, and Corinth. From the east came the Alabama & Mississippi Rivers road, and to the west ran the Southern road, extending toward Jackson. Military stores of every sort filled its warehouses and overflowed onto the platforms of neighboring stations. To Sherman, Meridian looked like big game; if it could be seized with all its stores and rolling stock, the whole Confederate position west of the Tombigbee would be untenable.

Sherman's plans were expertly drawn. He left Vicksburg on February 3, 1864, with two columns of infantry, twenty thousand strong. Simultaneously, a force of seven thousand cavalry, under the command of General W. Sooy Smith, was directed to sweep down from Tennessee along the line of the Mobile & Ohio, to wreck railroad and public property from Okolona southward, and rendezvous with Sherman at Meridian. Smith was especially primed to destroy the troublesome Nathan Bedford Forrest.[1]

Fortunately for the Confederates the Federal program miscarried —in part. Thanks to fumbling management and to the incredible effrontery of Forrest (whose effectives numbered less than half those of the enemy), Smith was hustled back into Tennessee, having penetrated no closer to Meridian than West Point, one hundred miles short of his goal. And though Sherman's infantry had little difficulty in reaching their objective, their massive approach could not be kept secret.[2]

Though not yet associated with Sims's Railroad Bureau, Major George Whitfield already was directing military railroad transportation at Meridian under General Leonidas Polk. Whitfield's reaction to the emergency was prompt and vigorous. On the eighth, as soon as Sherman was well past Jackson and had thus advertised his intentions, Whitfield directed the Mobile & Ohio and the Alabama & Mississippi Rivers road to bring every engine and car they could find to Meridian for the evacuation of stores. By the thirteenth most government property already had been removed, and on the following day Sherman's scouts listened helplessly to the rumble of the last Mobile & Ohio train as it bore away the final load. Altogether about twelve million dollars' worth of military property was saved, not to mention the rolling stock, all of which was gotten away save some condemned units. Included in the salvage were thirteen cars belonging to the Western & Atlantic which now, after two years of exile in Mississippi, were pulled to Mobile, ferried over the bay, and returned to their own rails. Nor was this all. At Enterprise, fourteen miles south of Meridian, Whitfield remained for two days, saving two thousand bales of government cotton and a quantity of railroad shop material. The thud of Federal musketry was sounding in his ears as he swung aboard the final southbound train.[3]

Whitfield had turned in a creditable performance, but the prospect, following the withdrawal of Sherman, was gloomy enough. The Federal commander tarried undisturbed at Meridian for a week, while his infantry wreaked upon the railroads of the vicinity the kind of vengeance for which they presently were to become famous. Sixteen miles of the Mobile & Ohio were torn up and the rails utterly ruined; over five additional miles the iron was pried loose. All bridges and trestles were gone upon a forty-seven-mile stretch between Lauderdale Springs and a point below Quitman. Even the blundering Smith had succeeded in wrecking considerable stretches of line between Okolona and West Point. On the Southern, the loss was fifty-one bridges, of an aggregate length of more than four thousand feet, and four miles of track. Destroyed on the Alabama & Mississippi Rivers were three bridges, five trestles, and nine miles of track. The Federals had also smashed (mostly at Canton, Mississippi) nineteen locomotives, twenty-eight cars, and 724 carwheels. Moreover, they had committed further vandalism upon the trackage of the New Orleans, Jackson & Great Northern and the Mississippi Central.[4]

The task of reconstruction was thus formidable. President Samuel Tate of the Memphis & Charleston was hurriedly summoned to Polk's headquarters and placed in general charge of the work, while Major Whitfield was ordered to direct the repairs upon the Mobile & Ohio. Both received authority to impress property and labor of every description.[5]

With the active aid of Superintendent Fleming (whom he pronounced "the best railroad worker in this or any other country"), Whitfield soon had large gangs at work upon the Mobile & Ohio. His chief difficulty seems to have been a supply of spikes, which had to be ordered from the Railroad Bureau. But after the arrival of three hundred kegs restoration proceeded rapidly. General Polk shouted down the inevitable objections of planters over the impressment of their slaves, and by noon of March 19 the road was open from Tibbee, Mississippi, to Meridian, a distance of nearly one hundred miles. By April 1 trains were running over as much of the Mobile & Ohio as had been in use before the Sherman raid. Just 25½ days had elapsed since Whitfield had first gone to work. Under Confederate conditions this was excellent time; Whitfield himself, with his profound lack of modesty, termed it "extraordinary." [6]

The breaks in the Alabama & Mississippi Rivers road east of Meridian were quickly restored; but work on the Southern proceeded more slowly. A squadron of cavalry which General Polk had placed at Tate's disposal to aid in the impressment of labor, was ordered elsewhere; and reconstruction did not get well under way until April. Petty arguments arose as to where the repair effort should start, and after the completion of the Mobile & Ohio, Whitfield was transferred to Jackson to hasten matters. On April 14 he suffered a fractured leg, which physically incapacitated him until July, but he continued to direct operations from his bed. Two days after his accident he reported that the Southern should be open from Meridian to Brandon by May 6. His estimate was not inaccurate. "Trains got through to Brandon today," he telegraphed Polk on the seventh. [7]

Yet Sherman's expedition to Meridian had disrupted the whole Confederate position in east-central Mississippi for a month or more. It had depleted further the southern supply of rail and fastenings. Thereafter, the railroads serving Jackson operated upon a day-to-day basis only. Military supply routine had been broken asunder. As late as May quantities of bacon were stranded in both north-central and southwestern Mississippi, while heavy shipments of salt, just arrived from Virginia, could find no satisfactory places of storage. And Major W. H. Dameron, regional Chief Commissary of Subsistence, failed to secure sufficient wagon transportation to offset the breakdown in rail service. [8]

Any respectable Union force that cared to do so could now occupy Mississippi at leisure. And though Sherman would not afflict the state again, he was by no means finished with the railroads of the Confederacy.

III

The possession of Richmond meant the mastery of Virginia. Therein lay the principal significance of the Confederate capital city. As the seat of government, its moral value was enormous, and its manufacturing facilities were by no means unimportant. But also vital was its position upon a circlet of railroads that gave access to almost every portion of the Old Dominion. It was Richmond and its sister city of Petersburg that gathered up the threads of iron which brought supplies from the west and south. He who held Richmond in suitable force could do with Virginia what he would. And Virginia had been, for three years, the steel helmet of the Confederacy.

It was not merely for sentimental reasons, then, that the Federal war effort had again and again been concentrated against the southern capital. Whoever held the city, controlled a large proportion of the Confederacy's lines of communication, and conversely an army which could occupy the chief railroads of Virginia controlled the city. A primary Confederate task was to prevent northern seizure of either.

The record of the final year of Virginia's defense is heroic, colorful, and highly complex. Our concern here is the manner in which the steam railroad served as an element of southern resistance.

The story is the familiar one of concentration upon interior lines. By early spring the Confederate command had ascertained the basic elements of Union strategy: an attack upon Lee in the well-worn Fredericksburg-Rapidan theater, a push in force from maritime bases, either in North Carolina or upon the lower James, and a complex of raids and diversions both in the Valley and against the principal southern channels of supply. In north Georgia, Sherman was preparing his drive upon Atlanta, and even in the far southwest, Shreveport was the objective of General Banks. Grant, now commander in chief of all the northern forces, began the general advance in northern Virginia on May 4, 1864.

To meet so multifarious a threat the Confederacy possessed insufficient manpower. The situation in Virginia seemed especially grim. Even the return of Longstreet's twelve thousand from east Tennessee was not enough. Before mid-April the Government was obliged to reach into the lower South for reinforcements.

In the beginning the men were brought forward only hesitantly. Charleston still lay under siege, and the War Department was likewise haunted by nightmares of a Federal sweep across North Carolina. Some of the first units (Evans' Brigade and, from Savannah, Holcomb's Legion) moved only to Wilmington. For a time Charleston endeavored to maintain its full strength by drawing in men from Florida.[9]

But the tension at the capital swiftly became unbearable. In mid-April, P. G. T. Beauregard was relieved of the command of the Department of South Carolina, Georgia, and Florida and ordered north to cope with an enemy advance which was known to be developing to the southeast of Petersburg; he established his new headquarters at Weldon, North Carolina, on the twenty-second. Soon a cascade of telegrams flashed down the wires to his successor at Charleston, Sam Jones, ordering unit after unit onto the first available northbound trains.[10]

This was to be no carefully organized transit to Chickamauga. The Railroad Bureau evidently had little to do with arrangements, which promptly fell into chaos. Cross-currents of reinforcements were running simultaneously to Johnston in upper Georgia. Fourteen hundred Federal prisoners enroute to Andersonville further clogged traffic. Moreover, Virginia's appeals for men were interspersed with calls for trainloads of corn. The emergency caught the carriers badly off balance. The first unit (the 21st South Carolina Volunteers of Hagood's Brigade) did not pull out of Charleston until the morning of April 28, and the railwaymen were unable to accommodate Hagood's other three regiments until the following day. The next brigade, Wise's, could not board the cars until the evening of May 3, while the entraining of Colquitt's Brigade, the last regiment of which had arrived exhausted from Florida on April 27, consumed the whole of May 5 and 6.[11]

Frantic as were the messages from Richmond, they had not been dispatched swiftly enough. Time, traffic, and deferred maintenance had sadly reduced the capacity of the carriers. The 21st South Carolina was dragged, shunted, unloaded, and reloaded for eight long days before its first train, bearing three hundred infantry, steamed into Petersburg through the early morning darkness of May 6. In upper Virginia, the Battle of the Wilderness had already begun. The remaining half of the regiment did not come up the road from Weldon until nearly noon. When Hagood's other units rolled into the station, night had fallen again. Already it looked like a case of too little and too late. Two days before, an enormous Federal flotilla had steamed up the James to debouch infantry and artillery by the thousand at Port Walthall, north of the Appomattox and flanking the railroad to Richmond. To oppose them, there had been in Petersburg only one infantry regiment, the City Battalion, and the Washington Artillery, plus militia in vague quantities. That instant doom did not fall upon the Confederates could be ascribed to the famed incompetence of the Union commander, Benjamin F. Butler. Even so, after all of Hagood's elements had arrived and been thrown into the breach, the bluecoats briefly occupied and tore up a short stretch of the Richmond & Petersburg.[12]

Nor was this all. The news came that Federal cavalry had burned the railroad bridges over Stony Creek and the Nottoway River, respectively twenty-one and twenty-six miles *below* Petersburg. To the north, facing Lee, Grant refused to release his pressure, and the Wilderness holocaust re-erupted into Spotsylvania. In Richmond there was momentary panic and Jefferson Davis talked of diverting the oncoming brigades to the circuitous and yet unfinished Danville route. Quartermasters worked frenziedly to set up a wagon-ferry across the five-mile break, but on the ninth a cluster of trains waited at Stony Creek for more than eighteen hours before expected troops and supplies could get across. Nevertheless, the worst was over. The Union cavalry drew off and Butler remained miraculously apathetic.

Once the railroads could establish an operating momentum, reinforcements came forward more quickly. Wise's Brigade had not left Charleston until late on the third, but on the night of the eighth it was beyond Weldon, and three of its regiments had passed over the bridgeless gap and were in Petersburg by noon of the tenth. Moreover, the trains were picking up additional brigades in North Carolina—Hoke's, Evans', Clingman's, and Ransom's. Many of the delays had occurred upon the demoralized trackage below Wilmington; north thereof, the trains ran fairly smoothly. On the night of May 9 the Weldon telegraph informed Richmond that a total of five brigades had passed through and that two more— Kemper's and Corse's—were expected hourly. By the following morning the carriers, bridge damage and all, had brought into Petersburg nearly five thousand men. By the twelfth Colquitt had arrived, six days from Charleston, and only three from Wilmington.[13]

But it had been a close thing. Richmond remained in a state of nervous exhaustion, and the telegraph south continued to tap out demands for reinforcements. On May 15 the President ordered north practically all of the organized infantry and cavalry in the South Carolina department. In the end the region was not laid quite bare, but for a full month the rumble of troop trains seldom ceased. A typical movement was that of the 12th Georgia Battalion, 410 men, which pulled out of Charleston on May 18, and was reported passing Weldon at seven o'clock on the morning of the twenty-first. This was not fast running, but at least the reinforcements came on steadily. However, the current did not maintain its volume indefinitely. Early in June, because of Union demonstrations along the coast, a counterflow was established in the direction of Charleston again.[14]

Though the railroads had been of unquestionable aid in staving off disaster at Petersburg, a disquieting trend was evident. The carriers could not transport men as rapidly as theretofore. In September, 1863, they had taken Benning's Brigade 775 miles from Richmond to Atlanta in about four days, but in May, 1864, it required six days for Colquitt's command to cover the 433 miles from Charleston to Petersburg. The Nottoway-Stony Creek gap served, of course, to delay matters, but the comparison was frightening. The return of Longstreet from east Tennessee to Charlottesville had been nearly as slow. In Richmond it was reported that the Virginia Central possessed sufficient rolling stock for 5,400 infantry only, without heavy baggage or horses.[15]

Railroads proved useful in John C. Breckinridge's picturesque little victory at New Market on May 15, but they performed appallingly at Lynchburg the following month. The latter incident was especially disturbing in that it involved neither long haul nor junction point. The task was to move General Jubal Early's Second Corps, now shrunk to scarcely eight thousand men, over sixty miles of the Orange & Alexandria from Charlottesville to Lynchburg, where Breckinridge faced the superior numbers of General David Hunter. But the Orange & Alexandria had lately been raided; all its rolling stock had been withdrawn to the comparative safety of Lynchburg. Before it could be used, it must be brought back to Charlottesville.[16]

This was awkward, but Early promptly made it worse. He nursed a profound distrust of Orange & Alexandria Superintendent Vandegrift and refused to leave Charlottesville until every piece of motive power and rolling equipment first had been brought in from Lynchburg. Breckinridge had supposed the whole Second Corps would arrive by noon of June 17, but the first train did not leave Charlottesville until eight that morning. Moreover, its speed averaged only twelve miles per hour and it did not reach Lynchburg until one o'clock. The remaining trains straggled in much later, many of them in the course of the night. Even then only half of Early's command had been brought forward, and it was necessary to run the empty cars back for the remaining troops. These did not all arrive until the evening of the eighteenth, and even then the Corps artillery still remained in Charlottesville. The leading elements had come in time to repulse a Federal assault, but the succeeding units steamed in so tardily that Early dared not counterattack while the time was ripe. Lynchburg had indeed been saved, but the opportunity of a Union defeat of the first order had been missed. Probably Early should not have insisted upon one-way train dispatching, but the sickly condition of the Orange & Alexandria had been equally to blame.[17]

By the end of 1864 signs of impotence were stronger still. On December 22 a heavy Federal raid upon Gordonsville was reported, and two brigades were withdrawn from the Richmond trenches and ordered up the Virginia Central to meet it. General Longstreet wanted the trains to leave at midnight, so that the troops might arrive in Gordonsville by daylight. Both brigades—3,300 strong—came tramping through the suburbs, but at the station they found but a single train waiting. This did pull out at midnight and reach Gordonsville shortly after dawn, but most of the soldiers were obliged to wait out the remainder of a chilly night before additional trains were provided. The Union advance was beaten off, but close calls of this nature were becoming too frequent.[18]

IV

While Grant battered at the Confederacy's head, William T. Sherman was slicing through its heart.

General Sherman had assumed command of the Military Division of the Mississippi on March 18, 1864. His responsibilities extended from the Appalachians into Arkansas, but already he had fixed his attention upon the state in which he was to find his real destiny—Georgia. Facing him there, its outposts strung along a low ridge known as Tunnel Hill, stood the Confederate Army of Tennessee, commanded now by Joseph E. Johnston.

Here began one of the decisive campaigns of the War Between the States. From the start it had a railroad background. From their positions on Tunnel Hill the southern pickets could look out over the rusting track of the Western & Atlantic as it curved away toward Ringgold and the Federal lines. As a result of last November's debacle at Chattanooga, twenty-five miles of the state road lay in enemy hands. The Western & Atlantic had become two railroads, each a supply artery for an army, and it was to remain in this divided condition until the fall of Atlanta ended its Confederate career.

Under Federal military operation the role of its partitioned section was a happier one than that of the portion remaining in southern hands. Above Ringgold the trains were operated briskly under the direction of the United States Military Railroad superintendent at Chattanooga. When additional rolling stock was required, it was provided. Upon Western & Atlantic land in Chattanooga rose a perfectly equipped machine shop. Beyond, far back into Tennessee and Kentucky, an elaborate defense system assured the uninterrupted passage of the trains from the banks of the Ohio, Cumberland, and Tennessee to the most advanced Federal depots.[19]

On May 7, in perfect campaigning weather, Sherman struck with 100,000 men. To oppose him the Army of Tennessee could at first muster no more than 45,000. But behind it, locomotives still could pull trains of decaying cars. From Mobile and eastern Mississippi they brought reinforcements—Cantey's Division and Loring's Division, more than ten thousand muskets, with the sturdy soldier-priest, Leonidas Polk, at their head. Cantey's men used the classic troop-train route through Montgomery and Atlanta and came swaying up through the hills just as the first rumble of battle drifted into Johnston's headquarters at Dalton. Loring's Division probably traveled through Selma to Blue Mountain, whence Polk himself directed them across country to the opposite railhead at Rome, where equipment from Atlanta had been concentrated. Loring's soldiers poured from the trains at Resaca on the tenth, eleventh, and twelfth. An extra contingent, French's Brigade, was past the Blue Mountain gap by the night of the sixteenth and were climbing aboard the cars at Rome, even taking with them some artillery. They detrained again at Calhoun, perhaps before dawn.[20]

Although Joseph E. Johnston was unquestionably skillful, he was painfully cautious. Finding before him a foe who feared to commit himself against superior numbers, Sherman had only to threaten a flank movement in order to force the Army of Tennessee backward along the Western & Atlantic Railroad from one defensive line to another. Tunnel Hill, Buzzard's Roost Gap, Dalton, Resaca, Kingston, were successively abandoned without decisive fighting.[21]

Nevertheless, Joseph E. Johnston was no fool. His disengaging movements were carried out expertly, and he was careful to move all Western & Atlantic rolling stock southward in advance of his withdrawals. He even made an effort to destroy the track he left behind. But delaying measures like these made little difference to the men of the United States Military Railroad. Reported General O. O. Howard of the Federal Army: "The rapidity with which the badly broken railroad was repaired seemed miraculous. We had hardly left Dalton before trains with ammunition and other supplies arrived. While our skirmishing was going on at Calhoun, the locomotive whistle sounded in Resaca. The telegraphers were nearly as rapid: the lines were in order to Adairsville on the morning of the eighteenth. While we were breaking up the state arsenal at Adairsville, caring for the wounded, and bringing in Confederate prisoners, word was telegraphed from Resaca that bacon, hardbread and coffee were already there at our service." [22]

Mid-June saw Johnston pushed fairly into the Georgia Piedmont. Despite a costly frontal attack upon the Confederates occupying the isolated peak called Kennesaw Mountain, Sherman's progress encountered no serious check, and July 17 found his advance columns across the Chattahoochee within sight of the church spires of Atlanta. Even here, four hundred miles from really friendly territory, the Federal pressure proved superior to that of a Confederate army ten miles from its principal base. For this President Davis blamed Johnston, and he was abruptly relieved of the command of the Army of Tennessee in favor of the brave but uncircumspect John B. Hood.[23]

The elevation of Hood saw the role of the Western & Atlantic as a part of the southern war effort nearly finished. A large part of its rolling stock already had been sent into the interior of the state. And now, among the gullied hills that fringed Atlanta, Sherman's divisions edged closer like enormous pincers. Against them the impetuous new commander hurled his veterans in vain. By the evening of July 22 the Federal left wing stood solidly across the track of the Georgia Railroad, midway between Atlanta and Decatur, breaking the best interior communication line remaining to the Confederacy. From this time forth transportation from Virginia and the Carolinas into Alabama and Mississippi would be confined to the uncertain route via Macon and Columbus. At month's end the Georgia Railroad could operate no farther west than Buck Head, ninety-six miles from Augusta.[24]

In a plea to Jefferson Davis for reinforcements Governor Brown had declared on June 28 that "[Atlanta] is to the Confederacy almost as important as the heart is to the human body." But now the heart remained connected with the rest of the South by only two overtaxed arteries: the Atlanta & West Point and the Macon & Western. Militia levies residing along the Georgia Railroad were obliged to proceed to the front via Augusta, Millen, and the line of the Central. Even the roads approaching Atlanta from south and west were found to be in deadly peril.[25]

Like Joseph E. Johnston, Sherman was not a man to fight unnecessary battles; he preferred to destroy his enemy's ability to make war. He was in no mood to carry Atlanta by storm, for he knew it was only a question of time before his pincers would impinge upon the city's last rail communications; when that happened, Hood would have to evacuate. In the meantime he might profitably vary his siege operations with slashing cavalry raids deep into the Confederate rear.

The first came without warning. On July 15, even before Sherman's masses had quite closed up to the defenses of Atlanta, a cloud of Federal horsemen, commanded by General Lovell H.

Rousseau, burst out of the hills of upper Alabama. At Talladega they paused long enough to destroy two small ordnance factories, the depot of the Alabama & Tennessee Rivers road, and several cars. But their real objective was the Montgomery & West Point. Moving rapidly through sparsely settled country, they descended upon the road at the lonely little station of Loachapoka on the seventeenth, nearly capturing Braxton Bragg, who had passed en-route to Montgomery only a few hours before. Rousseau found the line utterly unguarded, and his men turned to its ruin with gusto. Much of its track was of the "stringer" variety, as if designed for easy destruction. Before their departure the Federal troopers had wrecked no less than thirty miles, from a point near Chehaw all the way to Opelika and for a short distance down the Columbus branch. A scouting locomotive, running light with three employees aboard, steamed directly into their arms. The station buildings at Loachapoka, Notasulga, Auburn, and Opelika went up in smoke. At Opelika the Federal horsemen feasted upon government stores, put the torch to the remainder, destroyed six loaded freight cars, broke up a turntable and wye, and finally trotted off the way they had come.[26]

For the defenders of Atlanta this was serious; in two days they had lost their railroad connection to the grain-producing Black Belt and the munitions factories at Selma. The Quartermaster Office at Montgomery frantically advertised for two hundred wagons with teams and drivers to detour the destroyed section. The local department commander, General D. H. Maury, cut through command channels and ordered Major Whitfield of the Railroad Bureau to supervise the necessary reconstruction, using the iron of the Newbern branch of the Alabama & Mississippi Rivers road. The Engineer Bureau sent Lieutenant Colonel Meri-wether and, from Atlanta, Captain L. P. Grant. Even General Bragg endeavored to take charge; from Columbus, Georgia, he suggested, with the backing of interested citizens, the completion of the unfinished Montgomery-Union Springs-Girard route in lieu of the reconstruction of the narrow gauge Montgomery & West Point. Bragg's recommendation was echoed by General Hood.[27]

From the confusion one fact swiftly emerged: repair of the damage would consume less iron than the building of a new rail-road. The Union Springs scheme was quietly dropped, and by

August 14 Whitfield found himself back at his old task of track re-laying. With the aid of his Bureau colleague, Major Hottel, he pushed his gangs steadily forward. Before the end of the month the trains were running again over the whole Montgomery & West Point.[28]

But the Atlanta supply lines were not to suffer from Rousseau alone. On July 26 Sherman ordered two cavalry columns under Generals McCook and Stoneman to sweep southward on either side of the Macon railroad. Although the bulk of both units eventually was surrounded and captured, they did inflict considerable damage. At Lovejoy's, a small station twenty-six miles below Atlanta on the Macon & Western, McCook wrecked a mile and one-half of track and burned a wagon train. Following a brief shelling of Macon from the opposite bank of the Ocmulgee, Stoneman's raiders pounded eastward along the Central of Georgia main line. They left the bridges over Walnut Creek and the Oconee in flames. Between Macon and Oconee Station all brick depot buildings, water tanks and pumps were put to the torch, as was the station at Eatonton. At Gordon, where the Central's spur to Milledgeville and Eatonton left the main stem, they seriously damaged a collection of Western & Atlantic rolling stock which had been forwarded thence for safety. Saved only by the efforts of local citizens was a priceless consignment of shop machinery.[29]

Near Griswoldville, between Macon and Gordon, the Union horsemen seized a freight train, consisting of locomotive and twenty-seven cars. The cars they burned to their axles; the engine they detached and set rolling unattended down the line with open throttle. Without warning, it hurtled into Griswoldville and crashed into a standing passenger train crammed with refugees from the fighting zone. The rear coach was torn completely in two; most of the others were overturned or derailed. Yet none of the passengers sustained serious injury. The last car had been empty when the renegade locomotive ripped through it and had taken up most of the force of the impact.[30]

Although the raiders did not wreck Georgia communications beyond repair, their adventure had not been in vain. No trains could operate from the crossing of the Oconee to Macon for four weeks, and service could hardly have been restored even then had not duplicate bridge frames, prepared by the Engineer Bureau, been available in Macon. Seventeen passenger and thirty freight cars belonging to the Western & Atlantic had been ruined, and four engines of the same road had been seriously injured. For the remainder of the siege of Atlanta the defending army was denied the use of its last complete railroad connection with the Confederate northeast, and the effect of Stoneman's operations was alleviated only by the fact that the reinforcements which the destroyed equipment and bridges might have brought were not available

ing force were proving
c Macon & Western.
d by the delay of trains
graphed Hood's Chief
aac Scott on August 1.
g the run from Atlanta
rove a situation that al-
l days of August even
cuation of Atlanta was
rect, if ill-advised, action
tire passenger train was
ndaged casualties, put in
ut notifying any Macon
ere summarized later by
September, a collision oc-
een the Engine Dispatch
n, and the Engine Gover-
for Griffin, both being ir-
ary direction; both engines
x and one passenger car
many more seriously in-
office been regarded, the

ast kept in nearly constant
, nor a similar mission on
ceeded in interrupting the
road for more than a few days, ...gh Kilpatrick removed another mile or so of track and burned the depot at Jonesboro. When on the twenty-third the hoarse wail of the engines again announced the resumption of rail service to Atlanta, Sherman realized that he

must directly threaten the line with a substantial force of infantry if he were ever to force the evacuation of the city.[33]

Moreover, the northern army was in a theoretically dangerous position; it maintained contact with its bases at Nashville and Louisville only by several hundred miles of single-track railroad. Thrust deep into a hostile countryside, the isolation of Sherman invited a blow upon his communication line. Despite his love of frontal attacks, General Hood realized this as clearly as anyone else. Early in August, as the Federal grip upon Atlanta grew tighter, he ordered General Wheeler, with the greater part of the available southern cavalry, to sweep northward and wreck the Western & Atlantic and Nashville & Chattanooga roads. The Confederate horsemen embarked upon their mission with a will. A new Yankee bridge over the Etowah was burned out, the Confederate flag waved again briefly in Resaca and Dalton, and some thirty-five miles of Yankee iron were demolished. But the raiders were nowhere numerous enough to effect a permanent lodgment. "So vast were the facilities of the Federal commander," commented Hood after the war, "that we could not bring together a sufficient force of cavalry to accomplish the desired object . . . no sufficiently effective number of cavalry could be assembled in the Confederacy to interrupt the enemy's line of supplies to an extent to compel him to retreat." It is perhaps unnecessary to add that the reconstruction of thirty-five miles of railroad proved a routine matter to the United States Military Railroad. Once again the fighting spirit of the southern soldier broke itself against the rock of northern determination and industrial capacity.[34]

Time was running out for the Confederates in Atlanta. As the city shook to the explosions of his shells, Sherman steadily extended the right arm of his pincers about the southwestern outskirts until on August 29 it was in striking distance of the Macon & Western at Jonesboro. That the end was near was now apparent to all, although General Hardee's corps was sent hastily toward Jonesboro in a last effort to ward off the inevitable. Hood later declared that he foresaw the evacuation of Atlanta as early as August 28, at which time he instructed his chief quartermaster, ordnance officer, and commissary to load their stores upon railroad cars in preparation for a speedy departure. But the withdrawal, when it came, was carried out in panic. Over the city the night sky of August 31 pulsated with flashes as twenty-eight boxcars crammed with ammunition were fired by excited soldiers and blown from their wheels in a series of concussions that jarred the Union trenches in the suburbs. Over the Atlanta Rolling Mill a pillar of ruddy smoke rolled toward the stars. At the Macon & Western locomotive shed the engine N. C. Monroe, the famous General, and two other units belonging to the Western & Atlantic, were reduced to uselessness by maintenance crews under military order. Fifty-three additional freight cars, many of them loaded with quartermaster's stores, flamed in the yards. The troops scarcely noticed them as they shuffled dejectedly away.[35]

When the Federal columns swung into Atlanta on September 2, they were carrying out a mere formality. For the turntable of the Confederacy had ceased to function more than a month before, when Sherman's men had first bivouaced along the Georgia Railroad and had ended the operation of trains over the most direct route between the deep South, its grain fields and its armories, and Richmond.

CHAPTER

～ 20 ～

To Sea and Tennessee

"This may seem a hard species of warfare."—General
William Tecumseh Sherman, January 1, 1865.

I

"IT IS NOT TO BE DISGUISED," ASSERTED THE LEADING EDITORIAL
in the *Southern Recorder* of September 13, 1864, "that the possession of Atlanta by the enemy is a severe blow to Georgia and, we
may say, to the military operations of the Confederate Government." "A severe loss," commented Governor Brown two months
later. "It was most unfortunate," he continued, "that the Richmond
authorities had not concentrated upon Sherman's rail lines of communication," but "the powers that be determined upon a different
policy. The world knows the results." [1]

The fall of the city indeed was a terrible blow to what little hope
remained within the Confederacy. But the end was not yet. Sherman
may have dislocated the transportation net of the South; but he
had not directly injured Hood's army of forty thousand men,
which even then was reorganizing in the vicinity of Lovejoy's,
twenty-six miles south of Atlanta on the Macon & Western. Although Hood seems for the moment to have lost something of his
aggressive spirit (he was currently tearing up the track of the
Macon & Western as far as Barnesville and talked of destroying the
Georgia road as far east as its crossing of the Oconee), it still could
be argued that the military situation was not so hopeless as it
appeared. [2]

But southern optimists reckoned without General Sherman.

256

A prisoner of war. One of the locomotives abandoned by the Confederates when they evacuated Atlanta. This is probably an Atlanta & West Point machine and is not the famous General of the Western & Atlantic. From the Pictorial Supplement of *Official Records of the War of the Rebellion.*

Above, the roundhouse of the Georgia Railroad at Atlanta, from a photograph taken by G. N. Barnard in the summer of 1865. The locomotive in the foreground is the Telegraph; on the turntable, the O. A. Bull. Under arch (to right of center) is the E. Y. Hill; thence (from right to left) the Hercules, the M. P. Stovall, and the E. L. Ellsworth. The Hercules and the Stovall are the property of the Georgia Railroad; the Hill (a Federal re-name) belongs to the Western & Atlantic. The others are Atlantic & West Point units. University of North Carolina Library.

Below, ruins of rolling mill and wrecked tracks of the Georgia Railroad, Atlanta, after Hood's evacuation, showing the remnants of exploded boxcars. From a photograph by G. N. Barnard. Library of Congress. "Over the city the night sky of August 31 pulsated with flashes as twenty-eight boxcars crammed with ammunition were fired by excited soldiers and blown from their wheels in a series of concussions that jarred the Union trenches in the suburbs."

Solidly ensconced in Atlanta, from which he presently expelled the civilian population, the Federal commander harbored no serious intention of bringing Hood to battle. He understood, perhaps better than any other man, the real implications of modern warfare and selected the slower, but far safer, course: so to wreck the southern capacity to supply and renew the Confederate armies that they would be unable to exert an effective pressure upon the field of battle. Such a program involved, of course, the destruction of railroads on an unprecedented scale.

Before Sherman could perfect his plan, he was obliged to await some indication of what Hood would do. And the latter dawdled for nearly a month, seemingly uncertain of his next move. But there remained, after all, only one strategy which could promise success: a descent not merely by cavalry squadrons, but by the entire Confederate force, upon the Federal supply artery.

With this in view, the Army of Tennessee at last began to move northward on the first of October, marching through the tangled country to the west of the Western & Atlantic. Although a diversion against the line in the vicinity of Allatoona proved unsuccessful, Hood's columns continued their trudge, again veered temporarily in the direction of the road, captured Dalton with its garrison of seventeen hundred men, and destroyed more than twenty miles of track between Resaca and Tunnel Hill.[3]

Still uncertain of Hood's intentions, Sherman followed warily with the bulk of his army, and had carried his pursuit into northeastern Alabama before he became convinced that the Confederates planned no early return to Georgia. On October 26, he turned about and marched rapidly back to Atlanta.[4]

The Confederate progress in the direction of central Tennessee was apparently a serious threat, but Sherman had by this time decided upon his specific plan of campaign. As Hood pressed westward through the Cumberlands, the personnel of the United States Military Railroad labored to repair the damage to the Western & Atlantic. Presently the exhaust of the Federal locomotives echoed again from the hills as final consignments of food and ammunition moved into Atlanta and the residue of the Federal sick and wounded was carried away toward Chattanooga and Nashville. For Sherman now envisaged no less than a march to the sea, in the course of which he proposed not only to live off the country, but to destroy once and for all the capacity of middle Georgia to make war.[5]

That destruction he applied first to his old line of communication. For the last time the Western & Atlantic felt the hand of war as Federal wrecking parties carried ruin to eighty-four miles of track between Atlanta and Resaca, heating the rails upon flaming piles of ties and twisting them into uselessness. Above Resaca the iron was pried loose for twenty miles more and deposited at Dalton and beyond, where it would remain in Union hands. Every station, save that at Allatoona, was burned to the ground. The Etowah River bridge was dismantled and carried to the rear for storage. Every piece of rolling stock except two cars was either removed or smashed beyond repair. The derelict munitions plants at Rome were put to the torch. And as the columns of smoke rolled across the autumn sky, they marked the funeral pyres not merely of a railroad, but of a cause.[6]

Nor did Atlanta escape the holocaust. Everything in the city that possibly could prove useful in the waging of war was set afire, including the residue of rolling stock, the already half-ruined car and locomotive facilities, and the odd, barnlike Union Station. When on November 16 the Federal commander marched out of the city for the last time at the head of sixty-eight thousand selected veterans, all that remained of the chief transportation center of the Confederate States was a blackened shell, over which a pall of smoke still hung.[7]

II

The story of Sherman's March to the Sea requires no retelling here except as it involved the railroads of Georgia and their capacity to serve the Confederacy. Sherman's "bummers" have been accused of impartial destruction wherever they went, but their special prey was certainly railroads. Along practically the whole of their route the fate of the Western & Atlantic was re-enacted; tracks were torn up with a terrible precision; stations and bridges and rolling stock were consigned to the flames. Reported Sherman: "In the destruction of the iron rails, mechanical skill vied with native ingenuity in doing most effective work. The chief engineer designed a machine for twisting the rails after heating them in the fires made from burning cross ties, carrying them red hot and twisting them around the trunks of trees, or warping them in such fantastic ways that they were useless except for old iron. About three hundred miles of railroad were destroyed in this way." [8]

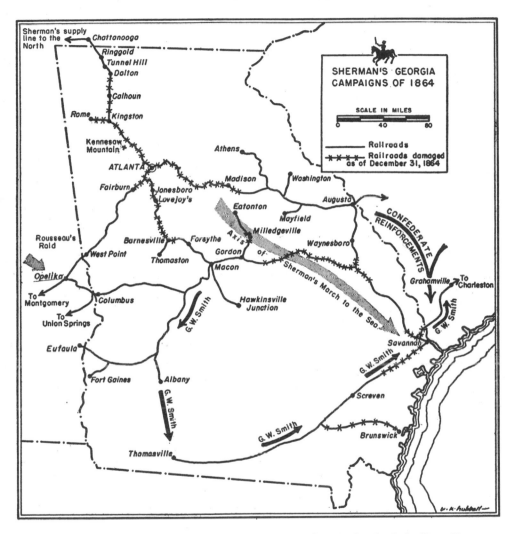

Of the trackage thus worked over, the Federals left literally nothing but the embankments. Complete ruin marked the line of the West Point road between Atlanta and Fairburn, and the Georgia Railroad presented a similar picture from the same city to its crossing of the Oconee beyond Madison. Eastward from Walnut Creek, the Georgia Central main stem was completely demolished to the Little Ogeechee, forty-six miles from Savannah. Upon its Eatonton branch, six miles of track were destroyed, plus the passenger and freight stations at Milledgeville, the station and engine houses at Eatonton, and the bridges over Fishing Creek and Little River. Along the old Augusta & Savannah road between Augusta and Millen, the toll was ten miles of track, three stations, one locomotive, and several cars. And when in December the Yankee divisions closed in on Savannah, fourteen additional miles of main line experienced similar destruction. All told, 139 miles of the Central system were practically obliterated. The Macon & Western fared a little better, but between the efforts of Hood and Sherman all but five and one-half miles of the road between Forsythe and Atlanta were torn up.[9]

This, not Appomattox, was the Confederate Götterdämmerung.

Southern resistance was little more than a formality. Hood's Army was now far away and was presently to waste its substance in futile frontal assaults at Franklin and Nashville. The three thousand Georgia Militia, cowering upon the sidelines at Macon, could not possibly fight in the open field. The thin squadrons of Wheeler's cavalry that clung to the Federal flanks could deliver no more than fleabites. From Atlanta to the coastal marshes, Sherman moved virtually unopposed.

There was considerable uncertainty at first as to the Federal objective. Until November 19 Governor Brown's principal move was to devote some of the state road's equipment to the removal of the sick and wounded from the immediate vicinity of the enemy. But by that date Sherman's intentions became clearer, and from Milledgeville came a ringing proclamation of a levy-en-masse of the male population of Georgia. It is interesting to note that even this scraping of the manpower barrel exempted railroad employees, though their status was subject to the following qualification: "All railroad companies in this State will transport all persons applying for transportation to the front, and in case anyone refuses, its president, superintendent, agents and employees will be immediately sent to the front."[10]

With Sherman's seasoned infantry advancing at a rate of from ten to fifteen miles per day, even desperate measures were not enough. There remained neither the time nor the resources to collect, organize, equip, and train the whole of a state's male population. Moreover, not many men of military age were left. And so the weight of the defense fell upon the handful of Georgia militia already mobilized near Macon, upon the relatively small Confederate force under General Hardee in Savannah, and upon whatever casuals could be assembled from the vicinity of Augusta, Charleston, and adjacent regions of South Carolina. The sole hope, though a forlorn one, lay in the concentration of these scattered elements. And with Sherman heading straight for the sea, they could be placed in front of him only by rail.

The position of the Georgia militia at Macon was especially awkward. It could not move directly to Savannah; Sherman interposed, and a large portion of the Central main line already was a shambles. But there remained a lengthy and discontinuous alternative: the 104 miles of the Southwestern road from Macon to Albany, thence an empty gap of 62 miles to Thomasville, beyond which the Atlantic & Gulf led toward Savannah through a portion of the state as yet remote from Union patrols. It was scarcely a satisfactory route, but no other existed. On November 25 General Gustavus W. Smith packed the militia into as much Southwestern rolling stock as could be assembled and went rattling off toward Albany.[11]

The Southwestern road occupied the calmest backwater of the state; its track and equipment had suffered no damage save that incident to wear and tear. Its trains drew into Albany almost like clockwork, and by noon of the twenty-eighth the last regiment was tramping into Thomasville. Then came the inevitable flaw. Instead of the five trains ordered, the Atlantic & Gulf had provided only two, and it was long after dark before these could wheeze off with a single brigade of twelve hundred men. And their progress was so creeping that they did not reach Savannah until two o'clock on the morning of the thirtieth.[12]

They came none too soon. The Charleston & Savannah road was at that moment threatened by raiding parties from the enemy coastal command, and Smith was instructed to keep his first two trainloads aboard the cars and continue to Grahamville, South Carolina. When informed that they were being taken out of Georgia in violation of state regulations, some of the men expressed certain unmilitary, and very American, opinions, but within a few minutes their trains were lumbering over the connecting track across the city to the Central and Charleston lines. Confronted with a *fait accompli*, the soldiers ceased their grumbling and were in high spirits when they issued from the cars at Grahamville at about eight o'clock. They accomplished their mission: as the Union advance approached the vital railroad, the moss-hung forest exploded with musketry, and the Charleston & Savannah remained a Confederate artery a little longer. The victorious militia were safely back on Georgia soil at ten that night.[13]

Once started, the reinforcements from Augusta and Charleston came in more rapidly, and in greater numbers. Three thousand left Augusta on the afternoon of the twenty-ninth, and others left Charleston at the same time. Two thousand passed Summerville, South Carolina, at noon on December 1. Thirteen hundred more drew out of Augusta on the second. On the morning of the sixth two trains of infantry from Wilmington and one loaded with light artillery from Georgia were reported standing on the Charleston side of the Ashley River, waiting for the Savannah road to clear. A shipment of North Carolina state troops was expected there shortly after midnight. Twenty cars of Georgia soldiers crossed the Ashley at 10:00 p.m. Another contingent came down the South Carolina road in the early morning hours of the eighth. All were hurried forward as fast as the railroaders and quartermasters could send them. Already Hardee had telegraphed that Sherman's advance threatened the line between Savannah and the Savannah River bridge, and by the tenth the bluecoats had poured across the track almost within sight of the city. They reached, and burned, the bridge on the following day.[14]

Just how many reinforcements the railways managed to deliver to Hardee is difficult to estimate. It does not matter; they were not enough. Leaving behind them a trail of destruction, Sherman's divisions early in December reached the Ogeechee salt marshes. Even in faraway Richmond, pessimism reigned. On the fifth, Quartermaster General Lawton quietly telegraphed his old business friend, President Cuyler of the Central of Georgia, to move the equipment of the Central and Gulf roads out of Savannah to Columbia, via Charleston. Cuyler complied only in part; he had the trains withdrawn, but in the opposite direction, down the Atlantic & Gulf. While fleeing in one of them on the seventh, he and his brother were taken prisoners by a fast-driving Federal column and presently were enjoying an interview with Sherman himself. It was not an unpleasant meeting; another Cuyler had been a surgeon in the old army and an intimate friend of the Federal commander. After a brief chat, wherein the Central's president incautiously divulged some military information, the brothers were released.[15]

The treatment accorded the Gulf Railroad was not so kind. Federal wrecking parties tore it to pieces as far as the Altamaha, and for the remainder of the war its eastern terminus was at Screven, Georgia, seventy miles short of Savannah. "Even if I do not take Savannah," Sherman wrote Grant on December 18, "I will leave it in a bad way."[16]

But the city already was practically bagged. When a brave attempt to defend the bastion of Fort McAllister collapsed within fifteen minutes in the face of overwhelming numbers, Hardee began his preparations for evacuation. Before the Union columns had cut the Charleston railroad, he had directed the irreplaceable machinery in the old Central of Georgia shops removed to Madison, Georgia, for safekeeping. The few engines and cars remaining in the city he ordered burned or smashed. He had insufficient time to destroy his artillery and ammunition and some twenty-five thousand bales of cotton, and on the night of December 20 his dejected garrison crossed the river into South Carolina. They could not utilize railroad transportation now until they reached Hardeeville. Sherman entered Savannah the following day and presently was sending his famous "Christmas gift" telegram to President Lincoln.[17]

III

While Sherman was as yet only toying with his idea of a march to the sea, Hood had already embarked upon an even more grandiose program. He would move into Tennessee, smash the Union forces there, sweep to the Ohio, turn to Virginia, join Lee, crush Grant, march on Washington, dictate terms. Hood's eyes glowed as his tattered columns swung into the Cumberlands through the October sunshine.

There existed, apparently, a single difficulty—logistics. The plateaus of northern Alabama were not mid-Georgia, fat with food and forage, and as yet untouched by enemy hands. The Army of

Tennessee, though little more than half as large as the force Sherman took to Savannah, could not live off the country. It must be supplied from elsewhere. That meant railroads; even the sanguine Hood realized that wagon transportation could hardly carry the burden alone.

The local railroad picture was not satisfactory. In northeastern Alabama the Memphis & Charleston and the Nashville & Chattanooga were either wrecked or guarded by well-fortified Federal garrisons that would be costly to dislodge. The Alabama & Tennessee Rivers road still extended no further than Blue Mountain. The Mobile & Ohio survived as far north as Corinth, and a disused fragment of the Memphis & Charleston thence ran eastward thirty-six miles to Cherokee, Alabama; but the former had suffered from recent washouts, and the latter was overgrown with brambles and briars.[18]

Yet these lines through Corinth furnished the most promising route of supply for a Confederate advance into Tennessee. As early as October 8 Hood, while still maneuvering through the Georgia hills, telegraphed General Bragg requesting the repair of the Mobile & Ohio and Memphis & Charleston as far as Decatur, Alabama. And instead of marching directly on Nashville, he swung his army in a long westward detour, so as to have their rails behind him before he began his final drive.[19]

Major George Whitfield was by now the recognized authority upon railroad rehabilitation in the States of Alabama and Mississippi. Yet he received no inkling of Hood's intentions until certain heavy equipment arrived at Blue Mountain for shipment around the Selma-Meridian-Corinth circle. The whole Confederate chain of command had become, in fact, hopelessly tangled. Bragg was only a "military adviser" to Jefferson Davis, and Hood himself was not quite supreme in his own sphere. He now directed the Army of Tennessee under the broad supervision of General Beauregard, whom Richmond had recently sent down as commander of the "Military Division of the West." It was Beauregard who at last, on October 23, issued formal orders for the repair of the Mobile & Ohio and the Memphis & Charleston. By then Hood's infantry were fast approaching their proposed railhead.[20]

As was inevitable, the task was delegated to Whitfield. With a small force of impressed Negroes, loaned by Engineer detachments at Mobile and Demopolis, he went so earnestly to work that on the sixth of November he had put existing trackage in "tolerably safe" condition as far as Cherokee, Alabama. But he lacked the means to extend the iron rapidly to the point where Hood most needed it—to Decatur and a junction with the direct line to Nashville. "The Negroes and white men I have worked on railroads,"

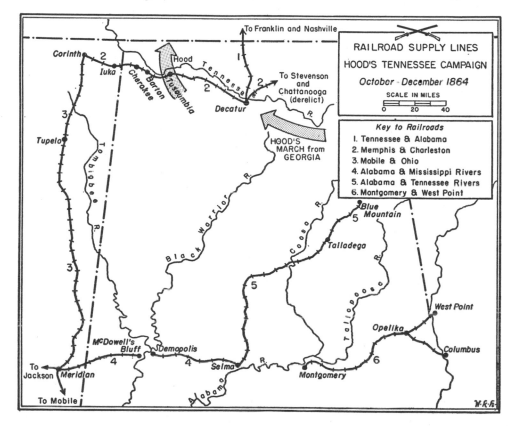

he wrote Sims, "have been badly clothed and fed and never paid. This was because I was dependent upon the Medical Director for medical attention, to the Commissary for provisions, and to other officers for clothing and paying the men." But if he thus blamed others for his difficulties, he was always ready to receive credit for his accomplishments. "I am happy to say," he remarked in the same letter, "that we moved the stores as rapidly as they were ready and no blame can be attached to your Department, having the papers to show that we did our whole duty." [21]

Whatever Whitfield's failings, he was persistent. On November 18 the trains were running nearly to Barton, five miles beyond Cherokee, and day by day, bar by bar, the track crept eastward. He became so absorbed that he neglected the movement of freight over existing rails, and for all his happy statements to Sims, supplies came in very slowly. General Hood complained that the Mobile & Ohio would not permit the operation of its cars over the Memphis & Charleston, and stores of all sorts began to choke wayside stations. With Whitfield deep in his construction program, the task of traffic control fell to Major Edward Willis, Beauregard's staff quartermaster. But the real trouble was the customary lack of rolling stock, especially boxcars; canvas was scarce, and flats could not be used in many cases because of the autumn rains. By the end of November the situation on the M. & O. had become so bad that even Whitfield was obliged to give it his personal attention. Hood at last departed upon his great adventure, but the tardy flow of supplies had delayed him for three exasperating—and vital—weeks.[22]

Worse was to come. The Federals were quick to realize the significance of the Mobile & Ohio, and from late November onward took pains to pepper it with raids. The first thrusts did little damage, but the southern defensive response was pitifully insufficient. The tatterdemalion Mississippi militia rushed up and down the threatened road, always two or three days behind the Federal troopers. Clanton's Brigade of 350 dismounted cavalry received orders to move from Opelika, Alabama, to Meridian on November 24, but despite repeated appeals for haste, it had proceeded, by December 3, only as far as Montgomery, and the remainder of its journey—down the Alabama River to Selma, the train ride to Demopolis, the ferrying of the Tombigbee, and the final railroad move into Meridian—consumed three additional days. Even when concentrated, no such rag-tag and bobtail force could parry any businesslike Union blow, and this came in the final week of December. Though of brief duration, the raid of Brigadier General B. H. Grierson was reminiscent of Sherman. His command did not advance in a solid mass, but in scattered parties which hit and ran over the whole of northern Mississippi. Their movements threw the Confederates into turmoil. Attempts to bring up reinforcements by rail were marked by mechanical breakdowns, garbled schedules, locomotives running out of water, and the actual capture of some of the troop trains. When the Yankees had galloped off again, they left behind destroyed bridges and trestles of an aggregate length of four miles, fourteen smashed locomotives, ninety-five gutted cars, and ten miles of ruined track. Although part of the damage had been borne by the Mississippi Central, the worst destruction had been dealt the Mobile & Ohio between Tupelo and Okalona.[23]

This was serious. Even before the coming of Grierson the wreck of Hood's army had begun its retreat from the fields of Franklin and Nashville. And now, on Christmas Day, as it recrossed the Tennessee, it found its rail communications gone. There was momentary panic at Confederate headquarters, which pondered briefly whether the remnant could be supplied by wagon train from Blue Mountain. But in the end the army staggered on, past Tuscumbia, Iuka, and the ancient bastion of Corinth, thence southward to Tupelo. It was a miserable march, but the situation would have been even worse had it not been for Major Whitfield and Colonel J. C. Cole, commanding the infantry reserves in northeastern Mississippi. Together they put gangs of Negroes to work upon the Mobile & Ohio while its bridges yet smouldered, and within six days the trains were running once more into Corinth. So excellent a performance brought commendation from above and served, of course, as the occasion for another exercise in self-praise by Whitfield.[24]

Back on an operating railroad, Hood's decimated brigades could rest and reorganize. The engines coughed like consumptives, but they brought supplies—more supplies than any wagon train could carry. The Army of Tennessee survived to fight one more day.

❧ 21 ❧

The Final Effort

I

By December, 1864, the decision against the Confederacy already had been rendered. The Federal power not only was pounding its armies to pieces from without; it was tearing the southern structure apart from within. In the course of his march to the sea, Sherman had well-nigh eliminated the lingering advantage of interior lines; of the approximately one thousand miles of railroad in Georgia, nearly 450 had been reduced to ruin. Every carrier entering Atlanta and Savannah had suffered heavily, the Western & Atlantic probably worst of all. Indeed, this road scarcely existed any longer, and it was not until the middle of March, 1865, that an attempt was made merely to replace the tracks in its Atlanta yards to hold the remnant of its rolling stock. Much of the equipment of the Central road had been saved, but 139 miles of its track, plus a large proportion of its fixed property, had been obliterated. Moreover, Sherman presently would quit the soil of Georgia to march with fire and sword through the Carolinas. Yet in the face of everything—burned plantations, disintegrating armies, famine, and casualties—many of the southern people strove to rebuild and fight on.[1]

Significantly, the military turned first to the shattered Georgia railroads. Gutted homes, ravaged crops, even smashed rolling mills, could wait. But if the Confederacy was to survive for more than a few weeks, the trains would have to run again. There lacked not volunteers for the task; indeed, they were so numerous as to get in each other's way. From Augusta General Bragg blandly ordered the "immediate" repair of the Georgia Railroad to Atlanta. Beaure-

gard hastened to get the work under way by appropriating the
services of Major Hottel of the Railroad Bureau. The Engineer
Bureau entered the field with Lieutenant Colonel Meriwether of
the Iron Commission and Captain L. P. Grant of its Atlanta office.
They later were supplemented by Major E. T. D. Myers. Someone
asked Sims to take over. Beauregard added his chief quartermaster,
Major Edward Willis, to the stew, with jurisdiction over Hottel.
The War Department endeavored to place Captain Grant in charge
of everything. Late in December President Cuyler of the Central
of Georgia appeared in Macon and brought forth a program of
his own.[2]

This could be disastrous. Beauregard's adjutant, Colonel George
William Brent, noted that Hottel and Meriwether were engaged
upon the same project, but under different orders. Willis resented
the competition of Captain Grant. When Meriwether desired to
seize the rails of the Mobile & Girard, and approached Brent for
the necessary authority, the administrative confusion was such that
Brent feared to grant it, and the matter was kicked through channels to the Secretary of War. A *modus vivendi* was finally established, wherein Beauregard assumed general direction of activities
through Major Willis, Major Hottel was charged with the reconstruction of the Atlanta & West Point, Captain Grant confined
himself to the Georgia road, and Meriwether and Myers selected
the trackage from which iron was to be taken. Repairs upon the
Central fell chiefly upon company forces. Thereafter things progressed more smoothly.[3]

Under the circumstances it was obvious that all of the wrecked
Georgia roads could not be restored. Even Cuyler despaired of
placing his line back in operation in its original form. The best he
could propose was the rehabilitation of the main stem as far east
as Gordon, plus repair of the branch that ran thence to Milledgeville and Eatonton. From the latter a space of only about twenty-
five miles intervened to Madison upon the Georgia road. Nothing
could be done below Gordon, and on the thirty-first of December
the Central simply discharged the majority of its employees.[4]

With Savannah in Union hands, the Central no longer loomed
large as a military route, and the army devoted most of its energy
to the Atlanta & West Point and Georgia roads. Early in January,
1865, the Engineer Bureau estimated that these could be rebuilt

by February 20. The Atlanta & West Point was actually opened for limited operation by January 20, but progress upon the Georgia road lagged, a fact due (it was alleged) to the inefficiency of Captain Grant as well as to the greater extent of the work. Grant announced plaintively that he would be unable to finish until mid-April, and Hottel was instructed to transfer his laborers to the other side of Atlanta and work eastward until he met Grant's force. The end of the Confederacy had come, however, before trains could run again from Augusta to Atlanta. The stump of the Central did better; it re-established service between Macon and Milledgeville before the New Year.[5]

The presence of the Federals in Savannah likewise lent urgency to the construction of two entirely new roads. One, a direct line from Columbia to Augusta, had been the subject of casual discussion since 1858 and the object of equally desultory construction since the summer of 1864. Now its management, and the South Carolina Assembly, cited Sherman as justification for immediate government aid. The other scheme, a connection between Thomasville and Albany, Georgia, was urged by President John Screven of the Atlantic & Gulf as a through interior route from Florida; it was endorsed by Lieutenant Colonel Sims and actually authorized by the Georgia legislature on March 11, 1865. Needless to say, neither of these lines ever carried a car of Confederate property.[6]

The work actually accomplished was difficult enough. Ordinary labor could be impressed—an appeal from Beauregard to Governor Brown brought in a thousand Negroes before the end of December. But bridge-carpenters were scarce and had to be searched for in the army. Certain tasks required real specialists, and to remove the unexploded shells that lay buried in certain cuttings on the Atlanta & West Point, Beauregard attempted to utilize Federal prisoners. This, however, was prevented by the regional commandant of prisons, General John H. Winder, an act which belied his reputation for brutishness.[7]

But the chief stumbling-block was, inevitably, rail and fastenings. By this time no one expected to secure any new iron; from the first it was assumed that materials would have to be taken from existing lines. But which should be sacrificed? Every railroad official in Georgia knew the answer: the other fellow's road. When informed that the army desired the rails of his Warrenton, Washington, and Athens branches, President King of the Georgia Railroad filled the air with lamentations, though a portion of the impressed iron was intended for use upon his own main stem. The seizure of twelve miles of rail and fastenings from the Augusta branch of the Central literally killed Richard Cuyler; exhausted and heartbroken, he died suddenly on April 19. The Macon & Brunswick, with the active support of the mayor of Macon, so stubbornly defended its iron that the army ultimately secured only two and one-half miles. Even the military were unable always to agree upon whose track should be taken. Colonel Sims provided some iron from the government connections in Augusta and Montgomery. In the end, the most satisfactory iron mine was the Fort Gaines branch of the Southwestern road, twenty miles of which were commandeered during February.[8]

II

With Sherman triumphant in Savannah, the Army of Northern Virginia withering slowly in the Petersburg trenches, and the Army of Tennessee encamped half-shattered at Tupelo, the Confederate command could only return to the strategy it had used so often—concentration. Even this provided little more than a forlorn hope. But unless the remaining southern armies east of the Mississippi could combine against either Grant or Sherman, or keep Grant and Sherman apart, the day of the Confederacy was done.

Hood, his confidence gone, and soon to retire from active command, took little part in the planning, which fell primarily to Beauregard. That the Army of Tennessee should turn east to confront its old adversary, Sherman, seems to have occurred to him before the March to the Sea was over, and by the end of 1864 he already was discussing the project with Richmond. In mid-January Major Whitfield completed a survey of railroad capabilities in Mississippi and Alabama; he found the carriers alarmingly decrepit and suggested that the artillery be shipped by river as far as Montgomery. Nevertheless, he remained hopeful. "I think we should be able to move from 2,500 to 3,000 men a day, easy," he concluded.[9]

The size of this last major troop move by rail in the Southern Confederacy remains uncertain. An "official return" of January 20 showed 17,709 infantry and artillery in the Army of Tennessee, but 4,000 of these were left behind to help in the defense of Mobile. The number on furlough also was large, and General Joseph E. Johnston later declared that only about 5,000 actually reached North Carolina. Whatever their real strength, the three corps that gathered beside the Mobile & Ohio tracks to depart upon their last campaign, were but shadows.[10]

Much of their route, even their destination, remained vague. For the moment their orders directed them to proceed to Augusta, not via Atlanta, which still was a shambles, but through Columbus, Macon, and Milledgeville. Over a portion of the way they would have to march on foot.[11]

Lee's Corps was first to leave Tupelo at dawn on January 19. Additional trains were at first provided fairly rapidly, but once the men were started, they encountered constant delays. Lee's Corps was routed over the Alabama & Mississippi Rivers road, and five days later its vanguard was hardly beyond Montgomery. Soon the congestion at Demopolis and Selma was such that the current corps commander, General Stevenson, recommended that all succeeding units move via Mobile. The soldiers were reported to be misbehaving in the course of the tedious stop-overs. In the end the central route was practically abandoned in favor of that through Mobile.[12]

Thenceforth things went more smoothly, though not sufficiently so to satisfy the military. By the twenty-sixth all of Lee's and one division of Cheatham's Corps were on their way, but the quartermasters at Tupelo complained of the "great irregularity" of the trains. Even along the Mobile route, enormous confusion developed when troops arrived at junction points (Pollard, Alabama, especially) without advance notice. There was, in fact, no proper supervision, although Beauregard's quartermaster, Major Willis, was supposed to exercise a general control. Even with the best of coordination, physical deficiencies would have caused delays. All of Stewart's and much of Cheatham's Corps were obliged to march from Tupelo down the Mobile & Ohio to West Point, fifty-one miles, before trains could be found for them.[13]

Beyond Augusta the Army of Tennessee encountered chaos. Sherman was in motion again, cutting a swath through South Carolina. By mid-February whole sections of the South Carolina Railroad had been torn up by the roots, and the Union infantry were closing in on Columbia. The little city gave way to panic,

Above, Confederate Life Line. The Western & Atlantic Railroad at Allatoona Pass, Georgia. Note piles of locomotive wood beside shed at right. From a photograph by G. N. Barnard. Library of Congress.

Below, Northern soldiers and civilians pose beside a derelict Richmond & Petersburg locomotive in fallen Richmond, April, 1865. The Virginia State House appears in background at right. Library of Congress.

Above, Lee's last supply line. The South Side Railroad at Appomattox Station, Virginia, shortly after the surrender. Note condition of track and remains of train destroyed by Sheridan's troopers. Library of Congress.

Below, Sheridan leaves a momento. Wreckage of the Richmond, Fredericksburg & Potomac Railroad bridge over the North Anna River, Virginia, May, 1864. Library of Congress.

amid scenes suggestive of Atlanta. Civilians and military mobbed the railroad stations. To evacuate the machinery of the arsenal, ordnance officers ordered thirty boxcars; they got four, which never were moved. They did make away with some ammunition, but only by virtue of strong-arm methods. "I returned to the cars at twelve at night," one of them later reported, "and attempted to get a car, but found it impossible. My mechanics came up with their personal effects, and we found a car (freight) filled with some Treasury employees and their baggage. These we turned out by force, put aboard the ammunition (no easy task) and by dint of threats succeeded in getting the car switched on the train then about to start. In the meantime the city was in the wildest terror. The army had been withdrawn, the straggling cavalry and rabble were stripping warehouses and railroad depots, and the city was illuminated by burning cotton." [14]

Sherman demolished the railroads of South Carolina as thoroughly as those of Georgia. When he quitted the state its steam communications had been utterly disrupted. He had nearly erased the South Carolina road from the map. The old main line was gone between the Edisto and Windsor; its Columbia branch was little more than a smoking scar through the woods. Terminal facilities in Columbia had suffered the same fate as those in Atlanta. Above the capital the tracks were gone from the Spartanburg & Union, from Alston to its crossing of the Broad River. Northern wrecking parties had obliterated the Charlotte & South Carolina as far as Black Stocks Depot. The Cheraw & Darlington was broken up in a score of places. All told, the state lost, at the hands of Sherman, nearly two hundred line miles of railroad.[15]

When the first trains bearing the Army of Tennessee rolled into Augusta, the soldiers could only clamber from the cars and start trudging across country. Neither they nor their officers knew clearly where they were going. The Confederate answer to Sherman was at first little more than a confused effort to get cotton and military stores out of his way and to concentrate scattered military units against him. The latter seemed a particularly hopeless task. The Tennessee corps soon were wandering all over the Piedmont. From Charleston came Hardee with the sweepings of the old coastal forces. Strewn over the countryside was a peppering of local defense organizations. "It would scarcely have been possible," said General Wade Hampton, "to disperse a force more effectively." [16]

For the moment Beauregard remained in general command. He planned at first to assemble the available troops at Chester, South Carolina, or at Charlotte, both railroad points above Columbia. Two days later he thought that Greensboro would be better. Two more days and he chose Salisbury. By this time the situation appears to have rather unbalanced him, for we find him telegraphing President Davis that he fully intended to crush Sherman, move against Grant, then "march on Washington to dictate a peace." [17]

The fall of Wilmington served to bring Beauregard back into focus. Though a disaster of major proportions, it at least simplified the picture. No longer could the Confederates in South Carolina hope to use the coastal railways to get in front of Sherman. If they were to utilize steam at all, they would have to assemble quickly at the nearest up-country railhead. Realizing this, Beauregard on February 23 designated Chester again as the assembly point for the majority of his units.[18]

Even the inland route around Sherman's advance had its difficulties. From Chester the five-foot Charlotte & South Carolina led to Charlotte, whence the four-foot-eight-and-one-half-inch North Carolina Railroad ran in a crescent through Salisbury, Greensboro, and Raleigh to Goldsboro. Not only did this require a change of cars, but a considerable quantity of rolling stock salvaged from the South Carolina carriers could not be run through. To get the equipment further from danger, Beauregard requested authority from Quartermaster General Lawton to widen the tracks to Danville. Lawton obliged, and within a day or so, military details were shifting the rails along the forty-three-mile leg to Salisbury. But Beauregard and Lawton reckoned without the North Carolina Governor, Zebulon Vance. From Salisbury the narrow-gauge Western North Carolina road ran west toward the Blue Ridge and, Vance, a son of the hill counties, had no intention of seeing it cut off. Even the Confederate field command feared to defy him and when the squabble was referred to the new Secretary of War, John C. Breckinridge, it was the Governor who showed the better staying power. Breckinridge endeavored to explain, but to no avail. He did not attempt to override Vance. Even in its death agony, the

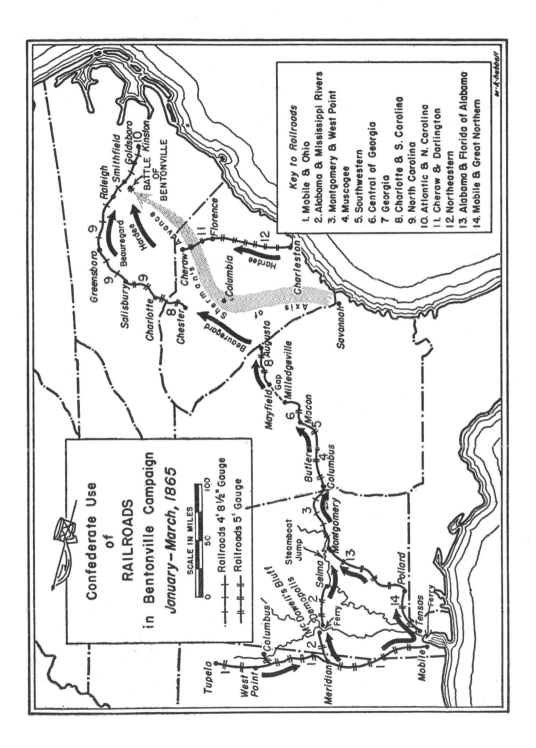

Confederate Use
of
RAILROADS
in Bentonville Campaign
January–March, 1865

SCALE IN MILES

0   50   100

+—+—+ Railroads 4' 8½" Gauge

==+== Railroads 5' Gauge

Key to Railroads
1. Mobile & Ohio
2. Alabama & Mississippi Rivers
3. Montgomery & West Point
4. Muscogee
5. Southwestern
6. Central of Georgia
7. Georgia
8. Charlotte & S. Carolina
9. North Carolina
10. Atlantic & N. Carolina
11. Cheraw & Darlington
12. Northeastern
13. Alabama & Florida of Alabama
14. Mobile & Great Northern

W. R. Herbert

Davis Administration remained faithful to the dogma of States' Rights.[19]

Meanwhile Joseph E. Johnston had been recalled to his old place as commander of the Army of Tennessee. Beauregard retained his somewhat meaningless "Military Division of the West," and the two generals, architects of the Confederacy's first major troop movement by rail at Manassas, together directed its last. Beauregard suggested that Sherman might swing east to unite with Federal columns moving inland from Newbern and Wilmington, and that the southern counter-concentration should take place at Smithfield, a small lumber and turpentine village west of Goldsboro on the North Carolina Railroad. Smithfield seemed to be on Sherman's route; the trains could carry the greater part of the Army of Tennessee directly to it, and the Confederates facing Wilmington, now under the command of Bragg, could fall back upon it—likewise by rail. Johnston agreed. On March 4 he started for eastern North Carolina to gather the scattered units there, leaving Beauregard in Charlotte to bring forward the Tennessee Army.[20]

At once Beauregard directed the commands of Stewart and Cheatham, and any troops of Lee's Corps that were in Chester, to proceed by rail to Smithfield. Even the artillery, wagons and animals, were to accompany them. As the five-foot gauge had reached Salisbury, his orders forbade a change of cars at Charlotte. He placed Major Willis in immediate charge of the loading operations, instructing him to remain at Chester "until troops commence leaving and things are working systematically" and then to proceed to Salisbury to supervise the change to the narrow-gauge portion of the North Carolina road.[21]

But things did not work systematically. Bragg had retreated to the vicinity of Goldsboro and Kinston, where he hourly expected a Federal assault, and on March 6 Johnston directed the troops to detrain not at Smithfield, but at Goldsboro. The following day he learned that Sherman's main body was advancing rapidly on Fayetteville, and abruptly ordered the trains halted at Smithfield again. But Bragg simultaneously found Schofield's Federal Corps in his front and arbitrarily instructed all arriving units to continue on through, past Goldsboro, to Kinston. He significantly warned that Major W. H. Harvey, the local military railroad superintendent, should be informed of the movement of all trains, "so as

to avoid collisions." So deep was the confusion into which operations had been thrown already.[22]

At first, soldiers and impedimenta were carried away from
Chester with dispatch; Stewart's Corps passed Charlotte on March
8 and Cheatham's was expected to move through on the tenth. But
thereafter everything seemed to go wrong. The chaos which
marked the eastern portion of the line spread swiftly. Whole brigades piled up in Salisbury; by the eleventh, troops, artillery, and
wagons equal to 120 carloads clogged the yards. Sixty-five cars of
casuals stood immobile at Chester, waiting for the Salisbury bottleneck to clear. At Kinston Bragg fought a little battle, retreated, and
Smithfield was again designated as the detraining point. From
Richmond came plaintive telegrams asserting that the troop movements in North Carolina were disrupting grain shipments to Virginia. Major Willis requested the loan of extra equipment from the
Piedmont Railroad, but the response was half-hearted. From Smithfield General Johnston complained that "this railroad [the North
Carolina] with its enormous amount of rolling stock has brought
us only about five hundred men a day." [23]

With all the orders and counter-orders, lack of engines and cars,
and rising tempers, the Confederates could manage only a partial
concentration. As late as March 19 only Stewart's Corps had come
down from Salisbury. Bragg's men, of course, were available, and
Hardee's kaleidoscopic elements were about to arrive, following a
rail and road journey from Florence, South Carolina. Johnston had
to be content with these, for Sherman's advance was sweeping
toward Smithfield. He formed his line of battle near a backwoods
hamlet called Bentonville and smote the approaching Federal Fourteenth Corps with such fury as to send it reeling back upon its
supports. But when, the following day, the trains at last brought
Cheatham's infantry, it was too late to press the little victory, for
the Confederates now were confronted by Sherman's entire army.
Johnston could only order a retreat—his last.[24]

The southern effort in North Carolina went swiftly to pieces.
Johnston tried to get his supplies out of Smithfield by rail, but the
cars were loaded in panic, and much property was wasted. At
Raleigh railway officials prepared to remove their remaining equipment westward. But even the up-country was no longer safe, for
from behind the Blue Ridge came the cavalry of the Union Gen-

eral Stoneman. The Confederates were in an uproar. Johnston considered another concentration near Smithfield; Beauregard issued contrary orders massing every available man between Greensboro and Charlotte. Further efforts to use the railroads fell into chaos. Certain units found themselves proceeding in opposite directions. The resistance offered Stoneman was negligible; his raiders bore down upon the North Carolina, Western North Carolina, and Piedmont roads, and to the crash of sledgehammers and the crackle of flames abruptly ended their military usefulness. "This was fatal," Stoneman reported with blunt accuracy, "to the hostile armies of Lee and Johnston, who depended upon that road for supplies and as their ultimate line of retreat." Already the news had come that Richmond had been abandoned and that Lee had surrendered the remnants of the Army of Northern Virginia. And hardly had the whistle of the last Confederate locomotive died away when what remained of the southern edifice came tumbling down in a heap.[25]

III

While Sherman hacked his way up the Atlantic seaboard, the Confederate Congress was holding its last session in the classic temple on Capitol Hill. Superficially the proceedings were marked with all the dignity and protocol of a permanent legislative body, but between the lines of its acts and resolutions ran a current of hysteria. As report followed black report, senators and representatives alike displayed an increasing willingness to forget ancient shibboleths. They approved the drafting of slaves, not merely into the services of supply, but into the fighting arms. And when they read of the uprooted tracks and smashed locomotives in Georgia and South Carolina, they handed the Executive a new and improved transportation law—better, even, than the enactment of May, 1863, the kind of law which should have been placed upon the books, and enforced, from the beginning. Moreover, they indicated clearly to Davis that he need fear no political reprisals for any action he might take to restore the South's communications.

The congressional change of heart was first marked by a House resolution, offered by James McCallum of Tennessee on January 11. It instructed the House Military Affairs Committee to inquire "into the expediency" of (1) the Government's taking possession of indispensable railroads and repairing them, (2) a large-scale seizure of rail, rolling stock, and other materials, and (3) a renewed program of railroad construction for military purposes. There was little that was really new in the resolution, and it seems to have been adopted without debate. But while the House Military Committee was still deliberating, the Senate went a step further. On the twenty-fourth it asked the President to furnish information as to the numbers of white men and Negroes required for the reconstruction and operation of the railroads of the country, together with a list of routes deemed vital enough to justify direct government aid.[26]

President Davis referred the request to the War Department, whence it filtered down to Lieutenant Colonel Sims and to the Iron Commission. Sims's reply was dated February 10. It quoted no precise figures; indeed, it contained little more than a restatement of his known views. The worst difficulties, he declared, arose from the everlasting shortage of mechanics and materials. The Iron Commission had partially relieved the rail problem, but the situation had not improved with respect to other materials, such as copper, pig-tin, steam gauges, cast steel, files and so on. Equally discouraging was the continued independence of railroad managers. "Your earnest attention," he wrote, "is called to the entire absence of responsibility of railroad officers to any military authority [although] the public and indeed most of the officers are under the impression that your Bureau has supreme power over all the railroads and trains in the Confederacy, and has but to order them at your will to any point you desire." This, of course, was not so. On the other hand, he continued, the roads themselves were receiving little protection from the Armed Forces, and he pointed ruefully to the recent losses in Georgia, totaling "probably 25 engines and 400 cars, or an equipment greater than we now have to work the Richmond and Danville Railroad."[27]

For its part, the Iron Commission recommended public aid for five railroad connections: Columbia to Augusta, Albany to Thomasville, Union Springs to Montgomery, Montgomery to Selma, and the Tombigbee River bridge. These, and the repair of damaged lines, would, it was estimated, require 825 military details and 4,800 impressed Negroes. The cost of both rehabilitation and new construction would total about $21,000,000.[28]

All this information was laid before the Senate on February 28. It found the legislators little disposed to quibble. The indicated appropriation of $21,000,000, which would have set a political hurricane to whirling a few months before, passed both houses of Congress within the week. It received Mr. Davis's signature on March 9, just a month before Appomattox.[29]

Meanwhile the need for public control of the roads had grown so overwhelming that Congress had gone ahead with a measure of its own, without waiting for the Executive. When on February 15 the House Military Affairs Committee at last replied to the original McCallum resolution, it unwrapped no less than a full-grown transport regulation bill. Styled "an act to provide for the more efficient transportation of troops, supplies and munitions of war upon the railroads, steamboats and canals in the Confederate States, and to control telegraph lines employed by the Government," it did not merely threaten companies which refused to cooperate, but thrust the employees of all common carriers of military significance directly into the army. It authorized government aid to needy railroads, and provided for the repayment of damages resulting from the law, but as to the military responsibilities of railroad men, it left no doubt. "After the passage of this act," read Section 4, "when the Secretary of War shall take charge of any railroad...line, the officers, agents, and employees of such company, or companies, shall be considered as forming part of the land forces of the Confederacy and as serving with armies in the field while such road...is employed for the use of the Government." Only imminent disaster could have wrung from a Confederate congressional committee a measure like this.[30]

Stern as it was, the bill passed both houses of Congress in four days. The only opposition worth mentioning came from a minority of the same House committee which had drawn it up, and they proposed a substitute law of equally rigorous character. The final House vote was 52 to 18. In the Senate, not a voice was raised against it. In the end the only stumbling block seems to have been President Davis—he whom half the Confederacy had called tyrant and dictator, but who now so hesitated to use the fragment of autocratic power being placed in his hands that he did not approve it for ten days.[31]

But even the prerogatives of an Egyptian Pharaoh could not have saved the Confederacy in the winter of 1865. Nearly everyone, save Jefferson Davis, knew that the end was not far off. Perhaps that is why a jealous legislature could freely vote despotic authority to the Executive, only to find him fearful to use it.

CHAPTER

~ 22 ~

End of Track

I

For the South the War Between the States, to its last weeks, remained a railroad war. By January of 1865 the effective Confederacy had been virtually reduced to a man and a city, both supported by a thin web of iron. To Lee and Richmond alike, the remaining railroads of southern Virginia were indispensable. From Lynchburg and the west, the South Side continued to serve Petersburg; from Danville and the Carolina Piedmont the Richmond & Danville still carried supplies to the seat of government. Together they traced across the map a tremulous X, at the intersection of which lay the village of Burkeville. Connecting its eastern termini, and affording direct access between the bulk of Lee's army and the capital, ran the Richmond & Petersburg. The loss of any of these lines meant the collapse of the whole Confederate position in Virginia.

They were badly clotted arteries. So meager was the nourishment provided by the Danville road that the War Department suspended its passenger trains on the second day of the new year, and service was not resumed until January 30. Even so, neither the Richmond & Danville nor the South Side was willing to interchange rolling stock, and when Colonel Sims attempted to work out a system of through freight-car lines, the managements demurred for a month, until "neutral" equipment could be brought in from the now derelict Virginia & Tennessee.[1]

But in Richmond the paper prospects of the Railroad Bureau had never seemed brighter. Sims at last had the assistance of an executive officer, Captain W. G. Gray, and the transportation act

282

of February provided him with the kind of power which he had
come to regard as essential. But with the best spirit in the world the
carriers could hardly perform efficiently with the means at their

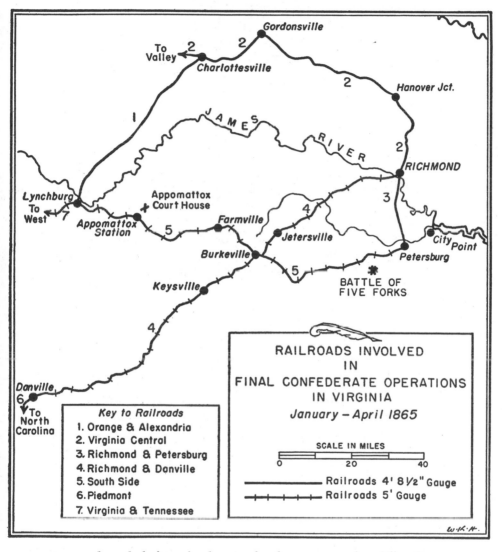

RAILROADS INVOLVED
IN
FINAL CONFEDERATE OPERATIONS
IN VIRGINIA
January – April 1865

SCALE IN MILES

Key to Railroads
1. Orange & Alexandria
2. Virginia Central
3. Richmond & Petersburg
4. Richmond & Danville
5. South Side
6. Piedmont
7. Virginia & Tennessee

———— Railroads 4' 8½" Gauge
+++++ Railroads 5' Gauge

command, and their attitude remained uncooperative. The Orange
& Alexandria and the Virginia Central, which in combination provided an alternate, if lengthy and hazardous, troop-train route from
Lynchburg to the capital, maintained that a longer ride justified a
higher fare. Congestion on the South Side road steadily worsened;

on March 22 the topographical engineer, Captain Jedidiah Hotchkiss, consumed fourteen hours upon the 123-mile journey from Petersburg to Lynchburg. But when the Government announced it would take over the line west of Burkeville and exchange its locomotives for heavier power, President Lemuel Peebles condemned the action as a "high-handed measure, calculated to result in no good for either the Government or this company." [2]

And now disaster snowballed to the inevitable climax. Sheridan's cavalry came pouring from the Shenandoah Valley and put the Virginia Central and the Richmond, Fredericksburg & Potomac out of the war for good. At Petersburg starvation and attrition reached such a point that Lee was driven to a forlorn attempt to roll up Grant's line by a surprise assault upon Fort Stedman. To push home the attack it was intended to bring down Pickett's Division from the Richmond defenses. But the Richmond & Petersburg road could not provide equipment to move the eight thousand men in less than twenty-four hours; only a single brigade actually got off, and this failed to reach Petersburg in time to participate. The attack was delivered with fury, but Union countercharges turned even this last hope into a bloodbath wherein the Confederates lost, in killed and wounded and captured, a sickening total of 3,500 men. [3]

The end was at hand. The cars did carry Pickett's Division over the James on the twenty-sixth, but even this reinforcement could not prevent the crushing of the Confederate position at Five Forks on April 1. The Union masses now were behind Petersburg; the South Side Railroad lay at their mercy. With his hand at last around the southern egg, Grant did not hesitate to squeeze. The shell crumpled; and from Petersburg in the dawn of a beautiful spring Sunday, a courier departed hastily for the Richmond War Department. [4]

Upon Richmond's most terrible twenty-four hours, we need not dwell. It is sufficient to say that the city ceased temporarily to be a railroad center at the same time it ceased permanently to be the capital of the Confederate States. As the Federals swung into its avenues on the morning of April 3, the blazing Danville and Petersburg bridges still were crashing, span by span, into the James. At the foot of Eighth Street the shop and depot facilities of the Petersburg road already were a mass of ruins; its treasurer lay wounded, after vainly endeavoring to save the company's records. Across the river most of its remaining passenger equipment stood abandoned on a siding, stripped by vandals. Near by, the last train of the Richmond & Danville took aboard the naval rearguard of Admiral Raphael Semmes; the remainder of its engines and cars were straining toward Danville as fast as reduced steam-pressure could carry them. On one of the trains rode Jefferson Davis, calm but white-lipped, and all of his cabinet save Breckinridge. Other cars—flat, box, baggage, and a scattering of ruinous coaches—carried the rank and file of the Confederate bureaucracy, including Sims of the Railroad Bureau, who guarded a hurriedly packed bundle of his records. He had not had the time to save them all; the greater part already were ashes in the smoldering shell of Belvin's Block.[5]

From Petersburg the Army of Northern Virginia groped westward in misery. It endeavored to cover the track to Danville, but Union cavalry swerved around it with ease; and on the afternoon of the fourth of April an excited operator at Farmville, Virginia, telegraphed that the Yankees had overrun Burkeville Junction at 3:10 P.M. The route to Danville was blocked; but beyond the junction the South Side road still operated. It was Lee's only hope, and he shifted his line of march from southwest to west. Progress was a nightmare; ill-fed for months, the troops were starving; many of those who dropped from the ranks did not so much desert as find it physically impossible to continue. At Farmville, upon which they at last converged, their spirits briefly soared when they saw a South Side train, filled with rations, waiting at the station. But the pursuit was relentless; hardly had the advance Confederates gotten their bacon to frying when the train had to chug hastily away to avoid being cut off. It was whispered that it was the only train the South Side had left.[6]

The railroad had not, in fact, been reduced to such extremity, but the steam locomotive nevertheless had served the Army of Northern Virginia for the last time. Early on April 8 four additional trainloads of supplies came down the line from Lynchburg; at an obscure siding called Appomattox Station they ground to a halt and began to discharge their precious freight. But the task had not been half-completed before Sheridan's cavalry came charging. A brisk little battle developed as a southern force attempted to cut its way through to the cars, but the northerners clung to their prize. After the Confederates had been repulsed and night had fallen, a number of the Union command, former railroaders, "amused themselves by running the trains to and fro, creating much confusion, and keeping up such an unearthly screeching with the whistles that I [Sheridan] was on the point of ordering the cars burned." One of the trains actually was put to the torch; the others were run in triumph into the Federal lines. That night Lee could see the glow of enemy campfires along the *western* horizon, between his position and Lynchburg. The end had come, though his army was to make one more convulsive effort in the gray dawn.[7]

Appomattox practically finished the career of the Virginia railroads as carriers of the Confederacy. Just two days after Lee's surrender, the United States Military Railroad had narrowed the gauge of the South Side as far as Burkeville and was operating trains from the Federal tidewater base at City Point. Only the Richmond & Danville remained Confederate for a few brief days. It had managed to salvage all of its rolling equipment—twenty-two engines and "trains of cars"—in the course of the Richmond evacuation, and it ventured to maintain schedules as far east as Keysville until April 12, when the Staunton River bridge was burned by order of a stray southern officer. At Danville, President Harvie, Jefferson Davis, and the Engineer Bureau argued fruitlessly whether it would be better to change the width of the Piedmont Railroad —the project died hard—so as to save the Richmond & Danville equipment, or to erect fortifications to defend it. Neither was really an alternative. Already Stoneman was jabbing through the roads at Greensboro and beyond; soon the Federal Sixth Corps would be moving on Danville like a juggernaut.[8]

The head and shoulders of the Confederacy, most sturdy of its parts, were first to die. The withdrawal of the southern government became undisguised flight. Many of its military members—from Breckinridge downward—endeavored half-heartedly to follow, but soon mingled with the forces which the realistic Joseph E. Johnston was surrendering to Sherman. We may pass over the lengthy, and at times disheartening, negotiations, noting only the formal parole on May 12, 1865, of Quartermaster General Lawton and Lieutenant Colonel F. W. Sims at Charlotte, North Carolina. By this time all that remained of the Confederate States Railroad Bureau was a mass of rain-sodden papers which the Federal quartermasters were packing for shipment to Washington with the rest of the captured "rebel archives." [9]

II

Though the mid-section of the Confederacy still writhed, the end of organized resistance was at hand. Too many transportation arteries had been cut. Nearly one hundred miles of the South Carolina Railroad had suffered obliteration during February; and on April 19 much of its remaining equipment, 13 locomotives and 147 cars, taken for refuge to the upper end of its Camden branch, was destroyed by a Federal expedition under General Potter. The road could operate only between Aiken and Augusta, seventeen miles. In Georgia the work of reconstruction was hardly well begun; the Western & Atlantic remained utterly desolate, and early in March Governor Brown was obliged to meet a serious food famine in the mountain counties with wagon trains.[10]

And now the Federal knife slashed through the Confederate transportation system for the last time. From Pensacola a flying column late in March severed the old Mobile route at Pollard, Alabama. The Mobile & Great Northern gave up the struggle; its remaining equipment was taken across Mobile Bay and sought safety on the iron of the Mobile & Ohio. For a day or two longer, the connecting Alabama & Florida continued to run, though it led nowhere.[11] Then came the *coup de grâce*—the cavalry thrust of General James H. Wilson.

Wilson's raid practically destroyed the last southern ability to carry on the conflict east of the Mississippi. Primary objectives were the munitions plants at Selma, Alabama, and Columbus, Georgia, heretofore untouched and still producing for the Confederacy. The operation was thus by no means wholly directed against railroads, but the effect upon the carriers was as devastating as Sherman's. When the General had finished, few trains were running in either Alabama or Georgia.

Wilson's squadrons did not come unheralded. As early as February Confederate spies were sending in reports of an impending blow, and on March 2 the southern commander at Selma was advised to move the rolling stock of the "Montgomery & Mobile" railroad to the supposed safety of Columbus. But when the Union horsemen came charging down from the hills, the counter-moves had been imperfectly advanced. While hysterical telegrams flashed over the state in a vain effort to gather troops, yard crews still were loading the rolling stock of the Alabama & Florida road on flatcars for shipment east over the narrow-gauge Montgomery & West Point. Much of the A. & F. company's other property had to be left behind.[12]

At Selma only part of the stores and machinery, both government and railroad, could be carried away before the Union formations crashed through its defences, and soon a large proportion of the remaining Confederate war potential was rolling in pillars of smoke across the April sky. The carriers suffered notably. For the Alabama & Mississippi Rivers road the toll was one roundhouse, one stationary engine, most of its shop machinery, twenty boxcars and two passenger cars; the Alabama & Tennessee Rivers lost a fully equipped roundhouse, five locomotives, nineteen boxcars and fifty flatcars.[13]

At Montgomery the Federals committed miscellaneous depredations, but they wreaked their worst havoc at West Point and Columbus, whither most of the engines and cars had been sent. The Montgomery & West Point equipment was hopelessly cornered. "Its narrow gauge, which had during four years of fearful war prevented its outfit from being scattered throughout the Southern States, proved in the end to be the certain means of its destruction," reported Superintendent Cram. "All the effective locomotives, 19 in number, owned by the company at the beginning of the year, were as nearly destroyed as fire and a liberal use of the sledge hammer could accomplish it." Similar ruin befell the Alabama & Florida; all its property of a destructible nature was ripped, smashed, and burned. The Federal score at Columbus totaled 13 locomotives, 10 passenger, 45 box, 24 flat and 9 coal cars, plus a roundhouse with complete machine shop. Across the Chattahoochee River the little Mobile & Girard road yielded another "extensive roundhouse and railroad machine shop," two engines, and 15 boxcars. Even more elaborate was the destruction at West Point: 20 engines and 350 cars of all kinds, loaded with stores and machinery.[14]

The Confederates were stunned. Even where railroads continued to run, they seemed unable to concentrate troops in the face of

Wilson's advance. When he first appeared across the Chattahoochee from Columbus, General Robert Toombs appealed for militia reinforcements, but Governor Brown could only answer that there were no trains to bring them. Mobile was abandoned, and the remnants of General Richard Taylor's command collected in pitiful array at Meridian, where they found themselves completely cut off from communication to Georgia and the east. So smashed were the railroads that casuals from the seaboard armies who came wandering in were reorganized into a new division on the spot; there would be no purpose in trying to return them to their proper units. The Yankee storm now was surging across the helpless waist of Georgia; and behind it southern railroaders were turning to the rehabilitation of their property with evident listlessness.[15]

Even firebrands like Joseph E. Brown had now to accept defeat. Indeed the news of Johnston's capitulation must have come as a relief. On April 28, when a dispatch arrived from General Wilson, then occupying Macon, requesting his cooperation in the reopening of the Western & Atlantic between Dalton and Atlanta, his reply was almost cordial: "Will be glad to have interview with you . . . will direct superintendent of the road at Atlanta to give you any aid in his power to facilitate the work." One week more, and General Taylor's headquarters at Meridian was informing the last functioning member of the Confederate States Railroad Bureau, Major George Whitfield, that all was over.[16]

All was over! But not quite. For three more weeks a vague Confederate authority lingered on in Texas, the state wherein, oddly enough, the rule of Richmond had seemed most shadowy. There the last land engagement of the war, Palmetto Ranch, was fought on May 11, and what is more, was won by the Confederates. And so late as the twentieth and twenty-first, one still could see Texan locomotives hauling troops under Confederate orders. They were evacuating Galveston—the last southern troop trains.[17]

III

The War Between the States was at an end. The South was prostrate; its people in mourning; its incipient industries wrecked; its fields neglected; its future clouded with a race problem to which the passage of a century would bring no solution. But the condition of its railroads seemed especially appalling. "It was no easy task," wrote the superintendent of the Montgomery & West Point, "surrounded by the blackened walls of buildings and amid the smoking debris of a hundred loaded cars, to select or even distinguish what belonged to the company." In 1861 the New Orleans, Jackson & Great Northern had possessed 45 locomotives, 37 passenger cars, 10 baggage and express cars, and 503 freight and handcars of all types. In May, 1865, it owned three locomotives—two damaged and partly burned—three passenger cars, one baggage car, and 18 freight cars. The 81 cars lost by the Mississippi & Tennessee seemed impossible of replacement; as of May 6, 1865, the road held in its treasury $12,300 in Confederate currency, $72,820 in Confederate 4 per cent bonds, and Confederate Government accounts-payable totaling $54,429.07. General Wilson had so damaged the Alabama & Tennessee Rivers road that the company suspended all service for two months from April 1, 1865. Three years after Appomattox, only twelve and one-half miles of the original 45.2 miles of the Alabama & Florida of Florida were yet in running order—the volatile Avery had not exaggerated his troubles after all. The prospects of the Mobile & Ohio were as grim. Emancipation had deprived the company of fifty Negroes, said to have been worth $119,691. It held $125,000 of Alabama State War Bonds, which were promptly repudiated. All of its bridges and buildings, from Union City, Tennessee, to Okolona, Mississippi, 184 miles, were in ruins.[18]

In Georgia the carriers faced equally evil days. Even those which had escaped the worst vengeance of Stoneman and Sherman and Wilson had been bled white. Reported the superintendent of the Southwestern road on August 1, 1865: "After being cut off from the balance of the world for over four years, and thrown upon our own resources, with no possibility of procuring materials necessary to keep up our rolling stock, it is not surprising that it has greatly deteriorated, particularly as we have been more pressed with freight and more tonnage has passed over the Road during the last three years than ever before in the same length of time. Our cars are failing for want of wheels, axles and springs." [19]

The Central of Georgia in the first year of peace could quote no figures for miles run per cord of wood and cost per mile for fuel. "In our present condition," said the management, "it would be impossible to make them correctly." Even with the help of northern money and northern iron, its first through train from Savannah to Macon did not run until June 12, 1866. The engines and cars of the Western & Atlantic were strewn, in varying stages of dilapidation, all over the Atlantic seaboard; in the winter of 1866 certain of its bridges still had not been replaced, and every shop belonging to the road had been wrecked. The whole of the Brunswick & Albany, from Tebeauville to St. Simon's Sound, was reported in ruinous condition as late as 1868.[20]

The roads of the Carolinas and Virginia seemed no better off. On September 1, 1865, the shops of the Western North Carolina road at Salisbury "consisted of a shed boarded on one side and end, . . . stocked with one pair of small bellows, one old anvil and a forge built of brick and mud." Only one station had been left standing on the Virginia & Tennessee between Lynchburg and Bristol. The Virginia Central held in its treasury just $100 in gold. Its labor force was utterly disorganized; its corporate debt stood at $1,637,118.08. Its line showed damage of varying kinds throughout its length.[21]

And yet, for the iron horse in Dixie, things were not so bad as they seemed. Certain roads, especially those long established, began to make speedy recoveries. The Federal Government, burdened with the now unneeded property of the United States Military Railroad, proved generous about selling it at low prices. "Seldom do we see," asserted John M. Robinson of the Seaboard & Roanoke in the spring of 1867, "in the history of any road so shattered by war—its costly bridges burned, its rails torn up and taken away, its shops rifled—such rapid renovation." "Our earnings have already increased greatly," Superintendent James W. Wilson of the Western North Carolina reported from the ruins of his shops in August, 1865, "and they will this month compare favorably with any corresponding one previous to the war." President Hawkins of the Raleigh & Gaston congratulated his stockholders upon their apparently good prospects. Samuel Tate of the Memphis & Charleston, over which the armies had struggled for three full years, thought his road should resume dividend payments by 1868. Much of this talk was only whistling in the dark; yet the Virginia Central reopened its entire line from Richmond to Jackson's River on

July 23, 1865 without any Federal aid whatever. In Georgia the shattered Central was actually facing its golden age.[22]

IV

But what of the Confederate railroaders? Generally speaking, they kept on railroading. Few of them seem to have become men of distinction. An exception was Barbour of the Orange & Alexandria. Another was Mahone of the Norfolk & Petersburg, who emerged from the war with dazzling plans for a new and expanded system. He presently mismanaged his dream, and ultimately plunged into politics in a fashion that hardly enhanced his popularity with Virginians. But his vision of a railroad revived; today it is the Norfolk & Western.[23]

Most successful as a practical railroader was William Wadley. For him the future appeared darkest of all in the spring of 1865. He was penniless, and his Vicksburg, Shreveport & Texas was both wrecked and bankrupt. Heartbroken over the failure of southern independence, he thought seriously of emigrating with his family to South America. He even was deprived of his position on the Shreveport road, by methods said to have been scarcely honorable. And then the directors of the Central of Georgia called him back to Savannah as president of their half-moribund property. He had not been installed for more than a few weeks before the company's stock rose from 68 to 75.[24]

Wadley perceived the advantages inherent in the consolidation of small railroads into unified systems. It was under his supervision that the Central formally annexed the Macon & Western and Southwestern roads, thus acquiring direct entries into Atlanta and the still developing agricultural regions of lower Georgia. Nor did he permit such transactions to serve as shields for financial piracy; he remained enough of a back-country Yankee to emphasize the solid rather than the clever. When the panic of 1873 brought down the jerry-built structure of one carrier after another, both in the South and elsewhere, his Central of Georgia stood firm.

He died at Saratoga Springs, New York, on August 10, 1882. A less conscientious man would have lived longer. He never attained national stature, but in Georgia his memory has not been forgotten. In front of the union station at Macon, within sound of the trains, his officers and employees erected a statue of him, inscribed to "Our President and Friend." And on the line of the original old Central, midway between Savannah and Macon, the village which the time-tables of the sixties called Bostwick is today known as Wadley, Georgia.[25]

Unlike Wadley, Sims did not remain a railroader. He returned to Savannah and re-entered the life of the community with characteristic gusto. He does not appear to have engaged again in newspaper work, but became a cotton factor, and in 1868 established a general brokerage business under the name of F. W. Sims & Co. He had a flair for business promotions and became successively a director of the Ransome Stone Manufacturing Company of Georgia and the Southern Insurance and Trust Company. In 1867 he was elected a vice-president of the Savannah Merchants' Exchange, and in the same year became interested in furthering a street railway—his only reversion to type. He dabbled, too, in politics, and from 1867 to 1869 was a member of the City Council, wherein he espoused the white-conservative viewpoint.[26]

Sims never lost his interest in charitable and community projects. In 1866-67 he had the pleasure of serving as vice-president of the Union Society under his old chief, Wadley, and the work likewise carried him into close association with another familiar personality of Richmond days, Alexander R. Lawton. He also acquired an interest in yachting and in 1869 he helped organize and was elected steward of the Regatta Association of Chatham County.[27]

Sims's last years were clouded with sorrow. Of his six children, four died in infancy. Moreover, he suffered from a common failing of the period—he waded too deep into business speculation. The circumstances of his death tell the story all too clearly. He died in that favorite land of the second-chance, California, on May 25, 1875. To his wife and two surviving daughters, he left less than $1,000. And thus F. W. Sims passed from the scene, still in the prime of life, a minor victim of the great depression of the seventies. Perhaps that is why he has been so completely forgotten.[28]

V

Lastly, what does the experience of the railroads of the Confederacy teach us? Did they play a role of any significance in the

American War Between the States? It is the opinion of the present writer that they did. Railroads formed the backbone, though not the whole structure, of the southern apparatus of supply and communication, just as they have done in the continental phase of every American war effort since. *They afforded a principal Confederate advantage—interior lines.* So long as the majority of those lines remained intact, the southern front might give ground, but it did not suffer general collapse.

Yet the Confederate States did not win the Civil War. Were the carriers of the South in any degree responsible for that failure? To this question the author can only answer—yes. Railroad transportation in the Confederacy suffered from a number of defects, all of which played a recognizable part in the southern defeat:

1. There were not enough railroads in the South, in terms of line miles, and they were not always in the right places, strategically.

2. There existed far too many gaps in what should have been continuous lines. Included here should be differences of gauge, though this was not an exclusively Confederate deficiency.

3. The southern ability to manufacture railroad supplies was much too low. In the face of a general lightness of construction, a distinct *initial* shortage of rolling stock, and an increasingly effective Federal blockade, this was an extremely serious, if not fatal, matter.

The shortcomings named above might have proved decisive in themselves, always assuming that the Federal power never lifted its pressure. So often does the advantage of interior lines entail a beleaguered fortress, suffering from shortages of everything except mobility! Germany has twice discovered this, to her sorrow. *But the Confederates by no means made the best use of what they had.* It is men who are most at fault when a war is lost—not locomotives, or cars, or even economic geography. And in so far as railroad logistics were concerned, the Confederates committed two major sins:

1. Railroad owners, managers, and even employees were unwilling to make serious sacrifice of their personal interests.

2. The Confederate Government was loath to enforce the kind of transportation policy the war effort demanded.

Calhoun's glorification of the individual state and his doctrine of the concurrent majority may have provided a satisfactory political philosophy for outnumbered southerners in the old Union, but they were hardly an effective engine of unity in the face of military attack. Such theories had, over the decades, so permeated the thinking of southerners that they stood in terror of their own creation at Richmond. Even the Confederate Government was too frequently afraid of itself. And in no field was it more pusillanimous than in its handling of the railroad problem. This inability to face unpleasant measures affected in some degree every person involved —Ashe, Wadley, Sims, Seddon, the Congress, even Jefferson Davis himself, "Southern nationalist" though he was. Indeed, the Confederate President was not to acquiesce in the enforcement of really rigid transportation regulations until Appomattox was hardly a month off.

Without either wholehearted public cooperation, or government coercion, it is practically impossible to wage a modern war. It is well to possess both of these things. The Confederacy had too little of either. The North could claim at least one of them in good measure—a powerful government that understood its own potentialities and was comparatively unafraid to use them.

It is here, if anywhere, that the story of the railroads of the Confederacy assumes a distinctive meaning. And though it be but a minor chapter in a huge tragedy, it still may be worth the telling as an object lesson for Americans. For it perhaps has not been sufficiently emphasized how extraordinarily *American* the Confederates were. Even their locomotives were of the western continent. Their clanging bells proclaimed their nativity.

APPENDIX

NOTES

BIBLIOGRAPHY

Appendix

A Note on Texas Railroads

BECAUSE OF A GENERAL DEARTH OF SOURCE MATERIAL AND, ES-pecially, their remoteness from the primary theaters of military activity, the railroads of Texas have received scant mention in this book. Yet, for the sake of balance, a brief reference to them appears desirable.

Confederate use of the Texas carriers was largely of a routine nature. The lines serving Houston, Galveston, and the coastal plain to the eastward proved valuable, however, in the face of Federal raids.[1] Moreover, the Trans-Mississippi command, finding itself for long intervals practically beyond the control of Richmond, could make use of the roads in an arbitrary fashion impossible further east. Thus General Magruder could tear up the entire lines of the San Antonio & Mexican Gulf and Indianola Railroads early in 1863 with a minimum of argument. Much of the Eastern Texas road and the Beaumont-Orange segment of the Texas & New Orleans were similarly despoiled to provide material for coastal fortifications. In 1864, General Kirby Smith required the Southern Pacific road to take up the iron upon its Caddo Lake branch and re-lay it in the direction of Shreveport, upon a promise (never fulfilled) of physical and financial assistance.[2]

Probably because they all were new companies, the Texas carriers suffered financially even in the midst of the war. Early in 1862 the Washington County road already was in the hands of its principal creditor. Not a single Texas railroad company paid a dime in dividends during the Confederate period. Especially near the end, payments for transportation on government account were seldom forthcoming. The collapse of the South left the Texas & New Orleans holding the bag to the extent of $33,000.00. Most of the freight traffic handled by the Southern Pacific from June, 1864, to June, 1865, was Confederate property, but practically all the bills therefor remained permanently unpaid.[3]

299

Notes

Chapter One

RAILROADS THROUGH DIXIE

1. Oxford (Miss.) *Mercury*, February 2, 1860, quoted in Vicksburg *Weekly Whig*, February 8, 1860.
2. The South began to dabble with railroads at about the same time as the North. The South Carolina Railroad was chartered as early as 1828. Various Virginia projects, including the Richmond, Fredericksburg & Potomac, and the Petersburg Railroad date from the early thirties. Of equally early vintage were the Central of Georgia and a variety of minuscule companies in lower Louisiana. The Central of Georgia, when completed from Savannah to Macon in the fall of 1843, had the honor of being the longest (190 miles) line under a single management in the world. See John B. Mordecai, *A Brief History of the Richmond, Fredericksburg & Potomac Railroad* (Richmond, 1938), pp. 1 ff.; *Virginia, A Guide to the Old Dominion* (Va. W. P. A. Writers Project) (New York: 1940), pp. 287, 249; Charles S. Sydnor, *The Development of Southern Sectionalism 1819-1848* (Baton Rouge, 1948), pp. 267-74; Central of Georgia Railway Co., *The First Hundred Years* (1943), pp. 1 ff.; Samuel M. Derrick, *Centennial History of the South Carolina Railroad* (Columbia, 1930), pp. 1 ff. A good general study for the entire ante-bellum period is Ulrich B. Phillips' *A History of Transportation in the Eastern Cotton Belt to 1860* (New York, 1908). See also, Walter Prichard, ed., "A Forgotten Louisiana Engineer: G. W. R. Bayley and his 'History of the Railroads of Louisiana,'" *The Louisiana Historical Quarterly*, Vol. 30, No. 4 (October, 1947).
3. *American Railroad Journal*, January 5, 1861; *Hunt's Merchant's Magazine and Commercial Review*, March, 1861, p. 371; *Preliminary Report of the Eighth Census* (Ex. Doc. No. 116, 37th Congress, 2nd Session, Washington, Government Printing Office, 1863) pp. 236-37.
4. *DeBow's Review*, May, 1860, pp. 594-95.
5. *DeBow's Review*, May, 1860, pp. 593-94; *Hunt's Merchant's Magazine and Commercial Review*, March, 1861, p. 371.
6. *American Railroad Journal*, January 5, 1861.
7. *Ibid.* See also *Hunt's Merchant's Magazine and Commercial Review*, March, 1861, p. 371.
8. *American Railroad Journal*, January 5, 1861. The average expenditure per mile of track in Arkansas was actually the highest for any of the Southern States, amounting to $46,153. This figure, however, is of little meaning, as the State possessed, at the outbreak of the war, a single railroad, and this was not yet half finished.

9. *Ibid.*

10. *Annual Report*, Mobile & Ohio Railroad Co., May, 1861, quoted in *American Railroad Journal*, May 25, 1861.

11. *Appleton's Railway and Steam Navigation Guide*, December, 1860, pp. 242-62. Even the Southern Railroad of Mississippi had not been completed to Meridian by the beginning of 1861. As late as January 9 trains were operated only to Newton, whence stage connections provided service eastward. Vicksburg *Weekly Whig*, January 9, 1861.

12. *American Railroad Journal*, March 23, 1861; Vicksburg *Weekly Whig*, January 16, 1861.

13. *Appleton's Railway and Steam Navigation Guide*, December 1860, p. 263; Houston *Telegraph*, April 9, 1861, quoted in *American Railroad Journal*, April 27, 1861.

14. Houston *Telegraph*, quoted in *American Railroad Journal*, June 22, 1861.

15. *Journal of Proceedings*, Florida House of Representatives, 12th Session, 1863, pp. 27-28; *Proceedings*, Florida Board of Internal Improvements, Vol. I, p. 213.

16. MS Report of President R. W. Hughes, Virginia & Kentucky Railroad, to Virginia Board of Public Works, February 6, 1862, Archives Division, Virginia State Library; "Report of Chief Engineer of Western Extension," *Annual Report*, Richmond & Danville Railroad, 1859.

17. *American Railroad Journal*, January 26, 1861.

18. MS Abstract of Annual Report, Spartanburg & Union Railroad, October 1, 1861, in South Carolina Historical Dept.; MS letter, Edward Frost, President, Blue Ridge Railroad to James Simms, November 26, 1860, in *ibid.*

19. *Proceedings*, Florida Board of Internal Improvements, Vol. I, p. 220; p. 207.

20. *Acts of the Alabama General Assembly*, 1859-60, pp. 704-5.

21. Knoxville *Whig*, quoted in *American Railroad Journal*, April 13, 1861.

22. *Annual Report*, New Orleans Jackson & Great Northern Railroad, 1861.

23. The separation of the Florida and Georgia lines amounted to less than 50 miles. It persisted to the Civil War period primarily because of the local jealousy of Floridians, who feared that their trade would otherwise flow out of the State to the port of Savannah. Arrangements for so obvious a link were not completed until March, 1861. "Whatever may have been the prejudices against a connection among our Florida friends," commented the Savannah *Republican* when the agreement was announced, "we feel sure they will disappear..." See *American Railroad Journal*, March 30, 1861.

24. Interests promoting the development of Wilmington and other North Carolina ports had blocked plans for a connecting railroad to Virginia as early as 1835. When, in 1858, Governor Morehead of North Carolina attempted to subsidize a Greensboro-Danville road, a certain William S. Ashe of Wilmington, of whom more shall be said, succeeded in preventing any action in the matter. S. A. Ashe, "William Shepperd Ashe," S. A. Ashe and others, eds., *Biographical History of North Carolina* (8 Vols., Greensboro, 1917), Vol. VIII, pp. 31-36.

25. Montgomery *Weekly Confederation*, May 10, 1861; Thomas McAdory Owen, *History of Alabama and Dictionary of Alabama Biography*, Vol. I, pp. 506-10; Vol. II, p. 1013; *American Railroad Journal*, April 27, 1861.

26. *The War of the Rebellion, the Official Records of the Union and Con-*

federate Armies, Series IV, Vol. I, pp. 485-86. Hereafter cited as *Official Records.*

27. *Official Records,* IV, I, p. 394; Richmond *Daily Examiner,* April 21, 1861.
28. Major W. S. Ashe to Jefferson Davis, November 27, 1861. MS copy in
    C. S. Railroad Documents, War Department Collection of Confederate
    Records, War Records Division, National Archives.
29. Colton's *Map of Savannah,* 1855.
30. Thomas W. Chadwick, ed., "Diary of Samuel Edward Burges, 1860-
    1862," *South Carolina Historical and Genealogical Magazine,* Vol.
    XLVIII, No. 3 (July, 1947), p. 157.
31. I.e., the Richmond & Danville, the South Side, the Virginia & Tennes-
    see, the Norfolk & Petersburg in Virginia; the Wilmington & Man-
    chester, the Atlantic, Tennessee, & Ohio, and the Charlotte & South Carolina.
    The Seaboard & Roanoke, with a gauge of four feet, eight and one-half
    inches did, indeed, enter South Side Virginia from a generally westerly
    direction, but this was an essentially North Carolina road. H. V. Poor,
    Manual of the Railroads of the United States, 1869-70 (New York, 1869).
32. Poor's *Manual,* 1869-70; *Proceedings,* Florida Board of Internal Improve-
    ments, Vol. I, pp. xv-xxxvi; "Map of United States Military Railroads,
    1866," *Official Records,* III, V, pocket; Walter Prichard, *op. cit.,* p. 1156.
33. *Official Records,* IV, I, p. 1085-87.

Chapter Two

OF TRACKS AND TRAINS

1. *Annual Report,* Atlantic & Gulf Railroad, May 1, 1861, pp. 19-20.
2. *Annual Report,* Virginia & Tennessee Railroad, September, 1861.
3. *Annual Report,* Macon & Western Railroad, December 1, 1859.
4. Walter Prichard, *op. cit.,* p. 1159.
5. The 68-lb. rail used almost everywhere upon the Mobile & Ohio seems
   to have been the heaviest in the Confederacy. The heaviest rail of the
   period in use upon northern roads is said to have been that of the Hudson
   River Railroad—70 lbs. to the yard. "T" rail weight varied considerably
   through the South; on the Richmond Fredericksburg & Potomac there were
   62 miles of 50-lb. rail; on the Macon & Western the weight was 52½ lbs.; in
   Florida, a legal provision required, for practical purposes, the use of at least
   60-lb. iron. Report of Mobile & Ohio Railroad, 1865 in *Report No. 34,
   Affairs of Southern Railroads* (House of Representatives, 39th Congress, 2nd
   Session), 1867, p. 856 (hereafter cited as *Affairs of Southern Railroads*);
   Appleton's Railway & Steam Navigation Guide, July, 1860, p. 76; MS letter
   W. H. Irwin to Thomas H. Dewitt, Virginia Board of Public Works Papers
   (July 16, 1860); MS report F. McD. Goldsborough to Virginia Board of
   Public Works, March 22, 1859, in *ibid.; American Railroad Journal,* Nov. 23,
   1861; *Proceedings,* Florida Board of Internal Improvements, Vol. I, pp. xv-
   xxxvi; *Annual Report,* Macon & Western Railroad, December, 1859.
6. MS letter, P. V. Daniel, Jr., to Jefferson Davis, April 22, 1862, Papers of
   C.S. Secretaries of War, War Records Division, National Archives.
7. Mordecai, *op. cit.,* p. 28; *American Railroad Journal,* November 23, 1861;
   Annual Report, Richmond & Danville Railroad, December, 1861; *Annual*

Report, Nashville & Chattanooga Railroad, August, 1861; Thomas Weber, The Northern Railroads and the Civil War (unpublished doctoral dissertation, Columbia University, 1949), p. 322; *Annual Report,* Georgia Railroad, May, 1859; *Official Records,* Series I, Vol. XXXVIII, Part II, pp. 904-9; Charles G. Woodward, *The Southwestern Railroad,* pp. 9, 15.

8. *Annual Report,* Macon & Western Railroad, 1859. References to chairs are scattered profusely through the railroad correspondence and reports of the period.

9. *Annual Report,* Virginia & Tennessee Railroad, 1858; *American Railroad Journal,* August 9, 1862. Some of the reports of the northern roads were impressive. In 1861, for example, the Hartford & New Haven had 65 miles of second track and siding as against 61 miles of main line. Between Albany and Buffalo the New York Central possessed a system of about 550 line miles; it also could boast 314 miles of secondary track.

10. Seventh Annual Statement, Atlantic & Gulf Railroad, July 31, 1861, MS in Georgia Railroad papers, Georgia Archives, Atlanta; *Annual Report,* Georgia Railroad, May, 1864; MS Statement of Richmond Fredericksburg & Potomac Railroad, March 31, 1864, Virginia Board of Public Works Papers.

11. For example, the famous "General," although formally called "freight" power, was hauling a passenger train at the time of the Andrews raid.

12. *Annual Reports:* Macon & Western Railroad, 1859; Seaboard & Roanoke Railroad, February, 1862; Virginia Central Railroad, October, 1864; Virginia & Tennessee Railroad, July, 1858.

13. *Annual Reports:* Savannah Albany & Gulf Railroad, May, 1861; Macon & Western Railroad, 1859; Western & Atlantic Railroad, October, 1861; Virginia & Tennessee Railroad, July, 1858; Virginia Central Railroad, October, 1864; Seaboard & Roanoke Railroad, February, 1862; Charleston & Savannah Railroad, 1860.

14. *Ibid.* See also *Annual Report,* Nashville & Chattanooga Railroad, 1866. The northern names quoted above besmirched the power of the Central of Georgia. In another and greater conflict the modern road of the same name suitably honored tradition by renaming its "Mikado" class of power "McArthur."

15. *Ibid.* See also *Annual Report,* North Carolina Railroad, July, 1860.

16. Although conversion to coal was already underway in the North, all southern carriers seem to have depended exclusively upon wood as fuel.

17. *Annual Report,* Macon & Western Railroad, 1859.

18. *Georgia Railroad Local Tariff,* December 3, 1867, p. 6.

19. A modern steam freight locomotive may exert 70,000 lbs., or much more, of tractive effort "at the drawbar."

20. *Annual Reports:* Central of Georgia Railroad, December, 1862; Seaboard & Roanoke Railroad, February, 1862; Charleston & Savannah Railroad, February, 1861; North Carolina Railroad, May, 1860; Montgomery & West Point Railroad, April, 1862.

21. A good example of Civil War bogie construction can be seen upon the tender of the engine "Texas," now preserved in the cyclorama building in Grant Park, Atlanta. The bogie truck was a characteristically American feature made necessary by the excessive curvature of American track.

22. *Annual Report,* Montgomery & West Point Railroad, April, 1862.

23. *Annual Report,* Macon & Western Railroad, 1859; *Annual Report,*

Memphis & Charleston Railroad, June, 1860; *Annual Report,* North Carolina Railroad, 1860.

24. Private Journal of Sarah L. Wadley, Part I, p. 50. (Typewritten copy in possession of Mrs. William Burt, Bolingbroke, Ga.); Vicksburg *Weekly Whig,* January 9, 1861.

25. *American Railroad Journal,* January 19, 1861, January 26, 1861, March 23, 1861, and August 9, 1862; *Annual Reports* of Central of Georgia, December, 1860, and Savannah, Albany & Gulf, May, 1861; *Journal* of Florida House of Representatives, 12th Session, 1863, pp. 27-28.

26. *American Railroad Journal,* August 9, 1862.

27. *American Railroad Journal,* August 9, 1862; *Annual Report,* Southwestern Railroad, August, 1861; *Annual Report,* Montgomery & West Point Railroad, April, 1862; *Proceedings,* Florida Board of Internal Improvements, Vol. I, p. 213.

28. Balloon stacks acted, with somewhat dubious efficiency, as spark catchers. Most northern machines were still wood-burners in 1861.

29. *Annual Reports:* Western & Atlantic Railroad, October, 1861; Central of Georgia Railroad, December, 1860; Seaboard & Roanoke Railroad, February, 1862; Macon & Western Railroad, 1859; New Orleans Jackson & Great Northern Railroad, January, 1861; Southwestern Railroad, August, 1861.

30. *Annual Reports:* Virginia & Tennessee Railroad, 1858; Charleston & Savannah Railroad, February, 1861; *Rules and Regulations for the Government of the South Carolina Railroad* (1855, Revised 1869), p. 38.

31. *Dictionary of American Biography,* Allen Johnson and Dumas Malone, eds., Vol. I, p. 268; *Annual Reports:* Virginia & Tennessee Railroad, 1858; Virginia Central Railroad, September, 1864; Richmond & Danville Railroad, October, 1863; Nashville & Chattanooga Railroad, July, 1861; MS Petition of Confederate Railroads to Government at Richmond, February, 1863, Railroad Papers, Georgia Archives; Annual message of Gov. Joseph E. Brown of Georgia, November 7, 1860, Georgia Executive Minutes; Private Journal of Sarah L. Wadley, Part I, p. 101.

32. Mordecai, *op. cit.,* p. 26; *Annual Reports:* Richmond & Danville Railroad, 1859; Montgomery & West Point Railroad, April, 1862; Central of Georgia Railroad, December, 1860; Savannah *Republican,* December 31, 1860.

33. *Annual Reports:* South Side Railroad, 1866; Virginia Central Railroad, 1861; Memphis & Charleston Railroad, June, 1860; Montgomery & West Point Railroad, April, 1862; Milton S. Heath, Public Cooperation in Railroad Construction in the Southern United States to 1861 (unpublished doctoral thesis, Harvard University, 1937), p. 24.

Chapter Three

OF MEN AND METHODS

1. *Dictionary of American Biography,* Vol. I, pp. 592-93.

2. T. B. Catherwood, ed., *The Life and Labors of William M. Wadley* (Savannah, 1885), pp. 3-13; *Official Records,* I, LI, Part II, pp. 276-78; Walter Prichard, *op. cit.,* pp. 1065 ff.; State Proxy Holder from Clarke

County Virginia to Thos. H. Dewitt, Secretary of Virginia Board of Public Works, Nov. 23, 1861, MS in Virginia Public Works Papers.

3. *Annual Reports:* Virginia & Tennessee Railroad, 1858; Richmond & Danville Railroad, 1862; Virginia Central Railroad, 1861; Petersburg Railroad, 1866; Georgia Railroad, 1859.

4. *Ibid.* See also *Annual Report,* Atlantic & North Carolina Railroad, 1861, and of Raleigh & Gaston Railroad, 1861.

5. *Ibid.* See also MS copy of Minutes of Richmond Railroad Convention, January 9, 1863, Confederate Railroad Papers, War Records Division, National Archives.

6. *Annual Reports:* Nashville & Chattanooga Railroad, August, 1866; Raleigh & Gaston Railroad, July, 1861; South Carolina Railroad, 1859; Central of Georgia Railroad, December, 1860; Macon & Western Railroad, December, 1864; Georgia Railroad, 1859; Montgomery & West Point Railroad, April, 1862; Charles G. Woodward, *op. cit.,* p. 10; Walter Prichard, *op. cit.,* p. 1212.

7. *Annual Reports:* Virginia & Tennessee Railroad, 1858; Richmond & Danville Railroad, 1859, 1862; Virginia Central Railroad, 1864. Many MS copies of slave contracts are in the railroad papers of the Virginia Board of Public Works. An advertisement in the Richmond *Daily Examiner,* December 16, 1861, informs the slaveholding public that the Virginia & Tennessee Railroad wishes to "hire, for the ensuing year, to work on the repairs of their road and in their shops, the following described slaves, viz: 400 laborers, 50 train hands, 33 carpenters, 20 blacksmiths and strikers . . . E. H. Gill, Superintendent."

8. *Annual Report,* Virginia & Tennessee Railroad, 1858; *Annual Report,* Richmond & Danville Railroad, 1861.

9. *Appleton's Railway Guide,* December, 1860, p. 252.

10. *Appleton's Railway Guide,* December, 1860, pp. 245, 253, 261; South Carolina Railroad, *Rules & Regulations,* 1855-69, Rule 18, p. 22; *DeBow's Review,* November, 1860, p. 671.

11. "Comptroller General's Reports," *Reports and Resolutions of the General Assembly of the State of South Carolina,* 1861; MS Abstract Report, Wilmington & Manchester Railroad, for year ending October 1, 1861, Railroad Papers, South Carolina Historical Department; *W. & A. R. R. Time Table No. 20,* effective May 12, 1868, Railroad Papers, Georgia Archives; *Weekly* Montgomery *Confederation,* May 24, 1861.

12. *Appleton's Railway Guide,* December, 1860, pp. 242, 250; *Hill & Swayze's Confederate States Railroad & Steamboat Guide,* May, 1863, p. 2. William M. Wadley, then Chief Engineer and General Superintendent of the Southern Railroad of Mississippi, advised the readers of the Vicksburg *Weekly Whig* on January 9, 1861 that, while his road would attempt earnestly to fulfill its published schedules, "for any failures or omissions to comply therewith, or to carry any freight which may be hauled to any depot for transportation on the road, the Company will not hold itself responsible."

13. *DeBow's Review,* February, 1860, p. 230, March, 1861, p. 376; (Eighth Census) *Statistics of the United States in 1860,* Government Printing Office, p. 216.

14. *Annual Report,* Virginia & Tennessee Railroad, September, 1861.

15. South Carolina Railroad, *Rules and Regulations,* pp. 17, 19, 24, 33, 47.

16. Walter Prichard, *op. cit.,* p. 1160.

17. *Annual Report,* Richmond & Danville Railroad, 1862. In 1864 the Orange & Alexandria Railroad was partially controlling its freight and extra trains by telegraph. Orange & Alexandria timetable, February 10, 1864, Virginia Board of Public Works Papers.

18. *Annual Report,* North Carolina Railroad, July, 1860.

Chapter Four

OF DOLLARS AND CENTS

1. *Annual Reports,* Central of Georgia Railroad, December, 1860, December, 1861.

2. *Annual Reports:* Georgia Railroad, 1859; North Carolina Railroad, 1860; Petersburg Railroad, January, 1862; Memphis & Charleston Railroad, June, 1860; Western & Atlantic Railroad, October, 1861; *Hunt's Merchant's Magazine and Commercial Review,* March, 1861, p. 373; Charles G. Woodward, *op. cit.,* p. 11.

3. *Annual Reports:* Central of Georgia Railroad, December, 1860; Petersburg Railroad, January, 1862; Seaboard & Roanoke Railroad, February, 1862; North Carolina Railroad, July, 1860.

4. *Annual Reports:* Georgia Railroad, 1859; Macon & Western Railroad, 1859; Western & Atlantic Railroad, October, 1861; Memphis & Charleston Railroad, June, 1860; Richmond, Fredericksburg & Potomac Railroad, May, 1861; *American Railroad Journal,* April 20, 1861.

5. *Annual Report,* Western & Atlantic Railroad, October, 1861; *DeBow's Review,* February, 1860, pp. 225-26. A promising break in this ridiculous system was arranged in the winter of 1861 by the Central of Georgia and the Charleston & Savannah, whereby "cotton...be brought from Macon to Charleston, and goods sent back, without changing cars in Savannah." This required real foresight, especially in view of the simmering jealousy of Charleston long cultivated by Savannah commercial interests. *Annual Report,* Charleston & Savannah Railroad, February, 1861.

6. *Appleton's Railway Guide,* December, 1860, pp. 242, 243, 258; *Annual Report,* Atlantic & North Carolina Railroad, 1861; *American Railroad Journal,* March 23, 1861; *DeBow's Review,* March, 1860 (advertisement section).

7. *Annual Report,* Nashville & Chattanooga Railroad, August, 1861; *Annual Report,* Virginia Central Railroad, 1858; *Appleton's Railway Guide,* December, 1860, p. 245; *Annual Report,* Macon & Western Railroad, 1859; C. S. Engineering Department, MS Map of part of Eastern North Carolina, 1864, North Carolina Archives.

8. Charles G. Woodward, *op. cit.,* p. 6; *Farrow's & Dennett's Mobile City Directory,* 1861; p. 25; Joseph E. Brown to R. R. Cuyler, June 15, 1861, Georgia Executive Letters; *Annual Report,* Virginia Central Railroad, p. 26.

9. *Annual Report,* North Carolina Railroad, July, 1860.

10. All of the fares quoted above were published in *Appleton's Railway Guide,* December, 1860.

11. Vicksburg *Weekly Whig,* January 9, 1861; Western & Atlantic Commutation Ticket Ledger Record, June 1, 1855–October 31, 1861, Georgia Railroad Papers, Georgia Archives.

12. *Rules and Regulations*, South Carolina Railroad, 1855, revised 1869.

13. Milton S. Heath, *op. cit.*, p. 17.

14. *Annual Report*, Atlantic & North Carolina Railroad, 1861; *Annual Report*, Nashville & Chattanooga Railroad, August, 1861; *Journal* of Florida House of Representatives, 12th Session, 1863, pp. 26-27; Certificate of F. C. Barrett, Secretary and Treasurer of Florida Railroad Company, Sept. 8, 1862, Yulee Papers, University of Florida Library; *Annual Report*, Richmond, Fredericksburg & Potomac Railroad, May, 1861; Charles G. Woodward, *op. cit.*, p. 5.

15. *H. R. Report No. 34, Affairs of Southern Railroads*, 1867, 39th Congress, 2nd Session, p. 76; Georgia Executive Minutes (1860-66), October 7, 1861, pp. 244-45.

16. Charles G. Woodward, *op. cit.*, p. 6; Milton S. Heath, *op. cit.*, p. 54.

17. Milton S. Heath, *op. cit.*, provides an excellent survey of the subject. Unfortunately, it has never been published.

18. Milton S. Heath, *op. cit.*, pp. 39, 46-49, 63-70; Poor's *Manual*, 1869-70, p. 217.

19. By September 30, 1865, Virginia had expended more than $18,000,000 in the purchase of railroad stock. When the Virginia Central experienced trouble in penetrating the Blue Ridge, the State built that section of the road itself and thereafter charged the railroad a rental for its use. Heath, *op. cit.*, pp. 114-22; MS List of Stockholders of the Richmond & Danville Railroad Company, September 22, 1866, Virginia Board of Public Works Papers; MS correspondence as to directors and proxies of other roads in *ibid.*; MS Statements of charges due from Virginia Central Railroad for traffic passing over the Blue Ridge Railroad, in *ibid.*; *Biennial Report of the Board of Public Works to the General Assembly of Virginia* (1860-61), p. 17.

20. Heath, *op. cit.*, pp. 156-61; U. S. *Statutes at Large*, Ch. XXXI, 1856, Vol. II, pp. 15-16; *Proceedings* of Trustees of Florida Internal Improvement Fund (26 vols., Tallahassee, 1902-1949), Vol. I, pp. xv-xxxvi; *Journal* of the Florida House of Representatives, 12th Session, 1863, pp. 27-28; *Journal* of the Florida House of Representatives, 1860, p. 73.

21. *Proceedings* of Trustees of Florida Internal Improvement Fund, Vol. I, pp. xv-xxxvi, 200; *Journal* of Florida House of Representatives, 12th Session, 1863, pp. 27-28.

22. Annual Message of Governor Brown of Georgia, Georgia Executive Minutes, November 7, 1860; *Annual Report*, North Carolina Railroad, July, 1860; Heath, *op. cit.*, pp. 102-5; Comptroller General of South Carolina to Governor M. L. Bonham, October 4, 1863, MS in Railroad Papers, South Carolina Historical Dept.

23. State "2% and 3% funds were established for the development of desirable internal improvements and were based upon Federal land cessions. Mississippi utilized a similar device. Heath, *op. cit.*, pp. 144-50, 188-96; *American Railroad Journal*, February 3, 1861.

24. *American Railroad Journal*, February 16, 1861, March 30, 1861; Heath, *op. cit.*, pp. 220-22; Prichard, *op. cit.*, pp. 1165, 1213; Meridian (Miss.) *Daily Clarion*, August 8, 1865.

25. Heath, *op. cit.*, pp. 86, 95-98, 125-29, 152, 175, 197; *Annual Report*, Mobile & Great Northern Railroad, April, 1866; *Laws of Florida*, 1860-61, Ch. 1, 149 (No. 56), p. 108; *Annual Report*, Knoxville & Kentucky

Railroad, March, 1861; *Annual Report*, Charleston & Savannah Railroad, 1861.

26. *Annual Report*, Atlantic & North Carolina Railroad, 1861; Heath, *op. cit.*, pp. 95-98, 131; 198-200, 203, 226.

27. William H. Irwin to Thomas H. Dewitt of Virginia Board of Public Works, July 16, 1860, MS in Virginia Board of Public Works Papers; Heath, *op. cit.*, pp. 109, 198-200, 226; *Journal* of Florida House of Representatives, 12th Session, 1863, pp. 27-28; Georgia Executive Minutes, pp. 81, 199; *Annual Report*, Mobile & Great Northern Railroad, April, 1866.

28. Comptroller General of South Carolina to Gov. M. L. Bonham, October 4, 1863, MS in Railroad Papers, South Carolina Historical Dept.; Heath, *op. cit.*, pp. 252-53.

29. *Annual Report*, Georgia Railroad, May, 1859.

30. *Annual Reports:* Central of Georgia Railroad, December, 1860; Memphis & Charleston Railroad, June, 1860; Richmond, Fredericksburg & Potomac Railroad, May, 1861; *Hunt's Merchant's Magazine and Commercial Review*, July, 1860, p. 115; *American Railroad Journal*, April 20, 1861, August 9, 1862; Samuel M. Derrick, *Centennial History of the South Carolina Railroad*, p. 222.

31. *Annual Report*, New Orleans, Jackson & Great Northern Railroad, 1861; Walter Prichard, *op. cit.*, p. 1161; *Annual Report*, Charleston & Savannah Railroad, February, 1861; Paulding (Miss.) *Eastern Clarion*, May 24, 1861.

32. Charles G. Woodward, *op. cit.*, p. 7; *Appleton's Railway Guide*, December, 1860, pp. 251, 255, 257; *Annual Reports:* Montgomery & West Point Railroad, April, 1862; Wilmington & Weldon Railroad, 1863; Seaboard & Roanoke Railroad, February, 1862; Charleston & Savannah Railroad, 1861; Vicksburg *Weekly Whig*, February 8, 1860.

33. *Annual Reports:* Roanoke Valley Railroad, October, 1861; Richmond, Fredericksburg & Potomac Railroad, May, 1861; *Official Records*, IV, I, p. 1024.

Chapter Five

THE IRON HORSE GOES FORTH TO WAR

1. *Official Records*, IV, I, pp. 120, 132, 224, 228, 236-37; Walter Prichard, "G. W. R. Bayley," p. 1069; *American Railroad Journal*, May 25, 1861.

2. *Acts* of Alabama Assembly, Called Session, 1861, No. 49, p. 52; *Florida Laws*, 1860-61, Sec. 8, Ch. I, 138 (No. 45), p. 84.

3. *Official Records*, IV, I, pp. 114-15.

4. Gen. Henry C. Wayne to Maj. E. R. Harden, First Regiment, Georgia Army, February 27, 1861, Georgia Adj. General Letter Book, Part I, p. 150, Georgia Archives.

5. *Official Records*, IV, I, pp. 175, 176-77.

6. *Official Records*, IV, I, pp. 191, 192, 193.

7. Thomas McAdory Owen, *op. cit.*, II, p. 1013; Montgomery *Weekly Confederation*, May 10, 1861, May 24, 1861; A. C. Myers, Acting Quartermaster General, C.S.A., to L. P. Walker, May 21, 1861, Confederate Secretaries of War Papers; Montgomery *Mail*, May 4, 1861.

8. "Appendix G" of MS Reports of Montgomery Railroad Convention, C. S. Railroad Papers, War Records Division, National Archives.
9. August Dietz, *The Confederate States Post Office Department, Its Stamps and Stationery* (Richmond, 1948), p. 6.
10. Montgomery *Daily Mail*, April 29, 1861.
11. *Ibid.* See also *Official Records*, IV, I, p. 269.
12. Montgomery *Daily Mail*, April 29, 1861; *Acts and Resolutions of the First Three Sessions of the Provisional Congress of the Confederate States* (Richmond, 1862), Second Session, No. 111, pp. 7-8.
13. Montgomery *Daily Mail*, April 29, 1861.
14. *Report of Railroad Convention*, Chattanooga, Tennessee, June 4-5, 1861, copy in Georgia State Library, Atlanta. No evidence of the actual publication of the common tariff has been found by the author.
15. *Annual Report*, Virginia Central Railroad, 1861.
16. *Annual Report*, Richmond, Fredericksburg & Potomac Railroad, May, 1861; *Official Records*, IV, I, pp. 240-41, 724-25.
17. *Official Records*, I, LI, II, pp. 98-99.
18. *Official Records*, I, L, pp. 858, 866, 917.
19. Report of E. C. Marshall, Agent of the Board of Public Works of Virginia, November 13, 1865, MS in Virginia Board of Public Works Papers.
20. *Annual Report*, Southwestern Railroad, August, 1861; R. A. Anderson to Dr. J. W. Lewis, July 1, 1861, MS letter in Georgia Railroad Papers; *Official Records*, I, LII, II, pp. 78-79.
21. *Official Records*, IV, I, pp. 274-75; Richmond *Daily Examiner*, May 3 and May 25, 1861.
22. *Official Records*, IV, I, pp. 240-41; Richmond *Daily Examiner*, April 30, 1861.
23. Brown to Judah P. Benjamin, October 2, 1861, Georgia Executive Letters.
24. Gov. Moore to Charles T. Pollard, October 24, 1861, MS in Alabama Quartermaster Papers, Military Records Division, Alabama Department of Archives and History; Bill of Lading Form and Vouchers for Transportation of the South Carolina Railroad in *ibid;* Tennessee Transportation Requests in Thomas Peters Papers, War Records Division, National Archives; Soldier's Tickets of Alabama & Florida and Atlanta & West Point Railroads, C. S. Railroad Papers, in *ibid.*
25. Gov. Brown to R. R. Cuyler, June 8, 1861, Georgia Executive Letters; *Annual Report*, Central of Georgia Railroad, December, 1861; Richmond *Semi-Weekly Examiner*, December 20, 1861; D. C. Campbell to H. C. Wayne, Adj. Gen. of Georgia, November 16, 1861, MS in Georgia Railroad Papers; Abstract of Field Return, Dist. of Alabama, C. S. Army, December 2, 1861, in John W. Goodwin Papers, War Records Division, National Archives; Goodwin to Capt. H. Oladowski, January 17, 1862, MS in Goodwin Papers; Annual Message, Gov. Brown of Georgia, November 6, 1861, Georgia Executive Minutes.
26. Douglas Southall Freeman, *Lee's Lieutenants* (3 Vols., New York, 1946), Vol. I, pp. 40-44.
27. *Official Records*, I, II, p. 566.
28. *Ibid.*, I, II, pp. 470-78, 486, 569.
29. *Ibid.*, I, II, pp. 566, 980-81, 983, 985, 986.

Chapter Six

TRANSPORTATION EMERGENCY—FIRST PHASE

1. E. Merton Coulter, *The Confederate States of America, 1861-1865* (Louisiana State University Press, 1950) pp. 374 ff.
2. *Ibid.*, pp. 401 ff.
3. S. A. Ashe and others, *Biographical History of North Carolina*, VIII, pp. 30-36; see also sketch in *Dictionary of American Biography*, Vol. I, p. 388; for Ashe's appointment by Davis, see Register of Appointments, C. S. Army, Ch. I, File No. 86, p. 171, War Records Division, National Archives.
4. Ashe caused to be printed a "requisition for transportation of freight," whereon his name appeared in large block letters, followed by a blank for the signature of an assistant and for the name of the point at which the assistant was stationed. Ashe's subordinate at Wilmington was his own General Ticket Agent, S. D. Wallace. Confederate transportation requests for both passengers and freight are available in great numbers at the National Archives. The regulations for the transportation of the sick were repeatedly published in the Richmond *Examiner* during the late fall of 1861; an official printing of the same survives in the Keith M. Read Confederate Collection, Emory University Library.
5. *Official Records*, I, V, pp. 770, 833.
6. *Ibid.*, I, V, pp. 857-58, 867, 871.
7. *Ibid.*, I, V, pp. 875-76.
8. More than 2,000 fresh troops, intended for Johnston's army, loitered in Richmond through a whole November week before they could be sent on by rail; even then they were routed to Fredericksburg over the Richmond, Fredericksburg & Potomac, and marched thence to Manassas. See telegrams of Benjamin to Johnston, November 7, 1861, *Official Records*, I, V, p. 940; Benjamin to Johnston, November 13, 1861, *ibid.*, p. 953; Cooper to Johnston, November 15, 1861, *ibid.*, pp. 954-55. For Haupt's estimate see Weber, *op. cit.*, p. 274.
9. Bruce, *Virginia Iron Manufacture*, pp. 363-64; Lewis E. Harvie, President of Richmond & Danville Railroad to R. M. T. Hunter, Confederate Secretary of State, October 9, 1861, MS in C. S. Railroad Papers, National Archives; *Annual Report*, Virginia Central Railroad, 1861; *Official Records*, I, IV, pp. 401 and 402.
10. Ashe to Brown, October 3, 1861, Georgia Executive Letters; *Official Records*, IV, I, pp. 617, 634.
11. Benjamin to Brown, October 1, 1861, Georgia Executive Letters; Ashe to Brown, October 3, 1861, in *ibid.*, Brown to Ashe, October 3, 1861, in *ibid.*
12. Harvie to Hunter, October 9, 1861, MS in C. S. Railroad Papers, National Archives; Report of Brig. Gen. John B. Floyd, November 7, 1861, *Official Records*, I, V, p. 285; Gov. Isham G. Harris of Tennessee to Gen. A. S. Johnston, November 1, 1861, in *ibid.*, p. 496; Reuben Davis to Jefferson Davis, November 4, 1861, in *ibid.*, pp. 510-11; Georgia Executive Minutes, November 6, 1862; MS letter and map, Supt. Rowland of Western and Atlantic to Gov. Brown, November 13, 1861, Georgia Railroad Papers;

Par. I, Special Orders No. 216, Adj. and Insp. General's Office, C.S.A., November 11, 1861, *Official Records*, I, IV, p. 538.

13. *Official Records*, I, VII, p. 733.

14. *Official Records*, I, LII, II, pp. 227-28, I, VI, p. 768.

15. *Official Records*, I, LI, II, pp. 276, 278, 304-5; Ashe to Davis, April 16, 1862, MS in C. S. Railroad Papers, National Archives; *Dictionary of American Biography*, I, p. 398; S. A. Ashe, *op. cit.*, I, pp. 34-36. The circumstances of Ashe's death were horrible. In the late summer of 1862 he had commenced the construction of some salt works at Wrightsville Sound. On the evening of September 12 he was returning home over the track of his Wilmington & Weldon road upon a handcar, when it was run down by a southbound freight train without a headlight. No one else on the handcar with Ashe was hurt, but he was so terribly mutilated that he "when discovered could not for some time be recognized." Following the amputation of his right leg, he died on September 14. Wilmington *Journal*, September 13, 1862, quoted in Raleigh *Weekly Register*, September 17, 1862.

16. Stanley F. Horn, *The Army of Tennessee* (Indianapolis and New York, 1941), p. 61. It is said that only three boats in operating condition were left upon the Cumberland at Nashville.

17. See map, p. 141.

18. Stanley F. Horn, *op. cit.*, pp. 55, 56, 61.

19. *Official Records* I, IV, pp. 437, 438, 439, 445, 539, 553; I, VII, pp. 818-19; L. B. Northrup to Sec. of War J. A. Seddon, May 2, 1863, MS in Hottel Papers, War Records Division, National Archives.

20. Richmond *Daily Examiner*, May 1, 1861; *Official Records*, IV, I, p. 394; Richmond *Daily Examiner*, June 14 and 25, 1862.

21. *Official Records*, IV, I, pp. 405, 417-18, 484-85.

22. Richmond *Dispatch*, December 23, 1861; Carter S. Anderson, "Train Running for the Confederacy" (Part IV), *Locomotive Engineering*, November, 1892.

23. A. T. Bledsoe, Chief of Bureau of War, to J. P. Benjamin, October 30, 1861, MS in C. S. Secretaries of War Papers, National Archives; William Mahone to Sec. of War Randolph, May 2, 1862, MS in *ibid*. As a general officer in the Army of Northern Virginia, Mahone repeatedly displayed his willingness to sacrifice his life for the Confederate cause, but as president of the Norfolk & Petersburg, he showed himself equally indisposed to sacrifice the interests of his railroad. Even before the completion of the link, he demanded that Ashe change its location, and when, the following spring, a shift was being considered, he denounced the new alignment as "selfishly stupid" and a display of "morbid taste." (The relocation proposed would have encroached even further upon his own property.)

24. Ashe to J. Davis, November 27, 1861, MS in C. S. Railroad Papers, National Archives; *Acts* of Alabama General Assembly, Regular Session, 1861, No. 125, p. 106; C. T. Pollard to Q. M. General A. C. Myers, December 16, 1861, MS in C. S. Secretaries of War Papers, National Archives; C. J. McRae to Benjamin, December 13, 1861, in *ibid.*, Pollard to Benjamin, December 5, 1861, in *ibid*.

25. Vicksburg *Weekly Whig*, February 27, 1861.

26. *DeBow's Review*, May and June, 1861, p. 679.

27. Ashe to Davis, November 27, 1861, MS in C. S. Railroad Papers, National Archives; Ashe to Davis, December 13, 1861, MS in *ibid*.

28. *Journal* of C. S. Congress, I, pp. 358 and 379; Milton S. Heath, *op. cit.*, p. 147.
29. For material on the early phases of the Danville-Greensboro scheme, see John A. Washington to B. M. Jones, May 11, 1861, *Official Records*, I, II, pp. 830-31; *Annual Report*, Richmond & Danville Railroad, December, 1862; *Journal* of C. S. Congress, I, pp. 477, 548, 566, 586; Harvie to Hunter, October 9, 1861, MS in C. S. Secretaries of War Papers, National Archives; Richmond *Daily Dispatch*, December 13, 1861.
30. Material upon the progress and completion of the Mobile & Great Northern can be found in *American Railroad Journal*, April 27, 1861; Montgomery *Weekly Confederation*, June 7, 1861; President William D. Dunn to J. M. Withers, October 2, 1861, MS in C. S. Railroad Papers, National Archives; Montgomery *Daily Mail*, November 18, 1861, *et. seq.*; *Official Records*, I, VI, p. 766; I, LII, II, pp. 164-65; IV, I, p. 732.
31. *Journal* of C. S. Congress, I, pp. 226, 477.
32. Harvie to R. M. T. Hunter, October 9, 1861, MS in C. S. Secretaries of War Papers, National Archives; *Journal* of C. S. Congress, I, pp. 290, 379; MS "Bill Authorizing the President to regulate and take control of railroads in certain cases," F. W. Sims Papers, National Archives.
33. *Official Records*, I, V, p. 7.

Chapter Seven

PROFITS, LOSSES, AND SHORTAGES

1. Market Report of John A. Lancaster & Son, Richmond *Daily Dispatch*, May 3, 1861.
2. Quoted in *American Railroad Journal*, June 1, 1861.
3. *Annual Report*, Nashville and Chattanooga Railroad, August, 1861; *American Railroad Journal*, May 25, 1861.
4. *Annual Reports:* Nashville & Chattanooga Railroad, August, 1861; Richmond & Danville Railroad, December, 1861; Central of Georgia Railroad, December, 1860, 1861; also *American Railroad Journal*, August 10, 1861; Samuel M. Derrick, *op. cit.*, p. 222. In virtually no instance did a southern railroad enjoy a higher gross income in 1861 than in 1860. To be sure, the North Carolina road could show a paper increase of more than $362,000, but its fiscal period ran from June to June. *Annual Report*, North Carolina Railroad, July, 1864.
5. *Annual Reports:* Seaboard & Roanoke Railroad, February, 1862; Mobile & Ohio Railroad, May, 1861; Richmond & Danville Railroad, December, 1861; Central of Georgia Railroad, December, 1861; Montgomery & West Point Railroad, April, 1862; Southwestern Railroad, August 1861, 1862.
6. *Annual Reports:* Virginia Central Railroad, October, 1861; Virginia & Tennessee Railroad, September, 1861; North Carolina Railroad, July, 1864; Central of Georgia Railroad, December, 1861; Southwestern Railroad, August, 1861, 1862; Thomas W. Chadwick, ed., "Diary of Samuel Edward Burges, 1860-1862," *South Carolina Historical and Genealogical Magazine*, July, 1947, p. 161.
7. *Annual Reports:* Virginia Central Railroad, October, 1861; North Carolina Railroad, July, 1864; Samuel M. Derrick, *op. cit.*, p. 222.

8. *Annual Report*, Virginia Central Railroad, October, 1861; "Comptroller General's Reports," *Reports and Resolutions of the General Assembly of the State of South Carolina*, 1861; MS dividend data, Petersburg Railroad, Virginia Board of Public Works Papers; Richmond *Daily Examiner*, September 6, November 18, December 18, 1861; Richmond *Dispatch*, May 3, 1861; *Annual Report*, Virginia & Tennessee Railroad, September, 1861; *Georgia Senate Journal*, 1861, p. 210; *Appleton's Railway Guide*, December, 1860; Savannah *Daily Morning News*, January 30, 1862, August 21, 1862.

9. *Annual Report*, Petersburg Railroad, January, 1862.

10. *Annual Report*, Petersburg Railroad, January, 1862.

11. *Ibid.;* MS report of Lt. Col. Larkin Smith, January 13, 1862, Sims Papers, National Archives.

12. *Eighth Census of the United States* (Population), Washington, Government Printing Office, 1864, pp. 672-73.

13. Richmond *Daily Examiner*, April 24, 1861; *Official Records*, IV, I, p. 616; Georgia Executive Letters, March 24, 1862.

14. Owen to Davis, November 18, 1861, MS in C. S. Secretaries of War Papers, National Archives.

15. *Annual Report*, Atlantic & Gulf Railroad, February, 1861; *Monroe Register*, January 31, 1861, quoted in *American Railroad Journal*, March 9, 1861; *Annual Report*, Vicksburg, Shreveport & Texas Railroad, January, 1861, quoted in *ibid.;* Poor's *Manual*, 1869-1870, p. 196; *Annual Report*, Western North Carolina Railroad, 1861; J. W. Lapsley to Secretary of War Randolph, May 5, 1862, MS in C. S. Secretaries of War Papers, National Archives.

16. *DeBow's Review*, February, 1866, pp. 205-6; *Annual Report*, Mississippi & Tennessee Railroad, November, 1865; *American Railroad Journal*, April 27, 1861, May 18, 1861; Milledgeville (Ga.) *Southern Recorder*, August 20, 1861.

17. Alex. R. Holladay, Pres. of (Va.) Board of Public Works to Barbour, November 27, 1861, MS in Virginia Board of Public Works Papers; Thomas McA. Owen, *op. cit.*, I, pp. 507-8; *Acts* of Alabama Assembly Called Session, 1861, No. 11, p. 19; *Acts* of Alabama Assembly, Regular Session, 1861, No. 36, p. 41.

18. *Annual Report*, Virginia & Tennessee Railroad, September, 1861.

19. *Annual Reports:* Virginia & Tennessee Railroad, September, 1861; Southwestern Railroad, August, 1861; Virginia Central Railroad, October, 1861; Gov. Brown to Supt. Rowland of Western & Atlantic Railroad, December 3, 1861, Georgia Executive Minutes.

20. Adv. of Theodore Dehon in *American Railroad Journal*, March 9, 1861; *Annual Report*, Macon & Brunswick Railroad, February, 1866; *Acts and Resolutions of the First Three Sessions of the Provisional Congress of the Confederate States*, Richmond, 1862, Second Session, No. 179, p. 92; *Official Records* (Navy), II, I, p. 754.

21. Quartermaster-General A. C. Myers to Sec. of War Benjamin, January 31, 1862, MS in C. S. Secretaries of War Papers, National Archives.

22. *Journal* of C. S. Congress, I, pp. 46, 59-60, 123, 148, 151; *Acts & Resolutions of the First Three Sessions of the Provisional Confederate Congress*, 1st Session, No. 88, p. 135; *ibid.*, 2nd Session, No. 162, p. 54, No. 163, pp. 62-63.

23. *Statutes at Large,* Provisional Government of the Confederate States, Provisional Congress, 4th Session, Ch. III, January 23, 1862, p. 285; *Journal* C. S. Congress, I, pp. 252, 832; *Acts & Resolutions of the Third Session of the Provisional Congress of the Confederate States,* Richmond, 1861, No. 238, p. 39; *Acts & Resolutions,* 4th Session of Provisional Congress of C. S., Richmond, 1862, No. 401, pp. 100-1.

24. *Official Records,* I, VI, pp. 781-82.

25. *Annual Reports:* Central of Georgia Railroad, December, 1860; Southwestern Railroad, August, 1861, 1862.

26. *Annual Report,* Virginia Central Railroad, October, 1861; *Official Records,* I, V, pp. 587, 858-59; I, LI, II, pp. 248-49, 258-59. Stonewall Jackson is said to have bagged a fine lot of Baltimore & Ohio rolling stock as early as May and to have moved it to Winchester. Just how much of this was carried south remains obscure. Myers in his letter of August 29 refers to the movement of Baltimore & Ohio cars to the Manassas Gap road.

27. *Annual Reports,* Central of Georgia Railroad, December, 1860, December, 1861.

28. *Annual Report,* Virginia Central Railroad, October, 1861.

29. *Annual Report,* Central of Georgia Railroad, December, 1861; *Annual Report,* Richmond & Danville Railroad, December, 1861.

30. Report of Supt. John M. Robinson, *Annual Report,* Seaboard & Roanoke Railroad, February, 1862.

31. Richmond *Daily Examiner,* December 18, 1861; *Official Records,* IV, I, p. 868.

32. Mobile *Register and Advertiser,* June 30, 1861; Richmond *Semi-Weekly Examiner,* September 4, 1861; *Annual Report,* Seaboard & Roanoke Railroad, February, 1862; "Comptroller General's Report," *Reports and Resolutions,* South Carolina General Assembly, 1861.

33. *Acts & Resolutions* of C. S. Provisional Congress, 3rd Session, No. 223, pp. 20-21.

34. Examples of "railroad money," by no means confined to the Civil War period, are to be found in many places. A fifty-cent Mobile & Ohio, plus a two-dollar and a fifteen-cent Central of Georgia, are displayed in the Georgia Room of the Confederate Museum, Richmond.

35. Francis T. Willis, President of Augusta & Savannah Railroad to Governor Brown, December 23, 1861, MS in Georgia Railroad Papers; *Official Records,* I, LI, II, p. 451; telegrams of Gov. Brown of Georgia, November 20, 21, 1861, letter of Gov. Brown to G. W. Adams, December 16, 1861, Georgia Executive Letters; Richmond *Daily Examiner,* December 19, 1861, January 25, February 1 and 3, 1862.

36. Georgia Executive Minutes, October 7, 1861. Charles S. Schlatter was appointed State Superintendent of the Road at a salary of eighteen hundred dollars per year; the name of the road was changed to Brunswick & Albany on December 16, 1861; see Georgia *Laws,* 1861, p. 113.

37. Brown to R. Hazlehurst and Charles L. Schlatter, October 7, 1861; Brown to R. R. Cuyler, December 9, 1861, Brown to Gen. H. M. Mercer, December 9, 1861, Brown to R. R. Cuyler, December 12, 1861, Georgia Executive Letters.

38. *Annual Report,* Augusta & Savannah Railroad, 1861.

39. *Annual Report,* Seaboard & Roanoke Railroad, February, 1862.

Chapter Eight

COLONEL MYERS FACES CHAOS

1. *Journal,* Confederate States Congress, I, pp. 654, 720-21; *Official Records,* IV, I, pp. 884-85.
2. Confederate States Quartermaster General's Office *Circular,* Richmond, Va., February 10, 1862; Adv. as to transportation of recruits, Richmond *Daily Examiner,* March 10, 1862.
3. *Journal,* Confederate States Congress, V, pp. 82, 122; II, p. 87.
4. *Ibid.,* V, pp. 251-53.
5. Sarah L. Wadley, *A Brief Record of the Life of William M. Wadley, Written by His Eldest Daughter* (New York, 1884), p. 39.
6. *Journal,* Confederate States Congress, V, pp. 152, 188, 215, 253-54, 269.
7. *Ibid.,* II, pp. 195, 198, 215.
8. *Official Records,* IV, I, p. 1052; IV, II, p. 51; Smith to Myers, January 13, 1862, MS in Sims Papers.
9. *Official Records,* IV, II, pp. 48-49.
10. *Ibid.,* p. 54.
11. *Official Records,* IV, II, pp. 200, 210; *Journal* Confederate States Congress, II, pp. 330-31.
12. *Official Records,* IV, I, pp. 839, 843-45, 868, 880-82, 896-97.
13. *Journal,* Confederate States Congress, I, p. 701.
14. Richmond *Daily Examiner,* February 6, 1862; *Official Records,* IV, II, pp. 505-8; Raleigh *Weekly Register,* February 12, 1862; *DeBow's Review,* May-August, 1862, p. 95.
15. Richmond *Daily Examiner,* February 6, 8, 1862.
16. *Annual Report,* North Carolina Railroad, July, 1865.
17. *Annual Report,* Virginia Central Railroad, 1863; *Journal,* Confederate States Congress, II, p. 267; Mason Morfit to A. C. Myers, October 14, 1862, MS in Confederate States Railroad Papers, National Archives; Barbour to Randolph, October 11, 1862, two MSS in Confederate States Secretaries of War Papers, National Archives.
18. Mason Morfit to A. C. Myers, October 14, 1862, MS in Confederate States Railroad Papers, National Archives; *Annual Report,* Virginia Central Railroad, 1863.
19. Col. William M. Wadley to Secretary of War Seddon, May 27, 1863, MS in Confederate States Railroad Papers, National Archives; *Annual Report,* Richmond & Petersburg Railroad, May, 1863; Capt. Thomas R. Sharp to Kemp R. Battle, January 29, 1863; MS in Confederate States Secretaries of War Papers, National Archives.
20. *Annual Report,* North Carolina Railroad, July, 1862; *Annual Report,* Petersburg Railroad, January, 1866; *Annual Report,* Richmond & Petersburg Railroad, May, 1863.
21. *Official Records,* II, I, p. 676; I, XVIII, p. 859.
22. *Circular,* Quartermaster General's Office, C. S. A., September 12, 1862; Jackson *Daily Mississippian,* Sept. 12, 1862.
23. Savannah *Daily Morning News,* October 7, 1862.
24. *Annual Report,* Petersburg Railroad, March, 1863; Jones *Diary,* I, p. 207; Charles Ellis to G. W. Randolph, April 14, 1862, MS in Confederate

States Secretaries of War Papers, National Archives; George Dowden to Lieut. McHenry, October 19, 1862, MS in *ibid.*; Dowden to Col. J. Gorgas, October 19, 1862, MS in *ibid.*; *Official Records*, I, XX, II, p. 407.

Chapter Nine

WILLIAM M. WADLEY

1. There is, unfortunately, no full-length biography of Wadley. Probably the best account is Sarah L. Wadley, *A Brief Record of the Life of William M. Wadley, Written by His Eldest Daughter* (New York, 1884). Though the author displays a natural filial bias and at times turns sentimental, her account is valuable because of her personal knowledge of many of the principal episodes of her father's life. T. B. Catherwood, ed., *The Life and Labors of William M. Wadley* (Savannah, 1885) is very brief and highly eulogistic, but contains some interesting supplementary material. The article on Wadley in W. J. Northen, ed., *Men of Mark in Georgia* (Atlanta, 1911, Vol. III of seven volumes) adds nothing of note and is marred by inaccuracies. The author is especially obligated to Mrs. William Burt of Great Hill Place, Bolingbroke, Georgia, for the loan of additional manuscript sources, without which even this sketchy treatment of the most significant railroad man of the Southern Confederacy would not have been possible.
2. Private Journal of Sarah L. Wadley (Typed Volume No. I, in possession of Mrs. William Burt, Great Hill Place, Bolingbroke, Georgia), pp. 65, 91, 95; Sarah L. Wadley, *Brief Record of William M. Wadley*, p. 35; *Official Records*, I, XIX, II, p. 717.
3. Sarah Wadley Journal (Typed Vol. I), pp. 95-97, 99; *Official Records*, IV, II, p. 225.
4. *Official Records*, IV, II, pp. 231-32, 304-5, 372-73.
5. Sarah Wadley Journal (Typed Vol. II), p. 100; typewritten resumé of military record of Frederick W. Sims, Sims Papers, National Archives; Savannah *Daily Morning News*, December 12, 1862.
6. Notice of Augusta Convention in Montgomery *Daily Mail*, December 6, 1862; Editorial in Richmond *Daily Examiner*, December 10, 1862.
7. *Official Records*, IV, II, pp. 270-78.
8. Except where otherwise noted, the material for this sketch of the Augusta Railroad Convention has been taken from Wadley's report to Gen. S. Cooper, December 31, 1862, *Official Records*, IV, II, pp. 270-78.
9. The author is in possession of one of Wadley's circulars, dated Augusta, Georgia, December 17, 1862. A small supply of them is likewise in the Valentine Museum, Richmond.
10. *Official Records*, IV, II, pp. 271-72. The effect of conscription upon the railroads of the Confederacy will be treated in a later chapter.
11. *Official Records*, IV, II, pp. 295-96.
12. Bently D. Hasell to Wadley, December 24, 1862, MS in Valentine Museum Library, Richmond.
13. *Official Records*, IV, II, p. 348; *Journal*, Confederate States Congress, III, p. 15.
14. Seddon to Wadley, January 8, 1863, MS telegraphic receipt in Valentine

Museum, Richmond; *Official Records,* I, XXI, p. 1110; I, LI, II, pp. 674-75.

15. *Official Records,* I, XVIII, p. 859; *Affairs of Southern Railroads,* p. 70.
16. *Official Records,* I, XXV, II, pp. 610-11; IV, II, pp. 384-85.
17. *Official Records,* I, XXV, II, pp. 610-11; I, XVIII, p. 874; Sarah Wadley Journal (Typed Vol. II), p. 112.
18. *Official Records,* I, XXV, II, pp. 610-11; IV, II, pp. 373-74.
19. *Official Records,* IV, II, pp. 609-10, 638-39.
20. *Journal,* Confederate States Congress, IV, pp. 72, 95, 103, 402, 443-44.
21. *Republished General Orders as to railroads,* March 23, 1863, printed notice in Confederate State Railroad Papers, National Archives; Wadley to W. S. Downer, Superintendent of Armories, February 18, 1863, MS in Wadley Papers, National Archives; Wadley to Seddon, May 27, 1863, MS in Confederate States Railroad Papers, National Archives.
22. Under the absurd system existing, most stray railway equipment and supplies coming into the hands of the Confederate Government passed to Raleigh through *Quartermaster* channels, where it was turned over by Sharp to Sims. A number of the receipts issued therefor survive among the Sims Papers, National Archives.
23. *Official Records,* I, XVIII, p. 859; Northrup to Seddon, May 2, 1863; MS in Hottel Papers, War Records Division, National Archives; Sims to Gen. S. Cooper, June 4, 1863, MS in *ibid.*
24. Sarah Wadley Journal (Typed Vol. II), pp. 119, 123; *Official Records,* I, XXIV, I, pp. 289-90, 298; I, XXIV, III, pp. 598, 625. The role of the railroads in the Vicksburg campaign and its aftermath will be briefly treated in a later chapter.
25. *Official Records,* IV, II, p. 457; Jones *Diary,* I, p. 290; C. O. Sanford, Superintendent of Petersburg Railroad, to President W. T. Joynes, April 4, 1863, MS in Confederate States Railroad Papers, National Archives; Joynes to Wadley, April 29, 1863, MS in *ibid.; Annual Report,* Western North Carolina Railroad, 1863, pp. 14-17. MS (fragment) of Colonel A. C. Myers, probably to Seddon in late April, 1863, Confederate States Railroad Papers, National Archives.
26. MS copy of minutes of Convention of the Railroads of Virginia, Richmond, January 8 and 9, 1863, Confederate States Railroad Papers, National Archives; MS copy of petition of officials of thirteen Confederate railroad companies to Secretary of War, February, 1863, Georgia Railroad Papers, Georgia Department of Archives; MS petition of same to Legislature of Georgia, March, 1863, in *ibid.; Official Records,* IV, II, pp. 394-95, 409-10, 841-42.
27. Wadley to Seddon, April 14, 1863, MS in Confederate States Railroad Papers, National Archives; *Official Records,* IV, II, pp. 483-85; I, XXV, II, pp. 735-36.
28. Wadley to Seddon, April 17, 1863, MS in Confederate States Railroad Papers, National Archives; "Memo of proposed agreement between R. R. Co's & Government," MS in Wadley's handwriting in Valentine Museum, Richmond; *Official Records,* IV, II, pp. 508-10; MS Resolutions of Richmond Railroad Convention, 1863, Confederate States Secretaries of War Papers, National Archives.
29. *Official Records,* IV, II, pp. 509-10.
30. Jones *Diary,* I, p. 302; *Official Records,* IV, II, p. 508.

31. *Journal*, Confederate States Congress, III, pp. 259, 291, 317, 350-51.
32. Seddon to Wigfall, April 26, 1863, MS in Confederate States Railroad Papers, National Archives.
33. *Journal*, Confederate States Congress, III, pp. 354-55, 429; VI, pp. 472-73.
34. Charles W. Ramsdell, *Laws and Joint Resolutions of the last Session of the Confederate Congress* (Durham, 1941), pp. 167-69, text from original bill, as amended, in National Archives.
35. *Journal*, Confederate States Congress, III, p. 409.
36. *Ibid.*, pp. 412, 426.
37. Letter of Mrs. F. W. Altstetter to the author, July 12, 1949.
38. *Ibid.*, p. 20; T. B. Catherwood, *op. cit.*, pp. 3-13.

Chapter Ten

EXPANDING DIFFICULTIES

1. *Official Records*, I, XVIII, pp. 951-52; *Annual Report*, South Side Railroad, November, 1863; *Annual Report*, Richmond & Petersburg Railroad, May, 1863; *Annual Report*, Virginia Central Railroad, October, 1863; Bentley D. Hasell to William M. Wadley, December 24, 1862, MS in Valentine Museum, Richmond; G. H. Arms, Chief Engineer, Southern Railroad, to W. C. Smedes, December 24, 1862, MS in Confederate States Secretaries of War Papers, National Archives.
2. *Annual Report*, Central of Georgia Railroad, December, 1862; *Annual Report*, Wilmington & Weldon Railroad, October, 1863.
3. *Annual Reports:* Southwestern Railroad, August 1, 1861-2-3; Central of Georgia Railroad, December, 1860-63; Montgomery & West Point Railroad, April, 1862; Virginia Central Railroad, October, 1863, 1864; Jones *Diary*, I, p. 304; *Annual Report*, North Carolina Railroad, July, 1863.
4. Bentley D. Hasell to William M. Wadley, December 24, 1862, MS in Valentine Museum; *Annual Report*, Virginia Central Railroad, October, 1862; Annual Message, Gov. Brown of Georgia, November 6, 1862, Georgia Executive Minutes; *Annual Reports*, Central of Georgia Railroad, December, 1862; Macon & Western Railroad, 1859, 1863.
5. C. Wallace to John S. Rowland, July 29, 1863, MS in Georgia Railroad Papers.
6. *DeBow's Review*, January-February, 1862, p. 169; *Annual Report*, Central of Georgia Railroad, December, 1862, 1863.
7. Gov. Brown of Georgia to Supt. Rowland of Western & Atlantic, August 26, 1862, Georgia Executive Letters; *Annual Report*, Central of Georgia Railroad, December, 1860, 1863; Gov. Brown to Gen. H. C. Wayne, October 12, 1863, Georgia Executive Letters; Gov. Brown to Dr. George D. Phillips, Supt. of Western & Atlantic, November 30, 1863, Georgia Executive Minutes; *Official Records*, I, XXV, II, pp. 683-84.
8. *Annual Reports*, Macon & Western Railroad, 1859, 1863, 1864; Montgomery *Daily Mail*, December 30, 1862, *et seq.; Annual Report*, South Side Railroad, 1863.
9. H. D. Whitcomb to E. Fontaine, November 7, 1862, MS in Virginia Board of Public Works Papers, Virginia State Library; Raleigh *Weekly Register*, February 12, 1862.

10. Lewis E. Harvie to James A. Seddon, March 31, 1863; Georgia Senate
    Journal, 1862, p. 266; Georgia *Laws,* 1862-63, p. 63; Work Account
Book, Western & Atlantic Railroad, Georgia Railroad Papers, Georgia Dept.
of Archives and History; Special Message, Governor Brown to Georgia
General Assembly, December 2, 1863, Georgia Executive Minutes; *Annual
Reports,* Virginia Central Railroad, 1861, 1862, 1863.

11. *Journal,* Confederate States Congress, V, pp. 90, 95; *Official Records,*
    IV, I, p. 1081.

12. Telegrams, Brown to Maj. Gen. H. R. Jackson, April 11, 12, 1862,
    Georgia Executive Letters; Brown to Davis, April 22, 1862, in *ibid.* See
also *Official Records,* IV, I, p. 1084; IV, II, p. 642. Brown's attitude was
abundantly summed up the following spring (1863) when he wrote Col.
Wadley as follows: "We have no employees upon the State Road who are
subject to conscription. Every man employed has been regularly mustered
into the military service of the State of Georgia and detailed under my authority to the service of the Road. I do not therefore recognize the right of
the Confederate Government to interfere with them in any way whatever,
nor can I permit any such interference."—Brown to Wadley, April 23, 1863,
Georgia Executive Letters.

13. MS Chart of Exemptions and Details of Railroad Employees, August 12,
    1862, Confederate States Secretaries of War Papers, National Archives,
Official Records, IV, II, p. 162; *Journal,* Confederate States Congress, II, p.
218; V, pp. 432-34, 457, 477, 487, 491, 561.

14. *Annual Report,* Western & Atlantic Railroad, October, 1862. The pleas
    of individual roads for the detail of their employees never ceased
throughout the remainder of the war, and their demands became more in-
sistent as time went on. Specific examples of the army-railroad struggle over
manpower will be noted in a later chapter. For northern draft policy with
respect to railway workers, see Thomas Weber, *op. cit.,* pp. 224-29; also,
Secretary of War Stanton to Thomas A. Scott, August 12, 1862, *Official
Records,* III, II, p. 358.

15. Richmond *Daily Examiner,* November 19 and 25, 1862, March 22, 1863,
    August 3, 1863; Minutes of Board of Directors, Virginia Central Rail-
road, MS in possession of Chesapeake & Ohio Railway Company, Richmond;
Annual Report, Virginia Central Railroad, October, 1863.

16. For material upon Pemberton's food order see *Official Records,* I, XV,
    pp. 937-38, 971.

17. *Public Laws,* C.S.A., 1st Congress, 3rd Session, 1863, Ch. 38, pp. 120-21.

18. Mary G. Cumming, *op. cit.,* p. 80; *Annual Report,* Central of Georgia
    Railroad, December, 1863.

19. L. P. Ellis to J. R. MacMurdo, Treasurer, Richmond, Fredericksburg &
    Potomac Railroad, June 16, 1862, MS in Joseph Gentry papers; MS
Treasurer's Account, Mississippi, Gainesville & Tuscaloosa Railroad, April
18, 1864, Confederate States Railroad Papers, National Archives; Testimony
of Charles C. Shackleford, Director of New Orleans, Jackson & Great
Northern Railroad, February 2, 1867, *Affairs of Southern Railroads,* pp.
128-29; Joseph E. Brown to Secretary of Treasury Memminger, December
20, 1862, Georgia Executive Letters.

20. Message of Gov. Brown to Georgia House of Representatives, April 3,
    1862. Georgia Executive Minutes; Annual Message, Gov. Brown, No-
vember 5, 1863, in *ibid.;* Special Message, Gov. Brown, March 25, 1863, in

ibid.; Gov. Brown to Supt. Rowland of Western & Atlantic, May 1, 1862, in *ibid.*; Executive Order, Gov. Brown, November 29, 1862, Georgia Executive Letters; Jones *Diary*, I, p. 350. A persistent and serious problem in the Confederacy was the supply of common salt. Not only did the blockade cut the South off from northern sources; the production of the Kanawah Valley of western Virginia was early denied by Federal military advances. The chief remaining beds were at Saltville near Bristol, Virginia, to which ran a branch of the Virginia & Tennessee Railroad. How critical the matter became can be imagined when it is remembered that the preservation of meat by refrigeration was then almost unknown.

21. *Annual Report*, Central of Georgia Railroad, December, 1862, December, 1863; *Affairs of Southern Railroads*, p. 70 (testimony of Gustavus W. Smith to House Committee on Affairs of Southern Railroads, January 30, 1867).

22. *Annual Report*, Virginia Central Railroad, 1862; "Comptroller General's Reports," *Reports and Resolutions* of South Carolina Assembly, 1861, 1863; *Appleton's Railway Guide*, December, 1860; *Hill & Swayze's Confederate States Railroad & Steamboat Guide*, May, 1863; Richmond *Daily Examiner*, August 2, 1862.

23. *Annual Report*, Wilmington & Weldon Railroad, September, 1863; *Official Records*, IV, II, pp. 381, 382, 388-89; Georgia Executive Letters, 1860-65, p. 473; Mary G. Cummings, *op. cit.*

24. *Annual Report*, South Side Railroad, November, 1863; MS Account to Confederate States Government, Mississippi, Gainesville & Tuscaloosa Railroad, April 18, 1864; Confederate States Railroad Papers, National Archives; Mobile *Daily Advertiser and Register*, November 20, and 22, 1863.

25. *Annual Report*, Atlantic & North Carolina Railroad, 1863; Thomas McAdory Owen, *History of Alabama*, I, pp. 1013-14; *Annual Report*, Virginia & Tennessee Railroad, October, 1863; Annual Message, Gov. Brown, Georgia Executive Minutes, November 5, 1863; *Annual Reports*: Southwestern Railroad, 1863; Central of Georgia Railroad, December, 1863; Macon & Western Railroad, December, 1863; Mississippi & Tennessee Railroad, November, 1865.

26. *Annual Report*, Wilmington & Weldon Railroad, 1863; *Annual Report*, Petersburg Railroad, 1864; "Comptroller General's Report," *Reports and Resolutions* of the General Assembly of South Carolina, 1863.

27. MS replies of railroads entering Richmond to Virginia Board of Public Works in Virginia Board of Public Works Papers, Virginia State Library; Montgomery *Daily Mail*, December 25, 1862 *et seq.*; *ibid.*, January 17, 1863.

28. *Annual Report*, Central of Georgia Railroad, December, 1862; "Comptroller General's Reports," *Reports and Resolutions* of the South Carolina Assembly, 1861 and 1863. It must not be assumed that the South Carolina and Laurens roads operated precisely upon schedule in all instances save those noted. The figures quoted involved *failure to make connections* only and did not embrace simple tardiness.

Chapter Eleven

CONCENTRATIONS

1. Stanley F. Horn, *The Army of Tennessee*, p. 99; *Official Records*, I, VII, pp. 881, 887, 897-98; Brown to Rowland, February 12, 1862, Georgia Executive Letters.
2. Rowland to Brown, February 15, 1862, Georgia Executive Letters.
3. *Official Records*, I, VII, pp. 428-31.
4. *Official Records*, I, VI, pp. 398, 824, 828; I, VII, p. 897.
5. *Official Records*, I, VII, p. 889; I, VI, p. 398.
6. *Ibid.*, I, VII, p. 878.
7. *Official Records*, I, X, II, pp. 297-99, 318; I, VI, pp. 660-62, 828, 829, 838-39, 874-75.
8. *Official Records*, I, X, II, pp. 297-99, 304-5, 339-40.
9. *Official Records*, I, XI, pp. 848-49, 847; I, X, II, pp. 327, 332, 341-42, 370.
10. Annual Message, Governor Brown, November 6, 1862, Georgia Executive Minutes; Special Message, Governor Brown, December 2, 1863, in *ibid.*; *Annual Report*, Memphis & Charleston Railroad, July, 1866.
11. *Annual Report*, Memphis & Charleston Railroad, July, 1866; *Official Records*, I, X, II, pp. 441-42, 429. Larcombe's guilt seemed definitely established when it was reported that he had entered General Mitchell's service as superintendent of that part of the road controlled by the Federal military, but stories of a general disaffection among the officers of the company appear to have been without foundation.
12. *Annual Report*, Memphis & Charleston Railroad, July, 1866; *Official Records*, I, X, II, pp. 358, 364, 376, 418.
13. Now Kennesaw, Georgia.
14. Robert Selph Henry, *The Story of the Confederacy* (New York, 1936), pp. 131-35, furnishes a good brief account of the episode. The *General*, restored to its original condition, is now on exhibition at the Union Station, Chattanooga. The *Texas*, commandeered by Fuller at Adairsville, and in which he completed the chase, is displayed in the Cyclorama Building, Grant Park, Atlanta. This engine is reported to have covered nine miles in nine minutes over a portion of the pursuit. Speed of that kind on the Western & Atlantic track of the period required something more than courage.
15. Atlanta *Southern Confederacy*, April 15, 1862, quoted in report of Judge Advocate General J. Holt, U. S. A., March 27, 1863, *Official Records*, I, X, I, p. 631; Annual Message, Governor Brown, November 6, 1862, Georgia Executive Minutes.
16. *Official Records*, I, X, II, pp. 436, 456-57, 466-67, 476-77; Horn, *op. cit.*, p. 145.
17. *Official Records*, I, X, II, p. 465; Horn, *op. cit.*, p. 150.
18. *Official Records*, I, X, II, pp. 557, 562; *Annual Reports*, Memphis & Charleston Railroad, July, 1866.
19. *Official Records*, I, X, II, pp. 569-70, 576; *Annual Report*, Memphis & Charleston Railroad, July, 1866.
20. *Affairs of Southern Railroads*, pp. 128-29; Walter Prichard, ed., "G. W. R. Bayley, *Louisiana Historical Quarterly*, Vol. XXX, No. 4 (October, 1947), p. 1137; *Official Records*, I, VI, pp. 578-79.

21. *Annual Report,* Atlantic & North Carolina Railroad, 1862, 1863; *Official Records,* I, IX, p. 47.
22. *Official Records,* I, V, p. 1093; I, XL, II, pp. 1073-74.
23. *Proceedings of a Convention of Rail Roads held at Goldsboro April 1, 1862* (Raleigh, 1862), printed pamphlet in North Carolina Archives, Raleigh; *Official Records,* I, IX, p. 463; I, XI, III, pp. 490, 507, 508.

Chapter Twelve

WARTIME CONSTRUCTION PROGRAMS

1. *Official Records,* IV, I, p. 859; James W. Wilson to Giles Mebane, January 29, 1862; and Charles D. Slaughter to Jefferson Davis, February 6, 1862, MS in Confederate States Secretaries of War Papers, National Archives.
2. Richmond *Daily Examiner,* February 8, 1862; Richmond *Semi-Weekly Examiner,* February 7, 1862; Raleigh *Weekly Register,* February 12, 1862; *Annual Report,* Richmond & Danville Railroad, 1862; *Official Records,* IV, I, p. 912; *Acts and Resolutions,* 4th Session of Confederate States Provisional Congress, No. 385, pp. 72-73. *Journal,* Confederate States Congress, I, pp. 731-34, 737, 762, 764, 766-68, 770, 781-82, 784.
3. *Annual Report,* Richmond & Danville Railroad, December, 1862.
4. *Annual Report,* Richmond & Danville Railroad, December, 1863.
5. Par. 22, Special Orders 50, Adj. Gen. Office, C.S.A., March 4, 1862, MS extract in E. T. D. Myers' Papers, War Records Division, National Archives; *Annual Report,* Richmond & Danville Railroad, December, 1862; *Official Records,* IV, I, pp. 947, 1022-27, 1055, 1107.
6. *Annual Report,* Richmond & Danville Railroad, December, 1862; Extract of Par. 19, Special Orders 138, Adj. Gen. Office, C.S.A., June 16, 1862, MS in E. T. D. Myers' Papers.
7. *Annual Report,* Richmond & Danville Railroad, December, 1862.
8. *Ibid.*
9. *Annual Report,* Richmond & Danville Railroad, December, 1862; *Journal,* Confederate States Congress, V, pp. 333, 356; Jones *Diary,* I, p. 176; *Official Records,* I, XIX, II, p. 681; *ibid.,* IV, II, p. 73.
10. Jones *Diary,* I, p. 183; *Official Records,* I, XVIII, p. 779; *ibid.,* IV, II, pp. 175-76, 386-87, 393-94.
11. Harvie to Randolph, May 24, 1862, MS in Confederate States Secretaries of War Papers, National Archives; *Annual Report,* Richmond & Danville Railroad, December, 1862.
12. *Official Records,* I, XVIII, p. 825; *ibid.,* IV, II, pp. 845-46; Jones *Diary,* I, p. 287; *Journal,* C. S. Congress, III, p. 171; *Annual Report,* Richmond & Danville Railroad, December, 1863; Harvie to Seddon, April 13, 1863; MS in C. S. Secretaries of War Papers, National Archives. A part of the Tredegar Works' difficulty was a shortage of basic pig iron. See Bruce, *Virginia Iron Manufacture,* pp. 413-14.
13. MS receipt for blasting powder, June 26, 1863, Myers Papers, National Archives; Myers to Gilmer, July 6, 1863, MS in Confederate States Secretaries of War Papers, National Archives.
14. *Annual Report,* Richmond & Danville Railroad, December, 1863.
15. *Official Records,* IV, I, pp. 1048-49.

16. *Ibid.* See also Poor's *Manual,* 1869-70, p. 121.
17. *Official Records,* IV, I, p. 859.
18. *Journal,* Confederate States Congress, I, pp. 701, 810, 821-22, 832; *Official Records,* IV, I, p. 941. Rhett's city of Charleston owned a large block of Memphis & Charleston stock, while all Georgians were part owners of the Western & Atlantic.
19. *Official Records,* IV, I, pp. 1048-49.
20. *Official Records,* IV, I, pp. 1054-55; *Journal,* Confederate States Congress, II, pp. 121-22; V, p. 165; *Public Laws* of the Confederate States (1st Congress, 1st Session), Ch. XVIII, p. 11; Richmond *Daily Examiner,* April 3, 1862; Mortgage Agreement and Promissory Note of the Alabama & Mississippi Rivers Railroad Company, April 23, 1862, MS in Confederate States Railroad Papers, National Archives; Bond of the President and Directors of the Alabama & Mississippi Rivers Railroad Company, April 23, 1862, MS in *ibid.*
21. *Official Records,* IV, I, p. 1048.
22. F. S. Lyon to J. Davis, September 24, 1862, MS in Confederate States Secretaries of War Papers, National Archives; *Official Records,* IV, I, pp. 1089-91, 1171-73.
23. *Official Records,* IV, I, pp. 1145-46, 1171-73.
24. *Official Records,* IV, I, pp. 1171-73; G. G. Griffin to Capt. P. H. Thompson, June 24, 1862, MS in Confederate States Railroad Papers, National Archives.
25. *Official Records,* I, XVII, pp. 624-25, 627, 637, 644.
26. Tate to Bragg, August 23, 1862, MS in Confederate States Secretaries of War Papers, National Archives; Bragg to F. S. Lyon, August 24, 1862, MS in *ibid.;* F. S. Lyon to Randolph, August 30, 1862, MS in *ibid.;* R. G. H. Kean to Randolph, September 8, 1862, MS in *ibid.;* F. S. Lyon to J. Davis, September 24, 1862, MS in *ibid.;* Memorandum, Davis to Secretary of War in the matter of the Selma-Meridian railroad connection (undated), MS in Confederate States Railroad Papers, National Archives; O. M. Avery to Sec. Randolph, August 7, 1862, MS in *ibid.;* Tate to Randolph, July 19, 1862, MS in *ibid.*
27. Randolph to Shorter, October 2, 1862, *Official Records,* IV, II, p. 106; Moore to Shorter, October 24, 1862, Shorter to Randolph, October 27, 1862, in *ibid.,* pp. 148-49.
28. Gaines to Randolph (Seddon), December 10, 1862, MS in Confederate States Secretaries of War Papers, National Archives.
29. J. W. Lapsley to Secretary Randolph, May 5, 1862, MS in Confederate States Secretaries of War Papers, National Archives.
30. *Ibid.; Journal,* Confederate States Congress, V, p. 302; Bragg to F. S. Lyon, August 24, 1862, MS in Confederate States Secretaries of War Papers, National Archives.
31. *Journal,* Confederate States Congress, II, pp. 398-99, 407-8; V, pp. 485, 362, 434, 455-56, 479-80; *Official Records,* IV, II, pp. 139-40, 200-1; Duff Green to Davis, September 6, 1862, MS in Confederate States Secretaries of War Papers, National Archives; *Public Laws* of Confederate States (1st Congress, 2nd Session), Ch. XX, p. 66 (October 2, 1862).
32. *Official Records,* IV, II, pp. 144-45; *Acts* of Alabama Assembly, 1862, No. 118, pp. 143-44; Owen, *History of Alabama,* I, p. 508.

33. Indorsement of Sec. Randolph on letter Alfred Shorter to J. Davis, October 25, 1862, *Official Records*, IV, II, pp. 144-45; Chief Engineer Gilmer to Secretary Seddon, October 10, 1863, *Official Records*, I, XXVIII, II, pp. 410-11.

34. *Journal*, Confederate States Congress, V, p. 45; *Official Records*, IV, I, pp. 1013-14.

35. *Journal*, Confederate States Congress, V, pp. 260-61; *ibid.*, II, pp. 195-99.

36. *Official Records*, IV, I, pp. 1073-74; *Public Laws*, Confederate States Congress (1st Congress, 1st Session), Ch. XXXVI, pp. 34-35.

37. *Official Records*, IV, I, pp. 1108-9, 1113; *ibid.*, IV, II, pp. 107-8; *Journal*, Confederate State Congress, II, pp. 335, 409.

38. *Official Records*, I, VI, p. 397; Lee to J. W. Hayne, Chief of (S. C.) Justice & Police, February 28, 1862, MS in Confederate States Secretaries of War Papers, National Archives.

39. *Official Records*, I, VI, pp. 407, 428, 431; *ibid.*, I, XIV, p. 484; Pemberton to Governor Brown, April 25, 1862, Georgia Executive Letters.

40. Bently D. Hasell, President of Charleston & Savannah Railroad, to Colonel J. W. Hayne, December 12, 1862, and Hasell to Governor M. L. Bonham of South Carolina, January 10, 1863, MSS in S. C. Hist. Dept., Columbia; F. W. Sims to General A. R. Lawton, September 12, 1863, Quartermaster General's Office Letter Book, Ch. 5, Vol. 8, S. 438, National Archives; *Official Records*, I, XIV, p. 503; Map of Augusta, 1864-65, Map Supplement, *Official Records*.

41. *Acts* of Alabama Assembly, Regular Session, 1862, No. 119, pp. 145-47; *Official Records*, I, XXIII, II, p. 761.

42. *Journal*, Confederate States Congress, II, pp. 332-33; V, pp. 200, 440; Pres. H. W. Guion of Wilmington, Charlotte & Rutherford to Secretary Randolph, August 20, 1862, with indorsements, MS in Confederate States Secretaries of War Papers, National Archives; Richmond *Semi-Weekly Examiner*, February 8, 1862.

43. (Raleigh) *North Carolina Standard*, February 26, 1862; *Private Laws* of North Carolina, 1863, Ch. 26, p. 27; Adv. for bids, Chatham Railroad Company, Raleigh *Weekly Register*, October 8, 1862; *Official Records*, IV, I, pp. 944-46; *Proceedings* of Trustees of Florida Internal Improvement Fund, I, pp. 200, 229-30, 244; *Journal* of Florida House of Representatives, 1862, pp. 32-33.

Chapter Thirteen

FREDERICK W. SIMS

1. MS note directing appointment of Captain Sims in handwriting of Secretary Seddon, June 2, 1863, Confederate States Railroad Papers, National Archives; *Official Records*, IV, II, p. 579.

2. Letters of Sims's great-grandnephew, Mr. Calder W. Payne, to the author, October 21 and 28, 1949; Letter of Mrs. Lilla M. Hawes, Director of Georgia Historical Society, to the author, June 8, 1949; Savannah *Daily Morning News*, July 12, 1856.

3. List of Members, *Minutes of the Union Society*, 1860; *Proceedings of Union Society*, 1859-60; *ibid.*, 1860-61; Savannah *Daily Morning News*, July 26, 1856; Mrs. Lilla M. Hawes to author, June 8, 1949.

4. Typewritten military record of Sims, Sims Papers, National Archives.
5. Whitford to Quartermaster General Lawton, November 24, 1863, MS in
   Confederate States Quartermaster General's Office Papers, S-333, National
   Archives; MS pay voucher of Capt. J. H. Hottel, June, 1863, Hottel Papers,
   National Archives; *Official Records*, I, XX, II, p. 445; Major George Whit-
   field to Major B. F. Jones, September 9, 1864, MS in Whitfield Papers, Na-
   tional Archives.
6. Sims to Sec. Seddon, July 9, 1863 (with indorsements), MS in Sims
   Papers, National Archives; Gen. A. R. Lawton to Seddon, December 19,
   1863, MS in Confederate States Railroad Papers in National Archives;
   Journal, Confederate States Congress, III, pp. 613, 619, 628-29; Sims to Gen.
   A. R. Lawton, September 5, 1863, Quartermaster General's Office Letter
   Book, Ch. 5, Vol. 8, S. 365, National Archives; Major M. B. McMicken to
   Major Peters, August 19, 1863, MS copy in Peters Papers, National Archives;
   Sims to Hottel, November 22, 1863, MS copy in Hottel Papers, National
   Archives; Memorandum of F. W. Sims, as to Peters, MS in *ibid.; Official
   Records*, I, XXIX, II, p. 773; I, LI, II, p. 732. The precise date of Sims's trans-
   fer to the Quartermaster Department is unknown, but it had been effected
   prior to his promotion to Lieutenant Colonel in December, 1863.
7. *Dictionary of American Biography* (edition of 1946), Vol. XI, pp. 61-62;
   Jones *Diary*, II, p. 134.
8. Sims to Cooper, June 4, 1863, MS in Sims Papers, National Archives;
   The Stranger's Guide and Official Directory for the City of Richmond,
   Vol. I, No. 1, October, 1863, p. 13; "List of Railroads and quartermasters by
   whom their accounts are audited," MS in Sims Papers, National Archives.
9. MS mileage voucher, F. W. Sims, December 14, 1863, in Confederate
   States Railroad Papers, National Archives; MS mileage vouchers, July-
   September, 1863, Hottel Papers, National Archives; MS mileage vouchers,
   November, 1863–January, 1864, Peters Papers, National Archives.
10. Sims to A. C. Myers, June 19, 1863, MS in Sims Papers, National
    Archives; see also Q. M. General's Office Letter Book, Ch. 5, Vol. 7,
    S. 364, in National Archives.
11. Sims to Sec. of War, June 10, 1863, Q. M. General's Office Letter Book,
    Ch. 5, Vol. 7, S. 310, National Archives; Sims to Col. Myers, June 24,
    1863, MS in C. S. Railroad Papers, National Archives.
12. Sims to Hottel, June 24, 1863, MS in Hottel Papers, National Archives;
    Official Records, IV, II, pp. 881-83; Capt. F. W. Holt to Sims, Septem-
    ber 12, 1863, MS telegraph receipt form, Railroad Bureau telegraphic file,
    Valentine Museum, Richmond; Sims to Q. M. General, August 12, 1863,
    Q. M. General's Office Letter Book, Ch. 5, Vol. 8, S. 170, National Archives;
    Sims to Maj. J. L. Calhoun, February 9, 1864, MS telegraph receipt form,
    Confederate States Railroad Papers, National Archives.
13. MS telegraphic receipt blanks, Railroad Bureau telegraphic file, Valen-
    tine Museum, Richmond: G. Jordan to Sims, August 28, 1863, W. H.
    McDowell to Sims, September 17; McDowell to Sims, October 26; G. J.
    Fulton to Sims, October 29; McDowell to Sims, October 12; E. B. Walker
    to Sims, December 7; T. R. Sharp to Sims, October 19; see also Lewis E.
    Harvie to Sec. Seddon, December 19, 1863, with indorsements, MS in Con-
    federate States Secretaries of War Papers, National Archives.
14. Sims to Supt. Cole of Nashville & Chattanooga Co., undated MS telegram

in Confederate States Railroad Papers, National Archives; *Official Records*, IV, II, pp. 881-83.

15. *Official Records*, IV, II, pp. 881-83.
16. Gov. Brown to Sims (addressed to Wadley), June 17, 1863, Georgia Executive Letters; *Proceedings of the Southern Railroad Convention*, Macon, Georgia, November 25, 1863, printed pamphlet in Sims Papers, National Archives.
17. Sims to Lawton, September 2, 1863, Q. M. General's Office Letter Book, Ch. 5, Vol. 8, S. 351, National Archives; Brown to Sims, November 27, 1863, Georgia Executive Letters.
18. J. M. Seixas to Maj. T. L. Bayne, August 13, 1863, MS telegraphic receipt; Seixas to Bayne, October 25, 1863, MS telegram; George D. Phillips to Sims, December 18, 1863, MS telegram, all in Railroad Bureau file, Valentine Museum, Richmond.
19. A. F. Ravenal to Sims, December 22, 1863, MS telegraphic receipt; G. W. Adams to Sims, December 11, 1863, MS telegraphic receipt; Maj. R. J. Echols to Sims, December 28, 1863, MS telegraphic receipt, all in Railroad Bureau file, Valentine Museum, Richmond.
20. *Official Records*, IV, II, p. 792; *The Weekly Register* (Lynchburg, Va.), Vol. I, No. 1 (January 2, 1864), p. 5.
21. James Yonge to Major F. W. Sims, September 28, 1863, MS telegram; B. S. Guerin to Major C. S. Carrington, October 17, 1863, MS telegram; G. Jordan to Sims, October 21 and 26, 1863, MSS telegrams, all in Railroad Bureau file, Valentine Museum, Richmond. See also Sims's correspondence in Q. M. General's Office Letter Books, National Archives.
22. *Official Records*, I, XXVIII, II, pp. 295-96; I, XXX, IV, pp. 713-14.
23. Sims to Cruger, January 8, 1864, MS in Sims Papers, National Archives.
24. Cruger to W. P. Miles, January 8, 1864, with attached draft bill for the establishment of a Railroad Bureau, MS in Sims Papers, National Archives.

Chapter Fourteen

STEAM CARS TO GLORY

1. Abraham Dudley to Thomas H. Dewitt, January 9, 1863, MS in Virginia Board of Public Works Papers, Virginia State Library; Thomas Weber, *op. cit.*, pp. 235-36; *Annual Report*, Richmond & Danville Railroad, December, 1862; Jones *Diary*, I, p. 126; Correspondence of Joseph Gentry during his stay at Lynchburg, Virginia, MSS in Valentine Museum, Richmond; *Official Records*, I, XI, III, pp. 501-2; E. Fontaine to Randolph, May 10, 1862, MS in Confederate States Secretaries of War Papers, National Archives; Carter S. Anderson, "Train Running for the Confederacy," Part IV, "Locomotives Climb Broad Street Hill in Richmond, 1862," *Locomotive Engineering*, November, 1892; *Annual Report*, Richmond, Fredericksburg & Potomac Railroad, May, 1863.
2. *Official Records*, I, XI, III, pp. 555, 574; Alfred Hoyt Bill, *The Beleagured City* (New York, 1946), p. 131.
3. Bill, *op. cit.*, p. 129; Freeman, *Lee's Lieutenants*, I, p. 465.
4. Freeman, *op. cit.*, I, p. 466; Bill, *op. cit.*, p. 131; G. F. R. Henderson,

Stonewall Jackson and the American Civil War (authorized American edition, London and New York, 1949), p. 297; John Esten Cooke, *Stonewall Jackson, A Military Biography* (New York, 1866), p. 201; *Official Records*, I, LI, II, p. 1074.

5. *Official Records*, I, XI, III, p. 598; Capt. Mason Morfit to Randolph, August 18, 1862, MS in Confederate States Secretaries of War Papers, National Archives.

6. Chester R. Anderson, *op. cit.*, Part I, *Locomotive Engineering*, July, 1892; *Official Records*, I, XI, III, p. 598.

7. Cooke, *op. cit.*, p. 201; Henderson, *op. cit.*, p. 298; Freeman, *op. cit.*, I, p. 466, citation No. 148. Oddly enough, Freeman makes no direct mention of Supt. Bird's letter of June 13 to Secretary Randolph.

8. Cooke, *op. cit.*, p. 201; Freeman, *op. cit.*, I, p. 468; Chester R. Anderson, *op. cit.*, Part I.

9. Freeman, *op. cit.*, I, pp. 468-69.

10. Freeman, *op. cit.*, I, pp. 489 ff.; Henderson, *op. cit.*, pp. 300 ff.; Decatur Axtell, "History of Chesapeake & Ohio Railroad," Ch. V, MS in Public Relations Department, Chesapeake & Ohio Railway, Richmond; Anderson, *op. cit.*, Part II, *Locomotive Engineering*, August, 1892.

11. *Official Records*, I, XVI, II, p. 695; I, XVI, I, p. 710.

12. Horn, *op. cit.*, p. 159; *Official Records*, I, XVII, II, pp. 629, 645.

13. *Official Records*, I, XVI, II, pp. 708, 710, 714, 718, 725-27.

14. *Official Records*, I, XVII, II, p. 648.

15. *Ibid.*, pp. 655, 656.

16. *Official Records*, I, XVII, II, pp. 656-57, 648.

17. *Ibid.*, pp. 656-57, 660.

18. *Official Records*, I, XVII, II, pp. 655-57, 660; I, XVI, II, pp. 738-39, 741.

19. Horn, *op. cit.*, p. 248.

20. James B. Longstreet, *From Manassas to Appomattox* (Philadelphia, 1896), pp. 433-34; *Official Records*, I, XXIX, II, pp. 693-94, 699-701.

21. Lee to Davis, September 6, 1863, in *ibid.*

22. Whitford to Sims, September 7, 1863, MS telegraph receipt, Valentine Museum, Richmond; H. M. Drane to Sims, September 8, 1863, MS telegraph receipt, in Valentine Museum; Sims to Lawton, September 9, 1863, Q. M. General's Office Letter Book, Ch. V, Vol. 8, S. 403, National Archives; South Carolina Railroad notices in Columbia *Tri-Weekly South Carolinian*, September 11 and 24, 1863; see also file of telegraphic passing reports from carriers in North and South Carolina, MS receipts in Valentine Museum.

23. *Official Records*, I, XXIX, II, p. 706; Longstreet, *op. cit.*, p. 436; Jones *Diary*, II, p. 37; Longstreet's Corps was formally detached from the Army of Northern Virginia on September 9. *Official Records*, I, XXIX, I, p. 398.

24. *Official Records*, I, XXIX, II, pp. 682-83, 706; I, XXX, IV, p. 652.

25. Freeman, *Lee's Lieutenants*, III, p. 224; *Official Records*, I, XXIX, II, pp. 708, 713; Longstreet, *op. cit.*, pp. 436-37.

26. *Official Records*, I, XXIX, II, p. 710; MS telegraphic passing reports, Railroad Bureau telegraph file, Valentine Museum, Richmond; *Diary of Dr. J. F. Shaffner, Sr., September 13, 1863–February 5, 1865* (privately published, no date; copy in North Carolina State Library), entry for September 13, 1861.

27. General Moxley Sorrel and Augustus Dickert, quoted in Freeman, *op. cit.*, III, pp. 227-28; Dr. J. F. Shaffner, *op. cit.*, entry for September 14, 1863; Longstreet, *op. cit.*, p. 437.
28. *Official Records*, I, XXIX, II, pp. 720-21, 725-26.
29. New York *Herald*, September 8, 1863, *et seq.* The New York *Tribune* asserted as late as September 18 that stories of Longstreet's transfer to Bragg were disbelieved by most officers of the Army of the Potomac, who thought them a "ruse."
30. *Official Records*, I, XXIX, II, p. 710; I, LI, II, pp. 763-65. The *Standard*, which hardly was a strenuous advocate of the Confederate cause, was reported to have published "crude misstatements" at the expense of non-North Carolina troops. Benning never denied that his command had been implicated in the outbreak, but he placed the weight of the blame upon certain North Carolina units which had hitched a ride upon his cartops from Weldon. Nevertheless, the Georgians seem not to have been kept under proper control; at the time of the incident, the exhausted commander lay asleep in the railroad yards with his head on a crosstie. See *Official Records*, I, XXIX, II, p. 723, and I, LI, II, pp. 770-71.
31. Telegraphic passing reports, Railroad Bureau telegraphic file, Valentine Museum, Richmond.
32. *Official Records*, I, XXX, IV, pp. 643, 647-49, 652.
33. *Official Records*, I, XXX, II, p. 290; I, XXX, IV, p. 672.
34. *Official Records*, I, XXX, II, pp. 287, 451, 503, 509; I, XXX, IV, pp. 672, 675.
35. Supt. H. T. Peake to Major Sims, September 16, 1863, MS telegraphic receipt in Railroad Bureau telegraphic file, Valentine Museum, Richmond. The figures quoted herein have been derived from an estimate compiled by John O. Littleton, Park Historian, Chickamauga—Chattanooga National Military Park, in January, 1950. Some further hint as to the extent of the movement, including the two brigades for Charleston, is given by the fact that the Richmond & Petersburg carried 8,556 southbound white passengers in August, 1863, and 29,925 in September. See *Annual Report*, Richmond & Petersburg Railroad, April, 1864.
36. Railroads carried more than just the two divisions of Longstreet's corps to Bragg. Late in August three brigades had come from Johnston's army in Mississippi. Subsequent appeals brought two more, which moved by the old route via Mobile and arrived in Atlanta on September 11. They departed north the following evening. When Johnston learned of the arrival of the Virginia troops, he called lustily for their return, but all brigades took part at Chickamauga. *Official Records*, I, XXX, IV, pp. 538, 608, 635, 645; I, XXX, II, p. 17.
It is interesting to note that the Federal reaction to Chickamauga was an even greater railroad move. To reinforce the badly-mauled Rosecrans, 16,000 men were carried from Culpeper, Virginia, to Bridgeport, Alabama, in eight days.
Years after Chickamauga, E. P. Alexander, Longstreet's Chief of Artillery, published the schedule of his command from Petersburg to Ringold (it arrived nearly a week after the battle was over). Its very detail is evidence of its essential accuracy:

Lv. Petersburg	4 p.m.	Sept. 17
Ar. Wilmington	2 a.m.	20th. (change of cars)
Lv. Wilmington	2 p.m.	20th.
Ar. Kingsville	6 p.m.	21st. (change of cars)
Lv. Kingsville	12 midnight	21st.
Ar. Augusta	2 p.m.	22nd.
Lv. Augusta	7 p.m.	22nd.
Ar. Atlanta	2 p.m.	23rd. (change of cars)
Lv. Atlanta	4 a.m.	24th.
Ar. Ringold	2 a.m.	25th.

See E. P. Alexander, *Military Memoirs of a Confederate* (New York, 1907). pp. 448-50.

Chapter Fifteen

THE IRON HORSE STUMBLES

1. *Tri-Weekly South Carolinian*, September 25, 1863.
2. *Official Records*, I, XX, II, pp. 453, 462, 479; I, XXIII, II, p. 745; I, XX, II, pp. 453-62, 479; I, XXIII, II, p. 745.
3. *Official Records*, I, XIV, pp. 741-42, 774-75.
4. *Official Records*, I, XXXIII, pp. 1177-78.
5. Bruce, *Virginia Iron Manufacture*, p. 368; *Official Records*, I, VI, p. 626; I, XXIV, I, pp. 289-90, 307, 309; I, XXIV, III, p. 625; Major George Whitfield to Pemberton, March 24, 1863, MS in Whitfield Papers, National Archives; Jones *Diary*, I, p. 346.
6. Quoted in Natchez *Daily Courier*, March 24, 1863.
7. Brown to Rowland, March 16, 1863, Georgia Executive Letters; *Official Records*, I, LII, II, pp. 434, 435, 438. Governor Brown, when aroused, sometimes lapsed into the vernacular of his up-country boyhood.
8. Major M. B. McMicken to Major Thomas Peters, July 27, 1863, MS in Peters Papers, National Archives; Brown to General W. W. Mackall, July 27, 1863, Georgia Executive Letters; Supt. Phillips of Western & Atlantic to Brown, November 18, 1863, in *ibid.*
9. Bragg to Brown, November 15, 1863, Georgia Executive Letters; *Official Records*, I, XXXI, III, pp. 698-99.
10. Brown to Bragg, November 16, 1863, Georgia Executive Letters.
11. Brown to Johnston, December 30, 1863, Georgia Executive Letters; Johnston to Brown, January 12, 1864, in *ibid.*; Brown to Johnston, January 13, 1864, in *ibid.*; Brown to Lawton, January 15, 1864, in *ibid.*; Phillips to Brown, January 14, 1864, in *ibid.* Johnston's complaints became savage. To Adj. Gen. Henry C. Wayne of Georgia he asserted that the Western & Atlantic "seems to be entirely unmanaged." (See *Official Records*, I, XXXII, II, p. 552.)
12. Johnston to General Wayne, January 14, 1864, *Official Records*, I, XXXII, II, p. 557; Special Message, Governor Brown, to Georgia Assembly, December 2, 1863, Georgia Executive Minutes.
13. *Official Records*, I, XXXII, II, pp. 591-92; I, LII, II, pp. 607-8, 615, 621-23.
14. Davis to Brown, March 7, 1864, Georgia Executive Letters; Brown to Davis, March 7, 1864, in *ibid.*

15. *Southern Historical Society Papers*, II (July-December, 1876), p. 101; E. M. Coulter, *The Confederate States*, pp. 241-42.
16. S. B. French to Northrup, January 12, 1864, in *Southern Historical Society Papers*, II, p. 101; *Annual Report*, Richmond & Petersburg Railroad, April, 1864; Jones *Diary*, II, p. 9.
17. *Southern Historical Society Papers*, II, p. 102; *Official Records*, I, XXXIII, p. 1077; Jones *Diary*, II, pp. 84, 161.
18. Jones *Diary*, II, pp. 9, 167, 173, 182; *Official Records*, I, XXXIII, pp. 1077-78. Davis was quite ready to re-employ Wadley as a civilian "agent," but Seddon noted sadly that "I fear Colonel Wadley's services are not now obtainable."
19. *Official Records*, IV, III, pp. 92-93.
20. Railroad Bureau telegraphic file, Valentine Museum, Richmond; *Official Records*, IV, III, p. 209; I, XXXIII, p. 1236; Arney Robinson Childs, ed., *The Private Journal of Henry William Ravenal 1859-1887* (Columbia, 1947), p. 195.

Chapter Sixteen

THE TREASURE HUNT FOR IRON

1. P. V. Daniel, Jr., to Davis, April 22, 1862 (with indorsements), MS in Confederate States Secretaries of War Papers, National Archives.
2. L. M. Merritt, Francis Bobe, Joseph Sierra, O. M. Avery and Jones Abercrombie to Confederate States Secretary of War, May 17, 1862, MS in Confederate States Secretaries of War Papers, National Archives.
3. *Ibid.;* Avery to Secretary of War, May 31, 1862, MS in Confederate States Secretaries of War Papers, National Archives.
4. Avery to Secretary of War, May 31, 1862, MS in Confederate States Secretaries of War Papers, National Archives; Avery to Secretary of War, August 7, 1862, MS in *ibid.*
5. Telegram, Avery to Brown, July 18, 1862, Telegram Brown to Avery, July 18, 1862, Georgia Executive Letters; Avery to Randolph, August 7, 1862, MS in Confederate States Secretaries of War Papers, National Archives.
6. Tate to Randolph, July 19, 1862, MS in Confederate States Railroad Papers, National Archives.
7. O. M. Avery to Gen. Forney, November 21, 1862, MS in Confederate States Secretaries of War Papers, National Archives; Avery, A. E. Maxwell, R. B. Hilton and John M. Martin to Secretary of War Seddon (no date, but with indorsement of May 5, 1863), MS in *ibid.;* Avery to Mallory, August 14, 1863, MS in *ibid.*
8. *Private Acts* of First Congress, Confederate States of America, 4th Session, Ch. II, p. 13; *Journal*, Confederate States Congress, III, pp. 514, 521, 603, 623, 624, 719, 732, 783.
9. Jones *Diary*, I, p. 195.
10. Mallory to Randolph, July 25, 1862, MS in Confederate States Secretaries of War Papers, National Archives.
11. *Annual Report*, Atlantic & North Carolina Railroad, 1863; Poor's *Manual*, 1869-70, p. 371; Gov. Brown to R. R. Cuyler, November 25, 1863, Georgia Executive Letters; *Official Records*, I, XVIII, pp. 875, 912.

12. *Official Records,* IV, II, pp. 365-66.
13. *Official Records,* IV, II, p. 393.
14. Report of Iron Commission concerning Railroads, March 28, 1863, MS in C. S. Railroad Papers, National Archives; Col. Rives to Major Meriwether, November 6, 1863, MS in Meriwether Papers, National Archives; Typewritten summary of Military Record of Minor Meriwether in Meriwether Papers; Meriwether to Gen. Gilmer, October 24, 1863, MS in Meriwether Papers; MS extract of personal record of E. T. D. Myers, Myers Papers, National Archives.
15. Report of Iron Commission concerning Railroads, March 28, 1863, MS in Confederate States Railroad Papers, National Archives.
16. Col. A. L. Rives to Meriwether, November 6, 1863, MS in Meriwether Papers, National Archives.
17. Adjutant and Inspector General's Office, Richmond, *General Orders No. 115,* August 70, 1863, *General Orders No. 128,* September 30, 1863, *General Orders No. 129,* October 1, 1863, *General Orders No. 160,* December 7, 1863, original imprints in Rare Books Section, Emory University Library, Atlanta.
18. Telegram, G. Jordan to Capt. Richardson, August 13, 1863, MS in Confederate States Secretaries of War Papers, National Archives; "Abstract of Articles sold up to the end of 3rd Quarter 1864 for which payment has not been received," MS signed by Minor Meriwether, Minor Meriwether Papers, National Archives.
19. E. T. D. Myers to Major F. W. Sims, October 27, 1863, MS telegraphic receipt, Valentine Museum, Richmond; Minor Meriwether to Lieut. Gen. L. Polk, May 19, 1864, MS in Meriwether Papers, National Archives; Meriwether to Maj. Gen. S. D. Lee, June 15, 1864, MS in *ibid.;* "Report of Operations" of Iron Commission, November, 1864, MS in *ibid.; Official Records,* I, III, XXXII, p. 745; I, XVIII, pp. 951-52.
20. *Official Records,* IV, II, p. 655; Meriwether to Polk, May 19, 1863, MS in Meriwether Papers, National Archives; J. W. Simpson and S. R. Todd to Seddon, August 21, 1863, MS in Confederate States Railroad Papers, National Archives; Petition of Alabama Citizens to the Confederate Government against the removal of iron from the Northwestern Railroad of Alabama (1863), MS in *ibid.; Lloyd's Southern Railroad Guide,* June, 1864, p. 19.
21. *Official Records,* IV, I, pp. 777-79; *Annual Report,* Atlantic & Gulf Railroad, February, 1863; Florida *Senate Journal,* 1863, p. 25.
22. *Official Records,* IV, I, pp. 777-79.
23. *Dictionary of American Biography,* XX, p. 638.
24. *Official Records,* IV, II, pp. 650, 651; Milton to Yulee, June 8, 1863, Florida *Senate Journal,* pp. 209-15.
25. *Official Records,* I, LIII, p. 358.
26. Milton to Finegan, May 7, 1863, in Florida *Senate Journal,* 1863, p. 202.
27. Finegan to Milton, May 12, 1863, in *ibid.,* p. 206.
28. Yulee to Milton, May 23, 1863, in *ibid.,* p. 206; Milton to Yulee, May 30, 1863, in *ibid.,* pp. 207-8; Yulee to Milton, June 4, 1863, in *ibid.,* pp. 208-9; Milton to Yulee, June 8, 1863, in *ibid.,* pp. 209-15.
29. Yulee to Milton, June 19, 1863, in *ibid.,* pp. 215-17; Milton to Beauregard, June 29, 1863, in *ibid.,* p. 217; Beauregard to Milton, July 6, 1863, in *ibid.,* pp. 217-18; Milton to Yulee, July 10, 1863, in *ibid.,* pp. 218-24.

30. Yulee to Milton, July 17, 1863, in *ibid.*, p. 225.
31. *Official Records*, IV, II, pp. 649-50, 809; I, XXXI, III, pp. 787-88; *Annual Report*, Atlantic & Gulf Railroad, February, 1866.
32. *Official Records*, I, XXXV, I, p. 618; I, XXXV, II, p. 334; I, LIII, pp. 309-10.
33. *Official Records*, I, LIII, pp. 353-54, 363-64.
34. *Official Records*, I, XXXV, II, p. 484; I, LIII, pp. 358, 359, 364.
35. *Ibid.*, I, LIII, pp. 353-54, 363.
36. *Ibid.*, pp. 355, 362-63.
37. *Ibid.*, pp. 353-55, 358, 359, 362-63.
38. *Ibid.*, pp. 363-64; *ibid.*, IV, III, pp. 560-62; *Proceedings*, Florida Internal Improvement Board, I, pp. 268-69.
39. Reports of Railroad Iron Commission, October and November, 1864, MSS in Meriwether Papers, National Archives; *Official Records*, I, XXXV, II, pp. 594, 607; I, XLIX, I, p. 1029.

Chapter Seventeen

THE DOWNGRADE STEEPENS

1. *Annual Reports:* Georgia Railroad, May, 1864; Virginia Central Railroad, October, 1864; Western & Atlantic Railroad, October, 1864; *Official Records*, IV, III, pp. 508, 514; Jones *Diary*, II, p. 138; MS Statement of Railroad Supply Prices, Richmond, Fredericksburg & Potomac Railroad, April 1, 1864, Virginia Board of Public Works Papers, Virginia State Library; Supt. H. D. Whitcomb of Virginia Central to President E. Fontaine, July 11, 1864, MS in *ibid.*; Abner J. Strobel, *The Old Plantations and Their Owners*, quoted in S. G. Reed, *A History of the Texas Railroads* (1941), p. 79.
2. *Annual Report*, Virginia Central Railroad, October, 1864; *Acts* of Alabama Assembly, Called Session, 1864, No. 26, p. 21; Montgomery *Daily Advertiser*, September 3, 1864.
3. *Annual Report*, Virginia Central Railroad, October, 1864; *Official Records*, I, XXXIII, pp. 1073-74; Richmond *Daily Examiner*, December 14, 1864, *et seq.*
4. *Journal*, Confederate States Congress, VI, p. 529; printed memorial of P. V. Daniel, Jr., and Charles Ellis to the Senate and House of Representatives of the Confederate States, C. S. Railroad Papers, National Archives.
5. Par. V., Sec. 10, of Extended Draft Act of February 17, 1864, *Official Records*, IV, III, p. 180.
6. *Annual Report*, Georgia Railroad, May, 1864; *Annual Report*, North Carolina Railroad, July, 1864; *Official Records*, IV, III, pp. 598-601.
7. Sims to Col. Preston, Chief of Conscription Bureau, January 27, 1865; Sims to Hugh Rice, February 13, 1865; Rail Road Bureau Letter Book, National Archives.
8. *Official Records*, IV, III, pp. 1099-1110. However, all details were summarily revoked in October, 1864. *Ibid.*, I, LI, II, pp. 1064-65.
9. H. D. Whitcomb to E. Fontaine, July 11, 1864, MS in Virginia Board of Public Works Papers, Virginia State Library; *Annual Report*, Virginia

Central Railroad, October, 1864; *Annual Report*, Raleigh & Gaston Railroad, July, 1864; *Official Records* (Navy), I, XXI, p. 870. Governor Brown of Georgia proved an especially benevolent employer to the men of the State-owned Western & Atlantic. The $10 daily wage was among the highest paid in Atlanta and instantly created resentment among the workers at the neighboring Naval Ordnance Works, who struck for equally generous pay. In his report of the incident, the works Superintendent, Lt. McCorkle, termed Brown a "miserable devil."

10. *Appleton's Railway and Steam Navigation Guide*, December, 1860, p. 255; Montgomery *Weekly Advertiser*, April 1, 1864; *Lloyd's Southern Railroad Guide*, October, 1863, p. 37; *ibid.*, June, 1864, pp. 26, 28. The roster of marvelously slow trains in the last year of the Confederacy could be extended almost indefinitely.

11. "Rates of Tariff for Tonnage Transportation," Norfolk & Petersburg Railroad, March 1, 1864, printed poster in Virginia Board of Public Works Papers; William Mahone to Thomas H. Dewitt, April 15, 1864, MS in *ibid.*; H. D. Whitcomb to E. Fontaine, July 11, 1864, MS in *ibid.*; MS "Freight Tariff of the Orange & Alexandria Railroad," April 1, 1864, in *ibid.*; MS Orange & Alexandria Freight Tariff, "to take effect September 5, 1864," in *ibid.*

12. Mahone to Thomas Dewitt, April 15, 1864, MS in Virginia Board of Public Works Papers; *Official Records*, IV, III, p. 616; *Lloyd's Southern Railroad Guide*, June, 1864. The surviving correspondence of the Virginia Board of Public Works for this period is filled with requests for boosts in both freight and passenger rates.

13. *Official Records*, I, LI, II, p. 851; *Annual Report*, Virginia Central Railroad, October, 1864; Capt. John Frizzell to General Lawton, May 1, 1864, MS in John Frizzell Papers, National Archives; Sims to Frizzell, January 30, 1865, Railroad Bureau Letter Book, National Archives.

14. *Official Records*, IV, III, pp. 616-18; Printed House Committee Report upon a bill disallowing railroad refusal of liability, in South Carolina Historical Department, Columbia; MS Senate Committee, December, 1864, in South Carolina Historical Department.

15. *Annual Reports:* Atlantic & North Carolina Railroad, June, 1864; Southwestern Railroad, August, 1864; Mississippi & Tennessee Railroad, October, 1864; Petersburg Railroad, January, 1865; Raleigh & Gaston Railroad, July, 1864; also Samuel M. Derrick, *Centennial History of the South Carolina Railroad*, p. 222. Only in Texas, where the disruption of ordinary business was little assuaged by military traffic, do the carriers appear to have been in general financial difficulties. At the end of 1863 six companies there were in arrears in their interest payments upon State loans to the extent of $442,097.60. See MS "Statement of Interest and Sinking Fund, due upon Bonds of Railroad Companies up to and for November 1, 1863, and remaining unpaid," Texas Archives.

16. *Annual Report*, Georgia Railroad, May, 1864; H. D. Whitcomb to E. Fontaine, July 11, 1864, Virginia Board of Public Works Papers; *Annual Report*, Alabama & Florida Railroad, January, 1866.

17. *Public Laws*, Confederate States of America, 1st Congress, 4th Session, Ch. 66, p. 221; *The Weekly Register*, Vol. I, No. 5, March 5, 1864; *Journal*, Confederate States Congress, VII, p. 108; Printed Memorial of

Committee of Columbia Railroad Convention, May 9, 1864, Sims Papers, National Archives.

18. *Annual Reports:* Virginia Central Railroad, October, 1864; Raleigh & Gaston Railroad, July, 1864; North Carolina Railroad, July, 1864; Nashville & Chattanooga Railroad, August, 1866.

19. Marietta *Rebel,* April 15, 1864, quoted in Milledgeville *Southern Recorder,* April 26, 1864; *Acts* of Alabama Assembly, Regular Session, 1864, No. 90, p. 77; *Annual Report,* North Carolina Railroad, July, 1864.

20. Mary Boykin Chesnut, *A Diary from Dixie,* ed. Ben Ames Williams (Boston, 1950), pp. 323 ff.; Richmond *Daily Examiner,* November 17, 1863.

21. *Annual Report,* New Orleans, Jackson & Great Northern Railroad, January, 1869; *Annual Report,* Mississippi & Tennessee Railroad, November, 1865; *Affairs of Southern Railroads,* pp. 769 ff.; *Official Records,* I, XXX, I, pp. 8-11.

22. *Official Records,* I, LII, II, pp. 510-13; Jones *Diary,* I, p. 386. Goodman posed as an amateur strategist eager to do the right thing, but his true attitude was presently revealed when the Government proposed seizing his rolling stock outright; then his cries echoed from one end of Mississippi to the other. See Seddon to Johnston, October 1, 1863, *Official Records,* I, XXX, IV, p. 720.

23. Sarah L. Wadley, *Brief Record of the Life of William M. Wadley,* pp. 41-42; Brown to Davis, May 25, 1863, Georgia Executive Letters; Brown to Capt. L. P. Grant, July 31, 1863, in *ibid.;* Georgia Adjutant General Letter Book No. 18, pp. 279-82, 377-80 (typewritten copy in Georgia Department of Archives & History); *ibid.,* No. 19, pp. 182, 184-86, 386-89.

24. *Annual Report,* Richmond & Danville Railroad, October, 1864; Richmond *Daily Examiner,* June 24, 1864; Natchez *Courier,* July 12, 1864.

25. *Battles and Leaders of the Civil War,* IV, pp. 553 ff., 568 ff., 577; Whitcomb to Secretary Seddon, June 28, 1864, *Official Records,* I, XL, II, pp. 697-98; General J. F. Gilmer to Seddon, July 1, 1864, in *ibid.,* I, LI, II, pp. 1029-30.

Chapter Eighteen

THE FAILURE OF A BUREAUCRACY

1. Sims traveled on official business from Richmond to Augusta and returned between April 10 and 23, 1864. See MS mileage voucher in Sims Papers, National Archives.

2. *Official Records,* I, LII, II, pp. 660, 850-52; IV, III, pp. 228-29.

3. *Official Records,* I, XXXII, II, p. 581; I, LI, II, p. 852. President Robert Owen of the Virginia & Tennessee was appointed Government superintendent of the ailing East Tennessee & Virginia. The supervision of military traffic upon his own line was undertaken in March by Major John W. Goodwin, who had been Military Superintendent of Railroads on the staff of the Army of Tennessee. Goodwin seems to have neglected his duties, and perhaps absented himself without leave, because of family worries. He was permitted to resign in March, 1865. See correspondence in John W. Goodwin Papers, National Archives.

4. *Official Records,* I, LI, II, p. 942.

5. Richmond *Daily Examiner*, July 4, 1863; John Brannon to Gov. William Smith of Virginia, August 20, 1864, MS in Virginia Board of Public Works Papers, Virginia State Library; *Annual Report*, Virginia Central Railroad, October, 1864.

6. E. Merton Coulter, *The Confederate States of America*, p. 132; Charles W. Ramsdell, ed., *Laws and Joint Resolutions of the Last Session of the Confederate Congress* (Durham, N. C., 1941), p. 31.

7. "Comptroller's Statement of Difference in the Settlement of the Account of Capt. E. D. T. Myers, *Engineer's Corps*," MS in Myers Papers, National Archives; *Official Records*, IV, III, pp. 392-93.

8. Capt. Thomas Butler to General Bragg, May 25, 1864, *Official Records*, I, LI, II, p. 959; Jones *Diary*, II, p. 217.

9. *Annual Report*, Richmond & Danville Railroad, October, 1864.

10. *Official Records*, I, XLII, III, pp. 1334-35; I, XLVI, II, pp. 1026-27; Jones *Diary*, II, p. 363. The Hoke report had an interesting career. It was captured by the enemy before it reached Lee, then was recaptured in the course of a skirmish before Petersburg on January 9, on which date it was finally delivered. It must have made interesting reading in the Federal trenches.

11. *Official Records*, I, XLII, III, pp. 1346-49; Jones *Diary*, II, pp. 381, 401, 406; Sims to Hugh Rice, January 30, 1865, Railroad Bureau Letter Book, National Archives; Sims to President of Piedmont Railroad, January 13, 1865 in *ibid.*

12. Sims to President of Piedmont Railroad, January 13, 1865, Railroad Bureau Letter Book, National Archives; Sims to J. R. Anderson, January 20, 1865, in *ibid.*; Sims to Superintendent Dodamead of Piedmont Road, January 30, 1865, in *ibid.*; Sims to Superintendent Talcott of Richmond & Danville Railroad, February 10 and 11, 1865, in *ibid.*; *Official Records*, I, XLVI, II, pp. 1166-67.

13. *Official Records*, I, LII, II, pp. 641, 647; IV III, pp. 312, 742-43; *Journal*, Confederate States Congress, IV, p. 33.

14. *Official Records*, I, XXXI, III, p. 788; I, XXXII, III, p. 745; J. W. Taylor to G. G. Ly and T. G. Cornish, March 7, 1864, MS in Military Records Division, Alabama Dept. of Archives and History; Meriwether to General R. Taylor, April 13, 1865, MS in Minor Meriwether Papers, National Archives.

15. *Official Records*, IV, III, pp. 575-76; I, XLII, II, p. 1257; *Journal*, Confederate States Congress, VII, pp. 135, 240, 441.

16. Jones *Diary*, II, p. 132; *Official Records*, IV, III, pp. 339-40, 570-71.

17. *Official Records*, I, XXXIX, II, pp. 737-38; IV, III, pp. 339-40; Seddon to Davis, November 3, 1864, quoted in *The Weekly Register*, Vol. I, No. 37, November 26, 1864.

18. *Journal*, Confederate States Congress, IV, pp. 63, 70, 119, 219-20; VII, pp. 231-32, 234-38, 281; Richmond *Daily Examiner*, June 15, 1864.

19. MS per diem vouchers, F. W. Sims, dated June-November, 1864, Sims Papers, National Archives.

20. *Official Records*, I, XXXVI, II, p. 987; Par. XV, Special Orders, No. 122, May 26, 1864, MS in George Whitfield Papers, National Archives; Whitfield to Seddon, January 31, 1864, with endorsements by Polk, Lawton and Seddon, MS in *ibid.*; Lawton to General S. Cooper, May 3, 1864, MS in

ibid.; Whitfield to Sims, July 5, 1864, July 20, 1864, December 10, 1864, January 13, 1864, MSS in *ibid.*

21. MS Abstract of Peters' personal military files, Peters Papers, National Archives; Lieut. Col. Minor Meriwether to General Leonidas Polk, May 19, 1864, MS in Meriwether Papers, National Archives. For the Sims-Peters friction, see the tone of their correspondence in the Peters Papers and elsewhere.

22. MS commutation, forage and fuel vouchers, Hottel Papers, National Archives. In fairness to Hottel it should be noted that his rank entitled him to maintain a private mount at Government charge.

23. Smith to Sims, December 27, 1864, with endorsements by Sims and Lawton, MS in Sims Papers, National Archives; "Statement relative to payments and loss and damage on Western & Atlantic Railroad, No. 4," MS in John Frizzell Papers, National Archives.

24. Whitfield to Sims, July 20, 1864, and December 10, 1864, MSS in Whitfield Papers, National Archives; Sims to Major Peters, February 1, 1865, and to Whitfield, February 2, 1865, Railroad Bureau Letter Book, National Archives.

25. *Official Records,* IV, III, pp. 226-29, 253; *Annual Report,* Richmond & Petersburg Railroad, April, 1864.

26. *Official Records,* IV, III, p. 77; II, VI, pp. 925-26; II, VII, pp. 422-23; Sims to Supt. H. T. Peake of South Carolina Railroad, February 13, 1864, MS telegram, Confederate States Railroad Papers, National Archives.

27. Major Hottel to Sims, March 2, 1864, and to W. T. Harrison, March 2, 1864, MS copies in Hottel Papers, National Archives; MS Railroad Bureau accounts in Sims Papers, National Archives; Sims to C. T. Pollard, March 17, 1864, MS in *ibid.*

28. Bruce, *Virginia Iron Manufacture,* p. 425; Ira Van Pelt to Sims, May 25, 1864, MS in Valentine Museum, Richmond; Sims to Colonel W. R. Hunt, January 21, 1865, and to Captain G. A. Cuyler, January 30, 1865, Railroad Bureau Letter Book, National Archives.

Chapter Nineteen

HARD FAITH AND SOFT IRON

1. *Battles and Leaders,* IV, pp. 247, 416.

2. *Ibid.,* pp. 247, 416-17; Major George Whitfield to Major Thomas Peters, February 9, 1864, MS telegraphic record book, Whitfield Papers, National Archives.

3. *Memoirs of General W. T. Sherman, Written by Himself* (Fourth Edition, 2 Vols., New York, 1891), Vol. I, pp. 418 ff.; Whitfield to Fleming, February 8, 1864, Whitfield to Peters, February 9, 1864, Whitfield to General S. G. French, February 10, 1864, Whitfield to M. B. Prichard and Major Peters, February 13, 1864, in MS telegraphic record book, Whitfield Papers; Whitfield to Lieut. Col. Sims, March 19, 1864, MS in *ibid.; Official Records,* I, XXXII, II, pp. 733-34.

4. *Official Records,* I, XXXII, I, pp. 209-13, 344-45; Sherman, *Memoirs,* I, p. 420.

5. *Official Records,* I, XXXII, I, pp. 344-45; Par. VI, Special Orders No. 56,

Hqs., Demopolis, Alabama, February 25, 1864, MS copy in Whitfield Papers, National Archives.

6. Whitfield to General Polk, March 19, 1864, MS copy of telegram in Whitfield Papers; Whitfield to Sims, March 19, 1864, MS letter in *ibid.;* Whitfield to Major B. F. Jones, September 9, 1864, MS in *ibid.;* MS receipt for spikes, Whitfield to Sims, in *ibid.*

7. *Official Records,* I, XXXII, I, pp. 344-45; I, LII, II, pp. 653-54; MS telegram record book, Whitfield Papers, National Archives.

8. *Lloyd's Southern Railroad Guide,* June, 1864; *Official Records,* I, XXXIX, II, p. 607.

9. *Official Records,* I, XXXV, II, pp. 425, 426, 441. Tebeauville is the present-day Waycross, Georgia.

10. Freeman, *Lee's Lieutenants,* III, pp. 450-53.

11. *Official Records,* I, XXXV, II, pp. 451, 453, 454, 462, 472.

12. Freeman, *op. cit.,* III, pp. 455-64; *Official Records,* I, LI, II, p. 899.

13. Freeman, *op. cit.,* III, pp. 466-67; *Official Records,* I, LI, II, pp. 902, 903, 904, 906, 908-9, 915, 927.

14. *Official Records,* I, LI, II, p. 933, 955; I, XXXV, II, pp. 494-95, 496, 526, 561.

15. *Official Records,* I, LI, II, p. 903; Freeman, *op. cit.,* III, pp. 336-37.

16. *Official Records,* I, XXXVII, II, pp. 672-73.

17. *Official Records,* I, XXXVII, II, pp. 160, 763; 765; I, XXXVII, I, pp. 96-100; Freeman, *Lee's Lieutenants,* III, pp. 524-27; *Battles and Leaders,* IV, pp. 492-94.

18. *Official Records,* I, XLIII, II, pp. 938, 943, 946, 947.

19. Minutes of Western & Atlantic Railroad, September 21, 1865, MS in Georgia Dept. of Archives & History; Maj. Gen. O. O. Howard in *Battles and Leaders,* IV, p. 294.

20. Horn, *Army of Tennessee,* p. 325; *Battles and Leaders,* IV, pp. 265, 281; *Official Records,* I, XXXVIII, IV, pp. 693, 694, 695, 708, 718.

21. Horn, *op. cit.,* pp. 326 ff.

22. *Battles and Leaders,* IV, p. 305.

23. Horn, *op. cit.,* pp. 340 ff.

24. Annual Message, Governor Brown, November 3, 1864, Georgia Executive Minutes; Montgomery *Weekly Advertiser,* August 3, 1864.

25. Governor Brown to Davis, June 28, 1864, Georgia Executive Letters; Instructions, Governor Brown to Militia of Georgia, July 21, 1864, Georgia Executive Minutes.

26. *Official Records,* I, XXXVIII, II, pp. 904-5; Montgomery *Weekly Advertiser,* July 27, 1864.

27. Montgomery *Daily Advertiser,* July 25, 1864; *Official Records,* I, XXXIX, II, pp. 771-72; I, XXXVIII, V, pp. 904-5, 908.

28. Whitfield to Major B. F. Jones, September 9, 1864, MS in Whitfield Papers, National Archives; Montgomery *Weekly Advertiser,* August 26, 1864.

29. Horn, *op. cit.,* p. 362; *Annual Report,* Central of Georgia Railroad, December, 1865; Macon *Telegraph,* quoted in Milledgeville *Southern Recorder,* August 9, 1864.

30. Macon *Telegraph,* quoted in Milledgeville *Southern Recorder,* August 9, 1864.

31. *Annual Report,* Central of Georgia Railroad, December, 1865; *Official Records,* I, XXXVIII, V, p. 937; Annual Message, Gov. Joseph E. Brown, November 3, 1864; Georgia Executive Minutes.
32. *Official Records,* I, XXXI, V, p. 938; *Annual Report,* Macon & Western Railroad, December, 1864.
33. General J. B. Hood, "The Defense of Atlanta," *Battles and Leaders,* IV, p. 342; Sherman, *Memoirs,* II, p. 104.
34. Hood, "The Defense of Atlanta," *Battles and Leaders,* IV, p. 342.
35. *Ibid.,* p. 343; *Annual Report,* Macon & Western Railroad, December, 1864. In a dispatch dated September 4 to General Bragg in Richmond, Hood asserted that the rolling stock had had to be destroyed "owing to the wanton neglect of Chief Quartermaster of this Army [who] I am informed is too much addicted to drink of late to attend to his duties." *Official Records,* I, XXXI, V, p. 1018. A Court of Inquiry which investigated the matter the following winter, agreed with Hood and roundly condemned the Quartermaster. It reported in part: "The twenty-eight carloads of ammunition, the quartermaster's stores, and the cars and engines were destroyed principally in consequence of the failure of Lieutenant Colonel McMicken, Chief Quartermaster, to comply with the specific and repeated instructions from the chief of staff to have all such stores removed by daylight; that Lieutenant Colonel McMicken had at his disposal sufficient cars and engines to move all the trains as ordered, and they were not so moved because proper instructions were not given by him to the railroad agents. We consider him highly culpable for not having promptly complied with said orders from the chief of staff ..." See Special Orders No. 51, Adj. & Insp. General's Office, Richmond, March 2, 1865, *Official Records,* I, XXXVIII, III, pp. 991-92. Hottel does not appear to have been at Atlanta at the time of the evacuation. He may still have been working upon the Montgomery & West Point. Captain Frizzell already had moved his office to Macon.

Chapter Twenty

TO SEA AND TENNESSEE

1. Annual Message, Governor Brown, Georgia Executive Minutes, November 3, 1864.
2. *Official Records,* I, XXXIX, II, pp. 860, 867; Mary G. Cumming, *Georgia Railroad and Banking Company, 1833-1945* (Augusta, 1945), p. 80.
3. General J. B. Hood, "The Invasion of Tennessee," *Battles and Leaders,* IV, p. 425; Horn, *Army of Tennessee,* p. 378.
4. Horn, *op. cit.,* p. 381.
5. Sherman, *Memoirs,* II, pp. 167-70.
6. Jacob D. Cox, *The March to the Sea* (New York, 1882), p. 23; Milledgeville *Southern Recorder,* December 20, 1864.
7. Horn, *op. cit.,* p. 381; Sherman, *Memoirs,* II, pp. 171-79.
8. *Official Records,* I, XLIV, p. 13.
9. *Ibid.; Annual Report,* Macon & Western Railroad, December, 1865.
10. Governor Brown to E. B. Walker, November 17, 1864, Georgia Executive Letters; Georgia Executive Minutes, November 19, 1864. Governor Brown likewise loaned Western & Atlantic equipment to the State of North

Carolina and to the Confederate Government to help remove cotton belonging to them from southwestern Georgia. It was thought at first that Sherman was headed in that direction. See Special Message, Governor Brown, November 17, 1864, Georgia Executive Minutes.

11. G. W. Smith, "The Georgia Militia During Sherman's March to the Sea," *Battles and Leaders,* IV, p. 667; *Official Records,* I, XLIV, pp. 413, 899.

12. *Ibid.,* p. 413; G. W. Smith, *op. cit.,* p. 667.

13. Smith, *op. cit.,* pp. 667-68; *Official Records,* I, XLIV, pp. 413-17. But it had been another southern close-call. Furthermore, the last of the Georgia militia did not reach Savannah from Thomasville until nearly noon on December 2. See Col. L. Von Zinken to Col. T. B. Roy, *Official Records,* I, XLIV, p. 921.

14. *Official Records,* I, XLIV, pp. 908, 911, 918, 920, 923, 935, 938, 939, 946, 952.

15. Lt. Col. Sims to R. R. Cuyler, January 2, 1865, Railroad Bureau Letter Book, National Archives; *Official Records,* I, XLIV, pp. 668-69.

16. *Annual Report,* Atlantic & Gulf Railroad, January, 1866; Sherman to Grant, December 18, 1864, *Official Records,* I, XLIV, pp. 742-43.

17. *Annual Report,* Central of Georgia Railroad, December, 1865; O. O. Howard, *op. cit.,* p. 666; *Official Records,* I, XLIV, pp. 964-65, 967.

18. *Official Records,* I, LII, II, p. 749; Major George Whitfield to Lt. Col. Sims, December 10, 1864, MS in Whitfield Papers, National Archives.

19. Horn, *op. cit.,* pp. 378-80.

20. Whitfield to Sims, December 10, 1864, MS in Whitfield Papers; Horn, *op. cit.,* pp. 373-75; *Official Records,* I, XXXIX, II, pp. 844-45.

21. *Official Records,* I, XXXIX, II, pp. 855-56, 903; Whitfield to Sims, December 10, 1864, MS in Whitfield Papers.

22. *Official Records,* I, XLV, I, p. 1219; I, XXXIX, II, p. 871; J. C. Berry to Major Willis, November 18, 1864, MS telegram in Willis Papers, Library of Congress; MS Memo Book No. 3, 1864-1865, in *ibid.;* Willis to Brent, December 2, 1864, MS Memo Book No. 3; Horn, *op. cit.,* pp. 382-83.

23. *Official Records,* I, XLV, I, pp. 844-47, 865-75, 1244, 1256, 1261; I, XLV, II, pp. 642, 643, 644.

24. Horn, *op. cit.,* p. 420; *Official Records,* I, XLV, II, pp. 742, 753; I, XLV, I, pp. 871-72; Whitfield to Lt. Col. Sims, January 13, 1865, MS in Whitfield Papers, National Archives.

Chapter Twenty-One

THE FINAL EFFORT

1. *Annual Report,* Western & Atlantic Railroad, October, 1864; Governor Brown to Martin J. Dooly, March 15, 1865; Georgia Executive Letters; Annual Message, Governor Brown, November 3, 1864, Georgia Executive Minutes; *Annual Report,* Central of Georgia Railroad, December, 1865.

2. Jones *Diary,* II, p. 344; *Official Records,* I, XLV, II, pp. 640, 705-6; I, LIII, pp. 383-84; I, XLIV, pp. 995-96; Capt. W. G. Gray (for F. W. Sims) to Major Whitfield, January 5, 1865, Railroad Bureau Letter Book, National Archives; Major Willis, to Colonel Brent, December (no date), 1864, MS

Memo Book No. 3, 1864-1865, Willis Papers, Library of Congress; Willis to G. W. Adams, December 20, 1864, Willis to General Lawton, December 29, 1864, Willis to Beauregard, January 2, 1865, in *ibid.*

3. *Official Records*, I, XLV, II, pp. 705-6; II, VII, p. 49; I, XLVII, II, p. 1108; Willis to General Lawton, December 29, 1864, and Willis to Beauregard, January 2, 1865, MS Memo Book No. 3, Willis Papers, Library of Congress.

4. *Official Records*, I, XLIV, pp. 995-96. The personnel of the Western & Atlantic were luckier; Governor Brown retained them even after the loss of the road, their wages being paid, for the time being, by "the proceeds of cotton purchased, shipped and sold speculatively by the State." *Annual Message*, Governor Brown, November 3, 1864. Cuyler of the Central, however, did accept a substantial cut in his annual salary of $8,000.

5. *Official Records*, I, XLIV, p. 996; I, XLV, II, p. 786; I, XLVII, II, p. 1323.

6. *Acts* of South Carolina General Assembly, September and December, 1863, pp. 200-9; MS Resolutions of South Carolina Senate and House of Representatives as to Columbia & Hamburg Railroad Co., December, 1864, in South Carolina Historical Dept., Columbia; *Official Records*, IV, III, pp. 968-70, 1006-7, 1053-54; Jones *Diary*, II, p. 370; Sims to John Screven, February 3, 1865, Railroad Bureau Letter Book, National Archives; Georgia Executive Minutes, March 11, 1865; Georgia Senate *Journal*, Extra Session, 1865, p. 56.

7. MS Memo Book No. 3, 1864-1865, Willis Papers, Library of Congress; *Official Records*, II, VIII, p. 49.

8. MS Memo Book No. 3, 1864-1865, Willis Papers, Library of Congress; *Annual Report*, Central of Georgia Railroad, December, 1865; T. B. Catherwood, *The Life and Labors of William M. Wadley*, p. 9; *Annual Report*, Macon & Brunswick Railroad, February, 1866; MS Abstract of Railroad Bureau property, December 31, 1864, Sims Papers, National Archives; *Annual Report*, Southwestern Railroad, August, 1865; *Official Records*, I, XLVII, III, pp. 714, 727; I, XLV, II, pp. 705-6; I, XLVII, II, p. 1108.

9. *Official Records*, I, XLV, II, pp. 757-58, 786-87.

10. Horn, *op. cit.*, pp. 422-23.

11. *Official Records*, I, XLV, II, pp. 792-93.

12. *Official Records*, I, XLIX, I, pp. 930, 932, 936. However, the local quartermaster at Selma protested that no delays were occurring at that point. Major S. Hillyer to Major E. Willis, January 26, 1865, MS telegram in Willis Papers, Library of Congress.

13. Major W. F. Ayer, to Major E. Willis, January 26, 1865, MS telegram in Willis Papers, Library of Congress; Willis to Major Whitfield, January 26, 1865, MS Memo Book No. 3, Willis Papers; *Official Records*, I, XLIX, I, p. 946; Horn, *op. cit.*, p. 423.

14. *Official Records*, I, LIII, pp. 1052-53, 1049-50.

15. *Official Records*, I, XLVII, I, pp. 19-23.

16. See "Correspondence, etc.—Confederate" in *Official Records*, I, XLVII, II; also Horn, *op. cit.*, p. 424.

17. *Official Records*, I, XLVII, II, pp. 1209-10, 1222-23, 1238.

18. *Ibid.*, pp. 1259-60.

19. *Official Records*, I, XLVII, II, pp. 693-94, 724, 1239, 1311, 1312, 1425; F. W. Sims to Major E. Willis, February 24, 1864, MS in Willis Papers.

20. *Official Records*, I, XLVII, II, pp. 1247, 1298, 1316.
21. *Official Records*, I, XLVII, II, pp. 1321, 1323.
22. *Official Records*, I, XLVII, II, pp. 1334, 1339, 1343.
23. *Official Records*, I, XLVII, II, pp. 1353, 1361, 1364, 1371, 1374, 1376, 1377, 1406; J. L. Morrow to Willis, March 15, 1865, MS telegram in Willis Papers.
24. Horn, *op. cit.*, p. 425; Wade Hampton, "The Battle of Bentonville," *Battles and Leaders*, IV, pp. 700-5; *Official Records*, I, XLVII, II, pp. 1450-51.
25. Space does not permit here the citing of all the *Official Records* sources for the final days of Confederate railroading in North Carolina. A reading of Series I, Vol. XLVII, Part II, pp. 1449 ff., and Part III, pp. 695 ff. will give a sufficient impression of confusion and disaster. Stoneman's official account of the wrecking of the lines operating through Salisbury and Greensboro will be found in *Official Records*, I, XLVII, I, p. 29. See also *Annual Report*, Western North Carolina Railroad, August, 1865, and *Annual Report*, North Carolina Railroad, July, 1865. On the Western North Carolina road, the total damage (in U. S. currency) exceeded $110,000.
26. *Journal*, Confederate States Congress, VII, p. 442; *Official Records*, IV, III, p. 1095.
27. *Official Records*, IV, III, pp. 1091-93.
28. Gilmer to Breckinridge, February 11, 1865, MS copy in Sims Papers, National Archives.
29. *Official Records*, IV, III, pp. 1095-96; Davis to the Senate and House, February 28, 1865, MS in Sims Papers, National Archives; *Journal* Confederate States Congress, IV, p. 619, 642, 649, 709; Charles W. Ramsdell, *Laws and Joint Resolutions of the Last Session of the Confederate Congress*, p. 101.
30. *Journal*, Confederate States Congress, VII, pp. 584-86.
31. *Journal*, Confederate States Congress, IV, pp. 571, 573-74, 660.

Chapter Twenty-Two

END OF TRACK

1. Richmond *Daily Examiner*, January 3, and 31, 1865; Sims to Major E. B. Branch, January 2, 1865, to H. D. Bird, January 2, 1865, to Capt. H. M. Waller, February 7, 1865, to R. L. Owen, February 7, 1865, Railroad Bureau Letter Book, National Archives. The Virginia & Tennessee had been wrecked by Stoneman.
2. Capt. W. G. Gray to H. W. Vandegrift, January 23, 1865, Railroad Bureau Letter Book, National Archives; *Official Records*, I, XLVI, I, p. 519; I, XLVI, III, p. 1335.
3. *Battles and Leaders*, IV, p. 521; Jones *Diary*, II, p. 444; *Annual Report*, Richmond, Fredericksburg & Potomac Railroad, November, 1865; *Official Records*, I, XLVI, III, pp. 1341, 1342, 1365; Freeman, *Lee's Lieutenants*, III, pp. 650-51.
4. Bill, *The Beleaguered City*, pp. 268-69.
5. *Annual Report*, Richmond & Petersburg Railroad, 1865; *Annual Report*,

Richmond & Danville Railroad, 1865; Clifford Dowdey, *Experiment in Rebellion* (New York, 1946), pp. 402-3.

6. *Official Records*, I, XLVI, III, pp. 1383-84, 1387; Freeman, *op. cit.*, III, pp. 712-16.

7. Authorities do not precisely agree upon the details of the capture of Lee's last railroad trains. See *Personal Memoirs of P. H. Sheridan* (2 vols., New York, 1888), II, pp. 188-90; Sheridan to Grant, April 8, 1865 (9:20 P.M.) quoted in *ibid.*, II, p. 199; Freeman, *op. cit.*, III, pp. 720 ff.; F. T. Miller and R. S. Lanier, eds., *Photographic History of the Civil War* (10 vols., New York, 1911), III, p. 313; Lee to Jefferson Davis, April 12, 1865, *Battles and Leaders*, IV, p. 724.

8. Thomas Weber, "The Northern Railroads in the Civil War," MS cit., p. 294; *Annual Report*, Richmond & Danville Railroad, 1865; *Official Records*, I, XLVI, III, pp. 1391-92.

9. Typewritten extracts from military records of F. W. Sims, Sims Papers, National Archives.

10. *Affairs of Southern Railroads*, pp. 1041-42; Arney Robinson Childs, ed., *The Private Journal of Henry William Ravenal, 1859-1887*, pp. 225-26; Governor Brown to Capt. R. L. Rodgers, March 7, 1865, Georgia Executive Minutes.

11. *Affairs of Southern Railroads*, pp. 896, 904.

12. *Official Records*, I, XLIX, I, pp. 1023, 1154-56; *Affairs of Southern Railroads*, pp. 895-96.

13. *Official Records*, I, XLIX, I, p. 484.

14. *Affairs of Southern Railroads*, pp. 895-96; *Annual Report*, Montgomery & West Point Railroad, April, 1866; *Official Records*, I, XLIX, I, pp. 369, 486-87.

15. Governor Brown to General Toombs, April 16, 1865, Georgia Executive Letters; *Official Records*, I, XLIX, II, pp. 1233, 1244, 1257; I, LII, II, p. 814.

16. Governor Brown to General Wilson, Georgia Executive Letters, April 28, 1864; *Official Records*, I, XLIX, II, p. 1281.

17. *Official Records*, I, XLVIII, II, pp. 1316-17.

18. *Annual Report*, Montgomery & West Point Railroad, April, 1866; *Annual Report*, New Orleans, Jackson & Great Northern Railroad, January, 1869; *Annual Report*, Mississippi & Tennessee Railroad, November, 1865; *Annual Report*, Alabama & Tennessee River Railroad, April, 1866; Poor's *Manual*, 1869-70, p. 359; *Annual Report*, Mobile & Ohio Railroad, April, 1866.

19. *Annual Report*, Southwestern Railroad, August, 1865.

20. *Annual Report*, Central of Georgia Railroad, December, 1865; Central of Georgia Railway, *The First Hundred Years*, p. 7; Supt. Robert Baugh of Western & Atlantic to Governor James Johnson of Georgia, December 5, 1865, MS in Georgia Dept. of Archives and History; Report of Gov. Charles J. Jenkins of Georgia to Georgia Legislature on Western & Atlantic Railroad, January 30, 1866, MS in *ibid.*; Poor's *Manual*, 1869-70, p. 371.

21. *Annual Report*, Western North Carolina Railroad, 1866; North Carolina *Document No. 23*, Session 1866-67; Robert L. Owen to Gov. F. H. Pierpont of Virginia, June 23, 1865, MS in Virginia Board of Public Works

Papers, Virginia State Library; *Annual Report,* Virginia Central Railroad, 1865.

22. See various reports, *Affairs of Southern Railroads; Annual Reports:* Seaboard & Roanoke Railroad, April, 1867; Western North Carolina Railroad, August, 1865; Memphis & Charleston Railroad, 1866; Virginia Central Railroad, 1865; Sarah L. Wadley, *Life of William M. Wadley,* p. 58.

23. *Dictionary of American Biography,* XII, pp. 211-12.

24. Sarah L. Wadley, *Brief Record of William M. Wadley,* p. 47; Private Journal of Sarah L. Wadley, September 26, November 14, 1865, January 30, 1866, MS in Southern Historical Collection, University of North Carolina Library.

25. T. B. Catherwood, *The Life and Labors of William M. Wadley.*

26. Letter to the author from Mrs. Lilla M. Hawes of Georgia Historical Society, June 8, 1949; Savannah *Daily Morning News,* September 1, 1868, August 18, 1868, July 8, 1869, October 18, 1867, October 31, 1867, March 25, 1868.

27. *Proceedings of the Union Society,* 1866-67; Savannah *Daily Morning News,* June 21, 1869.

28. Savannah *Daily Morning News,* October 1, 1869, October 7, 1869; Letter from Mr. Calder W. Payne of Macon, Georgia, to the author, October 28, 1949; MS letter of Guardianship of the surviving children of F. W. Sims, October 25, 1875, Ordinary's Office, Chatham County, Georgia.

Appendix

1. *Official Records,* I, XV, pp. 814-85; I, XXXIV, III, p. 796, S. G. Reed, *A History of Texas Railroads* (Houston, 1941), p. 126.

2. *Official Records,* I, XV, p. 909; Poor's *Manual* (1869-70), p. 196; Annual Report, Eastern Texas R. R., May, 1865, MS in Texas State Archives; Reed, *op. cit.,* pp. 86, 126; Annual Reports, Southern Pacific Railroad, June, 1864, January, 1866, MSS in Texas State Archives.

3. Annual Report, Washington County Railroad, October, 1863; Annual Report, Texas & New Orleans Railroad, June, 1866; Annual Report, Southern Pacific R. R., January, 1866, MSS of all in Texas State Archives.

Bibliography

OFFICIAL PUBLICATIONS

ALABAMA

Acts of the Alabama Assembly (1859-60; First Called Session, 1861; Regular Session, 1861; Regular Session, 1862; Called Session, 1863; Regular Session, 1863; Called Session, 1864; Regular Session, 1864).

CONFEDERATE STATES

Acts and Resolutions of the First Three Sessions of the Provisional Congress of the Confederate States (Richmond, 1862).

Acts and Resolutions of the Third Session of the Provisional Congress of the Confederate States (Richmond, 1861).

Acts and Resolutions of the Fourth Session of the Provisional Congress of the Confederate States (Richmond, 1862).

Circulars of Quartermaster General's Office, Richmond, February 10, 1862, September 12, 1862, and April 1, 1864.

Confederate Army Regulations (1863).

General Orders of Adjutant & Inspector General's Office, Richmond, 1863 (No. 13, January 31, 1863; No. 58, May 11, 1863; No. 115, August 24, 1863; No. 128, September 30, 1863; No. 129, October 1, 1863; No. 160, December 7, 1863).

Private Acts of First Congress, Confederate States of America (Richmond, 1864).

Public Laws of the Confederate States of America (1st Congress, 1st Session —Richmond, 1862).

Public Laws of the Confederate States of America (1st Congress, 3rd Session —Richmond, 1863).

Public Laws of the Confederate States of America (1st Congress, 4th Session—Richmond, 1864).

Public Laws of the Confederate States of America (2nd Congress, 1st Session—Richmond, 1864).

Public Laws of the Confederate States Congress (Richmond, 1862).

Regulations for the Care and Transportation of the Sick in the Army of the Potomac (Dept. of War, Richmond, October 21, 1861).

Statutes at Large, Provisional Government of the Confederate States (Richmond, 1862).

FLORIDA

Florida Senate Journal (1863).

Journal of Proceedings of the House of Representatives (1860, 1862, 1863).

Laws of Florida (1860-1861; 1862).

Proceedings of the Board of Internal Improvements (26 Vols., Tallahassee, 1902-1949).

GEORGIA

Georgia Senate Journal (1861, 1862, 1863, Extra Session 1865).
Laws of Georgia (1862, 1863).

NORTH CAROLINA

Document No. 31, Session 1860-61.
Document No. 23, Session 1866-67.
Private Laws of North Carolina (1863).

SOUTH CAROLINA

Acts of South Carolina General Assembly (September & December, 1863).
Reports and Resolutions, South Carolina General Assembly, (1861 & 1863).

UNITED STATES

Eighth Census of the United States (Population) (Washington, Government Printing Office, 1864).
Preliminary Report of the Eighth Census (Ex. Document No. 116, 37th Congress, 2nd Session) (Washington, Government Printing Office, 1862).
Journal of the Congress of the Confederate States of America (58th Congress, 2nd Session, Senate Document No. 234) (7 Vols., Washington, Government Printing Office, 1904-1905).
Affairs of Southern Railroads. See Report No. 34.
Official Records. See *The War of the Rebellion*, etc.
Official Records of the Union and Confederate Navies in the War of the Rebellion (30 Vols., Washington, Government Printing Office, 1894-1922).
Report No. 34, Affairs of Southern Railroads (House of Representatives, 39th Congress, 2nd Session) (Washington, Government Printing Office, 1867).
The War of the Rebellion: The Official Records of the Union and Confederate Armies (128 Vols., Washington, Government Printing Office, 1880-1901).
United States Statutes at Large.

VIRGINIA

Biennial Report of the Board of Public Works to the General Assembly of Virginia (1860-1861).
Annual Report, Board of Public Works (1866).

RAILROAD ANNUAL REPORTS

These reports, usually in the form of small printed pamphlets, were issued under various names. For purposes of convenience, they are all designated herein as *Annual Reports*.

Alabama & Florida R. R. (of Alabama) (January, 1866).
Alabama & Tennessee River R. R. (April, 1866).
Atlanta & West Point R. R. (July, 1866).

Atlantic & Gulf R. R. (February, 1861; February, 1862; February, 1863; January, 1864; January, 1866).
Atlantic & North Carolina R. R. (1861, 1862, 1863, 1864, 1865).
Augusta & Savannah R. R. (1861).
Central of Georgia R. R. (December, 1860, 1861, 1862, 1863, 1865).
Charleston & Savannah R. R. (February, 1861).
Georgia R. R. (May, 1859; May, 1864).
Knoxville & Kentucky R. R. (March, 1861).
Macon & Brunswick R. R. (February, 1862; February, 1866).
Macon & Western R. R. (December, 1859, 1863, 1864, 1865).
Memphis & Charleston R. R. (June, 1860, 1866).
Memphis & Ohio R. R. (1861).
Mississippi & Tennessee R. R. (1864, 1865).
Mobile & Great Northern R. R. (April, 1866).
Mobile & Ohio R. R. (April, 1866).
Montgomery & West Point R. R. (April, 1862; April, 1866).
Nashville & Chattanooga R. R. (August, 1861; August, 1866).
New Orleans, Jackson & Great Northern R. R. (January, 1861; January, 1866).
North Carolina R. R. (July, 1860, 1862, 1863, 1864, 1865).
Petersburg R. R. (1859, 1860, 1861, 1862, 1863, 1864, 1866).
Raleigh & Gaston R. R. (July, 1861, 1864, 1865, 1866).
Richmond & Danville R. R. (December, 1859, 1861, 1862, 1863, 1864, 1865).
Richmond, Fredericksburg & Potomac R. R. (May, 1861, 1863; November, 1865, 1866).
Richmond & Petersburg R. R. (May, 1862, 1863; April, 1864; November, 1865).
Savannah, Albany & Gulf R. R. (May, 1861).
Seaboard & Roanoke R. R. (February, 1861, 1862; April, 1867).
Selma & Meridian R. R. (January, 1866).
South Side R. R. (November, 1863, 1866).
Southwestern R. R. (August, 1861, 1862, 1863, 1864, 1865).
Tennessee & Alabama R. R. (1866).
Virginia Central R. R. (1858, 1861, 1862, 1863, 1864, 1865).
Virginia & Tennessee R. R. (September, 1858, 1861; October, 1863).
Western R. R. (of North Carolina) (1858).
Western & Atlantic R. R. (October, 1861, 1862).
Western North Carolina R. R. (August, 1861, 1862, 1863, 1865).
Wills Valley R. R. (May, 1866).
Wilmington & Weldon R. R. (September, 1863).

Manuscript Collections, etc.

Alabama Department of Archives & History (Military Records Division) Montgomery
  Files of Alabama State Quartermaster's Department
Chesapeake & Ohio Ry. Co. (Public Relations Dept., Richmond)
  Minutes of Board of Directors, Virginia Central R. R. Co., September 26, 1861, October 1, 1863

Confederate Museum, Richmond
  Collection of papers of C. S. Quartermaster Department
Emory University Library (Rare Books Division) Atlanta
  Keith M. Read Confederate Collection
University of Florida Library, Gainesville
  Yulee Papers
Georgia Department of Archives and History, Atlanta
  Business Record Ledger, Western & Atlantic R. R. (1860-1862)
  Georgia Adjutant General Letter Books, Nos. 1, 14, 15, 16, 18, 19
  Georgia Executive Letter Books (1860-1865)
  Georgia Executive Minutes (1860-1866)
  Georgia Railroad Papers (Brown administration, 1861-1865)
  Opinion of Attorney General A. J. Hammond in re. State Aid to Rail-
    roads, August 22, 1872
  Western & Atlantic R. R., Ledger Record of Commutation Ticket Sales,
    June 1, 1855–October 31, 1861
Library of Congress, Washington
  E. Willis Papers
National Archives (War Records Division), Washington
  Register of Appointments, C. S. Army
  John Frizzell Papers
  John W. Goodwin Papers
  John M. Hottel Papers
  Minor Meriwether Papers
  E. T. D. Myers Papers
  Thomas Peters Papers
  C. S. Quartermaster General's Office Letter Books
  C. S. Railroad Bureau Letter Book
  C. S. Railroad Bureau Papers
  C. S. Railroad Papers
  C. S. Secretaries of War Papers
  F. W. Sims Papers
  William M. Wadley Papers
  George Whitfield Papers
South Carolina Historical Department, Columbia
  South Carolina Railroad Papers
Office of Ordinary of Chatham County, Georgia, Savannah
  Estate Records of F. W. Sims
Texas State Archives
  Manuscript Texas Railroad Reports, 1860-1866
Valentine Museum, Richmond
  Joseph Gentry Papers
  Valentine Collection of C. S. Quartermaster Dept. Papers
  C. S. Railroad Bureau Telegraphic File (in part)
Virginia State Library (Division of Archives), Richmond
  Papers of Virginia Board of Public Works

DIARIES

Chesnut, Mary Boykin, *A Diary from Dixie*, ed. Ben Ames Williams (Boston, 1950).

Jones, John B., *A Rebel War Clerk's Diary*, ed. Howard Swiggett (2 Vols., New York, 1935).

Ravenal, H. W., *The Private Journal of Henry William Ravenal, 1859-1887*, ed. Arney Robinson Childs (Columbia, 1947).

Shaffner, J. F., *Diary of Dr. J. F. Shaffner, Sr., Sept. 13, 1863—Feb. 5, 1865* (Privately published, no date. Copy in N. C. State Library).

Wadley, Sarah L., Private Journal of Sarah L. Wadley (Typewritten copy in University of N. C. Library).

NEWSPAPERS AND PERIODICALS

American Railroad Journal
Appleton's Railway and Steam Navigation Guide
Columbia *Tri-Weekly South Carolinian*
DeBow's Review
Harper's Weekly
Hill & Swayze's Confederate States Rail-Road and Steamboat Guide
Hunt's Merchant's Magazine and Commercial Review
Jackson *Weekly Mississippian* and *Daily Mississippian*
Journal of Southern History
Lloyd's Southern Railroad Guide
Locomotive Engineering
The Louisiana Historical Quarterly
Meridian *Daily Clarion*
Milledgeville *Southern Recorder*
Mobile *Register and Advertiser*
Mobile *Tribune*
Montgomery *Daily Mail*
Montgomery *Daily Post*
Montgomery *Weekly Advertiser* and *Daily Advertiser*
Montgomery *Weekly Confederation*
Natchez *Daily Courier*
New York *Herald*
New York *Tribune*
Paulding (Miss.) *Eastern Clarion*
Poor's *Manual of the Railroads of the United States*
Raleigh *Standard*
Raleigh *Weekly Register*
Richmond *Daily Dispatch*
Richmond *Daily Examiner, Semi-Weekly Examiner,* and *Weekly Examiner*
Richmond *Enquirer*
Richmond *Whig*
Savannah *Daily Morning News*
Savannah *Republican*
South Carolina Historical and Genealogical Magazine
Vicksburg *Whig* and *Weekly Whig*
The Weekly Register (a newsmagazine, published at Lynchburg)

Maps

It is not to be assumed that the maps cited herein are recommended as accurate portrayals of the railroad system of the Confederacy. Most of them contain singular errors, due primarily to the fact that the period just before the war was one of extremely rapid railroad extension in many parts of the South. Of the maps listed, the most reliable are the manuscript productions of Confederate Army Engineers. They were actually on the ground and had no reason to draw upon their imaginations. Unfortunately, their maps cover only limited areas. The most satisfactory of all the maps examined were those provided in Milton S. Heath's MS doctor's thesis, "Public Cooperation in Railroad Construction in Southern United States to 1861."

G. T. Berg's *Map of Columbia* (186?)

Colton's *Map of Savannah* (J. H. Colton, New York, 1855).

W. M. Robertson's *Plan of the City of Mobile* (1853).

Map of Selma (by unknown publisher from data in "War Dept. Records"—copy in Map Division, Alabama State Library).

Railroad and Plank Road Map of North Carolina (publisher unknown; date about 1861; copy in North Carolina Archives, Raleigh).

U. S. Coast Survey, *Map of North Carolina* (1863).

U. S. Coast Survey, *Map of Southern Georgia and Part of South Carolina* (1865).

U. S. Coast Survey, *Map of Southern Mississippi and Alabama* (1863).

Virginia Board of Public Works, *A Map of the Rail Roads of Virginia* (1858).

Cooke's *Map of the Routes to the Virginia Springs* (1858).

Appleton's *Railway Map of the United States and the Canadas* (1860).

E. Ezekial, *Map of the Seat of War with the Lines of R. Roads leading thereto* (New Orleans, 1861).

MS Map of Petersburg, Va. (C. S. Engineers Bureau, 1863—in Confederate Museum, Richmond).

MS Map of Richmond and Vicinity (C. S. Engineers Bureau, 1862—in Confederate Museum, Richmond).

MS Map of Part of Eastern North Carolina (C. S. Engineers Bureau, 1864—in North Carolina Archives, Raleigh).

MS Location Map of Cheraw & Coal Fields R. R. (by F. C. Harris, 1860—in North Carolina Archives, Raleigh).

MS Map of Marietta, Ga., and Vicinity (Engineer Office, C. S. Cavalry Corps, June 24, 1864—in Map Division, Alabama Department of Archives, Montgomery).

MS Map of Lafayette and Dalton, Ga., and Vicinity (probably same source and date as above—in Map Division, Alabama Department of Archives).

MS Map of Atlanta, Ga., and Vicinity (Engineer Office, C. S. Cavalry Corps, July 10, 1864—in Map Divison, Alabama Department of Archives).

MS Map of Burned Bridges, Western & Atlantic R. R. (by Supt. John S. Rowland, in Georgia Dept. of Archives and History, Atlanta).

Secondary Works

Alexander, E. P., *Military Memoirs of a Confederate* (New York, 1907).

Avery, I. W., *The History of the State of Georgia from 1850 to 1881* (New York, 1881).

Axtell, Decatur, "History of the Chesapeake & Ohio Railroad" (MS in possession of Public Relations Dept., Chesapeake & Ohio Ry., Richmond).

Bill, Alfred Hoyt, *The Beleaguered City* (New York, 1946).

Bradlee, Francis B. C., *Blockade Running in the Confederacy* (Salem, Mass., 1925).

Bruce, Kathleen, *Virginia Iron Manufacture in the Slave Era* (New York, 1931).

Butler, John C., *Historical Record of Macon and Central Georgia* (Macon, 1879).

Catherwood, T. B., ed., *The Life and Labors of William M. Wadley* (Savannah, 1885).

Central of Georgia Railway Co., *The First Hundred Years* (1943).

Cooke, John Esten, *Stonewall Jackson, A Military Biography* (New York, 1866).

Coulter, E. Merton, *The Confederate States of America, 1861-1865* (Vol. VII of *A History of the South*, Louisiana State University Press, 1950).

Cumming, Mary G., *Georgia Railroad & Banking Company, 1833-1945* (Augusta, 1945).

Cox, Jacob D., *The March to the Sea* (New York, 1882).

Derrick, Samuel M., *Centennial History of the South Carolina Railroad* (Columbia, 1930).

Dietz, August, *The Confederate States Post Office Department, Its Stamps and Stationery* (Richmond, 1948).

Dowdey, Clifford, *Experiment in Rebellion* (New York, 1946).

Easterby, J. H., ed., *The South Carolina Rice Plantation as revealed in the Papers of Robert F. W. Allston* (Chicago, 1945).

Fiske, John, *The Mississippi Valley in the Civil War* (Boston & New York, 1900).

Freeman, Douglas Southall, *Lee's Lieutenants, A Study in Command* (3 Vols., New York, 1946).

Heath, Milton S., Public Cooperation in Railroad Construction in the Southern United States to 1861 (unpublished doctoral thesis, Harvard University, 1937).

Henderson, G. F. R., *Stonewall Jackson and the American Civil War* (Authorized American edition, London & New York, 1949).

Henry, Robert Selph, *The Story of the Confederacy* (New York, 1936).

Horn, Stanley F., *The Army of Tennessee* (Indianapolis & New York, 1941).

Johnston, James Houstoun, *The Western and Atlantic Railroad of the State of Georgia* (Atlanta, 1931).

Longstreet, James B., *From Manassas to Appomattox* (Philadelphia, 1896).

Mordecai, John B., *A Brief History of the Richmond, Fredericksburg and Potomac Railroad* (Richmond, 1938).

Owen, Thomas McAdory, *History of Alabama and Dictionary of Alabama Biography* (4 Vols., Chicago, 1921).

Phillips, Ulrich B., *A History of Transportation in the Eastern Cotton Belt to 1860* (New York, 1908).

Ramsdell, Charles W., *Laws and Joint Resolutions of the Last Session of the Confederate Congress* (Durham, 1941).

Reed, St. Clair G., *A History of Texas Railroads and of Transportation conditions under Spain and Mexico and the Republic and the State* (Houston, 1941).

Sherman, William T., *Memoirs of General W. T. Sherman, Written by Himself* (Fourth Edition, 2 Vols., New York, 1891).

Sheridan, P. H., *Personal Memoirs of P. H. Sheridan* (2 Vols., New York, 1888).

Sydnor, Charles S., *The Development of Southern Sectionalism 1819-1848* (Baton Rouge, 1948).

Virginia W. P. A. Writers Project, *Virginia, A Guide to the Old Dominion* (New York, 1940).

Wadley, Sarah L., *A Brief Record of the Life of William M. Wadley, Written by his Eldest Daughter* (New York, 1884).

Weber, Thomas, The Northern Railroads and the Civil War (unpublished doctoral dissertation, Columbia University, 1949).

Woodward, Charles G., *The South-Western Railroad, A Common Carrier of the South before and during the War Between the States* (published by Central of Ga. Ry. Co., 1947).

Encyclopaedias, etc.

Robert Underwood Johnson and Clarence Clough Buel, eds., *Battles and Leaders of the Civil War* (4 Vols., New York, 1884, 1887, 1888).

S. A. Ashe and others, eds., *Biographical History of North Carolina* (8 Vols., Greensboro, 1917).

Allen Johnson and Dumas Malone, eds., *Dictionary of American Biography* (22 Vols., New York, 1946).

James Truslow Adams, editor-in-chief, *Dictionary of American History* (5 Vols., New York, 1940).

William J. Northern, ed., *Men of Mark in Georgia* (7 Vols., Atlanta, 1911).

Francis Trevelyan Miller and Robert S. Lanier, eds., *The Photographic History of the Civil War* (10 Vols., New York, 1912).

Miscellaneous

Proceedings of a Convention of Railroads held at Goldsboro, April 1, 1862 (copy in N. C. Dept. of Archives, Raleigh).

Farrow and Dennett's Mobile City Directory (1861).

The Stranger's Guide and Official Directory for the City of Richmond (1863).

Proceedings of the Union Society (1859-60).

Minutes of the Union Society, 1750-1858 (Savannah, 1860).

Rules and Regulations for the Government of the South Carolina Rail Road (January, 1855, revised 1869).

Proceedings of the Southern Railroad Convention (Macon, Ga., November 25, 1863).

Memorial of Columbia Railroad Convention to C. S. Congress, April, 1864.
Proceedings of Petersburg Railroad Convention (March 12, 1862).
Local Rates of Transportation (Central R. R. of Georgia, Macon & Western R. R., Southwestern R. R. and Muscogee R. R., June 15, 1863).
Southern Historical Society Papers.
Low's Railway Directory for 1862 (New York, 1862).
Georgia Railroad Local Tariff (December 3, 1867).
Report of Railroad Convention (held at Chattanooga, June 4-5, 1861).
J. Houstoun Johnston, *Report to Georgia Public Service Commission* (December, 1929).
Time Table No. 20, Western & Atlantic Railroad (May 12, 1868).
Various wartime tariffs of Virginia railroads, contained in Virginia Board of Public Works Papers, Archives Division, Virginia State Library.

INDEX

As you can see from the source code, the algorithm steps through (iterates) the numbers 1 through 5, building the factorial with each successive multiplication.

A Recursive Approach

You can use a recursive approach to solve the same problem. For starters, you'll need a function to act as a base for the recursion, a function that will call itself. There are two things you'll need to build into your recursive function. First, you'll need a mechanism to keep track of the depth of the recursion. In other words, you'll need a variable or a parameter that changes, depending on the number of times the recursive function calls itself.

Second, you'll need a terminating condition, something that tells the recursive function when it's gone deep enough. Here's one version of a recursive function that calculates a factorial:

```
int    factorial( int num )
{
   if ( num > 1 )
      num *= factorial( num - 1 );

   return( num );
}
```

factorial() takes a single parameter, the number whose factorial you are trying to calculate. First, factorial() checks to see whether the number passed to it is greater than 1. If it is not, factorial() calls itself, passing 1 less than the number passed into it. This strategy guarantees that, eventually, factorial() will get called with a value of 1.

Figure 11.2 shows this process in action. The process starts with a call to factorial():

```
result = factorial( 3 );
```

Take a look at the leftmost factorial() source code in Figure 11.2. factorial() is called with a parameter of 3. The if statement checks to see whether the parameter is greater than 1. Since 3 is greater than 1, the following statement is executed:

```
num *= factorial( num - 1 );
```

291

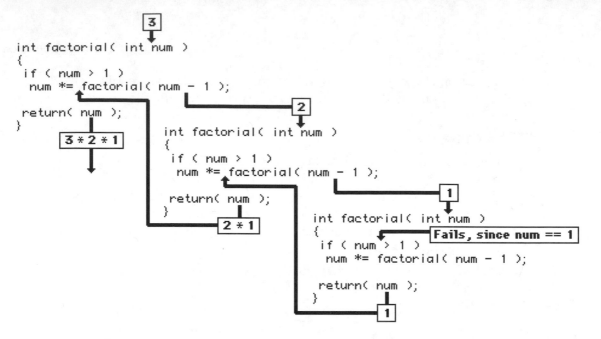

Figure 11.2 The recursion process caused by the call `factorial(3)`.

This statement calls `factorial()` again, passing a value of n–1, or 2, as the parameter. This second call of `factorial()` is pictured in the center of Figure 11.2.

Important

> It's important to understand that this second call to `factorial()` is treated just like any other function call that occurs in the middle of a function. The calling function's variables are preserved while the called function runs. In this case, the called function is just another copy of `factorial()`.

This second call of `factorial()` takes a value of 2 as a parameter. The `if` statement compares this value to 1 and, since 2 is greater than 1, executes the statement:

```
num *= factorial( num - 1 );
```

This statement calls `factorial()` yet again, passing num–1, or 1, as a parameter. The third call of `factorial()` is portrayed on the rightmost side of Figure 11.2.

The third call of `factorial()` starts with an `if` statement. Since the input parameter was 1, the `if` statement fails. Thus, the recursion termination condition is reached. This third call of `factorial()` now returns a value of 1.

At this point, the second call of `factorial()` resumes, completing the statement:

```
num *= factorial( num - 1 );
```

Since the call of `factorial()` returned a value of 1, this statement is equivalent to:

```
num *= 1;
```

This leaves num with the same value it came in with, namely, 2. This second call of `factorial()` returns a value of 2.

At this point, the first call of `factorial()` resumes, completing the statement:

```
num *= factorial( num - 1 );
```

Since the second call of `factorial()` returned a value of 2, this statement is equivalent to:

```
num *= 2;
```

Since the first call of `factorial()` started with the parameter num taking a value of 3, this statement sets num to a value of 6. Finally, the original call of `factorial()` returns a value of 6. This is as it should be, since 3 factorial = 3 * 2 * 1 = 6.

> The recursive version of the factorial program is also provided on disk. You'll **Important**
> find it in the `Learn C Projects` folder, under the subfolder named `11.02`
> `- recurse`. Open the project and follow the program through, line by line.

Binary Trees

As you learn more about data structures, you'll discover new applications for recursion. For example, one of the most-used data structures in computer programming is the binary tree (Figure 11.3). As you'll see later, binary trees were just made for recursion. The binary tree is similar to the linked list. Both consist of `structs` connected by pointers embedded in each `struct`.

Linked lists are linear. Each `struct` in the list is linked by pointers to the `struct` behind it and in front of it in the list. Binary trees always start with a single `struct`, known as the root `struct`, or **root node**. Where the linked-list `structs` we've been working with contain a single pointer, named `next`, binary-tree `structs` each have two pointers, usually known as `left` and `right`.

Check out the binary tree in Figure 11.3. Notice that the root node has a left **child** and a right child. The left child has its own left child, but its `right` pointer is set to NULL. The left child's left child has two NULL pointers. A node with two NULL pointers is known as a **leaf node,** or **terminal node**.

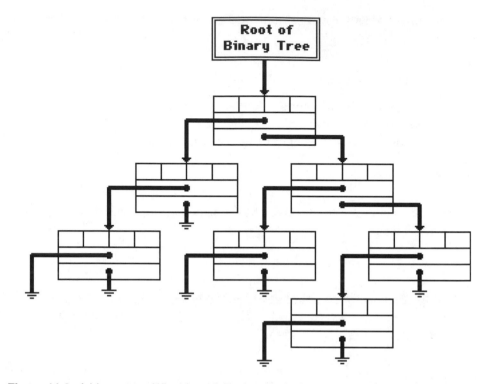

Figure 11.3 A binary tree. Why binary? Each node in the tree contains two pointers.

Binary trees are extremely useful. They work especially well when you are trying to sort data having a **comparative relationship**. This means that if you compare two pieces of data, you'll be able to judge the first piece as greater than, equal to, or less than the second piece. For example, numbers are comparative. Words in a dictionary can be comparative, if you consider their alphabetical order. The word *iguana* is greater than *aardvark* but less than *xenophobe*.

Here's how you might store a sequence of words, one at a time, in a binary tree. We'll start with this list of words:

```
opulent
entropy
salubrious
ratchet
coulomb
yokel
tortuous
```

Figure 11.4 shows the word `opulent` added to the root node of the binary tree. Since it is the only word in the tree so far, both the left and right pointers are set to NULL.

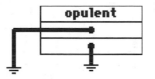

Figure 11.4 The word `opulent` is entered into the binary tree.

Figure 11.5 shows the word `entropy` added to the binary tree. Since `entropy` is less than `opulent` (that is, comes before it alphabetically), `entropy` is stored as `opulent`'s left child.

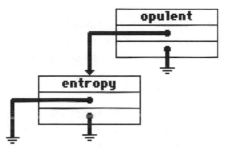

Figure 11.5 The word `entropy` is less than the word `opulent` and is added as its left child in the binary tree.

Next, Figure 11.6 shows the word `salubrious` added to the tree. Since `salubrious` is greater than `opulent`, it becomes `opulent`'s right child.

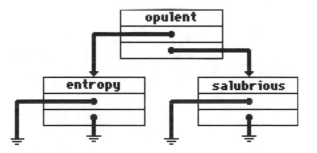

Figure 11.6 The word `salubrious` is greater than the word `opulent` and is added to its right in the tree.

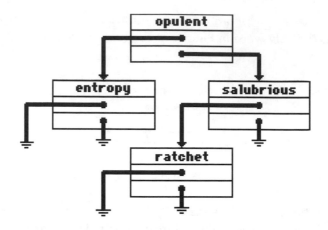

Figure 11.7 The word `ratchet` is greater than `opulent` but less than `salubrious` and is placed in the tree accordingly.

Figure 11.7 shows the word `ratchet` added to the tree. First, `ratchet` is compared to `opulent`. Since `ratchet` is greater than `opulent`, we follow the right pointer. Since there's a word there already, we'll have to compare `ratchet` to this word. Since `ratchet` is less than `salubrious`, we'll store it as `salubrious`'s left child.

Figure 11.8 shows the binary tree after the remainder of the word list has been added. Do you understand how this scheme works? What would the binary tree

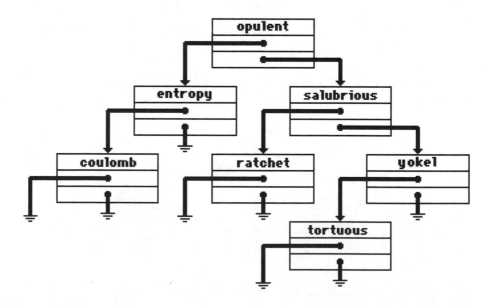

Figure 11.8 The words `coulomb`, `yokel`, and `tortuous` are added to the tree.

look like if `coulomb` were the first word on the list? The tree would have no left children and would lean heavily to the right. What if `yokel` were the first word entered? As you can see, this particular use of binary trees depends on the order of the data. Randomized data starting with a value close to the average produces a **balanced tree**. If the words had been entered in alphabetical order, you would have ended up with a binary tree that looked like a linked list.

By the Way

Data structure theory is one of my favorite topics in all of computer science. I'd like to rattle on and on about variant tree structures and binary tree balancing algorithms, but my editors would like me to get this book out sometime this year. This shouldn't stop you, though. Go to your library and check out a book on data structures and another on sorting and searching algorithms (which we'll get to in a minute). My favorite books on these topics are listed in the bibliography in Appendix G.

Searching Binary Trees

Now that your word list is stored in the binary tree, the next step is to look up a word in the tree. This is known as **searching** the tree. Suppose you wanted to look up the word `tortuous` in your tree. You'd start with the root node, comparing `tortuous` with `opulent`. Since `tortuous` is greater than `opulent`, you'd follow the right pointer to `salubrious`. You'd follow this algorithm down to `yokel` and finally `tortuous`.

By the Way

Searching a binary tree is typically much faster than searching a linked list. In a linked list, you search through your list of nodes, one at a time, until you find the node you are looking for. On average, you'll end up searching half of the list. In a list of 100 nodes, you'll end up checking 50 nodes on average. In a list of 1000 nodes, you'll end up checking 500 nodes on average.

In a balanced binary tree, you reduce the search space in half each time you check a node. Without getting into the mathematics (check Knuth's *The Art of Computer Programming*, Volume 3, for more info), the maximum number of nodes searched is approximately $\log_2 n$, where n is the number of nodes in the tree. On average, you'll search $\log_2 n/2$ nodes. In a list of 100 nodes, you'll end up searching 3.32 nodes on average. In a list of 1000 nodes, you'll end up checking about 5 nodes on average.

As you can see, a binary tree provides a significant performance advantage over a linked list.

A binary tree that contained just words may not be very interesting, but imagine that these words were names of great political leaders. Each `struct` might contain a leader's name, biographical information, and, perhaps, a pointer to another data structure containing great speeches. The value, name, or word that determines the order of the tree is said to be the **key**.

You don't always search a tree based on the key. Sometimes, you'll want to step through every node in the tree. For example, suppose that your tree contained the name and birth date of each of the presidents of the United States. Suppose that also that the tree was built using each president's last name as a key. Now suppose that you wanted to compose a list of all presidents born in July. In this case, searching the tree alphabetically won't do you any good. You'll have to search every node in the tree. This is where recursion comes in.

Recursion and Binary Trees

Binary trees and recursion were made for each other. To search a tree recursively, the recursing function has to visit the current node, as well as call itself with each of its two child nodes. The child nodes will do the same thing with themselves and their child nodes. Each part of the recursion stops when a terminal node is encountered.

Check out this piece of code:

```
struct Node
{
    int         value;
    struct Node *left;
    struct Node *right;
} myNode;


Searcher( struct Node *nodePtr )
{
    if ( nodePtr != NULL )
    {
        VisitNode( nodePtr );
        Searcher( nodePtr->left );
        Searcher( nodePtr->right );
    }
}
```

The function `Searcher()` takes a pointer to a tree node as its parameter. If the pointer is `NULL`, we must be at a terminal node, and there's no need to recurse any deeper. If the pointer points to a `Node`, the function `VisitNode()` is called. `VisitNode()` performs whatever function you want performed for each node in the binary tree. In our current example, `VisitNode()` could check to see whether the president associated with this node was born in July. If so, `VisitNode()` might print the president's name in the console window.

Once the node is visited, `Searcher()` calls itself twice, once passing a pointer to its left child and once passing a pointer to its right child. If this version of `Searcher()` were used to search the tree in Figure 11.8, the tree would be searched in the order described in Figure 11.9. This type of search is known as a **preorder search**, because the node is visited before the two recursive calls take place.

Here's a slightly revised version of `Searcher()`. Without looking at Figure 11.10, can you predict the order in which the tree will be searched? This version of `Searcher()` performs an **inorder search** of the tree:

```
Searcher( struct Node *nodePtr )
{
    if ( nodePtr != NULL )
```

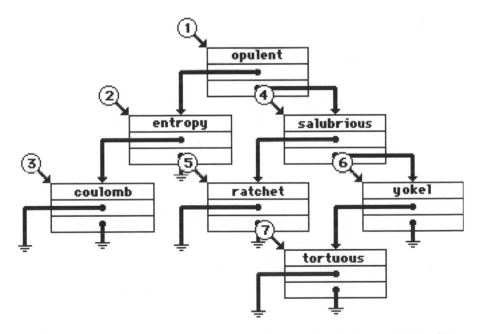

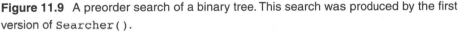

Figure 11.9 A preorder search of a binary tree. This search was produced by the first version of `Searcher()`.

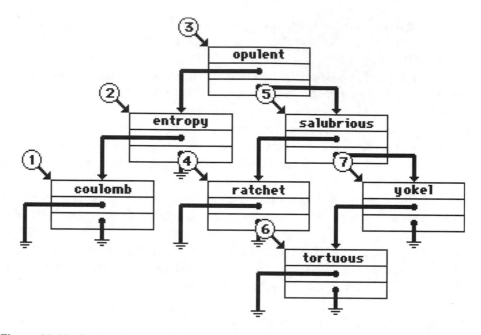

Figure 11.10 An inorder search of the same tree.

```
    {
        Searcher( nodePtr->left );
        VisitNode( nodePtr );
        Searcher( nodePtr->right );
    }
}
```

Here's a final look at `Searcher()`. This version performs a **postorder search** of the tree (Figure 11.11):

```
Searcher( struct Node *nodePtr )
{
    if ( nodePtr != NULL )
    {
        Searcher( nodePtr->left );
        Searcher( nodePtr->right );
        VisitNode( nodePtr );
    }
}
```

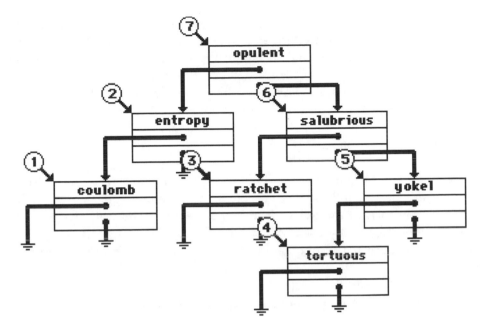

Figure 11.11 A postorder search of the same tree.

Recursion and binary trees are two extremely powerful programming tools. Learn how to use them—they'll pay big dividends.

Function Pointers

Next on the list is the subject of **function pointers**. Function pointers are exactly what they sound like: pointers that point to functions. Up to now, the only way to call a function was to place its name in the source code:

```
MyFunction();
```

Function pointers give you a new way to call a function. Function pointers allow you to say, "Execute the function pointed to by this variable." Here's an example:

```
int(*myFuncPtr)( float );
```

This line of code declares a function pointer named myFuncPtr, which is a pointer to a function that takes a single parameter, a float, and that returns an int. The parentheses in the declaration are all necessary. The first pair tie the * to myFuncPtr, ensuring that myFuncPtr is declared as a pointer. The second pair surround the parameter list and distinguish myFuncPtr as a function pointer.

Suppose we had a function called DealTheCards() that took a float as a parameter and returned an int. This line of code assigns the address of DealTheCards() to the function pointer myFuncPtr:

```
myFuncPtr = DealTheCards;
```

Notice that the parentheses were left off the end of DealTheCards(). This is critical. If the parentheses were there, the code would have called DealTheCards(), returning a value to myFuncPtr. You may also have noticed that the & operator wasn't used. When you refer to a function without using the parentheses at the end, the compiler knows that you are referring to the address of the function.

Now that you have the function's address in the function pointer, there's only one thing left to do—call the function. Here's how it's done:

```
int    result;

result = (*myFuncPtr)( 3.5 );
```

This line calls the function DealTheCards(), passing it the parameter 3.5 and returning the function value to the int result. You could also have called the function this way:

```
int    result;

result = myFuncPtr( 3.5 );
```

Some older (non-ANSI compliant) compilers can't handle this form, but it is easier on the eye.

By the Way

There's a lot you can do with function pointers. You can create an array of function pointers. How about a binary tree of function pointers? You can pass a function pointer as a parameter to another function. Taking this one step further, you can create a function that does nothing but call other functions. Cool!

For your enjoyment, there's a function-calling example on the source code disk. You'll find the project in the Learn C Projects folder, inside the 11.03 – funcPtr subfolder. The program is pretty simple, but it should serve as a useful reference when you start using function pointers in your own programs.

Initializers

When you declare a variable, you can also provide an initial value for the variable at the same time. The format for integer types, floating-point types, and pointers is as follows:

```
type   variable = initializer;
```

In this case, the initializer is just an expression. Here are a few examples:

```
float    myFloat = 3.14159;
int      myInt = 9 * 27;
int      *intPtr = &myInt;
```

If you plan on initializing a more complex variable, such as an array, struct, or union, you'll use a slightly different form of initializer, embedding the elements used to initialize the variable between pairs of curly braces. Consider these two array declarations:

```
int     myInts[] = { 10, 20, 30, 40 };
float   myFloats[ 5 ] = { 1.0, 2.0, 3.0 };
```

The first line of code declares an array of four ints, setting myInts[0] to 10, myInts[1] to 20, myInts[2] to 30, and myInts[3] to 40. If you leave out the array dimension, the compiler makes it just large enough to contain the listed data.

The second line of code includes a dimension but not enough data to fill the array. The first three array elements are filled with the specified values, but myFloats[3] and myFloats[4] are initialized to 0.0.

By the Way

If you don't provide enough values in your initializer list, the compiler initializes all the remaining elements to their **default initialization value**. For integers, the default initialization value is 0; for floats, 0.0; and for pointers, NULL.

Here's another example:

```
char   s[ 20 ] = "Hello";
```

What a convenient way to initialize an array of chars! Here's another way to accomplish the same thing:

```
char   s[ 20 ] = { 'H', 'e', 'l', 'l', 'o', '\0' };
```

Once again, if you leave out the dimension, the compiler will allocate just enough memory to hold your text string, including a byte to hold the 0 terminator. If you include the dimension, the compiler will allocate that many array elements, then fill the array with whatever data you provide. If you provide more data than will fit in the array, your code won't compile.

Here's a struct example:

```
struct Numbers
{
    int    i, j;
    float f;
}

struct Numbers myNums = { 1, 2, 3.01 };
```

As you can see, the three initializing values were wrapped in a pair of curly braces. This leaves myNums.i with a value of 1, myNums.j with a value of 2, and myNums.f with a value of 3.01. If you have a struct, union, or array embedded in your struct, you can nest a curly wrapped list of values inside another list. For example:

```
struct Numbers
{
    int    i, j;
    float f[ 4 ];
}

struct Numbers myNums1 = { 1, 2, {3.01, 4.01, 5.01, 6.01} };
```

The Remaining Operators

If you go back to Chapter 5 and review the list of operators shown in Figure 5.7, you'll likely find a few operators you are not yet familiar with. Most of the ones we've missed were designed specifically to set the individual bits within a byte. For example, the | operator (not to be confused with its comrade, the logical || operator) takes two values and "ORs" their bits together, resolving to a single value. This operator is frequently used to set a particular bit to 1.

Check out this code:

```
short    myShort;

myShort = 0x0001 | myShort;
```

This code sets the rightmost bit of myShort to 1, no matter what its current value is. This line of code, based on the |= operator, does the exact same thing:

```
myShort |= 0x0001;
```

The & operator takes two values and "ANDs" their bits together, resolving to a single value. This operator is frequently used to set a particular bit to 0 (more frequently referred to as **clearing a bit**).

Check out this code:

```
short    myShort;

myShort = 0xFFFE & myShort;
```

This code sets the rightmost bit of myShort to 0, no matter what its current value is. It might help to think of 0xFFFE as 1111111111111110 in binary. The next line of code, based on the &= operator, does the exact same thing:

```
myShort &= 0xFFFE;
```

The ^ operator takes two values and "XORs" their values together. It goes along with the ^= operator. The ~ operator takes a single value and turns all the 1s into 0s and all the 0s into 1s. The &, |, ^, and ~ operators are summarized in Figure 11.12.

A	B	A&B	A I B	A^B	~A
1	1	1	1	0	0
1	0	0	1	1	0
0	1	0	1	1	1
0	0	0	0	0	1

Figure 11.12 A summary of the &, |, ^, and ~ operators.

By the Way

The previous examples assumed that a `short` is 2 bytes (16 bits) long. Of course, this makes for some implementation-dependent code. Here's a more portable example.

```
short    myShort;

myShort = (~1) & myShort;
```

This code sets the rightmost bit of `myShort`, no matter how many bytes are used to implement a `short`. You could also write this as:

```
myShort &= (~1);
```

The last of the binary operators, <<, >>, <<=, and >>=, are used to **shift bits** within a variable, either to the left or to the right. The left operand is usually an `unsigned` variable, and the right operand is a positive integer specifying how far to shift the variable's bits.

For example, this code shifts the bits of `myShort` 2 bits to the right:

```
unsigned short    myShort = 0x0100;

myShort = myShort >> 2; /* equal to myShort >>= 2; */
```

Notice that `myShort` starts off with a value of 0000000100000000 and ends up with a value of 0000000001000000 (in hex, that's 0x0040). Notice that zeros get shifted in to make up for the leftmost bits that are getting shifted over and that the rightmost bits are lost when they shift off the end.

These operators were designed to work with unsigned values only. Check with your compiler to see how it handles shifting of signed values.

The last two operators we need to cover are the , and :? operators. The , operator gives you a way to combine two expressions into a single expression. The , operator is binary, and both operands are expressions. The left expression is evaluated first and the result discarded. The right expression is then evaluated and its value returned. Here's an example:

```
for ( i=0, j=0; i<20 && j<40; i++,j+=2 )
   DoSomething( i, j );
```

This for loop is based on two variables instead of one. Before the loop is entered, i and j are both set to 0. The loop continues as long as i is less than 20 and j is less than 40. Each time through the loop, i is incremented by 1, and j is incremented by 2.

The ? and : operators combine to create something called a **conditional expression**. A conditional expression consists of a logical expression (an expression that evaluates to either true or false), followed by the ? operator, followed by a second expression, followed by the : operator, followed by a third expression:

```
logical-expression ? expression2 : expression3
```

If the logical expression evaluates to true, expression2 gets evaluated, and the entire expression resolves to the value of expression2. If the logical expression evaluates to false, expression3 gets evaluated, and the entire expression resolves to the value of expression3. Here's an example:

```
IsPrime( num ) ? DoPrimeStuff( num ) : DoNonPrimeStuff( num );
```

As you can see, a conditional expression is really a shorthand way of writing an if-else statement. Here's the if-else version of the previous example:

```
if ( IsPrime( num ) )
   DoPrimeStuff( num );
else
   DoNonPrimeStuff( num );
```

Some people like the brevity of the ?: operator combination. Others find it difficult to read. As always, make your choice and stick with it.

Warning

A word of advice: Don't overuse the ?: operator. For example, suppose that you wanted to use ?: to generate a number's absolute value. You might write code like this:

```
int    value;

value - (value<0) ? (-value) : (value);
```

Although this code works, take a look at this code translated into its if-else form:

```
int    value;

if ( value<0 )
     value = (-value);
else
     value = (value);
```

As you can see, the ?: operator can lead you to write source code that you would otherwise consider pretty darn silly.

Creating Your Own Types

The typedef statement lets you use existing types to create brand new types you can then use in your declarations. You'll declare this new type just as you would a variable, except that you'll precede the declaration with the word typedef, and the name you declare will be the name of a new type. Here's an example:

```
typedef   int    *IntPointer;

IntPointer  myIntPointer;
```

The first line of code creates a new type named IntPointer. The second line declares a variable named myIntPointer, which is a pointer to an int.

Here's another example:

```
typedef  float (*FuncPtr)( int * );

FuncPtr  myFuncPtr;
```

The first line of code declares a new type named `FuncPtr`. The second line declares a variable named `myFuncPtr`, which is a pointer to a function that returns a `float` and that takes a single `int` as a parameter.

Enumerated Types

In a similar vein, the `enum` statement lets you declare a new type known as an enumerated type. An enumerated type is a set of named integer constants, collected under a single type name. A series of examples will make this clear.

```
enum Weekdays
{
   Monday,
   Tuesday,
   Wednesday,
   Thursday,
   Friday
};

enum Weekdays  whichDay;

whichDay = Thursday;
```

This code starts off with an `enum` declaration. The `enum` is given the name `Weekdays` and consists of the constants `Monday`, `Tuesday`, `Wednesday`, `Thursday`, and `Friday`. The second line of code uses this new enumerated type to declare a variable named `whichDay`, an integer variable that can take on any of the `Weekdays` constants, as evidenced by the last line of code, which assigns the constant `Thursday` to `whichDay`.

Here's another example:

```
enum Colors
{
   red,
   green = 5,
   blue,
```

```
        magenta,
        yellow = blue + 5
} myColor;

myColor = blue;
```

This code declares an enumerated type named `Colors`. Notice that some of the constants in the `Colors` list are accompanied by initializers. When the compiler creates the enumeration constants, it numbers them sequentially, starting with 0. In the previous example, `Monday` has a value of 0, `Tuesday` has a value of 1, and so on, with `Friday` having a value of 4.

In this case, the constant `red` has a value of 0. But the constant `green` has a value of 5. Things move along from there, with `blue` and `magenta` having values of 6 and 7, respectively. Next, `yellow` has a value of `blue+5`, which is 11.

This code also declares an enumeration variable named `myColor`, which is then assigned a value of `blue`.

By the Way

You can declare an enumerated type without the type name:

```
enum
{
    chocolate,
    strawberry,
    vanilla
};

int iceCreamFlavor = vanilla;
```

This code declares a series of enumeration constants with values of 0, 1, and 2. We can assign the constants to an `int`, as we did with `iceCreamFlavor`. This comes in handy when you need a set of integer constants but have no need for a tag name.

Static Variables

Normally, when a function exits, the storage for its variables is freed up, and their values are no longer available. By declaring a local variable as `static`, the variable's value is maintained across multiple calls of the same function. Here's an example:

```
int    StaticFunc( void )
{
    static int  myStatic = 0;

    return myStatic++;
}
```

This function declares an int named myStatic and initializes it to a value of 0. The function returns the value of myStatic and increments myStatic after the return value is determined. The first time this function is called, it returns 0, and myStatic is left with a value of 1. The second time StaticFunc() is called, it returns 1, and myStatic is left with a value of 2.

By the Way

Take a few minutes and try this code out for yourself. You'll find it in the Learn C Projects folder in the subfolder 11.04 – static.

One of the keys to this function is the manner in which myStatic received its initial value. Imagine if the function looked like this:

```
int    StaticFunc( void )
{
    static int  myStatic;

    myStatic = 0;  /* <- Bad idea.... */

    return myStatic++;
}
```

Each time through the function, we'd be setting the value of myStatic back to 0. This function will always return a value of 0. Not what we want, eh?

The difference between the two functions? The first version sets the value of myStatic to 0 by initialization (the value is specified within the declaration). The second version sets the value of myStatic to 0 by assignment (the value is specified after the declaration). If a variable is marked as static, any initialization is done once and once only. Be sure that you set the initial value of your static variable in the declaration and not in an assignment statement.

By the Way

> One way to think of `static` variables is as global variables that are limited in scope to a single function.

More on Strings

The last topic we'll tackle in this chapter is **string manipulation**. Although we've done some work with strings in previous chapters, there are a number of Standard Library functions that haven't been covered. Each of these functions requires that you include the file `<string.h>`. Here are a few examples.

strcpy()

The function `strcpy()` is declared as follows:

```
char *strcpy( char *dest, const char *source );
```

This function copies the string pointed to by `source` into the string pointed to by `dest`, copying each of the characters in `source`, including the terminating 0 byte. That leaves `dest` as a properly terminated string. The function returns the pointer `dest`.

An important thing to remember about `strcpy()` is that you are responsible for ensuring that `source` is properly terminated and that enough memory is allocated for the string returned in `dest`. Here's an example of `strcpy()` in action:

```
char  name[ 20 ];

strcpy( name, "Dave Mark" );
```

This example uses a string literal as the source string. The string is copied into the array `name`. The return value was ignored.

strcat()

The function `strcat()` is declared as follows:

```
char *strcat( char *dest, const char *source );
```

The function `strcat()` appends a copy of the string pointed to by `source` onto the end of the string pointed to by `dest`. As was the case with `strcpy()`, `strcat()` returns the pointer `dest`. Here's an example of `strcat()` in action:

```
char   name[ 20 ];

strcpy( name, "Dave " );
strcat( name, "Mark" );
```

The call of `strcpy()` copies the string `"Dave "` into the array `name`. The call of `strcat()` copies the string `"Mark"` onto the end of `dest`, leaving `dest` with the properly terminated string `"Dave Mark"`. Again, the return value was ignored.

strcmp()

The function `strcmp()` is declared as follows:

```
int   strcmp( const char *s1, const char *s2 );
```

This function compares the strings `s1` and `s2` and returns 0 if the strings are identical, a positive number if `s1` is greater than `s2`, and a negative number if `s2` is greater than `s1`. The strings are compared one byte at a time. If the strings are not equal, the first byte that is not identical determines the return value. Here's a sample:

```
if ( strcmp( "Hello", "Goodbye" ) )
    printf( "The strings are not equal!" );
```

Notice that the `if` succeeds when the strings are not equal.

strlen()

The function `strlen()` is declared as follows:

```
size_t   strlen( const char *s );
```

This function returns the length of the string pointed to by `s`. Look at this call, for example:

```
length = strlen( "Aardvark" );
```

The value returned is 8, the number of characters in the string, not counting the terminating zero.

More Standard Library

There is a lot more to the Standard Library than what we've covered in the book. Having made it this far, consider yourself an official C programmer. You now have a sworn duty to dig in to the C Library Reference that came on the CD in back of this book. Start off with Chapter 15, which covers the functions declared in <string.h>. Find out what the difference is between strcmp() and strncmp(). Wander around. Get to know the Standard Library. You will be making extensive use of it.

If you haven't done so already, go out and buy a copy of *C: A Reference Manual* by Harbison and Steele. When it comes to a definitive answer to a C programming question, having Harbison and Steele by your side is the next best thing to having Keith Rollin's home phone number.

What's Next?

Chapter 12 answers the question, Where do you go from here? Do you want to learn to create programs with that special Macintosh look and feel? Would you like more information on data structures and C programming techniques? Chapter 12 offers some suggestions to help you find your programming direction.

Exercises

1. What's wrong with each of the following code fragments:

   a.
```
struct Dog
{
    struct Dog      *next;
} ;

struct Cat
{
    struct Cat *next;
} ;

struct Dog   myDog;
struct Cat   myCat;
```

```
      myDog.next = (struct Dog)&myCat;
      myCat.next = NULL;
b.  int    *MyFunc( void );
    typedef  int (*FuncPtr)();

    FuncPtr  myFuncPtr = MyFunc;
c.  union Number
    {
       int        i;
       float f;
       char   *s;
    } ;

    Number    myUnion;

    myUnion.f = 3.5;
d.  struct Player
    {
       int          type;
       char     name[ 40 ];
       int          team;
       union
       {
          int      myInt;
          float myFloat;
       } u;
    } myPlayer;

    myPlayer.team = 27;
    myPlayer.myInt = -42;
    myPlayer.myFloat = 5.7;
e.  int       *myFuncPtr( int );

    myFuncPtr = main;
    *myFuncPtr();
f.  char   s[ 20 ];

    strcpy( s, "Hello " );
```

```
        if ( strcmp( s, "Hello" ) )
            printf( "The strings are the same!" );
g.  char *s;

    s = malloc( 20 );
    strcpy( "Heeeers Johnny!", s );
h.  char *s;

    strcpy( s, "Aardvark" );
i.  void DoSomeStuff( void )
    {
        /* stuff done here */
    }

    int main( void )
    {
        int    ii;

        for ( ii = 0; ii < 10; ii++ )
            DoSomeStuff;

        return 0;
    }
```

2. Write a program that reads in a series of integers from a file, storing the numbers in a binary tree in the same fashion as the words were stored earlier in the chapter. Store the first number as the root of the tree. Next, store the second number in the left branch if it is less than the first number or in the right branch if it is greater than or equal to the first number. Continue this process until all the numbers are stored in the tree.

   Now write a series of functions that print the contents of the tree using preorder, inorder, and postorder recursive searches.

Where Do You Go from Here?

Now that you've mastered the fundamentals of C, you're ready to dig into the specifics of Macintosh programming. As you've run the example programs in the previous chapters, you've probably noticed that none of the programs sport the look and feel that make a Mac program a Mac program.

For one thing, all of the interaction between you and your program focuses on the keyboard and the console window. None of the programs take advantage of the mouse. None offer color, pull-down menus, or a selection of different fonts. These are all part of the Macintosh **user interface.**

The Macintosh Graphical User Interface

User interface is the part of your program that interacts with the user. So far, your user interface skills have focused on writing to and reading from the console window, using such functions as printf(), scanf(), and getchar(). The advantage of this type of user interface is that each of those functions is available on every machine that supports the C language. Programs written using the Standard C Library are extremely portable.

However, console-based user interfaces tend to be limited. With a console-based interface, you can't use an elegant graphic to make a point. Text-based interfaces can't provide animation or digital sound. In a nutshell, the console-based interface is simple and, at the same time, simple to program. The Macintosh's **graphical user interface (GUI)** offers an elegant, more sophisticated method of working with a computer.

A Macintosh just wouldn't be the same without windows, pull-down and pop-up menus, icons, push buttons, and scroll bars. You can and should add these user interface elements to your C programs. The difficult part is deciding which features to use and where to use them.

Once you've identified the pieces of the Mac interface you want in your program, you're ready to take advantage of the Mac's version of the Standard Library: the **Macintosh Toolbox.**

The Macintosh Toolbox

Every Mac that rolls off the assembly line comes with a slew of built-in user interface functions. Each Mac comes with a **read-only memory (ROM)** chip that contains the more than 2000 functions that make up the Macintosh Toolbox. The Mac Toolbox contains functions that create windows on the screen and others that draw text in these windows. There are functions for drawing shapes, lines, and dots in color and in black and white. There's a set of functions that allows you to implement your own pull-down menus. The Mac Toolbox is huge.

Every program that supports the standard Macintosh interface relies on the Mac Toolbox. That's why Macintosh programs have such a consistent look and feel. Take a look at the pull-down menu in Figure 12.1. Notice the close resemblance to every other Mac pull-down menu. That's because the Toolbox provides a set of functions that implements a standard Macintosh pull-down menu bar. When Mac programmers want to implement a pull-down menu, they always turn to this set of functions, collectively known as the **Menu Manager**. The Menu Manager follows a set of rules when pulling down a menu. For example, a standard Macintosh menu is always drawn using the **Chicago** font. The **Chicago** font is built into the Mac's ROM.

By the Way

This particular menu comes from the **Finder,** the application that runs when your Macintosh first starts up. The Finder is the application containing all of the windows and icons you use to launch other applications.

```
┌─────────────────────────┐
│ Edit                    │
├─────────────────────────┤
│ Undo              ⌘Z    │
│ ·····················   │
│ Cut               ⌘H    │
│ Copy              ⌘C    │
│ Paste             ⌘U    │
│ Clear                   │
│ Select All        ⌘A    │
│ ·····················   │
│ Show Clipboard          │
└─────────────────────────┘
```

Figure 12.1 An **Edit** menu. Do you know where it came from?

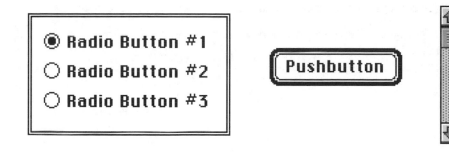

Figure 12.2 A set of radio buttons, a push button, and a scroll bar. Each of these is created and maintained with the Control Manager.

The Toolbox is divided into a series of managers. As you learn to implement a standard Mac interface, you'll learn about the functions that make up each manager. For example, you'll learn how to use the functions that make up the **Window Manager** to create and maintain your program's windows. You'll use the **Control Manager** to manage scroll bars, push buttons, and other standard Macintosh controls, like the ones shown in Figure 12.2.

windowMaker.μ

Our final project, windowMaker, presents a complete Mac Toolbox application. Although windowMaker doesn't do much, it does demonstrate some of the user interface concepts you've been reading about.

Go into the Learn C Projects folder, then into the subfolder named 12.01 – windowMaker, and open the project named windowMaker.μ.

Run the project by selecting **Run** from the **Project** menu. Once CodeWarrior recompiles your source code, the menu bar in Figure 12.3 will appear at the top of your screen. If you have a color Macintosh with the color turned on, the should appear in color.

For starters, select the first item in the menu, **About WindowMaker . . .** You should hear a short beep; then the window shown in Figure 12.4 should appear on the screen. This window is known as an "about box" and tells you a little

Figure 12.3 windowMaker's menu bar.

Figure 12.4 This window appears when you select **About WindowMaker...** from the menu.

bit about WindowMaker. When you get tired of staring at this work of art, click on the **OK** button to make the window disappear.

Next, click on the **File** menu. The menu shown in Figure 12.5 will appear. Note the command-key equivalents located to the right of each menu item. A command-key equivalent equates a keyboard sequence to a menu item. For example, if you hold down the command key (the key with the ⌘ on it) and type an N, the item **New** will be selected.

Select the first item, **New**. A window will appear, bearing the title **WindowMaker** (Figure 12.6). A jazzy picture of the sun will appear, centered in the window. Select **New** several more times. Several more windows will appear. Try clicking on a window's close box. The window should close. Open a few more windows. Select **Close** to close a window. Click on a back window to bring it to the front. Notice that as a window is uncovered, its picture is automatically re-drawn. When you are done, select **Quit** from the **File** menu to exit the program.

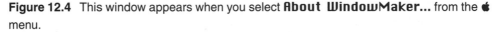

Figure 12.5 windowMaker's **File** menu.

Figure 12.6 A `windowMaker` window.

Getting Started with the Mac Toolbox

The next step in your programming education is to learn how to use the Macintosh Toolbox in your own programs. The first thing you should do is go out and get yourself a real development environment. As you've probably noticed, the version of CodeWarrior we've been using won't let you create new projects. Although it's just fine for running the programs in this book, this limited version of CodeWarrior definitely won't cut it when it comes to developing your own applications.

By far, the two leading Macintosh development environments are CodeWarrior and Symantec C++ for Macintosh. Both environments can compile source code written in C and C++ (more on C++ in a minute), and both environments are capable of producing native 680x0 and PowerPC object code. Although there are differences between the two products, it would be difficult to recommend one over the other.

If you know a group of people who use a specific development environment, that's the one you should go with. If your best friend is a Mac programmer, stick with what that person uses. It is much easier to learn if you use the same development environment as your teacher.

Symantec makes a C and 680x0 only (no C++, no native PowerPC code) version of its compiler for $199. MetroWerks has a 680x0-only version of its compiler that *does* compile C++ for $99. Competition being what it is, these prices will probably have changed by the time you read this, but if you are a hobbyist and have no plans for moving beyond C, one of these deals might be a good bet. On the other hand, if you plan on moving to C++ eventually (and you should), investing in C++ now might not be a bad idea.

C++ is a superset of C and is the language of choice for Macintosh software development. If you are serious about learning to program the Macintosh (and since you are still reading this far into the book, this is probably a pretty reasonable assumption), you should first spend some time with C and learn the basics of Macintosh Toolbox programming, then move on to C++. Don't worry. Most everything you learn in C will carry over into C++, and all of the Mac Toolbox stuff will still work in the C++ universe. Learn the Toolbox. Master C. Then dig into C++.

By the Way

> If you just can't wait to get started with C++, check out the sequel to this book, called *Learn C++ on the Macintosh*. It assumes that you know C and gets you started with C++.

Once you've purchased your copy of CodeWarrior or Symantec C++ for Macintosh, you're ready to start using the Toolbox. Fortunately, there's a lot of literature available to help ease you through the Toolbox learning curve.

Useful Resources

If there is one item found on every Macintosh programmer's bookshelf, it's a well-worn copy of *Inside Macintosh*, Apple's official Macintosh programmer's reference guide. *Inside Macintosh* covers the Toolbox in depth, listing every Toolbox function, along with the function's parameters and that function's place in the Mac universe.

Inside Macintosh is broken out as a series, starting with *Inside Macintosh: Macintosh Toolbox Essentials*, with more than 30 volumes in the complete set. Get a copy of *Macintosh Toolbox Essentials* and *More Macintosh Toolbox*. These two volumes introduce the Macintosh graphical user interface and describe most of the Toolbox functions you'll need to get started.

Once you get comfortable with the Toolbox, you'll probably want to pick up the rest of the *Inside Macintosh* series. Unfortunately, unless your company is picking up the tab, the entire series is probably not in this year's programming budget. Fortunately, the entire *Inside Macintosh* series is available on CD-ROM. You can find the electronic version at most of the places that sell CodeWarrior and Symantec C++ for Macintosh, including the MacTech mail-order store (310-575-4343) and through Apple's Developer Tools Catalog (800-282-2732).

Another tool well worth checking out is Apple's Toolbox Assistant (also known as TBA). Toolbox Assistant is a database filled with all the functions and constants from the entire *Inside Macintosh* series. Type in the name of a Toolbox function or constant, enter a return, and Toolbox Assistant displays a page showing you everything you could want to know about the function or constant. Even better, Toolbox Assistant can communicate with both CodeWarrior and with Symantec C++ for Macintosh. Hold down the command key and double-click on a Toolbox function or constant in your code, and the Toolbox Assistant automatically jumps to the correct page. This tool is absolutely worth the investment.

Although *Inside Macintosh* is an invaluable resource, it can be pretty intimidating when you are first learning about the Toolbox. There are a number of books out there that help bridge the gap for first-time Macintosh programmers.

If you like the writing style in this book, check out the *Macintosh C Programming Primer* by Dave Mark and Cartwright Reed. (This book is frequently referred to as the *Primer* or the *Mac Primer*.) The *Primer* offers a step-by-step tour through the mysteries of the Toolbox, punctuating each chapter with a variety of sample programs. The *Mac Primer* takes the sting out of learning to program using the Mac Toolbox.

The *Primer* also offers a lot of advice for programmers looking to get involved with the Macintosh development community. Whether you are interested in developing your own best-selling Macintosh application or just want to hook up with other Mac developers, the *Mac Primer* can help. Inside, you'll find descriptions of Apple's developer relations programs, designed to help you get your products out the door. You'll learn where the developers hang out, whether on CompuServe, America Online, eWorld, or on the Internet.

In general, Cartwright and I tried to put everything into the *Primer* that we were looking for when we were first learning to program the Macintosh. We hope you enjoy it.

A book that I frequently turn to is *Macintosh Programming Secrets* by Scott Knaster and Keith Rollin. This book is full of Macintosh programming tips, tricks, and techniques. Scott and Keith take their years of experience as Apple employees and put them to good use, revealing some of the deep, dark secrets that only a Mac aficionado could know. Once you've mastered the basics of Macintosh Toolbox programming, give this book a try.

Get On-line

All of the major on-line services have a Macintosh development area where you can get all your questions answered. For example, on CompuServe, type GO MACDEV and check out Section 11, called "Learn Programming." This section is an excellent place to meet other Mac programmers and post your questions.

On America Online, you can use the keyword "MDV" to jump to the Macintosh development area; eWorld has a Mac development area as well. Take the time to check out the Macintosh development forum on your online service. Explore the libraries to see what kinds of tools and sample source code are available. Find out if there are regular meetings for beginners. You'll find that most of the folks who populate these sections are friendly and more than willing to spend some time helping you through a difficult concept or pointing you in the right direction.

Go Get 'Em

Well, that's about it. I hope you enjoyed reading this book as much as I enjoyed writing it. Above all, I hope you are excited about C. Now that you have C under your belt, go out there and write some source code.

Enjoy!

Glossary

68000 emulator: Software that runs on a PowerPC-based machine designed to emulate a 68000 processor. The 68000 emulator allows you to run software compiled for a 68000 on a PowerMac.

algorithm: The technical approach used to solve a problem.

ANSI C: The standard version of the C programming language established by the American National Standards Institute.

append: A mode used when opening a file for writing. Append mode specifies that any data written to the file is written after any existing data.

argument: Another word for **parameter**.

array: A variable containing a sequence of data of a particular type. For example, you can declare an array of 50 `int`s.

array element: The smallest addressable unit of an array. In an array of 50 `int`s, each `int` represents an element of the array.

ASCII character set: A set of 128 standard characters defined by the American Standard Code for Information Interchange.

backslash combination or **backslash sequence:**   A single character represented by the combination of the backslash (\) and another character. For example, the sequence '\n' represents a new line character.

backward compatibility: A computer design that allows a newer generation of computers to run the previous generation of software. In this book, backward compatibility refers to software compiled for the 68000 that still runs on a 68020, 68030, 68040, and even on a PowerPC.

balanced tree: A binary tree that maintains a uniform depth. The more unbalanced a tree becomes, the less efficient some tree-searching algorithms become.

bell curve: A bell-shaped statistical curve that represents a normal probability distribution. Plotting the possible rolls of a pair of six-sided dice yields a bell curve.

binary: A system of mathematics based on the two digits 0 and 1. Computers use binary to represent the value stored in memory.

binary tree: A data structure that consists of a series of nodes, each of which features a left and right pointer. These two pointers point to other nodes, linking the group of nodes into a tree-like structure.

bit: The smallest unit of computer memory, a bit has a value of either 0 or 1.

bit bucket: A euphemism used to indicate a place where lost data goes. If your data went into the bit bucket, you'll never see it again—it is irretrievably lost.

block: A sequence of memory.

call: Cause a function to be executed. When a function is called, its code gets executed and control is then returned to the calling function.

case-sensitive: Sensitive to the difference between upper- and lower-case letters. C is a case-sensitive language and therefore distinguishes between names such as `MyFunction()` and `MYFUNCTION()`.

cast: See **typecast**.

Central Processing Unit (CPU):   The integrated circuit that controls the processing of a computer. The Macintosh family of computers is driven by either a 68000 series or PowerPC series CPU.

child: A node in a tree pointed to by another node. The node that points to a child node is known as the child's parent.

clearing a bit: Changing the value of a bit to 0.

code optimization: A process used by a compiler to increase the efficiency of the object code it generates.

Command-key equivalent: A key sequence tied to a specific pull-down menu item. Command-key equivalents always consist of a keyboard key combined with the Command (⌘) key.

comparative operator: An operator that compares its left side with its right side, producing a value of either TRUE or FALSE.

comparative relationship: The relationship between the two sides of a comparative operator that determines whether the operator returns a value of TRUE or FALSE.

compiler: A program that translates source code into the machine code understood by a computer.

compound statements: Statements made up of several parts, and possibly including other statements.

conditional expression: An expression built around the ? and : operators.

console: A terminal or window that receives the output from Standard Library functions, such as printf() and echoes the input from the keyboard.

constant: A program value that doesn't change: 27, 1.1414, and '\n' are all examples of constants.

Control Manager: The functions in the Macintosh Toolbox that deal with controls, such as radio buttons, push buttons, and scroll bars.

convention: A standard agreed upon by a group of people. For example, most Macintosh programmers follow the convention of starting their global variable names with the letter g.

counter: A variable whose sole purpose is to keep a running count of an event. The variable that changes each time through a for loop is a counter.

CPU: See **Central Processing Unit.**

deallocate: The opposite of allocate. Memory is typically allocated using malloc() and deallocated using free().

declaration: A statement used to define a new variable, function, or type. A variable declaration establishes both the name and type of the variable.

decrement: Decrease in value. Typically, decrementing a variable decreases its value by 1.

default initialization value: The value used to initialize a global variable. The default initialization value for an int is 0 and for a pointer is NULL.

definition: A declaration that causes memory to be allocated for the item being declared.

dereference: Use a pointer to retrieve the contents of the memory location that the pointer points to.

dictionary: The table used by the compiler to hold the list of #define substitutions contained in the source code being compiled.

dimension: The number of array elements associated with an array.

doping: The process of using a laser beam to create impurities in the silicon of an integrated circuit.

exceeding the bounds: Exceeding the bounds of an array means trying to access an inappropriate element of the array, such as the 51st int in an array of 50 ints.

expression: A combination of variables and operators that resolves to a single value.

fat binary or **fat application:**   An application that contains both 68000 and PowerPC object code.

field: An element of a struct. A field is normally accessed using either the . or -> operator.

file: A series of bytes residing on some storage media. For example, a file might be stored on a floppy disk, a hard drive, or even a CD-ROM.

file position: The current location in a file, indicating the next byte that will be returned by a read operation or the location where a read operation will place its first byte.

Finder: The application that runs when your Macintosh first starts up. The Finder is the application with all of the windows and icons you use to launch other applications.

floating-point numbers: Numbers that contain a decimal point. For example, 3.5, -27.6874, and 3.14159 are all floating-point numbers.

flow control: The ability to control the order in which your program's statements are executed.

format specifier: A sequence of bytes, starting with %, that determines the format of data being read or written.

format specifier modifier: A sequence of bytes that adds more detail to a format specifier. For example, %6d is a format specifier and the 6 in %6d is the format specifier modifier.

fractional part: The part of a floating point to the right of the decimal point.

function: A sequence of source code that accomplishes a specific task. C functions have a title and a body. The title contains the function's name and parameters. The body contains the function's code.

function declaration: A line containing a function's return value, name, and parameter list, followed by a semicolon. The function declaration is also known as a function prototype and is used by the compiler to perform type checking.

function parameter: A class of variable that allows data sharing between a calling function and a called function.

function pointer: A variable containing a pointer to a function. Function pointers can be used to call the function they point to.

function prototype: See **function declaration.**

function return value: The value returned by a function. Functions of type `void` are the only types of functions that do not return a value.

function specifier: The first line of a function, basically, a function declaration without the semicolon.

global variable: A variable that is accessible from inside every function in your program.

graphical user interface (GUI): A user interface that features graphical elements, such as pictures, icons, and windows. The Mac is a great example of a graphical user interface.

header file: A file that is included by another source code file using the `#include` mechanism. Header files typically end with `.h`.

hexadecimal notation or **hex notation:** A notation that represents numbers in base 16 instead of the traditional base 10.

HyperTalk: The programming language supported by HyperCard.

increment: Increase in value. Typically, incrementing a variable increases its value by 1.

index: The number used to refer to an individual array element. An array index usually appears between the brackets following the array name.

indices: The plural of index.

infinite loop: A loop that repeats indefinitely. This is usually a bad thing.

initialization: The process of assigning a value to a variable for the first time.

initialized: Containing a known value.

inorder search: A binary tree search that recursively searches a node's left child, visits the node itself, then recursively searches the node's right child.

input buffer: A block of memory designed to accumulate input from the keyboard for later retrieval by your program.

input device: A device that allows a user to provide input to your program. The mouse and the keyboard are both input devices.

integer: A whole number, such as 1, -26, or 3,876,560.

integer part: The part of a floating-point number to the left of the decimal point.

ISO C: The international standard for C established by the International Standards Organization. ISO C is based on ANSI C.

iteration: The process of stepping through a list or array. In C, iteration frequently starts at 0 and proceeds to some upper limit.

key: The field in a tree struct that determines the search order of the tree.

l-value: The left-hand side of an assignment statement.

leaf node: A terminal node of a tree. In a binary tree, a leaf node has two NULL pointers.

library: A file containing precompiled object code used as part of a project. The routines in the Standard Library are compiled into a series of libraries.

linked list: A data structure consisting of two or more `structs`, linked together by pointers.

linking: The process of joining the elements in a project into its ultimate form. For example, a series of compiled files might be linked into an application.

literal: A constant of any type. The number 123 is an example of an `int` literal. `"Hello"` is an example of a literal text string.

loading: The process of copying a library's object code into the project file.

local variable: A variable declared within a function (as opposed to a global variable).

localize: Customize your software so it is readable in a specific country, using a specific language. For example, you might localize your program for use in Japan by replacing the English, ASCII text by the multibyte character system used in Japan.

logical operator: The set of operators that resolve to either `true` or `false`. `!`, `&&`, and `||` are examples of logical operators.

loop: Any repeating source code sequence. `do`, `while`, and `for` are examples of C loop statements.

machine language: A machine readable translation of your source code. Machine language is also known as object code.

Macintosh Toolbox: The collection of functions that make a Macintosh program look and feel like a Macintosh program.

macro: A `#define` that takes a parameter.

master pointer: The pointer to the first element in a linked list.

memory: A portion of a computer, composed of specially designed integrated circuits, used for the temporary storage of programs and data.

Menu Manager: The functions in the Macintosh Toolbox that deal with the menu bar and pull-down and pop-up menus.

modification: The code within a loop that modifies the value of the loop's expression. Without modification, the loop will never terminate.

multi-dimensional array: An array declared with more than one index.

native mode: A program running on a PowerPC that was compiled into PowerPC object code.

object code: See **machine language**.

open a file: Perform the necessary work prior to accessing a file's data. Files can be opened using several different modes, among them read, write, and append.

operator: A special character (or set of characters) that represents a specific computer operation. `=`, `++`, and `/` are examples of operators.

out of bounds: See **exceeding the bounds**.

output: The result of your program. In this book, all the output appeared in a console window.

pad byte or **padding:** Characters appended to a block of memory used to bring the block up to a predetermined size. Space characters are frequently used to pad a string to a fixed record size. Pad bytes are used to bring a `struct` up to a specific alignment in memory.

parameter: See **function parameter**.

parameter list: The list of parameters associated with a function. A function's parameter list is found in the function specifier.

pointer: A special variable, designed specifically to hold the address of another variable.

pointer arithmetic: The process of incrementing or decrementing a pointer to point to a new memory location.

pointer variable: See **pointer**.

postfix notation: The use of the ++ or -- operator following a variable. In postfix notation, the value of the variable is returned before the variable is incremented or decremented.

postorder search: A binary tree search that recursively searches a node's left child, recursively searches the node's right child, then visits the node itself.

prefix notation: The use of the ++ or -- operator preceding a variable. In prefix notation, the variable is incremented or decremented before the value of the variable is returned.

preorder search: A binary tree search that visits a node, then recursively searches the node's left and right children.

prime number: A number whose only factors are 1 and itself. 2, 3, 5, and 7 are the only primes less than 10.

processor: See **Central Processing Unit**.

project file: A special file CodeWarrior and Symantec C++ use to gather information about your project. The project object code is stored in the project file.

project window: A window listing each of the source code files associated with the project. The project window also lists the current size of the object code associated with each source code file.

prompt: A text string that tells the user what your program expects him or her to do. For example, a prompt might ask the user to type in a number between 1 and 10.

Random Access Memory (RAM):   See **memory**.

random file access: Accessing the data in a file by seeking to a specific location, as opposed to reading a byte at a time from the beginning of the file.

read a file: The process of transferring the data stored in a file into your program.

Read-Only Memory (ROM):   A memory chip that can be read but not written to. The Macintosh Toolbox is found on a set of ROM chips mounted on the Mac's motherboard.

recursion: The process that occurs when a function calls itself. Recursive functions normally feature a parameter that keeps track of the depth of the recursion (the number of times the function has called itself). The recursive function will stop calling itself once a terminating condition has been met.

return: What a function does when it is ready to exit. When a function returns, its nonstatic local variables go out of scope (can no longer be accessed).

return type: The data type returned by a function.

ROM: See **Read-Only Memory**.

root node: The first node in a tree. A root node has no parents.

scientific or **exponential notation:**   A notation for representing numbers as a floating point number times a power of 10. For example, 2.5e3 is equal to 2.5 times 10 to the third power, which is equal to 2500.

scriptable program: A program designed to work with a scripting language like AppleScript. The Finder is scriptable. So is CodeWarrior.

searching: The process of traversing a tree or list to look for a particular feature or value.

sequential stream of bytes: A stream of bytes, one right after another. Accessing a stream sequentially is the opposite of random file access.

shift bits: Move the bits within a byte either to the left or to the right.

signed: A variable capable of storing both positive and negative values.

simple statement: An assignment statement or function call. Simple statements never have substatements.

source code: A sequence of statements that tells the computer what to do. Source code is written in a specific programming language, such as C or Pascal.

source code editor: A program that allows you to review and modify your source code. CodeWarrior has a built-in source code editor.

Standard Library: A set of built-in functions that comes with every ANSI standard compiler.

star operator: Another name for the * operator (the pointer dereferencing operator).

statement: A combination of function calls, operators, and variables that performs a set of computer operations. Statements are usually followed by a semicolon.

step through: Usually associated with an array or a linked list. Stepping through an array or linked list means performing an operation on each element of the array or linked list.

stream: A sequence of bytes, normally associated with a file.

string constant: A string literal, such as `"Hello"`.

string manipulation: The process of copying or altering a string variable. String manipulation is normally performed on a 0-terminated string embedded in an array of `chars`.

syntax error: An error in your source code that prevents the compiler from compiling your code. CodeWarrior reports syntax errors by printing an error message in a separate window.

terminal node: Another name for a **leaf node**.

termination: The condition within a loop that allows the loop to exit.

trace: A process that allows you to map the flow of your program's code. You can trace your program's execution using the CodeWarrior debugger.

traversal: The process of stepping through a linked list, binary tree, or similar data structure. Traversals usually follow a specific pattern, such as preorder, inorder, or postorder.

two's complement notation: The notation used by a compiler to represent `signed` integers.

type: The class a variable belongs to. A variable's type determines the type of data that can be stored in the variable. `char`, `int`, and `float` are examples of variable types.

typecast: A C mechanism for converting a variable from one type to another.

typecasting: The process of applying a typecast to a variable.

typo: Slang for a typographical error.

unary: Usually used with respect to an operator, this indicates that the operator has a single operand.

union: A data structure that allows multiple fields but dedicates all its memory to one of the fields.

unsigned: A variable capable of storing only values greater than or equal than zero.

update mode: The file opening modes that allow you to switch between reading and writing without reopening the file. Update modes are specified by including a + in the mode specifier.

user interface: The part of your program that interacts with the user.

variable: A container for your program's data. Variables have a name and a type.

variable scope: Within a program, a variable's scope determines where in the program the variable can be accessed. Local variables are only accessible within the function they are declared in. Global variables are accessible throughout the file they are declared in.

variable type: See **type**.

white space: An invisible character, such as a space, tab, or carriage return. White space is ignored by the compiler.

whole number: An integer, as opposed to a floating point number. -256, 22, and 1,000,000 are all whole numbers, but 3.14159 is not a whole number.

wide character data types: Data types designed to hold characters represented by more than one byte. ISO supports wide character types, ANSI does not.

wide string data types: String data types based on **wide character data types**. To learn more about these, see the writeup in Harbison and Steele's *C: A Reference Manual*.

Window Manager: The functions in the Macintosh Toolbox that deal with the display and management of windows on the Mac's screen.

write a file: The process of transferring data stored in your program's variables out to a disk file.

Source Code Listings

02.01 - hello _____ **hello.c**

```c
#include <stdio.h>

int main( void )
{
    printf( "Hello, world!\n" );

    return 0;
}
```

04.01 - hello2 _____ **hello2.c**

```c
#include <stdio.h>

void SayHello( void );

int main( void )
{
    SayHello();

    return 0;
}

void SayHello( void )
{
    printf( "Hello, world!\n" );
}
```

04.02 - hello3 _____ **hello3.c**

```c
#include <stdio.h>
```

```
void SayHello( void );


int main( void )
{
   SayHello();
   SayHello();
   SayHello();

   return 0;
}


void SayHello( void )
{
   printf( "Hello, world!\n" );
}
```

05.01 - operator _____ operator.c

```
#include <stdio.h>


int    main( void )
{
   int    myInt;

   myInt = 3 * 2;
   printf( "myInt ---> %d\n", myInt );

   myInt += 1;
   printf( "myInt ---> %d\n", myInt );

   myInt -= 5;
   printf( "myInt ---> %d\n", myInt );

   myInt *= 10;
   printf( "myInt ---> %d\n", myInt );

   myInt /= 4;
   printf( "myInt ---> %d\n", myInt );

   myInt /= 2;
   printf( "myInt ---> %d", myInt );

   return 0;
}
```

05.02 - postfix _____ **postfix.c**

```c
#include <stdio.h>


int    main( void )
{
   int        myInt;

   myInt = 5;
   printf( "myInt ---> %d\n", myInt++ );
   printf( "myInt ---> %d", ++myInt );

   return 0;
}
```

05.03 - slasher _____ **slasher.c**

```c
#include <stdio.h>


int    main( void )
{
   printf( "0000000000\r" );
   printf( "11111\n" );

   printf( "0000\b\b11\n" );

   printf( "Here's a backslash...\\...for you.\n" );
   printf( "Here's a double quote...\"...for you.\n" );

   printf( "Here are a few tabs...\t\t\t\t...for you.\n" );

   printf( "Here are a few beeps...\a\a\a\a...for you." );

   return 0;
}
```

06.01 - truthTester _____ **truthTester.c**

```c
#include <stdio.h>


int    main( void )
{
   int    hasCar, hasTimeToGiveRide;
   int    nothingElseOn, newEpisode, itsARerun;
```

```
        hasCar = true;
        hasTimeToGiveRide = true;

        if ( hasCar && hasTimeToGiveRide )
            printf( "Hop in - I'll give you a ride!\n" );
        else
            printf( "I've either got no car, no time, or both!\n" );

        nothingElseOn = true;
        newEpisode = true;

        if ( newEpisode || nothingElseOn )
            printf( "Let's watch Star Trek!\n" );
        else
            printf( "Something else is on or I've seen this one.\n" );

        nothingElseOn = true;
        itsARerun = true;

        if ( nothingElseOn || (! itsARerun) )
            printf( "Let's watch Star Trek!\n" );
        else
            printf( "Something else is on or I've seen this one.\n" );

        return 0;
}
```

06.02 - loopTester   loopTester.c

```
#include <stdio.h>


int     main( void )
{
    int     i;

    i = 0;
    while ( i++ < 4 )
        printf( "while: i=%d\n", i );

    printf( "After while loop, i=%d.\n\n", i );

    for ( i = 0; i < 4; i++ )
        printf( "first for: i=%d\n", i );

    printf( "After first for loop, i=%d.\n\n", i );
```

```
   for ( i = 1; i <= 4; i++ )
       printf( "second for: i=%d\n", i );

   printf( "After second for loop, i=%d.\n", i );

   return 0;
}
```

06.03 - isOdd _____ isOdd.c

```
#include <stdio.h>


int    main( void )
{
   int    i;

   for ( i = 1; i <= 20; i++ )
   {
      printf( "The number %d is ", i );

      if ( (i % 2) == 0 )
          printf( "even" );
      else
          printf( "odd" );

      if ( (i % 3) == 0 )
          printf( " and is a multiple of 3" );

      printf( ".\n" );
   }

   return 0;
}
```

06.04 - nextPrime _____ nextPrime.c

```
#include <stdio.h>
#include <math.h>


int main( void )
{
   int    startingPoint, candidate, last, i;
   int    isPrime;

   startingPoint = 19;
```

```
            if ( startingPoint < 2 )
            {
               candidate = 2;
            }
            else if ( startingPoint == 2 )
            {
               candidate = 3;
            }
            else
            {
               candidate = startingPoint;
               if (candidate % 2 == 0)   /* Test only odd numbers */
                  candidate--;
               do
               {
                  isPrime = true;        /* Assume glorious success */
                  candidate += 2;        /* Bump to the next number to test */
                  last = sqrt( candidate );/* We'll check to see if candidate */
                                          /* has any factors, from 2 to last */
                                          /* Loop through odd numbers only */
                  for ( i = 3; (i <= last) && isPrime; i += 2 )
                  {
                     if ( (candidate % i) == 0 )
                        isPrime = false;
                  }
               } while ( ! isPrime );
            }

            printf( "The next prime after %d is %d.  Happy?\n",
                    startingPoint, candidate );
            return 0;
         }
```

06.05 - nextPrime2 _____ nextPrime2.c

```
#include <stdio.h>
#include <math.h>


int    main( void )
{
   int      candidate, isPrime, i, last;

   printf( "Primes from 1 to 100: 2, " );

   for ( candidate=3; candidate<=100; candidate+=2 )
   {
```

```
        isPrime = true;
        last = sqrt( candidate );

        for ( i = 3; (i <= last) && isPrime; i += 2 )
        {
            if ( (candidate % i) == 0 )
                isPrime = false;
        }

        if ( isPrime )
            printf( "%d, ", candidate );
    }

    return 0;
}
```

06.06 - nextPrime3 _____ **nextPrime3.c**

```
#include <stdio.h>
#include <math.h>


int    main( void )
{
    int    primeIndex, candidate, isPrime, i, last;

    printf( "Prime #1 is 2.\n" );

    candidate = 3;
    primeIndex = 2;

    while ( primeIndex <= 100 )
    {
        isPrime = true;
        last = sqrt( candidate );

        for ( i = 3; (i <= last) && isPrime; i += 2 )
        {
            if ( (candidate % i) == 0 )
                isPrime = false;
        }

        if ( isPrime )
        {
            printf( "Prime #%d is %d.\n", primeIndex, candidate );
            primeIndex++;
        }
```

```
        candidate+=2;
    }

    return 0;
}
```

07.01 - drawDots _____ drawDots.c

```
#include <stdio.h>


/***********************/
/* Function Prototypes */
/***********************/
void   DrawDots( int numDots );

int    main( void )
{
    DrawDots( 30 );

    return 0;
}

void   DrawDots( int numDots )
{
    int     i;

    for ( i = 1; i <= numDots; i++ )
        printf( "." );
}
```

07.02 - squareIt _____ squareIt.c

```
#include <stdio.h>


/***********************/
/* Function Prototypes */
/***********************/
void   SquareIt( int  number, int   *squarePtr );


int    main( void )
{
    int    square;

    SquareIt( 5, &square );
```

```
   printf( "5 squared is %d.\n", square );

   return 0;
}


void  SquareIt( int  number, int  *squarePtr )
{
   *squarePtr = number * number;
}
```

07.03 - addThese _____ addThese.c

```
#include <stdio.h>


/***********************/
/* Function Prototypes */
/***********************/
int  AddTheseNumbers( int num1, int num2 );


int  main( void )
{
   int   sum;

   sum = AddTheseNumbers( 5, 6 );

   printf( "The sum is %d.", sum );

   return 0;
}


int  AddTheseNumbers( int num1, int num2 )
{
   return( num1 + num2 );
}
```

07.04 - listPrimes _____ listPrimes.c

```
#include <stdio.h>
#include <math.h>


/***********************/
/* Function Prototypes */
```

```
/**********************/
int    IsItPrime( int candidate );


int   main( void )
{
   int   i;

   for ( i = 1; i <= 50; i++ )
   {
      if ( IsItPrime( i ) )
         printf( "%d is a prime number.\n", i );
   }

   return 0;
}


int   IsItPrime( int candidate )
{
   int   i, last;

   if ( candidate < 2 )
      return false;
   else
   {
      last = sqrt( candidate );

      for ( i = 2; i <= last; i++ )
      {
         if ( (candidate % i) == 0 )
            return false;
      }
   }

   return true;
}
```

07.05 - power _____ **power.c**

```
#include <stdio.h>


/**********************/
/* Function Prototypes */
/**********************/
```

```c
void  DoPower( int *resultPtr, int base, int exponent );


/***********/
/* Globals */
/***********/
int     gPrintTraceInfo;


int   main( void )
{
   int    power;

   gPrintTraceInfo = false;

   if ( gPrintTraceInfo )
      printf( "---> Starting main()...\n" );

   DoPower( &power, 2, 5 );
   printf( "2 to the 5th = %d.\n", power );

   DoPower( &power, 3, 4 );
   printf( "3 to the 4th = %d.\n", power );

   DoPower( &power, 5, 3 );
   printf( "5 to the 3rd = %d.\n", power );

   if ( gPrintTraceInfo )
      printf( "---> Leaving main()...\n" );

   return 0;
}


void DoPower( int *resultPtr, int base, int exponent )
{
   int    i;

   if ( gPrintTraceInfo )
      printf( "\t---> Starting DoPower()...\n" );

   *resultPtr = 1;
   for ( i = 1; i <= exponent; i++ )
      *resultPtr *= base;

   if ( gPrintTraceInfo )
      printf( "\t---> Leaving DoPower()...\n" );
}
```

07.06 - power2 _____ power2.c

```c
#include <stdio.h>


/***********************/
/* Function Prototypes */
/***********************/
int    DoPower( int base, int exponent );


/***********/
/* Globals */
/***********/
int        gPrintTraceInfo;


int    main( void )
{
   int    power;

   gPrintTraceInfo = false;

   if ( gPrintTraceInfo )
      printf( "---> Starting main()...\n" );

   printf( "2 to the 5th = %d.\n", DoPower( 2, 5 ) );
   printf( "3 to the 4th = %d.\n", DoPower( 3, 4 ) );
   printf( "5 to the 3rd = %d.\n", DoPower( 5, 3 ) );

   if ( gPrintTraceInfo )
      printf( "---> Leaving main()...\n" );

   return 0;
}


int    DoPower( int base, int exponent )
{
   int    i, result;

   if ( gPrintTraceInfo )
      printf( "\t---> Starting DoPower()...\n" );

   result = 1;
   for ( i = 1; i <= exponent; i++ )
      result *= base;
```

```
    if ( gPrintTraceInfo )
        printf( "\t---> Leaving DoPower()...\n" );

    return result;
}
```

07.07 - nonPrimes _____ nonPrimes.c

```
#include <stdio.h>
#include <math.h>


/***********************/
/* Function Prototypes */
/***********************/
int    IsItPrime( int candidate );


int    main( void )
{
    int    i;

    for ( i = 1; i <= 50; i++ )
    {
        if ( ! IsItPrime( i ) )
        {
            if ( (i % 3) == 0 )
                printf( "%d is not a prime number and is a multiple of 3.\n", i );
            else
                printf( "%d is not a prime number.\n", i );
        }
    }

    return 0;
}


int    IsItPrime( int candidate )
{
    int    i, last;

    if ( candidate < 2 )
        return false;
    else
    {
        last = sqrt( candidate );

        for ( i = 2; i <= last; i++ )
```

```
        {
            if ( (candidate % i) == 0 )
                return false;
        }
    }

    return true;
}
```

08.01 - floatSizer   floatSizer.c

```
#include <stdio.h>


int    main( void )
{
    float        myFloat;
    double        myDouble;
    long double    myLongDouble;

    myFloat = 12345.67890123456789;
    myDouble = 12345.67890123456789;
    myLongDouble = 12345.67890123456789;

    printf( "sizeof( float ) = %d\n", (int)sizeof( float ) );
    printf( "sizeof( double ) = %d\n", (int)sizeof( double ) );
    printf( "sizeof( long double ) = %d\n\n", (int)sizeof( long double ) );

    printf( "myFloat = %f\n", myFloat );
    printf( "myDouble = %f\n", myDouble );
    printf( "myLongDouble = %f\n\n", myLongDouble );

    printf( "myFloat = %25.16f\n", myFloat );
    printf( "myDouble = %25.16f\n", myDouble );
    printf( "myLongDouble = %25.16f\n\n", myLongDouble );

    printf( "myFloat = %10.1f\n", myFloat );
    printf( "myFloat = %.2f\n", myFloat );
    printf( "myFloat = %.12f\n", myFloat );
    printf( "myFloat = %.9f\n\n", myFloat );

    printf( "myFloat = %e\n\n", myFloat );

    myFloat = 100000;
    printf( "myFloat = %g\n", myFloat );

    myFloat = 1000000;
```

```
    printf( "myFloat = %g\n", myFloat );

    return 0;
}
```

08.02 - intSizer _____ intSizer.c

```
#include <stdio.h>


int   main( void )
{
    printf( "sizeof( char ) = %d\n", (int)sizeof( char ) );
    printf( "sizeof( short ) = %d\n", (int)sizeof( short ) );
    printf( "sizeof( int ) = %d\n", (int)sizeof( int ) );
    printf( "sizeof( long ) = %d\n", (int)sizeof( long ) );

    return 0;
}
```

08.03 - typeOverflow _____ typeOverflow.c

```
#include <stdio.h>


int   main( void )
{
    unsigned char  counter;

    for ( counter=1; counter<=1000; counter++ )
        printf( "%d\n", counter );

    return 0;
}
```

08.04 - ascii _____ ascii.c

```
#include <stdio.h>


/***********************/
/* Function Prototypes */
/***********************/
void  PrintChars( char low, char high );


int   main( void )
```

```
{
   PrintChars( 32, 47 );
   PrintChars( 48, 57 );
   PrintChars( 58, 64 );
   PrintChars( 65, 90 );
   PrintChars( 91, 96 );
   PrintChars( 97, 122 );
   PrintChars( 123, 126 );

   return 0;
}


void  PrintChars( char low, char high )
{
   char  c;

   printf( "%d to %d ---> ", low, high );

   for ( c = low; c <= high; c++ )
      printf( "%c", c );

   printf( "\n" );
}
```

08.05 - dice _____ dice.c

```
#include <stdlib.h>
#include <time.h>
#include <stdio.h>


/***********************/
/* Function Prototypes */
/***********************/
int     RollOne( void );
void  PrintRolls( int        rolls[] );
void  PrintX( int howMany );


int   main( void )
{
   int      rolls[ 13 ], twoDice, i;

   srand( clock() );

   for ( i=0; i<=12; i++ )
```

```
      rolls[ i ] = 0;

   for ( i=1; i <= 1000; i++ )
   {
      twoDice = RollOne() + RollOne();
      ++ rolls[ twoDice ];
   }

   PrintRolls( rolls );

   return 0;
}


int   RollOne( void )
{
   return (rand() % 6) + 1;
}


void  PrintRolls( int       rolls[] )
{
   int      i;

   for ( i=2; i<=12; i++ )
   {
      printf( "%2d (%3d):  ", i, rolls[ i ] );
      PrintX( rolls[ i ] / 10 );
      printf( "\n" );
   }
}


void  PrintX( int howMany )
{
   int   i;

   for ( i=1; i<=howMany; i++ )
      printf( "x" );
}
```

08.06 - name _____ **name.c**

```
#include <string.h>
#include <stdio.h>


int   main( void )
```

```
{
    char      name[ 50 ];

    printf( "Type your first name, please: " );

    scanf( "%s", name );

    printf( "Welcome, %s.\n", name );
    printf( "Your name is %d characters long.", (int)strlen( name ) );

    return 0;
}
```

08.07 - wordCount _____ wordCount.c

```
#include <stdio.h>
#include <ctype.h>


#define kMaxLineLength        200
#define kZeroByte             0


/***********************/
/* Function Prototypes */
/***********************/
void   ReadLine( char *line );
int    CountWords( char *line );


/**************************************************> main <*/
int    main( void )
{
    char   line[ kMaxLineLength ];
    int      numWords;

    printf( "Type a line of text, please:\n" );

    ReadLine( line );
    numWords = CountWords( line );

    printf( "\n---- This line has %d word", numWords );

    if ( numWords != 1 )
        printf( "s" );

    printf( " ----\n%s\n", line );
```

```
      return 0;
}


/***********************************************> ReadLine <*/
void   ReadLine( char *line )
{
   while ( (*line = getchar()) != '\n' )
      line++;

   *line = kZeroByte;
}


/***********************************************> CountWords <*/
int   CountWords( char *line )
{
   int       numWords, inWord;

   numWords = 0;
   inWord = false;

   while ( *line != kZeroByte )
   {
      if ( ! isspace( *line ) )
      {
         if ( ! inWord )
         {
            numWords++;
            inWord = true;
         }
      }
      else
         inWord = false;

      line++;
   }

   return numWords;
}
```

08.08 - dice2 _____ **dice2.c**

```
#include <stdlib.h>
#include <time.h>
#include <stdio.h>
```

```
#define kMaxRoll  18
#define kMinRoll  3

/***********************/
/* Function Prototypes */
/***********************/
int     RollOne( void );
void  PrintRolls( int        rolls[] );
void  PrintX( int howMany );


int    main( void )
{
   int        rolls[ kMaxRoll + 1 ], threeDice, i;

   srand( clock() );

   for ( i=0; i<=kMaxRoll; i++ )
      rolls[ i ] = 0;

   for ( i=1; i <= 1000; i++ )
   {
      threeDice = RollOne() + RollOne() + RollOne();
      ++ rolls[ threeDice ];
   }

   PrintRolls( rolls );

   return 0;
}


int    RollOne( void )
{
   return (rand() % 6) + 1;
}


void  PrintRolls( int        rolls[] )
{
   int        i;

   for ( i=kMinRoll; i<=kMaxRoll; i++ )
   {
      printf( "%2d (%3d):  ", i, rolls[ i ] );
      PrintX( rolls[ i ] / 10 );
      printf( "\n" );
```

```c
   }
}


void  PrintX( int howMany )
{
   int    i;

   for ( i=1; i<=howMany; i++ )
      printf( "x" );
}
```

08.09 - wordCount2 _____ wordCount2.c

```c
#include <stdio.h>
#include <ctype.h>


#define kMaxLineLength        200
#define kZeroByte             0


/*********************/
/* Function Prototypes */
/*********************/
void  ReadLine( char *line );
int      CountWords( char *line );
void  PrintWords( char *line );


/***********************************************> main <*/
int   main( void )
{
   char   line[ kMaxLineLength ];
   int       numWords;

   printf( "Type a line of text, please:\n" );

   ReadLine( line );
   numWords = CountWords( line );

   printf( "\n---- This line has %d word", numWords );

   if ( numWords != 1 )
      printf( "s" );

   printf( " ----\n%s\n", line );
```

```
      printf( "\n---- Here are the words ----" );
      PrintWords( line );

      return 0;
   }


/**************************************************> ReadLine <*/
void  ReadLine( char *line )
{
   while ( (*line = getchar()) != '\n' )
      line++;

   *line = kZeroByte;
}


/**************************************************> CountWords <*/
int   CountWords( char *line )
{
   int      numWords, inWord;

   numWords = 0;
   inWord = false;

   while ( *line != kZeroByte )
   {
      if ( ! isspace( *line ) )
      {
         if ( ! inWord )
         {
            numWords++;
            inWord = true;
         }
      }
      else
         inWord = false;

      line++;
   }

   return numWords;
}


/**************************************************> PrintWords <*/
void  PrintWords( char *line )
```

```
{
    int      inWord;

    inWord = false;

    while ( *line != kZeroByte )
    {
        if ( ! isspace( *line ) )
        {
            if ( ! inWord )
            {
                putchar( '\n' );
                inWord = true;
            }
            putchar( *line );
        }
        else
            inWord = false;

        line++;
    }
}
```

09.01 - multiArray _____ multiArray.c

```
#include <stdio.h>


#define kMaxCDs                     300
#define kMaxArtistLength     50


/**********************/
/* Function Prototypes */
/**********************/
void  PrintArtists( short numArtists,
        char artist[][ kMaxArtistLength + 1 ] );


/***************************************************> main <*/
int   main( void )
{
    char   artist[ kMaxCDs ][ kMaxArtistLength + 1 ];
    short  numArtists;
    char   doneReading, *result;

    printf( "The artist array takes up %ld bytes of memory.\n\n",
```

```
                    sizeof( artist ) );

      doneReading = false;
      numArtists = 0;

      while ( ! doneReading )
      {
         printf( "Artist #%d (return to exit): ", numArtists+1 );
         result = gets( artist[ numArtists ] );

         if ( (result == NULL) ||
            (result[0] == '\0') )
            doneReading = true;
         else
            numArtists++;
      }

      printf( "----\n" );

      PrintArtists( numArtists, artist );

      return 0;
   }


/*************************************************> PrintArtists <*/
void  PrintArtists( short numArtists,
         char artist[][ kMaxArtistLength + 1 ] )
   {
      short i;

      if ( numArtists <= 0 )
         printf( "No artists to report.\n" );
      else
      {
         for ( i=0; i<numArtists; i++ )
            printf( "Artist #%d: %s\n",
               i+1, artist[i] );
      }
   }
```

09.02 - structSize _____ structSize.h

```
#define kMaxArtistLength      50
#define kMaxTitleLength       50
```

```
/**********************/
/* Struct Declarations */
/**********************/
struct CDInfo
{
    char   rating;
    char   artist[ kMaxArtistLength + 1 ];
    char   title[ kMaxTitleLength + 1 ];
};
```

09.02 - structSize _____ **structSize.c**

```
#include <stdio.h>
#include "structSize.h"


/***************************************************> main <*/
int    main( void )
{
    struct CDInfo  myInfo;

    printf( "rating field:    %ld byte\n",
            sizeof( myInfo.rating ) );

    printf( "artist field:   %ld bytes\n",
            sizeof( myInfo.artist ) );

    printf( "title field:    %ld bytes\n",
            sizeof( myInfo.title ) );

    printf( "                 ---------\n" );

    printf( "myInfo struct: %ld bytes",
            sizeof( myInfo ) );

    return 0;
}
```

09.03 - structSize2 _____ **structSize2.h**

```
/**********************/
/* Struct Declarations */
/**********************/

struct LongShortShort
{
    long   myLong;
    short  myShort1;
```

361

```
        short myShort2;
};

struct ShortLongShort
{
    short myShort1;
    long  myLong;
    short myShort2;
};

struct DoubleChar
{
    double   myDouble;
    char   myChar;
};

struct CharDoubleChar
{
    char   myChar1;
    double   myDouble;
    char   myChar2;
};

struct DoubleCharChar
{
    double   myDouble;
    char   myChar1;
    char   myChar2;
};
```

09.03 - structSize2 _____ structSize2.c

```c
#include <stdio.h>
#include "structSize2.h"


/***********************************************> main <*/
int   main( void )
{
    printf( "char:   %ld byte\n", sizeof( char ) );
    printf( "short:  %ld bytes\n", sizeof( short ) );
    printf( "long:   %ld bytes\n", sizeof( long ) );
    printf( "double: %ld bytes\n\n", sizeof( double ) );

    printf( "LongShortShort: %ld bytes\n",
        sizeof( struct LongShortShort ) );
```

```
    printf( "ShortLongShort: %ld bytes\n",
        sizeof( struct ShortLongShort ) );

    printf( "DoubleChar:     %ld bytes\n",
        sizeof( struct DoubleChar ) );

    printf( "CharDoubleChar: %ld bytes\n",
        sizeof( struct CharDoubleChar ) );

    printf( "DoubleCharChar: %ld bytes\n",
        sizeof( struct DoubleCharChar ) );

    return 0;
}
```

09.04 - paramAddress _____ paramAddress.h

```
/***********/
/* Defines */
/***********/
#define kMaxCDs                     300
#define kMaxArtistLength    50
#define kMaxTitleLength     50


/**********************/
/* Struct Declarations */
/**********************/
struct CDInfo
{
    char  rating;
    char  artist[ kMaxArtistLength + 1 ];
    char  title[ kMaxTitleLength + 1 ];
};


/**********************/
/* Function Prototypes */
/**********************/
void  PrintParamInfo( struct CDInfo *myCDPtr,
          struct CDInfo myCDCopy );
```

09.04 - paramAddress _____ paramAddress.c

```
#include <stdio.h>
#include "paramAddress.h"
```

```
/**********************************************> main <*/
int    main( void )
{
   struct CDInfo  myCD;

   printf( "Address of myCD.rating in main():              %ld\n",
          &(myCD.rating) );

   PrintParamInfo( &myCD, myCD );


   return 0;
}


/********************************> PrintStructAddresses <*/
void  PrintParamInfo( struct CDInfo *myCDPtr,
           struct CDInfo myCDCopy )
{
   printf( "Address of myCDPtr->rating in PrintParamInfo(): %ld\n",
          &(myCDPtr->rating) );

   printf( "Address of myCDCopy.rating in PrintParamInfo(): %ld\n",
          &(myCDCopy.rating) );
}
```

09.05 - cdTracker _____ cdTracker.h

```
/**********/
/* Defines */
/**********/
#define kMaxCDs                      300
#define kMaxArtistLength      50
#define kMaxTitleLength       50


/*********************/
/* Struct Declarations */
/*********************/
struct CDInfo
{
   char        rating;
   char        artist[ kMaxArtistLength + 1 ];
   char        title[ kMaxTitleLength + 1 ];
   struct CDInfo  *next;
} *gFirstPtr, *gLastPtr;
```

```
/***********************/
/* Function Prototypes */
/***********************/
char        GetCommand( void );
struct CDInfo  *ReadStruct( void );
void        AddToList( struct CDInfo *curPtr );
void        ListCDs( void );
void        Flush( void );
```

09.05 - cdTracker _____ cdTracker.c

```c
#include <stdlib.h>
#include <stdio.h>
#include "cdTracker.h"


/***********************************************> main <*/
int   main( void )
{
   char         command;

   gFirstPtr = NULL;
   gLastPtr = NULL;

   while ( (command = GetCommand() ) != 'q' )
   {
      switch( command )
      {
         case 'n':
            AddToList( ReadStruct() );
            break;
         case 'l':
            ListCDs();
            break;
      }
   }

   printf( "Goodbye..." );

   return 0;
}


/******************************************> GetCommand <*/
char  GetCommand( void )
{
   char      command;
```

```
      do
      {
         printf( "Enter command (q=quit, n=new, l=list):  " );
         scanf( "%c", &command );
         Flush();
      }
      while ( (command != 'q') && (command != 'n')
                 && (command != 'l') );

      printf( "\n----------\n" );
      return( command );
}


/********************************************> ReadStruct <*/
struct CDInfo   *ReadStruct( void )
{
      struct CDInfo    *infoPtr;
      int              num;

      infoPtr = malloc( sizeof( struct CDInfo ) );

      if ( infoPtr == NULL )
      {
         printf( "Out of memory!!!  Goodbye!\n" );
         exit( 0 );
      }

      printf( "Enter Artist's Name:  " );
      gets( infoPtr->artist );

      printf( "Enter CD Title:  " );
      gets( infoPtr->title );

      do
      {
         printf( "Enter CD Rating (1-10):  " );
         scanf( "%d", &num );
         Flush();
      }
      while ( ( num < 1 ) || ( num > 10 ) );

      infoPtr->rating = num;

      printf( "\n----------\n" );
```

```
      return( infoPtr );
}


/*********************************************> AddToList <*/
void  AddToList( struct CDInfo *curPtr )
{
   if ( gFirstPtr == NULL )
      gFirstPtr = curPtr;
   else
      gLastPtr->next = curPtr;

   gLastPtr = curPtr;
   curPtr->next = NULL;
}


/*********************************************> ListCDs <*/
void  ListCDs( void )
{
   struct CDInfo  *curPtr;

   if ( gFirstPtr == NULL )
   {
      printf( "No CDs have been entered yet...\n" );
      printf( "\n----------\n" );
   }
   else
   {
      for ( curPtr=gFirstPtr; curPtr!=NULL; curPtr = curPtr->next )
      {
         printf( "Artist:   %s\n", curPtr->artist );
         printf( "Title:    %s\n", curPtr->title );
         printf( "Rating:   %d\n", curPtr->rating );

         printf( "\n----------\n" );
      }
   }
}


/*********************************************> Flush <*/
void  Flush( void )
{
   while ( getchar() != '\n' )
      ;
}
```

```c
#include <stdio.h>


#define kMaxCDs                    300
#define kMaxArtistLength      50


/**********************/
/* Function Prototypes */
/**********************/
void   ReadLine( char *line );
void   Flush( void );
void   PrintArtists( short numArtists,
           char artist[][ kMaxArtistLength + 1 ] );


/***************************************************> main <*/
int     main( void )
{
   char    artist[ kMaxCDs ][ kMaxArtistLength + 1 ];
   short numArtists;
   char   doneReading;

   printf( "The artist array takes up %ld bytes of memory.\n\n",
           sizeof( artist ) );

   doneReading = false;
   numArtists = 0;

   while ( ! doneReading )
   {
      printf( "Artist #%d (return to exit): ", numArtists+1 );
      ReadLine( artist[ numArtists ] );

      if ( artist[numArtists][0] == '\0' )
         doneReading = true;
      else
         numArtists++;
   }

   printf( "----\n" );

   PrintArtists( numArtists, artist );

   return 0;
```

```
}


/************************************************> ReadLine <*/
void  ReadLine( char *line )
{
   char   c;
   short  numCharsRead;

   numCharsRead = 0;

   while ( ((c = getchar()) != '\n') &&
      (++numCharsRead <= kMaxArtistLength))
   {
      *line = c;
      line++;
   }

   *line = 0;

   if ( numCharsRead > kMaxArtistLength )
      Flush();
}


/************************************************> Flush <*/
void  Flush( void )
{
   while ( getchar() != '\n' )
      ;
}


/************************************************> PrintArtists <*/
void  PrintArtists( short numArtists,
         char artist[][ kMaxArtistLength + 1 ] )
{
   short i;

   if ( numArtists <= 0 )
   {
      printf( "No artists to report.\n" );
      return;
   }
   else
   {
      for ( i=0; i<numArtists; i++ )
```

```
            printf( "Artist #%d: %s\n",
               i+1, artist[i] );
      }
}
```

09.07 - cdTracker2 _____ cdTracker2.h

```
/**********/
/* Defines */
/**********/
#define kMaxCDs                         300
#define kMaxArtistLength      50
#define kMaxTitleLength       50


/**********************/
/* Struct Declarations */
/**********************/
struct CDInfo
{
   char        rating;
   char        artist[ kMaxArtistLength + 1 ];
   char        title[ kMaxTitleLength + 1 ];
   struct CDInfo  *next;
} *gFirstPtr, *gLastPtr;


/**********************/
/* Function Prototypes */
/**********************/
char        GetCommand( void );
struct CDInfo *ReadStruct( void );
void        AddToList( struct CDInfo *curPtr );
void        InsertInList( struct CDInfo *afterMeCDPtr, struct CDInfo *newCDPtr );
void        ListCDs( void );
void        Flush( void );
```

09.07 - cdTracker2 _____ cdTracker2.c

```
#include <stdlib.h>
#include <stdio.h>
#include "cdTracker2.h"


/***************************************************> main <*/
int   main( void )
```

```
{
    char        command;

    gFirstPtr = NULL;
    gLastPtr = NULL;

    while ( (command = GetCommand() ) != 'q' )
    {
        switch( command )
        {
            case 'n':
                AddToList( ReadStruct() );
                break;
            case 'l':
                ListCDs();
                break;
        }
    }

    printf( "Goodbye..." );

    return 0;
}


/*****************************************> GetCommand <*/
char  GetCommand( void )
{
    char   command;

    do
    {
        printf( "Enter command (q=quit, n=new, l=list):  " );
        scanf( "%c", &command );
        Flush();
    }
    while ( (command != 'q') && (command != 'n')
                && (command != 'l') );

    printf( "\n----------\n" );
    return( command );
}


/*****************************************> ReadStruct <*/
struct CDInfo  *ReadStruct( void )
{
```

```
        struct CDInfo  *infoPtr;
        int            num;

        infoPtr = malloc( sizeof( struct CDInfo ) );

        if ( infoPtr == NULL )
        {
            printf( "Out of memory!!!  Goodbye!\n" );
            exit( 0 );
        }

        printf( "Enter Artist's Name:  " );
        gets( infoPtr->artist );

        printf( "Enter CD Title:  " );
        gets( infoPtr->title );

        do
        {
            printf( "Enter CD Rating (1-10):  " );
            scanf( "%d", &num );
            Flush();
        }
        while ( ( num < 1 ) || ( num > 10 ) );

        infoPtr->rating = num;

        printf( "\n----------\n" );

        return( infoPtr );
    }


/*******************************************> AddToList <*/
void  AddToList( struct CDInfo *curPtr )
{
    struct CDInfo  *beforePtr;

/* First check to see if the list is empty */
    if ( gFirstPtr == NULL )
        InsertInList( NULL, curPtr );
    else if ( curPtr->rating <= gFirstPtr->rating )
/* Next check to see if curPtr should be the new first item */
        InsertInList( NULL, curPtr );
    else
/* Walk through the list till you find the first rating higher than us */
    {
```

```
      beforePtr = gFirstPtr;

      while ( (beforePtr->next != NULL) &&
         (beforePtr->next->rating < curPtr->rating) )
      {
         beforePtr = beforePtr->next;
      }
      InsertInList( beforePtr, curPtr );
   }
}


/*********************************************> InsertInList <*/
void  InsertInList( struct CDInfo *afterMeCDPtr, struct CDInfo *newCDPtr )
{
   if ( afterMeCDPtr == NULL )
/* This means we want to insert the new one as the first in the list */
   {
      newCDPtr->next = gFirstPtr;
      gFirstPtr = newCDPtr;
      if ( gLastPtr == NULL )
         gLastPtr = newCDPtr;
   }
   else if ( afterMeCDPtr == gLastPtr )
/* This means we want to insert the new one as the last in the list */
   {
      gLastPtr->next = newCDPtr;
      newCDPtr->next = NULL;
      gLastPtr = newCDPtr;
   }
   else
   {
      newCDPtr->next = afterMeCDPtr->next;
      afterMeCDPtr->next = newCDPtr;
   }

}


/*********************************************> ListCDs <*/
void  ListCDs( void )
{
   struct CDInfo  *curPtr;

   if ( gFirstPtr == NULL )
   {
      printf( "No CDs have been entered yet...\n" );
```

```
            printf( "\n----------\n" );
        }
        else
        {
            for ( curPtr=gFirstPtr; curPtr!=NULL; curPtr = curPtr->next )
            {
                printf( "Artist:  %s\n", curPtr->artist );
                printf( "Title:   %s\n", curPtr->title );
                printf( "Rating:  %d\n", curPtr->rating );

                printf( "\n----------\n" );
            }
        }
}


/********************************************> Flush <*/
void  Flush( void )
{
    while ( getchar() != '\n' )
        ;
}
```

09.08 - cdTracker3 _____ **cdTracker3.h**

```
/**********/
/* Defines */
/**********/
#define kMaxCDs                         300
#define kMaxArtistLength      50
#define kMaxTitleLength       50


/**********************/
/* Struct Declarations */
/**********************/
struct CDInfo
{
    char        rating;
    char        artist[ kMaxArtistLength + 1 ];
    char        title[ kMaxTitleLength + 1 ];
    struct CDInfo  *next, *prev;
} *gFirstPtr, *gLastPtr;


/**********************/
/* Function Prototypes */
```

```
/**********************/
char        GetCommand( void );
struct CDInfo  *ReadStruct( void );
void        AddToList( struct CDInfo *curPtr );
void        ListCDs( void );
void        ListCDsInReverse( void );
void        Flush( void );
```

09.08 - cdTracker3   cdTracker3.c

```
#include <stdlib.h>
#include <stdio.h>
#include "cdTracker3.h"


/*************************************************> main <*/
int    main( void )
{
   char         command;

   gFirstPtr = NULL;
   gLastPtr = NULL;

   while ( (command = GetCommand() ) != 'q' )
   {
      switch( command )
      {
         case 'n':
            AddToList( ReadStruct() );
            break;
         case 'l':
            ListCDs();
            break;
         case 'r':
            ListCDsInReverse();
            break;
      }
   }

   printf( "Goodbye..." );

   return 0;
}


/*******************************************> GetCommand <*/
char  GetCommand( void )
```

```c
{
    char  command;

    do
    {
        printf( "Enter command (q=quit, n=new, l=list, r=list reverse): " );
        scanf( "%c", &command );
        Flush();
    }
    while ( (command != 'q') && (command != 'n')
           && (command != 'l') && (command != 'r') );

    printf( "\n----------\n" );
    return( command );
}


/******************************************> ReadStruct <*/
struct CDInfo  *ReadStruct( void )
{
    struct CDInfo  *infoPtr;
    int            num;

    infoPtr = malloc( sizeof( struct CDInfo ) );

    if ( infoPtr == NULL )
    {
        printf( "Out of memory!!!  Goodbye!\n" );
        exit( 0 );
    }

    printf( "Enter Artist's Name:  " );
    gets( infoPtr->artist );

    printf( "Enter CD Title:  " );
    gets( infoPtr->title );

    do
    {
        printf( "Enter CD Rating (1-10):  " );
        scanf( "%d", &num );
        Flush();
    }
    while ( ( num < 1 ) || ( num > 10 ) );

    infoPtr->rating = num;
```

```
   printf( "\n----------\n" );

   return( infoPtr );
}


/*******************************************> AddToList <*/
void  AddToList( struct CDInfo *curPtr )
{
   if ( gFirstPtr == NULL )
      gFirstPtr = curPtr;
   else
      gLastPtr->next = curPtr;

   curPtr->prev = gLastPtr;

   gLastPtr = curPtr;
   curPtr->next = NULL;
}


/*******************************************> ListCDs <*/
void  ListCDs( void )
{
   struct CDInfo  *curPtr;

   if ( gFirstPtr == NULL )
   {
      printf( "No CDs have been entered yet...\n" );
      printf( "\n----------\n" );
   }
   else
   {
      for ( curPtr=gFirstPtr; curPtr!=NULL; curPtr = curPtr->next )
      {
         printf( "Artist:  %s\n", curPtr->artist );
         printf( "Title:   %s\n", curPtr->title );
         printf( "Rating:  %d\n", curPtr->rating );

         printf( "\n----------\n" );
      }
   }
}


/*******************************************> ListCDsInReverse <*/
void  ListCDsInReverse( void )
```

```
{
    struct CDInfo  *curPtr;

    if ( gLastPtr == NULL )
    {
        printf( "No CDs have been entered yet...\n" );
        printf( "\n----------\n" );
    }
    else
    {
        for ( curPtr=gLastPtr; curPtr!=NULL; curPtr = curPtr->prev )
        {
            printf( "Artist:  %s\n", curPtr->artist );
            printf( "Title:   %s\n", curPtr->title );
            printf( "Rating:  %d\n", curPtr->rating );

            printf( "\n----------\n" );
        }
    }
}


/*****************************************> Flush <*/
void  Flush( void )
{
    while ( getchar() != '\n' )
        ;
}
```

10.01 - printFile   printFile.c

```
#include <stdio.h>


int   main( void )
{
    FILE  *fp;
    int   c;

    fp = fopen( "My Data File", "r" );

    if ( fp != NULL )
    {
        while ( (c = fgetc( fp )) != EOF )
            putchar( c );

        fclose( fp );
```

```
    }

    return 0;
}
```

10.02 - cdFiler _____ cdFiler.h

```
/**********/
/* Defines */
/**********/
#define kMaxArtistLength       50
#define kMaxTitleLength        50

#define kCDFileName                    "cdData"


/**********************/
/* Struct Declarations */
/**********************/
struct CDInfo
{
   char         rating;
   char         artist[ kMaxArtistLength + 1 ];
   char         title[ kMaxTitleLength + 1 ];
   struct CDInfo  *next;
};


/**********************/
/* Global Declarations */
/**********************/
 extern struct CDInfo    *gFirstPtr, *gLastPtr;


/******************************/
/* Function Prototypes - main.c */
/******************************/
char         GetCommand( void );
struct CDInfo *ReadStruct( void );
void         AddToList( struct CDInfo *curPtr );
void         ListCDs( void );
void         ListCDsInReverse( void );
void         Flush( void );


/******************************/
/* Function Prototypes - files.c */
/******************************/
```

```
void  WriteFile( void );
void  ReadFile( void );
char  ReadStructFromFile( FILE *fp, struct CDInfo *infoPtr );
```

10.02 - cdFiler _____ files.c

```
#include <stdlib.h>
#include <stdio.h>
#include "cdFiler.h"


/*********************************************> WriteFile <*/
void  WriteFile( void )
{
   FILE         *fp;
   struct CDInfo   *infoPtr;
   int           num;

   if ( gFirstPtr == NULL )
      return;

   if ( ( fp = fopen( kCDFileName, "w" ) ) == NULL )
   {
      printf( "***ERROR: Could not write CD file!" );
      return;
   }

   for ( infoPtr=gFirstPtr; infoPtr!=NULL; infoPtr=infoPtr->next )
   {
      fprintf( fp, "%s\n", infoPtr->artist );
      fprintf( fp, "%s\n", infoPtr->title );

      num = infoPtr->rating;
      fprintf( fp, "%d\n", num );
   }

   fclose( fp );
}


/*********************************************> ReadFile <*/
void  ReadFile( void )
{
   FILE       *fp;
   struct CDInfo *infoPtr;
   int           i;

   if ( ( fp = fopen( kCDFileName, "r" ) ) == NULL )
```

```c
   {
      printf( "***ERROR: Could not read CD file!" );
      return;
   }

   do
   {
      infoPtr = malloc( sizeof( struct CDInfo ) );

      if ( infoPtr == NULL )
      {
         printf( "Out of memory!!!  Goodbye!\n" );
         exit( 0 );
      }
   }
   while ( ReadStructFromFile( fp, infoPtr ) );

   fclose( fp );
   free( infoPtr );
}


/***********************************> ReadStructFromFile <*/
char  ReadStructFromFile( FILE *fp, struct CDInfo *infoPtr )
{
   int      num;

   if ( fscanf( fp, "%[^\n]\n", infoPtr->artist ) != EOF )
   {
      if ( fscanf( fp, "%[^\n]\n", infoPtr->title ) == EOF )
      {
         printf( "Missing CD title!\n" );
         return false;
      }
      else if ( fscanf( fp, "%d\n", &num ) == EOF )
      {
         printf( "Missing CD rating!\n" );
         return false;
      }
      else
      {
         infoPtr->rating = num;
         AddToList( infoPtr );
         return true;
      }
   }
   else
```

```
                return false;
    }


10.02 - cdFiler _____ main.c
#include <stdlib.h>
#include <stdio.h>
#include "cdFiler.h"


/***********************/
/* Global Definitions */
/***********************/
struct CDInfo    *gFirstPtr, *gLastPtr;


/*************************************************> main <*/
int    main( void )
{
    char         command;

    gFirstPtr = NULL;
    gLastPtr = NULL;

    ReadFile();

    while ( (command = GetCommand() ) != 'q' )
    {
        switch( command )
        {
            case 'n':
                AddToList( ReadStruct() );
                break;
            case 'l':
                ListCDs();
                break;
        }
    }

    WriteFile();

    printf( "Goodbye..." );

    return 0;
}
```

```
/*****************************************> GetCommand <*/
char  GetCommand( void )
{
   char   command;

   do
   {
      printf( "Enter command (q=quit, n=new, l=list):  " );
      scanf( "%c", &command );
      Flush();
   }
   while ( (command != 'q') && (command != 'n')
              && (command != 'l') );

   printf( "\n----------\n" );
   return( command );
}



/*****************************************> ReadStruct <*/
struct CDInfo  *ReadStruct( void )
{
   struct CDInfo  *infoPtr;
   int            num;

   infoPtr = malloc( sizeof( struct CDInfo ) );

   if ( infoPtr == NULL )
   {
      printf( "Out of memory!!!  Goodbye!\n" );
      exit( 0 );
   }

   printf( "Enter Artist's Name:  " );
   gets( infoPtr->artist );

   printf( "Enter CD Title:  " );
   gets( infoPtr->title );

   do
   {
      printf( "Enter CD Rating (1-10):  " );
      scanf( "%d", &num );
      Flush();
   }
   while ( ( num < 1 ) || ( num > 10 ) );
```

```
       infoPtr->rating = num;

       printf( "\n----------\n" );

       return( infoPtr );
    }


    /*****************************************> AddToList <*/
    void  AddToList( struct CDInfo *curPtr )
    {
       if ( gFirstPtr == NULL )
          gFirstPtr = curPtr;
       else
          gLastPtr->next = curPtr;

       gLastPtr = curPtr;
       curPtr->next = NULL;
    }


    /*****************************************> ListCDs <*/
    void  ListCDs( void )
    {
       struct CDInfo  *curPtr;

       if ( gFirstPtr == NULL )
       {
          printf( "No CDs have been entered yet...\n" );
          printf( "\n----------\n" );
       }
       else
       {
          for ( curPtr=gFirstPtr; curPtr!=NULL; curPtr = curPtr->next )
          {
             printf( "Artist:  %s\n", curPtr->artist );
             printf( "Title:   %s\n", curPtr->title );
             printf( "Rating:  %d\n", curPtr->rating );

             printf( "\n----------\n" );
          }
       }
    }


    /*****************************************> Flush <*/
    void  Flush( void )
```

```
{
   while ( getchar() != '\n' )
      ;
}
```

10.03 - dinoEdit _____ dinoEdit.h

```
/**********/
/* Defines */
/**********/
#define kDinoRecordSize      20
#define kMaxLineLength       100
#define kDinoFileName        "My Dinos"


/******************************/
/* Function Prototypes - main.c */
/******************************/
int    GetNumber( void );
int    GetNumberOfDinos( void );
void   ReadDinoName( int number, char *dinoName );
char   GetNewDinoName( char *dinoName );
void   WriteDinoName( int number, char *dinoName );
void   Flush( void );
void   DoError( char *message );
```

10.03 - dinoEdit _____ main.c

```
#include <stdlib.h>
#include <stdio.h>
#include <string.h>
#include "dinoEdit.h"


/**************************************************> main <*/
int    main( void )
{
   int     number;
   FILE   *fp;
   char   dinoName[ kDinoRecordSize+1 ];

   while ( (number = GetNumber() ) != 0 )
   {
      ReadDinoName( number, dinoName );

      printf( "Dino #%d: %s\n", number, dinoName );

      if ( GetNewDinoName( dinoName ) )
```

```
            WriteDinoName( number, dinoName );
   }

   printf( "Goodbye..." );

   return 0;
}


/*******************************************> GetNumber <*/
int    GetNumber( void )
{
   int    number, numDinos;

   numDinos = GetNumberOfDinos();

   do
   {
      printf( "Enter number from 1 to %d (0 to exit): ",
         numDinos );
      scanf( "%d", &number );
      Flush();
   }
   while ( (number < 0) || (number > numDinos) );

   return( number );
}


/*******************************> GetNumberOfDinos <*/
int    GetNumberOfDinos( void )
{
   FILE    *fp;
   long    fileLength;

   if ( (fp = fopen( kDinoFileName, "r" )) == NULL )
      DoError( "Couldn't open file...Goodbye!" );

   if ( fseek( fp, 0L, SEEK_END ) != 0 )
      DoError( "Couldn't seek to end of file...Goodbye!" );

   if ( (fileLength = ftell( fp )) == -1L )
      DoError( "ftell() failed...Goodbye!" );

   fclose( fp );

   return( (int)(fileLength / kDinoRecordSize) );
```

```c
}


/********************************> ReadDinoName <*/
void  ReadDinoName( int number, char *dinoName )
{
    FILE      *fp;
    long      bytesToSkip;

    if ( (fp = fopen( kDinoFileName, "r" )) == NULL )
        DoError( "Couldn't open file...Goodbye!" );

    bytesToSkip = (long)((number-1) * kDinoRecordSize);

    if ( fseek( fp, bytesToSkip, SEEK_SET ) != 0 )
        DoError( "Couldn't seek in file...Goodbye!" );

    if ( fread( dinoName, (size_t)kDinoRecordSize,
        (size_t)1, fp ) != 1 )
        DoError( "Bad fread()...Goodbye!" );

    fclose( fp );
}


/*****************************> GetNewDinoName <*/
char  GetNewDinoName( char *dinoName )
{
    char  line[ kMaxLineLength ];
    int     i, nameLen;

    printf( "Enter new name: " );

    gets( line );

    if ( line[0] == '\0' )
        return false;

    for ( i=0; i<kDinoRecordSize; i++ )
        dinoName[i] = ' ';

    nameLen = strlen( line );

    if ( nameLen > kDinoRecordSize )
        nameLen = kDinoRecordSize;

    for ( i=0; i<nameLen; i++ )
```

387

```
            dinoName[i] = line[i];

      return true;
}



/*******************************> WriteDinoName <*/
void  WriteDinoName( int number, char *dinoName )
{
   FILE      *fp;
   long      bytesToSkip;

   if ( (fp = fopen( kDinoFileName, "r+" )) == NULL )
      DoError( "Couldn't open file...Goodbye!" );

   bytesToSkip = (long)((number-1) * kDinoRecordSize);

   if ( fseek( fp, bytesToSkip, SEEK_SET ) != 0 )
      DoError( "Couldn't seek in file...Goodbye!" );

   if ( fwrite( dinoName, (size_t)kDinoRecordSize,
      (size_t)1, fp ) != 1 )
      DoError( "Bad fwrite()...Goodbye!" );

   fclose( fp );
}



/*********************************************> Flush <*/
void  Flush( void )
{
   while ( getchar() != '\n' )
      ;
}



/*********************************************> DoError <*/
void  DoError( char *message )
{
   printf( "%s\n", message );
   exit( 0 );
}
```

10.04 - fileReader _____ fileReader.c

```
#include <stdio.h>
#include <stdlib.h>
```

```
/***********************/
/* Function Prototypes */
/***********************/
void  DoError( char *message );
int     ReadLineOfNums( FILE *fp, int numsPerLine, int *intArray );
void  PrintLineOfNums( int numsPerLine, int *intArray );


/*****************************************> main <*/
int   main( void )
{
   FILE  *fp;
   int      *intArray, numsPerLine;
   size_t   arraySize;

   fp = fopen( "My Data File", "r" );

   if ( fp == NULL )
      DoError( "Couldn't open file!" );

   if ( fscanf( fp, "%d", &numsPerLine ) != 1 )
      DoError( "Bad fscanf() call!" );

   if ( numsPerLine <= 0 )
      DoError( "Too few items per line!" );

   arraySize = numsPerLine * sizeof( int );

   if ( (intArray = malloc( arraySize )) == NULL )
      DoError( "Couldn't malloc() int array!" );

   while ( ReadLineOfNums( fp, numsPerLine, intArray ) )
      PrintLineOfNums( numsPerLine, intArray );

   free( intArray );

   return 0;
}


/***********************************> ReadLineOfNums <*/
int   ReadLineOfNums( FILE *fp, int numsPerLine, int *intArray )
{
   int   i;

   for ( i=0; i<numsPerLine; i++ )
   {
```

389

```
        if ( fscanf( fp, "%d", &(intArray[ i ]) ) != 1 )
           return false;
   }

   return true;
}


/**********************************> PrintLineOfNums <*/
void  PrintLineOfNums( int numsPerLine, int *intArray )
{
   int    i;

   for ( i=0; i<numsPerLine; i++ )
      printf( "%d\t", intArray[ i ] );

   printf( "\n" );
}


/******************************************> DoError <*/
void  DoError( char *message )
{
   printf( "%s\n", message );
   exit( 0 );
}
```

10.05 - cdFiler2 _____ cdFiler2.h

```
/**********/
/* Defines */
/**********/
#define kMaxLineLength          200
#define kCDFileName                     "cdData"


/*********************/
/* Struct Declarations */
/*********************/
struct CDInfo
{
   char        rating;
   char        *artist;
   char        *title;
   struct CDInfo  *next;
};
```

```
/***********************/
/* Global Declarations */
/***********************/
 extern struct CDInfo   *gFirstPtr, *gLastPtr;


/******************************/
/* Function Prototypes - main.c */
/******************************/
char        GetCommand( void );
struct CDInfo  *ReadStruct( void );
void        AddToList( struct CDInfo *curPtr );
void        ListCDs( void );
void        ListCDsInReverse( void );
void        Flush( void );
char        *MallocAndCopy( char *line );
void        ZeroLine( char *line );


/******************************/
/* Function Prototypes - files.c */
/******************************/
void  WriteFile( void );
void  ReadFile( void );
char  ReadStructFromFile( FILE *fp, struct CDInfo *infoPtr );
```

10.05 - cdFiler2 _____ **files.c**

```
#include <stdlib.h>
#include <stdio.h>
#include "cdFiler2.h"


/**********************************************> WriteFile <*/
void  WriteFile( void )
{
   FILE          *fp;
   struct CDInfo  *infoPtr;
   int           num;

   if ( gFirstPtr == NULL )
      return;

   if ( ( fp = fopen( kCDFileName, "w" ) ) == NULL )
   {
      printf( "***ERROR: Could not write CD file!" );
      return;
```

```
         }

         for ( infoPtr=gFirstPtr; infoPtr!=NULL; infoPtr=infoPtr->next )
         {
            fprintf( fp, "%s\n", infoPtr->artist );
            fprintf( fp, "%s\n", infoPtr->title );

            num = infoPtr->rating;
            fprintf( fp, "%d\n", num );
         }

         fclose( fp );
}


/***********************************************> ReadFile <*/
void  ReadFile( void )
{
   FILE          *fp;
   struct CDInfo  *infoPtr;

   if ( ( fp = fopen( kCDFileName, "r" ) ) == NULL )
   {
      printf( "***ERROR: Could not read CD file!" );
      return;
   }

   do
   {
      infoPtr = malloc( sizeof( struct CDInfo ) );

      if ( infoPtr == NULL )
      {
         printf( "Out of memory!!!  Goodbye!\n" );
         exit( 0 );
      }
   }
   while ( ReadStructFromFile( fp, infoPtr ) );

   fclose( fp );
   free( infoPtr );
}


/***********************************> ReadStructFromFile <*/
char  ReadStructFromFile( FILE *fp, struct CDInfo *infoPtr )
{
```

```c
   int      num;
   char  line[ kMaxLineLength ];

   ZeroLine( line );
   if ( fscanf( fp, "%[^\n]\n", line ) != EOF )
   {
       infoPtr->artist = MallocAndCopy( line );
       ZeroLine( line );

       if ( fscanf( fp, "%[^\n]\n", line ) == EOF )
       {
           printf( "Missing CD title!\n" );
           return false;
       }
       else
       {
           infoPtr->title = MallocAndCopy( line );

           if ( fscanf( fp, "%d\n", &num ) == EOF )
           {
               printf( "Missing CD rating!\n" );
               return false;
           }
           else
           {
               infoPtr->rating = num;
               AddToList( infoPtr );
               return true;
           }
       }
   }
   else
       return false;
}
```

10.05 - cdFiler2 _____ main.c

```c
#include <string.h>
#include <stdlib.h>
#include <stdio.h>
#include "cdFiler2.h"


/**********************/
/* Global Definitions */
/**********************/
```

```c
struct CDInfo  *gFirstPtr, *gLastPtr;


/************************************************> main <*/
int    main( void )
{
   char         command;

   gFirstPtr = NULL;
   gLastPtr = NULL;

   ReadFile();

   while ( (command = GetCommand() ) != 'q' )
   {
      switch( command )
      {
         case 'n':
            AddToList( ReadStruct() );
            break;
         case 'l':
            ListCDs();
            break;
      }
   }

   WriteFile();

   printf( "Goodbye..." );

   return 0;
}


/*******************************************> GetCommand <*/
char  GetCommand( void )
{
   char   command;

   do
   {
      printf( "Enter command (q=quit, n=new, l=list):  " );
      scanf( "%c", &command );
      Flush();
   }
   while ( (command != 'q') && (command != 'n')
```

```
                    && (command != 'l') );

    printf( "\n----------\n" );
    return( command );
}



/*******************************************> ReadStruct <*/
struct CDInfo  *ReadStruct( void )
{
    struct CDInfo  *infoPtr;
    int            num;
    char           line[ kMaxLineLength ];

    infoPtr = malloc( sizeof( struct CDInfo ) );

    if ( infoPtr == NULL )
    {
        printf( "Out of memory!!!  Goodbye!\n" );
        exit( 0 );
    }

    printf( "Enter Artist's Name:  " );
    gets( line );
    infoPtr->artist = MallocAndCopy( line );

    printf( "Enter CD Title:  " );
    gets( line );
    infoPtr->title = MallocAndCopy( line );

    do
    {
        printf( "Enter CD Rating (1-10):  " );
        scanf( "%d", &num );
        Flush();
    }
    while ( ( num < 1 ) || ( num > 10 ) );

    infoPtr->rating = num;

    printf( "\n----------\n" );

    return( infoPtr );
}



/*******************************************> AddToList <*/
```

```
void  AddToList( struct CDInfo *curPtr )
{
   if ( gFirstPtr == NULL )
      gFirstPtr = curPtr;
   else
      gLastPtr->next = curPtr;

   gLastPtr = curPtr;
   curPtr->next = NULL;
}


/*******************************************> ListCDs <*/
void  ListCDs( void )
{
   struct CDInfo  *curPtr;

   if ( gFirstPtr == NULL )
   {
      printf( "No CDs have been entered yet...\n" );
      printf( "\n----------\n" );
   }
   else
   {
      for ( curPtr=gFirstPtr; curPtr!=NULL; curPtr = curPtr->next )
      {
         printf( "Artist:  %s\n", curPtr->artist );
         printf( "Title:   %s\n", curPtr->title );
         printf( "Rating:  %d\n", curPtr->rating );

         printf( "\n----------\n" );
      }
   }
}


/********************************************> Flush <*/
void  Flush( void )
{
   while ( getchar() != '\n' )
      ;
}


/*************************************> MallocAndCopy <*/
char  *MallocAndCopy( char *line )
{
```

```
/*
   This function takes a string as a parameter and malloc()s
   a new block of memory the size of the string, with an
   extra byte for the 0-terminator.

   strcpy() is called to copy the string into the new
   block of memory and the pointer to the new block is
   returned...
*/
   char  *pointer;
   if ( (pointer = malloc( strlen(line)+1 )) == NULL )
   {
      printf( "Out of memory!!!  Goodbye!\n" );
      exit( 0 );
   }
   strcpy( pointer, line );

   return pointer;
}


/*********************************> ZeroLine <*/
void  ZeroLine( char *line )
{
   int      i;

   for ( i=0; i<kMaxLineLength; i++ )
      line[ i ] = 0;
}
```

11.01 - iterate _____ iterate.c

```
#include <stdio.h>


int main( void )
{
   int      i, num;
   long  fac;

   num = 5;
   fac = 1;

   for ( i=1; i<=num; i++ )
      fac *= i;
```

```
        printf( "%d factorial is %ld.", num, fac );

        return 0;
}
```

11.02 - recurse _____ recurse.c

```
#include <stdio.h>

long  factorial( long num );

int main( void )
{
   long   num = 5L, fac;

   printf( "%ld factorial is %ld.", num,
       factorial( num ) );

   return 0;
}


long  factorial( long num )
{
   if ( num > 1 )
      num *= factorial( num - 1 );

   return( num );
}
```

11.03 - funcPtr _____ funcPtr.c

```
#include <stdio.h>

int    SquareIt( int num );

int main( void )
{
   int      (*myFuncPtr)( int );
   int      num = 5;

   myFuncPtr = SquareIt;
   printf( "%d squared is %d.", num,
       (*myFuncPtr)( num ) );

   return 0;
```

```
}


int    SquareIt( int num )
{
   return( num * num );
}
```

11.04 - static _____ static.c

```
#include <stdio.h>

int    StaticFunc( void );

int main( void )
{
   int        i;

   for ( i=1; i<=5; i++ )
      printf( "%d\n", StaticFunc() );

   return 0;
}


int    StaticFunc( void )
{
   static int  myStatic = 0;

   return myStatic++;
}
```

11.05 - treePrinter _____ treePrinter.h

```
/***********/
/* Defines */
/***********/
#define kNumbersFileName        "treePrinter numbers"


/**********************/
/* Struct Declarations */
/**********************/
struct Node
{
   int              number;
```

```
        struct Node    *left, *right;
    };


    /**********************/
    /* Global Declarations */
    /**********************/
     extern struct Node      *gRootNodePtr;


    /******************************/
    /* Function Prototypes - main.c */
    /******************************/
    void  BuildTree( void );
    int     GetNumberFromFile( int *numPtr, FILE *fp );
    void  DoError( char *message );


    /******************************/
    /* Function Prototypes - tree.c */
    /******************************/
    void  AddNumberToTree( int num );
    void  AddNodeToTree( struct Node *newNodePtr, struct Node **curNodePtrPtr );
    void  DescendTreePreorder( struct Node *nodePtr );
    void  DescendTreeInorder( struct Node *nodePtr );
    void  DescendTreePostorder( struct Node *nodePtr );
    void  VisitNode( struct Node *nodePtr );
```

11.05 - treePrinter _____ main.c

```
#include <stdlib.h>
#include <stdio.h>
#include "treePrinter.h"


/**********************/
/* Global Definitions */
/**********************/
struct Node *gRootNodePtr;


/***************************************************> main <*/
int   main( void )
{
   gRootNodePtr = NULL;
```

```
   BuildTree();

   printf( "Preorder:   " );
   DescendTreePreorder( gRootNodePtr );

   printf( "\nInorder:    " );
   DescendTreeInorder( gRootNodePtr );

   printf( "\nPostorder: " );
   DescendTreePostorder( gRootNodePtr );

   printf( "\n\nGoodbye..." );

   return 0;
}


/*****************************************> BuildTree <*/
void  BuildTree( void )
{
   int      num;
   FILE  *fp;

   if ( ( fp = fopen( kNumbersFileName, "r" ) ) == NULL )
      DoError( "Could not read numbers file!\n" );

   printf( "Numbers:    " );

   while ( GetNumberFromFile( &num, fp ) )
   {
      printf( "%d, ", num );
      AddNumberToTree( num );
   }

   printf( "\n-------\n" );

   fclose( fp );
}


/*********************************> GetNumberFromFile <*/
int   GetNumberFromFile( int *numPtr, FILE *fp )
{
   if ( fscanf( fp, "%d\n", numPtr ) == EOF )
      return false;
   else
      return true;
```

```
   }


/****************************************> DoError <*/
void  DoError( char *message )
{
   printf( "%s\n", message );
   exit( 0 );
}
```

11.05 - treePrinter _____ tree.c

```
#include <stdlib.h>
#include <stdio.h>
#include "treePrinter.h"


/*********************************> AddNumberToTree <*/
void  AddNumberToTree( int num )
{
   struct Node *nodePtr;

   nodePtr = malloc( sizeof( struct Node ) );

   if ( nodePtr == NULL )
      DoError( "Could not allocate memory!\n" );

   nodePtr->number = num;
   nodePtr->left = NULL;
   nodePtr->right = NULL;

   AddNodeToTree( nodePtr, &gRootNodePtr );
}


/*********************************> AddNodeToTree <*/
void  AddNodeToTree( struct Node *newNodePtr, struct Node **curNodePtrPtr )
/*
   This recursive function inserts a new tree node (pointed to by newNodePtr)
   into the subtree pointed to by the pointer pointed to by curNodePtr. We use
   two levels of pointer here so we can change the value of the pointer passed
   in. See the call to AddNodeToTree a few lines up.

   Here's the algorithm: AddNodeToTree first checks to see if *curNodePtrPtr
   is NULL. If so, this is where the new node belongs: *curNodePtrPtr is
   set to point to the new node and we are done.

   If not, we'll check the node *curNodePtrPtr does point to and repeat the
```

```
         search in either the left or right child, depending on whether the new
         number being added to the tree is less than or greater than/equal to the
         current node.

         To help with the notation, think of:

             *curNodePtrPtr

         as equivalent to

             gRootNodePtr
*/
{
   if ( *curNodePtrPtr == NULL )
       *curNodePtrPtr = newNodePtr;
   else if ( newNodePtr->number < (*curNodePtrPtr)->number )
       AddNodeToTree( newNodePtr, &( (*curNodePtrPtr)->left ) );
   else
       AddNodeToTree( newNodePtr, &( (*curNodePtrPtr)->right ) );
}


/**********************************> DescendTreePreorder <*/
void  DescendTreePreorder( struct Node *nodePtr )
{
   if ( nodePtr == NULL )
       return;

   VisitNode( nodePtr );
   DescendTreePreorder( nodePtr->left );
   DescendTreePreorder( nodePtr->right );
}


/**********************************> DescendTreeInorder <*/
void  DescendTreeInorder( struct Node *nodePtr )
{
   if ( nodePtr == NULL )
       return;

   DescendTreePreorder( nodePtr->left );
   VisitNode( nodePtr );
   DescendTreePreorder( nodePtr->right );
}


/**********************************> DescendTreePostorder <*/
```

```
void  DescendTreePostorder( struct Node *nodePtr )
{
   if ( nodePtr == NULL )
      return;

   DescendTreePreorder( nodePtr->left );
   DescendTreePreorder( nodePtr->right );
   VisitNode( nodePtr );
}



/********************************> VisitNode <*/
void  VisitNode( struct Node *nodePtr )
{
   printf( "%d, ", nodePtr->number );
}
```

12.01 - windowMaker _____ windowMaker.c

```
/*************************************************/
/*                                               */
/*   WindowMaker Code from Chapter 12 of         */
/*                                               */
/*      *** Learn C on the Macintosh ***         */
/*                                               */
/* Copyright 1995, Dave Mark, All Rights Reserved */
/*                                               */
/*************************************************/


#include <limits.h>


#define   kMoveToFront        (WindowPtr)-1L
#define kSleep                LONG_MAX
#define   kLeaveWhereItIs     false

#define mApple                128
#define iAbout                1

#define mFile                 129
#define iNew                  1
#define iClose                2
#define iQuit                 4

#define mEdit                 130

#define kPICTResID            128
```

```
#define  kAboutAlertResID       128
#define  kWINDResID             128
#define  kAppleMenuResID        128
#define  kMBARResID             128
#define  kErrorAlertResID       129

#define  kErrorStrNoMBAR        128
#define  kErrorStrNoMENU        129
#define  kErrorStrNoPICT        130
#define  kErrorStrNoWIND        131

#define  kWindowHomeLeft        5
#define  kWindowHomeTop         45
#define  kNewWindowOffset       20
#define  kRightEdgeThreshold    200
#define  kBottomEdgeThreshold   200

#define    kFatalErrorString    "\pGame over, man!"

void    ToolBoxInit( void );
void    MenuBarInit( void );
void    EventLoop( void );
void    DoEvent( EventRecord *eventPtr );
void    HandleMouseDown( EventRecord *eventPtr );
void    HandleMenuChoice( long menuChoice );
void    HandleAppleChoice( short theItem );
void    HandleFileChoice( short theItem );
void    CreateWindow( void );
void    DoUpdate( EventRecord *eventPtr );
void    DrawMyPicture( PicHandle pic, WindowPtr window );
void    CenterPict( PicHandle picture, Rect *srcRectPtr, Rect *destRectPtr );
void    ErrorHandler( short stringNum );


Boolean        gDone;
short       gNewWindowLeft = kWindowHomeLeft, gNewWindowTop = kWindowHomeTop;


/***************************** main *********/

int     main( void )
{
   ToolBoxInit();
   MenuBarInit();

   EventLoop();

   return 0;
```

```
    }


/******************************** ToolBoxInit */

void  ToolBoxInit( void )
{
   InitGraf( &qd.thePort );
   InitFonts();
   InitWindows();
   InitMenus();
   TEInit();
   InitDialogs( 0L );
   InitCursor();
}


/********************************        MenuBarInit    */

void  MenuBarInit( void )
{
   Handle      myMenuBar;
   MenuHandle  menu;

   if ( ( myMenuBar = GetNewMBar( kMBARResID ) ) == NULL )
      ErrorHandler( kErrorStrNoMBAR );

   SetMenuBar( myMenuBar );

   if ( ( menu = GetMHandle( kAppleMenuResID ) ) == NULL )
      ErrorHandler( kErrorStrNoMENU );

   AddResMenu( menu, 'DRVR' );
   DrawMenuBar();
}


/****************************** EventLoop ********/

void  EventLoop( void )
{
   EventRecord    event;

   gDone = false;
   while ( gDone == false )
   {
      if ( WaitNextEvent( everyEvent, &event, kSleep, nil ) )
```

```
        DoEvent( &event );
    }
}


/*********************************** DoEvent     */

void  DoEvent( EventRecord *eventPtr )
{
    char  theChar;

    switch ( eventPtr->what )
    {
        case mouseDown:
            HandleMouseDown( eventPtr );
            break;
        case updateEvt:
            DoUpdate( eventPtr );
            break;
        case keyDown:
        case autoKey:
            theChar = eventPtr->message & charCodeMask;
            if ( (eventPtr->modifiers & cmdKey) != 0 )
                HandleMenuChoice( MenuKey( theChar ) );
            break;
    }
}


/*********************************** HandleMouseDown */

void  HandleMouseDown( EventRecord *eventPtr )
{
  WindowPtr    window;
  short      part;
  long int  menuChoice, windSize;

    part = FindWindow( eventPtr->where, &window );

    switch ( part )
    {
        case inMenuBar:
            menuChoice = MenuSelect( eventPtr->where );
            HandleMenuChoice( menuChoice );
            break;
        case inSysWindow:
            SystemClick( eventPtr, window );
            break;
        case inDrag:
```

```
                    DragWindow( window, eventPtr->where, &qd.screenBits.bounds );
                    break;
                case inGoAway:
                    if ( TrackGoAway( window, eventPtr->where ) )
                        DisposeWindow( window );
                    break;
                case inContent:
                    SelectWindow( window );
                    break;
            }
    }


/************************************** HandleMenuChoice */

void  HandleMenuChoice( long menuChoice )
{
    short theMenu;
    short theItem;

    if ( menuChoice != 0 )
    {
        theMenu = HiWord( menuChoice );
        theItem = LoWord( menuChoice );
        switch ( theMenu )
        {
            case mApple:
                HandleAppleChoice( theItem );
                break;
            case mFile:
                HandleFileChoice( theItem );
                break;
        }
        HiliteMenu( 0 );
    }
}


/******************************** 	HandleAppleChoice   *******/

void  HandleAppleChoice( short item )
{
    MenuHandle   appleMenu;
    Str255       accName;
    short     accNumber;

    switch ( item )
    {
```

```
      case iAbout :
         NoteAlert( kAboutAlertResID, NULL );
         break;
      default:
         appleMenu = GetMHandle( mApple );
         GetItem( appleMenu, item, accName );
         accNumber = OpenDeskAcc( accName );
         break;
   }
}


/******************************    HandleFileChoice    *******/

void  HandleFileChoice( short item )
{
   WindowPtr   window;

   switch ( item )
   {
      case iNew :
         CreateWindow();
         break;
      case iClose :
         if ( ( window = FrontWindow() ) != NULL )
            DisposeWindow( window );
         break;
      case iQuit :
         gDone = TRUE;
         break;
   }
}


/********************************** CreateWindow  */

void  CreateWindow( void )
{
   WindowPtr   window;

   if ( ( window = GetNewWindow( kWINDResID, NULL,
            kMoveToFront ) ) == NULL )
      ErrorHandler( kErrorStrNoWIND );

   if ( ( (qd.screenBits.bounds.right - gNewWindowLeft) < kRightEdgeThreshold ) ||
       ( ( qd.screenBits.bounds.bottom - gNewWindowTop) < kBottomEdgeThreshold ) )
   {
```

```
        gNewWindowLeft = kWindowHomeLeft;
        gNewWindowTop = kWindowHomeTop;
    }

    MoveWindow( window, gNewWindowLeft, gNewWindowTop, kLeaveWhereItIs );
    gNewWindowLeft += kNewWindowOffset;
    gNewWindowTop += kNewWindowOffset;

    ShowWindow( window );
}


/*********************************** DoUpdate     */

void  DoUpdate( EventRecord *eventPtr )
{
    short     pictureID;
    PicHandle     picture;
    WindowPtr     window;

    window = (WindowPtr)eventPtr->message;

    BeginUpdate( window );

    picture = GetPicture( kPICTResID );

    if ( picture == NULL )
        ErrorHandler( kErrorStrNoPICT );

    DrawMyPicture( picture, window );

    EndUpdate( window );
}


/******************************** DrawMyPicture *********/

void  DrawMyPicture( PicHandle pic, WindowPtr window )
{
    Rect   myRect;

    CenterPict( pic, &window->portRect, &myRect );

    SetPort( window );

    DrawPicture( pic, &myRect );
}
```

```
/***************** CenterPict *****************/

void  CenterPict( PicHandle picture, Rect *srcRectPtr, Rect *destRectPtr )
{
   Rect  pictRect;

   pictRect = (**( picture )).picFrame;

   OffsetRect( &pictRect, srcRectPtr->left - pictRect.left,
                       srcRectPtr->top - pictRect.top);
   OffsetRect( &pictRect,(srcRectPtr->right - pictRect.right)/2,
                    (srcRectPtr->bottom - pictRect.bottom)/2);

   *destRectPtr = pictRect;
}


/***************************** ErrorHandler *********/

void  ErrorHandler( short stringNum )
{
   StringHandle   errorStringH;

   if ( ( errorStringH = GetString( stringNum ) ) == NULL )
      ParamText( kFatalErrorString, "\p", "\p", "\p" );
   else
   {
      HLock( (Handle)errorStringH );
      ParamText( *errorStringH, "\p", "\p", "\p" );
      HUnlock( (Handle)errorStringH );
   }
   StopAlert( kErrorAlertResID, NULL );
   ExitToShell();
}
```

CSyntax Summary

The if Statement _____

syntax:

```
if ( expression )
      statement
```

example:

```
if ( numEmployees > 20 )
      BuyNewBuilding();
```

alternate syntax:

```
if ( expression )
      statement
else
      statement
```

example:

```
if ( temperature < 60 )
      WearAJacket();
else
      BringASweater();
```

The while Statement _____

syntax:

```
while ( expression )
      statement
```

example:

```
while ( FireTooLow() )
        AddAnotherLog();
```

The for Statement

syntax:

```
for ( expression1 ; expression2 ; expression3 )
        statement
```

example:

```
int   i, myArray[ 100 ];

for ( i=0; i<100; i++ )
      myArray[ i ] = 0;
```

The do Statement

syntax:

```
do
    statement
while ( expression ) ;
```

example:

```
do
      CallMeAtLeastOnce();
while ( KeepGoing() ) ;
```

The switch Statement

syntax:

```
switch ( expression )
{
      case constant:
            statements
```

```
    case constant:
        statements
    default:
        statements
}
```

example:

```
switch ( theYear )
{
    case 1066:
        printf( "Battle of Hastings" );
        break;
    case 1492:
        printf( "Columbus sailed the ocean blue" );
        break;
    case 1776:
        printf( "Declaration of Independence\n" );
        printf( "A very important document!!!" );
        break;
    default:
        printf( "Don't know what happened during this year"
);
}
```

The break Statement _____

syntax:

```
break;
```

example:

```
i=1;

while ( i <= 9 )
{
    PlayAnInning( i );
    if ( ItsRaining() )
            break;
    i++;
}
```

The return Statement _____

syntax:

```
return;
```

example:

```
if ( FatalError() )
      return;
```

alternate syntax:

```
return( expression );
```

example:

```
int   AddThese( int num1, int num2 )
{
      return( num1 + num2 );
}
```

Selections from the Standard Library

This appendix contains excerpts reprinted from the *C Library Reference* found on the CodeWarrior disk and is being reprinted with permission from MetroWerks. This is only part of the *C Library Reference* so make sure you check out the original.

atof(), atoi(), atol()

Purpose	Convert a character string to a numeric value.
Synopsis	`#include <stdlib.h>`
	`double atof(const char *nptr);`
	`int atoi(const char *nptr);`
	`long int atol(const char *nptr);`
Remarks	The `atof()` function converts the character array pointed to by `nptr` to a floating point value of type double.
	The `atoi()` function converts the character array pointed to by `nptr` to an integer value.
	The `atol()` function converts the character array pointed to by `nptr` to an integer of type `long int`.
	All three functions skip leading white space characters.
	All three functions set the global variable `errno` to `ERANGE` if the converted value cannot be expressed in their respective type.
Return value	`atof()` returns a floating point value of type double.
	`atoi()` returns an integer value of type int.
	`atol()` returns an integer value of type `long int`.
See also	`errno.h`
	`stdio.h:` `scanf()`

bsearch()

Purpose	Efficient sorted array searching.
Synopsis	`#include <stdlib.h>`
	`void *bsearch(const void *key,`

```
                                    const void *base,
                                    size_t nmemb,
                                    size_t size,
                                    int (*compare)
                                    (const void *,
                                    const void *))
```

Remarks   The bsearch() function efficiently searches a sorted array for an
            item using the binary search algorithm.
            The key argument points to the item to search for.
            The base argument points to the first byte of the array to search.
            The array must already be sorted in ascending order based on the
            comparison requirements of the function pointed to by the com-
            pare argument.
            The nmemb argument specifies the number of array elements to
            search.
            The size argument specifies the size of an array element.
            The compare argument points to a programmer-supplied function
            that takes two pointers to different array elements and compares
            them based on the key. If the two elements are equal, compare
            must return a zero. The compare function must return a negative
            value if the first element is less than the second. Likewise, the func-
            tion must return a positive value if the first argument is greater
            than the second.

Return value bsearch() returns a pointer to the element in the array matching
            the item pointed to by key. If no match was found, bsearch()
            returns a null pointer (NULL).

See also stdlib.h: qsort()

---

exit() _____

Purpose   Terminate a program normally.
Synopsis #include <stdlib.h>
            void exit(int status);
Remark   The exit() function calls every function installed with atexit()
            in the reverse order of their installation, flushes the buffers and
            closes all open streams, then calls the Toolbox system call
            ExitToShell.
Return value exit() does not return any value to the operating system. The
            status argument is kept to conform to the ANSI C Standard Library
            specification.
See also stdlib.h: abort(), atexit()

fclose() _____

Purpose	Close an open file.
Synopsis	`#include <stdio.h>` `int fclose(FILE *stream);`
Remarks	The `fclose()` function closes a file created by `fopen()`, `freopen()`, or `tmpfile()`. The function flushes any buffered data to its file and closes the stream. After calling `fclose()`, stream is no longer valid and cannot be used with file functions unless it is reassigned using `fopen()`, `freopen()`, or `tmpfile()`. All of a program's open streams are flushed and closed when a program terminates normally. `fclose()` closes then deletes a file created by `tmpfile()`.
Return value	`fclose()` returns a zero if it is successful and returns a -1 if it fails to close a file.
See also	`stdio.h:  fopen(), freopen(), tmpfile()` `stdlib.h:  exit(), abort()`

feof() _____

Purpose	Check the end-of-file status of a stream.
Synopsis	`#include <stdio.h>` `int feof(FILE *stream);`
Remarks	The `feof()` function checks the end-of-file status of the last read operation on stream. The function does not reset the end-of-file status.
Return value	`feof()` returns a nonzero value if the stream is at the end-of-file and return zero if the stream is not at the end-of-file.
See also	`stdio.h:  clearerr(), ferror()`

ferror() _____

Purpose	Check the error status of a stream.
Synopsis	`#include <stdio.h>` `int ferror (FILE *stream);`
Remarks	The `ferror()` function returns the error status of the last read or write operation on stream. The function does not reset its error status.
Return value	`ferror()` returns a nonzero value if stream's error status is on, and returns zero if stream's error status is off.
See also	`stdio.h:  clearerr(), feof()`

fflush()

Purpose	Empty a stream's buffer to its file.
Synopsis	`#include <stdio.h>`
	`int fflush(FILE *stream);`
Remarks	The `fflush()` function empties stream's buffer to the file associated with stream.
Return value	`fflush()` returns a nonzero value if it is unsuccessful and returns zero if it is successful.
See also	`stdio.h:  setvbuf()`

fgetc()

Purpose	Read the next character from a stream.
Synopsis	`#include <stdio.h>`
	`int fgetc(FILE *stream);`
Remarks	The `fgetc()` function reads the next character from stream and advances its file position indicator.
Return value	`fgetc()` returns the character as an `int`. If the end-of-file has been reached, `fgetc()` returns `EOF`.
See also	`stdio.h: getc(), getchar()`

fgetpos()

Purpose	Get a stream's current file position indicator value.
Synopsis	`#include <stdio.h>`
	`int fgetpos(FILE *stream,`
	`            fpos_t *pos);`
Remarks	The `fgetpos()` function is used in conjunction with the `fsetpos()` function to allow random access to a file. The `fgetpos()` function gives unreliable results when used with streams associated with a console (`stdin, stderr, stdout`).
	While the `fseek()` and `ftell()` functions use long integers to read and set the file position indicator, `fgetpos()` and `fsetpos()` use `fpos_t` values to operate on larger files. The `fpos_t` type, defined in `stdio.h`, can hold file position indicator values that do not fit in a `long int`.
	The `fgetpos()` function stores the current value of the file position indicator for stream in the `fpos_t` variable pos points to.

Return value   `fgetpos()` returns zero when successful and returns a nonzero value when it fails.

See also   `stdio.h:  fseek(), fsetpos(), ftell()`

fgets() ───

Purpose   Read a character array from a stream.

Synopsis   `#include <stdio.h>`
```
char *fgets(char *s, int n,
                FILE *stream);
```

Remarks   The `fgets()` function reads characters sequentially from stream beginning at the current file position, and assembles them into s as a character array. The function stops reading characters when n characters have been read. The `fgets()` function finishes reading prematurely if it reaches a newline (`'\n'`) character or the end-of-file. Unlike the `gets()` function, `fgets()` appends the newline character (`'\n'`) to s. It also null terminates the character array.

Return value   `fgets()` returns a pointer to s if it is successful. If it reaches the end-of-file before reading any characters, s is untouched and `fgets()` returns a null pointer (`NULL`). If an error occurs `fgets()` returns a null pointer and the contents of s may be corrupted.

See also   `stdio.h:  gets(), fprintf(), printf()`

fopen() ───

Purpose   Open a file as a stream.

Synopsis   `#include <stdio.h>`
```
FILE *fopen(const char *filename,
                const char *mode);
```

Remarks   The `fopen()` function opens a file specified by filename, and associates a stream with it. The `fopen()` function returns a pointer to a `FILE`. This pointer is used to refer to the file when performing I/O operations.

The mode argument specifies how the file is to be used. Table 7 describes the values for mode. A file opened with an update mode (`"+"`) is buffered, so it cannot be written to and then read from (or vice versa) unless the read and write operations are separated by an operation that flushes the stream's buffer or the last read or write reached the end-of-file. The `fseek()`, `fsetpos()`, `rewind()`, and `fflush()` functions flush a stream's buffer.

All file modes, except the append modes ("a", "a+", "ab", "ab+"), set the file position indicator to the beginning of the file. The append modes set the file position indicator to the end-of-file.

Return value   fopen( ) returns a pointer to a FILE if it successfully opens the specified file for the specified operation. fopen( ) returns a null pointer (NULL) when it is not successful.

See also   stdio.h: fclose( )

fprintf( )

Purpose   Send formatted text to a stream.

Synopsis   #include <stdio.h>
               int fprintf(FILE *stream,
                              const char *format, ...);

Remarks   The fprintf( ) function writes formatted text to stream and advances the file position indicator. Its operation is the same as printf( ) with the addition of the stream argument. Refer to the description of printf( ).

Return value fprintf( ) returns the number of arguments written or a negative number if an error occurs.

See also   stdio.h: printf( ), sprintf( ), vfprintf( ),
               vprintf( ), vsprintf( )

fputc( )

Purpose   Write a character to a stream.

Synopsis   #include <stdio.h>
               int fputc(int c, FILE *stream);

Remarks   The fputc( ) function writes character c to stream and advances stream's file position indicator. Although the c argument is an int, it is converted to a char before being written to stream. fputc( ) is written as a function, not as a macro.

Return value fputc( ) returns the character written if it is successful, and returns EOF if it fails.

See also   stdio.h: putc( ), putchar( )

fputs( )

Purpose   Write a character array to a stream.

Synopsis   #include <stdio.h>
               int fputs(const char *s,
                              FILE *stream);

Remarks   The fputs() function writes the array pointed to by s to stream and advances the file position indicator. The function writes all characters in s up to, but not including, the terminating null character. Unlike puts(), fputs() does not terminate the output of s with a newline ('\n').

Return value fputs() returns a zero if successful, and returns a nonzero value when it fails.

See also   stdio.h: puts()

fread()

Purpose   Read binary data from a stream.

Synopsis   ```
#include <stdio.h>
size_t fread(void *ptr,
                        size_t size,
                        size_t nmemb,
                        FILE *stream);
```

*Remarks*     The fread() function reads a block of binary or text data and updates the file position indicator. The data read from stream are stored in the array pointed to by ptr. The size and nmemb arguments describe the size of each item and the number of items to read, respectively.

The fread() function reads nmemb items unless it reaches the end-of-file or a read error occurs.

*Return value*  fread() returns the number of items read successfully.

*See also*      stdio.h:  fgets(), fwrite()

## free()

*Purpose*     Release previously allocated memory to heap.

*Synopsis*    ```
#include <stdlib.h>
void free(void *ptr);
```

Remarkss   The free() function releases a previously allocated memory block, pointed to by ptr, to the heap. The ptr argument should hold an address returned by the memory allocation functions calloc(), malloc(), or realloc(). Once the memory block ptr points to has been released, it is no longer valid. The ptr variable should not be used to reference memory again until it is assigned a value from the memory allocation functions.

See also   stdlib.h: calloc(), malloc(), realloc()
              Refer to the example for calloc()

freopen() _____

Purpose	Redirect a stream to another file.
Synopsis	`#include <stdio.h>`
	`FILE *freopen(const char *filename,`
	`                      const char *mode,`
	`                      FILE *stream);`
Remarks	The `freopen()` function changes the file stream associated with another file. The function first closes the file the stream is associated with, and opens the new file, filename, with the specified mode, using the same stream.
Return value	`fopen()` returns the value of stream, if it is successful. If `fopen()` fails it returns a null pointer (NULL).
See also	`stdio.h:  fopen()`

fscanf() _____

Purpose	Read formatted text from a stream.
Synopsis	`#include <stdio.h>`
	`int fscanf(FILE *stream,`
	`                      const char *format, ...);`
Remarks	The `fscanf()` function reads programmer-defined, formatted text from stream. The function operates identically to the `scanf()` function with the addition of the stream argument indicating the stream to read from. Refer to the `scanf()` function description.
Return value	`fscanf()` returns the number of items read. If there is an error in reading data that is inconsistent with the format string, `fscanf()` sets `errno` to a nonzero value. `fscanf()` returns EOF if it reaches the end-of-file.
See also	`errno.h`
	`stdio.h:  scanf()`

fseek() _____

Purpose	Move the file position indicator.
Synopsis	`#include <stdio.h>`
	`int fseek(FILE *stream,`
	`                      long offset,`
	`                      int whence);`
Remarks	The `fseek()` function moves the file position indicator to allow random access to a file.

The function moves the file position indicator either absolutely or relatively. The whence argument can be one of three values defined in `stdio.h`: SEEK_SET, SEEK_CUR, SEEK_END.

The SEEK_SET value causes the file position indicator to be set offset bytes from the beginning of the file. In this case offset must be equal or greater than zero.

The SEEK_CUR value causes the file position indicator to be set offset bytes from its current position. The offset argument can be a negative or positive value.

The SEEK_END value causes the file position indicator to be set offset bytes from the end of the file. The offset argument must be equal or less than zero.

The `fseek()` function undoes the last `ungetc()` call and clears the end-of-file status of stream.

Return value `fseek()` returns zero if it is successful and returns a nonzero value if it fails.

See also stdio.h: fgetpos(), fsetpos(), ftell()

fsetpos()

Purpose Set the file position indicator.

Synopsis
```
#include <stdio.h>
int fsetpos(FILE *stream,
                    const fpos_t *pos);
```

Remarks The `fsetpos()` function sets the file position indicator for stream using the value pointed to by pos. The function is used in conjunction with `fgetpos()` when dealing with files having sizes greater than what can be represented by the long int argument used by `fseek()`.

`fsetpos()` undoes the previous call to `ungetc()` and clears the end-of-file status.

Return value `fsetpos()` returns zero if it is successful and returns a nonzero value if it fails.

See also stdio.h: fgetpos(), fseek(), ftell()

ftell()

Purpose Return the current file position indicator value.

Synopsis
```
#include <stdio.h>
long int ftell(FILE *stream);
```

Remarks   The `ftell()` function returns the current value of stream's file position indicator. It is used in conjunction with `fseek()` to provide random access to a file.

The function will not work correctly when it is given a stream associated to a console file, such as `stdin`, `stdout`, or `stderr`, where a file indicator position is not applicable. Also, `ftell()` cannot handle files with sizes larger than what can be represented with a `long int`. In such a case, use the `fgetpos()` and `fsetpos()` functions.

Return value `ftell()`, when successful, returns the current file position indicator value. If it fails, `ftell()` returns –1L and sets the global variable `errno` to a nonzero value.

See also   `errno.h`
          `stdio.h: fgetpos()`

fwrite()

Purpose   Write binary data to a stream.
Synopsis   `#include <stdio.h>`
          ```
          size_t fwrite(const void *ptr,
                        size_t size,
                        size_t nmemb,
                        FILE *stream);
          ```
Remarks   The `fwrite()` function writes `nmemb` items of `size` bytes each to stream. The items are contained in the array pointed to by `ptr`. After writing the array to stream, `fwrite()` advances the file position indicator accordingly.

Return value `fwrite()` returns the number of elements successfully written to stream.

See also   `stdio.h:  fread()`

getc()

Purpose   Read the next character from a stream.
Synopsis   `#include <stdio.h>`
          `int getc(FILE *stream);`
Remarks   The `getc()` function reads the next character from stream, advances the file position indicator, and returns the character as an `int` value. Unlike the `fgetc()` function, `getc()` is implemented as a macro.

Return value	getc() returns the next character from the stream or returns EOF if the end-of-file has been reached or a read error has occurred.
See also	stdio.h: fgetc(), fputc(), getchar(), putchar()

getchar() ———————————————————————

Purpose	Get the next character from stdin.
Synopsis	#include <stdio.h> int getchar(void);
Remarks	The getchar() function reads a character from the stdin stream.
Return value	getchar() returns the value of the next character from stdin as an int if it is successful. getchar() returns EOF if it reaches an end-of-file or an error occurs.
See also:	stdio.h: fgetc(), getc(), putchar()

gets() ———————————————————————

Purpose	Read a character array from stdin.
Synopsis	#include <stdio.h> char *gets(char *s);
Remarks	The gets() function reads characters from stdin and stores them sequentially in the character array pointed to by s. Characters are read until either a newline or an end-of-file is reached. Unlike fgets(), the programmer cannot specify a limit on the number of characters to read. Also, gets() reads and ignores the newline character ('\n') so that it can advance the file position indicator to the next line. The newline character is not stored s. Like fgets(), gets() terminates the character string with a null character. If an end-of-file is reached before any characters are read, gets() returns a null pointer (NULL) without affecting the character array at s. If a read error occurs, the contents of s may be corrupted.
Return value	gets() returns s if it is successful and returns a null pointer if it fails.
See also	stdio.h: fgets()

malloc() ———————————————————————

Purpose	Allocate a block of heap memory.
Synopsis	#include <stdlib.h> void *malloc(size_t size);

Remarks   The `malloc()` function allocates a block of contiguous heap memory-size bytes.

Return value `malloc()` returns a pointer to the first byte of the allocated block if it is successful and returns a null pointer if it fails.

See also   `stdlib.h:  calloc(), free(), realloc()`

memchr()

Purpose   Search for an occurrence of a character.

Synopsis
```
#include <string.h>
void *memchr(const void *s, int c,
                            size_t n);
```

Remarks   The `memchr()` function looks for the first occurrence of c in the first n characters of the memory area pointed to by s.

Return value `memchr()` returns a pointer to the found character, or a null pointer (`NULL`) if c cannot be found.

See also   `string.h:  strchr(), strrchr()`

memcmp()

Purpose   Compare two blocks of memory.

Synopsis
```
#include <string.h>
int memcmp(const void *s1,
                       const void *s2,
                       size_t n);
```

Remarks   The `memcmp()` function compares the first n characters of s1 to s2 one character at a time.

Return value `memcmp()` returns a zero if all n characters pointed to by s1 and s2 are equal.

`memcmp()` returns a negative value if the first nonmatching character pointed to by s1 is less than the character pointed to by s2.

`memcmp()` returns a positive value if the first nonmatching character pointed to by s1 is greater than the character pointed to by s2.

See also   `string.h:  strcmp(), strncmp()`

memcpy()

Purpose   Copy a contiguous memory block.

Synopsis
```
#include <string.h>
void *memcpy(const void *dest,
```

```
                           const void *source,
                           size_t n);
```

Remarks The `memcpy()` function copies the first n characters from the item pointed to by source to the item pointed to by dest. The behavior of `memcpy()` is undefined if the areas pointed to by dest and source overlap. The `memmove()` function reliably copies overlapping memory blocks.

Return value `memcpy()` returns the value of dest.

See also `string.h:  memmove(),  strcpy(), strncpy()`
Refer to the example for `memchr()`.

memmove() _____

Purpose Copy an overlapping contiguous memory block.

Synopsis
```
#include <string.h>
void *memmove(void *dest,
                      const void *source,
                      size_t n);
```

Remarks The `memmove()` function copies the first n characters of the item pointed to by source to the item pointed to by dest.
Unlike `memcpy()`, the `memmove()` function safely copies overlapping memory blocks.

Return value `memmove()` returns the value of dest.

See also `string.h:  memcpy(), memset(), strcpy(), strncpy()`

perror() _____

Purpose Output an error message to stderr.

Synopsis
```
#include <stdio.h>
void perror(const char *s);
```

Remarks The `perror()` function outputs the character array pointed to by s and the value of the global variable errno to stderr.

See also `abort.h: abort()`
`errno.h`

printf() _____

Purpose Output formatted text.

Synopsis
```
#include <stdio.h>
int printf(const char *format,  ...);
```

Remarks   The `printf()` function outputs formatted text. The function takes one or more arguments, the first being format, a character array pointer. The optional arguments following format are items (integers, characters, floating point values, etc.) that are to be converted to character strings and inserted into the output of format at specified points.

The `printf()` function sends its output to `stdout`.

The format character array contains normal text and conversion specifications. Conversion specifications must have matching arguments in the same order in which they occur in format.

A conversion specification describes the format its associated argument is to be converted to. A specification starts with a percent sign (`%`), optional flag characters, an optional minimum width, an optional precision width, and the necessary, terminating conversion type. Doubling the percent sign (`%%`) results in the output of a single `%`.

An optional flag character modifies the formatting of the output; it can be left or right justified, and numerical values can be padded with zeroes or output in alternate forms. More than one optional flag character can be used in a conversion specification. Table 8 describes the flag characters.

The optional minimum width is a decimal digit string. If the converted value has more characters that the minimum width, it is expanded as required. If the converted value has fewer characters than the minimum width, it is, by default, right justified (padded on the left). If the `-` flag character is used, the converted value is left justified (padded on the right).

The optional precision width is a period character (`.`) followed by decimal digit string. For floating point values, the precision width specifies the number of digits to print after the decimal point. For integer values, the precision width functions identically to, and cancels, the minimum width specification. When used with a character array, the precision width indicates the maximum width of the output.

A minimum width and a precision width can also be specified with an asterisk (`*`) instead of a decimal digit string. An asterisk indicates that there is a matching argument, preceding the conversion argument, specifying the minimum width or precision width.

The terminating character, the conversion type, specifies the conversion applied to the conversion specification's matching argument. Table 9 describes the conversion type characters.

A conversion type can be prefixed with an h, l, or L. Using h indicates that the corresponding argument is a short int or unsigned short int. The l indicates the argument is a long int or unsigned long int. The L indicates the argument is a long double.

Return value   printf(), like fprintf(), sprintf(), vfprintf(), and vprintf(), returns the number of arguments that were successfully output. printf() returns a negative value if it fails.

See also   stdio.h: fprintf(), sprintf(), vprintf(), vprintf()

---

putc()

Purpose	Write a character to a stream.
Synopsis	#include <stdio.h>
	int putc(int c, FILE *stream);
Remarks	The putc() function outputs c to stream and advances stream's file position indicator.
	The putc() works identically to the fputc() function, except that it is written as a macro.
Return value	putc() returns the character written when successful and return EOF when it fails.
See also	stdio.h: fputc(), putchar()

---

putchar()

Purpose	Write a character to stdout.
Synopsis	#include <stdio.h>
	int putchar(int c);
Remarks	The putchar() function writes character c to stdout.
Return value	putchar() returns c if it is successful and returns EOF if it fails.
See also	stdio.h: fputc(), putc()

---

puts()

Purpose	Write a character string to stdout.
Synopsis	#include <stdio.h>
	int puts(const char *s);
Remarks	The puts() function writes a character string array to stdout, stopping at, but not including, the terminating null character. The function also appends a newline ('\n') to the output.

Return value   `puts()` returns zero if successful and returns a nonzero value if it fails.

See also   `stdio.h:  fputs()`

qsort()

Purpose   Sort an array.

Synopsis
```
#include <stdlib.h>
void qsort(void *base,
                   size_t nmemb,
                   size_t size,
                   int (*compare)
                   (const void *,
                   const void *))
```

Remarks   The `qsort()` function sorts an array using the quicksort algorithm. It sorts the array without displacing it; the array occupies the same memory it had before the call to `qsort()`.

The base argument is a pointer to the base of the array to be sorted. The `nmemb` argument specifies the number of array elements to sort.

The size argument specifies the size of an array element.

The compare argument is a pointer to a programmer-supplied compare function. The function takes two pointers to different array elements and compares them based on the key. If the two elements are equal, compare must return a zero. The compare function must return a negative number if the first element is less than the second. Likewise, the function must return a positive number if the first argument is greater than the second.

See also   `stdlib.h:  bsearch()`

rand()

Purpose   Generate a pseudo-random integer value.

Synopsis
```
#include <stdlib.h>
int rand(void);
```

Remarks   A sequence of calls to the `rand()` function generates and returns a sequence of pseudo-random integer values from 0 to RAND_MAX. The RAND_MAX macro is defined in `stdlib.h`.

By seeding the random number generator using srand(), different random number sequences can be generated with rand().

Return value rand() returns a pseudo-random integer value between 0 and RAND_MAX.

See also stdlib.h: srand()

---

remove() _____

Purpose Delete a file.

Synopsis #include <stdio.h>
int remove(const char *filename);

Remarks The remove() function deletes the named file specified by filename.

Return value remove() returns 0 if the file deletion is successful, and returns a nonzero value if it fails.

See also stdio.h: fopen(), rename()

---

rename() _____

Purpose Change the name of a file.

Synopsis #include <stdio.h>
int rename(const char *old,
                          const char *new);

Remarks The rename() function changes the name of a file, specified by old to the name specified by new.

Return value rename() returns a nonzero if it fails and returns zero if successful

See also stdio.h: freopen(), remove()

---

rewind() _____

Purpose Reset the file position indicator to the beginning of the file.

Synopsis #include <stdio.h>
void rewind(FILE *stream);

Remarks The rewind() function sets the file indicator position of stream such that the next write or read operation will be from the beginning of the file. It also undoes any previous call to ungetc() and clears stream's end-of-file and error status.

See also stdio.h: fseek(), fsetpos()

scanf() _____

Purpose   Read formatted text.

Synopsis
```
#include <stdio.h>
int scanf(const char *format,
                    ...);
```

Remarks   The `scanf()` function reads text and converts the text read to programmer specified types.

The format argument is a character array containing normal text,
white space (space, tab, newline), and conversion specifications.
The normal text specifies literal characters that must be matched in
the input stream. A white space character indicates that white space
characters are skipped until a non-white-space character is reached.
The conversion specifications indicate what characters in the input
stream are to be converted and stored.

The conversion specifications must have matching arguments in the
order they appear in format. Because `scanf()` stores data in memory, the matching conversion specification arguments must be
pointers to objects of the relevant types.

A conversion specification consists of the percent sign (`%`) prefix,
followed by an optional maximum width or assignment suppression, and ending with a conversion type. A percent sign can be
skipped by doubling it in format; `%%` signifies a single `%` in the input
stream.

An optional width is a decimal number specifying the maximum
width of an input field. `scanf()` will not read more characters for
a conversion than is specified by the width.

An optional assignment suppression character (`*`) can be used to
skip an item by reading it but not assigning it. A conversion specification with assignment suppression must not have a corresponding
argument.

The last character, the conversion type, specifies the kind of conversion requested. Table 10 describes the conversion type characters.
The conversion type may be preceded by u, U, l, or L. When used
with integer conversion types, u and U specify unsigned integers.
The l and L , when used with integer conversions, signify long
integers. When used with floating point conversions, l signifies a
double and L signifies a long double.

Return value scanf() returns the number of items successfully read and returns EOF if a conversion type does not match its argument or and end-of-file is reached.

See also stdio.h: printf(), sscanf()

setbuf()

Purpose Change the buffer size of a stream.

Synopsis
```
#include <stdio.h>
void setbuf(FILE *stream,
                         char *buf);
```

Remarks The setbuf() function allows the programmer to set the buffer size for stream. It should be called after stream is opened, but before it is read from or written to.

The function makes the array pointed to by buf the buffer used by stream. The buf argument can either be a null pointer or point to an array of size BUFSIZ, defined in stdio.h.

If buf is a null pointer, the stream becomes unbuffered.

See also stdio.h: setvbuf()
stdlib.h: malloc()

setvbuf()

Purpose Change the buffering scheme for a stream.

Synopsis
```
#include <stdio.h>
int setvbuf(FILE *stream,
                        char *buf,
                        int mode,
                        size_t size);
```

Remarks The setvbuf() allows the manipulation of the buffering scheme as well as the size of the buffer used by stream. The function should be called after the stream is opened but before it is written to or read from.

The buf argument is a pointer to a character array. The size argument indicates the size of the character array pointed to by buf. The most efficient buffer size is a multiple of BUFSIZ, defined in stdio.h.

If buf is a null pointer, then the operating system creates its own buffer of size bytes.

The mode argument specifies the buffering scheme to be used with stream. mode can have one of three values defined in stdio.h: _IOFBF, _IOLBF, and _IONBF.
_IOFBF specifies that stream be buffered.
_IOLBF specifies that stream be line buffered.
_IONBF specifies that stream be unbuffered.

Return value setvbuf() returns zero if it is successful and returns a nonzero value if it fails.

See also stdio.h: setbuf()
stdlib.h: malloc()

sprintf()

Purpose Format a character string array.

Synopsis
```
#include <stdio.h>
int sprintf(char *s,
            const char *format,
            ...);
```

Remarks The sprintf() function works identically to printf() with the addition of the s parameter. Output is stored in the character array pointed to by s instead of being sent to stdout. The function terminates the output character string with a null character.
For information on how to use sprintf() refer to the description of printf().

Return value sprintf() returns the number of characters assigned to s, not including the null character.

See also stdio.h: fprintf(), printf()

srand()

Purpose Set the pseudo-random number generator seed.

Synopsis
```
#include <stdlib.h>
void srand(unsigned int seed);
```

Remarks The srand() function sets the seed for the pseudo-random number generator to seed. Each seed value produces the same sequence of random numbers when it is used.

See also stdlib.h: rand()

sscanf() _____

Purpose	Read formatted text into a character string.

Synopsis	`#include <stdio.h>`
	`int sscanf(char *s,`
	       `const char *format,`
	       `...);`

Remarks	The `sscanf()` operates identically to `scanf()` but reads its input from the character array pointed to by s instead of `stdin`. The character array pointed to s must be `null terminated`. Refer to the description of `scanf()` for more information.
Return value	`scanf()` returns the number of items successfully read and converted and returns `EOF` if it reaches the end of the string or a conversion specification does not match its argument.
See also	`stdio.h:  fscanf(), scanf()`

strcat() _____

Purpose	Concatenate two character arrays.

Synopsis	`#include <string.h>`
	`char *strcat(char *dest,`
	       `const char *source);`

Remarks	The `strcat()` function appends a copy of the character array pointed to by source to the end of the character array pointed to by dest. The dest and source arguments must both point to `null terminated` character arrays. `strcat()` null terminates the resulting character array.
Return value	`strcat()` returns the value of dest.
See also	`string.h:  strncat()`

strchr() _____

Purpose	Search for an occurrence of a character.

Synopsis	`#include <string.h>`
	`char *strchr(const char *s,`
	       `int c);`

Remarks	The `strchr()` function searches for the first occurrence of the character c in the character array pointed to by s. The s argument must point to a `null terminated` character array.

Return value   `strchr()` returns a pointer to the successfully located character. If it fails, `strchr()` returns a null pointer (`NULL`).

See also   `string.h: memchr(), strrchr()`

strcmp()

Purpose   Compare two character arrays.

Synopsis
```
#include <string.h>
int strcmp(const char *s1,
        const char *s2);
```

Remarks   The `strcmp()` function compares the character array pointed to by `s1` to the character array pointed to by `s2`. Both `s1` and `s2` must point to null terminated character arrays.

Return value   `strcmp()` returns a zero if `s1` and `s2` are equal, a negative value if `s1` is less than `s2`, and a positive value if `s1` is greater than `s2`.

See also   `string.h: memcmp(), strcoll(), strncmp()`

strcpy()

Purpose   Copy one character array to another.

Synopsis
```
#include <string.h>
char *strcpy(char  *dest,
            const char *source);
```

Remarks   The `strcpy()` function copies the character array pointed to by `source` to the character array pointed to `dest`. The source argument must point to a null terminated character array. The resulting character array at `dest` is null terminated as well.

If the arrays pointed to by `dest` and `source` overlap, the operation of `strcpy()` is undefined.

Return value   `strcpy()` returns the value of `dest`.

See also   `string.h: memcpy(), memmove(), strncpy()`

strcoll()

Purpose   Compare two character arrays according to locale.

Synopsis
```
#include <string.h>
int strcoll(const char *s1,
            const char *s2);
```

Remarks   The `strcoll()` function compares two character arrays based on the collating sequence set by the `locale.h` header file.

The MetroWerks C implementation of `strcoll()` compares two character arrays using `strcmp()`. It is included in the string library to conform to the ANSI C Standard Library specification.

Return value   `strcoll()` returns zero if `s1` is equal to `s2`, a negative value if `s1` is less than `s2`, and a positive value if `s1` is greater than `s2`.

See also   `locale.h`
`string.h:   memcmp(), strcmp(), strncmp()`

strcspn()

Purpose   Count characters in one character array that are not in another.

Synopsis
```
#include <string.h>
size_t strcspn(const char *s1,
                        const char *s2);
```

Remarks   The `strcspn()` function counts the initial length of the character array pointed to by `s1` that does not contain characters in the character array pointed to by `s2`. The function starts counting characters at the beginning of `s1` and continues counting until a character in `s2` matches a character in `s1`.

Both `s1` and `s2` must point to null terminated character arrays.

Return value   `strcspn()` returns the length of characters in `s1` that does not match any characters in `s2`.

See also   `string.h:   strpbrk(), strspn()`

strerror()

Purpose   Return an error message in a character array.

Synopsis
```
#include <string.h>
char *strerror(int errnum);
```

Remarks   The `strerror()` function returns a pointer to a null terminated character array that contains an error message. The `errnum` argument has no effect on the message returned by `strerror()`; it is included to conform to the ANSI C Standard Library specification.

Return value   `strerror()` returns a pointer to a null terminated character array containing an error message.

strlen()

Purpose   Compute the length of a character array.

Synopsis
```
#include <string.h>
size_t strlen(const char *s);
```

Remarks   The `strlen()` function computes the number of characters in a null terminated character array pointed to by `s`. The null character (`'\0'`) is not added to the character count.

Return value `strlen()` returns the number of characters in a character array not including the terminating null character.

strncat()

Purpose   Append a specified number of characters to a character array.

Synopsis
```
#include <string.h>
char *strncat(char *dest,
              const char *source,
              size_t n);
```

Remarks   The `strncat()` function appends a maximum of n characters from the character array pointed to by source to the character array pointed to by `dest`. The `dest` argument must point to a null terminated character array. The source argument does not necessarily have to point to a null terminated character array.

If a null character is reached in source before n characters have been appended, `strncat()` stops.

When done, `strncat()` terminates `dest` with a null character (`'\0'`).

Return value `strncat()` returns the value of `dest`.

See also   `string.h:` `strcat()`

strncmp()

Purpose   Compare a specified number of characters.

Synopsis
```
#include <string.h>
int strncmp(const char *s1,
            const char *s2,
            size_t n);
```

Remarks   The `strncmp()` function compares n characters of the character array pointed to by `s1` to n characters of the character array pointed to by `s2`. Both `s1` and `s2` do not necessarily have to be null terminated character arrays.

The function stops prematurely if it reaches a null character before n characters have been compared.

Return value   `strncmp()` returns a zero if the first n characters of s1 and s2 are equal, a negative value if s1 is less than s2, and a positive value if s1 is greater than s2.

See also   `string.h:  memcmp(), strcmp()`

strncpy()

Purpose   Copy a specified number of characters.

Synopsis
```
#include <string.h>
char *strncpy(char *dest,
              const char *source,
              size_t n);
```

Remarks   The `strncpy()` function copies a maximum of n characters from the character array pointed to by `source` to the character array pointed to by `dest`. Neither `dest` nor `source` must necessarily point to null terminated character arrays. Also, `dest` and `source` must not overlap.

If a null character (`'\0'`) is reached in source before n characters have been copied, `strncpy()` continues padding `dest` with null characters until n characters have been added to `dest`.

The function does not terminate `dest` with a null character if n characters are copied from source before reaching a null character.

Return value   `strncpy()` returns the value of `dest`.

See also   `string.h:  memcpy(), memmove(), strcpy()`

strpbrk()

Purpose   Look for the first occurrence of an array of characters in another.

Synopsis
```
#include <string.h>
char *strpbrk(const char *s1,
              const char *s2);
```

Remarks   The `strpbrk()` function searches the character array pointed to by s1 for the first occurrence of a character in the character array pointed to by s2.

Both s1 and s2 must point to null terminated character arrays.

Return value   `strpbrk()` returns a pointer to the first character in s1 that matches any character in s2, and returns a null pointer (NULL) if no match was found.

See also   `string.h:  strcspn()`

strrchr() _____

Purpose	Search for the last occurrence of a character.

Synopsis	`#include <string.h>`
	`char *strrchr(const char *s,`
	                  `int c);`

Remarks	The `strrchr()` function searches for the last occurrence of `c` in the character array pointed to by `s`. The `s` argument must point to a null terminated character array.
Return value	`strrchr()` returns a pointer to the character found or returns a null pointer (`NULL`) if it fails.
See also	`string.h:  memchr(), strchr()`

strspn() _____

Purpose	Count characters in one character array that are in another.

Synopsis	`#include <string.h>`
	`size_t strspn(const char *s1,`
	               `const char *s2);`

Remarks	The `strspn()` function counts the initial number of characters in the character array pointed to by `s1` that contains characters in the character array pointed to by `s2`. The function starts counting characters at the beginning of `s1` and continues counting until it finds a character that is not in `s2`. Both `s1` and `s2` must point to null terminated character arrays.
Return value	`strcspn()` returns the number of characters in `s1` that matches the characters in `s2`.
See also	`string.h:  strpbrk(), strscpn()`

strstr() _____

Purpose	Search for a character array within another.

Synopsis	`#include <string.h>`
	`char *strstr(const char *s1,`
	               `const char *s2);`

Remarks	The `strstr()` function searches the character array pointed to by `s1` for the first occurrence of the character array pointed to by `s2`. Both `s1` and `s2` must point to null terminated (`'\0'`) character arrays.

Return value strstr() returns a pointer to the first occurrence of s2 in s1 and returns a null pointer (NULL) if s2 cannot be found.

See also string.h: memchr(), strchr()

strtok()

Purpose Extract tokens within a character array.

Synopsis
```
#include <string.h>
char *strtok(char *str,
                const char *sep);
```

Remarks The strtok() function tokenizes the character array pointed to by str. The sep argument points to a character array containing token separator characters. The tokens in str are extracted by successive calls to strtok().

The first call to strtok() causes it to search for the first character in str that does not occur in sep. The function returns a pointer to the beginning of this first token. If no such character can be found, strtok() returns a null pointer (NULL).

If, on the first call, strtok() finds a token, it searches for the next token.

The function searches by skipping characters in the token in str until a character in sep is found. This character is overwritten with a null character to terminate the token string, thereby modifying the character array contents. The function also keeps its own pointer to the character after the null character for the next token. Subsequent token searches continue in the same manner from the internal pointer.

Subsequent calls to strtok() with a NULL str argument cause it to return pointers to subsequent tokens in the original str character array. If no tokens exist, strtok() returns a null pointer. The sep argument can be different for each call to strtok().

Both str and sep must be null terminated character arrays.

Return value When first called strtok() returns a pointer to the first token in str or returns a null pointer if no token can be found.

Subsequent calls to strtok() with a NULL str argument causes strtok() to return a pointer to the next token or return a null pointer (NULL) when no more tokens exist.

strtok() modifies the character array pointed to by str.

tmpfile() _____

Purpose	Open a temporary file.
Synopsis	`#include <stdio.h>`
	`FILE *tmpfile(void);`
Remarks	The `tmpfile()` function creates and opens a binary file that is automatically removed when it is closed or when the program terminates.
Return value	`tmpfile()` returns a pointer to the `FILE` variable of the temporary file if it is successful. If it fails, `tmpfile()` returns a null pointer (`NULL`).
See also	`stdio.h:  fopen(), tmpnam()`

tmpnam() _____

Purpose	Create a unique temporary filename.
Synopsis	`#include <stdio.h>`
	`char *tmpnam(char *s);`
Remarks	The `tmpnam()` functions creates a valid filename character string that will not conflict with any existing filename. A program can call the function up to `TMP_MAX` times before exhausting the unique filenames `tmpnam()` generates. The `TMP_MAX` macro is defined in `stdio.h`.
	The `s` argument can either be a null pointer or pointer to a character array. The character array must be at least `L_tmpnam` characters long. The new temporary filename is placed in this array. The `L_tmpnam` macro is defined in `stdio.h`.
	If `s` is `NULL`, `tmpnam()` returns with a pointer to an internal static object that can be modified by the calling program.
	Unlike `tmpfile()`, a file created using a filename generated by the `tmpnam()` function is not automatically removed when it is closed.
Return value	`tmpnam()` returns a pointer to a character array containing a unique, nonconflicting filename. If `s` is a null pointer (`NULL`), the pointer refers to an internal static object. If `s` points to a character array, `tmpnam()` returns the same pointer.
See also	`stdio.h:  fopen(), tmpfile()`

tolower(), toupper()

Purpose	Character conversion macros.
Synopsis	`#include <ctype.h>`
	`int tolower(int c);`
	`int toupper(int c);`
Remarks	The `tolower()` macro converts an uppercase letter to its lowercase equivalent. Non-uppercase characters are returned unchanged. The `toupper()` macro converts a lowercase letter to its uppercase equivalent and returns all other characters unchanged.
Return value	`tolower()` returns the lowercase equivalent of uppercase letters and returns all other characters unchanged.
	`toupper()` returns the uppercase equivalent of a lowercase letter and returns all other characters unchanged.
See also	`ctype.h:  isalpha(), islower(), isupper()`

ungetc()

Purpose	Place a character back into a stream.
Synopsis	`#include <stdio.h>`
	`int ungetc(int c,`
	`        FILE *stream);`
Remarks	The `ungetc()` function places character c back into stream's buffer. The next read operation will read the character placed by `ungetc()`. Only one character can be pushed back into a buffer until a read operation is performed.
	The function's effect is ignored when an `fseek()`, `fsetpos()`, or `rewind()` operation is performed.
Return value	`ungetc()` returns c if it is successful and returns EOF if it fails.
See also	`stdio.c:  fseek(), fsetpos(), rewind()`

vfprintf()

Purpose	Write formatted output to a stream.
Synopsis	`#include <stdio.h>`
	`int vfprintf(FILE *stream,`
	`                const char *format, va_list arg);`
Remarks	The `vfprintf()` function works identically to the `fprintf()` function. Instead of the variable list of arguments that can be passed to `fprintf()`, `vfprintf()` accepts its arguments in the

array of type `va_list` processed by the `va_start()` macro from the `stdarg.h` header file.

Return value   `vfprintf()` returns the number of characters written or `EOF` if it failed.

See also   `stdio.h:` `fprintf()`, `printf()`
            `stdarg.h`

vprintf()

Purpose   Write formatted output to `stdout`.

Synopsis
```
#include <stdio.h>
int vprintf(const char *format,
        va_list arg);
```

Remarks   The `vprintf()` function works identically to the `printf()` function. Instead of the variable list of arguments that can be passed to `printf()`, `vprintf()` accepts its arguments in the array of type `va_list` processed by the `va_start()` macro from the `stdarg.h` header file.

Return value   `vprintf()` returns the number of characters written or a negative value if it failed.

See also   `stdio.h:` `fprintf()`, `printf()`
            `stdarg.h`

vsprintf()

Purpose   Write formatted output to a string.

Synopsis
```
#include <stdio.h>
int vsprintf(char *s,
            const char *format,
            va_list arg);
```

Remarks   The `vsprintf()` function works identically to the `sprintf()` function. Instead of the variable list of arguments that can be passed to `sprintf()`, `vsprintf()` accepts its arguments in the array of type `va_list` processed by the `va_start()` macro from the `stdarg.h` header file.

Return value   `vsprintf()` returns the number of characters written to `s` or `EOF` if it failed.

See also   `stdio.h:` `printf()`, `sprintf()`
            `stdarg.h`

About CodeWarrior . . .

Although you've spent a lot of time with CodeWarrior as you've made your way through these pages, you've only skimmed its surface. This appendix (written by Avi Rappoport, one of Metrowerks's finest!) offers a closer look at one of the leading Macintosh development environments.

Important

It's important to note that this appendix describes the commercial version of CodeWarrior, not the "Lite" version that came with the book. For example, CodeWarrior Lite will not allow you to create a new project, whereas the commercial version obviously does.

Using CodeWarrior

As you've seen throughout this book, CodeWarrior provides you with an integrated programming environment, including an editor, a project window, a compiler, and a linker. When you launch your program from within CodeWarrior, it runs as a separate application. Alternatively, the Metrowerks Debugger allows you to view and modify your variables as you step through your source code.

Projects

To write a program using CodeWarrior, you'll first need to create a project to store the source file names, preferences, and object code. Choose **New Project** from the **File** menu, and a dialog box will appear, allowing you to name your new project. A pop-up menu will appear at the bottom of the dialog, allowing you to select from a list of stationery that determine the files that are added to your new project. The projects in this book were all built using the stationery **~ANSI 68K (2i)C.µ** (ANSI library, 68K version of CodeWarrior, C language, and 2-byte `int`s). Figure E.1 shows the stationery for new 68K-based projects, and Figure E.2 shows the stationery for new PowerPC-based projects.

447

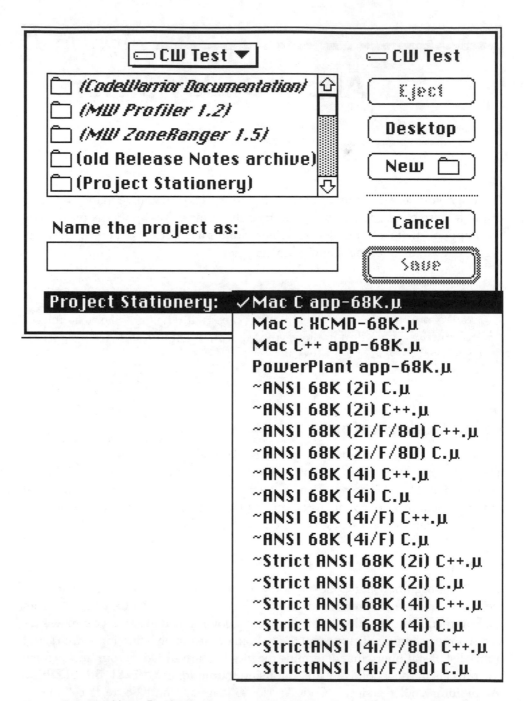

Figure E.1 The **New Project** dialog box showing the list of stationery available in the 68K version of CodeWarrior.

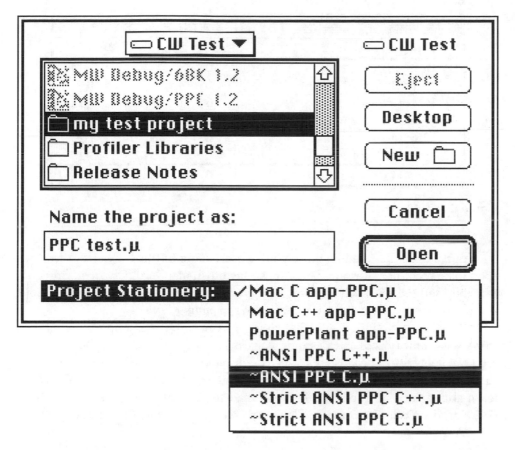

Figure E.2 The **New Project** dialog box showing the list of stationery available in the PowerPC version of CodeWarrior.

Stationery automatically sets the preferences and includes the correct libraries for your project. We have stationery for making both ANSI console applications and Macintosh graphical user interface applications. Once you name your new project, the project window will appear, with the temporary source files and the correct libraries installed (see Figures E.3 and E.4).

Projects include placeholder source code files and resource files, as well as appropriate CodeWarrior libraries. You'll notice that you can use almost any Mac character in the file names, including spaces. Most CodeWarrior projects end in "μ" (mu, option-m), making the name distinct from other kinds of files, but this is not required.

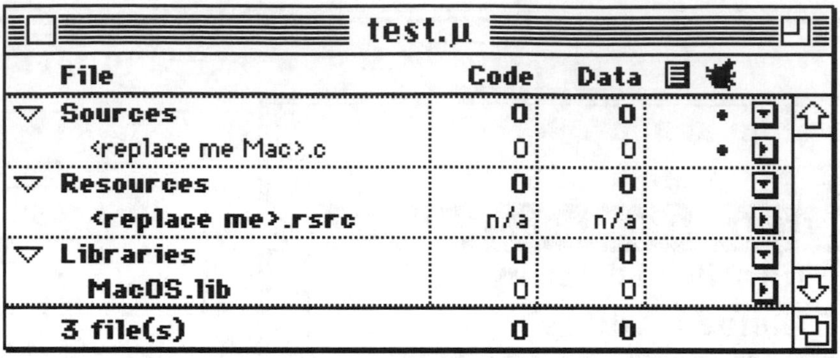

Figure E.3 A 68K project window.

Source code files are like those you've been using in this book: text files with code to be compiled. Resource files are a Macintosh-standard way of storing data that the user will see, such as icons, strings, and alert boxes. You'll learn all about resources when you read the *Macintosh C Programming Primer*.

Libraries are compiled code that your code can call. For example, a function in the ANSI C library is `printf()`, and you can call it from your code, but you can't see how it's written, because it's already compiled. The Mac Toolbox libraries are called `MacOS.lib` on the 68K and `InterfaceLib` on the PowerPC. Again, you'll learn about the Mac Toolbox when you read the *Primer*. The *CodeWarrior User's Guide* on the CodeWarrior CD tells you about all of the libraries that come with CodeWarrior.

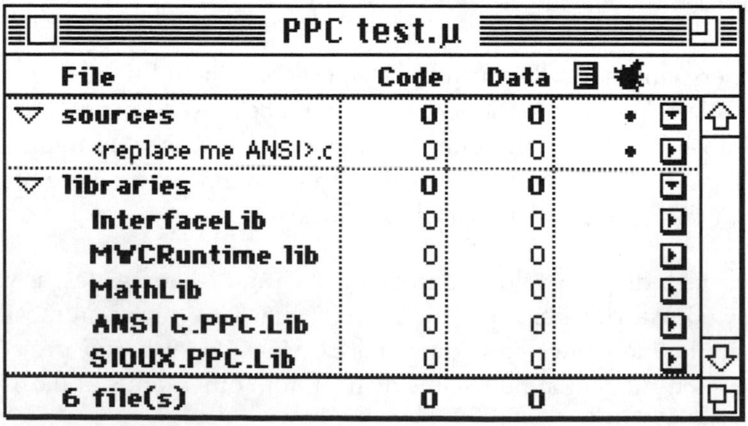

Figure E.4 A PowerPC project window.

In general, your source code file names will end in either ".c" or ".cp". CodeWarrior uses the suffix to determine which compiler to use to compile the source code in the file. C source code is in ".c" files; and C++ source code is in ".cp" files.

You can add any number of source, resource, and library files to your project by using the **Add Files** command in the project menu or by dragging the file or folder onto the Project window from the desktop. If you use the **Save As** command from the **File** menu to save a source file, the new version with its new name will be included in your project.

When you compile, CodeWarrior will parse the code in each source file, locate the headers, and generate an intermediate object format, which is stored in the project. If you change a few files or a header file included in several files, those will be updated, but the rest of the project does not have to be recompiled. When you select **Make**, the linker connects the object with the Mac Toolbox and other libraries and generates an executable program on your disk.

Editing

The CodeWarrior Editor lets you work on up to 32 source code files at one time. You can't see it here, but the editor automatically colors comments and C/C++ keywords, such as void and while. (Use the Preferences to add new words and change colors.) The Editor automatically converts DOS and UNIX line endings, so if you are using source code from these systems, you don't have to worry about the format. The Editor also handles large amounts of text, up to several megabytes.

There are up to four icons in the lower-left corner of each Editor window (Figure E.5). Three of these icons are connected to pop-up menus. The leftmost icon (sideways triangle) shows all headers included in the file. When you select one, that include file is opened for you. The curly-brace icon lists all the function names found in the file. When you select a function name, the source code window scrolls so that the function appears in the window. The document icon allows you to set the line-end format (Mac, DOS, UNIX) and toggle the syntax coloring. The lock or pencil icon shows whether the file is write-only or has Projector source code control status.

CodeWarrior features a sophisticated search-and-replace mechanism. You can also search and replace text in a single file, in sources and headers, and in saved sets of files (Figure E.6). The **Batch** option lets you see the results of your search in a list.

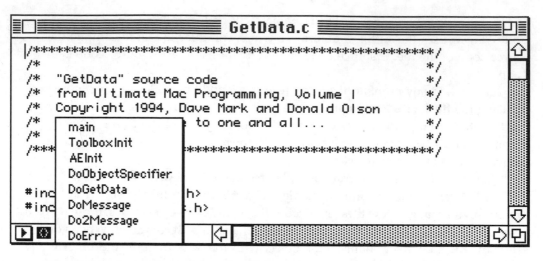

Figure E.5 A sample source code editing window.

Compiling, Linking, and Running

As you write code, you should save and compile to see whether you're getting it right. The fast CodeWarrior compiler will list all errors, so you can fix them up before going on.

Using the stationery will automatically include the correct libraries in your project. All you have to do is choose **Make** (or **Run**) from the **Project** menu, and CodeWarrior will compile any uncompiled source files, and locate and link in the libraries. If your code calls a function that is in a header file but not in any of the libraries, you'll see an error message during this phase and will have to add a library.

If you choose **Run**, CodeWarrior will automatically launch the application that you've just created. Or, you can double-click on the application on the desktop—it's a real Mac program now.

Debugging

To track your program's execution and variables, choose **Enable Debugging** from the **Project** menu, and CodeWarrior will automatically set all the debugging options. Then, when you choose **Run** from the **Project** menu or double-click on the symbol file (which ends in ".SYM" on 68K and ".xSYM" on PowerPC), you'll launch the Metrowerks Debugger and be able to see your source code as your program runs (Figure E.6).

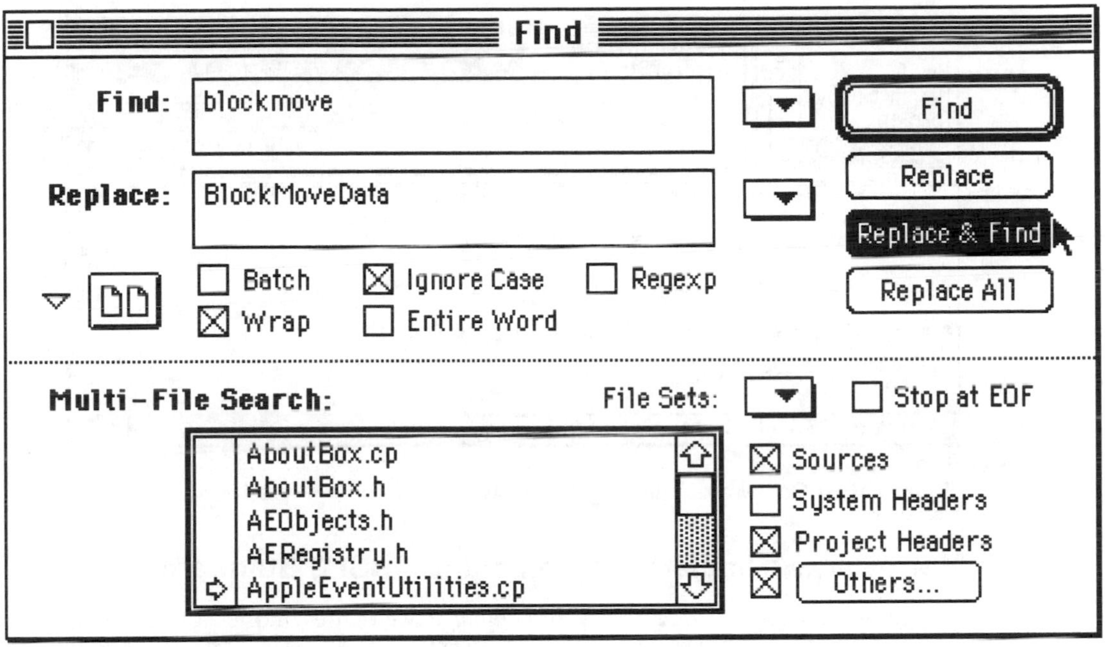

Figure E.6 The dialog box to find and replace.

The debugger window allows you to set breakpoints, allowing you to stop the program at any line in your source code. The upper-left pane shows the current chain of function calls. The upper-right pane shows all variables in scope (along with their current values). The lower section shows the source. You can control the debugging process from the menu or the floating toolbar.

The Metrowerks Debugger shows variables in many useful formats, includings strings and structures; supports expression evaluation, conditional breakpoints, hex dump of various memory locations, assembler, threads; and includes many other features. The interface is the same on the 68K and PowerPC, so you can debug both versions of your program easily. The Debugger will even debug code resources and libraries.

CodeWarrior and ANSI C programming

As you know from this book, CodeWarrior includes the standard ANSI libraries and allows you to write command-line, console-oriented programs. You can compile and run programs written for other systems (with some changes) or use code for statistics, data analysis, and other functions that do not require a Mac interface. Then, you can write a Mac program that calls these functions but includes a standard graphical user interface.

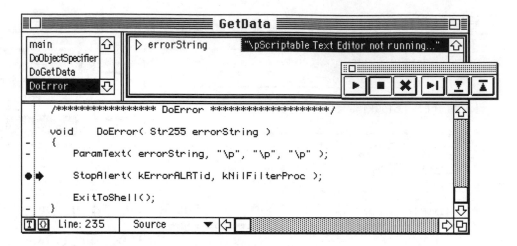

Figure E.7 A CodeWarrior debugger window.

Metrowerks's Implementation of the ANSI C Standard

Metrowerks's *C, C++, and Assembly Language Manual* explains how the compiler and linker implement the ANSI C standard. The standard leaves many definitions, such as the length of an integer, "compiler-dependent," and this manual explains how CodeWarrior will treat these options.

The *C Library Reference* document describes the ANSI C Library shipped on the CodeWarrior CD. It describes each call, its parameters, and return value and provides general information on usage. This document also covers the Metrowerks SIOUX console library, as well as the unix functions, which allow CodeWarrior programs to use standard UNIX calls, such as creat(), to make a new file.

Notes on which ANSI library to include in your project, as well as error messages for the C compiler and linker, are described in the CD's *CodeWarrior User's Guide*.

ANSI C++

C++ is an extension of C, designed for object-oriented programming. C++ allows you to organize your programs in classes based on the data rather than the kind of function and to reuse code rather elegantly. CodeWarrior supports C++, as described in the Metrowerks's *C, C++ and Assembly Language Manual*, and the *C++ Library Reference* (on the CodeWarrior CD, in QuickView interactive document format).

To learn ANSI Standard C++, you can follow the tutorials in *Learn C++ on the Macintosh*.

Writing Mac Programs

As you've probably noticed by now, ANSI C is only part of programming the Macintosh. You have to learn all about the Mac Toolbox to create programs with the Mac user interface and functionality. The *Macintosh C Programming Primer* describes this kind of programming.

CodeWarrior makes it easy for you to write Mac programs with Macintosh Toolbox headers and libraries, together with your resource files. The 68K and PowerPC CodeWarrior environments are identical, so you can use the same project organization and even the same source code (libraries are different). When you're done programming, merge the applications, and you'll have a fat binary that runs in native mode on both 68K and PowerPC Macintosh systems, just like our CodeWarrior environment. The *CodeWarrior User's Guide* and CodeWarrior *Tutorials* will help you with making Mac programs.

Beyond the standard libraries, the CodeWarrior CD includes special libraries for QuickTime, Sound, XTND, Thread Manager and QuickDraw GX.

You can also write code resources, such as HyperCard XCMDs; After Dark screensaver modules; and Photoshop, Illustrator, and Freehand plug-ins. This is an easy way to start programming the Mac. Libraries for each of these external formats are on the CodeWarrior CD.

The PowerPlant framework uses C++ and multiple inheritance to provide many Macintosh standard elements, including menus, windows, controls, simple file handling, and memory management. More esoteric features include QuickTime movies, off-screen bitmaps, Apple Events, and drag-and-drop.

What You Get with CodeWarrior

The CodeWarrior CD comes with:

- C, C++, Pascal, and Object Pascal compilers and linkers (68K code generation only in CW Bronze, 68K, PowerPC, and Intel code generation in CW Gold)
- Standard ANSI libraries
- SIOUX input-output console library (for command-line programs)
- Macintosh Toolbox libraries
- Source-level debugger
- Profiling and memory-tracking tools
- MPW shell and Metrowerks compiler and linker tools for 68K and PowerPC

- PowerPlant application framework
- More than 2500 pages of documentation
- Tutorials and examples
- APIs for various Mac applications
- Helpful source code and libraries
- Demos of various programmer tools

CodeWarrior Subscription

When you buy CodeWarrior, you get the first CD and two update CDs within the first year; you can then renew your subscription at a reduced rate. CodeWarrior releases are in January, May, and September.

You will also get free, responsive technical support by phone, fax, or e-mail.

Prices

- $99 for Bronze (680x0 Mac native code only)
- $399 for Gold (680x0, PowerPC Mac, and Intel x86/Pentium native code)

If you are affiliated with an educational institution, you are eligible for the academic version, at $99, with all the features of the Gold version.

To order, contact your local software store, university computer store, or Metrowerks Mail Order at (800) 377-5416 or fax (419) 281-6883.

Hardware and System Requirements

Metrowerks CodeWarrior CW6 requires a Macintosh computer with a Motorola MC68020, MC68030, MC68040, or PowerPC processor; 8 megabytes of RAM; Color QuickDraw; Mac OS System 7.1 or later; and a CD-ROM drive to install the software.

Other Cool Stuff

The CodeWarrior CD includes many additional programming tools and documentation files. For a printed version of the core documentation, you can buy *Inside CodeWarrior* from your computer bookstore or Metrowerks Mail Order (see above).

CodeWarrior Information

Up-to-date information and help with CodeWarrior is available on various on-line services, including:

- Internet newsgroup: comp.sys.mac.programmer.codewarrior

- Web site: http://www.iquest.com/~fairgate/cw/cw.html

- America Online forum: metrowerks

Information is also available directly from Metrowerks:

Metrowerks Corporation
The MCC Building, Suite 310
3925 West Braker Lane
(at Mopac Expressway)
Austin, TX 78759-5321
Telephone: (512) 305-0400
Fax: (512) 346-0440

Answers to Selected Exercises

Chapter 4

1.

2.

3.

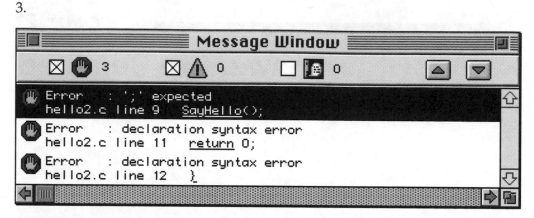

4.

Chapter 5

1. a. Missing quotes around "`Hello, World`".
    b. Missing comma between two variables.
    c. `=+` should be `+=` (although this will compile with some older compilers).
    d. Missing second parameter to `printf()`. Note that this error won't be caught by the compiler and is known as a run-time error.
    e. Another run-time error. This time, you are missing the `%d` in the first argument to `printf()`.
    f. This time, we've either got an extra `\` or are missing an n following the `\` in the first `printf()` parameter.
    g. The left- and right-hand sides of the assignment are switched.
    h. The declaration of `anotherInt` follows a nondeclaration.

2. a. 70
    b. −6

c. −1
d. 4
e. −8
f. 2
g. 14
h. 1

Chapter 6

1. a. The `if` statement's expression should be surrounded by parentheses.
   b. We increment i inside the `for` loop's expression, then decrement it in the body of the loop. This loop will never end!
   c. The `while` loop has parentheses but is missing an expression.
   d. The do statement should follow this format:

```
do
statement
while ( expression ) ;
```

   e. Each `case` in this `switch` statement contains a text string, which is illegal. Also, `case default` should read `default`.
   f. The `printf()` will never get called.
   g. This is probably the most common mistake made by C programmers. The assignment operator (=) is used instead of the logical equality operator (==). Since the assignment operator is perfectly legal inside an expression, the compiler won't find this error, an annoying little error you'll encounter again and again!
   h. Once again, this code will compile, but it likely is not what you wanted. The third expression in the `for` loop is usually an assignment statement—something to move i toward its terminating condition. The expression `i*20` is useless here, since it doesn't change anything.

2. Look in the folder `06.05   nextPrime2`.

3. Look in the folder `06.06 - nextPrime3`.

Chapter 7

1. a. Final value is 25.
   b. Final value is 512. Try changing the `for` loop from 2 to 3. Notice that this generates a number too large for a 2-byte `int` to hold.
   c. Final value is 1024.

2. Look in the folder `07.06 - power2`.

3. Look in the folder `07.07 - nonPrimes`.

Chapter 8

1. a. If the `char` type defaults to `signed` (very likely), `c` can hold values only from –128 to 127. Even if your `char` does default to `unsigned`, this is dangerous code. At the very least, use an `unsigned char`. Even better, use a `short`, `int`, or `long`.

    b. Use `%f`, `%g`, or `%e` to print the value of a `float`, not `%d`.

    c. The text string `"a"` is composed of two characters: `'a'` and the terminating zero byte. The variable `c` is only a single byte in size. Even if `c` were 2 bytes long, you can't copy a text string this way. Try copying the text one byte at a time into a variable large enough to hold the text string and its terminating zero byte.

    d. Once again, this code uses the wrong approach to copying a text string, and there is not enough memory allocated to hold the text string and its zero byte.

    e. The `#define` of `kMaxArraySize` must come before the first non-`#define` reference to it.

    f. The following definition creates an array ranging from `c[0]` to `c[kMaxArraySize-1]`:

    ```
    char c[ kMaxArraySize ];
    ```

    The reference to `c[kMaxArraySize]` is out of bounds.

    g. The problem occurs in the line:

    ```
    cPtr++ = 0;
    ```

    This line assigns the pointer variable `cPtr` a value of 0 (making it point to location 0 in memory), then increments it to 1 (making it point to location 1 in memory). This code will not compile. Here's a more likely scenario:

    ```
    *cPtr++ = 0;
    ```

    This code sets the `char` that `cPtr` points to to 0, then increments `cPtr` to point to the next `char` in the array.

    h. The problem here is with the statement:

    ```
    c++;
    ```

    You can't increment an array name. Even if you could, if you increment `c`, you no longer have a pointer to the beginning of the array! A more proper approach is to declare an extra `char` pointer, assign `c` to this `char` pointer, then increment the copy of `c`, rather than `c` itself.

    i. You don't need to terminate a `#define` with a semicolon. This statement defines "kMaxArraySize" to "200;", probably not what we had in mind.

2. Look in the folder `08.08 - dice2`.

3. Look in the folder `08.09 – wordCount2`.

Chapter 9

1. a. The semicolon after `employeeNumber` is missing.
   b. This code is really pretty useless. If the first character returned by `getchar()` is '\n', the ; will get executed; otherwise, the loop just exits. Try changing the == to != and see what happens.
   c. This code will work, since the double quotes around the header file name tell the compiler to search the local directory in addition to the places it normally searches for system header files. On the other hand, it is considered better form to place angle brackets around a system header file: `<stdio.h>`.
   d. The `name` field is missing its type. As it turns out, this code will compile, but it might not do what you think it does. Since the type is missing, the C compiler assumes that you want an array of `int`s. Even though it compiles, this is bad form!
   e. Both `next` and `prev` should be declared as pointers.
   f. There are several problems with this code. First, the `while` loop is completely useless. Also, the code should use '\0' instead of 0 (although that's really a question of style). Finally, by the time we get to the `printf()`, `line` points beyond the end of the string!

2. Look in the folder `09.06 - dice2`.

3. Look in the folder `09.07 - cdTracker2`.

4. Look in the folder `09.08 – cdTracker3`.

Chapter 10

1. a. The arguments to `fopen()` appear in reverse order.
   b. Once again, the arguments to `fopen()` are reversed. In addition, the first parameter to `fscanf()` contains a prompt, as if you were calling `printf()`. Also, the second parameter to `fscanf()` is defined as a `char`, yet the %d format specifier is used, telling `fscanf()` to expect an `int`. This will cause `fscanf()` to store a value of size `int` in the space allocated for a `char`. Not good!
   c. The `line` is declared as a `char` pointer instead of as an array of `char`s. No memory was allocated for the string being read in by `fscanf()`. Also, since `line` is a pointer, the & in the `fscanf()` call shouldn't be there.
   d. This code is fine except for one problem. The file is opened for writing, yet we are trying to read from the file by using `fscanf()`.

2. Look in the folder `10.04 – fileReader`.

3. Look in the folder `10.05 – cdFiler2`.

Chapter 11

1. a. In the next-to-last line, the address of myCat is cast to a struct. Instead, the address should be cast to a (struct Dog *).

   b. The typedef defines FuncPtr to be a pointer to a function that returns an int. MyFunc() is declared to return a pointer to an int, not an int.

   c. The declaration of Number is missing the keyword union. Here's the corrected declaration:

   ```
   union    Number    myUnion;
   ```

   d. The Player union fields must be accessed using u. Instead of myPlayer.myInt, refer to myPlayer.u.myInt. Instead of myPlayer.myFloat, refer to myPlayer.u.myFloat.

   e. First off, myFuncPtr is not a function pointer and not a legal l-value. As is, the declaration just declares a function named myFuncPtr. This declaration fixes that problem:

   ```
   int     (*myFuncPtr)( int );
   ```

   Next, main() doesn't take a single int as a parameter. Besides that, calling main() yourself is a questionable practice. Finally, to call the function pointed to by myFuncPtr, use either myFuncPtr(); or (*myFuncPtr)(); instead of *myFuncPtr();.

   f. The function strcmp() returns zero if the strings are equal. The if would fail if the strings were the same. The message passed to printf() is wrong.

   g. The parameters passed to strcpy() should be reversed.

   h. No memory was allocated for s. When strcpy() copies the string, it will be writing over unintended memory.

   i. This is a common problem that tons of people, including battle-scarred veterans, run into. The function call in the loop is not a function call. Instead, the address of the function DoSomeStuff is evaluated. Because this address is not assigned to anything or used in any other way, the result of the evaluation is discarded. The expression "DoSomeStuff;" is effectively a no-op, making the entire loop a no-op.

2. Look in the folder 11.05 – treePrinter.

Bibliography

1. *The C Programming Language*, Brian W. Kernighan and Dennis M. Ritchie, 1988, Prentice Hall, Englewood Cliffs, NJ.

2. *C: A Reference Manual*, Fourth Edition, Samuel Harbison, 1994, Prentice Hall, Englewood Cliffs, NJ.

3. *Macintosh C Programming Primer*, Volume I, Second Edition, Dave Mark and Cartwright Reed, 1992, Addison-Wesley Publishing Company, Reading, MA.

4. *Macintosh C Programming Primer*, Volume II, Dave Mark, 1990, Addison-Wesley Publishing Company, Reading, MA.

5. *Danny Goodman's AppleScript Handbook*, Second Edition, Danny Goodman, 1995, Alfred A. Knopf, New York, NY.

6. *Macintosh Human Interface Guidelines*, Apple Computer, Inc., 1992, Addison-Wesley Publishing Company, Reading, MA.

7. *Inside Macintosh: PowerPC System Software*, Apple Computer Inc., 1994, Addison-Wesley Publishing Company, Reading, MA.

8. *Algorithms in C*, Robert Sedgewick, 1990, Addison-Wesley Publishing Company, Reading, MA.

9. *Data Structures and C Programs*, Second Edition, Christopher J. Van Wyk, 1990, Addison-Wesley Publishing Company, Reading, MA.

10. *The Art of Computer Programming, Volume 1: Fundamental Algorithms*, Second Edition, Donald E. Knuth, 1973, Addison-Wesley Publishing Company, Reading, MA.

11. *Learn C++ on the Macintosh*, Dave Mark, 1993, Addison-Wesley Publishing Company, Reading, MA.

12. *The Art of Computer Programming, Volume 3: Sorting and Searching*, Donald E. Knuth, 1973, Addison-Wesley Publishing Company, Reading, MA.

13. *Inside Macintosh: Macintosh Toolbox Essentials*, Second Edition, Apple Computer, Inc., 1992, Addison-Wesley Publishing Company, Reading, MA.

14. *Inside Macintosh: More Macintosh Toolbox*, Second Edition, Apple Computer, Inc., 1993, Addison-Wesley Publishing Company, Reading, MA.

15. *Macintosh Programming Secrets*, Second Edition, Scott Knaster, 1992, Addison-Wesley Publishing Company, Reading, MA.